PENGUIN BOOKS
MEMORIES OF MALGUDI

R.K. Narayan was born in Madras in 1906 and educated there and at Maharajah's College in Mysore. His first novel *Swami and Friends* (1935) was set in the enchanting fictional territory of Malgudi. Narayan's other novels are *The Bachelor of Arts* (1937), *The Dark Room* (1938), *The English Teacher* (1945), *Mr Sampath* (1949), *The Financial Expert* (1952), *Waiting for the Mahatma* (1955), the Sahitya Akademi award-winning *The Guide* (1958), *The Man-eater of Malgudi* (1962), *The Vendor of Sweets* (1967), *The Painter of Signs* (1976), *A Tiger for Malgudi* (1983), *Talkative Man* (1986) and *The World of Nagaraj* (1990).

Besides six collections of short stories (*A Horse and Two Goats, An Astrologer's Day and Other Stories, Lawley Road, Malgudi Days, Grandmother's Tale* and *Under the Banyan Tree*), Narayan published two travel books (*My Dateless Diary* and *The Emerald Route*), five collections of essays (*Next Sunday, Reluctant Guru, A Writer's Nightmare, A Story-teller's World* and *Salt and Sawdust*), translations of Indian epics and myths (*The Ramayana, The Mahabharata* and *Gods, Demons, and Others*, published together as *The Indian Epics Retold*) and a memoir, *My Days*. *A Town Called Malgudi, The World of Malgudi, The Magic of Malgudi* and *Memories of Malgudi*, collections of Narayan's fiction, and *Malgudi Landscapes*, a selection of his best writings, are available from Penguin Books. *Malgudi Schooldays*, a volume of Narayan's children's writing, is available in Puffin, while *The Writerly Life*, a volume of his selected non-fiction, is available in Viking.

In 1980 R.K. Narayan was awarded the A.C. Benson medal by the Royal Society of Literature and was made an Honorary Member of the American Academy and Institute of Arts and Letters. In 1989 he was made a member of the Rajya Sabha. In 2000 the Government of India conferred on him the Padma Vibhushan.

R.K. Narayan died in May 2001.

S. Krishnan taught English literature at Madras Christian College and at Annamalai University. He spent many years with the United States Information Agency in their educational and cultural programmes. He is now a weekly columnist for the *Hindu*, consulting editor with the *Indian Review of Books* and senior editor of *Shruti*, a music and dance magazine. Krishnan has edited several volumes of R.K. Narayan's writings for Penguin Books. He lives in Chennai.

By R.K. Narayan in Penguin Books India

The Emerald Route

The Indian Epics Retold

Indian Thought: A Miscellany

The Magic of Malgudi

Malgudi Landscapes

Malgudi Schooldays

Memories of Malgudi

My Dateless Diary

The Ramayana

Salt and Sawdust

A Story-teller's World

A Town Called Malgudi

The World of Malgudi

A Writer's Nightmare

The Writerly Life: Selected Non-fiction

R. K. NARAYAN

Memories of Malgudi

The Dark Room
The English Teacher
Waiting for the Mahatma
The Guide
The World of Nagaraj

Edited with an introduction by
S. Krishnan

PENGUIN BOOKS
An imprint of Penguin Random House

PENGUIN BOOKS

USA | Canada | UK | Ireland | Australia
New Zealand | India | South Africa | China | Singapore

Penguin Books is part of the Penguin Random House group of companies
whose addresses can be found at global.penguinrandomhouse.com

Published by Penguin Random House India Pvt. Ltd
4th Floor, Capital Tower 1, MG Road,
Gurugram 122 002, Haryana, India

Penguin
Random House
India

First published in Viking by Penguin Books India 1999
Published in Penguin Books 2002

Copyright © R.K. Narayan 1999
Introduction copyright © S. Krishnan 1999

The *Man-eater of Malgudi* was first published by William Heinemann Ltd. 1961
Talkative Man was first published by William Heinemann Ltd. 1986
The short stories were first published as part of *Malgudi Days* (first published by
WilliamHeinemann Ltd. 1982), *Under the Banyan Tree* (first published by
William HeinemannLtd. 1985) and Salt and Sawdust (first published by
Penguin Books India 1993).

ISBN 9780141002453

For sale in the Indian Subcontinent and Singapore only

Typeset in Sabon by SÜRYA, New Delhi

Printed at Manipal Technologies Limited, India

www.penguin.co.in

MIX
Paper | Supporting
responsible forestry
FSC® C043100

Contents

Contents

Introduction

WITH *Memories of Malgudi*, Penguin India completes its omnibus editions of all of R.K. Narayan's Malgudi novels and his finest short stories. *A Town Called Malgudi*, the first in the series, comprises *The Man-eater of Malgudi, Talkative Man*, and sixteen of his best short stories. *The World of Malgudi* includes four novels: *Mr Sampath, The Financial Expert, The Painter of Signs* and *A Tiger for Malgudi*. The third in the series, *The Magic of Malgudi*, contains the perennial favourite, *Swami and Friends*, as well as two other novels, *The Bachelor of Arts* and *The Vendor of Sweets*. The present volume includes the remaining five novels. The novella, *Grandmother's Tale*, is the only one to be left out, for two reasons. One is that it is not set in Malgudi. The second reason is that it is not so much fiction as 'faction', to use a current term. It tells a true family story as a fascinating piece of fiction.

The first novel in the present volume, *The Dark Room*, was the third that Narayan wrote. Not only does it lack the exuberance of his first two novels (*Swami and Friends* and *The Bachelor of Arts*), it is actually a bleak, one might even say haunting, story of a woman in a middle-class family, who is ignored by her husband, or, when she is not ignored, is treated humiliatingly. The story line is quite simple. Ramani, a company executive, pompous and full of himself, his position and his Chevrolet, has little use for his long-suffering wife and children. As if things were not bad enough already, he becomes infatuated with Shanta Bai, who works in his company.

His wife, Savitri, puts up with all of this for a while, taking refuge in 'the dark room' when she has had more than she can take. In old-fashioned Hindu houses, the dark room was usually the storeroom, to which women had recourse when they wanted to get over some trauma, or when they just wanted to be alone. As always it is the children who suffer whenever their mother keeps away from the family by going into the dark room. They know something is wrong between their parents, but are too young to understand what it is all about. Eventually, Savitri decides to leave the house, but she does not go very far, only to another part of the town. In a few days the thought of how difficult her children might find it to cope without her overpowers Savitri, and she returns home. The children are of course overjoyed, the puzzled servants remain puzzled, and Ramani acts as if he was not aware of her absence from the house, and remains indifferent as before; Savitri finds herself in the same old rut. The book was a critical success, especially in the UK, though some Indian reviewers were disturbed by its portrayal of Indian marriages which seemed to survive only on the basis of the loyalty and integrity of the wife. But Narayan himself said of the novel: 'I was somehow obsessed with a philosophy of Woman as opposed to Man, her constant oppressor. (This must have been an early statement of the 'Women's Lib' movement.) Man assigned her a secondary place and kept her there with such subtlety and cunning that that she herself began to lose all notion of her independence, stature and strength. A woman in an orthodox milieu of Indian society was an ideal victim of such circumstances. My novel dealt with her, with this philosophy broadly in the background.' Despite the sombre nature of the book, it has many light moments as always with Narayan, such as getting dolls ready for the annual Navarathri festival; and the sharp characterization of even minor characters, such as the burglarious locksmith and his wife who provide refuge for Savitri during her flight, and take care of her with the deference and respect due to someone from the upper crust.

In 1934 Narayan married Rajam. In a society in which boys and girls were segregated, Narayan found himself in love with any pretty girl he saw but could not of course talk to. 'After the false starts, the real thing occurred . . . One day I saw a girl drawing water from the street tap and immediately fell in love with her . . . I could not really stand and stare; whatever impressions I had of her would be through a side glance while passing the tap. I suffered from a continually melting vision. The only thing I was certain of was that I loved her, and I suffered agonies of restraint imposed by the social conditions in which I lived.' She was the local headmaster's daughter, and finally Narayan mustered up enough courage to tell him that he wanted to marry her. Despite gloomy astrological forebodings, Narayan insisted on having his way, and the wedding took place. They had a blissful time together, a baby girl was born to them, but the stars had their way in the end. Within six years of their marriage, Rajam died of typhoid, and Narayan was overwhelmed with grief, the little girl being his only solace.

He went to Madras for a change, where he met a couple who conducted psychic experiments. His experiences with them and his association with Paul Brunton, the mystic, finally brought him a measure of peace, and he was ready to write again. He then ran an enjoyable but ill-fated magazine called *Indian Thought* which folded up after three issues. He was now ready to write *The English Teacher*, which true Narayan aficionados consider the best novel ever written by him.

It is basically an account of his married life, his wife's death, and his efforts to reach her through spiritual experiments. He says in his autobiography:

> More than any other book, *The English Teacher* is autobiographical in content, very little part of it being fiction . . . The toll that typhoid took and all the desolation that followed, with a child to look after, and the psychic adjustments are based on my own experience. That book falls into two parts—one is domestic life and the other half is 'spiritual'. Many readers have gone through the first half with interest and the second half with bewilderment and even resentment, perhaps feeling that they have been baited with the domestic picture into tragedy, death, and nebulous, impossible speculations. The dedication of the

book to the memory of my wife should to some extent give the reader a clue that the book may not be all fiction; still, most readers resist, naturally, as one always does, the transition from life to death and beyond.

The above excerpt from Narayan's autobiography, *My Days*, seems really to tell all there is about the novel, but it is a typical understatement. The novel is an outstanding accomplishment, and a perfect example of emotion recollected in tranquillity. Narayan's clone in the novel is named Krishna. He is a college teacher, living in the hostel and eagerly awaiting the return of his wife from her parental home where she has gone to deliver their first baby. In joyous anticipation, Krishna finds a house where they can all stay once the mother and child return. It is quite a pleasant house, but when his father offers to advance some money for them to buy a new house, his wife Susila is delighted. Krishna finds a particularly attractive house, where she goes to inspect the lavatory, which is incredibly filthy, and is stricken with typhoid by the flies swarming there. Despite the best medical efforts she dies. The second part of the book narrates Krishna's attempts to keep his daughter from missing her mother, and in participating in the psychical experiments, which he feels bring Susila and him together. The novel ends with the words: 'A cool breeze lapped our faces. The boundaries of our personalities suddenly dissolved. It was a moment of rare, immutable joy—a moment for which one feels grateful to Life and Death.'

It is odd that though one grieves with Krishna and suffers along with him, one realizes after reading the story completely that it is remarkably unsentimental. The early scenes of Krishna as a lecturer, life in the hostel, the panic with which Krishna behaves in the railway station, wondering whether the train would stop long enough for Susila and the baby to alight safely . . . are all written with a deft touch, with great humour and an economy in words. The description of Krishna and Susila staying together in the new house, the details of domestic life and their minor squabbles are all depicted in a masterly manner. The joys and amusements that the little girl provides keep the book from getting unduly morbid in the second part. With this book, Narayan reaches a watershed in his writing.

Though as 'a writer immersed in his materials'—as John Updike described him—he uses personal experiences and characters he has known in real life, there was never to be any going back. From here on, he is on the outside of events, viewing his characters and their antics benevolently. With *The English Teacher* Narayan arrives on the literary scene as a truly great writer.

Waiting for the Mahatma is an unreasonably underrated book, for no tenable reason. Some objected to the Mahatma being brought in as a character in a novel. Others felt that the national struggle should not have formed the background to a love story. I am among those who believe firmly that it is exactly these two factors that enhance the value of the novel. Narayan wrote this novel several years after the Mahatma's assassination, and I don't think it was just a novelist's desire to do something different. The stirring events of the struggle for Indian independence had all taken place during the years of his growing up and adolescence. It was inevitable that he should want to pay his own tribute to the country's greatest contemporary leader in his own fashion. In the novel Gandhiji never speaks or acts out of character. And there was nothing incongruous in making him a party to the fulfilment of the love of the protagonists because of his interest in young people.

It is actually the story of a sheltered young man coming of age and finding himself and his own worth. Sriram, an orphan, lives an undisturbed life with his grandmother. When Gandhiji arrives in Malgudi, Sriram's quiet existence takes a turn for the unexpected as he runs into one of Gandhiji's followers, a bright, beautiful young girl named Bharati, and falls passionately in love with her. The novel tracks the development of the relationship between Sriram and Bharati, under whose influence he takes part in the freedom struggle. Sriram is also impressed by terrorist activities, but stays with the mainstream movement. Both Sriram and Bharati are imprisoned, and when they are released they go to the Mahatma for his blessings. He actually agrees to conduct the wedding himself, then hurries to his prayer meeting where he is shot by Nathuram Godse.

The novel ends right there, but earlier, because of some premonition he feels, Gandhiji tells the young couple that they

should go ahead with their wedding, whether he is present at it or
not. In addition to the absorbing story, Narayan fills it with some
remarkable characters and scenes—Sriram's grandmother who
is a powerful personality within the house 'but seemed to shrink
in stature under an open sky'; the shopkeeper Kanni, 'a parched,
cantankerous, formidable man, who sat on his haunches all day
briskly handing out goods to his customers'; the arguments among
the big men of the place as to where Gandhiji should stay (he of
course prefers to stay in the Harijan colony); the Collector, who,
as the custodian of the British heritage, pointedly refers to the
Mahatma as Mr Gandhi; and innumerable others.

Waiting for the Mahatma is really one of Narayan's outstanding
novels in which he crafts a personal story against the backdrop
of the nation's struggle, creates almost real-life characters and
intersperses grim moments with his special brand of gentle humour,
without striking a single false note.

The Guide is Narayan's most popular work which won him the
Sahitya Akademi Award. It has been translated into many languages
ranging from Hebrew to Japanese (proving the universality of its
appeal), dramatized and filmed. In 1956 Narayan was awarded a
grant by the Rockefeller Foundation to travel widely in the US, and
meet writers, publishers and academics. When he reached Berkeley,
he decided to finish the writing of *The Guide*, the ideas for which
had been developing in his mind for quite a while. He took a room
in Hotel Carlton near the University of California, bought a hotplate
for cooking his simple meals, and, writing in longhand, completed
the book in three months. He says in his autobiography:

> At this time I had been thinking of a subject for a novel—a
> novel about someone suffering enforced sainthood. A
> recent situation in Mysore offered a setting for such a story.
> A severe drought had dried up all the rivers and tanks;
> Krishnaraja Sagar, an enormous reservoir feeding channels
> that irrigated thousands of acres, had also become dry, and
> its bed, a hundred and fifty feet deep, was now exposed
> to the sky with fissures and cracks, revealing an ancient
> submerged temple, coconut stumps, and dehydrated

crocodiles. As a desperate measure, the municipal council organized a prayer for rains. A group of Brahmins stood knee-deep in water (procured at great cost) on the dry bed of Kaveri, fasted, prayed and chanted certain mantras continuously for eleven days. On the twelfth day it rained. It was really the starting point of *The Guide*.

In leading up to this idea of parched earth yielding water, Narayan makes up a brilliant story about Raju, the railway guide, the sinner who became a saint, willy-nilly. Raju, who was earning a reasonable living as a railway guide, with, one presumes, no greater ambitions, suddenly finds his life turning topsy-turvy with the arrival of an intrepid seeker of old inscriptions and old monuments, accompanied by his wife, a beautiful dancer. 'Marco', the archaeological enthusiast, spends so much time in his pursuit that he leaves Rosie, his wife, to amuse herself as best as she can. The inevitable happens, and after a while Rosie leaves Marco and joins Raju, who builds her up as a great dancer. She gets many engagements, but Raju comes a cropper when Marco initiates a criminal misappropriation suit. He serves a jail term, and afterwards, thoroughly disenchanted, settles down under a tree near a temple by the river—he really has no place to go. A villager, Velan, takes him to be a holy man, and through his word-of-mouth publicity, the villagers throng around Raju, and provide him with milk and fruits. Even when Raju tells his life story to Velan, the latter listens politely, but it is obvious that he has no interest in what Raju has to say—as far as he is concerned Raju is a 'Swami'. When a drought occurs some time later, everybody looks to Raju to do something to propitiate the gods. He goes on a fast provisionally but the villagers, respecting what they think is his wish, make sure that no food is provided to him. The crowds grow larger, with the press too assembling in full strength. Raju slowly loses his energy, but now something unexpected happens—he refuses to be helped back to normality. On the eleventh day, he asks Velan to help him to his feet, staggers down to the river-bed with two men at his side, then says: 'Velan, it's raining in the hills. I can feel it coming up under my feet, up my legs . . .' and collapses.

It is an extraordinary story, written on two levels—Raju talking to Velan, and Raju talking to the readers. The two narratives mesh seamlessly. As I said earlier, the book was filmed and dramatized, and both versions were utter failures. The well-known actor-producer, Dev Anand, did the film, shooting much of the story in Jaipur and places like that, and introducing a tiger fight. (Narayan has a hilarious article, titled 'Misguided *Guide*', which describes the entire painful episode with great good humour. This article is included in *Malgudi Landscapes* and *A Writer's Nightmare*, both of which have been published by Penguin.) The theatrical version, written by Harvey Breit of the *New York Times*, was an equal flop—he tried to drop Rosie from the script altogether. The inevitable conclusion one can derive from these experiences is that Narayan's stories are gentle tales about simple people in a simple setting, and do not really lend themselves to melodramatization.

The World of Nagaraj is the most recent of Narayan's full-length novels. I repeat here what I recently wrote about the book. It has a serious theme in that it deals with both the generation gap and family dissensions. Nagaraj is conservative and well to do. Respected by the citizens of Malgudi, childless and living with his mother and wife, his great ambition in life is to write a book on the sage Narada. This desire never really translates into actuality, but he derives a lot of pleasure from talking about it, tracking down reference books and other sources of information, and generally doing research for the book which, he cannot admit to himself, he will neither finish or in fact even begin to write. In his free hours, he helps out with the book-keeping of a friend's saree company. His placid life is suddenly disrupted when Tim, the rebellious son of his elder brother, suddenly appears to stay with him, escaping his own ambitious father. What should Nagaraj do now? He is in a quandary as he loves Tim—and, whatever the latter's fault, he *has* come to Nagaraj seeking refuge. On the other hand, Nagaraj has the deepest respect for his elder brother who is the head of the family. This dilemma, and the attitudes moulded by generations, the expectations of the joint family—all leave Nagaraj in a conflicting welter of emotions. Nagaraj is the distilled essence of all the nice and good but feckless people whom Narayan has created. The writing as usual is limpid, the humour unaffected, and there is a mysterious 'Narayan aura' that surrounds the book like perfume from a garden of flowers—not overpowering but gentle, though penetrating.

When I was sixteen, and beginning to read for my MA in Literature, I was introduced to Narayan's works by one of my professors, James Russel Macphail. My thoughts always go back to him whenever I read something by or about Narayan. I had the privilege of meeting Narayan for the first time in the spring of 1957 in New York. Since then I have been in regular and close touch with him. In my view, he is quite simply our greatest fiction writer in the English language; humour and humanity, love for the oppressed and sympathy for the underdog, and a general overall kindness mark his literary persona. Not only myself but all of us should feel privileged to have known him, and to have known his work.

November 2000   **S. Krishnan**

The Dark Room

The Dark Room

1

AT SCHOOLTIME BABU suddenly felt very ill, and Savitri fussed over him and put him to bed. And in bed he stayed till Ramani came in and asked, 'What is this?'

'Nothing,' said Savitri, and passed into the kitchen. Ramani questioned the patient himself and called 'Savitri!' Before she could answer, he called her twice again, and asked, 'Are you deaf?'

'I was just—'

'What is the matter with Babu?'

'He is not well.'

'You are too ready with your medical certificate. Babu, get up! Don't miss your school on any account.'

Babu turned on his mother a look of appeal. She said, 'Lie down, Babu. You are not going to school today.'

Ramani said, 'Mind your own business, do you hear?'

'The boy has fever.'

'No, he doesn't. Go and do any work you like in the kitchen, but leave the training of a grown-up boy to me. It is none of a woman's business.'

'Can't you see how ill the boy is?'

'All right, all right,' Ramani said contemptuously. 'It is getting late for my office.' He went to the dining-room.

Babu dressed and slunk off to school. Savitri gave him a tumbler of milk and saw him off. She returned to the kitchen. Her husband had already begun his meal, served by the cook.

She asked again, 'Can't you see how ill the boy is?'

Ramani did not deign to hear the question but asked, 'Who selected the vegetables for this meal?'

'Why?'

'Brinjals, cucumber, radish, and greens, all the twelve months in the year and all the thirty days in the month. I don't know when I shall have a little decent food to eat. I slave all day in the office for this mouthful. No lack of expenses, money for this and money for that. If the cook can't cook properly, do the work yourself. What have you to do better than that?'

Savitri hovered between the cook and her husband, watching every item on his dining-leaf, and instructing the cook to bring a second or a third helping. This was by no means an easy task, for Ramani was eccentric and lawless in his taste. 'Why do you torment

me with this cucumber for the dozenth time? Do you think I live
on it?' Or he would say, if there was the slightest delay, 'Ah, ah!
I suppose I'll have to apply to my office for leave and wait for
this salted cucumber! A fine thing. Never knew people could be so
niggardly with cucumber, the cheapest trash in the market. Why not
cut up a few more, instead of trying to feed the whole household on
a quarter of it? Fine economy. Wish you'd show the same economy
in other matters.' Savitri never interrupted this running commentary
with an explanation, and her silence sometimes infuriated her
husband. 'Saving up your energy by being silent! Saving it up for
what purpose? When a man asks you something you could do
worse than honour him with a reply.' Sometimes, if she offered an
explanation, as occasionally happened, she would be told, 'Shut up.
Words won't mend a piece of foul cooking.'

After the meal he hurried away to his room and dressed for
his office. This was an elaborate ritual, complicated by haste.
Ramani would keep calling the servant Ranga in order to tell him
what he was and where he ought to be for not polishing the boots
properly, for folding the trousers with a wrong crease, for leaving
the coat on the frame with all the pockets bulging out. Savitri, too,
would sometimes be told what her husband thought of her for not
attending to buttons or sock-holes, and for not keeping an eye on
Ranga. Every item of dress infuriated Ramani and incited him to
comment, with the exception of ties, which received his personal
attention. He kept them carefully pressed between the leaves of
three bulky books which he had on his table: a heavy Annandale's
Dictionary, a *Complete Works* of Byron, and an odd volume of the
Encyclopaedia Britannica contained between them all his best ties.

Dressed in a silk suit, and with a sun-hat on, he stood at the
street door and called, 'Who is there?' which meant, 'Savitri, come
here and see me off.' When Savitri came he said, 'Close this door.'

'I have finished all the change. I shall have to buy some
vegetables for the evening.'

'Will a rupee do?' He gave her the money and strode out. For
a moment Savitri lingered in the doorway to hear the protests and
growls of the old Chevrolet as it was taken out of the garage. When
the noise of the engine ceased, a calm fell on the house.

Now Savitri had before her a little business with her god. She
went to the worshipping-room, lit the wicks and incense, threw on
the images on the wooden pedestal handfuls of hibiscus, jasmine

and nerium, and muttered all the sacred chants she had learnt from her mother years ago. She prostrated herself before the god, rose, picked up a dining-leaf, and sat down in the kitchen. The cook served her with a doleful face. He asked, 'Are the preparations very bad today, madam?' He was very sensitive to criticism and every day he smarted while his master talked at dinner.

'We ought not to have repeated the brinjal today. We had it yesterday,' Savitri said. 'No more of it this week, whatever happens.'

'All right, madam. Are the preparations very bad this morning?'

'Not exactly bad. Perhaps you would have done well to reduce the tamarind in the sauce. Your master doesn't like tamarind very much.'

The cook served her in sullen silence. Every day this happened. He was affected acutely both by criticism and by hunger, and criticism hurt him all the more because he lived in a state of protracted hunger, being the last to eat. Other cooks might have eased the situation by snatching a gulp of milk or curd when the mistress was not looking their way, but not he; Savitri locked up these commodities in the kitchen cupboard and served them out herself.

'I don't know, master is never satisfied. I do my best, and what more can a human being do?'

As this was almost a daily lament as regular as her husband's lecture, Savitri ceased to pay attention to it and ate in silence. Her thoughts reverted to Babu. The boy looked unwell, and perhaps at that moment was very ill in his class. How impotent she was, she thought; she had not the slightest power to do anything at home, and that after fifteen years of married life. Babu did look very ill and she was powerless to keep him in bed; she felt she ought to have asserted herself a little more at the beginning of her married life and then all would have been well. There were girls nowadays who took charge of their husbands the moment they were married; there was her own friend Gangu who had absolutely tethered up her poor man.

After food she went to her bench in the hall and lay down on it, chewing a little arecanut and a few betel leaves, and browsed over the pages of a Tamil magazine. In half an hour the house became perfectly still. The servant had finished the day's washing and gone to a nearby shop for a smoke; the cook was out for an hour in order to meet his friends at a coffee-house and compare kitchen politics. Odd noises, crows and sparrows in the garden broke the stillness of the hour. Over the pages of the magazine Savitri snatched a brief nap.

The clatter of the one o'clock bell from the Extension Elementary School reached her drowsing mind and woke her up. It was the recess hour and her two daughters, Sumati and Kamala, would be here presently, jumping about in their haste. Savitri went to the kitchen to mix curd and rice for the girls. Just as she was opening the kitchen cupboard she heard footsteps in the hall and almost immediately Kamala, a plump little girl with a springy pigtail, burst into the kitchen and sat down with her plate before her. She was panting for breath.

'How often am I to tell you not to come running in the sun? Where is Sumati?'

'She is coming with her friends.'

'Why couldn't you have come with her?'

'She won't allow me in her company. They are all in the Eighth Class.'

Kamala stuffed a few mouthfuls and tried to rise. Savitri pushed her down in her seat and said, 'You have got to eat the whole of it. I mixed only a little.' Kamala wriggled and protested.

'It is getting late, Mother. I must go. I can't go on eating all day.'

'I will give you three pies. Finish it.'

'All right,' said Kamala, and related to her mother some of the day's events in the school.

'Our teacher caned Sambu today. He is a bad boy, Mother. He threw a big stone at another boy's toes. Every day he threatens to snatch away my notebooks.'

Kamala had picked up her slate and books and was ready to start when her elder sister Sumati came in. 'Are you going back to school already, Kamala?' she asked authoritatively.

'Yes.'

'Mother,' Sumati cried, 'why do you let Kamala go back so early? We have still half an hour.'

Savitri said, 'Here, Kamala, what is the hurry?'

'I have some work. I have to go,' said Kamala, and vanished.

Sumati went to her desk, carefully put away her books of the morning, and took out her afternoon lessons; she arranged her notebooks in a pile and placed on top the yellow cardboard box in which she kept a number of pencils, a rubber and some pieces of coloured thread. She was examining the points of her pencils when Savitri came to her desk and exclaimed, 'So leisurely!'

'Our music-teacher said he would come late today—'

'Your rice is ready.'

At the mention of rice Sumati made a wry face. 'I'm not hungry, Mother.'

Savitri glared at her. 'Don't annoy me, madam.'

'I'm tired of eating rice, nothing but rice morning, noon, and night.'

Sumati went to the kitchen and sat down before her plate. Savitri watched her as she ate and wondered why this girl was getting thinner every day. She was eleven years old and still looked as she did three years ago, as if a whiff of wind could push her off her feet, frail and floating. Perhaps nothing wrong in it; must be hereditary, must be taking after her grandmother: every feature, the dusky colour, the small mouth, rather small eyes, and straight hair. 'As my mother must have looked about forty years ago.'

'Mother, I shall want four annas on Monday,' said Sumati.

'What for?'

'I have to buy an embroidery pattern book.'

'All right. By the way, why don't you keep Kamala with you and see that she doesn't come running through the streets?'

'She doesn't listen to me, Mother.'

'But she said you wouldn't allow her in your company.'

'She is such a nuisance to my friends. She keeps asking everyone for pencils and ribbons. It is disgraceful.'

'All the same, keep an eye on the girl.'

After Sumati went back to school Savitri sat down for a moment fretting about the cook. It was two and he hadn't come yet. How often had she to tell him to be back before two o'clock? He never returned before two-thirty and delayed coffee and tiffin till three-thirty—and close on its heels would come the planning of the night dinner, and on and on endlessly. Was there nothing else for one to do than attend to this miserable business of the stomach from morning till night?

The cook walked in at about two-thirty. 'I was about to light the oven for coffee,' said Savitri.

'Why, madam? Not at all necessary.'

'If you can't be back at two o'clock, you can tell me. I will do this tiffin business myself. I do so many things already, one more will make no difference. You can come at your leisure and do whatever is left undone.'

The cook went to the kitchen in a rage, muttering, 'One always comes back, one never goes out to be gone for ever. How is one to know whether it is two or two-thirty? No two clocks agree. When the school bell went off at two o'clock, the clock in the hotel showed only one forty-five. If you want me to be punctual, why can't you buy a watch for me?' When Savitri entered the kitchen a little later he told her, 'From tomorrow I propose to stay here in the afternoon and not go out anywhere.' Savitri said, 'I have no objection to your going out, but if you don't come back at two o'clock this miserable business for the stomach will continue the whole day—' She issued a few instructions in regard to the night dinner and said, 'I'm going out. If the children come from school before I return, give them coffee and tiffin. Babu will come in the evening. He is not quite well. Give him coffee. Don't compel him to take tiffin if he doesn't want it.'

She dressed her hair, washed her face, renewed the vermilion mark on her forehead, looked at her saree for a moment, wondering whether she should wear another and dismissing the thought with, 'This is quite good; I'm not going outside the Extension.' She was ready to go out on her afternoon round of visits at three-thirty. She called the cook and told him: 'Tell the children I'll be back very soon. Don't forget about Babu's coffee.'

At eight-thirty savitri's ears, as ever, were the first to pick up the hoarse hooting of the Chevrolet horn. She shouted to the servant, 'Ranga, open the motor shed!' Ramani as a rule sounded his horn at about a furlong from his gate, two long hoots which were meant to tell the household, 'Ranga, keep the shed door open when I reach there, if you value your life,' while to Savitri it said, 'It is your business to see that Ranga does his work properly. So take warning.' Some days the hooting would be less emphatic, and Savitri's ears were sufficiently attuned to the nuances and she could tell a few minutes in advance what temper her husband was in. Today the hooting was of the milder kind. It might mean that he was bringing home a guest for dinner or that he was in a happy mood, possibly through a victorious evening at the card table in his club. In either case they could await his arrival without apprehension. If he was happy he treated everyone tolerantly, and even with a kind of aggressive kindness; if he had a guest, he attended on him with such persistence and concentration that he would not notice the failings of his family. Savitri had a qualm for a moment, because a guest would mean a great deal of messing about with oil and frying pan and stove and getting some extra dish ready within the shortest possible time. Ramani was never in the habit of announcing in advance the arrival of a guest or of tolerating any poor show in the dining room. He just picked up a friend at the club and brought him home for dinner. It made him furious if it was suggested that he should give notice: 'We are not so down-and-out yet as not to afford some extra food without having to issue warnings beforehand.'

'But if we should have a lot of food left over every day?' Savitri had asked once or twice.

'Throw it into the gutter.'

'Or we can give it to the beggars?' Savitri suggested.

'Certainly. By all means. Make it a rule every day to give some food to the beggars. Remember, if I see any beggar turned away from our door, I shall be very wild.'

Savitri, however, had other methods of dealing with sudden guests. She had a genius for making the existing supply elastic and transforming an ordinary evening course, with a few hurriedly fried trimmings, into a feast.

Today, however, the soft hooting was not due to the presence of a guest. Savitri was greatly relieved to see her husband come into the house alone from the shed. Her alternative inference that he was in a happy mood was confirmed by the fact that he did not pass off into the right wing of the house with bent head, but stood at the doorway wiping his shoes on the mat and looking about. Again he did not say to Savitri, 'See if the fellow has locked the garage door,' but merely asked, 'Have the children had their food?' And again, after going to the room he did not shout in the dark, 'Who is trying to save the electric bill by keeping the house as dark as a burial ground?' but quietly switched on the lights.

Savitri felt relieved; the same relief ran through the children, who were all at their desks in another room, waiting, keyed up. They had now caught the signals. Ah, Father was going to be pleasant. It meant they could just hang about the dining-hall and listen to their elders' talk; otherwise they would have had to keep to their books for some time and then crawl away to their pillows.

After undressing and changing, Ramani came very quickly towards the dining-hall and said to Savitri, 'Hope you have finished your dinner.'

'Not yet.'

'What a dutiful wife! Would rather starve than precede her husband. You are really like some of the women in our ancient books.'

'And you?' Savitri asked. She could take any liberties with him now. She could say anything. She could be recklessly happy and free.

'I? I'm like—you'd have to write a new epic if you wanted anyone like me in an epic.' And he laughed and patted her on the back. She understood what it meant: he would make love to her, a kind of heavy, boisterous love, even before the cook and the children.

While eating he caught sight of Babu lurking behind the door, and said, 'Hello, you are still alive? The way your mother protected you this morning I thought—'

'My headache left me in the afternoon, Father.'

'Certainly, so that you might not miss the cricket in the evening; isn't it so?' Babu was silent. Ramani persisted in asking till he confessed that he went to play cricket in the evening.

'Look here, young fellow. I've been your age and played all these dodges in my time. So you can't trick me,' said Ramani, and turned to Savitri. 'Which of us was right?'

Savitri blushed. 'The boy did have a headache in the morning,' she said, and felt ashamed of herself for her excessive concern.

'Listen,' Ramani said to Savitri. 'Bear this in mind. There is a golden law of headaches. They come in time for school and leave in time for cricket.' He laughed heartily, well pleased with his epigram. Babu tiptoed away. Ramani said to Savitri: 'You have to learn a lot yet. You are still a child, perhaps a precocious child, but a child all the same.'

The beginning of love-making—Savitri understood and changed the subject. 'What happened to Ramaswami? You never told me what you did with him.'

'Oh, him? We disposed of that affair a long time ago. I didn't want to report the fellow to the head office. I called him up and warned him. He has made good the amount.'

'You won't get into trouble for that?'

'Trouble? Isn't it enough if I don't get them in to it? After all, he's only a poor fellow. Some temptation. A small amount. He has a good record of service.'

'But they may not like your disposing of the question so easily?'

'If they don't like it, here is Mr Ramani's resignation, and you can look out for another secretary for your blessed branch.'

'And suppose they accept the resignation?'

'Madam, the Engladia Insurance Company is a big one, I admit, but it is not the only insurance company in the world. Before I took charge, Malgudi district was not giving them even ten rupees' worth of policies a year, and now ten lakhs of business is passing through my hands every year. What do you say to that?'

Savitri's tactics never failed. If she wanted to divert his attention she had only to work him up into a professional mood. He was going on, expatiating on his work, on the offers he received from other companies, and so on. It saved her from his romantic attentions till the two girls came in.

'Ah, dear lady,' Ramani said to Kamala. 'Why have you neglected us?'

'I was doing my lessons.'

'Lessons! Lessons! You are a great woman. Didn't you hear your father come home?'

'Yes, Father.'

'That's all you care for us poor folk,' Ramani said with an elaborate mischievousness. 'What about you, lady?' he said, turning to his first daughter. 'Ah, how serene you look! You already look as if you had grandchildren.' The children giggled, looked at each other and giggled again. Savitri laughed. He would have been hurt if she hadn't. Ramani looked at his daughters benevolently and then looked at his wife and said with a wink, 'I wonder which of them will grow up like you? In any case, if any of them become half so— h'm, h'm!—as you are . . . I rather like the way you have arranged the jasmine in your hair today.'

Savitri said, rising, 'Get up. Time to go and wash our hands.'

2

THOUGH SAVITRI WAS on visiting terms with about a score of houses in the South Extension, she had only two real friends— Gangu and Janamma.

Savitri found Gangu fascinating. She had humour, abundant frivolity, and picturesque ambitions. She was the wife of a schoolteacher, and had four children. It was her ambition to become a film star, though she lacked any striking figure or features or acting ability; she wanted to be a professional musician, though she had no voice; she hoped to be sent some day as Malgudi delegate to the All-India Women's Conference; to be elected to various municipal and legislative bodies; and to become a Congress leader. She spent her days preparing for the fulfilment of one ambition or another. For serving on public bodies she felt she ought to know a little more English than she needed to read fairy tales and write letters to her husband at the beginning of their married life. Hence she engaged a tutor, who made her go through Scott's novels and trained her in conversation by putting inane questions to her in English. She prepared for her film career by attending two Tamil pictures a week and picking up several screen songs, in addition to wearing flimsy crêpe sarees and wearing her hair and flowers in an eccentric manner. She talked irresponsibly and enjoyed being unpopular in the elderly society of South Extension. She left home when she pleased and went where she liked, moved about without an escort, stared back at people, and talked loudly. Her husband never interfered with her but let her go her own way, and believed himself to be a champion of women's freedom; he believed he was serving the women's cause by constantly talking about votes and divorce.

Gangu was tolerated in the Extension.' she was interesting with all her talk, she was very religious, visiting the temple regularly, and she was not immoral.

Savitri's other friend, Janamma, was a different type altogether. She was rotund, elderly, and rich. Her husband was a public prosecutor. She never moved very freely among people. Savitri had a great regard for her, and consulted her whenever she was seriously worried.

Savitri was friendly with both Janamma and Gangu, though the two found each other intolerable. Janamma said of Gangu, 'That restless rat,' and Gangu said of Janamma, referring to her size and deportment, 'That temple chariot.' Janamma asked Savitri, 'Why do you allow that silly pup to worry you with her company?' Gangu often asked Savitri, 'How do you manage to remain alone with that creature? Isn't her face frightening at close quarters? She looks like a headmaster we had when we were at school.'

Between these two implacable enemies Savitri maintained a subtle balance. Only once did she find herself in a very difficult situation—when both of them met in her house. It happened that Gangu was on a visit to Savitri's house and Janamma dropped in later in the evening. Savitri was sitting on the bench in the hall with Gangu by her side. At the sight of Janamma, Gangu lost her voice but was too proud to get up and go away. Janamma stopped short as if a trap had caught her foot. Savitri said, Ah, come in, *mami*,' and edged away a little and made space for her on the bench on her other side. The enemies sat one on each side of her. There was an uneasy silence. Savitri made a vacuous remark on the heat during the day. The remark was in danger of extinction without a response. Shuddering at the prospect of having to invent another equally innocuous one, Savitri turned to Gangu and asked anxiously, 'Didn't you feel it?'

'Yes, I did,' replied Gangu cheerlessly.

Savitri, fearing that she might appear to be bestowing more attention on one than on the other, quickly turned to Janamma and inquired, 'It's unusually hot for the time of year, isn't it?'

'I suppose so,' said Janamma.

Then once again silence. Savitri felt the whole situation was thoroughly ridiculous—all three sitting on the same bench side by side like schoolchildren, and only one being able to talk. Janamma suddenly rose from the bench and sat on the floor, muttering an explanation, 'I always feel more comfortable on the floor.' Savitri found herself in a dilemma: she couldn't sit on the bench herself while an elderly visitor was sitting down on the floor, and she couldn't leave Gangu for the other. Savitri solved the problem by getting up, moving away from the bench, and standing at a spot which wasn't too near to either Gangu or Janamma. Gangu stared fixedly at a picture on the wall and Janamma kept looking at the door, and Savitri stood completely baffled. How was this to be brought to an end? Neither was willing to be the first to leave. Savitri kept on talking as best as she could of that day's menu for breakfast, the price of vegetables, scarcity of good vegetables, the impudence and avarice of some vegetable-vendors, the difficulties of going to the market every day, and all the bother with servants and cooks. She had to talk looking at neither in particular, and standing. She was invited twice to sit down, and twice did she complain of acute discomfort at the knee-joint.

This terrible situation only came to an end by the passage of time. It was nearing seven and Janamma could not stay any longer because it was time for the public prosecutor to return home and she would have to be there. When she was gone Gangu said triumphantly, 'Did she think that I would be afraid of her and scramble out of the house?'

3

SAVITRI WAS IN Janamma's house one evening when Kamala came and said, 'Father wants you to come home immediately.'

'Father! Has he come home?'

It was very unusual. Savitri's heart beat fast. Was he terribly ill? Or had anything happened to him or to the house? Why had he not gone to the Club? 'Why has he come home so soon, Kamala?'

'I don't know, Mother. I was playing in Kutti's house when he called me up and told me to find you at once. I couldn't stop and talk to Father: he looked so angry.'

Savitri rose, saying to Janamma, 'I must be going.' She almost ran out of the house. Kamala went prancing before her. 'Why don't you walk like a normal female, Kamala? You will break your neck some day.'

'Mother, shall we see which of us can reach home first?'

When she turned into her street, she saw that the car was still parked in the road. 'Didn't he tell you why he wants us so urgently?' she asked, and Kamala shook her head and said, 'He was very angry that Sumati and Babu were not at home.'

'How can the children be at home in the evenings? Doesn't he know that they have to go out and play?'

Savitri's throat went dry at the sight of her husband. He was pacing the front veranda; he had changed his coat and was wearing a blue blazer. He looked fixedly at her as she came up from the gate and said, 'You have made me wait for half an hour.' He added, 'A fellow comes home from the office, dog-tired, and he has only the doors and windows to receive him. Where is everybody gone? Anyone could walk in and walk out with all the things in the house.'

'I left the cook in charge of the house.'

'He is not a watchman. Perhaps you'd like him to put up his

oven at the street gate so that he can look after the house and cook at the same time.'

Her suspense had relaxed. He wasn't ill, and nothing else was wrong anywhere. She knew that he was either going to tell her that he was dining out or ask her to go out with him in the car. He said, looking at his watch, 'It is getting late. Are you coming with me to the cinema or not?'

'Now?'

'Immediately.'

'Where is Sumati, Kamala? Babu will be in the field. Send Ranga to fetch them while I dress.'

'The children can go some other day. Not a fly extra now.'

'Oh,' she said unhappily. She knew it would be useless to plead. All the same she could not restrain herself. 'The poor things, let them come, they will enjoy it.' Kamala was already making some indistinct impatient notes.

'It is very bad for the children to be taken out every time their elders go out.'

'At least let Kamala come with us,' said Savitri.

'Father, let me come to the cinema too.'

'You must never ask to be taken out.'

'If I don't ask, nobody will take me out,' said Kamala, and turned to her mother: 'Please let me come too. Sumati and Babu won't mind.'

Ramani was infuriated at the sight of the girl appealing to her mother and thundered, 'Learn not to whimper before your mother.' To Savitri he said, 'Are you coming out at all or shall I go alone? You can stay here and pet the little darling.'

'Let us go some other day,' she said.

'No. I want you to come now. Children some other day. I have not come all the way to be told "Some other day". I am not a vagabond to come in and go out without a purpose. Go and dress quickly. It is already six-fifteen. We can't fool about on the veranda all day.'

Savitri went in. Kamala went behind her, showing symptoms of stamping her feet and crying. Ramani said, 'If I hear you squeal, I will thrash you, remember. Be a good girl.' He shouted a moment later, 'Savitri, I will count sixty. You must dress and come out before that.' Instead of counting sixty he went on talking: 'Women are exasperating. Only a fool would have anything to do with them.

Hours and hours for dressing! Why can't they put on some decent clothes and look presentable at home instead of starting their makeup just when you are in a hurry to be off? Stacks of costly sarees, all folded and kept inside, to be worn only when going out. Only silly-looking rags to gladden our sight at home. Our business stops with paying the bill. It is only the outsider who has the privilege of seeing a pretty dress.'

Malgudi in 1935 suddenly came into line with the modern age by building a well-equipped theatre—the Palace Talkies—which simply brushed aside the old corrugated-sheet-roofed Variety Hall, which from time immemorial had entertained the citizens of Malgudi with tattered silent films.

Ramani sat in a first-class seat with his wife by his side, very erect. He was very proud of his wife. She had a fair complexion and well-proportioned featurend her sky-blue saree gave her a distinguished appearance. He surveyed her slyly, with a sense of satisfaction at possessing her. When people in the theatre threw looks at her, it increased his satisfaction all the more, and he leant over and said, 'They are showing *Kuchela*.'

'Yes. I read the notice while coming up.'

'It is a Tamil film. I thought you would like it.' He spoke to her because he was in a position to do it, and it made him feel important. He enjoyed his role of a husband so much that he showed her a lot of courtesy, constantly inquiring if her chair was comfortable, if she could see the screen properly, and if she would like to have a sweet drink.

The hall became dark and the show began. Savitri, like the majority of those in the hall, knew the story, had heard it a number of times since infancy, the old story from the epics, of Krishna and his old classmate Kuchela, who was too busy with his daily prayers and meditation to work and earn, and, hence left to his wife the task of finding food for their twenty-seven children . . .

Everything was there: Krishna's boyhood—he and his gawky classmates waylaying curdsellers and gorging themselves. A feat it was to consume so many pots of curds. An endless procession of rustic women with pots on their heads passed under the trees, in the branches of which a gang was waiting; the women halted under the trees and nearly asked to be robbed of their pots. How they wrung their hands at the broken pots and chased Krishna. As the curds spread on the ground, 'What a lot of curd wasted!' Savitri could not help thinking. And then Krishna's classroom jokes and the various ways in which he tormented his monitor; nobody was in a mood to question why the monitor, a perfectly timid and harmless man, deserved this treatment. Savitri enjoyed the sight of the troubled monitor and the triumph of the saucy-looking Krishna so much that she laughed aloud and whispered to her husband, 'Babu should have seen this, he would have enjoyed it.'

'Don't keep bothering about Babu, otherwise you won't be able to enjoy the show,' said her husband.

She was enchanted by the picture. It ran for nearly four hours. The film people had shown no hurry: they had a slow, spacious way of handling a story which gave a film-fan three times his money's worth. There were songs which characters sang as long as they liked, there were scenes of 'domestic humour' which threatened to last the whole evening, a procession complete with elephants and pipers and a band that took half an hour to pass, a storm which shook the theatre, a court scene with a dancer which was an independent programme by itself; there were irrelevant interludes which nearly made one forget the main story.

Savitri sympathized intensely with the unfortunate woman, Kuchela's wife. 'The poor girl!' she muttered to her husband.

'Note how patient she is, and how uncomplaining,' Ramani remarked.

Savitri was embarrassed by a suggestive conversation between a very fat husband and his wife at bedtime; she was thrilled by the magnificence of the procession; and she was immensely pleased when in the end Krishna heaped on his old friend wealth and honour. The whole picture swept her mind clear of mundane debris and filled it with superhuman splendours. Unnoticed by her passed the fumbling and faltering of the tinsel gods and the rocking of the pasteboard palaces in the studio wind, and all the exaggeration, emphasis, and noise. The picture carried Savitri with it, and when in the end Kuchela stood in his *puja* room and lighted camphor and incense before the image of God, Savitri brought her palms together and prayed.

The first show ended at ten o'clock.

The switching-on of the lights, the scurry of feet, and a blue-coated husband yawning, had the air of a vulgar anti-climax. 'You must bring the children tomorrow,' she said. The old Chevrolet

groaned and started. She loathed the dull drab prospect of changing
her saree, dining, and sleeping. The night air blew on her face and
revived her earthly senses a little. As she sat beside her husband, she
felt grateful to him and loved him very much, with his blue coat and
the faint aroma of a leather suitcase hanging about him.

When she reached home, she found Ranga and the cook sitting
up in the front veranda. Sumati and Babu were there too. Kamala
had slept on the hall bench. 'The poor girl has fallen asleep on the
bench!' exclaimed Savitri. 'Have the children had their food? Did
Kamala cry long after we went? Babu, you must see this picture. It
is very good.'

'An Indian film!' sneered Babu.

'You must see the little boy who acts Krishna. How can a small
boy act so well! He is wonderful.'

Babu smiled indulgently. 'That shows you have never seen
Shirley Temple. They pay her one thousand pounds a week to act. If
you see *Curly Top* you will never like any other picture.'

'Mother, he has not seen that picture. He is lying,' said Sumati.

'I never said I saw it. A friend of mine has seen it twice, and he
told me all about it.'

'You see this picture and then say. Your father has promised to
send you all to it tomorrow.'

'I don't like Indian films, Mother. I would like to be sent to
Frankenstein, which is coming next week,' Babu said.

'I don't like English films. Let us go to this tomorrow,' Sumati
said.

'It is because you don't understand English films,' said Babu.

'As if you were a master of English and understood all that they
say in the films! Why do you pretend?' said Sumati.

This threatened to develop into a quarrel, but Savitri stepped
between them and said, 'Sh! Don't start fighting.'

4

IN THE MONTH of September, the streets rang with the cries
of hawkers selling dolls—the earliest intimation of the coming
Navaratri festival.

'Mother, aren't we buying some dolls this year for the festival?'

'What's the use of buying them year after year; where are we
to keep them?'

'In the next house they have bought for ten rupees a pair of Rama and Sita, each image as large as a real child.'

'We have as many as we can manage. Why should we buy any more?'

'Mother, you must buy some new dolls.'

'We have already three casks full of dolls and toys.'

A day before the festival the casks were brought into the hall from an obscure storing-place in the house. Ranga had now a lot of work to do. It was an agreeable change for him from the monotony of sweeping, washing clothes, and running errands. He enjoyed this work. He expressed his gay mood by tying a preposterous turban round his head with his towel and tucking up his *dhoti*.

'Oh, look at Ranga's turban!' screamed Kamala.

'Hey, you look like a cow,' added Sumati.

'Do I?' Ranga bellowed like a cow, and sent the children into fits of laughter.

'Don't waste time in playing. Open the casks and take out the dolls,' said Savitri.

Ranga untied the ropes and brought out the dolls in their yellowing newspaper wrappings. 'Handle them carefully, they may break.' In a short while dust and sheets of old newspaper, startled cockroaches and silverfish were all in a heap on one side of Ranga, and, on the other, all the unwrapped dolls. Most of them had been given to Savitri by her mother, and the rest bought by her at various times. There they were—dolls, images, and toys of all colours, sizes, and shapes; soldiers, guards, and fat merchants; birds, beasts, and toys; gods and demons; fruits and cooking utensils; everything of clay, metal, wood, and cloth.

Ranga in his preposterous turban, stooping into the casks and bringing out the dolls, looked like an intoxicated conjurer giving a wild performance. The children waited, breathlessly watching for the next item, and shrieked at his absurd comments: 'Ah, here is my friend the parrot. He pecks at my flesh.' He would suck the blood on his finger and vow to break the parrot's beak before the end of the festival. He would hurriedly take out and put down a merchant or a grass-seller, complaining that they were uttering terrible swear-words and that he couldn't hold them. He would pretend to put the toy foods into his mouth and munch them with great satisfaction. Or he would scream at the sight of a cobra or a tiger. It was pure drama.

Savitri squatted down and wiped the dust off the dolls, and odd memories of her childhood stirred in her. Her eyes fell on a wooden rattle with the colour coming away in flakes, with which she had played when she was just a few months old. So her mother had told her. There was a toy flute into which she had wasted her babyhood breath. Savitri felt a sudden inexplicable self-pity at the thought of herself as an infant. She next felt an intense admiration for her mother, who never let even the slightest toy be lost but preserved everything carefully, and brought it all out for the Navaratri display. Savitri had a sudden longing to be back in her mother's house. She charged herself with neglecting her mother and not writing to her for several months now . . . How frightfully she (Savitri) and her sister used to quarrel over these dolls and their arrangements! She remembered a particular Navaratri which was completely ruined because she and her sister had scratched each other's faces and were not on speaking terms. Poor girl! Who would have dreamt that she would grow into a bulky matron; with a doctor husband and seven children, away from everybody in Burma? That reminded her, she had not answered her letters received a month ago; positively, next Thursday she would write so as to catch the Friday's steamer.

Now Ranga had put down a rosy-cheeked, auburn-haired doll which was eloquent with memories of her father. She remembered the evening when he had awakened her and given her the cardboard box containing this doll. How she adored this cardboard box and the doll and secretly used to thrust cooked rice into its mouth and steal sugar for it! Poor father, so decrepit now! . . .

A crash broke this reverie. Ranga had dropped a bluish elephant, as large as an ordinary cat.

'You ass, did you fall asleep?'

'Oh, it is broken!' wailed Sumati.

'Make him buy a new one, Mother. Don't give him his pay,' suggested Kamala.

Savitri felt very unhappy over the broken elephant: it was one of a pair that her mother had got from *her* mother, and it had been given to Savitri with special admonitions, and not to her sister, because she could not be depended upon to be so careful, and Savitri's mother had been very reluctant to separate the pair . . .

'I told you to be careful,' Savitri said, 'and yet, you ass—'

Ranga picked up the broken elephant. 'Oh, madam, only its

trunk is broken,' he announced gleefully.

'What is left of an elephant when its trunk is gone?' Savitri asked mournfully.

Ranga stood examining the trunkless elephant and said: 'It looks like a buffalo now. Why not have it in the show as a buffalo, madam?'

'Fool, stop your jokes.'

'He doesn't care a bit!' Kamala said, horrified.

Ranga said to Kamala, 'Little madam, I know now how buffaloes are made.'

'How?' asked Kamala, suddenly interested.

'By breaking off the trunks of elephants,' said Ranga. Then he said, 'Allow me to take this home, madam.'

'Impossible,' said Kamala. 'Mother, don't let him take it. Tell him he must pay for it.'

'It is broken. Why do you want it?' Savitri asked.

'My little boy will tie a string round its neck, drag it about, and call it his dog. He has been worrying me to get him a dog for a long time.'

Kamala said, 'You won't get it,' and snatched the elephant from his hand.

Now all the dolls and toys were there, over five hundred of them, all in a jumble, like the creations of an eccentric god who had not yet created a world.

Babu had given definite instructions that the arrangement of the platform for the dolls was to be left entirely to him, and they were to do nothing till he returned from school. The girls were impatient. 'It is not a boy's business. This is entirely our affair. Why should we wait for him?'

Babu burst in at five o'clock and asked, looking about impatiently, 'Have you put up the platforms yet?'

'No, we are waiting for you. There is no hurry. Eat your tiffin and come,' said Savitri.

In two minutes he was ready to do his work. The girls jeered: 'Are you a girl to take a hand in the doll business? Go and play cricket. You are a man.'

'Shut up, or I will break all the dolls,' he said, at which the girls screamed. Babu hectored Ranga and sent him spinning about on errands. With about eight narrow long planks, resting on raised supports at the ends, he constructed graduated step-like platforms.

He pulled out of the rolls of bedding in the house all the white bedsheets and spread them on the planks; he disturbed all the objects in the house and confiscated all the kerosene tins and stools, etc. for constructing supports for the planks. He brought in bamboo poles and built a pavilion round the platform. He cut up strips of coloured paper and pasted them round the bamboo poles and covered their nakedness. He filled the whole pavilion with resplendent hangings and decorations. He did his work with concentration, while the two girls sat down and watched him, not daring to make the slightest comment; for at the slightest word Babu barked and menaced the speaker. He gave Ranga no time to regale the company with his jokes, but kept him standing on a high table in order to execute decorations on the pavilion roof.

In a couple of hours a gorgeous setting was ready for the dolls. Babu surveyed his work from a distance and said to his mother, 'You can arrange your knick-knacks now.' He turned to his sisters and said, 'Move carefully within the pavilion. If I find you up to some mischief, tearing the decorations or disturbing the platforms, you will drive me to a desperate act.'

Savitri said to the girls, pointing to the pavilion, 'Could you have made a thing like this? You prated so much when he began the work.' Sumati was a little apologetic and appreciative, but Kamala said, 'If you had given me a little paste and paper I too could have done it. It is not a great feat.' Savitri said, 'Now lift the dolls carefully and arrange them one by one. Sumati, since you are taller than Kamala you will arrange the dolls on the first four platforms, and, Kamala, you will do it on the lower four platforms. Don't break anything, and don't fight.'

In an hour a fantastic world was raised: a world inhabited by all God's creations that the human mind had counted; creatures in all gay colours and absurd proportions and grotesque companies. There were green parrots which stood taller than the elephants beside them; there were horses of yellow and white and green colours dwarfed beside painted brinjals; there was a finger-sized Turkish soldier with not a bit of equipment missing; the fat, round-bellied merchant, wearing a coat on his bare body, squatted there, a picture of contentment, gazing at his cereals before him, unmindful of the company of a curly-tailed dog of porcelain on one side and a grimacing tiger on the other. Here and there out of the company of animals and vegetables and mortals emerged the gods—the great indigo-blue Rama, holding his mighty bow in one hand, and with his spouse, Sita, by his side, their serenity unaffected by the company about them, consisting of a lacquered wooden spoon, a very tiny celluloid doll clothed in a pink saree, a sly fox with a stolen goose in its mouth, and a balancing acrobat in leaf-green breeches; there stood the great Krishna trampling to death the demon serpent Kalinga, undistracted by the leer of a teddy bear which could beat a drum. Mortals and immortals, animals and vegetables, gods and sly foxes, acrobats and bears, warriors and cooking utensils, were all the same here, in this fantastic universe conjured out of coloured paper, wood, and doll-maker's clay.

'It is all very well now, but the trouble will be in putting them all back in their casks carefully after nine days. It is the most tedious work one could think of,' said Savitri.

'Mother, don't dismantle them again. Why can't we let them stay out for ever? It is always so terribly dull when the decorations are torn down and the dolls are returned to the casks.'

Next morning Babu took a look at his work and decided to improve it. It was all very well as far as gum and paper could go, but the lighting was defective. All the illumination that the pavilion got was from the bulb hanging a few yards from it in the hall. He would get his friend Chandru in, and fix up a festoon of ornamental coloured bulbs under the pavilion arch; he would transform the doll pavilion into something unique in the whole of Extension.

He brought Chandru in the afternoon. Chandru was very much his senior, but Babu spent much of his time with him. Chandru was studying in the Intermediate and had a genius for electricity. He had made miniature dynamos, electric bells, and telegraph sets.

Sumati and Kamala were delighted. 'It is going to beat the pavilion in the Police Inspector's house,' they said ecstatically. Chandru worked wonders with a piece of wire and a spanner. In a short while he had created a new circuit with an independent switch. When the switch was put on, a festoon of coloured bulbs twinkled in the archway and two powerful bulbs flooded all the dolls with a bluish light.

'When you switch on in the evening, do it very carefully,' warned Chandru, and left.

It was a great triumph for Babu. He felt very proud of being responsible for the illumination. 'If you like I will ask him to come and add an electric train to the dolls. That will be wonderful,' he said.

At five o'clock the two girls worried Babu to put the lights on. He told them he knew the right time to do it and warned them not to go near the switch. 'Lighting at six,' he said.

'We will be out at six,' they protested, 'inviting people. A lot of our friends will be coming now to invite us to their houses, and we would so love to have the illuminations at once. Please.'

'Will you leave that to me or not? I know when to do it, and I want you to mind your own business now.'

Savitri said to Babu, 'Don't be so strict. You have done everything for their sake, why should you grudge them the light now?'

'All right, at five-thirty,' said Babu.

At five-thirty nearly a dozen visitors had already arrived. Everyone wore bright silks, and sat gazing at the dolls. Finding so many ladies sitting in the hall, Babu hesitated at the door, wondering how he was to reach the switch in the pavilion. He called Sumati and said, 'With the tip of your finger push that small rod to one side, to the left. You must do it very gently.'

Sumati pushed the switch gently, then less gently, and then Babu shed his shyness and dashed to the switch. He rattled it but nothing happened. Not only were the pavilion lights not on, but the usual hall bulbs had also gone out. Babu looked at Sumati and said, 'I knew that if I let you touch it something or the other would happen.' He stood contemplating the new circuit, rattled the switch once more and said that somebody had tampered with it and that he would get at that person soon. Muttering that one couldn't plumb the depth of mischief in girls, he walked out of the hall. Nobody yet realized that anything was wrong because there was good sunlight.

At about seven-thirty the conditions were different. There was no light in the house. Visitors were received in the pale light of a hurricane lantern, and the pavilion was lit by flickering oil-lamps transferred from the *puja* room. The atmosphere was dim and gloomy. The sisters' rage knew no limits. 'Mother, do you understand now why we did not want any boy to come and interfere in our business? As if it wouldn't have been a pretty sight without those lights. Who wanted them anyway? We never asked him to come and fix the lights.'

Babu was in utter despair. Chandru had gone to the cinema and would not be back till nearly ten. And he had no friend who knew anything about electricity.

'Send someone to the electric office', said Savitri.

'Shall I go?' asked Babu.

Savitri hesitated. How could she send him out all alone so late? 'Take Ranga with you.'

And protected by Ranga's company, Babu set out to the electric office in Market Road—a distance of about two miles.

Babu stood before the entrance to the electric office and said to someone, 'There is no light in our house in the South Extension.'

'Go in and tell it to the people you will find there.'

Babu went in and was directed to a room in which three fellows were sitting, smoking and talking. One of them asked him, 'Who are you, boy?'

'The lights are out in our house in the South Extension.'

'Put the switches on,' somebody said, and all three laughed.

Babu felt awkward, but the light had to be set right. He pleaded: 'Can't you do something? We have tried the switches.'

'Probably the fuse has gone. Have you seen if the meter fuses are all right?'

'I haven't. There is nobody in the house.'

'Then, why do you want the lights? If the meter fuse is burnt, it is none of our concern. We will come only when the pole fuse is burnt. Go and see if the meter fuse is all right.'

When Babu reached home he found his father had already arrived. He was in a terrible temper. Ranga's absence had delayed the opening of the garage door and had infuriated him. In that state he entered the house and found it dark. Now failure of electric current was one of the things which completely upset him. He stood in the doorway and roared, 'What is this?' Savitri let the question wither without an answer. The girls did not dare to answer.

'Is everybody in this house dead?' he asked.

Savitri was angered by this, 'What a thing to say on a day like this, and at this hour! I have seen very few who will swear and curse at auspicious times as you do.'

'Then why couldn't you have opened your precious mouth and said what the matter was?'

'There is nothing the matter. You see that there is no current and that there are no lights, and that's all that's the matter.'

'Has anybody gone to the electric office?'

'Babu has gone there.'

'Babu, Babu, a very big man to go.'

This irrational pointless cynicism enraged Savitri, but she remained silent.

Ramani passed in to undress, grumbling all the way. Standing in the dark, he cursed the whole household and all humanity. 'Ranga! Here, Ranga!' he howled in the dark.

'I told you Ranga had gone to the electric office with Babu,' Savitri said.

'Why should everybody go to the electric office? Is Babu to be protected like a girl? Whose arrangement is it?' he raved. 'Bring some light, somebody.'

Savitri sent the hurricane lantern along with Kamala. Kamala set the lamp on the floor while her father looked at her fixedly. 'Here, that's not the place to put the lantern. Do I want illumination for my feet? Bad training, rotten training.' He lifted the lantern and looked about for a place and said, 'Don't you know that when you bring a lantern you have to bring a piece of paper to keep under it? When will you learn all this?'

'Very well, Father,' Kamala said, much intimidated by his manner.

This submissiveness pleased Ramani. He said, 'You must be a good girl, otherwise people won't like you.' He placed the lantern on the window sill. Kamala turned to go and took a few steps. 'Little girl, don't shuffle your feet while walking,' said Ramani.

'Hereafter I will walk properly, Father.'

He was thoroughly pleased with her. He felt he ought to bestow on her some attention—honour her with a little conversation. 'Have you been in the dark all the evening?'

'No, Father, we had current till six o'clock and then—' She hesitated.

'What happened?'

'Babu's friend put up new bulbs for the dolls, and when Babu pressed a switch something happened, and all the lights went out.'

When Babu returned from the electric office he found his father standing in the hall and shouting. As soon as he sighted Babu he asked, 'You blackguard, who asked you to tamper with the electric lights?' Babu stood stunned. 'Don't try to escape by being silent. Are you following your mother's example?'

'No, Father.'

'Who asked you to tamper with the electric lights?'

'I didn't touch anything. I brought in Chandru. He knows all about electricity.'

His father moved towards him and twisted his ear, saying, 'How often have I asked you to keep to your books and mind your business?'

'I'll try to set it right, Father, as soon as Chandru comes home.'

'Who asked you to go near the dolls' business? Are you a girl? Tell me, are you a girl?'

This insistent question was accompanied by violent twists of the ear. Babu's body shook under the grip of his father's hot fingers. 'No, Father, I am not a woman.'

'Then why did you go near the dolls?' He twisted the other ear too. 'Will you do a thing like this again? Tell me!'

In helpless anger Babu remained silent. His father slapped him on the cheek. 'Don't beat me, Father,' he said, and Ramani gave him a few more slaps. At this point Savitri dashed forward to protect Babu. She took him aside, glaring at her husband, who said, 'Leave him alone, he doesn't need your petting.' She felt faint with anger. 'Why do you beat him?' was all that she could ask, and then she burst out crying. At the sight of her tears, Babu could not control himself any longer. He sobbed, 'I didn't know . . . I didn't know it was wrong to add those lights.'

Ramani left, remarking that he was sick of this sentimental show. He came back after a wash. 'Now to dinner. We will manage with the available lights.' Savitri squatted down, her face covered with her hands. 'I see that you are holding a stage-show. I can't stand here and watch you. Are you coming in for food or not? . . . All right, you can please yourself.' He turned and walked to the dining-room calling, 'Has that effeminate boy eaten? Babu, come for your dinner!'

When he was gone, Savitri rose, went to the dark room next to the store, and threw herself on the floor. Later the cook tracked her down there and requested her to take her food, but she refused. The children came to her one by one and tried to coax her. She turned her face to the wall and shut her eyes.

The next morning the cook brought her a tumbler of coffee. She drank it. The cook took back the tumbler from her hand and asked nervously, 'What shall I cook?'

'Don't ask me,' she said.

'There are only a couple of potatoes. We will have to send for some vegetables and also for some mustard.'

'Do the cooking without the vegetables and the mustard or go and ask whoever is keen on having them for money. Don't come and mention them to me.'

The cook went away, his head bent in perplexity. Had anybody heard of cooking without mustard? Presently he got over his despair and began to enjoy the excitement of the situation. A part of his mind said, 'Go on, prepare the sauce and everything without mustard, and with only two potatoes, and if the master raves, tell him I waited long enough and got sufficient notice.' Another part of him said, 'Look here, this is an opportunity provided by the gods. Show them your worth.' In the backyard Ranga was splitting firewood. The cook said to him, 'When the master and the mistress quarrel it is we that suffer.'

'Not many words passed between them last night,' Ranga said. 'All the same, the situation appears to be very serious.'

'It is no business of a wife's to butt in when the father is dealing with his son. It is a bad habit. Only a battered son will grow into a sound man.'

'My wife is also like that,' admitted Ranga. 'I have only to look at my son and she will pounce on me. Last year when I went to the village my first boy did something or other. He skinned our neighbour's son's forehead with a sharp stone, and what should a father do?'

'You will have to run up to the shop now and bring vegetables,' said the cook.

'Certainly, but listen to this now,' persisted Ranga. 'What should a father do? I merely slapped the boy's cheek and he howled as I have never heard anyone howl before, the humbug. And the wife sprang on me from somewhere and hit me on the head with a brass vessel. I have sworn to leave the children alone even if they should be going down a well. Women are terrible.'

The servant-maid who was washing the vessels under the tap looked up and said, 'Wouldn't you like to say so! What do you know of the fire in a mother's belly when her child is suffering?'

The cook said, 'Only once has my wife tried to interfere, and then I nearly broke her bones. She has learnt to leave me alone now. Women must be taught their place.' With this he dismissed the subject and turned to the immediate business on hand. 'I'm responsible for the running of the house today. I'm going to show these people what I can do. The mistress of the house said, "Do anything, don't ask me," and I could well cook a dinner that a dog wouldn't touch. But is it a proper thing to do, after having been in the house for five years? Ranga, it is eight o'clock. Master will be coming for food in about two hours. Run to the Nair's shop and buy onions for two annas, potatoes for four annas, two lemons, coriander for one pie . . .' He knew what his master liked, and he was out to provide it. 'Tell the Nair that he will get the money by and by.'

Kamala went to her mother and asked, 'Mother, are you still angry?' Savitri did not reply.

'Father won't beat Babu again. Please don't go on lying there.' She hated to see her mother in this condition, during the Navaratri of all times. 'Mother, what sweets are we preparing for distributing in the evening?'

'We'll see,' said Savitri.

This reminder pained her. She cursed her own depression of spirits, which threatened to spoil the festival. 'I don't like these quarrels.' Kamala said, and left her. She felt indignant. Her school was closed so that they might remain in the doll-land, visit each other, and eat sweets; but Mother went on lying on the floor with her face to the wall. She traced the whole cause of the trouble to Babu, and threw furious looks at him.

Babu went about without so much as looking at the pavilion. His whole manner declared, 'This is what a man gets for helping in women's business. It is your school after all, not mine, that is closed for this silly festival. Please don't call me for anything.' He was troubled in his mind about his mother. It was he who had received the slaps, so why should she go on lying there as if a great calamity had befallen the house? Perhaps he ought not to have cried like a girl. The memory of his tears hurt him now. He loathed himself and resolved he would never cry again in his life. Before starting for school he went to the dark room and said to his mother, 'Why do you go on lying there? It was only a slight slap that he gave me after all. You make too much of it. I am going to school now.'

'Have you taken your food?' she asked.

'Yes, get up and go about your business.'

Ramani came in for food at his usual hour, before going to the office. He decided to ignore severely his wife's absence. He was

going to show her that sulking would not pay. He demonstrated his
calm indifference by humming a little song, whistling loudly, and by
talking to his daughters, whom he saw in the hall sitting near the
pavilion. He looked at the pavilion with condescending appreciation
and said, 'You must not keep them in such a jumble. You must have
all the animals in one line, all the human beings in another, and so
on. What sweets are you distributing this evening to your friends?'
     The girls looked at each other and said, 'We don't know yet.'
     'Don't you worry, I will buy sweets for two rupees.' He raised
his voice while saying it, which was a message to the dark room:
'Don't imagine that the festival can be spoilt by your sulking.'
     He whistled as he entered the dining-hall. He asked the cook
with a decided cheerfulness what he had prepared, and said 'Very
good' at the end of the list. The cook had prepared the meal very
well because he had the run of the kitchen cupboard, and he had
made unstinting use of rarities like pure ghee and parched coconut,
while Savitri would have allowed him to use only gingerly oil and
no coconut. Ramani ate his food with thorough enjoyment. He
shouted suddenly to his daughters in the hall, 'Kamala, did you eat
plenty of this potato and onion stuff?'
     'Yes, Father.'
     'Did your sister eat plenty of it?'
     'Yes, Father.'
     He then asked, 'Aren't the sauce and the plantain chips excellent?'
This was meant to convey to whomsoever it might concern that no
one was indispensable.
     The cook was very happy, which was due not only to his
master's compliments but also to the fact that the freedom of the
kitchen cupboard had enabled him to check his ten-thirty hunger
with a gulp or two of curd.
     Before leaving for the office Ramani called the girls and said,
'On my way I shall drop in at the electric office and send someone
from there. You will have lights this evening.'
     'Very good, Father. Can those coloured lights remain?'
     'All right, if you want them.'
     'But Babu said that he would ask Chandru to come and remove
them today.'
     'Ask him not to. Tell him that I want them there. When the
electric man comes, ask him to see if they are all right.'
     Just as the engine started Kamala ran to the car and shouted

above its din, 'Don't forget the sweets.'

'Certainly not,' he said, and wished that his engine made less noise so that his words might be heard in the dark room.

At two o'clock the girls began to feel scared. Mother had refused food and was still lying in the dark room. Sumati sat before the pavilion and wondered what to do. Mother's absence gave the house a still and gloomy appearance. Kamala returned to the hall after her tenth visit to the dark room.

'What does she say?' asked Sumati anxiously.

'She wouldn't answer me at all. "What jumper shall I wear this evening?" I asked, but she wouldn't answer.'

'You are a fool,' Sumati said. 'You ask the same question every time.'

'No. I've asked this question only three times. I've already asked her whom to invite this evening, when we are to go out, at what time to switch on the lights, and what sweets we are to have. I can't think of any more questions.'

The children believed that, if their mother could be made to answer some question and get involved in conversation, she could then be persuaded to come out of the dark room. This was a diplomatic step, but Savitri's answers were discouragingly to the point, and when she understood the purpose of the questions she stopped answering them.

'Why don't you go in and try?' suggested Kamala.

'Impossible,' replied Sumati. 'I'm afraid of anyone who lies in a dark room with her face to the wall.' She presently thought out a plan. 'I know how to get Mother out of this fearful state.'

Kamala was delighted, though she did not yet know what Sumati meant to do.

'I may have to go out for a moment,' Sumati said. 'I shall be back very soon. Look after the house and don't tell anyone that I am out.'

The mysterious air which she gave to the whole business thrilled her. Kamala became excited. 'Where are you going?'

Sumati hesitated and asked, 'Will you swear that you won't tell anyone?'

'I never swear. Isn't it enough if I tell you that I will keep the secret?'

'No,' said Sumati, and rose to go.

'I will come with you,' Kamala said.

'No. You will stay here.'

'Then I will go in and tell Mother that you are going out of the house.'

'If you do that, I will not go out and Mother will remain in the dark room for ever.'

Kamala was in despair. 'By our gods I swear I will not tell anyone where you have gone. Now tell me.'

'I am going to Janamma's house to bring her here. Mother will listen to her words.'

Kamala was doubtful. 'But don't you think that family secrets should not be allowed out of the house?'

This was a reasonable objection. Sumati remained thoughtful and said, 'I will merely tell her that she had better come and see Mother at once, and nothing more.'

'Do you think there will be anything wrong in it if you just mention that Babu spoiled the electric lights last night? I don't think if you merely asked her to come she would come.'

Janamma was enjoying a siesta on a mat in the front room of her house. Sumati stood on the edge of the mat silently. She hesitated for a moment whether to wake her up or not; left alone the *mami* would probably sleep till six in the evening. What was to happen to Mother? She leant over and softly called, '*Mami! Mami!*'

'Oh, Sumati! Come on, child, what do you want?'

'*Mami*, you had better come and see Mother at once.'

'What's the matter with her?'

'I don't know.'

'Is she ill?'

'I don't know. Perhaps.'

'What is she doing?'

'She may be sleeping. You must come at once and ask her to get up and bathe and eat.'

'Savitri,' Janamma said, standing over her in the dark room. Savitri opened her eyes. She took a few seconds to identify the visitor.

'Ah! come in, *mami*. Sit down. Bring a mat, Kamala.'

'I don't want a mat. I can sit on the floor. Do you know what the time is? It is past two, yet I see that you have not had your bath or food. What is the matter?'

Savitri said, 'I am not feeling well.'

'Is this where the sick people of your house usually sleep? Look here, child, I am your senior; you can't deceive me. When Sumati came and told me, I knew at once what it was. Don't contradict me.'

'Why did that girl run up to your house and trouble you?'

'What else could the poor thing do? When the elders quarrel it is the children who really suffer.'

'There is no quarrel. I never uttered a single word.'

'That makes it worse. You should either let your words out or feel that everything your husband does is right. As for me, I have never opposed my husband or argued with him at any time in my life. I might have occasionally suggested an alternative, but nothing more. What he does is right. It is a wife's duty to feel so.'

'But suppose, *mami*, he beats the child savagely?' Savitri explained the situation.

'Men are impetuous. One moment they will be all temper and the next all kindness. Men have to bear many worries and burdens, and you must overlook it if they are sometimes unreasonable.'

'I don't mind any treatment personally, but when a child—'

'After all they are better trainers of children than we can be. If they appear sometimes harsh, you may rest assured they will suffer for it later.' Janamma went on in this strain for an hour more, recounting instances of the patience of wives: her own grandmother who slaved cheerfully for her husband who had three concubines at home; her aunt who was beaten every day by her husband and had never uttered a word of protest for fifty years; another friend of her mother's who was prepared to jump into a well if her husband so directed her; and so on, till Savitri gradually began to feel very foolish at the thought of her own resentment, which now seemed very insignificant.

'Get up, Savitri. Bathe, and wear your best saree and take your food. You are a sight.'

Savitri murmured something about still being unwell and not wanting food.

'I am not going to leave this place till I see you out of this room,' Janamma said decisively. Savitri needed only a little more persuasion, and when Janamma said, 'What a foolish, inauspicious thing to do on a Navaratri day!' she felt guilty of a great crime. And then Janamma said, 'You are spoiling the happiness of these two girls. After all, Navaratri only comes once a year.'

Savitri hated herself for her selfish gloom.

'Girls, your mother wants to bathe. See if there is hot water.'

'I'll ask the cook to get it ready in a moment,' Sumati said, and ran out. Kamala ran behind her, almost dancing with joy. She screamed to the cook, 'Hot water! Mother is coming out of the dark room!'

5

IN THE NEW Year the Engladia Insurance Company decided to take a few women probationers into its branches, who were to be trained in office and field work, and later assist the Company in securing insurance policies on female lives. The Company advertised its new scheme with the maximum noise, and the response was very satisfying. A large number of applications poured into Ramani's office. 'We are not anxious to adorn our establishment with so many of the fair sex; we are more anxious to have them in as policyholders,' he observed with a dry official humour to Pereira, his office manager. 'What shall we do with these applications, sir?'

'Call them up for interviews between the fifteenth and twentieth instant. We can fix up the number of interviews per day accordingly.'

'Many of them have to come up from other towns, sir.'

'They must come at their own expense.'

'A nice treat the boss has arranged. You can have your pick for the harem between the fifteenth and the twentieth. Don't miss the office on any account,' he said to Kantaiengar, the accountant.

'Wouldn't it be enough if I kept my head above water with the family I have?' said Kantaiengar. He strongly disapproved of the new scheme. 'Do they want to convert the Company into a brothel?' he asked.

'A delightful idea,' Pereira remarked.

To Ramani, too, the scheme appeared novel and fantastic, but the Head Office at Madras pursued it with zest, and Ramani had to sit up and interview a lot of women between the fifteenth and twentieth of January. Out of the thirty or forty women he interviewed every day he couldn't find one that seemed to him likely to do any work for the Company. Some of them were just girls, educated up to Matriculation or Intermediate, young and bashful and pitifully trying not to give an impression of being too young or bashful. Some were widows, some were prostitutes out to take up a spare-time occupation. Ramani felt that these women would in no way add to the profits of the Company, though they added considerable colour to the office on the days when they were present. Kantaiengar bent over his accounts more than ever, resenting this intrusion and feeling self-conscious; the other clerks looked intimidated. Pereira made a festival of it. He arranged their accommodation in a spare corner of the office and flirted with them elegantly.

Ramani went through the interviews in a state of boredom, irritated with his Head Office for this infliction. He told the applicants after a number of questions that they would hear from him in due course.

On the very last day the last applicant entered. At the sight of her Ramani pushed his chair back and rose—a thing he had not done for anyone till now. Pereira, who followed the applicant in, delicately whisked his moustache with his little finger, and showed that he noticed this difference.

'Sit down, please,' Ramani said, and resumed his seat only after the visitor had sat down. He cleared his throat and asked, looking at a list before him, 'You are Mrs Shanta Bai?'

'Yes,' she said.

He looked at Pereira who was hovering about, and Pereira gave another delicate whisk to his moustache and made an unobtrusive exit. Outside, he winked at Kantaiengar and whispered, 'Of that houri in there we shall see a great deal, and, perhaps, hear also a great deal, yet.'

'Which district do you come from?' asked Ramani.

'I'm from Mangalore,' Shanta Bai said.

'Mangalore?' Ramani echoed, and added as a piece of courtesy, 'Some day I have planned to visit your district.'

'Oh,' she said, 'but it is a pretty dull place. I'm sure you won't like it.'

Ramani felt that he had been snubbed, but presently he appreciated the candour and smartness which had released the snub. He smiled and replied briskly that he was grateful for the timely warning, otherwise he would have wasted some money and time in going to Mangalore. She received the remark without interest. Ramani felt hurt. He suddenly asked himself angrily, 'Who is the master here?' Abruptly he shed all his unofficial humanity and asked severely, 'Do you live with your people there?'

'It is a difficult question, and it will take a lot of answering.'

Ramani once again felt his official manner slowly melting. He gathered himself together and said, 'I see you are married.'

'I am,' she said in a pathetic low voice, and Ramani did not dare put to her further questions about her private life. He said apologetically, 'I'm sorry to trouble you with personal questions, but I have to send a report to the Head Office. If they appoint you they will want to know all about you, whether your family is likely to hinder you in your work—'

'Oh, of that you can assure them. If I had a family to hinder me I shouldn't have come here with my application.'

'I shall want some more details and facts,' implored Ramani. While, till now, all the interviewers had been at his mercy, he found himself, to his distress, at the mercy of this applicant. He liked her pluck. Very seldom, he told himself, did such fair lips utter words without affectation or timidness. He admired her manners very much. She said as if taking pity on him, 'Well, here is my life story. I was born in Mangalore. I was married when I was twelve to a cousin of mine, who was a gambler and a drunkard. When I was eighteen I found he wouldn't change, and so I left him. My parents would not tolerate it and I had to leave home. I had studied up to the fifth form, and now I joined a Mission School. After completing my matriculation, with the help of an aunt, I came to Madras and joined the Women's College. I passed my BA three years ago. Since then I have been drifting about. I have had odd teaching jobs and I have also been companion to a few rich children. On the whole it has been a very great struggle. It is all nonsense to say that women's salvation lies in education. It doesn't improve their lot a bit; it leaves them as badly unemployed as the men.'

'I am really surprised to hear it,' said Ramani, feeling it was time he said something.

'So must anyone be, most of all we ourselves. We struggle hard, get our BA, and think that we are the first of our kind; but what happens? We find that there are thousands like us.'

Her tone was soft and pleasing. Ramani wanted to ask her if she could sing well, but restrained himself and said, 'Yours is a very interesting story. Then I suppose you saw our advertisement?'

'Yes, I did. I sent my application to all the branch offices, and

I was called up for interview only by you.'

'Where were you at the time?'

'I was in Bangalore, staying with some old college friends and looking for work. Now I am here. If you find me suitable for your office, I will be forever grateful to you.'

A thrill went through Ramani's being; this beautiful creature grateful to him! He swelled with importance as he said, 'I will do my best for you. Of course you know the final decision rests with the Head Office. I will do my very best for you.'

'Thank you very much,' she said.

'I must also tell you now,' he began in the orthodox style of the senior to the probationer, 'that an insurance career is not at all an easy one. It is one of the most exacting professions in the world. I've been in it for a decade and a half now . . .' The banalities and autobiography lasted till Pereira came in with a bundle of papers in his hand.

Ramani learnt that she lived in a hotel. That simply would not do. He called in Pereira next day and asked, 'What are you doing with that room in the passage?'

'Nothing very definite, sir. We have thrown in a few old chairs and records.'

'Can't you transfer that lumber to some other place, and make it habitable? Mrs Shanta Bai is staying in some dirty hotel; why shouldn't we give her that room till she gets settled in this place? There is no harm in it.'

'Oh, none whatever, sir.'

'It must be rather awkward for a lady to live in a hotel, you see.'

'You are right, sir. No decent hotel in the whole town. I will have the lumber turned out and stocked somewhere else. But the records? They are rather important. What about keeping them here?'

'Here?' Ramani didn't like the idea of anything intruding in his room. 'Put them away in some other place.'

'All right, sir. You will want the room ready tomorrow?'

'Yes, as soon as you can attend to it, thank you.'

Outside, Pereira told Kantaiengar, 'I shall have to fix up a nuptial chamber in the office, Iengar.'

'What is he driving at? It is absurd. This will be the talk of the town.'

'I am sure it will bring more people into the office.'

The other members of the staff also resented this feminine intrusion because a lot of lumber was brought into their room; and the old office watchman resented it because the passage room had been for years his home.

Ramani asked at home, 'What happened to the spare cot we had?'

'Krishnier's people borrowed it months ago when he was down with rheumatism, and they have not returned it.'

'Send for it. I want it for the office. We are going to fit up a guest's room.'

'What for?'

'We get a lot of outsiders; some important people come to us on business now and then, and we have to provide them with some decent accommodation.'

'If it is for the office, buy a cot with your office money. Why should we give ours?' She dared to suggest this amendment because it was one of his good-humoured evenings.

'But look here, my girl. If it comes to that, everything in this house, including the grain in the storeroom, belongs to the office, bought with the office money, you know.' She argued elaborately that they were not living on the charity of the Company, and declined to lend the cot. He pleaded and cajoled her. He liked to plead and cajole this evening. He said, 'I shall want it only for a time. I will return it as soon as we buy new furniture. There is no time now. An important guest is coming tomorrow. I shall also want your bench, a chair, and one or two vessels.'

'Oh, you want everything we have in the house.' The teakwood bench was her favourite piece of furniture. 'If you take away the bench, what am I to sleep on in the afternoons?'

'Oh, I will get you velvet couches, my dear,' he said, bringing his hands together in a romantic gesture. 'There is nothing that I wouldn't buy for you. Only say it.' It made her very happy.

The Head Office confirmed her appointment nearly a week later. Ramani's recommendation was so strong that the Head Office had no choice in the matter. Shanta Bai was to be on probation for six months, provided she did personal canvassing worth ten thousand rupees within the first two months (if she failed she was to be sent away and the next applicant on the list called up and given a chance). During the probationary period she was to receive a stipend of sixty rupees a month; after that she was to have a starting salary of a hundred and fifty rupees a month, with commission, and work as the chief woman agent for the branch.

On the day the confirmation came, Ramani sent for Shanta Bai and dramatically pushed the letter before her. He tried to look casual and unconcerned. He went through some papers while she read it. Though pretending to look at the letters he was secretly noting how artistic her chequered jumper was, and awaited eagerly her thanks for all his trouble.

'I am rather disappointed,' she said.

Ramani looked up, startled.

She said, 'I thought the starting salary would be two hundred.' She remained thoughtful for a moment and added, 'I had no business to imagine it because the advertisement never mentioned the amount.'

'What, is this girl going to reject the job for the sake of fifty rupees?' Ramani thought for a harrowing moment, and rushed to console her. 'You seem to overlook the fact that you will be drawing two hundred in two years. Please read carefully that increment clause. Besides, you will be getting your commission over your actual salary.'

'Well, I take your word for it. I will do whatever you advise me to do.'

He was pleased with the importance she gave him, and sat reflecting for a moment. How well a simple voile saree sat on her! Why couldn't one's wife dress as attractively?

Shanta Bai said, 'I thought that if I had a start of two hundred I could buy a tiny Baby Austin for myself.' She added with a sentimental sigh, 'But I suppose all one's dreams can never come true.'

'I am sure your commission on your personal work will enable you to have even a big Austin with a driver and all. Shall I wire to the Head Office that you accept the terms and ask them to post the agreement immediately?'

'As you please,' she said.

Such an exquisite complexion came only from Mangalore, Ramani thought; you could see the blood coursing in her veins. He said aloud, 'I will see if the probationary period cannot be cut down, and if the stipend cannot be put up a bit. But that's all by and by.

You may rest assured that your interests will have the best support and protection possible.'

'Excellent! When do I start work?'

'Tomorrow. Now you can go "home" if you like.' She rose and went out. Ramani looked after her and meditated. What a delightful perfume even after she was gone! What an impotent, boorish beggar that husband must be who couldn't hold this fair creature! What an innovation it would be to have a beauty on the office staff! The town was sure to talk about it. He hoped her presence wouldn't be too upsetting for the office staff to go on with their usual work: they must get used to it. It was all nonsense to keep men and women separate in water-tight compartments; women were as good as men and must be treated accordingly. He told Pereira, 'The Head Office has confirmed the lady's appointment.'

'It is pleasing news,' Pereira said.

'She is starting work tomorrow. I want you to arrange a table, etcetera, for her somewhere. Where are we to put her up?'

Pereira reflected for a moment and said, 'There is plenty of space in the office. We can make some kind of arrangement, sir.'

He had a vision of Kantaiengar: wouldn't it give him fits if he heard this? Ramani asked. 'Are you sure it wouldn't be an inconvenience?'

'Not at all. We are only a dozen in that large hall.' He paused, gave an elegant whisk to his moustache, and asked, 'Are we to put up a screen?'

'Is it necessary?'

'I do not know, sir, but I thought that the lady might want it.'

'Hm! You can get the screen if you feel that she might be a distraction to the typists.' He laughed as well as his official dignity would permit him.

Outside Pereira said to Kantaiengar, 'Clean up your table and go to that corner. I will give you another table.'

'What do you mean?'

'Orders from the boss. The fairy is taking her seat here. She is to be given the best place, and so you have to quit.'

'This is atrocious. I shall resign.'

'And leave your family on the streets, I suppose?'

'What does he mean by it?'

'Women and children first, my dear fellow. A rugged piece of timber like you can be kept anywhere, but wouldn't a fresh rose need a lot of air, light, and this large table, to keep it alive?'

Kantaiengar was wild. 'Isn't it enough that he has dumped all that lumber here, making the place unsightly and choking, that he should be bringing in this thing now?'

'The two are hardly alike except to your prejudiced mind. And that reminds me, we shall have to cover the lumber-heap with a Persian carpet when madam sits here.'

'What I can't understand is why he is thrusting her here. Why can't he have her in his room, on his lap if he likes?'

'All in due course. Meanwhile, may I tell you that the boss has asked me to arrange your chair to face a wall? He said, "Take care that the accountant does not lose himself in a trance and fail to add and subtract. Let his chair be arranged to face a wall."'

'Does he take me for a woman-hunter like himself? Remember that if only I cared for these things—'

'You could have had a hundred women at your beck and call? Likely too . . . Do you very much wish to stay where you are and not to be disturbed?'

'I will resign this job before I move out of this place,' said Kantaiengar furiously.

'We can't afford to lose you. So I will tell the boss not to worry you, if you promise you won't scowl at her when she is here. I don't see why you should be so sour. Personally, I rather welcome her; something to relieve this drabness, you know. But it will be a difficult job, all the same, for me to see that the typists and others do their work. The boss said, "Keep an eye on the typists, and on the accountant."'

6

ONE EVENING WHILE returning home from the Club, Ramani passed his office in Race Course Road, and had an impulse to stop his car and go in. He told himself that it would be improper, and passed on; but the car had hardly run a few yards when he told himself that he ought to inspect his office periodically at nights. That would make the watchman more alert. He had also to see if the safe and the file-chest were locked properly. One read in the papers of all sorts of thefts and rifling in the offices. By this time his car had nearly reached the junction of the Race Course Road with Market Road. He turned the car round, and drove towards his office.

He found the watchman sleeping soundly at the foot of the staircase. Ramani stood over him, musing indignantly: 'Fast asleep at eight o'clock! I will speak to Pereira about it tomorrow.' He climbed the stairs. He saw a light in the glass ventilator above the door of the room in the passage. He stood-gazing at it for a moment and then passed into his office room. He switched on the lights, went over to the file-chest and the safe, and tugged at their locks solemnly. He then wondered what to do. His inspection was over. He pulled out his drawer and idly looked at some of the envelopes in it; he spent some time pulling the pins out of the cushion and pushing them back; he examined the nibs of the pens on the table, went over to the chest and safe, tugged at their locks again, switched off the lights and came out of the room. He descended two steps, saying that he must really be hurrying away: why keep Savitri and the servants waiting unnecessarily? He paused suddenly, went up the two steps again, and gave a couple of gentle knocks on the door of the passage room.

'Who is that?'

Ramani had a momentary confusion as to who he should say he was. He said, 'Oh, don't disturb yourself. On my way home, I just remembered something and dropped in for a moment.'

Shanta Bai recognized his voice and opened the door. 'I was rather terrified, you know. Wondered if someone had come to abduct me.'

'Abduct you?' Ramani gave a slight inept laugh. 'I just began to doubt if I had locked the safe in the evening. Rather worrying, you see, such doubts. It brings to one's mind all the accounts of thefts and safe-breaking that one reads in the papers. A troublesome business having such a responsibility on one's head.'

'It must be awful. If anything goes wrong, I suppose you will be taken to task?'

'I shall be sent to jail. Not a paper must be lost, not an anna must escape the accounts.'

She listened to him with her eyes sparkling in the light of the bulb hanging in the passage. She was dressed in a white saree, and had jasmine in her hair. She asked abruptly, 'Why do you stand in the passage? Won't you step in?'

'I thought you might think it a bit unconventional.'

'Oh, I love unconventional things,' she said. 'Otherwise I shouldn't be here, but nursing children and cooking for a husband. Come in, come in, see how I have made a home for myself.'

Ramani stepped in, pleasantly excited, marvelling at Shanta Bai's ability to adapt herself. How meekly she accepted his official aloofness which he was of late practising in the office, and how warmly she now responded to a little friendliness! She had put up a few printed *khaddar* hangings on the doors and windows, a few group photos of her college days on the wall, a flowery counterpane on her bed, and a silk cushion on the chair. The door of an antechamber was covered with a curtain. 'She does her toilet and dressing in there,' Ramani thought with an inexplicable thrill. He looked about and exclaimed, 'What a transformation!'

'Please sit down.'

'Not when a lady is standing,' Ramani said.

'All right,' she said, and went over to her cot and sat on her counterpane. He sat down on the teakwood bench. She threw up her arms and stretched them, saying, 'My joints are becoming stiff. I think I am getting old.'

Ramani treated this remark as a great joke and laughed.

'Do you mind if I don't sit erect?' she asked.

'Oh, not at all, make yourself comfortable.'

She reclined on her pillows, stretched her legs, and said, 'I can't sit up. Even in my college days I used to lie in bed and study all night.'

Ramani's eyes followed every minute movement of her limbs. She tossed her head now and then, slightly pouted her lips, and raised her brow. Ramani felt now that his stiff aloofness with her during the office hours was a piece of cruelty and that some explanation was due to her: 'I have just remembered to tell you—if you have found me a little different in the office, please don't be hurt.'

'Oh no. Nothing can hurt me. In the office you are the chief, and now—'

'Your brother, if you will permit me to say so.'

'You have my fullest consent to think of me as your sister.'

'Oh, it is very good of you. In the office I don't want anyone to notice any difference. That's why I try not to give them any impression that my treatment is different—' He fumbled on elaborately.

After conferring on him the privilege of brotherhood, she grew intimate in her talk. The account of her life with her harsh husband was really moving. Ramani listened for a second time, with absorbing interest, to her account of her struggles after leaving home. He said that men deserved to be whipped when she hinted at a couple of attempts on her honour. He was in complete agreement with her philosophy of life (which cropped up at the end of every ten minutes thus: 'As for me life is . . .' something or other, some simple affair like Living Today and Letting Tomorrow Take Care of Itself or Honour being the One Important Possession, and so forth). He had known all these himself, but they had a new value for him when they issued from those fair lips. He assured her of his very best help when she told him what she hoped to achieve in the services of the Company. And bang into all this philosophy, autobiography, and hopes came the office clock's chime.

'It can't be ten!' he exclaimed, pulling out his watch. 'I thought it was just eight-thirty or nine.' He rose with a sigh.

'If I had had the slightest idea you were coming, I would have kept some food for you,' she said. 'It is very wrong of me to have kept you so long and to turn you out now on an empty stomach.'

She went down the stairs, and walked up to the car to see him off. He started the car and suddenly asked, 'Would you like a drive?'

'Now?'

'Yes, why not?'

'Aren't you hungry?'

He made a noise deprecating the idea of hunger, and suggested that a drive around with his sister would be more than food to him.

'No, I will really not trouble you now. I should have loved a drive if you had eaten something.'

He was deeply touched by her consideration and said: 'I had a very heavy tiffin at the Club. I don't think I can eat anything tonight.'

'Why have you stopped the engine?'

'The car won't start.'

'Really? What is wrong?'

'It needs another passenger besides myself to make it go,' he said.

She laughed at the joke and asked him if he was going to wait there all night till he could get a passenger. Yes, he said, with fervour, even if it was going to keep him there all night; and added, 'I suggest that we go round Race Course Road, and then, if you don't mind, to the river. Have you ever seen it at night?'

'Is it a very lovely sight?'

'Come and see it for yourself,' he said.

'You don't mind the trouble?'

'Don't ask ridiculous questions.'

She went up to lock her room. Ramani took out his handkerchief, dusted the seat lightly, got down, and waited for her. She came back to the car, and opened the door of the back seat. 'No, not there,' he said. 'Don't you see that the door is open here?'

'I prefer the back seat,' she said.

'You do, I am sure, but the engine won't start unless there are two passengers in the front seat. You are not afraid of me, are you?'

'Certainly not,' she said, and climbed in. He sat beside her and drove the car. The engine heaved, sputtered, and settled into a steady rattle, and above it she said, 'Aren't the stars in the sky beautiful? How delightful the night air is when it rushes on one's face!' She tossed her head and took a deep breath.

'Yes, yes,' he agreed with her, and asked, 'Are you fond of moonlit nights or dark nights?' feeling that he wanted to express something poetic himself.

At two o'clock he went home. He drove the car into the garage with as little noise as possible, opening the gate and then the garage door himself. He felt rather irritated afterwards, when he walked back into the house from the garage. 'I am not a thief getting into a house,' he said to himself, and loudly knocked on the door, calling 'Savitri, Savitri!' a dozen times before she could get up from her bed and come to the door.

She was still half-asleep as she followed him to his room and asked, 'Have you dined?' He threw an angry look at her drooping, nodding figure and said: 'I suppose you are too sleepy to serve me. You need not have sent the cook away. Sometimes a man may have to return home late. One can't always be rushing back, thinking of the dinner. Why do you send the cook away at night? You give the servants unheard-of privileges.'

Savitri shook off her sleep, went to the kitchen, and switched on the light.

Ramani was beginning to feel worried. Shanta Bai had been in the office now for a month and yet she exhibited no aptitude for canvassing work. The Head Office seemed to be fanatical in regard to the clause laying down the minimum of work to be done in the first two months. They had just sent a reminder. If Shanta Bai did not complete the amount in a month, she would have to be dismissed. Ramani looked down the list and noted that there was a Sharadamma of Gavipuram next to her. Would *she* have to be called up? It was a distasteful thought. When Pereira next came into the room Ramani said, 'Will you please ask the lady probationer to come in a moment?'

Shanta Bai came in. 'Please sit down,' Ramani said. 'You have been here for a month now. Do you feel you will be able to do ten thousand rupees' worth of canvassing in another month?'

'I hope to. Otherwise I suppose I shall be turned out?'

'It is a pretty rotten condition, I agree, but the Head Office sticks to it. Ten thousand rupees for two months is not very high either. I am rather worried because I have just received a reminder. I would advise you to reduce your office work and go about with the chief canvassing agent a little more. I will ask the office to relieve you of some portion of the work you are at present doing. That's all, thank you.'

She went to her table with bent head. Pereira followed her and asked, 'A troublesome interview?'

'A reminder from the HO.' She told him about it. 'What a horrid business to get the women of this town to insure! They simply won't do it. Either they do it or I walk out of the office.'

'If I may make a humble suggestion, madam, you may succeed better if you see the men themselves and persuade them to insure their wives.'

She turned over a few papers piled upon her table and said, 'Mr Kantaiengar, here are some accounts papers, I am sure brought by mistake. Please take them away.'

'Madam, from today you will try to learn something of the accounts too. Will you kindly check the figures in those papers?'

'I will do nothing of the kind. The boss said he would relieve me of office work for some time.'

'I was instructed yesterday to put you through the accounts. You can do what you please. Those are merely accounts of the daily agency reports. If you care to check the figures, it will be for your own benefit. Otherwise you can send the papers back to me tomorrow, but till tomorrow they will have to be with you, whether you look at them or not. I can't disobey the instructions that I have received. Thank you.'

'What a wicked ruffian!' Shanta Bai whispered to Pereira.

On the way home from the Club, Ramani halted at the office. This was threatening to become a daily habit. It was almost impossible to go home direct from the Club. Even the Club clung to him as a habit, perhaps as a necessity too—one had to leave the office premises at the closing of the day. At the Club he cut short his bridge a great deal nowadays, and never went near the billiard table. He left the Club early, put in a little unofficial attendance at the office, gave Shanta Bai a drive, and went home at ten at night.

Shanta Bai was in a bad mood today. The afternoon's interview had upset her. 'What a riddance it will be for you in a few weeks,' she said as soon as he came in and took a seat. She compressed her lips and jerked her head in the perfect Garbo manner: the temperamental heroine and the impending doom. Ramani had to be the soothing lover. He went near her and patted her shoulder gently. Shanta Bai refused to be comforted. She revelled in the vision of a blasted future. 'I know my fate, and I will not shirk it.' Ramani told her that he would somehow persuade the Head Office to cancel the troublesome clause. 'Don't be absurd,' she said. 'I won't have you do anything special for me.'

She freed herself from his arms and paced the room up and down. 'You shan't make yourself the laughing stock of the Company,' she said. She was steadily, definitely, methodically working herself up to a breakdown. Ramani knew it. He had already experienced it twice. She would start thus, and then sit with her face on the pillow, slight tremors shaking her back. In a moment she would rise, draw herself up, jerk her head and laugh at herself and at her moods. Such moments were very painful to Ramani. More than the breakdown, the subsequent heroic effort to master it stirred him deeply. He had never seen such things before; his wife's moods were different. She knew only one thing, a crude sulking in the dark room. She never made an effort to conquer her moods; that was why, he felt, women must be educated; it made all the difference. He felt unhappy at thinking disparagingly of his wife. Poor girl, she did her best to keep him happy and the home running. He told himself that he was not criticizing her but only implying that with a little education she might have been even better.

Shanta Bai went through her breakdown act and was just about to jerk her head and laugh at herself; Ramani rushed at her, locked her in his arms, and implored her to be courageous. She released herself from his arms and said: 'Tonight I feel like pacing the whole earth up and down. I won't sleep. I feel like roaming all over the town and the whole length of the river. I will laugh and dance. That's my philosophy of life. Laugh, clown, laugh—it was a film I saw years ago. Laugh, clown, laugh, though your heart be torn,' she said, unable to quote the exact words of the film. She asked suddenly, 'Shall we go to a picture tonight?' This was the first time she had suggested this, and Ramani sat more or less stunned. 'I said shall we go to a picture tonight?' she repeated with emphasis.

'Tonight?' Ramani asked in weak apprehension. There were already rumours abroad, and now to be seen together in public . . .

'Tonight. Answer in a word, yes or no.'

'Certainly, certainly,' Ramani said. 'I was just wondering what the picture was and if it was worth a visit. What is the picture tonight?'

'Whatever it is, I must see a picture tonight. If you are not coming with me, I am going alone. If you are coming, I am prepared to share my food with you.' She added, 'Perhaps you don't wish to be seen in public with me; perhaps your wife will perhaps—' All of which suggestions he indignantly repudi asserted with much bravado that he cared not a straw for public opinion, and that his wife was not the sort to question him or dictate to him.

He dallied till nine-thirty, when the picture should have started, so that he might make an unobtrusive entry into a dark hall and take his seat inconspicuously.

When they reached the theatre, she looked at the posters and exclaimed, 'A wretched Indian film! I'd have given my life to see a Garbo or Dietrich now.'

'What shall we do?'

'Anything is better than nothing.' She sat in the dark hall beside him, whispering criticisms of the picture before her: a stirring episode from the *Ramayana*, in which the giant monkey god set fire to Lanka . . .

'What rubbish the whole thing is!' she said. 'Our people can't produce a decent film. Bad photography, awful acting, ugly faces. Till our film producers give up mythological nonsense there is no salvation for our films . . . Let us get out. I can't stand this any more.'

Ramani followed her out. In the car she asked, 'Shall we go to the river?'

'Yes,' Ramani said.

'It is only ten. Let us sit on the bank and stay there till the dawn,' she said, and laughed as if she had uttered a huge joke.

Ramani laughed faithfully and drove the car towards the river. She sat nestling close to him as he drove, and said suddenly, 'Let us drive round the town once and then go to the river.' Ramani stopped, reversed, and drove the car into the town and about the streets. 'I'm rather mad tonight,' she said. 'I hope you don't mind it.'

'Not at all,' he said.

After driving the car along the principal thoroughfares of the town Ramani asked, 'What shall we do now?'

'To the river, to the river. You have a mad woman beside you tonight.' After about an hour at the river she suggested going back to her room. 'I can't sleep tonight,' she said as soon as she got down at Race Course Road. 'Would you care to step in? Shall we sit up and chat till dawn?'

'With pleasure,' Ramani said, and followed her into her room.

He returned home at five o'clock next morning. Savitri was in the veranda, watching the milkman milk the cow. When Ramani came up the veranda steps, she said, 'I was very anxious all night.'

'Oh?' he said.

'I wish you had sent word or something. Where have you been?'

'Can't you wait?' he cut in petulantly. 'Do you want me to stand at the street door and shout my explanation?' Savitri stepped aside and let him pass into the house.

She stood looking at the milkman, listening to the sound of milk squirting into the pail. Suddenly the sound ceased: the milkman looked up and asked, 'Master seems to have gone out very early today.' It stirred a disturbance in her mind. She tried to kill the question with her silence, but the milkman would not be silenced. He repeated, 'Master seems—'

Savitri replied, 'Yes. He had to go out very early in the morning to see someone.'

At about eight o'clock she took a tumbler of coffee and made it an excuse to meet her husband in his room. He was just back from a bath and was combing his hair. He saw her in the mirror but pretended not to have seen her. She saw his face in the mirror and doubted if any effort at peacemaking would be possible now. She hesitated whether she should place the coffee on the table and go away or should venture to ask a question. For the last few days disturbing doubts and a dull resentment had been gathering in her mind, and she hated herself for it. She felt angry with him and unhappy at being angry. It sapped all her energy. She would have given anything to lighten her mind of its burdens and to be able to think of her husband without suspicion. Just a word from him would do, just an unangry word; even a lie, a soothing lie. Unpleasant thoughts seemed to corrode her soul.

She set the tumbler on the table, threw a glance at the person engaged in hairdressing so intensely, and decided that it would be better to suffer in silence than to venture a question. She started out, turned once again at the threshold, caught him looking at her with a side glance. 'Shall I go out?' she asked, turning to him. Ramani pretended to be absorbed in his own thoughts. She said, 'I have put the tumbler on the table,' and went out. She saw the maidservant standing uncertainly about. 'Why are you idling there?' Savitri asked. 'Perhaps you are manoeuvring to ask for something or other, that you want the afternoon off and so on. If you want to absent yourself in the afternoon you had better absent yourself for ever. I can get scores of persons like you.'

'Why do you shout at me, my lady? What have I done?'

'I will shout as I please. You are not the person to question me. If you don't like it, you had better get out.'

'Madam knows only one thing, and that is saying "Get out" for everything. I was only waiting to ask if I may go home.'

'So soon! Have you done all your work?'

'Yes, madam.'

'Scrubbed the back yard?'

'Yes, madam.'

'Swept the whole house? Washed all the vessels? Have you removed the cow dung near the gate?'

'Yes, madam, I have done everything.'

'Why are you in such a hurry to finish your work and go home? Home, home; always dying to return home. Dust and grime everywhere, at every corner. Now listen to this. You shall not go home before ten from now on, whether you have work or not.

Understand me? If you don't like it, you can get out this moment.'

The servant was an old woman who had done a few years of service in the house and so knew her mistress's moods. Savitri went in and found everything in the kitchen irritating. 'Is this how you have been taught to slice brinjal?' she asked, throwing a fiery glance at the cook.

'The brinjals were rather large—' began the cook.

'Shut up, and don't try to invent an excuse for every blunder you commit! A set of useless, blundering, wasteful parasites in this house!'

Savitri went and sat on a carpet in the hall. Sumati came out of her little study. 'Why are you sitting down, Mother?' she asked.

'Why not? When there was the bench I could just rest on it for a moment when I felt tired; and now I have to squat down on the floor every time. The bench is gone. Nothing remains in this house. Everything has to be sent away to the office. Go and tell your father that I want the bench back immediately. He is in his room. Go and tell him.'

Sumati stood hesitating, and suggested weakly, 'Why don't you tell him that yourself, Mother? I'm afraid . . .'

'Afraid! Everybody is afraid of him.'

When he sat down for his dinner before going to the office she hovered about, attending mechanically. He ate very quietly, fixedly looking down at the rice on his leaf. She felt a sudden pity for him; there was something pathetic in the quietness with which he had accepted the ill-cut brinjals. Possibly Gangu might have lied. It might be nothing more than a scandal. The poor man was perhaps poring over account-books all night, and now without a moment's rest he would have to be rushing back once again in the hot day after heavy food. All for whose sake? She despised herself for listening to gossip. After all these years of life together, this was not the way to judge him. She was not going to let her foul mind spoil their life. She resolved not to ask him about the bench. She resolved to re-establish peace. She asked: 'Wouldn't you like a little more rice for the curd?'

'No,' he said.

She said, 'Babu has scored sixty marks out of one hundred in arithmetic. He stands fourth in his class this term.'

He displayed no enthusiasm over this news. She said again: 'I had a letter from my sister in Rangoon yesterday. All are well there.

It seems her husband's appointment was recently confirmed. And what do you think? My sister says that she is expecting her eighth child in a few months.'

'So your sister has gone far ahead of you?' he remarked hollowly.

Savitri succeeded in making a few sounds like laughter. Though her bitterness was now gone, she felt still a little uneasy. What would she not have given to be coaxed and cajoled a little now! All the same it was not so bad as it had been a few moments before.

When he was ready for the office she met him at the veranda steps. How well he looked in his silk suit! It was sheer envy that must have made Gangu and the rest talk scandal about him, they with their husbands all crooked and paunchy. She mustered up all her strength and asked, 'Will you be late tonight too?' He frowned at her without a reply. She at once said apologetically, 'I didn't mean to . . .'

'I can't be answering idiotic questions. You think I am just as old as Babu?' He strode furiously towards the garage.

Gangu flitted in in the afternoon. Savitri was lying on the carpet in the hall reading her magazine.

'What has happened to the bench which used to be here all these days? You are lying on the floor,' asked Gangu, and unwittingly started once again the very thoughts that Savitri had been at pains to smother since the morning.

'Something or other has happened to it,' Savitri said, discouraging all further reference to the subject.

Gangu said, 'I just asked because the hall looks so bare without it. I felt perfectly disgusted with the home, and so threw everything up and came out. Sometimes I do get into such a mood, you know.'

'I suppose you have finished the tiffin for the afternoon?'

'That's just what I haven't done. I said to my husband when he started for the school, "Don't expect any tiffin this evening when you come back from school. I would advise you to fill your stomach in a hotel."'

'What about the rest at home?'

'If he does not bring a packet for me and the children I will drive him out once again. He knows it.'

'Well, what is the news in the town?' asked Savitri.

'Nothing very special. Did you see the Tamil picture they are showing at the Palace? There are some good songs in it, but I could have played that heroine better. I will do it some day just wait . . . I think your husband went to the picture.'

'What!'

'He was sitting two or three chairs off mine.'

'So it was not the account-books that he had been poring over all night,' Savitri thought.

'Didn't you know?' Gangu asked.

'I don't usually bother him with questions as to his whereabouts.'

'But didn't he tell you that he had been to the picture?'

'He doesn't tell me anything unless I ask him; and he was so terribly busy the whole morning that I couldn't get a word with him.'

Savitri wanted all further talk about her husband to cease now, and switched on to, 'I heard that you were about to make records of some of your songs.'

'Yes, one of my husband's friends knows a person who knows some of the gramophone people in Madras. It is well under way. But it is all a secret yet.'

Savitri thought: so he had not been poring over accounts all night. Perhaps he had to go out and meet someone in the theatre. Gangu said unasked, 'Don't think I am gossiping, but there was another person with him; perhaps it is that person about whom people are talking all this nonsense. I didn't want to tell you, but I thought you might as well know, because what harm is there?'

Savitri sat gazing on the floor; she couldn't speak; she felt feverish. Gangu apologized. 'You mustn't let it affect you so much. I wouldn't have mentioned it if I had known you would be so foolish.'

Savitri still said nothing. The silence, to a person unaccustomed to it like Gangu, was very uncomfortable. She made a feeble effort to divert Savitri's thoughts by talking about the picture, its merits and demerits. Savitri did not lift her eyes from the floor. It was a monologue for Gangu. Savitri asked suddenly, 'What was she like?'

'Who? the heroine? They should have . . .'

'Not your heroine of the picture, but the real one.'

'Forget her. Don't brood over it like a fool. There can't be anything in it.'

'I must know what she was like. I never asked you to tell me about her. You have done it. Tell me everything. I must know!'

'There is nothing for you to know, that's all.'

'What was she like?'

'She is an old woman, very ugly, and no man would go near her.'

Savitri broke down. 'I know you are lying. She can't be old. Perhaps I am old and ugly. How can I help it? I have borne children and slaved for the house.'

'No, no, you are a darling. You are beautiful. You aren't old.'

Savitri said, 'I am middle-aged, old-fashioned, plain. How can I help it? She must be young and pretty. He has not been coming home before midnight for weeks. And yesterday he didn't come home at all; came only in the morning, and wouldn't talk to me.' She said, blowing her nose, 'He is indifferent even to the children. Tell me everything!'

Gangu wept a little herself and said, clearing her throat: 'I won't hide anything from you. They didn't stay very long in the theatre. She said something and both of them went out at ten o'clock.'

'And he couldn't come back home before the morning,' added Savitri.

She asked, 'Were they sitting very close to each other?'

'Yes.'

'Is she not young and better-looking than I am?'

'Her skin is white, but who cannot make herself up to look younger?'

Savitri saw herself in the mirror in the evening. Her eyes were swollen, her nose was red. The girls came home from school. Kamala cried, 'Mother, your eyes are very red. Have you been crying?'

'No. Why should I cry? I must have touched my eyes with the fingers I used for picking chillies, and I have a bad cold too.'

'Oh, I thought you had been crying, and I was so terrified, you know. I thought Father must have scolded you or something like that. I do hate Father scolding you, because you become so unhappy.'

'Why should your father scold me? He is so good. He only scolds when I do something wrong. How can one teach what is right without scolding?'

'That's what our teacher says. If she raps us on the knuckles when the arithmetic goes wrong and we cry out, she says nothing can be corrected without punishment. I am sure it is all a lie. Can't a sum be set right without a rap on the knuckles?'

'Mother, she gets thrashed every day at school,' said Sumati.

'It's a lie. It is she who gets thrashed every day. Today our teacher sent me out to fetch a piece of chalk, and I saw Sumati in her class standing, and somebody said that her teacher had made her stand the whole period.'

'It is a lie, Mother!' screamed Sumati. 'I was standing because our teacher had asked me to give a dictation to the class. I'm not like you,' she said, turning to Kamala.

They settled their differences very soon and went out to play. Babu came in from school. 'Mother, I won't touch the tiffin unless you promise to give me my cricket fee tomorrow. I must give four annas to the captain.'

'All right. I will give you the money.'

'And I want a rough notebook tomorrow.'

'You bought one only four days ago.'

'Yes. It is all filled. Can't we buy even rough notebooks liberally? There is my friend Gopal. His people buy him one dozen notebooks every month, and here you grumble at buying even two.'

After Babu left for the cricket ground, Savitri went to the mirror and scrutinized herself in it once again. The swelling of the eyes had subsided a little now. She smoothed out her hair with her fingers, turned her head, and looked at herself sideways. 'What is she like?' she asked herself. 'I'm not very bad, am I? Perhaps she is very good-looking. What is wrong with my face? These strumpets with their powder and paint! Has she as clear a skin as mine without her paints?' She remembered her husband's figure in the morning as he was dressed for the office. 'Perhaps I'm not good enough for him. Let me admit my complexion has become rather sooty, and these dark rings under the eyes. I am getting careless about my hair, and braid it anyhow; it's hardly his fault if he can't like my appearance very much.'

She applied a little scented oil to her hair, and combed it with great care. She braided and coiled it very neatly. She washed her face with soap and water, and applied very lightly a little face-powder. She had given up using face-powder and scented oil years ago. She stood before the mirror, applied a little perfumed paste between her eyebrows and pressed a very elegant pinch of vermilion on it, and trimmed its edges with her little finger to make it perfectly round. He always liked the forehead marking to be a little large. She stood close to the mirror, with her nose almost touching the glass. She was more or less satisfied with her appearance, except for two stray strands of grey hair which she had just discovered; she smoothed them out and tucked them cunningly into an under-layer. The glass clouded with the moisture of her breath; she wiped the moisture and saw herself once again. Perhaps the other one's cheeks were rosy, and her hair thicker and longer. 'My cheeks, too, were rosy and my hair came down to my hips before I had my two miscarriages and three childbirths . . .' She went out into the garden and plucked some jasmine, and red flowers, strung them together, and placed them in a curve on the coil at the back of her head—he always liked the red flowers to be interspersed with the white jasmine, and always admired the curved arrangement.

She wondered for a moment if she should dress herself in a new saree from the box; he always liked to see her in the blue one. But that might be too much. She felt a little shy to dress so well for the home.

The children had finished their dinner. They stood round and admired her and asked if she had been to a marriage-house. 'You smell lovely, Mother,' Kamala said.

'I don't like scents,' Babu said.

'Won't you coil my hair on my head like yours?' Kamala asked.

'I don't like this tight coiling,' Babu said, 'it makes the neck very ugly. I like the hair to fall on the ears a little.'

'You can ask your wife to braid her hair loose,' Savitri said.

'Don't talk rubbish, Mother. I am never going to marry.'

When the children went away for their study and sleep, Savitri sat up, her heart in a flutter: would he come back tonight? It would be impossible to bear it if he kept away again; the perfume and flowers to be wasted! She wrung her hands. She went to the mirror, stole another look at herself, and thought that if he saw her now he would certainly like her. Love her as boisterously as he had loved her in the first week of their marriage . . . 'No, no,' she told herself. 'He will not keep away tonight, not after I have asked him. He has great consideration for my feelings though he may appear rough outside. What did he say?—"Can't be answering idiotic questions"; of course he couldn't answer a question like that. Where was any sense in asking a man if he would return home? That was why he wouldn't waste his breath in answering such a question.'

She sat up quite late into the night. When overcome by fatigue she lay down, keeping her head lightly on the pillow for fear that she might crush the flowers or rumple the hair. He might come any time and she wanted to meet him fresh as she was in the evening; there was nothing more unsightly than rumpled hair and crushed flowers on one's head . . . She dreamt that her husband came home, held her in his arms, and swore that he had been carrying about only a coloured parasol, and silly people said that he had been going about with a woman . . .

And morning came. It was a Sunday and the children had no school. Their presence in the house was a check on Savitri's gloom. When she was alone and when the children's voices were not heard, her mind reverted to its obsession: he hasn't come, he hasn't come, he doesn't care for me now (before the mirror), perhaps she is better than I am.

At about midday Kamala asked, 'Mother, what has happened to Father?'

'He has gone out on business. He has so much work to do at the office.'

'Wouldn't he want to eat anything, or sleep?'

'No. When men have work they forget food, sleep, and home.'

Babu said, 'When I become a big man I will be a big officer, and I won't leave the office, but stay there night and day and do my work. I like being there so much.'

'What about your wife and children?' asked Savitri. Babu bared his teeth in disgust and said, 'Why do you always talk about marriage? I hate it. I am not going to marry even if it is going to cost me my life.'

'Very well, but what about me?' she asked. 'Shall I have to be at home all alone while you are away?'

'You! Oh!'

'You had forgotten me. Everybody forgets me. When you become a big man perhaps you won't even recognize your mother if you see her anywhere.'

Babu swore that he would always be at his mother's side, which comforted Savitri a great deal.

Ramani's car snorted and hooted at the gate at about nine that night. The children were already in their beds; the servant had dropped into a sleep in some part of the house. Savitri went to the garage and opened the door herself. Ramani came in and quietly went away to his room. The house had assumed a gloomy silence after the children had gone to bed. Savitri went about with a flush on her face. She decided not to open her mouth till he should finish his dinner. She hovered about him when he ate, and attended on him, while the sleepy cook served the food. Halfway through the dinner he seemed to notice suddenly that she was before him. 'Have you had your dinner?'

'Yes,' she said. 'You want me to sit up and wait for you, do you?' She was astonished at her own manner. Ramani looked up for a moment but said nothing.

When the cook had gone for the day, and she had shut the front door and put out the lights, she went to the bedroom, cleared her throat and said, 'This sort of thing has to stop, understand?' He was already in bed, with a novel shielding his face. He lowered the novel and scowled at her. 'Don't talk. Go and lie on your bed.'

'I'm not going to, till you promise to come to your senses.' She stood firmly beside his cot.

'Hush, don't talk so loudly. You will wake up the children and the neighbours,' he said.

'Ah, how considerate you are for the children!' she said.

He sat up, understood the terrific force that a woman about to be hysterical could muster, and tried to take her hands and draw her nearer. She pushed away his hand, crying, 'Don't touch me.'

'No, no! What's the matter with you, my pet? This is strange. What is wrong with you?'

He tried once again to hold her hands, and she shook her hands free, violently. 'I'm a human being,' she said, through her heavy breathing. 'You men will never grant that. For you we are playthings when you feel like hugging, and slaves at other times. Don't think that you can fondle us when you like and kick us when you choose.'

He tried to treat it as a joke and laugh it off. 'Very well, my dear. I grant here and now that you are a human being who can feel and think. All right. Now go to bed. I am sleepy.'

His endearing tone for a moment won her; his acquiescence momentarily satisfied her; and she was pleased that he had tried to fondle her. She burst into tears and allowed herself to be drawn to his side. She sat on the edge of his bed sobbing, and when he said, 'Now, now, be a good girl, don't! Lie down, my pet,' she felt that all her troubles had ceased, and blamed herself for exaggerating a little mistake that he might have committed.

She remained thus for a little while and, encouraged by his endearments, asked, 'Now, will you promise not to go near her again?' The first surprise was over, he had exhausted the little accommodation his nature was capable of, and he was once again his old self. He was irritated by the question and said, 'I don't want you to dictate to me.' She repeated her question and he said, 'Don't be a silly fool.' She understood the menace in his tone, drew herself away from him, and said, 'So you refuse?'

'Yes.'

'You won't give up this harlot?'

'Mind how you speak!' His head throbbed with anger.

'You are not having me and her at the same time, understand? I go out of this house this minute.'

'You can please yourself. Put out the light. I want to sleep.' He turned towards the wall.

He heard the banging of the door, turned, and found that she had gone out of the room. A terrific indignation welled up in him: so she was trying to nose-lead him with threats of leaving, like a damned servant! She could please herself, the ingrate. All the kindness and consideration wasted on her. When his bank balance was low he had somehow bought her that gold-laced saree and jumper because she desired it, and the diamond studs on her nose . . . the ingrate! He rose from bed and went out of the room. He found her waking up the three children sleeping in the hall. They sat rubbing their eyes, their minds in a whirl of confusion.

'Why have you disturbed them?'

'I'm taking them with me . . .'

'Shut up! Leave them alone! Are you mad?' Kamala began to cry. This was too much for him; he dragged Savitri away from the children, at which all three of them started crying. 'This is a fine scene!' he said. He thundered, 'Now keep quiet. Here, Kamala, if I hear your voice I will peel the skin off your back. Babu, Sumati, lie down and shut your eyes, and shut your mouths. Sleep at once. Obey!'

The children fell down, put their heads on their pillows, and shut their eyes fast, a sob occasionally bursting from one or the other.

Ramani turned to Savitri and said, 'Savitri, you are trying my patience. What madness is this? Go to bed. For the last time I tell you, go to bed.' He tried to take her by the hand and lead her to her bed.

'Don't touch me!' she cried, moving away from him. 'You are dirty, you are impure. Even if I burn my skin I can't cleanse myself of the impurity of your touch.' He clenched his teeth and raised his hands. She said, 'All right, strike me. I am not afraid.' He lowered his hands and said, 'Woman, get away now.'

'Do you think I am going to stay here? We are responsible for our position: we accept food, shelter, and comforts that you give, and are what we are. Do you think that I will stay in your house, breathe the air of your property, drink the water here, and eat food you buy with your money? No, I'll starve and die in the open, under the sky, a roof for which we need be obliged to no man.'

'Very well. Take your things and get out this moment.'

'Things? I don't possess anything in this world. What possession can a woman call her own except her body? Everything else that she has is her father's, her husband's, or her son's. So take these too . . .' She removed her diamond earrings, the diamond studs on her nose, her necklace, gold bangles and rings, and threw them at him. 'Now, come on, children, get up! Let us get out.' She tried to go near the children. He barred her way. 'Don't touch them or talk to them. Go yourself, if you want. They are *my* children.' She hesitated for a moment and then said, 'Yes, you are right. They are yours, absolutely. You paid the midwife and the nurse. You pay for their clothes and teachers. You are right. Didn't I say that a woman owns nothing?' She broke down, staring at their fidgeting forms on the beds. 'What will they do without me?'

'They will get on splendidly without you, don't you worry. No one is indispensable in this world.'

The diamonds and the gold lay at his feet on the floor. He picked them up. 'This ring and this necklace and this stud were not given by me. They are your father's.'

She shrank from them, 'Take them away. They are also a man's gift.'

Ramani said, 'I'm very sleepy. I'm waiting to bolt the street door and go to bed; that is, if you decide to go out.'

She threw a look at the children, at him, turned round and walked out, softly closing the door behind her.

Before she reached the gate she heard the sound of the bolting

of the front door. She opened the gate a little, let herself out, and
saw the light in the front hall put out. 'Will the children sleep there
in the dark without me?' She stood for a moment watching the light
in her husband's room, and moved on when it was also put out. It
was very nearly midnight. She walked down the silent street.

7

SHE WALKED ALL the way to the north end of the town and
reached the river an hour later. The Sarayu was flowing in the
dark, with a subdued rumble. Summer was still a few weeks ahead,
and now the water was fairly deep in some places, though in a
few weeks' time the river would shrink to a thin streak of water
furrowing the broiling sands.

Her mind was numb. Otherwise she could not have walked
through the town at midnight. Nothing seemed to matter now, not
even one's children. They were after all a husband's . . . Couldn't
she just go to the office, drag the other woman out, gash her face
with her fingernails? Wouldn't it be interesting to wait and see if he
would still grovel at the feet of that slut whose face was gashed and
whose hair was torn out?

Savitri sat on the last step with her feet in the dark moving
water. 'This is the end,' she said to herself, and felt very strange.
So strange indeed did this statement sound to her that she asked
herself: 'Am I the same old Savitri or am I someone else? Perhaps
this is just a dream. And I must be someone else posing as Savitri
because I couldn't have had the courage to talk back to my
husband. I have never done it in my life. I couldn't have had the
courage to walk through the streets at midnight. I am afraid to
go even a hundred yards from the house unescorted; yes, afraid,
afraid of everything. One definite thing in life is Fear. Fear, from
the cradle to the funeral pyre, and even beyond that, fear of torture
in the other world. Afraid of a husband's displeasures, and of the
discomforts that might be caused to him, morning to night and all
night too. How many nights have I slept on the bed on one side,
growing numb by the unchanged position, afraid lest any slight
movement should disturb his sleep and cause him discomfort.'
Afraid of one's father, teachers and everybody in early life, afraid of
one's husband, children, and neighbours in later life—fear, fear, in

one's heart till the funeral pyre was lit, and then fear of being sentenced by Yama to be held down in a cauldron of boiling oil . . . 'How many sins have I committed? . . . Not many, I have always performed my daily *puja* without fail. I've never lied in my life, except a few uttered in childhood. Didn't I and my sister finish off the honey in the bottle and then swear we didn't know what had happened to it? And then that scuffle after which I said that my brother had flung the ball at the glass chimney. Poor fellow, bearing patiently all our anger and vileness and never lifting his hand on us because we were girls. What ages since I saw him, never been the same man since he married that girl from Tayur, a vicious slattern. Far away there from everybody, in Hyderabad, led about by a nose-rope like a bullock. Years since he has written a line to anyone at home; perhaps he has forgotten all his sisters; must have quite a dozen children by now.'

Savitri felt an intense longing to see her brother and her parents. Wouldn't it be better to go round once, see everybody, and then die? Who was so dear to one, after all, as one's parents, one's brothers and sisters, really loving and affectionate? Not a husband but one's parents—theirs was the true affection, not even one's children's . . . Babu would perhaps not come home at all but spend his time in the office and not think of her; Sumati and Kamala would marry and go away and get wrapped up in their own family bothers and give their mother a thought once in a way when there was nothing else to think about . . .

'Must go and see my sister in Rangoon too. Perhaps I can see everybody, see her last, and jump into the sea while returning from Rangoon. What a happy couple those two are, never irritating each other, beautifully balanced. She has always been the luckier since childhood. She was the one to escape thrashing, to be given the first sweets and pencils, to be called up and petted by Father's friends; and no wonder the same luck persists in marriage too. Perhaps one gets the husband one deserves.' She now thought of her husband. Poor man, she said; not so bad by himself, only poisoned in mind now by that slut (was she such a heavenly creature that one should lose all one's senses?). Hadn't he said when they talked to each other for the first time, on the fifth day of marriage, up in the lonely upstairs room, that the moment he saw her he decided to marry her, and that he would have taken his life if he hadn't got her? How he had written to her in all the early letters that he hadn't met anyone with a skin as fair as hers, or with her eyes or hair or cheeks. She wished she had those letters with her now. She would throw them at him and say—'The woman in the office might be really good-looking. I'm not the Savitri that I was when he wrote those letters. Give the other one, too, three children and two miscarriages and see what she will come to; no one except me could have retained even so much of my early looks. Day before yesterday the mirror didn't depress me. I looked quite the same as I did before my nuptials, but it was his fault, he should have come home and seen me. All the flowers and trouble absolutely wasted. Not my fault, he came only a day after I looked my best.'

The Taluk office gong was being struck, and its notes came clearly through the still air. Savitri counted, one, two, three . . . 'I've never seen this hour before, always been asleep. Not always, when Babu had the chicken pox and Sumati had typhoid I've counted the gong at this hour on several nights. And also when he had his headache. How many nights have I sat up all night, yes, even at three o'clock, and held his throbbing head. Would the other one do it for an hour if he should have any pain now? Why do men have such a bad memory? He said, "Get out, I want to sleep."'

Three o'clock now, in an hour it would be four, then five, and six, and people would come and drag her back home or lock her up as being mad. What was the use of sitting on the river-step with a wandering mind and wasting one's time? No one who could not live by herself should be allowed to exist. 'If I take the train and go to my parents, I shall feed on my father's pension; if I go back home, I shall be living on my husband's earnings, and later, on Babu. What can I do by myself? Unfit to earn a handful of rice except by begging. If I had gone to a college and studied, I might have become a teacher or something. It was very foolish of me not to have gone on with my education. Sumati and Kamala must study up to the BA and not depend for their salvation on marriage. What is the difference between a prostitute and a married woman?—the prostitute changes her men, but a married woman doesn't; that's all, but both earn their food and shelter in the same manner. Yes, Kamala and Sumati must take their University course and become independent.' She laughed at herself for planning for her daughters. Who were they? His daughters, not hers. He had said that he had paid for their coming into the world and for their upkeep here.

No one who couldn't live by herself had a right to exist. It was three, in an hour it would be four, and then five . . . people would come and drag her away.

She rose and stepped down. There was still one step, the very last submerged under water, very slippery with moss; and then one felt the sand under one's feet; water reached up to one's hips, and as one went further down, to one's breasts; and now the running water tripped up one's legs from behind. She stood in the water and prayed to her God on the Hill to protect the children . . . 'In Yama's world the cauldron must be ready for me for the sin of talking back to a husband and disobeying him, but what could I do? What could I do . . . no, no, I can't die. I must go back home. I won't, I won't.' The last sensation that she felt was a sharp sting as the water shot up her nostrils, and something took hold of her feet and toppled her over.

8

BURGLARY WAS ONLY a side occupation for Mari. He was the locksmith, umbrella-repairer, and blacksmith of Sukkur village, which was a couple of miles from the other bank of the river. He was a burglar for various reasons; there was a predatory strain in his nature, perhaps handed down to him by his ancestors, which made him love the excitement of breaking into a house; he also valued the profits of the adventure; and he did it to please his wife. He was intensely devoted to her, and her one ambition in life was to fill a small brass pot with coins and precious metal and bury it at the root of a coconut tree which shot up from the back yard of their little home. Tinkering at iron things gave one a steady income but a small one; and if you put up your rates you might drive your customers to the next village; if you didn't put up your rates you had an inadequate income—which made a wife unhappy and quarrelsome. Mari cared a great deal for his wife, although he chased her about and threw things at her when he was drunk.

He sallied forth once a month or so across the river into Malgudi town, crying 'Locks repaired, sirs, umbrellas repaired!' in the streets. During these journeys, if any locked house caught his eye, he let himself into it at midnight and picked up any silverware or precious trifle that might be there.

On this day he was in town. It was a miserable day. He cried

'Locks repaired, sirs, umbrellas repaired!' till he felt as if a file were working inside his Adam's apple, and yet his only customer was a miser at the Market, who wouldn't give even an anna for a new rib to his umbrella; he wanted it to be done for six pies. Mari needed the six pies badly, and he did the work; and something else too: before handing back the umbrella, with a deft twist of the pliers somewhere he assured himself that it would be crippled at the next gust of wind; and then the heir of a miser could thank himself for the six pies saved!

What galled him most was that the wife at home expected a man to return laden with money. Time was when a man could earn at least a rupee in the town, but nowadays it was a mystery what people did with their broken umbrellas. Gone were the days when locks and keys were a luxury; now if a key was lost another with a lock (made in Japan) could be bought for an anna and a half!

Mari turned his steps from the crowded Market Road, Vinayak Mudali and Grove Streets, and with a last hope moved towards Lawley Extension. Here were rich bungalows; and people who never carried umbrellas but went about in cars. All the same occasionally there was a demand for a repairer, and payment was excellent . . .

His voice rang through the broad silent streets of Lawley Extension. He shouted louder here than anywhere else because every house had a compound, and the message had to get through the gates and reach the people living yards away from the road. This also proved to be a profitless excursion. Mari coughed and said to himself that he might cry till he spat blood but nobody would give him a pie.

He was in the Fourth Cross Road, cursing his luck, when he saw a locked house. He slackened his pace, observed the house more fully, paced the street up and down, and went away.

He sang as he walked back to Market Road. It seemed immaterial to him if his purse contained only half an anna.

There was an old woman squatting on the narrow pavement at the Market gateway selling fried groundnut, coloured edibles, and cucumber slices, arranged on a gunny-sack spread on the ground. Mari put down his small bundle of tools and sat down before the gunny-sack.

'Get out of the way,' the old woman cried.

'Ah, mother, you are really becoming blind,' Mari said, moving nearer. 'I am Mari.'

The old woman laughed and said: 'I can't see who is who at this hour. But what a nuisance the whole day, people coming and sitting down there every other minute! I am hoarse calling out . . .' She struck a match and lit the wick peeping out of a tin container. She placed the container on an inverted basket and brightened the surroundings with the wavering flare. 'I can see better now, can't I? When did you come to town, and why have you come so late, my son?'

'Have I not to earn some money before I come and spend it here? Would you give me a little pinch of anything unless I paid for it at once?'

'I am a poor wretch who has to add pie on pie; what can I do?'

'You have the cunning of a fox! You must have made a fortune by now, which you are salting and pickling somewhere, I know. Your days are nearly over, and yet your avarice has not ended; why should you not give your money to poor folk like me?' After these pleasantries Mari proceeded to business. He bought, after much haggling, groundnut for three pies, a curved slice of cucumber for a pie, and some fried stuff for two pies, and munched them with deliberate care and attention. 'A firelike hunger inside me and this is just a pinch in some corner,' he said at the end of the meal.

'Then buy some more. I have some nice things in this basket. . .'

'You tempt me. All right, but will you take the money tomorrow?'

'Credit day after tomorrow,' the old woman said.

Mari walked over to the fountain in the Market Square, took water in his hands, and drank it. 'Now it is better,' he said, coming back to the old woman. 'Oh, sister, give me a little tobacco and betel leaf. God will take you to heaven for it. I have given you all my money. I have no more. I shall go raving mad if I don't get a little piece of tobacco now.'

The old woman took out her greasy cloth purse, peered into it by the light of the smoky flare, picked up a piece of tobacco and a crumpled betel leaf, and flung them at Mari, grumbling, 'You are the biggest scoundrel God ever made. You spend half an anna but take goods for three-quarters of an anna.'

'Let me be smitten with leprosy if I have a pie more about me,' said Mari, receiving the gift and putting it in his mouth. He took his tool-bag and walked away. He crossed the road, went into the spacious rest-house before the Market, and lay down in the veranda.

Chewing the betel leaf and tobacco, he had a great sense of well-being; he shut his eyes and revelled in it for some time, and fell asleep.

He got up at midnight. The Market Road was silent; only the lights of a few late shops illuminated the road here and there. The last cinema shows were over and there was no traffic. Mari looked round; a number of others, travellers, adventurers, and mendicants, were lying about fast asleep; some were talking from unseen corners; and one or two were sitting and sucking at an enchanted clay pipe filled with opium leaf, the pipe glowing in the dark.

Mari moved down the road cautiously. He abandoned the main thoroughfare at the earliest possible moment, stole along by-ways and lanes, and reached Lawley Extension.

Not for him now the broad paved roads of the Extension. Here in this locality of government and police officials the constables went round with thoroughness on their beats. Mari slipped into an ill-lit conservancy lane, his ears cocked to catch the creaking of police boots. When he heard footsteps he flattened himself against a wall and stood still. The policeman appeared on the edge of the road, looking down the lane, lightly breathing through his whistle, and moved away after shouting, 'Stop, who are you? Don't run, stop! . . .'

Mari stood at the gate of the bungalow in the Fourth Cross Road, looked up and down, and vaulted over the compound wall. He closely examined the lock on the front door and squatted down so that he might not be seen from the road. He opened his tool-bag, took out a possible key, ran his file over it, and tried it on the lock. After filing it four or five times he was able to fit it into the lock. He never believed in breaking a lock open, it made things conspicuous. Opening a lock in the correct manner, and locking a house again when leaving it, was, Mari felt, a piece of courtesy which a man owed the absent householders.

Mari let himself into the house, shut the door again, and looked about by the light of a match. He was in a large furnished room. He saw a tray on a stool with betel leaves and arecanut in it. The leaves were stiff and dry, from which Mari concluded the family must have been away for at least three days. Mari transferred the leaves and nut to his tool-bag, and examined the tray: it looked like plated nickel. He put it down—it wasn't worth the risk a man ran in carrying it about.

He opened the shelves and cupboards. Some of them were empty, and some contained only books, clothes, and other useless stuff. So these people either possessed no silver or were the sneaky sort who kept it in iron safes!

He drifted towards the *puja* room; there at least one could pick up odd bits of silver—tiny images of gods, incense-holders, and such things. On the way he peeped into the kitchen safe. All the vessels were empty; only a little buttermilk, acrid and fermented, at the bottom of a vessel. He also found, wrapped in a piece of paper, a quarter loaf of bread, stiff as cardboard. Mari felt happy at the sight of it; so he needn't go away with an empty stomach. A handful of groundnut vended by that stingy hag was no food for a hungering stomach. He tried to bite the loaf of bread, but it scratched his gums and hurt the roof of his mouth;' he then soaked it in the sour buttermilk and thrust it into his mouth.

He felt contented and hoped that presently in the *puja* room he might find at least a half-inch-high god, not worth more than a rupee and eight annas, but better than nothing, some keepsake for the wife. These householders were cunning people all the world over: if they had large images and valuable pieces for worship they took care not to leave them about, the cunning hypocrites! Was there any true piety in a person who locked up the gods?

At this moment a noise like that of a terraced roof crashing down came through the darkness. Mari stood stock-still, not daring even to munch his bread. And then he heard groans, and a weak voice calling someone; and again another cascade of falling bricks, groans, and further sounds of choking.

Mari realized it was none of his business to find out what it was, but to clear out immediately if he didn't want to end up in jail. While moving towards the exit Mari saw a light through a window. Somebody was living in the back portion of the house. A young boy was administering medicine to an old man who was sitting up, choking and wheezing. 'Never thought for a moment you were all here, friends,' Mari said softly under his breath. 'Your cough will burst you soon, don't worry.'

He was out of the house very soon. His cheeks bulging with the dry bread, he threaded his way through dark alleys and was soon at Ellaman Street. In this part of the town a man could go about freely because the policemen slept on the *pyols* of houses or under the awnings of shop-fronts and got up only in the morning.

He approached the river, very much depressed. He wished he had brought away at least the tray. Now to be going home empty-handed after a full day out—his wife would spit in his face if she should see what he had brought from the town—a few withered betel leaves. He had better not show her the leaves but chew them off, as soon as he could take a mouthful of water from the river and wash down that terrible bit of bread and rid himself of the hiccups which had been torturing him at regular intervals all along: he had been afraid that in the still night his hiccups might stir up the town or awaken the policemen in Ellaman and North Streets.

He crossed the sands towards the steps; swimming across here saved distance, otherwise one would have to trudge all the way to Nallapa's Grove and cross the river . . .

The Taluk office gong struck three. Mari counted it and reckoned that he could be home at four: only a few strokes across the river and then two milestones.

Just as he reached the steps he saw, down below at the water's edge, an apparition. He stood petrified. Surely, this was Mohini, the Temptress Devil, who waylaid lonely wayfarers and sucked their blood . . . He watched it in fascination and horror, and presently the Mohini rose and walked into the river. 'Ah, the Devil can walk on water; at what inauspicious moment did I leave home today? She hasn't seen me yet. I dare not move . . .' By this time the apparition was in deep water and let out a cry: 'No, no, I can't die: I must go back home . . .' And then there was silence. Mari had by now got over his first fright, and said to himself, 'The Devil can't talk, and the Devil can't drown.' He ran down the steps.

He rescued Savitri before she had taken in too much water. Already the currents had carried her to the middle of the river and a little way down. Mari took hold of her hair and dragged her to the opposite bank. He rolled her over and very nearly jumped on her stomach. She opened her eyes and mumbled something.

Mari asked, 'What language are you speaking?'

She asked, 'When will you be back home?'

Mari replied, 'I should have been nearly there now but for you. I am sorry I ever left the village today.'

'Has Babu gone out to play? Did he drink the coffee?'

'I can't say. He might have. Can you get up?'

'Is it morning? Has the milkman come?'

'It is nearly morning, but I can't see the milkman anywhere.'

'What is the matter with him?'

'How can I tell? You didn't expect to find him in the river, did you?' With this Mari shook her, rolled her, twisted her limbs. Savitri stared at the dark face bending over her and screamed, 'Alas! Somebody help me! Thief, thief!' Mari said to himself, 'She has found me out. I am undone. This woman is uncanny,' and left her and broke into a run. He cursed her as he ran: 'This woman will see me in jail for my trouble. I should have let her drown herself ten times over . . .'

Savitri awoke next morning with a throbbing head and stiff aching limbs. She realized her position now. All the old bitterness and pain revived in her. On her right, beyond the stretch of water and sand, the Town Hall tower peeped over a cluster of roofs. Savitri gazed on it and reflected that, under some roof in the cluster, *he* must be with the woman; let him be. She must go on with her back to that cluster of roofs and never turn again towards them, never, unless he abandoned the woman and begged for pardon. She was an individual with pride and with a soul, and she wasn't going to submit to everything hereafter. Would *he* be searching for her now? It was more likely he had brought the other one and kept her in the house. Would she be ill-treating the children? Savitri wished that she had asked Janamma or Gangu to keep an eye on the children. But . . . children? Let them alone. They were his; he paid the midwife, and it was his duty to look after them. Hadn't he said that they would get on splendidly without her? 'Now what shall I do with myself? Shall I starve to death?'

A dark hefty man and a woman appeared before her. The woman asked, 'Are you all right now?'

'Who are you?'

'I am of Sukkur village and people call me Ponni My husband is a blacksmith. While he was returning home from—never mind where or why he had gone there, men have to go out and work, you know—he saw you in the river and he says that he saved your life and left you on the bank.'

'You should have left me alone,' Savitri said.

'Why do you say that? When he told me where he had left you, I shouted to him, "You can't leave a woman helpless, all alone there. Go there this minute and see if she is all right." But when he started someone came along to have a wheel-band set right; when it was over and just as we were starting someone else came

along with a battered lock. Oh, it is a nasty profession without
any rest, but we are poor people. We can't afford to say to anyone
"Come later." We have to live on their goodwill, you know.'

'You are right,' Savitri said.

'I am so happy to see you alive. You are so fair, and you look
rich. I can't understand how you came to be here. Why did you
jump into the river?'

'Is this your husband?'

'Yes.'

'Do you like him very much?'

At this Ponni looked shy and smiled. Savitri said, 'Suppose he
took another woman and neglected you, what would you do?'

Ponni threw a suspicious glance at her husband and asked,
'Have you been up to any such trick?'

'No, no,' Mari said, and asked, turning to Savitri, 'What do
you mean by this, madam?' Savitri explained to Ponni, 'I don't say
he has done it. Imagine for a moment . . .' Mari asked indignantly,
'Why should she imagine such a thing?'

Savitri persisted, 'If he did such a thing, what would you do?'

Ponni said, 'Let him try. Then he will know what he will get.'

'But that was all that I could do,' Savitri said, pointing at the
river. 'I have slaved for him all these years. We have children. And
now he is ensnared by a—by a—by some woman. He doesn't want
me.'

Ponni said, 'Sister, remember this. Keep the men under the rod,
and they will be all right. Show them that you care for them and
they will tie you up and treat you like a dog.'

'What do you mean?' Mari protested. 'When have I treated you
like a dog?'

'Don't talk now,' Ponni commanded. 'Don't butt in when
women are talking. Stay under that tree. I will call you when I want
you.' Mari hesitated to go. Ponni said: 'Look here. It is no use your
standing here. We are not going to talk to you. You have walked
two stones. Rest under that tree. You will hear soon enough when
you are wanted.' Mari faded out of the scene. Ponni said to Savitri,
'You see, that is the way to manage them. He is a splendid boy, but
sometimes he goes out with bad friends, who force him to drink,
and then he will come home and try to break all the pots and beat
me. But when I know that he has been drinking, the moment he
comes home, I trip him up from behind and push him down, and

sit on his back for a little while; he will wriggle a little, swear at me, and then sleep, and wake up in the morning quiet as a lamb. I can't believe any husband is unmanageable in this universe . . . Sister, I can't let you sit here all day, the sun is getting warm. Where would you like to go now?'

'Nowhere. I will stay here.'

'Shall I send my husband to the town and ask him to bring your people?'

Savitri shuddered at the suggestion.

'Or come with me to my house. My home is humble, but I will gladly clear a corner for you.' Savitri declined the offer.

Ponni said, 'I see you are a Brahmin and won't stay with us. I will ask someone of your own caste to receive you.'

'No. Leave me alone.'

'Or stay in our house. I will clear a part for you and never come there. I will buy a new pot for you, and rice, and you can cook your own food. I will never come that way. I will never cook anything in our house which may be repulsive to you. Please come with me.'

'No. I won't come anywhere.'

'Our village is only two stones from here. Let us walk slowly.'

'Please go away. Leave me alone.'

At this stubbornness Ponni lost her temper.

'I don't know what you are planning. You want to be neither here nor there. I don't know where you really want to go. A very fine person to deal with!'

'Why do you trouble yourself about me?'

'Why not? See here, my dear lady, either you will come with me to the village or go back to the town. I won't let you stay here. If you persist in moving neither way, I will send my husband to the town and bring someone from there to carry you back home.'

Savitri imagined someone coming from that cluster of roofs, tying her hand and foot, and carrying her back to the South Extension. She asked, 'Which way do we go?' in order to assure herself that it was away from the roofs and not towards them.

'I will come with you,' she said, 'on condition that you don't trouble me to come under your roof or any other roof. I will remain only under the sky.'

9

RAMANI GOT UP from bed after a night of disturbed sleep. With all his bravado before his wife, he was very much shaken by her manner. Such a thing had never happened to him at any time for fifteen years. She had always been docile and obedient, and the fire inside her was a revelation to him now. Though he had invited her to walk out of the house last night, he had not expected her to do it. He had expected she would go into the dark room and sulk for a few days, a few days more than usual; then she was bound to come to her senses and accept things as they were. He felt irritated when people made any fuss. A man had a right to a little fun now and then, provided it didn't affect his conduct at home. No doubt it took him home rather late, but that could have been rectified by a little persistent persuasion on her part; all this sullenness and dictation was not the right way to set about it; he expected to be coaxed and requested; he told himself that people could get anything from him if only they knew the proper way of approaching him. It would be a very bold person indeed who tried to dictate to him. He had never tolerated any advice from anyone—not even from his father, who, a few years before his death, when Ramani passed his Matriculation, had advised him to continue his studies and was told, 'I know better what I must do.'

Ramani was self-made. He hadn't waited for anybody's help or advice. If he had waited for other people to tell him what to do he might have earned a BA and become now a clerk in an office or a lawyer with a miserable practice. As it was, through his own, very own effort and enterprise, he was making a clear five hundred a month, in salary alone, and persons with double or treble degrees constantly applied to him for jobs worth fifty or sixty under him! (This last gave him a certain compensating satisfaction at being without a University degree. He sometimes regretted it because he had often seen BAs giving themselves airs, though they could not earn a hundred rupees a year, the ridiculous beings! He occasionally longed for a degree simply in order that he might snub the graduates a little more thoroughly, on their own ground.)

He was entirely self-made, and that proved one was right and needed no advice from others and least at all from a wife. Of course, he granted, there was some sense in the women's movement: let them by all means read English novels, play tennis, have their All-

India Conference, and go to pictures occasionally; but that should not blind them to their primary duties of being wives and mothers; they mustn't attempt to ape the Western women, all of whom, according to Ramani's belief, lived in a chaos of promiscuity and divorce. He held that India owed its spiritual eminence to the fact that the people here realized that a woman's primary duty (also a divine privilege) was being a wife and a mother, and what woman retained the right of being called a wife who disobeyed her husband? Didn't all the ancient epics and scriptures enjoin upon woman the strictest identification with her husband? He remembered all the heroines of the epics whose one dominant quality was a blind stubborn following of their husbands, like the shadow following the substance.

'Will you promise not to go near her again?' And what else? 'You are not having me and her at the same time.' A fine way to talk to a husband. Threatened to walk out like a servant. All the kindness and consideration entirely wasted. How could she forget the six-sovereign necklace he had bought for her at the beginning of his career, when he had not a bank account and was subsisting on insurance canvassing? How could she forget the misery and anxiety he suffered when she had labour pains and the rest? Like a servant threatening to leave, unless something or other was done! No one had any right to object to his friendship with Shanta Bai—that splendid creature with her understanding heart and cultured outlook. Savitri ought not to behave as if her husband was like some low-class fellow who kept a mistress . . .

He was decidedly not going to worry about her or search for her. She had walked out of her own will; she would have to face the consequences, of course; old enough to know what she was doing. Firmness was everything in life; that was the secret of success with women. If they found a man squeamish they would drive him about with a whip. He was certain she would return and apologize when her madness passed. This was only a different version of the sulking in the dark room. She might now be sulking in a dark corner of some friend's house. After all, where could she go? He was going to show that *he* wasn't the loser anyway.

In the morning the children sat up rather dazed. They were bewildered and unhappy. They huddled together in a corner of the hall. Sumati took upon herself the task of playing the mother. She went to the cook and said, 'You must give us coffee.'

'Where is your mother?' asked the cook.

Sumati, not being able to answer, said, 'Wait a moment,' and came to the hall to consult her brother. 'Babu, the cook asks where is Mother. What shall I tell him?'

'What will you tell him?'

'I don't know.'

'Tell him that it is none of his business.'

Kamala said, 'Perhaps he knows where she is: he might have seen her somewhere last night,' and burst into tears.

Ramani came that way. He now felt that all the responsibility of running the household had descended on him. He was going to prove that no one was indispensable in this world. He also felt that this was his opportunity to introduce certain reforms and economies which he had been suggesting for years to a deaf wife. (He was going to abolish the cooking of brinjals in the house, tell the cook to stay at night, have tea instead of coffee in the afternoons, cut the milk bill by half, and so on.)

He pinched Kamala's cheeks, rumpled Babu's hair, and patted Sumati's back. Decidedly, he was going to make them happy. They were not to miss their mother. 'Have you all had your coffee?' he asked with his brightest smile. His unusual affability comforted the children. 'Now, babies,' he said, 'come to my room.'

'All of us?' Babu asked, surprised. Admission to Father's room was a rare privilege, and only Kamala had it occasionally.

He seated them in a row on the floor, squatted before them like a village schoolmaster, and worked himself up to his best canvassing technique—a gift which made him net a lakh's worth of policies a year in the early days. 'Now, babies, you must not be miserable because your mother is not here.'

'Where is she?' Kamala asked.

'She has only gone to Talapur. Her father was suddenly taken ill. I had a telegram from Talapur at my office yesterday.'

The children listened to this story without enthusiasm, and Ramani asked, 'Why are you all silent?' Babu, being the eldest, believed the story the least. He wanted to ask several questions: why she had gone at midnight, why she had removed the jewels before going, why there had been so much of argument and tears; but he dared not put questions to his father. Kamala asked, 'Why didn't anyone go with her to the station?'

'There was no one to go with her. I couldn't, because you were all alone here.'

Sumati asked, 'Was a carriage brought to take her to the station?'

'Yes. It was waiting in the street.'

'But we didn't see it.'

'I thought, Father,' Kamala ventured, 'that you and Mother had a big quarrel because she cried so much when she went out.'

Ramani said, 'She wanted to take you all with her. I said "No". She became cross. You have school, you know.'

'Why did she cry so much, Father?'

'Her father was very ill. Wouldn't you cry very much if I should be very ill?' He looked at Babu and said, 'Why are you blinking? Do you want to ask anything?'

Babu felt obliged to ask, 'When will Mother be back?'

Ramani replied that it would depend on her father's health. 'Have you all bathed?'

'It is very difficult to make Kamala bathe,' said Sumati. 'Every day Mother had such a bother to make her bathe!'

Ramani looked at Kamala and said, 'No, no. You aren't like that, are you? You are a nice girl. Sumati will give you a bath. Now, will you be a nice little girl?'

'Yes, Father.'

Ramani changed his mind. 'Sumati, I think you had better leave her alone. She will bathe herself. Kamala, you are five years old; you must become self-reliant.'

'Yes, Father.'

Just when the children were starting for school he said, 'What do you do for tiffin?' The girls told him that they came home in the afternoons. Ramani said: i will tell the cook to stay. Come in the afternoon and see that he serves you properly. You must all learn to attend to your affairs yourselves. Self-reliance is the first thing you must learn in life. Do you also come home in the afternoon, Babu?'

'No, Father, I come home only in the evening.'

'Do you mean to tell me that you starve till the evening? It won't do.' What did she mean by letting Babu starve till the evening? 'You must carry a small tiffin packet for the afternoon, Babu.' Babu felt his father's attentions irksome. To him there was something shameful and degrading in carrying a packet and eating it in the school. His mother had given up the attempt as hopeless. Now Father was suggesting it. Why could not Father leave people alone?

'I will manage somehow today,' Babu said.

'What will you do? You can't starve,' said Ramani, and called the cook and told him, 'Make a tiffin packet for Babu.'

'The tiffin is not ready yet,' said the cook.

Ramani scowled at the cook. 'What do you mean by it? Don't you know that this boy is to have something for the afternoon? Wonderful work you are doing, to be sure. Let me not catch you at this sort of thing again. As soon as you prepare the tiffin, make a packet of it and take it to his school.' Babu was horrified at the prospect. His schoolfellows would surely stand round and grin at him and his cook as he swallowed the tiffin. It was simply not done. He protested mildly, but Father would not hear of it. 'I know what is best for you. Don't contradict your elders.' Babu accepted his fate with gloomy resignation. It was no use arguing with Father. Life was becoming messy and rotten. 'Now you may all go. Wait for me in the evening. I will take you all to a cinema.'

Sumati and Kamala clapped their hands in joy, but Babu asked, 'In the evening?'

'Yes, sir.'

'I have to play cricket, Father.'

'Not when your father wants you to go to the pictures with him.'

'We are playing against the YMU next week, and our captain will be very angry if I miss practice.'

'Look here, Babu, you are a very—' He was irritated and was about to begin a long analysis of Babu's character, but he checked himself as he remembered that he had to be very kind to the children. 'You must learn to be a nice boy, Babu. You must think of your sisters. They can't enjoy a picture without your company, can they? Don't refuse them that pleasure. You must also think of others; you must not be selfish.'

'I like pictures, Father, but I have to practise for a match. I said—'

'Well, well, well! Don't go on saying the same thing over and over again. Your match can wait.' Before going to the office he called the cook and told him, 'Make tea for everybody in the afternoon. Coffee only in the mornings.'

Ramani left the office at five o'clock in the evening. On the way he stopped before a restaurant and bought some sweets. The moment

he came home he asked if they had all had their afternoon curd and
rice and tiffin and tea correctly, and particularly if Babu had his
tiffin at school. Kamala said, 'I don't like the smell of tea, and so I
drank only half a tumbler.'

'No, that won't do. You must learn to like tea. It is a very good
drink.'

'All right, Father. From tomorrow I will try to like tea.'

Ramani was greatly pleased. He had not known till now that
his children were so manageable. 'Did you like your tea, Sumati?' he
asked, turning to the other. She said 'Yes,' and added that it didn't
make any difference to her whether it was tea or coffee.

He gave the packet of sweets to Sumati and said, 'Share it
among yourselves.'

He had bought rather a large quantity of the sweets, and so,
though the children started enthusiastically, they couldn't eat more
than half of what they took. Ramani shook his head disapprovingly:
'You mustn't get into the habit of wasting things. Babu, you have
left the largest quantity; that won't do. You are a sportsman. You
must eat a lot and grow strong. Polish it off, otherwise I will never
call you a cricket player. Go on.' Babu had been the first to arrive
at the stage of retching, but now he grabbed the stuff on the plate,
gulped it down, and looked at his father for approval. 'Great boy,'
Ramani said. 'You will be in the India Eleven some day.' Babu was
tremendously pleased though the sweets turned in his stomach.

He took them to the Palace Talkies, which was showing a
Laurel and Hardy film. The children sat completely absorbed. They
forgot this world, its troubles, and the absence of a mother, while
they watched the antics of the comedians.

Ramani got up in the middle of the show, whispering to them:
'Stay here till I come back and pick you up. Don't leave the theatre
even if I am delayed a bit.'

'I will look after them,' Babu said.

'Father, what shall we do if somebody comes and orders us out
of the theatre? Kamala asked.

'Life is one continuous boredom,' Shanta Bai said, locking her arms
behind her head and leaning back on the pillow. 'I started out in
life wanting to do things, but here I am vegetating. All day long
I listen to Pereira's humour and to Kantaiengar's rudeness, and
then come here and lie down on the couch. "As wind along the

waste—" Have you read Omar Khayyam?'

'Who is he?' Shanta Bai's literary allusions distressed him.

'The Persian poet.'

'I don't know the Mohammedan language,' Ramani said innocently, and Shanta Bai began to lecture him on Omar Khayyam and Fitzgerald.

'I can't exist without a copy of *The Rubá'iyár*; you will always find it under my pillow or in my bag. His philosophy appeals to me. Dead yesterday and unborn tomorrow. "What, without asking whither hurried hence" and so on. The cup of life must be filled to the brim and drained; another and another cup to drown the impertinence of this memory. In this world Khayyam is the only person who would have understood the secret of my soul. No one tries to understand me; that is the tragedy of my life. Khayyam says: "Into this Universe and why not knowing, etcetera, I am as wind along the waste."'

Ramani went over to the edge of her cot, sat down there, and tried to hold her hands. Shanta Bai took away her hands and pleaded: 'Please leave me alone. I am in no mood now.'

'Are you sure?'

'Absolutely. You may sit here if you like, but please don't touch me.'

Ramani folded his arms across his chest. Shanta Bai hummed a little tune to herself and said, tossing her head, 'I am so unhappy that I have not brought my violin with me. I am in a mood to play.'

'What a pity that I didn't know it!'

'Have you a violin at home?'

'No. I would have bought one for you.'

'Oh, you are so good to me. I don't know how I am ever going to repay your kindness.'

Ramani's heart thrilled at these words. 'I have told you not to talk of repayment. When I know I like a person, I like the person, that is all, and I will do anything for the person. Please don't talk of repayment on any account.'

Presently she said, 'Pereira told me that there is a Laurel and Hardy comic at the Palace. Shall we go there tonight?'

'I am so sorry, not tonight. I have to be with my children. My wife has gone to her parents.'

'Oh,' Shanta Bai said with resignation.

'H'm, just my luck, that is all. I would have so loved a picture tonight! Just my luck, that is all.'

'Don't mistake me, dear,' Ramani begged.

'Not at all. Your family duties first. I was only cursing my luck.' She dismissed the pictures with a sigh. She hummed a few tunes and Ramani said that she sang divinely. She said, 'Would you mind putting out the light? I feel that darkness would be more soothing to my soul now . . . I do so hate these electric bulbs . . .'

Ramani put out the light.

The Taluk office gong struck nine. Ramani counted it and jumped up, muttering: 'Goodness! I never thought it was nine. The children will be waiting: the poor things must be very hungry and sleepy.'

10

AS SOON AS they entered the village Savitri asked, 'Have we arrived?'

'Yes.'

'I will stay here. You may go to your house.'

'Here? On the roadside? You are not talking sensibly, if you will forgive me for saying so.'

'There is nothing wrong in it. Or I will go over to that field and stay there.'

'And get bitten by a cobra? You can't stay anywhere in the open. You are not the kind of person who ought to risk it. You will gather a crowd round you, and you will be suffocated by the crowd if nothing worse happens. Don't be foolish, madam. Come with me to our house and stay there just for this day. We will see if anything is possible tomorrow. God is great. He will show us a way.'

Savitri allowed herself to be taken to the house. She was too dazed and faint to persist.

Sukkur village consisted of about a hundred houses and six streets. Around the village there were immense stretches of paddy fields. Ponni lived in a hovel, with an extension of thatched shed abutting the crooked street, which served as Mari's workshop.

By this time they had gathered a small crowd of shepherds, urchins, and idlers behind them. People came out of their houses and stared at Savitri. One or two shouted to Ponni, 'Who is this lady?' Ponni passed on without replying.

Ponni said, as soon as they reached her house, 'You come from

the town. Perhaps you live in a palatial house there. I don't know if
you will find my hut tolerable.' Mari had come running in advance
and opened the door. He hurriedly pushed away odds and ends
and metal junk, which cluttered their small windowless front
room. Ponni entered the house, picked up a broom, and swept the
floor. She took out her best mat (which had a coloured pattern of
a Japanese girl holding an umbrella), unrolled it, and requested
Savitri to sit down on it. Savitri declined the mat and sat on the
floor. Ponni said, 'That is what I don't like about you, madam.' She
turned to her husband and said, 'Come with me.' Mari followed
her. They stood in the back yard where a tall coconut tree shot up
into the sky. She asked: 'Have you any money? None, of course, I
know.'

'What could I do?'

'You will see me in the streets before we have done with each
other,' she said. 'Here is the lady. We shall have to give her something
that she will accept from us. How do you propose to get it?' Mari
blinked desperately and looked away. She said, 'Now get up this tree
and pluck a couple of coconuts. We will beg her to drink at least the
water in them.' Mari hugged the tree and pulled himself up. 'Mind
you don't throw them on the tiles. Keep them ready. I will be back
soon,' she said, and went out. She hurried down the street and went
to a shop where a miscellany of goods were sold. Ranganna, the
shopman, was squatting amidst his articles. He asked, 'What can I
give you, good woman?'

'I hope I see you well. How are your children?'

'They are quite well.'

'Is your wife all right now?'

'Yes, yes, as well as she could be; that is all I can say. What can
I give you?'

'If you have plantains, please give me the four ripest ones.'

'With pleasure,' said the shopman, and held his hand for the
money.

Ponni looked hurt. 'Why should you be so suspicious? Will I
run away with your money?'

'Did I say so? I was just wondering if the fruits were ripe enough
for you.'

'I will see for myself,' said Ponni, and hopped up a platform
before the shop. She pulled up a bunch of plantains which was
hanging by a string. 'These are excellent,' she said. She selected

four, plucked them out, and jumped down the platform. She asked, 'How much?'

'Eight pies,' said the shopman.

'Too dear, too dear,' said Ponni shaking her head disapprovingly. 'How many fruits do you want at a quarter of an anna for six?'

'I will give you four pies, or, say, five pies for your sake.'

'I will bring the money tomorrow.'

'I can't give you anything on credit,' said the shopman; but Ponni was off. 'I don't know what to do with this frightful woman,' said the shopman.

Ponni set the coconut and the plantains before Savitri. Savitri said, 'I don't need these.'

'Only fruits and coconut. I knew that you wouldn't take anything else touched by me, so I have brought only fruits and coconut.'

'I am not hungry,' Savitri said.

Ponni persisted and argued, and there was no escape. And so Savitri had to confess, though she felt very awkward while doing it, 'I am resolved never to accept food or shelter which I have not earned.'

'A nice thing you are saying, my lady! What can you do, with your soft hands? I should be dragged to hell if I made you do any work for me . . .'

'It is a foolish thing to say. If you don't want me to starve, give me some work. I can cook, scrub, sew. I know a little gardening too. I had a beautiful garden once. I can look after children. Have you no children?'

'Ah, cursed me! We have been married for twenty years and I have promised offerings to all our gods, but I am not blessed yet.'

'What a pity! I have three children. My son is just thirteen. He is very intelligent and knows a lot of things about electricity. My two girls are reading in a school; very intelligent creatures.'

'You are a blessed being, my lady. God will protect you. The difficulty that has risen before you like a mountain will soon vanish like the dew . . . Please take this coconut, sister. It rends my heart to see you starve. You have been in the water a long time.'

'I am not hungry,' Savitri said.

Ponni sought her husband out in his workshop. He had just done a little riveting job on a barrow and was arguing his terms with some heat. Ponni called him aside and asked, 'Do you want a halter round your neck?'

'No.'

'Then do something about that lady in there. She has been starving since the morning, and if she dies the police will come on you for murder; and they will be right because you are going about as if she were none of your business but only mine. You were the person who found her, remember.'

'She is a lady, and so I thought I needn't come to that side.'

'Ah, a virtuous man indeed! You wouldn't speak to a lady, would you? Find out something for that lady to do so that she may take her food and live.'

'Let her come and work these bellows. It will be a good piece of work.'

'Wouldn't you like it? A fine high-caste lady to touch these worm-eaten bellows! Think of something else before I come again.' She turned to go. She added, 'If she dies I will tell the police that you killed her, and they will believe it, be sure.'

When she was gone Mari beat his brow and said to his customer, 'I sometimes think that it would be better to let the police take me and hang me than be married to that woman.'

'Why should the police hang you?'

'There is a mad woman in there who won't touch food unless she is given work. Hard enough for men to get work in these days.'

'What sort of woman is she?'

'Go and see her for yourself.'

The customer went in and saw Savitri. He came out and remarked, 'She is an eyeful. Won't somebody marry her? Or I will give her money.' And he made a ribald suggestion.

Mari, after disposing of the customer, went in and told his wife, 'I will go and see if there is anything for this lady, but what are the things she can do?'

'She can cook, sew, and scrub. What more does a woman need to know? She also says that she knows a little gardening.'

Mari went out.

He left the house briskly enough, but as soon as he came to the street he stopped, not having the faintest idea of what he should do. He didn't know how anyone set about getting a job, much less how a woman did it. He had inherited his foundry from his father, and had never applied to anyone for work; and now to go and beg for the sake of that woman . . . He resented the idea. For a moment he reflected how free he would have been now if he had let her float down the river: if her fate was good she would have survived it somehow, and if she had been destined to die she would have died in spite of any rescue, and he told himself that he would not have been particularly responsible for her death if he had left her alone. He felt angry with his wife for her fussing. Why couldn't she leave the woman alone? If she didn't want food it was entirely her business. This was what came of allowing too much liberty to women; they ought to be kept under proper control and then all would be well. He felt irritated with himself at his own helplessness before his wife . . .

'Did you start out only to stand in the street and meditate?' asked Ponni, peeping out of the house. Mari moved down the road without turning his head. 'You have started walking. Where do you intend to go?' she asked.

'You can leave it to me, and go in,' he shouted back, and felt a great relief at having said something of his own after all. He went down the street and stopped before Ranganna's shop. He occasionally enjoyed sitting on the platform before the shop and chatting with Ranganna and his customers; he had also a hope now that Ranganna might be able to suggest something.

Ranganna received Mari coldly. Mari did not notice it, but moved on to his favourite seat on the platform, and said, 'Well, well, well, how are you, brother?'

'If you let your wife come this way again I will call the police,' said Ranganna.

'That is a big word you are uttering. What has she done?'

'You already owe me an anna, which I don't know when you are going to pay. And that woman walks in as if she owned the shop . . .'

Mari saw that it was no time for companionship. He rose to his feet, saying: 'You talk too much. I fear you may suffer from sore throat tonight. You have not the guts to stop a woman from snatching a thing in your shop. Why do you come and complain to me?'

He crossed some of the lanes and cross-paths and went into the Brahmin street. She was a Brahmin lady and somebody might take her in. He stood at the beginning of the street, reflectively looking at the houses, wondering who was most likely to be useful to him.

There was the big landlord in whose house Ponni had, during certain seasons, done odd jobs; there was the teacher with whom Mari was familiar, having repaired the pulley over his well a number of times and soldered a leaky pot an equal number of times; then there was the other landlord, the young man with a violent temper; and his brother-in-law in the opposite house; and the police inspector; and the man who had married the big landlord's second daughter; and then the village accountant.

He drew a blank here. In the big landlord's house they wouldn't have anything to do with an adventuress, the teacher was too poor to burden himself with a guest or a servant, the young landlord was tight-fisted, and on the threshold of the police inspector's house Mari changed his mind. 'Keep out of his way,' his instinct told him.

Mari tramped the village streets up and down, spoke to all sorts of people about the woman, but received no help from anyone. Everyone was interested, curious, and even excited. They offered to go to his house and have a look at her, but none could give her work, though all offered her their charity.

Mari started back home, completely depressed. He resolved to suggest once again bellows-blowing for the lady. While passing before the old village temple, he stopped and fervently prayed for a way out. And an idea flashed on him.

The priest of the temple lived in the same street. The old man was sitting on the *pyol* of his house with a couple of his grandchildren playing about him. Mari stood before him and said, 'My salutations to you, my noble master.'

'Who are you?' asked the old man, half closing his eyes in his effort to catch the identity of his visitor.

'I am Mari, my master, your humble slave.'

'Mari, you are a vile hypocrite,' said the old man.

'What sin have I committed to deserve these harsh words?'

'I sent my boy thrice to your place, and thrice have you postponed and lied. It was after all for a petty, insignificant repair that I sent for you.'

'Nobody came and called me, master. I swear I would have dropped everything and come running if only the lightest whisper had reached me. Whom did you send?'

'Why should I send anyone? After all, some petty repair—I thought I might have a word with you about it if you came to the temple; but you are a godless creature; no wonder your wife is barren. How can you hope to prosper without the grace of Murugan?'

'Yours are words of wisdom. I promise that hereafter I will come to the temple twice a week and bring him a coconut once a month. Now, here I am awaiting your command.'

The old man was appeased by this submission and said, 'It is not ten minutes' work for a workman like you. Wait a minute.'

'I obey your command,' said Mari.

The old man got down from the *pyol*, looked at Mari, shading his eyes with his webbed, shrunken hands, and said, 'You don't look too well, not a quarter of what you were before.' It was only in the old man's eyes that Mari looked pulled down, but, for the sake of politeness, Mari felt obliged to agree. 'I too am growing old. All kinds of ills and bothers . . .'

The old man went in and returned half an hour later carrying three old umbrellas in his hands; behind him followed a youngster—employed in the house for cleaning the cowshed—carrying on his head a basket filled with junk. With difficulty the old man unfurled the umbrellas, and said: 'These are practically new, will be good enough to use for another ten years, if only a little rib or two is fixed up. I have been telling the boys to take these to you for ages, and they have all been postponing and lying. Everyone is a vile hypocrite.'

'I will make these brand new,' Mari said. He examined them, reflecting gloomily on the hours he would have to spend over these wretched things; and the old man was a miser.

The old man took out of the basket a bunch of grappling-hooks, four brass locks, a zinc bucket, and a blunt scythe, all of which needed Mari's healing touch very badly. Mari reflected, 'Two days of profitless labour,' and said, 'I will make these brand new for you, master.'

'What will you charge me for the whole lot?'

'I will take anything you give. What I value most is your blessing.'

'How long will you take to repair these?'

'Three days, master.'

'Can't you do it in a day?'

'I will try,' said Mari, and then opened the subject. 'Would you not like somebody to sweep the god's shrine, scrub it, and tend the garden?'

'No,' said the old man. 'What am I here for?'

'Ah,' began Mari, his wit sharpened by desperation, 'you have nobler work to do, my master,' and told him about Savitri.

'What have you to do with her?' asked the old man.

'Nothing, master, except that I have given her shelter in our humble home.'

'Why have you done it?'

'How can I say? Fate thrusts such troubles on us at times.'

'What do you care for her?'

'I really don't. My wife has taken a liking to her. It is really her doing, and she won't let me rest till I find some work for this woman.'

'If she won't let you rest, thrash her; that is the way to keep women sane. In these days you fellows are impotent mugs, and let your women ride you about.' After this homily the old man said, 'I won't have any woman in the temple. She will start some mischief or other and then the temple will get a bad name.' Mari took upon himself the task of assuring the old man of Savitri's character, but the old man would not accept it. 'There must be something wrong about her if she has no home and has to seek a livelihood outside; her husband must have driven her out. Why will a husband drive a wife out?'

'I know some sorrow has brought her out of her home,' said Mari. He had told everyone that Savitri had been found wandering on the outskirts of the village; he had not told anyone how she had really been found, fearing that it might lead to questions about his nocturnal movements. 'She is resolved to work and earn. It has grown in her as a madness. She has been starving and won't touch even fruit. I am afraid she may die in our house.'

'Drive her out and don't worry about her,' said the old man.

Mari felt desperate. He felt that it might be useful to remind the other of his debt. He said, 'I will repair these things in a day, and do any other work you may want me to do, but please let this woman work in your temple.'

'The iron bands around our grain-barrel are rather loose. Will you fix them up?'

'Yes, master, and you needn't give me an anna for all the work. Only, please employ this woman.'

'I am not unwilling to have a servant, but where am I to find the money to pay her? You fellows nowadays don't bring offerings to the god. In the days of your fathers and grandfathers I could have engaged ten such servants for the temple. Nowadays you fellows want to worship the god for free; no offerings, not even a piece of coconut.'

Mari promised to mend his irreligious ways and also undertook to reform some of his friends, and said, 'She won't demand much. Just give her something to live on, and she will be contented. Even rice will do, but please engage her. I will always be grateful to you for this kindness.' He significantly lifted the grappling-hooks and said, 'A little welding may also be necessary for this.' He then looked at the umbrellas fixedly.

The priest said, 'If I give her a half measure of rice and a quarter of an anna a day, will she be prepared to accept it and work?'

'I think she will, master.'

'If so, bring her here. I will have a look at her. If I don't see anything wrong—people can't deceive me, I can measure anyone at a glance—I will engage her. But not a grain more than a half measure.'

Ponni said to Savitri: 'My husband has found some work for you. I don't know if you will like it. I am sure if he had used his intelligence a little more he could have found a better job for you.'

Mari said fervently, 'I swear by all our gods that nothing better could be found. I searched everywhere and asked everyone.'

'Who are you to say what is good enough for this lady?'

'I never said any such thing. I saw everyone from the headman down.'

'Do you mean to imply that what you have found is the best for the lady?'

Savitri cut into the middle of this discussion: 'Any work which will keep my life in my body, though why it should I can't say, is suitable for me. I don't want to depend on anyone hereafter for the miserable handful of food I need every day.'

'You say hard words, my lady. May God grant that the sorrow which has risen before you like a mountain may soon vanish like the dew! May the God on the Hill dispel the pain in your soul!' With this prelude she told Savitri what work her husband had found for her.

Savitri felt very happy. She saw a new life opening before her. What more fitting life, she thought, could one choose than serving a god in his shrine? A half measure of rice was more than what she deserved, she felt. She could manage very well with it. She would dedicate her life to the service of God, numb her senses and memory, forget the world, and spend the rest of her years thus and die. No husband, home, or children. Ah, children! She would harden herself not to yearn for them. She would pray for them at the shrine night and day, and God would protect them: they could grow, go their ways, and tackle life as fate had ordained for each of them. What was this foolish yearning for children, this dragging attachment? One ought to do one's duty and then drift away. Did the birds and the animals worry about their young ones after they had learnt how to move? Why should she alone think of them night and day? Babu, Sumati, and Kamala were quite grown-up now; but Kamala gave no end of trouble over bath and food. Suppose she grew dirty and emaciated? Savitri dismissed this fear with a desperate effort. They were his children. He had paid for the midwife and for clothes, and for everything. He had said that she had no right to wake them up. Into this jumble of reflections Ponni intruded with, 'Madam, don't you like this work?'

'I do. I do like it very much. When shall we go there?'

'Tomorrow morning. It is late now . . . I beg of you not to fast any longer. Please eat at least two of these plantains and drink a little of the coconut water. Please rest here tonight. You will be making me very proud and happy if you will kindly accept my hospitality for just this night. You can go away tomorrow morning.' Ponni's eyes glistened with tears as she made this request. She added, 'I will prostrate myself at your feet and never rise unless you say "Yes".'

Savitri said, 'All right. I will take something.'

Eating food that was her own had grown into a perfect obsession, and so she needed some excuse for accepting the plantains and the coconut. She comforted her conscience by saying that this was the very last time in her life she would be doing it, and that it was her duty to show a little more regard for Ponni's feelings. She mentioned her hunger as the least urgent of the reasons.

Next morning mari and his wife escorted Savitri to the priest's house. Savitri went through it all as if in a trance, unconvinced of the reality of things. How could the one now tramping a village street with unknown people, in search of employment, like a boy just out of college, be the old Savitri of South Extension, wife of

So-and-so? Gangu, her old friend, could not have done a thing like this!

They stood before the priest's house. Mari shouted, 'Oh, master, master!' A little boy came to the street and said, 'Grandpa is at his prayers and asks you not to shout.'

After some time the old man came out, wrapped in a deep-red shawl. He went to the *pyol* and sat on it, muttering: 'Couldn't you wait till I finished my prayers? No chance for a man to meditate in this world with blackguards like you about. Why couldn't you have come a little later? Hm, let bygones be bygones. You are of course come about that woman. Am I right?'

'Absolutely right, my master, that is what I have come about.'

The old man laughed, rather pleased with himself at guessing Mari's mission so correctly. He shaded his eyes, looked at Ponni, and asked, 'Is this the woman?' And added, 'What is the matter with you, madam, that you should run away from home?'

'This is my wife, Ponni; she is not the one who wants to work. She has merely accompanied the other lady. This is the lady.' He whispered to Savitri, 'Please move a little to this side, madam, so that he may see you properly.' Savitri shifted her position, feeling awkward at having to exhibit herself. The old man said: 'What is the use of coming all the way if you keep yourself invisible? Come nearer. Let us have a look at you. I never decide without looking at a person, and no one can deceive me. I can measure a person at a glance, understand? Come nearer.' Savitri blushed, hung down her head, and felt very uneasy at having to display herself, with the sun's rays illuminating her on one side . . .

The old man looked at her and said he was surprised that a person like her was wandering in the world unattached. He put to her a number of questions which Savitri could not answer. When she opened her lips once or twice to say something, she found herself trembling and unable to say a word. Ponni intervened and said, 'Why should you ask these questions? There are wounds which must not be prodded.' Mari tried to check her. He whispered, 'Keep quiet. You will be irritating him.' To which she replied aloud, 'You can keep quiet if you like. I will talk to my master.' She asked the old man, 'Will you be offended if I talk to you?'

'Who are you? Oh, you are . . . I know. Why should I be offended? Anybody may talk to me. I am a servant of God. I am an old man.'

Saying this made him lose the thread of his previous talk with Savitri. Ponni said abruptly, 'Master, I am like a granddaughter to you, and I will talk to you freely. God has not blessed me with an artful tongue. I utter what I have in my soul.'

'True, true. One must utter the strictest truth,' said the old man.

'So will I. I want to ask you plainly whether you are going to engage this lady or not.'

'I am not,' said the old man promptly.

'All right, we will go home. Come on,' said Ponni. Savitri felt dejected. So back again to the life of charity and dependence. Mari apologized to the old man: 'Please don't be offended. She doesn't mean it.'

'I do mean it,' said Ponni. 'You promise one thing and do another. You are not fortunate enough to have a lady like this in your temple, that is all. And I will tell you another thing: send someone to fetch all the broken umbrellas and rubbish you have sent for repairs. If you don't send someone immediately I will throw it all into the manure dump . . .'

The mention of the old umbrellas had a good effect. The old man said, 'Woman, you are too impatient. Who said that this person would not be engaged?'

'You. Why do you ask things that are painful?'

'Just to know if I am dealing with the right person.'

'That is not the way, my master. I need not tell you, master, because you are learned and wise, whereas I am a stupid woman. You can see her, and take her in good trust and on our word, and if you find anything wrong with her later, you can dismiss her. There are questions which hurt one, you mustn't ask them.'

'I only want to know why she has run away from home. Without knowing it, how can I have her in the temple? If its reputation suffers . . .' Savitri shuddered at the implication of this remark.

Ponni said, 'There are a hundred reasons for a person to leave home. If this man by my side tries any new tricks I will walk out of home and that will be the last he will see of me, and people who ask why and what, how and when, will get the proper reply from me. You want us to do all sorts of things for you. Why should we do it? Just for the sake of friendship. And yet you won't do us a little good turn for the same friendship.'

'I never said I wouldn't do it, my good woman.'

'Will you engage this lady or not? That is what I want to know.'

'Of course I will. I am getting old. I really want somebody to keep the temple tidy.'

The temple had been built fifty years before by a local philanthropist, and dedicated to Subramanya, the peacock-enthroned god, the young son of Shiva. It was a small structure of brick and mortar, the inner shrine surmounted by a carved turret, now discoloured by time and weather, with an open circular corridor running between the shrine and the high outer wall.

Savitri and her friends waited in the street while the old man fumbled with a bunch of keys and opened the tall doors at the temple portal. Over it stood a mossy, dun-coloured peacock which once upon a time must have been as white as the plaster it was made of. The priest pushed the doors with his chest; they parted with a groan.

'Come in. Don't try to spend the whole day standing there,' the old man said, and walked in.

'Have you no kinder words to say, sir?' Ponni retorted.

'Hush!' Mari said. 'He doesn't mean any harm. You will irritate him if you speak like this.'

Ponni turned on her husband with a hiss.

'Go away and mind your own business, do you understand? We can look after ourselves quite well without you.' Mari hesitated. Ponni cried, 'Now begone! Go and open your tool-shed and earn some money. There may be people waiting for you. Don't waste the morning gaping at us. We can look after ourselves quite well.'

'Can't I wait till the shrine is opened, so that I may prostrate myself at God's feet before I begin the day's work?'

'All right. Sit down there. Don't follow us about with your remarks. Sit down there and wait till the shrine is opened and then disappear. I hope you understand simple words.'

Mari grunted something and sat down at the portal. Ponni said, 'It is no use losing one's temper.' And to Savitri, 'Come on, madam. Don't mind him; he doesn't know how to behave when there are respectable people about.' The priest had gone round the corridor once and was back again at the starting-point. He was furious. 'Do you want me to be telling you "Come on, come on" at every step? I go round thinking you are following me, and talking, and you are still here!'

'It will cost nothing to repeat your words to us again.'

'Here?' asked the old man, horrified. 'What can I tell you here? I was going round showing you where you have to do what, and you are content to stay behind. You people will kill me, one day, making me walk round and round this corridor till I am dizzy. I am not in the prime of life now. Keep it in mind.' He hobbled along, tapping his staff on the cobbled pavement. Savitri and Ponni followed him. He pointed at various corners saying, 'This is where you will have to do a little tidying.' He stopped at almost every bit of litter, saying, 'This must not be here, do you understand? This is what you will get paid for.' When they came to the portion of the corridor that was overshadowed by the branches of an immense mango tree growing in the field outside, he spent nearly half an hour pointing at every leaf which the tree had shed down. 'I have asked those rascals to do something about their tree and they won't do it. I will lop off these branches one day; let them drag me to a law court if they like. I am ready to spend my entire fortune on the lawyers.'

'Why?' Savitri ventured. 'These branches give very good shade here.'

'Do you like the shade?'

'Yes, very much.'

'Very well then,' said the old man as if Savitri's opinion decided the issue. 'I am glad to hear it, but be certain to keep the ground here clean; that is what you are getting your half measure of rice and a quarter of an anna for. Under this pile of withered leaves there may be cobras, and I don't like our devotees to be bitten to death here; devotees are rare enough without cobras.' Dry leaves on the cobbles crackled under their feet. At this corner there was a shanty created by enclosing the angles of the high wall with corrugated iron sheets and wooden boards. It had a rickety door. The old man unlocked it, saying, 'You have no home, I believe.'

'If she had a home here you would never have seen her,' Ponni said.

'You can live in this if you like,' the old man said. 'Come in and have a look. It is not bad.' Savitri stooped into it. It was very dark, light and air being admitted only by the chinks in the joints of the iron sheets. Rats jumped about, startled, and there was some flapping of wings above, which might be bats or sparrows. In a corner there was a gilded pedestal for carrying the image of God in

procession, two or three empty kerosene tins, and some gunny-
sacks. There was a blackened mud oven in another corner. Savitri
withdrew her head and breathed again. 'You can cook your food
there, and shut yourself in when you have no work,' said the old
man. 'But bear in mind that it is a special concession, and don't
imagine that you can demand it as a right. All that you can demand
is your half measure of rice and a quarter of an anna, and not this.'

'Are you giving it to me as a charity?'

'Absolutely. What doubt is there? If you have any doubt ask
anyone if anyone was ever given that room.'

Savitri said, 'I will do without the room. I will manage
somehow.'

'How will you manage? Do you think I will leave the shrine
open and that you can go and live there? I would never do that.'

'I never thought so, but I will manage. This corridor will be
home enough for me.'

'Here?' the old man exclaimed, looking up. 'With the wind and
sun and rain, not to mention any scoundrel who might think of
jumping over the wall . . . No, no. It won't do. The temple has a
name to maintain. I won't have you here if you refuse to have this
room; but don't demand it as a right.'

Ponni said, 'If you don't like this, come to my house when you
have no work to do here.'

Charity! Charity! Savitri was appalled by the amount of it that
threatened one. 'All right, I will live in this,' she said, choosing the
lesser charity.

The old man opened a back door and took them into the garden.
A few plants, nerium, jasmine, and one or two nondescripts, grew
there. There was a mud-walled well in the middle of the garden.

'I was told that you knew something of gardening. I should like
you to prove it,' said the old man. 'Here is the water, any amount
of it.'

Ponni protested: 'What do you mean by it, sir? You want her
to do the work of four persons. You want her to do this and that
endlessly in the temple; all right, we won't grumble about it. But
what is this? This is not the temple.'

'This is also a part of the temple. God must have His flowers
every day.'

'I know all that, but you can engage someone else to do the
gardening; we won't do it.'

'Very well,' said the old man. 'She need not do it; she needn't do anything.'

'What do you take her for? What do you think she is?'

'Whatever she is, we are not concerned with it now; she may be a king's wife or a judge's cousin. What do I care? I am a servant of Subramanya, and I don't care for anyone in this world.'

Finally Savitri intervened and said that she considered tending the garden the most agreeable part of the work. The old man spent nearly an hour in the garden. He stooped over every plant, and had a comment to make on every leaf.

When they came back to the portals he saw Mari squatting on the ground and asked, 'Fellow, why are you moping here?'

'I am waiting to prostrate myself before the god.'

'I am not opening the shrine now. Come in the evening. Don't imagine that I am at the beck and call of every guttersnipe in the place. Come in the evening.'

When they were about to start out Ponni asked, 'What are you doing for food today?'

'No need to think of it now. Time enough for it. I am getting my half measure of rice.'

'You will get it tomorrow,' Ponni said. 'Do you tell me that you are going to starve till tomorrow? You have starved enough, I think.'

'Why should anybody starve?' the old man asked. 'Come to my house. I will give you food.' Savitri declined the offer. Ponni suggested to the old man that he might give a measure of rice in advance. The old man revolved it in his mind and agreed. He added, 'But the quarter of an anna, she will get it only tomorrow. On no account will I give the money in advance.'

'What can she do sir, with bare rice? She has to buy a little salt and something else to go with the rice.'

The old man covered his ears with his hands. 'Don't talk. I am listening to too much talk. I won't, simply won't, give the money in advance, that is all. Don't stand there and talk till my ears ache.'

Ponni said, 'But, sir, my master, will you give her a little firewood and a small vessel?'

'All right. I never say "No" to a reasonable request.' Savitri was annoyed at the number of petty details that living demanded. Ponni was overjoyed. 'I will procure you a little buttermilk and salt.'

'No,' said Savitri emphatically. 'If you bring anything I will throw it into the well.'

'How are you going to eat plain rice?'

'I can do it. If I have to take buttermilk and salt from you, why should I work for the rice alone? You could give me that too!'

Before midday Savitri had swept the corridor clean not only of the dry leaves thrown down by the mango branches but also of all the coconut shells and faded flowers dropped there by devotees. She dug the plants and watered them. She felt a great thrill when she lit the oven and cooked a little rice for herself. 'This is my own rice, my very own; and I am not obliged to anyone for this. This is nobody's charity to me.' She felt triumphant, and a great peace descended on her as she drank a little water, came out of the kitchen, and lay down in the shade of the mango tree. She lay with her head on the threshold of the shanty, gazing at the blue sky and at the deep green of the mango foliage. Her satisfaction at having eaten food of her own was slightly spoilt by the memory of the concessions she had to accept. She soothed her mind by telling it that she would forgo a portion of her wage for some days to compensate for the vessel and the firewood. From tomorrow she would go out and gather faggots . . .

She felt happy to recollect the firmness with which she had declined Ponni's numerous offers . . .

It had been rather hard to swallow bare rice, cooked in water, without adding even salt, but it was worth it because it enhanced one's sense of victory.

The cool air, the mango shade, and the noonday glare induced a drowse. She fell asleep. The sound of a bamboo staff tapping the cobbles awoke her. 'Hey, get up, get up,' the old man cried. Savitri opened her eyes and sat up.

'It is four o'clock and you are still sleeping!'

Savitri got up and noticed that the sun had gone down the other side of the mango tree and was throwing a beam of light on the wall of the shrine.

'You think you are employed to sleep?' asked the old man, and hobbled about, peering closely at the ground. 'You have left the garbage of a week; why haven't you swept this properly?'

Savitri looked along the way he pointed. 'I don't see anything,' she said, determined to overcome her timidity.

'There, there,' the old man said, pointing with his stick. 'Don't tell me that you are blind.'

'I have good sight, but I don't see anything anywhere. I have swept the whole place thoroughly.'

'Have you? I am very glad to hear it. You appear to be a person who knows what to do. I like such persons. I don't like slackers. Come with me.'

He unlocked the door of the shrine. They entered the dark shrine, which smelt of burnt lamp-oil, flowers, incense, and bats. The old man lit a couple of tall bronze lamps. He asked, 'Where are the flowers?'

'Which flowers?'

'Which flowers!' the old man repeated. 'Flowers in the garden. Don't ask "Which garden?" Have you not gathered the flowers yet?'

Savitri went to the garden and brought a handful of flowers. The old man took the flowers and entered the inner shrine. Savitri brought together her palms and prayed to the idol: 'Protect Sumati, Babu, and Kamala. Let them all eat well and grow. Please see that they are not unhappy.' The old man said, 'This is the first day and so I don't mind if you are a little slack, but from tomorrow I won't show the same patience. Now take a rag and clean all the lamps and fill them with fresh oil.'

'Where can I find a rag?'

'Create one, young woman. You mustn't ask me where is this and what is that. I don't care if you have to tear a piece out of your saree. Work should not suffer, and the good name of the temple must be maintained at any cost. What is the use of having you here if you have got to be plaguing me like this? That blackguard and his wife and everybody comes to plead for you. I don't care for anyone here to know that. That woman may have the worst tongue in the village, but I am equal to it.' The old man went on talking as he bent over the idol and picked up the faded flowers on it, polished its ornaments, and decorated it with fresh flowers.

At five o'clock visitors began to arrive. Rumour had gone abroad that a mysterious woman was engaged in the temple, and this brought in more visitors than was usual. Everybody looked about, stared at Savitri, nudged each other, went round the corridor, prostrated before the image, and gave the old man the offerings. So many people kept staring at her that Savitri slipped out and shut herself in the shanty.

When the voices ceased, late in the evening, she came out. In the inner shrine the old man was bundling up the coconuts, fruits, and coins that he had collected. He was very pleased. 'People are once again becoming godly,' he said, his small face creased in a smile, and shining in the light near the idol. He threw a piece of coconut at her and said, 'Take it, it is your share.'

'I don't want it. My share is only a half measure of rice.'

'Take the coconut also. You are a good woman, you deserve it.'

'No. I never eat coconut.'

The old man was about to go home. As she saw him at the door, Savitri felt suddenly desolate. She would have to be all alone in this dark temple, with the dim oil-lamp, and stars, and the massive tree looming over the wall. The old man said, 'If you are afraid to remain here, you may come to my house. You can spend the night with the womenfolk in my house.'

'Of what should I be afraid?' asked Savitri. Was there no escape from fear and charity?

'How can I say?' said the old man.

'I am not afraid of anything,' said Savitri, and added, 'I am living in God's house and He will protect me.'

These brave words did not sustain her long. After the old man departed she regretted she had not accepted his offer. Everything terrified her. The whole air was oppressive; the surrounding objects assumed monstrous shapes in the solitary hour. She fled to her shanty and bolted the door. She lit a cotton wick floating on oil in a little mud pan.

As the hours advanced and the stillness grew deeper, her fears also increased. She was furious with herself at this: 'What despicable creations of God are we that we can't exist without a support. I am like a bamboo pole which cannot stand without a wall to support it . . .'

And she grew homesick. A nostalgia for the children, home, and accustomed comforts seized her. Lying here on the rough floor, beside the hot flickering lamp, her soul racked with fears, she couldn't help contrasting the comfort, security, and un-loneliness of her home. When she shut the door and put out the lights, how comforting the bed felt and how well one could sleep! Not this terrible state . . . And then the children. What a void they created! 'I must see them; I must see Babu, I must see Sumati, and I must see Kamala. Oh . . .' But what about the fiery vows, and the coming out at midnight?

The futility, the frustration, and her own inescapable weakness made her cry and sob. 'A wretched fate wouldn't let me drown first time. I can't go near the water again. This is defeat. I accept it. I am no good for this fight. I am a bamboo pole . . . Perhaps Sumati and Kamala have not had their hair combed for ages now . . .'

In the morning Savitri went over to the old man's house and told him, 'I am leaving.'

'What has happened?'

'I can't keep away from my children and home.'

'All right. I never asked you to come and work.'

'Here is the vessel I borrowed yesterday, here is the key of the room.'

'Are the things in it safe?'

'Yes. As you see, I am carrying nothing with me.'

'Hm! There is nothing there worth taking.'

They were silent for some time and he asked, 'Why are you standing there? I gave you your yesterday's wage in advance.'

'Yes,' she said, though he had given only the rice and not the money. 'I am only waiting to take leave of you.'

'All right, you can go. God's blessings be on you. Don't leave your children and wander about hereafter.'

She hesitated before Ponni's house for a moment. Her first impulse was to go away without telling her. A defeat needed no proclamation . . .

She knocked on the door. Ponni invited her in. 'No. I am going. I have just come to tell you I am going home.'

Ponni was overjoyed to hear it.

'At first I thought of going away without telling you.'

'Ah, how could you?'

'No, I couldn't. I will remember all my life your affection and help. God will reward you for your goodness. May He bless you with a child soon!'

'How are you going to reach the town?'

'Only two or three miles. I will manage; don't worry yourself.'

'Oh no, impossible,' said Ponni, and came out. She shouted to her neighbour: 'Sister, please keep an eye on this house. There is nobody in.'

They walked down the tree-flanked highway. Ponni explained her husband's absence. 'A cart broke down somewhere and people came and pulled the poor man right out of bed, even before dawn. Poor man, he really does work hard.' She stopped every passing bullock-cart to ask, 'Are you going townward? Will you take a passenger?' At last they found a cartman willing to take in a passenger. Ponni disputed with heat the fare the cartman demanded. It took nearly half an hour for a settlement to be reached.

'Now get into the cart, I will walk back home,' Ponni said. 'Go with a cheerful face. Don't look so sad. Remember: men are good creatures, but you must never give way to them. Be firm and they will behave.'

'All right,' Savitri said. 'I will remember it.' She was about to ask Ponni and her husband to visit her at South Extension, but checked herself. 'Who am I to invite a guest?'

'Murugan's blessings on you. He will protect you and your children. Mari occasionally comes to the town to earn an extra anna. I will ask him to see you,' said Ponni. She wiped her eyes and stood in the middle of the road, watching, till the cart was out of sight.

11

THE CHILDREN SAT round under the hall bulb.

Babu said, 'I don't like the look of things. We must do something. I don't believe Father.'

Kamala said. 'Father has told us that she has gone to see Grandfather.'

'I don't believe it, because if she has . . . You are still children. You may believe what he says, but I don't. Don't ask why.' At this Kamala showed signs of bursting into tears. Sumati put her arms around her and frowned at Babu. 'Why do you frighten the child by talking in this mysterious manner?'

Babu said, 'I was only joking. Don't cry. Mother has gone to see Grandpa, she will be back soon. Don't cry, little one. I will take you to Chandru's house tomorrow and show you the electric tram he has made.'

Kamala lifted her tear-filled eyes to him and asked, 'Is it a promise?'

'Yes.'

'Will you swear that you won't break it?'

'I never swear. If you don't believe me, don't believe me, that is all.'

'If you do, I will cry,' said Kamala, and showed signs of fulfilling the threat. Babu said, 'You mustn't cry. If you do, you will never be able to read your lessons, pass your exams, and become a doctor.'

'I don't want to be a doctor,' said Kamala petulantly.

'What else do you want to be? You said that when you were grown-up you wished to be a doctor like our lady doctor.'

'What do you care what I am going to be? It is none of your business.'

'Don't be impertinent. Learn to behave before your elders,' Babu said hotly, at which Kamala threatened to break down once again.

Sumati said, 'Now, will you leave us alone or not? I will call the cook.' She called the cook and told him, 'Babu is teasing me and Kamala, and won't leave us alone.'

The cook held up a finger and warned Babu: 'I will tell Father as soon as he comes home. Leave them alone, and go and read your books.'

'Mind your own business. Who are you to command me?'

The cook sat down on the carpet cross-legged and said, 'Look me in the eyes and say it.' He looked fixedly at Babu. Babu said, 'All right, I will. I am not afraid of your powers of magic.' The girls screamed and covered Babu's eyes with their hands, and also his mouth, in order to stop it from uttering further blasphemies.

'Take away your hands,' the cook said, looking wild.

'No, no. Forgive him for our sake. He won't say such things again. Please take your eyes off him.' The belief was that a person who looked into the cook's eyes at certain moments would be turned to stone. They had been told that many of the furlong and milestones in the place were once human beings who had dared to look into the cook's eyes; after they became stones the government people came along, chiselled them into shape, and carved miles and furlongs on them.

The girls very nearly threw Babu down and held him away from the cook's visual range. Babu was gasping for breath. Ranga came in from somewhere at the moment, and the cook appealed to him to decide whether Babu was to be petrified or not. Ranga, after a moment's thought, said, 'Leave him alone. He is more or less motherless now.' He then passed on to scandal: 'What is this that people are saying? I thought things looked rather queer . . .' He related how a friend of his working in the engineer's house overheard the engineer's wife saying that a certain lady's departure seemed to be rather abrupt, and as far as she knew (she also belonged to Talapur and received letters from there) there was nothing the matter with the old man; and then Ranga's friend had heard something about a new person in the office and complications at home.

The cook said, 'It may be true or it may not be. Why do you waste your time listening to gossip? Our business is to do our business. We don't care what happens to anybody. There was some talk about it this evening at the coffee-house, and I said that the departure was rather abrupt and as far as we knew there was neither letter nor telegram about the old man's health, and if that is so how could anyone be compelled to believe the story? It is no use compelling people to believe this or that, and I told them the truth, namely, that So-and-so has not been coming home punctually of late. Was there anything wrong in what I said?'

'No, none,' said Ranga. 'You spoke only the truth, didn't you?'

Kamala asked, 'Are you talking about Mother?'

'Why?'

'Because if it is about Mother we want to know what you are saying.'

'No. It is about someone else,' the cook said. 'Why should we talk about your mother? You were talking about someone else, weren't you, Ranga?'

'Yes, yes.'

it was about my uncle in the town who has a lot of money but is not coming home when he should, and so people want to shut him out of the house.'

'Where does he go?'

'He has a number of concubines and he stays with them.'

'What are concubines?' Kamala asked.

Babu warned Ranga: 'You are uttering bad words before the children. Take care.'

'What is bad about the word? Don't we say "wife"? It is a similar word.'

'Why don't you drop it if it is a bad word?' Sumati asked. Kamala said, 'We don't want to hear any bad word now, so leave it alone. Go on, tell me: if it was about your uncle and not about Mother you were speaking why did you mention Grandpa in Talapur?'

'My uncle's sister's grandfather is also in Talapur and she went to see him because he was unwell.'

'But you said that no letter or telegram arrived.'

'Yes. No letter or telegram arrived, yet she went off rather abruptly thinking that her grandfather was ill . . . I will tell you more about it while you eat. Come in for dinner. It is getting late.'

Father came home. He passed straight through to the kitchen, stood on the threshold, and watched the children eat.

'How many runs did you make this evening, Babu?'

'I got only one chance to bat, and I made twenty runs.'

'Is that all? When I was your age I never made anything under fifty. It was because I ate well and was strong. You are puny and won't eat. Look at the rice on your plate! It is a quarter of what I used to eat at your age. Eat well, young man, and you will be able to score more runs. Here, bring some more rice for this boy.'

Father looked at Kamala and said: 'Why is your hair so rumpled? Did you comb and braid it this evening?'

'I forgot to do it, Father,' said Kamala.

Sumati said, 'She gave such a lot of trouble that I couldn't do it. Every day Mother had such a lot of trouble . . .'

Ramani looked at Kamala reprovingly and said, 'Is this how you conduct yourself? Your hair is standing on end and you look like a sick person. You must be a good girl now. Sumati, you must attend to her properly. This won't do.' He watched them till they finished their dinner and then went in to change.

After they had washed their hands Babu managed to take Sumati aside, and said, 'Do you know what Janamma told me this evening?'

'No.'

'That Mother has not gone to Talapur. I suspected that there was some such thing.'

'Where is she?'

'Who can say? She might have been carried away by robbers or eaten by lions or tigers.'

Sumati trembled, and put her hands to her eyes. Babu sternly told her, 'None of that. Don't create a scene. If you cry I will never speak to you again.'

'What are we to do about it now?' Sumati asked.

'You leave it to me. I will speak to Father and ask him to search.'

'He may get angry with you.'

'If he gets angry I will do something else.' He had already made up his mind, as a last measure, to inform the police through his friend Chandru.

Babu waited till Kamala went to bed, and tiptoed to his father's room. He stood at the doorway and peeped in. Father was on his rattan lounge with a novel in his hand. Babu could see only Father's back and so was unable to foresee how he would be received. He wished he could get a view of his face, and tiptoed away back to his desk. Though he opened his geography and looked at it, he could not follow a single line. He felt restless. He felt that while he was sniffing at his cursed geography, his mother might be losing the last chance of being saved. He threw down the book and went once again to his father's room. He hesitated for a moment, looking at the back of Father's head . . . Suppose Father started beating him the moment Mother was mentioned? If he did, Babu would wrench away, run out of the house, and tell Chandru to tell the police . . . But why not wait a little while and try to catch Father some other time? He smothered this suggestion and resolutely walked in and stood before his father.

'Finished your studies for the night?' asked Father, looking over his book.

'Yes.'

'Then go and sleep.'

'All right, Father. But I have come to talk about Mother.'

'What about her?'

'Is she alive?' And saying this he burst into tears. Ramani was slightly frightened. He himself had not been quite easy in mind since the morning. It was three days since she had left, and still there was no sign of her. While the Strong Man in him said that she couldn't have gone far and that she was bound to return when she regained sense, the Weak Man, so long unnoticed by himself, constantly pricked him with the reminder that she had been gone two days and three nights now; and suppose she had done something very rash and foolish or something had happened to her, how was he to answer the children, her people, and everybody? People would talk: 'The wife of the Secretary of the Engladia Insurance Company . . .' He shuddered. If anything happened he would have to pack out of Malgudi . . . And now this boy.

'Why do you cry?' he asked. Babu sobbed that he had learnt

that Mother had not gone to Talapur and he had known that she hadn't gone there. Ramani felt angry. This little boy to come and cause a disturbance with his wild imaginings. 'Look here, I don't like this sort of thing. Don't listen to stupid lies. Go and sleep.' The boy stood still, showed no signs of moving, and his sobbing increased. Ramani looked at him in helpless anger. He felt like slapping him; he would have done it if Savitri had been there. Now he couldn't do it. The boy seemed to have inherited something of his mother's hysteria. He might create a very noisy scene with the other children joining in. He took Babu's hand, drew him nearer, and said, 'Don't cry. Your mother is safe. You are a big boy; you play cricket and all that. How can you cry like a baby if your mother is absent for a little while?'

'It is not that. It is because I suspect things,' Babu said, blowing his nose, considerably mollified by his father's manner. He told his father what he had heard from Janamma. Ramani felt very uncomfortable; he was frightened of the boy; he couldn't stay in his company any longer. He rose from his lounge and said, 'I never knew that you would feel so unhappy. I will go to the post office and send a telegram asking your mother to return at once.'

'Is she really there?'

'Of course. Why do you doubt it?' He dressed hurriedly and started out. 'I have some other business too. I may return late. If you are all afraid to be alone you can ask the cook to sleep in the hall.'

Babu announced to his sisters, 'Father will be late, and he says the cook may sleep in the hall.' Kamala threw up her pillow for joy. Sumati ran into inform the cook. Babu followed her and whispered, 'Father has gone to send a telegram to Mother. She will be here very soon. Father wasn't angry with me at all.'

Ramani drove about the streets aimlessly, wondering what steps he should take now. After some time it occurred to him that he might see his friend Naidu, the police inspector, and talk things over with him. He might be able to help. He drove the car to the inspector's quarters behind the Central Police Station in Market Road.

'Hello, Ramani!' the inspector said. 'What a rare bird you are nowadays! What brings you here, theft, larceny, or arson? What can I do for you?'

'I just passed this way and thought I might as well drop in,' said

Ramani. He stayed with the inspector for half an hour exchanging town gossip, and left.

He drove the car down Market Road and North Street, and reached the river. 'Why have I come here?' he asked himself. 'How does one search for a lost wife?' He sat in the car peering across the sands into the darkness as if expecting his wife to rise from the water and come to the car. He stayed for a long time thus. He hated himself for worrying about things. He hated Savitri for bringing him to this pass, and he hated Babu for disturbing his peace. 'Everything is a bother, no peace of mind in this life.' He brooded and speculated and then said, 'I will wait for a day longer.' He felt relieved at having found a way out of the present difficulty, however vague the exit might be. He reversed the car and retraced his way. His heart was lighter now as he drove up the silent Market Road. At the crossing he turned to his left, drove into Race Course Road, and stopped before his office.

12

IT WAS OVER an hour since she had arrived. The children's excitement had subsided. She ventured to ask, 'Where is your father?'

'Last night he went out to send the telegram and he hasn't yet come home. He said that the cook might sleep in the hall. What a fine story the cook told us! He went on till midnight, but Babu wouldn't let him continue . . .'

'Why did you interrupt the story, Babu?'

'What nonsense, Mother! Were we to keep awake all night?'

'You could have gone away from us and slept somewhere; you needn't have disturbed us.'

'Mother, he has promised to continue the story tonight. We weren't in the least afraid at being without you. We kept the light on all night.'

'Father took us all to a cinema and bought us such a lot of sweets.'

The car sounded its horn outside. Kamala and Sumati ran to the gate to announce, 'Mother has come!'

'Has she?' Ramani asked, and went into the house. He hesitated for a fraction of a second on the doormat and then passed on to his room. Savitri sat in the passage of the dining-room, trembling. What would he do now? Would he come and turn her out of the house?

An hour later Ramani came towards her. She started up. He threw a brief look at her, noted her ragged appearance, and went into the dining-room. He said to the cook, 'Hurry, up, I have to be at the office . . .' Savitri stood in the passage for some time. He had started eating. She stepped into the dining-room and stood before him, watching his leaf. She noticed a space in a corner of the leaf.

'Shall I call for some more beans?'

'No,' Ramani said without looking up.

'Curd?' Savitri asked.

'Yes.'

Savitri went to the cupboard and took hold of the curd vessel.

At eight-thirty in the evening the children had finished their dinner and were sitting round Savitri, ceaselessly talking, asking questions, and quarrelling. The hooting of the car a furlong off was heard—the long blast and the slight tremolo, which Savitri's accustomed ears picked up and interpreted, 'He is coming home in a sweet mood.' Her habit roused her. She was about to shout to Ranga to run to the garage, fretting and fussing so that the lord's homecoming might be smooth and without annoyance . . . She checked herself.

'The car has come,' the children said, jumping up.

'What if it has?' Savitri asked, as the car hooted continuously in front of the garage door.

'As usual Ranga is away somewhere, and the garage door is unopened,' Babu said.

'Find Ranga or go and open the door yourself,' said Savitri.

Ramani paused on the doormat and threw a genial look around. 'How are we all today?' he asked, and the children made some indistinct sounds in reply. 'What does your mother say?' he asked, and the children giggled. He went in to change.

Later he asked, 'Children finished their dinner?'

'Yes,' said Savitri.

'Haven't you finished yours?'

'No.'

'Waiting for me?'

'Yes.'

'What a dutiful wife you are,' he remarked, and laughed. He was granting her the privilege to laugh and joke and be happy.

'Oh, I should have bought some jasmine for you,' he said, looking at her mischievously. She tried to smile.

He watched her for a moment while she was eating. 'Oh, how poorly you eat!' he exclaimed. 'Have a little more ghee. Eat well, my girl, and grow fat. Don't fear that you will make me bankrupt by eating.'

She attempted to laugh, and muttered through it, 'If I grow too fat, people may not recognize me.' She knew it was a miserable joke. 'A part of me is dead,' she reflected.

He said, 'I came home early entirely for your sake, and now you won't talk to me properly. What is the matter with you?'

'I don't know. I am all right. I am tired and want to sleep.'

He pleaded with her, later: 'Just a pretty half an hour. You can go to bed at ten-thirty. Just a little talk. I came home early for your sake.'

'I can't even stand. I am very tired. I must sleep.'

'Please yourself,' he said, and went away to his room.

Days later, one afternoon she was lying on her carpet in the hall, half asleep. (The bench was still away at the office.) Her husband had gone to the office, the children had gone to school, the cook on his afternoon rounds, and Ranga was in the back yard washing clothes.

From somewhere came a voice crying, 'Locks repaired, sirs, umbrellas repaired!' Savitri rose from the carpet and sat on the sill of the window facing the street. The voice came nearer, and then she saw Mari passing in the dusty street, with his tool-bag slung over his shoulder and a couple of dilapidated umbrellas under his arm; his dark face was shining with sweat under the hot sun.

Savitri felt excited. She could give him food, water, and a magnificent gift, and inquire about her great friend Ponni; perhaps Ponni had sent him along now. Savitri almost called him through the window, but suddenly checked herself and let him pass. He had now passed the house. She felt unhappy at letting him go; she felt that it was very mean and unjust . . .

'Locks repaired, sirs . . .' came from the next street.

The poor fellow's face shone with sweat; perhaps he had been tramping the streets in the hot sun, foodless; perhaps he had not earned a pie yet in the town. How this man and Ponni had begged her to take the coconut and plantain . . .

'Very unjust to let him go, but what can I do?' she reflected.

She called Ranga and told him, 'Call that lock-repairer who was crying in the street just now. He must be in the next street.'

'Yes, madam.'

As Ranga was about to step out she changed her mind: 'Let him go, don't call him.' She thought: 'Why should I call him here? What have I?'

'Locks repaired, sirs, umbrellas repaired!' came from four or five streets off.

She sat by the window, haunted by his shining hungry face long after he was gone, and by his 'Locks repaired! . . .' long after his cry had faded out in the distance.

The English Teacher

1

I WAS ON the whole very pleased with my day—not many conflicts and worries, above all not too much self-criticism. I had done almost all the things I wanted to do, and as a result I felt heroic and satisfied. The urge had been upon me for some days past to take myself in hand. What was wrong with me? I couldn't say, some sort of vague disaffection, a self-rebellion I might call it. The feeling again and again came upon me that as I was nearing thirty I should cease to live like a cow (perhaps a cow, with justice, might feel hurt at the comparison), eating, working in a manner of speaking, walking, talking, etc.—all done to perfection, I was sure, but always leaving behind a sense of something missing.

I took stock of my daily life. I got up at at eight every day, read for the fiftieth time Milton, Carlyle and Shakespeare, looked through compositions, swallowed a meal, dressed, and rushed out of the hostel just when the second bell sounded at college; four hours later I returned to my room; my duty in the interval had been admonishing, cajoling and browbeating a few hundred boys of Albert Mission College so that they might mug up Shakespeare and Milton and secure high marks and save me adverse remarks from my chiefs at the end of the year. For this pain the authorities kindly paid me a hundred rupees on the first of every month and dubbed me a lecturer. One ought, of course, to be thankful and rest content. But such repose was not in my nature, perhaps because I was a poet, and I was constantly nagged by the feeling that I was doing the wrong work. This was responsible for a perpetual self-criticism and all kinds of things aggravated it. For instance what my good chief Brown had said to us that day might be very reasonable, but it irritated and upset me.

We were summoned to his room at the end of the day. Under normal conditions, he would welcome us with a smile, crack a joke or two, talk of nothing in particular for a couple of minutes and then state the actual business. But today we found him dry and sullen. He motioned us to our seats and said, 'Could you imagine a worse shock for me? I came across a student of English Honours, who did not know till this day that "honours" had to be spelt with a "u"?' He finished his sentence with a sharp, grim laugh. We looked at each other and were at a loss to know what to reply. Our Assistant Professor, Gajapathy, scowled at us as if it were we who had

induced the boy to drop the 'u'. Brown cleared his throat as a signal
for further speech, and we watched his lips. He began a lecture on
the importance of the English language, and the need for preserving
its purity. Brown's thirty years in India had not been ill-spent if they
had opened the eyes of Indians to the need for speaking and writing
correct English! The responsibility of the English department was
indeed very great. At this point Gajapathy threw us a further
furious look. The chief went on for forty-five minutes; and feeling
that it was time to leaven his sermon with a little humour, added:
'It would be a serious enough blunder even from a mathematics
honours man!'

When going out I was next to Gajapathy. He looked so heavily
concerned that I felt like pricking him so that he might vanish like
a bubble leaving no trace behind. But I checked myself. It would
be unwise: he was my senior in office, and he might give me an
hour of extra work every day, or compel me to teach the history
of language, of which I knew nothing. I had to bear with him till
we reached the hostel gate. He kept glancing at his own shoulder,
swelling with importance. He muttered: 'Disgraceful! I never knew
our boys were so bad . . . We cannot pretend that we come out of it
with flying colours . . .' I felt irritated and said, 'Mr Gajapathy, there
are blacker sins in this world than a dropped vowel.' He stopped on
the road and looked me up and down. He was aghast. I didn't care.
I drove home the point: 'Let us be fair. Ask Mr Brown if he can say
in any of the two hundred Indian languages: "The cat chases the
rat". He has spent thirty years in India.'

'It is all irrelevant,' said Gajapathy.

'Why should he think the responsibility for learning is all on our
side and none on his? Why does he magnify his own importance?'

'Good night,' said Gajapathy and was off. I felt angry and insulted,
and continued my discussion long after both Gajapathy and
Brown were out of my reach. Later when I went for a walk I still
continued the debate. But suddenly I saw illumination and checked
myself. It showed a weak, uncontrolled mind, this incapacity to
switch off. I now subjected myself to a remorseless self-analysis.
Why had I become incapable of controlling my own thoughts? I
brooded over it. Needless to say it took me nowhere. It left me
more exhausted and miserable at the end of the day. I felt a great
regret at having spent a fine evening in brooding and self-analysis,
and then reached a startlingly simple solution. All this trouble was

due to lack of exercise and irregular habits: so forthwith I resolved to be up very early next day, go out along the river on a long walk, run a few yards, bathe in the river and regulate my life thus.

After dinner my friends in the neighbouring rooms in the hostel dropped in as usual for light talk. They were my colleagues. One was Rangappa who taught the boys philosophy, and the other Gopal of the mathematics section. Gopal was sharp as a knife-edge where mathematical matters were concerned, but, poor fellow, he was very dumb and stupid in other matters. As a matter of fact he paid little attention to anything else. We liked him because he was a genius, and in a vague manner we understood that he was doing brilliant things in mathematics. Some day he hoped to contribute a paper on his subject which was going to revolutionize human thought and conceptions. But God knew what it was all about. All that I cared for in him was that he was an agreeable friend, who never contradicted and who listened patiently for hours, though without showing any sign of understanding.

Tonight the talk was all about English spelling and the conference we had with Brown. I was incensed as usual, much to the amazement of Rangappa. 'But my dear fellow, what do you think they pay you for unless it is for dotting the i's and crossing the t's?' Gopal, who had been listening without putting in a word of his own, suddenly became active.

'I don't follow you,' he said.

'I said the English department existed solely for dotting the i's and crossing the t's.'

'Oh!' he said, opening his eyes wide. 'I never thought so. Why should you do it?' His precise literal brain refused to move where it had no concrete facts or figures to grip. Symbols, if they entered his brain at all, entered only as mathematical symbols.

Rangappa answered: 'Look here, Gopal. You have come across the expression "raining cats and dogs"?'

'Yes.'

'Have you actually seen cats and dogs falling down from the sky?'

'No, no. Why?'

Rangappa would have worried him a little longer, but the college clock struck ten and I said: 'Friends, I must bid you good night.' 'Good night,' Gopal repeated mechanically and rose to go.

Not so the ever-questioning philosopher. 'What has come over you?'
he asked, without moving.

'I want to cultivate new habits . . .'

'What's wrong with the present ones?' he asked and I blinked
for an answer. It was a long story and could not stand narration.
Rangappa did not even stir from his seat; the other stood ready to
depart and waited patiently. 'Answer me,' Rangappa persisted.

'I want to be up very early tomorrow,' I said.

'What time?'

'Some time before five.'

'What for?'

'I want to see the sunrise, and get some exercise before I start
work.'

'Very good; wake me up too, I shall also go with you—' said
Rangappa rising. I saw them off at the door. I had an alarm clock
on which I could sometimes depend for giving the alarm at the
set time. I had bought it years before at a junk store in Madras. It
had a reddening face, and had been oiled and repaired a score of
times. It showed the correct time but was eccentric with regard to
its alarm arrangement. It let out a shattering amount of noise, and
it sometimes went off by itself and butted into a conversation, or
sometimes when I had locked the room and gone out, it started off
and went on ringing till exhaustion overcame it. There was no way
of stopping it, by pressing a button or a lever. I don't know if it had
ever had such an arrangement. At first I did not know about its
trouble, so that I suffered a great shock and did not know how to
silence it, short of dashing it down. But one day I learnt by some sort
of instinctive experiment that if I placed a heavy book like Taine's
History of English Literature on its crest, it stopped shrieking.

I picked up the clock and sat on my bed looking at it. I believe I
almost addressed it: 'Much depends upon you.' I set it at four-thirty
and lay down.

At four-thirty it shrieked my sleep away. I switched on the
light, picked up Taine hurriedly, and silenced it. I sent over to
Rangappa's room, stood at his window and called him a dozen
times, but there was no answer. As I stood looking at his sleeping
figure with considerable disgust and pity, he stirred and asked:
'Who is there?'

'It is nearing five, you wanted to be called out—'

'Why?'

'You said you would come out.'

'Not me—'

'It is about five—' I said.

'It looks to me like midnight; go back to bed, my dear fellow, don't hang about windows pestering people—' His voice was thick and the last words trailed off into sleep.

I stepped out of the hostel gates. Our college and hostel were not more than a couple of hundred yards from the river. There was a narrow lane to be crossed and at the end of it we were on the sands. As I walked down the lane a couple of municipal lamps were still burning, already showing signs of paling before the coming dawn. The eastern skyline was reddening and I felt triumphant. I could not understand how people could remain in bed when there was such a glory awaiting them outside. I thought of Rangappa. 'A dry philosopher I suppose—not susceptible to these influences. A hopeless man. In any case not my business . . .'

The sand was damp with the morning dew, but as I buried my feet, they felt deep down the warmth of the previous day's sun. In the half-dark dawn I saw some persons already out at work, fording the river, bathing and washing. There were immense banyan trees hanging over the river, and birds stirred and chirped in their nests. I walked on at an even pace, filling my lungs with morning air, and taking great strides. I felt I was really in a new world. I walked nearly four miles down the bank. Before turning back, I selected a clean spot, undressed, and plunged into the water. Coming on shore and rubbing myself with the towel, I felt I had a new lease of life. No doubt in my village home and in this very river I had often bathed, but at no other time could I remember such a glow of joy as that which filled me now. How could I account for it? There was something in the deliberate effort, and the hour and the air, and surroundings . . . Nature, nature, all our poets repeat till they are hoarse. There are subtle, invisible emanations in nature's surroundings: with them the deepest in us merges and harmonizes. I think it is the highest form of joy and peace we can ever comprehend. I decided to rush back to my table and write a poem on nature.

I was going to write of the cold water's touch on the skin, the cold air blowing on my chest and face, the rumble of the river, cries of birds, magic of the morning light, all of which created an alchemy of inexplicable joy. I paused for a moment and wondered how this poem would be received in a class-room—the grim tolerance with which boys listen to poetry, the annotator's desperate effort to convey a meaning, and the teacher's doubly desperate effort to wrest a meaning out of the poet and the annotator, the essence of an experience lost in all this handling . . .

I returned to my room before seven. I felt very well satisfied indeed with my performance. I told myself: 'I am all right. I am quite sound if I can do this every day. I shall be able to write a hundred lines of poetry, read everything I want to read, in addition to class-work . . .' This gave place to a distinct memory of half a dozen similar resolves in the past and the lapses . . . I checked this defeatism! 'Don't you see this is entirely different? I am different today . . .'

'How?' asked a voice. I ignored the question and it added, 'Why?'

'Shut up,' I cried. 'Don't ask questions.' I myself was not clear as to the 'Why?' except that my conscience perpetually nagged over arrears of work, books from libraries and friends lying in a heap on the table untouched, letters unanswered and accumulating, lines of poetry waiting for months to be put on paper, a picture of my wife meant to be framed and hung on the wall, but for months and months standing on the table leaning against the wall in its cardboard mount, covered with dust, bent by the weight of the books butting into it . . .

This table assailed my sight as soon as I entered and I muttered 'Must set all this right', as I sat down on my chair. I called Singaram our servant. He had been a hostel servant for forty years and known all of us as undergraduates and now as teachers—an old man who affected great contempt for all of us, including our senior professors and principal. He spoke to us with habitual rudeness. Somehow he felt that because he had seen all of us as boys, our present stature and age and position were a make-believe, to which he would be no party. 'Singaram,' I called, and he answered from somewhere, 'You will have to wait till I come. If you hurt your throat calling me, don't hold me responsible for it . . .' In a few minutes he stood before me, a shrunken old fellow, with angry wrinkles on his face. 'Now what is it this time? Has that sweeper not done her work properly? If she is up to her old tricks . . .'

'Tell the cook to bring my coffee . . .'

'So late! Why should you dally over your coffee so long, when you ought to be reading at your table . . .'

'I went for a bathe in the river, Singaram. I found it very fine . . .'
He was happy to hear it.

'I'm glad you are ceasing to be the sort who lounges before bathrooms, waiting for a hot bath. A river bath is the real thing for a real man. I am eighty years old, and have never had a day's sickness, and have never bathed in hot water.'

'Nor in cold water, I think,' I said as he went away to send me my coffee.

I made a space on the table by pushing aside all the books; took out a sheet of paper and wrote a poem entitled 'Nature', about fifty lines of verse. I read and re-read it, and found it very satisfying. I felt I had discharged a duty assigned to me in some eternal scheme.

I had four hours of teaching to do that day. *Lear* for the Junior BA class, a composition period for the Senior Arts; detailed prose and poetry for other classes. Four periods of continuous work and I hadn't prepared even a page of lecture.

I went five minutes late to the class, and I could dawdle over the attendance for a quarter of an hour. I picked out the attendance register and called out the first name.

'Here, sir—', 'Present', and I marked. Two boys in the front bench got up and suggested, 'Sir, take the attendance at the end of the period.'

'Sit down please, can't be done. I can't encroach into the next hour's work . . .'

A babble rose in the class, a section demanding that the attendance be taken immediately and another demanding postponement. I banged the table with my fist and shouted over the din: 'Stop this, otherwise I will mark everyone absent.'

'Attendance takes up most of our hours, sir.'

'We can't help it. Your attendance is just as important as anything else. Stop all noise and answer your names; otherwise, I will mark all of you absent . . .' At this the boys became quiet, because I outshouted them. The lion-tamer's touch! In a sober moment perhaps I would reflect on the question of obedience. Born in different households, perhaps petted, pampered, and bullied, by parents, uncles, brothers—all persons known to them and responsible for their growth and welfare. Who was I that they should obey my command? What tie was there between me and them? Did I absorb their personalities as did the old masters and merge them in mine? I was merely a man who had mugged earlier than they the

introduction and the notes in the Verity edition of *Lear*, and guided
them through the mazes of Elizabethan English. I did not do it out
of love for them or for Shakespeare but only out of love for myself.
If they paid me the same one hundred rupees for stringing beads
together or tearing up paper bits every day for a few hours, I would
perhaps be doing it with equal fervour. But such reflections do
not már our peace when we occupy the class-room chair. So that I
banged the table—shouted till they were silenced, and went through
the attendance; all this tittle-tattle swallowed up half an hour.

I opened my Verity. I had made a pencil mark where I had stopped
on the previous day: middle of the first scene in the third act.

I began in a general way: 'You will see that I stopped last time
where Lear faces the storm. This is a vital portion of this great
tragedy . . .' The words rang hollow in my ears. Some part of me
was saying: 'These poor boys are now all attention, cowed by your
superior force. They are ready to listen to you and write down
whatever you may say. What have you to give them in return?' I
noticed that some boys were already sitting up alert, ready to note
down the pearls dropping from my mouth . . . I felt like breaking
out into a confession! 'My dear fellows, don't trust me so much. I
am merely trying to mark time because I couldn't come sufficiently
prepared, because all the morning I have . . .' But I caught myself
lecturing: 'This is the very heart of the tragedy and I would like you
to follow this portion with the greatest attention . . .' I stole a look
at the watch . . . only fifteen minutes more. 'As usual I shall read
through this scene first, and then I shall take it up in detail . . .' I
looked at the page on the table—'Enter Lear and Fool. Blow winds
and crack your cheeks! Rage! Blow! You cataracts and hurricanes,
spout till you have drenched our steeples, drowned the cocks! . . .'
As I read on I myself was moved by the force and fury of the storm
compressed in these lines. The sheer poetry of it carried me on . . .

'. . . And thou, all-shaking Thunder
Strike flat the thick rotundity o' the world!'

I forgot all about the time, all about my unpreparedness.

'. . . Let the great gods
That keep this dreadful pother o'er our heads,
Find out their enemies now.'

I read on. The boys listened attentively. I passed on to the next
scene without knowing it. I could not stop.

'Poor naked wretches, wheresoe'er you are,
That hide the pelting of this pitiless storm,
How shall your houseless heads and unfed sides,
. . . defend you
From seasons such as these?'

At the thought of helpless humanity I nearly broke down. The bell rang, I shut my book with the greatest relief, and walked out of the class.

I managed the composition hour quite easily. The composition hour is a sort of relaxation for us, where we can sit looking at notebooks and do not demand too much attention from the boys. It was the small gallery room at the end of the southern corridor; I loved this room because the sun came through a ventilator, bringing in a very bright beam of light, and brilliant dust particles floated in it, and the two boys who sat on the second bench looked all aflame. Years and years ago I sat there on the bench as a student, and Gajapathy was then just a junior lecturer and not the big Assistant Professor he was now. I could still see where I used to sit assiduously cultivating correct language and trying to please the lecturer. And to my left would always sit Rangappa, who hated all composition. Little did I dream then that I would be a teacher in the same class.

The boys were making too much noise. I tapped the table lightly and said: 'Ramaswami, here is your notebook. See the corrections on it. There are more corrections on it than on any other paper . . .' It was a paraphrase of the poem beginning 'My days among the dead are past . . .' He hadn't understood a line of that poem, yet he had written down two pages about it. According to Ramaswami (though not according to Southey) the scholar when he said, 'My days among the dead are past' meant that he was no longer going to worry about his dead relations because wherever his eyes were cast he saw mighty minds of old (he just copies it down from the poem), and so on and on. I enjoyed this paraphrase immensely. I called, 'Ramaswami, come and receive your notebook . . .' My comments on the work could not be publicly shown or uttered. When he came near, I opened the notebook and pointed to my remark at the end of the notebook: 'Startling!' I put my finger on this and asked: 'Do you see what I mean?'

'Yes, sir . . .' whispered Ramaswami.

'You are very bad in English.'

'I am sorry, sir . . .'

'Does this poem make no sense as far as you are concerned?'

'No, sir . . .'

'Then why do you write so much about it?'

'I do not know, sir . . .'

'All right, go back to your seat . . . Come and see me sometime . . .'

'Yes, sir, when?'

I couldn't answer this question, because I visualized all my hours so thoroughly allotted for set tasks that I was at a loss to know when I could ask him to see me. So I replied: 'I will tell you, go to your seat.' I spent the rest of the period giving a general analysis of the mistakes I had encountered in this batch of composition—*rather for very, as such* for *hence*, split infinitives, collective nouns, and all the rest of the traps that the English language sets for foreigners. I then set them an exercise in essay-writing on the epigram 'Man is the master of his own destiny'. 'An idiotic theme,' I felt, 'this abstract and confounded metaphysic'; but I could not help it. I had been ordered to set this subject to the class. I watched with interest how the boys were going to tackle it. As a guidance it was my duty to puff up this theme, and so I wrote on the blackboard—'Man, what is man? What is destiny? How does he overcome destiny? How does destiny overcome him? What is fate? What is free will?'—a number of headings which reduced man and his destiny and all the rest to a working formula for these tender creatures to handle.

By the afternoon I had finished three hours of lecturing, and was with a faintly smarting throat, resting in a chair in the common room. There were a dozen other teachers. As each of them sat looking at a book or at the ceiling vacantly, there was a silence which seemed to me oppressive. I never liked it. I had my own technique of breaking it. I remarked to no one in particular: 'We have to decide an important issue before the examinations begin.' The others looked up with bored half-expectancy. 'We will have to call a staff meeting to decide how many marks are to be deducted for spelling honours with the middle u missing.'

'No, no, I don't think it is necessary,' said Sastri, the logic lecturer, who had a very straightforward, literal mind, looking up for a moment from the four-day old newspaper which he was reading. Gajapathy looked over his spectacles, and remarked from the farthest end of the room: 'You are joking over yesterday's meeting,

I suppose?' I replied, 'I am not joking, I am very serious.'

'What is it all about?' Dr Menon asked. He was Assistant Professor of Philosophy. Gajapathy explained, slowly, like an expert lawyer, what had happened the previous evening.

'No sense of proportion . . .' was the philosopher's verdict. Gajapathy removed his spectacles, folded the sides, and put them away as a preparation for dispute. 'How would you treat one of your students if he spelt *Kant, Cant?*'

'I wouldn't bother very much if he knew correctly what Kant had or hadn't said,' replied Dr Menon.

'Oh, I won't believe it,' said Gajapathy, 'there is a merit in accuracy, which must be cultivated for its own sake. I believe it wouldn't do to slacken anywhere.'

'Americans spell honours without the u,' I said and this diverted the subject, and deprived Gajapathy of the duel for which he was preparing. 'Americans are saner than their English cousins in most matters,' said Dr Menon, who had obtained his Ph.D at Columbia University.

'I think the American spelling is foolish buffoonery,' said Gajapathy with his loyalty of a lifetime to English language and literature.

'If we had Americans ruling us, I suppose we would say the same thing of the English people,' I said.

'Politics need not butt in everywhere. There are times when I wish there were no politics in the world and no one knew who was ruling and how,' said Gajapathy. 'This would help a little clearer, freer thinking in all matters. The whole of the West is in a muddle owing to its political consciousness, and what a pity that the East should also follow suit. It is like a weed choking all other human faculties. Shelley in his "Sensitive Plant" . . .'

'I am afraid your opinions are at least a thousand years behind the times; it is a one-sided view, Mr Gajapathy,' said Kumar, who lectured on political science to B.A. classes. 'Corporate life marks the beginning of civilized existence and the emergence of its values . . .'

'I am sure,' I said, finding the debate dull, 'a tormenting question can be framed for the boys at the next examination. "Corporate existence pulled the caveman out into the open. Discuss." If I have anything to do with the politics paper I'm going to insist on this question and make it compulsory. It will serve the young rascals right . . .'

'You haven't yet dropped the frivolous habits of your college days, Krishna,' said Gajapathy. 'You must cultivate a little more seriousness of outlook.'

'I have answered an advertisement I saw in an American paper where someone has offered to take on hand people who lack seriousness and turn them into better citizens. I have filled up the necessary coupon and have every hope you will find me passable ere long . . .'

'Don't you believe too much in these ads. In the United States there are any number of them. Once when I was in Chicago . . .' began Dr Menon of Columbia University, and the bell rang and all his audience rose to go to their different classes.

I returned to my room. The postman had slipped through the door two letters for me. I knew the pale blue envelope from my wife, who was in the habit of underlining the town three times; she seemed to be always anxious lest the letter should go off to some other town. And then my father's letter, from the village. Letters are very exciting things for me. I don't know why. By the time I open and see the contents, I feel an eon might have passed, and my heart goes thumping against my ribs. I looked through my father's letter first. He still wrote his fine, sharp hand, every letter put down with precision and care but without ornament, written closely on a memo pad of some revenue department. From time immemorial he had written only on those pads. No one knew how many pads he had or how he had come by them—perhaps through the favour of some friend in the Revenue Department. The paper had acquired an elegant tone of brown through years of storing but it was tough as parchment. My father had a steel pen with a fat green wooden handle, with which he had written for years. He had several bottles of ink—his own make from a recipe which was exclusively his and of which he was excessively proud. He would make up his store of ink once a year; and we little ones of the household waited for the event with tremendous enthusiasm—all the servants in the house would be present: a special brick oven was raised in the back yard, with a cauldron sizzling over it all day, and Father presiding. The most interesting part, however, would be the trip the previous evening for shopping to Kavadi—our nearest town, fifteen miles off. At three in the afternoon Father would yoke the big bulls to the wagon and we were dressed and ready for the expedition—I and my elder brother, and my two sisters. My elder brother would exact obedience and we would have to take our seats in the cart according to his directions. The way he handled us we always expected he would become a commander of an army or a police officer—but the poor fellow settled as an auditor in Hyderabad and was nose-led by his wife. He was always full of worries, being a father of ten, and having a haughty nagging wife. He seldom visited us in the village being so wrapped up in his own auditing and family.

We reached Kavadi at about two o'clock. Invariably I would fall to sleep lulled by the jingling of the bells around the neck of the bulls.

Kavadi was a wonderful place for one like me from the village—a street full of all sorts of shops, sewing machines rattling away, coloured ribbons streaming down from shop-fronts. My father had his favourite shop. The shopman would seat us all on the mat; and my father would buy us some edibles from the opposite shop, while the ink-ingredients were being packed. He would buy us each a toy—a ball, a monkey dangling at the end of a rubber-piece, and a doll, and invariably an exercise book and a pencil for my elder brother, declaring that he was past the age of having toys, a reminder which made him smart every time he heard it. The road would be ankle deep in bleached dust and the numerous cattle and country carts passing along stirred it up so much that a cloud always hung over the road, imparting an enchanting haze to the whole place, though by the time we started back, so much of this dust settled on our skins and hair that our mother had to give us a bath as soon as we reached home.

I don't know why my father took this ink business so very seriously, when we could buy all the ink we wanted in the shop and save ourselves all bother. He would be near his brick kiln the whole of the next day boiling up this potion, and distilling, and straining, and filling up huge mud jugs. He filled small glass pots for our use, and locked up the store in an almirah. We wrote our copies and lessons in this ink. It had a greenish tint which we didn't like, and which made us long for the blue or black ink sold in the shop. We never got over the feeling that this ink was not real ink—perhaps because of its pale greenish tinge, but my father seemed to appreciate it for that very reason, declaring that you couldn't buy that elegant shade even if you paid a fortune for it.

My father's letter brought back to me not only the air of the village and all my childhood, but along with it all the facts—home, coconut garden, harvest, revenue demand. He had devoted nearly a paragraph to my mother's health with a faint suggestion of complaint that she was not looking after herself quite properly—still keeping late hours for food—the last to eat in the house and still reluctant to swallow the medicines given to her . . .

And then came a paragraph of more immediate interest to me. 'Your father-in-law has written a letter today. I hear that by God's grace, your wife Susila, and the baby, are keeping well. He suggests that you should take her and the baby and set up a family and not live in a hostel any longer. He has my entire concurrence in this matter, as I think in the best interests of yourself you should set up a family. You have been in the hostel too long and I don't feel you ought to he wasting the best of your life in the hostel as it will affect your health and outlook. Your mother is also of the same view since your father-in-law's place is not a very healthy one for an infant. If you have no serious objection to this, your father-in-law suggests the tenth of next month as the most suitable and auspicious date . . .'

He was a BA of the olden days brought up on Pater and Carlyle and Scott and Browning; personally looked after by Dr William Miller, Mark Hunter and other eminent professors of Madras College; he was fastidious and precise in handling the English language, though with a very slight pomposity inevitable in the men of those days. After passing his BA he refused to enter government service, as many of his generation did, but went back and settled in his village and looked after his lands and property. I said to myself on reading his letter: 'God, what am I to do with a little child of seven months? . . .' This somehow seemed to terrify me. How did one manage these things? I had visited my wife's place three or four times since the baby was born. At the first trip I could hardly take notice of the child, although for my wife's sake I had to pinch its cheeks. I no doubt felt a mild affection for it, but there was nothing compelling or indispensable about it . . . . During the subsequent interviews I found more interest in the girl and began to feel that it would be nice to have her about the home, cooing and shouting . . . But I didn't bargain to accept her guardianship so suddenly. I had seen my sister's children of that age, seven months or eight months old, and they started howling and crying at nights till we felt that they would not survive whatever was afflicting them. But my mother was there, and she could take them in hand expertly: a fomentation, a rub with an oil, some decoction down their throats, and they were quietened.

My father's letter had a postscript: 'To help you set up the family your mother is quite willing to come and stay with you for a few weeks. I have not the slightest objection . . .'

I put down my father's letter. There was much food for thought in it.

I smelt my wife's letter before opening it. It carried with it the fragrance of her trunk, in which she always kept her stationery—a mild jasmine smell surrounded her and all her possessions ever since I had known her. I hurriedly glanced through her letter. In her uniform round hand, she had written a good deal about the child which made me want to see her at once. The baby was really too intelligent for her age, understood everything that was being said and done in the house. There was every indication that she was going to prove the most astonishingly intelligent person in the family. She crawled on her belly all over the place, and kept a spy-like watch on her mother's movements. Too cunning! She was learning to say 'Appa' (father); and with every look was asking her mother when Father proposed to take them home—I liked this, but was not prepared to accept it totally. She then referred to the letter from my father and her father and requested me to set up a house at the earliest moment possible. I felt I was someone whose plans and determinations were of the utmost importance to others . . .

I placed the letter on the table, locked the room, and went out for a wash. While crossing the quadrangle my eyes fell on a jasmine bush which completely covered our library wall. I had seen it as a very young sapling years and years ago. When I was a student, I had taken a special interest in its growth, and trained it up a small bamboo bower which I had put up with the help of Singaram the old peon . . . Many persons had laughed at me for this. 'Why should we grow a jasmine bush in a boys' hostel?' I was often asked. 'Just to remind us that there are better things in the world, that is all,' I replied. It was a struggle for existence for that plant, all kinds of cows trespassing into the compound and biting off the stalk. It went up and down several times causing me unending anxiety. And then one day I got the idea of entrusting it to Singaram's care with the suggestion that he might take its flowers, if they appeared, to his womenfolk at home and for the god during the celebration of the Vinayaka festival in the hostel. Since then it grew up under his personal care. He dealt severely with persons who went near it; and as a special favour, occasionally left half a dozen buds on the sill of my window. Now as I passed along to the bathroom I looked at it and said: 'I'm about to leave you . . . after all these years . . . after ten years'—the period I had spent in the hostel, first as student and then as teacher. I sighed as I passed it, the only object of any beauty hereabouts. The rest of the quadrangle was mere mud, scorched by the Malgudi sun.

I had to wait in the bathroom passage for some time, all the cubicles were engaged. Behind the doors, to the tune of falling water, a couple of boys were humming popular film songs. I paced the passage with the towel round my neck. It was a semi-dark, damp place, with a glass tile giving it its sole lighting. 'I shall soon be rid of this nuisance,' I reflected, 'when I have a home of my own. Hostel bathrooms are hell on earth . . . (God said to his assistants, 'Take this man away to hell', and they brought him down to the hostel bathroom passage, and God said, 'torture him', and they opened the room and pushed him in . . . No, no, at this moment the angels said 'the room is engaged'. . . . God waited as long as God can wait and asked 'Have you finished' and they replied 'still engaged', and in due course they could not see where their victim was, for grass had grown and covered him up completely while he waited outside the bathroom door. This promises to be a good poem. Must write it some day . . .)' At this moment a door opened and someone came out dripping. It was a student of the second-year class. He asked agitatedly: 'Sir, have I kept you waiting long?'

'Yes, my dear fellow, but how could you come out before finishing that masterpiece of a song?' The other held the door ostentatiously open and I passed in.

I was back in my room. I applied a little hair-cream, stood before the small looking glass hanging by the nail on the wall, and tried to comb. The looking glass was in the southern wall and I could hardly see my face. 'Nuisance,' I muttered, picked up the glass, and looked for a place to hang it on—not a place. Light at the window struck me in the face and dazzled me. 'The room is full of windows,' I muttered. 'These petty annoyances of life will vanish when I have a home of my own. My dear wife will see that the proper light comes at the proper angle.' I finally put the looking glass down on the table. It had a stand which would not support it. I picked up Taine's *History of Literature* and leaned the glass against it. 'Taine every time,' I muttered and combed my hair back, interrupting the operation for a moment to watch the spray from the comb wet-dotting the covers of books and notebooks on the table. I paused for a moment gazing at my face in the glass. 'This is how, I suppose, I appear to that girl and the little one. Yet they have confidence that I shall be able to look after them and run a home!'

I was ready to start out. I picked up the letters, smelt once again my wife's epistle, and sat back in the chair, and read the letter over again, without missing a single word. 'I want to see the baby and her mother very badly. How long am I to be in this wretched hostel?' I said to myself. I leaned back, reflecting. Through my window I could see the college tower and a bit of the sky. I had watched through this window the play of clouds and their mutation for a decade. All that was to be learnt about clouds was learnt by me, sitting in this place, and looking away, while studying for examinations or preparing lectures.

I started out. At the hostel gate I saw Rangappa standing. He was involved in a discussion with Subbaram—an assistant in the Economics department. I tried to go away pretending not to have seen him.

'Krishna, Krishna! Just a moment,' Rangappa cried on seeing me. He turned to his friend and said: 'Let us refer it to a third party.' I stopped. 'You see,' began Rangappa, 'the point is this . . .'

'No, let me first say what it is,' the other interrupted. 'What place would you give to economic values . . .' he began.

'It all depends,' I said ironically, without allowing him to finish the sentence.

'No, no, don't put it that way,' interrupted Rangappa.

'I will simplify it for you. Is a hundred per cent materialism compatible with our best traditions?' Just another of our numerous discussions going on night and day among my colleagues, leading God knew where. What pleasure or profit did they get by it? 'I will give the matter deep consideration and tell you in due course,' I said, and moved away. Rangappa cried: 'Wait, I will go with you.'

'I am not going for a walk but to search for a house,' I said, and went away.

'I must have a house,' I told myself, 'which faces south, for its breeze, keeps out the western sun, gets in the eastern, and admits the due measure of northern light that artists so highly value. The house must have a room for each one of us and a guest or two. It must keep us all together and yet separate us when we would rather not see each other's faces . . . We must have helpful people and good people near at hand, but obnoxious neighbours ten miles away. It must be within walking distance of college and yet so far out as to let me enjoy my domestic life free from professional intrusions.'

I spent the entire evening scouring various parts of the town watching for 'To Let' signs.

'The builder of this house must have been dead-drunk while doing the latter portion of the house. This is a house evidently intended for monkeys to live in. This house must have been designed by a tuberculosis expert so that his business may prosper for the next hundred years. This house is ideal for one whose greatest desire in life is to receive constant knocks on his head from door-posts. A house for a twisted pigmy.' Thus, variously, I commented within myself as I inspected the vacant houses in the east, west and south of the town. I scoured South Extension, Fort Area, Race Course Road, and Vinayak Mudali Street. I omitted Lawley Extension because it was expensive, and also the New Extension beyond it, because it was too far out of the way.

The search extended over three or four days. I could think of nothing but houses all the while. The moment I met anyone I asked: 'Can you suggest a good house?' I was becoming a bore, capable of talking of nothing but houses, houses, night and day. I got into the habit of taking aside my students and asking them about it. I was becoming anxious. The day was fast approaching when my wife and child would be arriving. There didn't appear to be a single house fit for their occupation in the whole town. Suppose fifteen days hence I was still in this state and they arrived and had nowhere to go outside the railway station! This vision was a nightmare to me. However I was spared. One of my students knew somebody who knew somebody else who had a house in Sarayu Street, and who was eager to have a good, cultured family as tenants. 'Am I good? Is mine a cultured family?' I asked myself immediately. Sarayu Street was a coveted spot in the town. It fulfilled almost all the conditions that are looked for in a residential locality, cheap houses, refined surroundings, and yet near enough to the market and the offices. I fell into feverish anxiety over this house. The boy promised to take me to the first link in the chain of introductions, on the following morning. I was too impatient to wait till then. I implored him: 'There is no sense in postponing these matters. Somebody else may be there before me. Let us go today.' I visualized the whole town waiting to crowd into the house and fight for it. The boy begged to be let off today since his evening was already committed to some other duty, but I brushed aside all his explanations and clung to him fast. He took me to his house behind the market, and then to someone a mile east of the market, and finally to an old man hunched up in a rag-covered cane chair on the veranda of a house in Ellaman Street. It was a narrow place with the tiles touching one's head, and the chair completely filled the veranda. The old man fussed about on my arrival and compelled me to sit on a stool, which was placed on the edge of the veranda, and I was in constant danger of being tipped off into the street if I moved my limbs a little carelessly. So I sat there holding my breath. He was a very shrunken palsied patriarch. His sight was dim. He strained his eyes to catch a glimpse of me, but did not succeed. A silence fell between us. I broke it by asking: 'Are you the owner of the house?'

'No,' he replied, promptly, in his querulous voice. 'God is the owner and I am his slave.'

'What is the rent?'

'First see the house and tell me if you like it.' I felt rather cowed by his authoritarian manner. I ventured: 'I can't do anything unless I know something about it. . .' He shook his head reflectively: 'Do you want the garage or not?'

'Has it a garage?' I asked.

'Don't ask all that now,' said the old man.

'Unless I know first if it has a garage . . .' I said.

'You want everything to be told first,' he snapped with disgust, 'before you say anything yourself. Go, go away. I am not prepared to talk to you any more. I don't want to give you my house. I have seen hundreds like you who come and ask questions and vanish out of sight.'

'What is the matter with you?' I asked indignantly. He bent close to my face and said: 'I am semi-blind. Till three months ago, I could see clearly, but it came on suddenly. And I can't talk without faltering: that's what paralysis has done for me: speaking is a strain to me. Otherwise I am prepared to sit here a whole day and wag my tongue to your heart's content, not caring whether you are a true tenant or one of the bogus ones who come and pester me by the score each day. I will send the boy along with the key. See the house and then come and talk to me.'

'All right,' I said. He called a boy, pressed into his hand a large rusty key and said: 'Show this master the bungalow. Show him every cupboard,' he commanded. I followed the boy out. On the way I tried to engage him in friendly conversation, but he did not want it. He had his pocket filled with fried nuts, and was ceaselessly transferring them to his mouth. He walked ten yards ahead. 'What class are you reading in?' 'I won't read,' he replied. He tossed the key up and caught it in mid-air. He led me through some maze of lanes and took me to Sarayu Street.

Mine was the last house in a particular row. I liked it at first sight. A small wooden gate, ten yards of garden space, and then four steps up to a gabled veranda. There was a small room opening on the veranda detached from the main house. I went in and threw the window open: 'A lovely view of Sarayu Street. When I have nothing else to do,' I told myself, 'I can watch the goings on of Sarayu Street. This room is evidently built for me, where I can study and write without disturbing the household or being disturbed.'

'Why has this been untenanted so long?' I asked the boy, without hoping for a reply as the boy waited for me tossing up the lock and key. But he seemed to have melted towards me; and promptly replied, 'Because Grandfather refuses to give it.'

'When was this last occupied?'

'Fifteen days ago,' he said.

'Is that all?' I asked, but he suddenly lapsed into his silent ways once again.

I liked the house very much. It had a central hall, 'where all of us can meet,' and a small room at one end of the hall. 'This must be her room and the child's,' I told myself. The kitchen and other portions of the house were very satisfactory. There was a coconut tree in the back yard. 'When a monkey goes up that tree, I can show it to the child,' I said, viewing it from the tiny back veranda.

I went back to the old man and said: 'I will take the house. What is the rent?'

'H'm,' he reflected, 'do you want it with or without a garage?' I studiously avoided asking if it had a garage at all and where. I merely said, with a trembling diplomacy: 'What'll be the difference with or without? Suppose I want a garage?'

'Hush!' He made a gesture of utter despair. 'I don't like you to brag about all that unnecessarily. Empty talk! Don't pretend you own a car. You have come walking. Even if I'm blind, do you think I can't notice it?'

'Look here,' I cried, losing all patience. 'If you are letting the house, let it, otherwise don't talk of matters which are not your concern. I'm not here to learn lessons from you. I am myself a teacher: and I teach a thousand boys in that college, mind you!' He was greatly impressed.

'College teacher!' He gave a salute with both hands and said, 'I revere college teachers, our gurus. Meritorious deeds in previous births make them gurus in this life. I'm so happy. I only wanted a good, cultured family.'

'Everybody knows how good we are, and how cultured our family is!' I replied haughtily. This had the desired effect. I added: 'Don't mistake me for an ordinary person!' I drew myself up proudly. He was tremendously impressed. His face beamed with relief. 'Do you know why I want a cultured family?' He whispered as if it were a State secret: 'I'm going away to live with my son after letting the house, and I want someone who will send me the rent without fail . . .'

'Depend upon me,' I said. 'What shall I have to pay you?'

'Twenty-five on the fifth of every month. It must reach me on that day at Bellary.'

'Very well. And what about the garage?' I asked haughtily.

'I'll build you one if you want, but ten rupees extra,' he said.

'All right, I will tell you when I need one,' I said.

Four days later my table and trunk and chair were loaded into a bullock cart, my old room was locked up and the key was handed to Singaram. My hostel friends stood on the veranda and cracked a joke or two. The hostel was a place where people constantly arrived and departed and it was not in anyone's nature there to view these matters pensively. Rangappa and the mathematics man stood on the veranda and said: 'Well, good-bye, friend. Good luck. Don't forget us for the house-warming,' and laughed. Singaram had been very busy the whole day packing up and loading my things. He had attended on me for ten years—sweeping my room, counselling me and running my errands. He walked behind the creaking cart warning the driver: 'When you unload, remove the trunk first and the table last. If I hear that you have broken any leg, I will break your head, remember . . .' I walked behind the cart. Singaram had come to the border of his domain—the hostel drive, and stopped. He *salaamed* me and said, 'Don't forget our hostel, keep visiting us now and then.' He hesitated for a moment and said: 'Now permit this old man to go . . .' It was his hint that the time had come for him to receive his reward. He nearly held out his hand for it. I took out my purse and put a rupee on his palm. He looked at me coldly and said: 'Is this all the value you attach to the old man?'

'Yes,' I replied. 'I should have given half of that to anyone else . . .'

'No, no, don't say so. Don't grudge an honest man his payment. I've been your servant for ten years. Do you know what Professor X gave me when he left this hostel?' 'I don't want all that information,' I said and added a nickel to the rupee. He said: 'Don't grudge an old servant his due. You will perhaps not see me again: I will perhaps be dead; next year I'm retiring and going back to my village. You will never see me again. You will be very sorry when you hear that old Singaram is dead and that you wouldn't give the poor fellow eight annas more . . .' I put in his hand an eight-anna coin. He bowed and said: 'God will make you a big professor one day . . .' and walked away. I passed out of the hostel gate, following my caravan and goods.

2

THE NEXT THREE days I was very busy. My table was placed in the front room of the new house. All my papers and books were arranged neatly. My clothes hung on a peg. The rest of the house was swept and cleaned.

My mother arrived from the village with a sack full of vessels, and helped to make up the house for me. She was stocking the store-room and the kitchen and spent most of her time travelling in a *jutka* to the market and coming back with something or other. She worked far into the night, arranging and rearranging the kitchen and the store. At night she sat down with me on the veranda and talked of her housekeeping philosophy. I liked this veranda very much. We had a cool breeze here. I felt immensely satisfied with my choice of the house now. I hoped my wife too would like it. But my mother, the moment she arrived from the village, said, 'What an awful kitchen! so narrow! And the dining room would have been better if they had added at least a yard in length that side . . .'

'We can't have everything our way in a house built by someone else . . .' I became rather impatient if anyone criticized this house. She understood it and said: 'I'm not saying it is a bad house . . .' She had been used to our large, sprawling home in the village, and everything else seemed to her small and choking. I explained this fact to her and she agreed it was so: 'But do you know how hard it is to keep a huge house like ours clean? It takes me a whole lifetime to keep it tidy, but I don't grudge it. Only I want a little more cooperation. Your father is becoming rather difficult nowadays . . .' She explained how impatient he became when he heard the swish of a broom or the noise of scrubbing, and shouted at her to stop it all. As he was growing old, these noises got on his nerves. And so every time she wanted to clean the house, she had to wait till he went away to the fields. 'And do you know, when I delay this, how many other things act out of routine? Unless I have cleaned the house I can't go and bathe. After bathing I have to worship, and only after that can I go near the cows . . . And if I fail to look at the cowshed for half an hour, do you know what happens?' She was completely wrapped up in her duties. Housekeeping was a grand affair for her. The essence of her existence consisted in the thrills and pangs and the satisfaction that she derived in running a well-ordered household. She was unsparing and violent where she met slovenliness. 'If a woman can't take charge of a house and run it sensibly, she must be made to get into man's dress and go out in a procession . . . I thought of my wife and shuddered at the fate that might be awaiting her in the few weeks my mother was going to stay and help us run the house. My wife was the last daughter of the family and was greatly petted by her parents, in her own house, where she spent most of her time reading, knitting, embroidering or looking after a garden. In spite of it, after my marriage my mother kept her in the village and trained her in housekeeping. My wife had picked up many sensible points in cooking and household economy, and her own parents were tremendously impressed with her attainments when she next visited them. They were thrilled beyond words and remarked when I went there, 'We are so happy, Susila has such a fine house for her training. Every girl on earth should be made to pass through your mother's hands . . .' which, when I conveyed it to my mother, pleased her. She said: 'I really do not mind doing it for everyone, but there are those who neither know nor learn when taught. I feel like kicking them when I come across that type.' I knew she was referring to her eldest daughter-in-law, my brother's wife, whom she detested heartily. I had half a suspicion that my eldest brother went away to seek his livelihood in Hyderabad solely for this reason, for there used to he very painful scenes at home while the first daughter-in-law was staying in our house, my mother's idiosyncrasy being what it was and the other being of a haughty disposition. She was the daughter of a retired High Court judge, and would never allow a remark or a look from my mother to pass unchallenged, and as a result great strife existed in the household for a number of years. My mother used to declare when my elder brother was not present, 'Whatever happens, even with a ten-thousand rupee dowry, I shall never accept a girl from a High Court judge's family again . . .'

It had always been my great anxiety that my wife should not share this fate. My mother seemed to feel that some reference of more immediate interest was due to me and said: 'Susila is a modest girl. She is not obstinate.' I was grateful for that negative compliment. That was at the beginning of our married years. They had constant contact after that, and with every effort Susila came out better burnished than before. And came a point when my mother declared: 'Susila has learnt how to conduct herself before guests.' At this point they separated; now they were meeting again, with Susila having a home of her own to look after, and my mother ready to teach the obedient pupil her business. It was really this which I secretly dreaded.

On the following Friday, I was pacing the little Malgudi railway station in great agitation. I had never known such suspense before. She was certain to arrive with a lot of luggage, and the little child. How was all this to be transferred from the train to the platform? And the child must not be hurt. I made a mental note, 'Must shout as soon as the train stops: "Be careful with the baby".' This seemed to my fevered imagination the all-important thing to say on arrival, as otherwise I fancied the child's head was sure to be banged against the doorway . . . And how many infants were damaged and destroyed by careless mothers in the process of coming out of trains! Why couldn't they make these railway carriages of safer dimensions? It ought to be done in the interests of baby welfare in India. 'Mind the baby and the door.' And then the luggage! Susila was sure to bring with her a huge amount of luggage. She required four trunks for her sarees alone! Women never understood the importance of travelling light. Why should they? As long as there were men to bear all the anxieties and bother and see them through their travails! It would teach them a lesson to be left to shift for themselves. Then they would know the value of economy in these matters. I wrung my hands in despair. How was she going to get out with the child and all that luggage! The train stopped for just seven minutes. I would help her down first and then throw the things out, and if there were any boxes left over they would have to be lost with the train, that was all. No one could help it. I turned to the gnarled blue-uniformed man behind me. He was known as Number Five and I had known him for several years now. Whatever had to be done on the railway platform was done with his help. I had offered him three times his usual wages to help me today. I turned to him and asked: 'Can you manage even if there is too much luggage?'

'Yes, master, no difficulty. The train stops for seven minutes.' He seemed to have a grand notion of seven minutes; a miserable flash it seemed to me. 'We unload whole wagons within that time.'

'I will tell the pointsman to stop it at the outer signal, if necessary,' he added. It was a very strength-giving statement to me. I felt relieved. But I think I lost my head once again. I believe, in this needless anxiety, I became slightly demented. Otherwise I would not have rushed at the station master the moment I set eyes on him. I saw him come out of his room and move down the platform to gaze on a far off signal post. I ran behind him, panting: 'Good morning, station master!' He bestowed an official smile and moved off to the end of the platform and looked up. I felt I had a lot of doubts to clear on railway matters and asked inanely: 'Looking at the signals?'

'Yes,' he replied, and took his eyes down, and turned to go back to his room. I asked: 'Can't they arrange to stop this train a little longer here?' 'What for? Isn't there enough trouble as it is?' I laughed sympathetic and said: 'I said so because it may not be possible for passengers to unload all their trunks.'

'I should like to see a passenger who carries luggage that will take more than six minutes. I have been here thirty years.'

I said: 'My wife is arriving today with the infant. I thought she would require a lot of time in order to get down carefully. And then she is bound to have numerous boxes. These women, you know,' I said laughing artificially, seeking his indulgence. He was a good man and laughed with me. 'Well, sometimes it has happened that the train was held up for the convenience of a second-class passenger. Are your people travelling second?' 'I can't say,' I said. I knew well she wouldn't travel second, although I implored her in every letter to do so. She wrote rather diplomatically: 'Yes, don't be anxious, I and the baby will travel down quite safely.' I even wrote to my father-in-law, but that gentleman preserved a discreet silence on the matter. I knew by temperament he disliked the extravagance of travelling second, although he could afford it and in other ways had proved himself no miser. I felt furious at the thought of him and told the station master: 'Some people are born niggards . . . would put up with any trouble rather than . . .' But before I could finish my sentence a bell rang inside the station office and the station master ran in, leaving me to face my travail and anguish alone. I turned and saw my porter standing away from me, borrowing a piece of tobacco from someone. 'Here, Number Five, don't get lost.' A small crowd was gathering unobtrusively on the platform. I feared he might get lost at the critical moment. A bell sounded. People moved about. We heard the distant puffing and whistling. The engine appeared around the bend.

A whirling blur of faces went past me as the train shot in and stopped. People were clambering up and down. Number Five followed me about, munching his tobacco casually. 'Search on that side of the mail van.' I hurried through the crowd, peering into the compartments. I saw my father-in-law struggling to get to the doorway. I ran up to his carriage. Through numerous people getting in and out, I saw her sitting serenely in her seat with the baby lying on her lap. 'Only three minutes more!' I cried. 'Come out!' My father-in-law got down. I and Number Five fought our way up, and in a moment I was beside my wife in the compartment.

'No time to be sitting down; give me the baby,' I said. She merely smiled and said: 'I will carry the baby down. You will get these boxes. That wicker box, bring it down yourself, it contains baby's bottle and milk vessels.' She picked up the child and unconcernedly moved on. She hesitated for a second at the thick of the crowd and said: 'Way please,' and they made way for her. I cried: 'Susila, mind the door and baby.' All the things I wanted to say on this occasion were muddled and gone out of my mind. I looked at her apprehensively till she was safely down on the platform, helped by her father. Number Five worked wonders within a split second.

I wouldn't have cared if the train had left now. The mother and child stood beside the trunks piled up on the platform. I gazed on my wife, fresh and beautiful, her hair shining, her dress without a wrinkle on it, and her face fresh, with not a sign of fatigue. She wore her usual indigo-coloured silk saree. I looked at her and whispered: 'Once again in this saree, still so fond of it,' as my father-in-law went back to the compartment to give a final look round. 'When will she wake up?' I asked pointing at the child, whom I found enchanting, with her pink face and blue shirt.

'Father is coming down,' she said, hinting that I had neglected him and ought to welcome him with a little more ceremony. I obeyed her instantly, went up to my father-in-law and said: 'I am very happy, sir, you have come . . .' He smiled and said: 'Your wife and daughter got comfortable places, they slept well.'

'Did they, how, how? I thought there was such a crowd . . .' My wife answered: 'What if there are a lot of others in the compartment? Other people must also travel. I didn't mind it.' I knew she was indirectly supporting her father, anticipating my attacks on him for travelling third. 'I only thought you might find it difficult to put the child to sleep,' I said.

'Oh, everybody made way for us, and we got a whole berth to ourselves,' she said, demanding of me by every look and breath that I should be sufficiently grateful to her for it. I turned to him and said: 'I'm so happy you managed it so well, sir.' He was pleased. He said: 'People are ever so good when they see Susila and the baby.'

'I hope you will stop with us for at least a week,' I said, and looked at my wife for approval. But her father declined the invitation with profuse thanks. He was to be back in his town next day and he was returning by the evening train. He said: 'There were three Bombay men, they liked Leela so much that they tried to give her a lot of biscuits. She was only too eager to accept, but I prevented. . .'

'Biscuits are bad for the baby,' I said. We moved on. I stretched out my hand: 'Let me carry her,' I said. My wife declined: 'You don't know how to carry a baby yet. You will sprain her.' She clasped her closer, and walked off the platform.

A Victoria carriage waited for us outside. Our trunks were stuffed into it, and we squeezed ourselves in. I shared the narrow seat behind the driver with my father-in-law, leaving the other seat for mother and child. Between us were heaped all the trunks and I caught patches of her face through the gaps in the trunks. She talked incessantly about the habits of the infant, enquired about the plan of our house, and asked the names of buildings and streets that we passed.

My mother came down and welcomed her at the gate. She had decorated the threshold with a festoon of green mango leaves and the floor and doorway with white flour designs. She was standing at the doorway and as soon as we got down cried: 'Let Susila and the child stay where they are.' She had a pan of vermilion solution ready at hand and circled it before the young mother and child, before allowing them to get down from the carriage. After that she held out her arms, and the baby vanished in her embrace.

A look at my mother, her eagerness as she devoured them with her look, and led them into the house, and I was moved by the extraordinary tenderness which appeared in her face. All my dread of yesterday as to how she would prove as a mother-in-law was suddenly eased.

My mother was swamped by this little daughter of mine. She found little time to talk or think of anything else. She fussed over the young mother and the child. She felt it her primary duty to keep the young mother happy and free to look after the little one. The child seemed to be their meeting point; and immediately established a great understanding and harmony between them. All day my mother compelled my wife to stay in her own room and spent her entire time in the kitchen preparing food and drink for her and the child. When the child cried at nights, my mother, sleeping in the hall, sprang up and rocked the cradle, before the young mother should be disturbed. The child still drew nourishment from its mother, and so the latter needed all the attention she could get.

My mother stayed with us the maximum time she could spare—two months—and then returned to the village.

I left the college usually at 4.30 p.m., the moment the last bell rang, and avoiding all interruptions reached home within about twenty minutes. As soon as I turned the street I caught a glimpse of Susila tinkering at her little garden in our compound, or watching our child as she toddled about picking pebbles and mud . . . It was not my wife's nature to be demonstrative, but I knew she waited there for me. So I said: 'I have taken only twenty minutes and already you are out to look for me!' She flushed when I said this, and covered it up with: 'I didn't come out to look for you, but just to play with the child . . .' My daughter came up and hugged my knees, and held up her hands for my books. I gave her the books. She went up the steps and put them on the table in my room. I followed her in. I took off my coat and shirt, picked up my towel and went to the bathroom, with the child on my arm, as she pointed at the various articles about the house and explained them to me in her own terms. Most of her expressions were still monosyllables, but she made up a great deal by her vigorous gesticulations. She insisted upon watching me as I put my head under the tap. The sight of it thrilled her and she shrieked as water splashed about. I put her safely away from the spray as I bathed, but she stealthily came nearer step by step and tried to catch some of the drops between her fingers. 'Ay, child, keep off water.' At this she pretended to move off, but the moment I shut my eyes under water and opened them again, she would have come nearer and drenched a corner of her dress, which was a signal for me to turn off the water and dry myself. I rubbed myself, lifted her on my arm, went to my room, and brushed my hair. I did this as a religious duty because I felt myself to be such a contrast to them when I returned in the evening, in my sagging grey cotton suit, with grimy face, and ink-stained fingers, while the mother and daughter looked particularly radiant in the evenings, with their hair dressed and beflowered, faces elegantly powdered.

By the time I reached this stage my wife came out and said: 'Your coffee is getting cold. Won't you come in?'

'Yes, yes,' and we moved off to our little dining room. An alcove at the end of the dining room served for a shrine. There on a pedestal she kept a few silver images of gods, and covered them with flowers; two small lamps were lit before them every morning. I often saw her standing there with the light in her face, her eyes closed and her lips moving lightly. I was usually amused to see her thus, and often asked what exactly it was that she repeated before her gods. She never answered this question. To this day I have never learnt what magical words she uttered there with closed eyes. Even when I mildly joked about it, 'Oh, becoming a yogi!' she never tried to defend herself, but merely treated my references with the utmost indifference. She seemed to have a deep secret life. There hung about this alcove a perpetual smell of burnt camphor and faded flowers.

I sat down on the plank facing the shrine, with the child on my lap. A little plate came up with some delicacy or titbit heaped on it—my tiffin. Susila placed this in front of me and waited to see my reaction. I looked up at her standing before me and asked: 'What is this?' She replied: 'Find out for yourself, let us see if you recognize it . . .' As I gazed at it wondering what it might be, the child thrust her hand out for it. I put a little into her mouth while the mother protested: 'You are going to spoil her giving her whatever she wants . . .'

'No, just a little . . .'

'It will make her sick, she has been eating all sorts of things lately. Don't blame me if she gets sick . . .'

'Oh, she won't, just a little won't do her any harm.' As Leela held up her hands for more, her mother cried: 'No, baby, it won't do. Don't trouble Father, come away come away,' and the little one stuck to me fast, avoiding her mother's gaze, and I put my left arm about her and said: 'Don't worry about her, I won't give her any more . . .' As I finished what was on the plate Susila asked: 'Do you want some more?' This was always a most embarrassing question for me. As I hesitated she asked, 'Why, is it not good?'

'It is good,' I groaned, 'but . . .'

'But smells rather smoky, doesn't it? But for the smell it would be perfect,' she said. And I couldn't but agree with her. 'I prepared such a large quantity thinking you would like it . . .'

She went in and brought out a little more and pushed it on to my plate and I ate with relish just because she was so desperately eager to get me to appreciate her handiwork!

She gave me coffee. We left the kitchen, and sat down in the hall. The child went over to her box in a corner and rummaged its contents and threw them about and became quite absorbed in this activity. My wife sat in the doorway, leaning against the door and watching the street. We spent an hour or more, sitting there and gossiping. She listened eagerly to all the things I told her about my college, work and life. Though she hadn't met a single person who belonged to that world, she knew the names of most of my colleagues and the boys and all about them. She knew all about Brown and what pleased or displeased him. She took sides with me in all my discussions and partisanships, and hated everyone I hated and respected anyone I respected. She told me a great deal about our neighbours, their hopes and fears, and promises and qualities. This talk went on till darkness crept in, and the lights had to be switched on. At the same time the clattering at the toy box ceased. This was a signal that the child would demand attention. She came towards us whimpering and uttering vague complaints. My wife got up and went in to light the oven and cook the dinner, while I took charge of Leela and tried to keep her engaged till her food was ready.

On the first of every month, I came home, with ten ten-rupee notes bulging in an envelope, my monthly salary, and placed it in her hand. She was my cash-keeper. And what a ruthless accountant she seemed to be. In her hands, a hundred rupees seemed to do the work of two; hundred, and all through the month she was able to give me money when I asked. When I handled my finances independently, after making a few routine savings and payments, I simply paid for whatever caught my eye and paid off anyone who approached me, with the result that after the first ten days, I went about without money. Now it was in the hands of someone who seemed to understand perfectly where every rupee was going or should go, and managed them with a determined hand. She kept the cash in a little lacquer box, locked it up in her almirah, and kept a minute account of it in the last pages of a diary, four years old.

We sat down at my table to draw up the monthly budget and list of provisions. She tore off a sheet of notepaper, and wrote down a complete list—from rice down to mustard. 'I have written down the precise quantity, don't change anything as you did once.' This was a reference to a slight change that I once attempted to make in her list. She had written down two seers of Bengal gram, but the National Provision Stores could not supply that quantity, and so the shopman suggested he would give half of it, and to make up the purchase, he doubled the quantity of jaggery. All done with my permission. But when I returned home with these, she saw the alterations and was completely upset. I found that there was an autocratic strain in her nature in these matters, and unsuspected depths of rage. 'Why has he made this alteration?' she had asked, her face going red. 'He didn't have enough of the other stuff,' I replied, tired and fatigued by the shopping and on the point of irritability myself. 'If he hasn't got a simple thing like Bengal gram, what sort of a shop has he?'

'Come and see it for yourself if you like,' I replied, going into my room. She muttered: 'Why should it make you angry? I wonder!' I lay down on my canvas chair, determined to ignore her, and took out a book. She came presently into my room with a paper sack full of sugar and said: 'This man has given underweight of sugar. He has cheated you.' I lowered the book, frowned at her and asked: 'What do you mean?'

'I fear to speak to you if you get angry,' she said.

'Who is angry?' I asked. 'What is the matter, tell me?'

'I wrote for two measures of sugar, and see this; he has billed for two measures and has actually given a measure and a half. I have measured it just now.' She looked at me victoriously, waiting to hear how I was going to answer this charge. I merely said: 'He wouldn't do such a thing. You must have some extraordinary measure with you at home.'

'Nothing wrong with my measure. Even your mother measured everything with it and said it was correct.' So this was a legacy from her mother-in-law. She had taught the girl even this. She had a bronze tumbler, which she always declared was a correct half measure, and she would never recognize other standards and measures. She insisted upon making all her purchases, ghee or oil or milk or salt, with the aid of this measure, and declared that all other measures, including the government stamped ones, were incorrect, and were kept maliciously incorrect because some municipal members were businessmen! She used the same tumbler for weighing too, placing it for weight in the scale pan, declaring that the curious thing about the vessel was that by weight too it was exactly half seer, and she would challenge anyone to disprove it. All tradespeople somehow succumbed to this challenge and allowed her to have her own way. She carried this tumbler about wherever she went, and I now found that she had procured a similar one for her daughter-in-law, and had trained her in the use of it.

'Throw away that tumbler and use an honest measure,' I said. Susila merely looked at me and said: 'Please don't speak so loudly. The child is asleep,' and tried to go out of the room. I called her back and said: 'If you use an honest measure you will find that others have also done so.'

'This National Provisions man is a thief,' she cried, 'the sooner you change the better.' This annoyed me very much. I had known the NPS man for years and liked him. I went all the way to South Extension to patronize his shop, and I liked the man because he was fat and talkative, and Sastri the logic man always said that it was the best shop in the town. I rather prided myself on going to the shop. I liked the fat, thoughtful proprietor. I said: 'There is nothing wrong with him. He is the best shop-man known. I won't change him . . .' 'I don't know why you should be so fond of him when he is giving under-measure and rotten stuff . . .' she replied. I was by this time very angry: 'Yes, I am fond of him because he is my second cousin,' I said with a venomous grin.

Her hatred of him was not mitigated. She said: 'You would pay cart hire and go all the way to South Extension to be cheated by him rather than go to a nearer shop. And his rates!' She finished the rest of her sentence with a shiver. 'I don't care if he overcharges—I won't drop him,' I declared. 'Hush, remember the child is sleeping,' she said and left the room. I lay in my chair fretting for fifteen minutes and then tried to resume my study, but could read only for five minutes. I got up and went over to the store-room as she was putting away the provisions and articles in their respective tin or glass containers. I stood at the doorway and watched her. I felt a great pity for her; the more because I had not shown very great patience. I asked: 'I will return the jaggery if it is too much. Have you absolutely no use for it?' In answer she pushed before me a glass goblet and said: 'This can hold just half a *viss* of jaggery and not more; which is more than enough for our monthly use. If it is kept in any other place, ants swarm on it,' she said. I now saw the logic of her indignation, and by the time our next shopping was done, she had induced me to change over to the Cooperative Stores.

Since then every time the monthly list was drawn up she warned me: 'Don't alter anything in it.' I followed her list with strict precision, always feeling that one could never be sure what mess any small change might entail. If there were alterations to be made, I rather erred on the side of omission and went again next day after taking her suggestion.

She was very proud of her list. It was precise. Every quantity was conceived with the correct idea as to how long it should last. There were over two dozen different articles to be indented and she listed them with foresight and calculation. She was immensely proud of this ability. She gave me twenty rupees or more for these purchases. I went out to the Cooperative Stores in the Market Road and returned home three hours later followed by a coolie carrying them all in paper bags and bundles, stuffed into a large basket. She always waited for them at the door with unconcealed enthusiasm. The moment I was at the gate she held out her hand for the bill, and hurriedly ran her eyes down the columns checking the figures and prices. 'Oh! you have got all the things, and the cost didn't go up above 22-80 total . . . slightly better than it was last month. Which item is cheaper this month?' She was in raptures over it. I loved to see her so pleased, and handed her the change to the last pie. She paid the coolie three annas; she would never alter this figure whatever happened. If any one had the hardihood to expect more she declared: 'Don't stand there and argue. Be off. Your master has offered you an anna more than you deserve. After all the market is only half a mile away!' She carried the packages to the store-room, and put each in its container, neatly labelled and ranged along a rack. She always needed my assistance to deal with rice. It was the bulkiest bag. It was my set duty on these days to drag the gunny sack along to the store, lift it and empty it into a zinc drum. I invited her displeasure if I didn't do it carefully. If any rice scattered accidentally on the floor, she said: 'I don't know when you will learn economic ways. You are so wasteful. On the quantity you throw about another family could comfortably live.'

She watched these containers as a sort of barometer, the level of their contents indicating the progress of the month. Each had to be at a particular level on a particular date and on the last date of the month—just enough for another day, when they would be replenished. She watched these with a keen eye like a technician watching an all-important meter at a power house.

All went very well as long as she was reigning supreme in the kitchen—till my mother sent an old lady from the village to cook for us and assist us.

One evening we were sitting as usual in the front veranda of the house when an old lady stood at our gate, with a small trunk under her arm, and asked: 'Is this teacher Krishna's house?'

'Yes, who are you, come in . . .' I opened the gate for her. She looked at me, wrinkling her eyes and said, 'Kittu . . . I have seen you as a baby and a boy. How big you have grown!' She came up to the veranda, peered closely into my wife's face and said: 'You are our daughter-in-law. I am an old friend of Kamu,' she said, referring to my mother by her maiden name. By this time Leela, who had been playing near her box, came out on hearing a new voice. At the sight of her the old lady cried: 'So this is Kamu's grandchild!' She picked her up in her arms and fondled her. Susila's heart melted at the sight of it and she said: 'Come into the house, won't you?' The old lady went in, sat under the lamp and took out of a corner of her saree a crumpled letter and gave it to me. It was from my mother: 'I am sending this letter with an old friend of mine, who was assisting me in household work when you were a baby. She then went away to live with her son. He died last year, and she has absolutely no one to support her. She came to me a few weeks ago in search of work. But I have no need for assistance nowadays. Moreover your father grows rather irritable if he sees any extra person in the house. So I have given her bus fare and sent her on to you. I have always felt that Susila needed an assistant in the house, the baby demanding all the attention she can give. My friend will cook and look after the child. And you can give her whatever salary you like.'

While the old lady kept fondling the child, sitting on the floor, I read the letter under the hall light and my wife read it over my shoulder. We looked at each other. There was consternation in her look. There were many questions which she was aching to ask me. I adjourned to my room and she followed me.

'What shall we do?' she asked, looking desperate.

'Why do you look so panicky? We will send her back if you do not want her.'

'No, no. How can that be? Your mother has sent her. We have got to have her.'

'I think it will be good to have her. All your time is now spent in the kitchen when you are not tending the baby. I don't like you to spend all your time cooking either tiffin or food.'

'But I like it. What is wrong in it?' she asked.

'You must spend some more time reading or stitching or singing. Man or woman is not born merely to cook and eat,' I said, and added: 'You have neglected your books. Have you finished

Ivanhoe?' She had been trying to get through *Ivanhoe* for years now, and Lamb's *Tales from Shakespeare*. But she never went beyond the fiftieth page. Her library also contained a book of hymns by a Tamil saint, a few select stanzas of the Kamban *Ramayana*, Palgrave's *Golden Treasury* and a leather-bound Bhagavad Gita in Sanskrit. I knew how fond she was of books. She was always planning how she was going to devour all the books and become the member of some library. But it never became more than an ambition.

In the earlier years of our married life we often sat together with one or other of the books, in the single top-floor room in her father's house, and tried to read. The first half an hour would be wasted because of an irresponsible mood coming over her, which made her laugh at everything: even the most solemn poem would provoke her, especially such poems as were addressed by a lover. 'My true love hath my heart and I have his.' She would laugh till she became red in the face. 'Why can't each keep his own or her own heart instead of this exchange?' She then put out her hand and searched all my pockets saying: 'In case you should take away mine!'

'Hush, listen to the poem,' I said, and she would listen to me with suppressed mirth and shake her head in disapproval. And then another line that amused her very much was 'Oh, mistress mine, where are you roaming?' She would not allow me to progress a line beyond, saying: 'I shall die of this poem some day. What is the matter with the woman loafing all over the place except where her husband is?'

However much she might understand or not understand, she derived a curious delight in turning over the pages of a book, and the great thing was that I should sit by her side and explain. While she read the Tamil classics and Sanskrit texts without my help, she liked English to be explained by me. If I showed the slightest hesitation, she would declare: 'Perhaps you don't care to explain English unless you are paid a hundred rupees a month for it?'

But all that stopped after the child was born. When the child left her alone, she had to be in the kitchen, and my argument now appealed to her. She said: 'But that will mean an extra expense. What shall we pay her?'

'About eight rupees, just what everyone pays, I think,' I said.

'Oh, too much,' she said. 'I'm sure she will waste another eight rupees' worth of things. This is an unnecessary expense,' she said.

I explained: 'Very necessary and we can afford it. In addition to the provident fund, why should we send thirty-five rupees to the savings bank? I think about twenty-five rupees a month for the bank will be more than enough. Many of my friends do not save even five rupees.'

'Why do you want to follow their example? We must live within our means, and save enough.' She often declared: 'When we are old we must never trouble others for help. And remember there is a daughter, for whose marriage we must save.'

'When we bring forth some more daughters and sons . . .' I began, and she covered my mouth with her fingers. 'You men! what do you care! You would think differently if God somehow made you share the bothers of bringing forth! Where is your promise?' I often reiterated and confirmed our solemn pact that Leela should be our only child. And anything I said otherwise, even in jest, worried her very much.

With the future so much in mind she planned all our finances. She kept a watch over every rupee as it arrived, and never let it depart lightly, and as far as possible tried to end its career in the savings bank.

But now our savings were affected to the extent of at least ten rupees—as she explained 'Six rupees, old lady's salary' (Susila stubbornly refused more than that for a year) and 'four rupees for all her waste, putting it at a minimum . . .' She was disconsolate over it a long time, till I appeased her by saying: 'Oh, don't worry about it. When I get some money from examination papers I will give you the whole of it for the savings bank.'

In course of time we found that we simply couldn't do without the old lady. She cooked the food for us, tended the child, gave us the necessary courage when the child had fever or stomach-ache and we became distraught; she knew a lot of tricks about children's health, she grew very fond of the child and took her out and kept her very happy. She established herself as a benign elder at home, and for us it meant a great deal. Her devotion to the child enabled me to take my wife twice or thrice a month to a picture, on a walk along the river, or out shopping. My wife grew very fond of her and called her 'Granny', so did Leela. But Susila had a price to pay for this pleasure. She lost her supremacy over the kitchen and the store. The levels in the containers at the store went down in other ways than my wife calculated. Susila protested and fought against it for some time, but the old lady had her own way of brushing aside our objections. And Susila adjusted her own outlook in the matter. 'Didn't I bargain for a waste of four rupees a month? Well, it is not so hard, because she wastes only three rupees . . .' Our provision bill fluctuated by only three rupees, and it was a small price to pay for the great company and service of the old lady, who lived on one meal a day, just a handful of cooked rice and buttermilk. It was a wonder how she found the energy for so much activity. My wife often sat down with her in order to induce her to eat well, but it was of no avail.

I sat in my room, at the table. It was Thursday and it was a light day for me at college—only two hours of work in the afternoon, and not much preparation for that either. *Pride and Prejudice* for a senior class, non-detailed study, which meant just reading it to the boys. And a composition class. I sat at my table as usual after morning coffee looking over the books ranged on the table and casually turning over the pages of some exercise books. 'Nothing to do. Why not write poetry? Ages since I wrote anything.' My conscience had a habit of asserting itself once in six months and reminding me that I ought to write poetry. At such moments I opened the bottommost drawer of my table and pulled out a notebook of about five hundred pages, handsomely bound. I had spent nearly a week at a local press getting this done some years ago. Its smooth pages contained my most cherished thoughts on life and nature and humanity. In addition to shorter fragments that I wrote at various times on a miscellany of topics, it contained a long unfinished poem on an epic scale to which I added a few dozen lines whenever my conscience stirred in me. I always fancied that I was born for a poetic career and some day I hoped to take the world by storm with the publication. Some of the pieces were written in English and some in Tamil. (I hadn't yet made up my mind as to which language was to be enriched with my contributions to its literature, but the language was unimportant. The chief thing seemed to be the actual effort.) I turned over the pages looking at my previous writing. The last entry was several months ago, on nature. I felt satisfied with it but felt acute discomfort on realizing that I had hardly done anything more than that. Today I was going to make up for all lost time; I took out my pen, dipped it in ink, and sat hesitating. Everything was ready except a subject. What should I write about?

My wife had come in and was stealthily watching the pages over my shoulder. As I sat biting the end of my pen, she remarked from behind me: 'Oh, the poetry book is out; why are you staring at a blank page?' Her interruption was always welcome. I put away my book, and said: 'Sit down,' dragging a stool nearer. 'No, I'm going away. Write your poetry. I won't disturb you. You may forget what you wanted to write.' 'I have not even thought of what to write,' I said. 'Some day I want to fill all the pages of this book and then it will be published and read all over the world.' At this she turned over the leaves of the notebook briskly and laughed: 'There seem to be over a thousand pages, and you have hardly filled the first ten.'

'The trouble is I have not enough subjects to write on,' I confessed. She drew herself up and asked: 'Let me see if you can write about me.'

'A beautiful idea,' I cried. 'Let me see you.' I sat up very attentively and looked at her keenly and fixedly like an artist or a photographer viewing his subject. I said: 'Just move a little to your left please. Turn your head right. Look at me straight here. That's right . . . Now I can write about you. Don't drop your lovely eyelashes so much. You make me forget my task. Ah, now, don't grin please. Very good, stay as you are and see how I write now, steady . . .' I drew up the notebook, ran the fountain pen hurriedly over it and filled a whole page beginning:

> 'She was a phantom of delight
> When first she gleamed upon my sight:
> A lovely apparition, sent
> To be a moment's ornament.'

It went on for thirty lines ending:

> 'And yet a spirit still, and bright
> With something of an angel-light.'

I constantly paused to look at her while writing, and said: 'Perfect. Thank you. Now listen.'

'Oh, how fast you write!' she said admiringly.

'You will also find how *well* I've written. Now listen,' I said, and read as if to my class, slowly and deliberately, pausing to explain now and then.

'I never knew you could write so well.'

'It is a pity that you should have underrated me so long; but now you know better. Keep it up,' I said. 'And if possible don't look at the pages, say roughly between 150 and 200, in the *Golden Treasury*. Because someone called Wordsworth has written similar poems.' This was an invitation for her to run in and fetch her copy of the *Golden Treasury* and turn over precisely the forbidden pages. She scoured every title and first line and at last pitched upon the original. She read it through, and said: 'Aren't you ashamed to copy?'

'No,' I replied. 'Mine is entirely different. He had written about someone entirely different from my subject.'

'I wouldn't do such a thing as copying.'

'I should be ashamed to have your memory,' I said. 'You have had the copy of the *Golden Treasury* for years now, and yet you listened to my reading with gaping wonder! I wouldn't give you even two out of a hundred if you were my student.' At this point our conversation was interrupted by my old clock. It burst in upon us all of a sudden. It purred and bleated and made so much noise that it threw us all into confusion. Susila picked it up and tried to stop it without success, till I snatched Taine and smothered it.

'Now, why did it do it?' she demanded. I shook my head. 'Just for pleasure,' I replied. She gazed on its brown face and said: 'It is not even showing the correct time. It is showing two o'clock, four hours ahead! Why do you keep it on your table?' I had no answer to give. I merely said: 'It has been with me for years, poor darling!'

'I will give it away this afternoon—a man comes to buy all old things.'

'No, no, take care, don't do it . . .' I warned. She didn't answer, but merely looked at it and mumbled, 'This is not the first time. When you are away it starts bleating after I have rocked the cradle for hours and made the child sleep, and I don't know how to stop it. It won't do for our house. It is a bother . . .'

That evening when I returned home from college the first thing I noticed was that my room looked different. My table had lost its usual quality and looked tidy, with all books dusted and neatly arranged. It looked like a savage, suddenly appearing neatly trimmed and groomed. The usual corner with old newspapers and magazines piled up was swept clean. The pile was gone. So was the clock on the table. The table looked barren without it. For years it had been there. With composition books still under my arm, I searched her out. I found her in the bathroom, washing the child's hands: 'What have you done with my clock?' I asked. She looked up and asked in answer: 'How do you like your room? I have cleaned and tidied it up. What a lot of rubbish you had gathered there! Hereafter on every Thursday . . .'

'Answer first, where is the clock?' I said.

'Please wait, I will finish the child's business First and then answer.'

I stood at the bathroom doorway and waited grimly. She finished the child's business and came out bearing her on her arm. While passing me she seized the child's hand and tapped me under the chin with it and passed on without a word to her room. She later met me in room as I sat gloomily at the table.

'Why have you not had your tiffin or wash?' she asked, coming up behind and gently touching my shoulder.

'I don't want any tiffin,' I snapped.

'Why are you so angry?' she asked.

'Who asked you to give away that clock?' I asked.

'I didn't give it away . . . That man gave me twelve annas for it—a very high price indeed.'

'Now you are a . . .' I began. I looked at the paper corner and wailed: 'You have given away those papers too! There were old answer papers there . . .'

'Yes, I saw them,' she said. 'They were four years old. Why do you want old papers?' she asked. I was too angry to answer. 'You have no business to tamper with my things,' I said. 'I don't want any tiffin or coffee.' I picked up my coat, put it on and rushed out of the house, without answering her question: 'Where are you going?'

I went straight back to the college. I had no definite plan. There was no one in the college. I peeped into the debating hall, hoping there might be somebody there. But the evening was free from all engagements. I remembered that I hadn't had my coffee. I walked about the empty corridors of the college. I saw the servant and asked him to open our common room. I sent him to fetch me coffee and tiffin from the restaurant. I opened my locker and took out a few composition books. I sat correcting them till late at night. I heard the college clock strike nine. I then got up and retraced my way home. I went about my work with a businesslike air. I took off

my coat, went at great speed to the bathroom and washed. I first
took a peep into my wife's room. I saw her rocking the baby in the
cradle. I went into the kitchen and told the old lady: 'Have the rest
dined?'

The old lady answered: 'Susila waited till eight-thirty.'

I was not interested in this. Her name enraged me. I snapped:
'All right, all right, put up my leaf and serve me. I only wanted to
know the child had eaten.' This was to clear any misconception
anyone might entertain that I was interested in Susila.

I ate in silence. I heard steps approaching, and told myself:
'Oh, she is coming.' I trembled with anxiety, lest she should be
going away elsewhere. I caught a glimpse of her as she came into
the dining room. I bowed my head, and went on with my dinner
unconcerned, though fully aware that she was standing before me,
dutifully as ever, to see that I was served correctly. She moved off to
the kitchen, spoke some words to the old lady, and came out, and
softly moved back to her own room. I felt angry: 'Doesn't even care
to wait and see me served. She doesn't care. If she cared, would she
sell my clock? I must teach her a lesson.'

After dinner I was back in my room and sat down at my table.
I had never been so studious at any time in my life. I took out some
composition books. I noticed on a corner of my table a small paper
packet. I found enclosed in it a few coins. On the paper was written
in her handwriting:

Time-piece	12 annas
Old paper	1 rupee
Total	One rupee and twelve annas.

I felt furious at the sight of it. I took the coins and went over to her
room. The light was out there. I stood in the doorway and muttered:
'Who cares for this money? I can do without it.' I flung it on her bed
and returned to my room.

Later, as I sat in my room working, I heard the silent night
punctuated by sobs. I went to her room and saw her lying with her
face to the wall, sobbing. I was completely shaken. I didn't bargain
for this. I watched her silently for a moment, and collected myself
sufficiently to say: 'What is the use of crying, after committing a
serious blunder?' Through her sobs, she sputtered: 'What do you
care what use it is or not? If I had known you cared more for a

dilapidated clock . . .' She didn't finish her sentence, but broke down and wept bitterly. I was baffled. I was in anguish myself. I wanted to take her in my arms and comfort her. But there was a most forbidding feeling within me. I merely said: 'If you are going to talk and behave like a normal human being, I can talk to you. I can't stand all this nonsense.'

'You go away to your room. Why do you come and abuse me at midnight?' she said.

'Stop crying, otherwise people will think a couple of lunatics are living in this house . . .'

I went back to my room—a very determined man. I lay on a mat, trying to sleep, and spent a miserable and sleepless night.

We treated each other like strangers for the next forty-eight hours—all aloof and bitter. The child looked on this with puzzlement, but made it up by attending to her toys and going to the old lady for company. It was becoming a torture. I could stand no more of it. I had hoped Susila would try to make it up, and that I could immediately accept it. But she confined herself to her room and minded her business with great concentration and never took notice of me. I caught a glimpse of her face occasionally and found that her eyes were swollen. I felt a great pity for her when I saw her slender neck, as she was going away from the bathroom. I blamed myself for being such a savage. But I couldn't approach her. The child would not help us either; she was too absorbed in her own activities. It came to a point when I simply could not stand any more of it. So the moment I returned home from college next evening I said to her, going to her room:

'Let us go to a picture . . .'

'What picture?' she asked.

'*Tarzan*—at Variety hall. You will like it very much . . .'

'Baby?'

'The old lady will look after her. We shall be back at nine. Dress up . . .' I was about to say 'Look sharp,' but checked myself and said: 'There is a lot of time. You needn't hustle yourself.'

'No, I'll be ready in ten minutes . . .' she said rising.

By the time we were coming out of the Variety hall that night we were in such agreement and showed such tender concern for each other's views and feelings that we both wondered how we could have treated each other so cruelly. 'I thought we might buy a new clock, that's why I gave away the old one,' she said.

'You did the best thing possible,' I said. 'Even in the hostel that wretched clock worried everyone nearabout. I am glad you have rid me of it.'

'They make such beautiful ones nowadays,' she said.

'Yes, yes, right. We will go out and buy one tomorrow evening,' I said. When we reached home we decided that we should avoid quarrelling with each other since, as she put it, 'They say such quarrels affect a child's health.'

3

ON THE OCCASION of our child's third birthday, my father wrote to say that he would advance me money to buy a house in Malgudi or to build one. He did not think it was very wise to go on living in a rented house. This offer made us very happy. My wife and I sat down and carried on endless discussions to decide which would be better, whether a built house or a site on which to build. 'A room all for myself where I can sit and spin out great poetry,' I said.

'Well, some place where you can be free from my presence?' she asked. 'Why don't you be plain?' 'No, no,' I replied awkwardly. 'I'm not eager to thrust my company on you either,' she said, 'I am as eager to have a separate room.'

'In that case, I don't want one,' I replied. 'Why should both of us have separate rooms?'

'Are you fighting?' the little one asked, gazing at us bewildered. 'You are always scolding Mother,' she said looking at me, and I felt unhappy at this thrust.

We agreed to go out on the following Sunday morning to Lawley Extension to choose a house or a site.

We were up with the sun. The old cook had gone out to see a relation on the previous evening. I had to light the fire and boil the water for coffee while Susila bathed, dressed, and prepared herself for the outing. As I sat struggling with smoke in my eyes and nostrils, she appeared at the kitchen doorway, like a vision, clad in her indigo saree, and hair gleaming and jasmine covered. I looked at her indigo saree and smiled to myself. She noticed it and asked, 'Why that?'

'Nothing, nothing,' I said with a cold damp in my nose. My

voice was thick. 'What is wrong with this saree? It is as good as another!' she said.

'Yes, yes,' I replied. 'That is why I say you should use it more sparingly, otherwise you will wear it out. . .' Her eyes sparkled with joy; she spread the fragrance of jasmine more than ever. 'The divine creature!' I reflected within myself, looking at her tall, slim figure.

'She was a phantom of delight
When first she gleamed upon my sight.'

My mind unconsciously quoted—the habit of an English teacher. The water reached boiling point and was lifting and throwing down the lid. All around the kitchen lay scattered faggots and burnt matchsticks and coal. Smoke still hung in the air. I smelt of coffee powder. 'Five spoons of powder and two tumblers of water, am I right?' I asked. She suddenly pushed me aside and said: 'Now, get ready. Let us be off. I will attend to this . . .'

I went away, and returned in half an hour ready and dressed. She gave me coffee. The maidservant had come. Susila placed a tumbler of milk on a teapoy outside and told the servant: 'Give this to the baby when she wakes up. Make her drink off the whole of it. Keep her engaged till the old lady returns. She will be back at about eight. Tell her that I will bring her fine toys and biscuits . . .'

She threw a look at the sleeping baby, drew a blanket over her, and said, 'Sit by her side, so that when she wakes up she may not cry.'

As we stepped out of the house, she said: 'I hope the child won't cry . . .'

'Don't keep bothering about her. She will be all right. You will be spoiling her if you bother so much. She must learn to exist by herself . . .' My wife merely smiled at me. 'I'm confident that the old woman will keep her happy, but she must come back in time.'

A fresh morning breeze blew. I took in a deep breath and said: 'Do you know how I used to love the early morning walk along the river when I was in the hostel . . . There is a magic in the atmosphere . . .' I was highly elated. The fresh sun, morning light, the breeze, and my wife's presence, who looked so lovely—even an unearthly loveliness—her tall form, dusky complexion, and the small diamond earrings—jasmine, jasmine . . . 'I will call you Jasmine, hereafter,' I said. 'I've long waited to tell you that . . .'

'Remember, we are in a public road, don't start any of your pranks here,' she warned, throwing at me a laughing glance. Her eyes always laughed—there was a perpetual smile in her eyes. 'The soul laughs through her eyes, it is the body which laughs with lips . . .' I remarked. 'What are you saying?' she asked. 'Nothing,' I replied.

'I hope you've not forgotten that we are in a public road?'

'What I say is perfectly innocent, no harm even if repeated on a public platform.' We were now in Market Road. Vehicles were moving about. The market was stirring into activity.

People as they passed threw a glance at us, some students saluted me. I said, 'My boys, good fellows . . .' 'Must be, because they salute you,' she said.

We were now passing before Bombay Anand Bhavan, a restaurant. 'Shall we go in?' she asked. I was only too delighted. I led her in. A number of persons were sitting in the dark hall over their morning coffee. There was a lot of din and clanging of vessels. Everybody turned and stared, the presence of a woman, particularly at that hour, being so very unusual. I felt rather shy. She went ahead, and stood in the middle of the hall not knowing where to go. A waiter appeared. 'Here Mani,' I hailed, knowing this boy, a youngster from Malabar, who had served me tiffin for several years now. I felt very proud of his acquaintance.

Mani said, 'Family room upstairs, follow me.' We followed him. There was a single room upstairs, with a wooden, marble-topped table and four chairs. The walls were lined as usual with fancy, coloured tiles.

'These marbles are so nice,' my wife said, running her fingers over them with simple joy. 'How smooth!'

'Do you know they are used only in bathrooms in civilized cities; they are called bathroom tiles.'

'They are so nice, why should these be used only for bathrooms?'

'Do you think those bathrooms are like ours?'

'Bathrooms are bathrooms wherever they may be . . .' she replied.

'No, no, a bathroom is very much unlike the smoke-ridden, wet, dripping bathing-place we have.'

'I try to keep it as neat as possible, and yet you think it is not good,' she remarked.

'I didn't mean that.'

'I think you did mean it.' I didn't like to spoil a good morning with a debate. So I agreed: 'I am sorry. Forgive and forget.'

'All right,' she said. She stretched her arms back and touched the wall behind her and said, 'I like these tiles, so fine and smooth! When we have a house of our own, won't you have some of them fixed like that on our walls?'

'With pleasure, but not in the hall, they are usually put up only in the bathrooms,' I pleaded.

'What if they are! People who like them for bathrooms may have them there, others if they want them elsewhere . . .'

At this moment Mani appeared carrying a tray of eatables. 'How quickly he has brought these!' she remarked: this was her first visit to Bombay Anand Bhavan. Its magnitude took her breath away. Her eyes sparkled like a child's.

She tried to eat with a spoon. She held it loosely and tipped the thing into her mouth from a distance. I suggested, 'Put it away if you can't manage with it.' She made a wry face at the smell of onion: 'I can't stand it—' she said. 'I know. I know,' I replied. 'What a pity.' It was careless of me. I knew that she hated onions but had taken no care to see that they were not given to her. I reproached myself. I called for the boy vociferously and commanded: 'Have that removed, bring something without onion.' I behaved as if I were an elaborate, ceremonial host. I wanted to please her. Her helplessness, innocence, and her simplicity moved me very deeply. 'I will give you something nice to eat.' I gave elaborate instructions to the boy. She mentioned her preference, a sweet, coloured drink—like a child's taste once again, I thought. I fussed about her till she said, 'Oh, leave me alone,' with that peculiar light dancing in her eyes. She said, 'Shall we take something for the child?' I didn't like to spoil a good morning with contradictions, but I did not approve of giving hotel stuff to the baby. So I said with considerable diplomacy: 'We will buy her some nice biscuits. She likes them very much.'

Nearly an hour later we came out of the hotel. I proposed that we should engage a *jutka* for going to Lawley Extension, but she preferred to walk. She said that she'd be happy to walk along the river. 'My dear girl,' I said, 'Lawley Extension is south and this river north of the town. We are going to the Extension on business.'

'Please, please,' she pleaded recklessly. 'I must wash my feet in the river today.' I was in the mood to yield completely to her wishes. So I agreed though it meant walking a couple of miles in the opposite direction.

It was a most exhilarating walk down the river. She splashed her feet in the water, rested under the banyan, heaped up sand and kept muttering, 'How the little girl would love it if only she could be brought here! I think she will simply roll in the sand. But we must take care not to let her go near the water.'

I watched her once again . . . 'Do you know how I used to spend all my morning here when I was in the hostel . . . I used to get up at dawn . . .'

'You could continue it even now . . . I hope you will not say I'm responsible for your giving up the good habit,' she said. I laughed. 'It doesn't look very important now, that is all; I did it for some time then; no compulsion to repeat the same thing for ever, even if it is good.'

When we were ready to go back I suggested, 'We must go on an all-India tour sometime. I will take you with me.'

'Promise?' she asked.

'Absolutely,' I said. 'I will take you also to England and Europe if I make a lot of money out of the books I am going to write.'

'What about the child?'

'She will be grown up by then,' I replied. 'We can leave her with her grandparents. You must see everything.' I imagined, even as I spoke, how she would touch the marble of the Taj, stand astounded before the snow-covered Himalayas, and before the crowd and magnitude of European cities.

We left the river and went to Lawley Extension in a *jutka*. When we got down there, she looked a little tired. Her face had a slight flush. 'We have to walk a little here,' I warned her. 'Do you think I can't?' she asked, and went forward.

Lawley Extension formed the southernmost portion of the town, and consisted of well laid-out residential buildings, lining the neat roads and crossroads. It was the very end of the town, beyond which passed the Trichy Trunk Road, shaded with trees. At one time, only those with very high incomes could have residences there, but about five years ago, under a new scheme, the Extension developed farther south; even beyond the Trunk Road the town was extending. There was a general scramble for these sites and houses, which received an uninterrupted southern breeze blowing across the fields, a most satisfactory outlook aesthetically, the corn fields, which were receding in the face of the buildings, waving in sunlight. 'I shall have to cycle up to the college, but it doesn't matter. We shall have a most enchanting view before us, we won't know that we are in a town.' I became very enthusiastic. A friend of mine, Sastri of the logic section, had promised me his help in choosing a house. He was the moving spirit of this New Extension, secretary of the Building and Acquisition Society, and a most energetic 'extender'. No one could have believed that he had so much business capacity—his main occupation being logic. He was a marvellous man—a strange combination of things, at one end 'undistributed middle', 'definition of knowledge', 'syllogisms', and at the other he had the spirit of a pioneer. His was the first building in the New Extension, and then he got together a few persons and formed his company, which was chiefly responsible for the growth of this New Extension.

We reached Sastri's house, a small bungalow in a vast compound overgrown with trees. Sastri—a thin grey-haired man—was sitting under a tree digging its roots.

'Hello, Sastri!' I cried. 'I am sorry I'm so late. This lady is responsible for it,' I said pointing to my wife. Sastri came up, picking the mud off his hands.

'So glad you have brought your wife, I hear lots of complaints that you don't bring her out,' said Sastri.

'Oh, there is a small child to be looked after,' I replied.

'You could bring her out too.'

'Oh, it is not so easy.' I began to visualize all the difficulties in an instant: the protection, ceaseless attention and all the rest of it. 'Father, take me up, I can't walk.' 'Father, put me down, I don't like to be carried.' 'I'm hungry,' and 'I won't eat anything.'

'It is not so easy,' I said.

'Why, why?' asked the logician.

'You see,' I began, but realized how utterly hopeless it would be to explain it all to him—this childless man would not understand the complications. I changed the subject: 'I hope you will take us to see some houses.'

'Come up, come up, we will discuss it.' He took me in and seated me in the veranda, on a discoloured rattan chair, which pricked my back. Sastri said: 'Still interested in houses? Why don't you buy a site and build a good house? I have a beautiful site for you up there.'

'Oh, I can't wait for all the bricks and mortar to take shape. I don't know anything of house building, too much bother.'

'Leave it all to me,' Sastri said. 'I will do it.' He had taken upon himself this task for scores of people, and some uncharitable ones remarked that he made a better living out of it than as a logic lecturer.

'I've no patience to wait, my dear fellow,' I pleaded. 'I can't stand all the nuisance. I want a house at the moment I think of it.'

'Very well, I'll show you some. See how you like them. If you don't like any of them, you may just accept my other suggestion.' He sent his servant to fetch the building contractor: a dark man, with a moustache, and a red vermilion hand. 'Sit down, Swamy, can those houses be seen today?' Sastri asked.

'Yes, yes, I will send the boy to keep them open.' He despatched a boy.

Sastri's wife had given us lemon squash to drink, and refreshed, Susila started out once again with us.

Sastri said: 'We will have to do a little walking. I hope the lady won't feel too fatigued.'

'No, no, not at all. I can walk miles,' Susila replied.

I was walking on between Sastri and the contractor, who were full of house-building talk. A little later I turned and noticed that Susila had fallen back, unable to keep pace with us. I stopped and joined her. Standing beside her, I felt like calling her 'Jasmine' once again. I whispered: 'We are going to see some very nice houses, are you pleased?'

'Yes, yes.'

'You must tell me which of them you like best . . .'

'Yes,' she replied. I whispered: 'Don't worry about the child, she will be quite happy.'

'If she starts crying for some reason or other, no one can stop her. The old lady will not be able to manage,' she said.

'Oh, don't imagine all those things,' I pleaded. I lowered my voice still further and said, 'Jasmine . . .' She suppressed a smile that came on her lips, her eyes flashed a mild reproof.

We came before a row of very small houses—each with a very narrow suffocating veranda, and a front garden, half a dozen monotonously alike.

'Do you like this pattern?' Sastri asked me. I looked at my wife.

She said: 'The child will lose her way not knowing which is her house—they are all alike. Why are these so alike?' She shook her head. Sastri added: 'The second house is for sale.' I said: 'Can't we see some other pattern? This is too small.' A young boy held the door open. Sastri said: 'Come in and see the house. No harm in seeing the house.' He was a connoisseur in houses and expected others to be the same. The contractor added: 'Yes, yes, you must see different types before deciding.' 'What an amount of banality surrounds the purchase of a house! How much we have to bear before we are through with it,' I reflected. The contractor commanded the boy: 'Are all the houses open?'

'Yes, master.'

'Don't say "yes"! Keep them open,' he said.

'Yes, master,' he said.

'You are a careless fool,' he added. 'I will pluck off your ear if you aren't careful!' 'Why does this man bully the young fellow unnecessarily?' I reflected. 'Some people are made that way. Perhaps, if a census on this subject were taken, ten thousand persons would be found to be bullying ten thousand others every minute all over the world . . .' I wanted the boy to be saved further persecution and so asked the contractor: 'What is the width of this veranda?'

'Forty-four inches . . .'

Sastri asked: 'What do you think of it?'

'I don't like it. It is no use having such a small house,' I replied.

'But the price!' Sastri said with a knowing smile. 'The best at twelve hundred!'

'Oh, Sastri, how did this house-salesmanship get into your blood, instead of logic?' I reflected.

At last we came to a house which seemed attractive. It had a wide compound, broad windows, and a general appearance of spaciousness and taste. All the doors and the walls looked fresh with paint. As we turned the street, Susila saw the contractor's boy standing at the gate, and asked with a great thrill: 'Is that also ours?' It was very attractive with two jasmine creepers trained over an arch on the gateway. It was full of flowers. The gates moved on silent hinges. As we were about to go under the arch I lightly touched her arm and pointed at the jasmine creeper. I told the contractor: 'I would love to call this the Jasmine House, its perfume greets us even as we enter.' The contractor was pleased. 'I hope you will like it inside too,' he said.

A few steps led up to the veranda—a fairly deep and cool veranda, with a short parapet. Susila sat on the parapet. I sat beside her and said: 'Someone with taste has planned it.' Sastri looked greatly pleased that a house of his selection had received such approval. The main door was opened, and we inspected the house room by room. A hall, four rooms, in addition to the kitchen, a pleasing light blue paint on all the walls inside the house. Susila and I were thrilled. We went away by ourselves, in every room, and visualized ourselves as its future occupants.

'What's the price?' she asked.

'Must be within our figure, otherwise they would not have brought us here.'

'Plenty of space for the child to play. She can simply run about just as she likes. Those parapets on the veranda are a good idea to prevent her from falling off.'

'There is plenty of space for guests too. The grandparents may also come and stay with us quite comfortably. The small room in the front veranda will be my study. I shall write immense quantities of poetry when I settle here, I think.'

'Sometime my mother must come and stay with us,' she said. 'She has always blamed us for living in a rented house. She will be very happy, I am sure.'

'You must also have the room next to mine as all your own—if you like I will have coloured marble tiles fitted along the walls.'

'So that you may call it the bathroom, I suppose,' she remarked. We joined the other two sitting on the veranda, and discussed the price and other details: 'It was occupied only for three months after it was built and changed hands.'

'Why?' I asked, trying to appear as a man of great business wisdom. Sastri replied, looking serious, 'I've not enquired. Have you any idea?' The contractor said: 'I built the house for the gentleman, and the family went away and settled in Madras. Rich people don't usually mind these things.'

'I hope it has a clear reputation,' Sastri said.

'Of course, without doubt,' replied the contractor. 'This is at the end of the town, that is the chief reason . . .' It was a fact. It was really the very last house, in the last crossroad of the New Extension. Fields of corn stretched away in front of the house, and far beyond it, a cluster of huts of the next village, and beyond it all stood up the blue outlines of Mempi Hills. It was a lovely prospect.

I stood looking at it and said: 'A magnificient view, only a buffalo could be insensible to it.'

'Is this a mosquito-ridden place?' I asked.

'Some parts of the year . . . The best thing to do is to sleep under a net.'

'I feel suffocated under a mosquito net. I prefer a mosquito bite,' Sastri said.

The contractor said: 'I am sixty-five years old and I have never been under a mosquito net! I've never had malaria even once.'

'Really.' Sastri asked, greatly impressed.

'A fact. You ask my old mother if you like,' replied the contractor. 'I think all stuff about mosquitoes is nonsense. As if there were no mosquitoes in the days of our grandfathers.' Susila found the talk boring: 'I'll go and have a look round the compound,' she said. I got up. Susila replied: 'No, you needn't come. I'll just see the compound and back yard, and return.' She started out. I followed her a few paces. 'Why do you want to go?' I asked. 'Shall I follow you?'

'Oh, won't you let me alone even for a few minutes?' she whispered. 'Nobody will carry me off. I can look after myself!' She went away. I returned to my friends, and continued our talk. I promised to write to my father, and complete the transaction at an early date. They fixed the coming Wednesday as a date for further discussions. I took Sastri aside and requested him to settle the price favourably. 'Leave it to me. I will cut down at least five hundred,' Sastri assured me. My mind was in a whirl—I was already tremendously excited. 'We must move in within a month, if possible,' I reflected.

Half an hour passed. 'What is Susila doing with herself so long?' I thought. I jumped down, saying: 'Wait a minute, please,' and ran round to the back yard.

I noticed as I went along what a lot of space there was for making a small manageable garden. The fertility of the surrounding fields had affected this place too and there was a growth of pleasant green grass and one or two uncared-for bushes of leucas— which put forth small, whitish flowers. 'This poor plant is the first to be removed whenever a garden is made, because it grows naturally—but I shall make a point of preserving it.' I stopped and plucked a flower. I wondered what ideas Susila had for the garden, and decided that the bulk of it should be left to her care and management. 'I am sure she is thinking of a very grand kitchen garden in the back yard . . .' I told myself. I went on to the back yard, where a few young coconut trees threw a sparse shade around. Susila was not to be seen. I looked for her and called, 'Susila! Susila!' She answered from somewhere. I called again, and she cried: 'Push the door open! I can't open it from this side.' I found that her voice came from the other side of a green-painted lavatory door. I gave it a kick and it flew open. Out she came—red and trembling. I looked at her and felt disturbed.

'What—what were you doing here?' I asked. She was panting with excitement. She was still shivering. I seated her on a stone slab nearby. 'What is the matter? What is the matter?'

'I went in there. The door was so bright and I thought it'd be clean inside . . . but oh!' she screwed up her face and shuddered, unable to bear the disgust that came with recollection. I felt agitated. 'Why did you go there?' I cried. She didn't answer. It was a sad anticlimax to a very pleasing morning. I looked at her feet. 'You went in barefoot?' She nodded.

'Where are your sandals?'

'I forgot them at home.' I shook my head in despair. 'I have told you a hundred times not to come out barefoot. And yet. . .' She merely looked at me without replying. Her face was beaded with perspiration. Her cheeks were flushed. She was still trembling. I melted at the sight of it: 'Oh, darling, why did you go there?'

'The door was so bright . . .' she replied softly. 'I thought it'd be clean inside too . . . but I couldn't come out after I went in—the door shut by itself with a bang. I thought something terrible had happened . . . Ah, the flies and other things there!' She was convulsed with disgust. 'Oh, oh . . . A fly came and sat on my lip.' She wouldn't bring her lips together. She kept rubbing them with her fingers in an effort to eradicate the touch of the fly . . . I said: 'There is the water tap. Rinse your mouth, and wash your feet, you will be all right. Don't think of it any more.' She jumped up on the stone slab, turned the tap on and washed her hands and feet and mouth, again and again. She rubbed her feet on the stone till they were red and till they smarted. It looked as though she would not stop this operation. I said: 'You'll hurt yourself, or you may catch a cold. Come away. Don't bother about it any more. You are all right.'

We came back to the veranda. Sastri and the contractor were waiting for us. I seated Susila in a clean corner of the veranda and advised her to lean on the wall, and rest. The others observed her flushed face and asked what the matter was. 'She visited that lavatory and found it rather unclean,' I said. 'Oh,' the contractor said: 'I wish the lady had told us, I'd have asked her not to go there. This is one of the curses of the place. It is so far out and so near the field and village that all kinds of people passing this way stop here for shelter, and they foul a lavatory beyond description . . . This is not the first time such a complaint has come to us.'

'When the house is occupied?' I asked.

'Oh no, no trouble then, only when it is vacant. It's so difficult to engage a caretaker for every little place, though there is a peon going round to see these things at least once a day.'

After resting for about half an hour Susila got up and said: 'I feel all right.'

Sastri and the contractor went ahead. I kept my wife company, watching her every movement anxiously. When we approached Sastri's house, he suggested: 'Won't you come in for a moment? The lady can have a little coffee. She looks tired.' Susila declined this with a smile.

'Oh no, thanks, we will be going, it is late,' I said. 'We will meet on Wednesday.'

We walked down the crossroad. When the presence of the other two was withdrawn, I grew elaborately fussy—I asked her for the hundredth time if she was feeling all right. As we were passing into the main road, we saw a small, newly-built temple. 'They have built a beautiful temple for this place, so near our house. So thoughtful of them . . .' I said. 'We will go in,' she said, 'and see the god.'

'Most certainly.'

There was an old woman sitting on a gunny sack at the temple gate, selling offerings. 'Buy something for the god,' she entreated.

'What temple is this?' Susila asked.

'Srinivasa—the greatest god; you need not visit Thirupathi Hills to see him, if you visit him here—he grants all your boons and blesses all your efforts . . .' She held up a coconut, a packet of camphor, plantain, and betel leaves.

'You are both so young and bright. He will bless you with numerous children and may they all be sons . . .' said the old lady.

'Hush,' Susila replied. 'We have one and we are satisfied with one . . .' she laughed and entered the temple. I was tremendously relieved to see her laugh. We entered the temple hall—a stone pillared hall, smelling of camphor and flowers, cool and shady. There were two bronze lamps burning in the inner sanctuary, illuminating a tall stone image of Srinivasa. A priest, wrapped in a shawl, sitting at the foot of the image, rose on seeing us and held up a plate. We placed the offerings on it.

'What a lovely image!' Susila remarked. She brought together her palms and closed her eyes in prayer. I stood watching her. The priest broke the coconut, and placed it and the other things at the foot of the image. He lit the camphor, sounded a bell, and circled the flame around the image. In this flickering light the image acquired strange shadows and seemed to stir, and make a movement to bless—I watched my wife. She opened her eyes for a moment. They caught the light of the camphor flame, and shone with an unearthly brilliance. Her cheeks glowed, the rest of her person was lost in the shadows of the temple hall. Her lips were moving in prayer. I felt transported at the sight of it. I shut my eyes and prayed: 'God bless this child and protect her.' She received the holy water from the priest and touched her lips and eyes, put a vermilion dot on her forehead, and tucked the flower offered to the god in her hair. We stepped out. As we descended the temple steps she muttered: 'Only now do I feel well again. We must make it a point to visit this temple as often as we can.'

'You can visit it every evening when we have taken the new house,' I said.

'Yes, yes.' I was greatly relieved to see her happy and fit once again. We hailed a passing *jutka*, climbed into it, and sat snugly close. The *jutka* wheels rattled over the cobbles and it lulled us into a mild drowse. We ceased to pass any remarks or comment and settled in a tranquil silence. I studied her face without her knowledge. A great peace had descended on her. 'It is God's infinite grace that has given me this girl.' The *jutka* was filled with the scent of the jasmine in her hair and the glare of the indigo-coloured saree.

As we passed the Market Road, she reminded me, 'You have promised to buy biscuits and a doll for the child.' We stopped the carriage before Novelty House. I dashed in and came out bearing a biscuit packet, a doll and a toy engine.

When we reached home we found the child playing very happily with the cook and a child from the next house. We heard her voice, over and above the rattle of the carriage wheels, when we were still two houses away. As soon as the carriage stopped, Leela came out running. Her mother took her up in her arms immediately, and gave her the doll, train and the biscuits. Leela's friend from the next house was also there. Leela said to her: 'You can go home now, my mother has come.' The friend said: 'All right . . .' and hesitated, casting a look on the game they had been playing . . . They had raised a building with wooden blocks, and various small utensils filled with water and grains and flowers and leaves were strewn about the small hall—they had been playing 'Homekeeping' and calling on each other.

'Yes, she was a very fine child today. When Mother is at home, she gives such a lot of trouble over food! She was my sweet child today,' said the old cook.

'Did she ask where we were?'

'Ah, didn't she? Every few minutes asking and asking why her mother had gone out without telling her. She is a smart child.'

'Why did you go away Mother, at night?' the little one asked. 'When I opened my eyes, I didn't see you but her.' The cook shook with laughter: 'What a lot of speech she has learnt! She is going to defeat all the others in your family in speech, madam.'

'Why did you go away, Mother?' the little girl asked. Her mother threw herself on the floor, even without changing her dress. 'Too tired for anything now. I won't get up, whatever happens, without resting for another half an hour . . .'

'You must eat your food first,' the old cook began.

'No, get up, get up, Susila,' I said. But she begged to be allowed to rest for half an hour.

'Where did you go, Mother, without telling me?'

'To buy a house for you.'

'What is it made of?'

'Stone and lime.'

'Is it so high?' she indicated with her hand a yard in height and said: 'I want one which is small and can be put in the trunk.'

'I mean a real big house like this,' said the mother.

'This is our house?' the child asked.

'Another one, more beautiful—Oh! You can play all day with plants.'

'Can I play in mud?'

'Oh, yes, it's very clean and nice . . .'

'My friend must also come with me.' She carried on this

conversation sitting on her mother, clutching the doll and the train, and eating a biscuit.

I busied myself for half an hour in my room, and came out. I still found my wife lying on the floor: 'Oh, why have you flung yourself down in this manner? Go and change. We will eat . . .'

'Leave me alone for a little, please,' she pleaded.

I felt her temples with my fingers: 'If this small excursion exhausts you so much, I don't know what I can do with you when we go on our North Indian travel.'

'I will be all right then.'

'You will be better if you eat a hearty meal at once.'

She begged, 'Please, don't compel me. The thought of food upsets me. Go and finish your food first, and don't wait for me.' I protested at the idea and went away to my room. 'I can also take it later with you. I'm not particularly hungry. I think the hotel stuff has not agreed with you.'

The child snuggled close to her mother and clung to her neck. I said: 'Don't trouble your mother.'

'I'm not troubling her. I'm making her headache go,' replied the child.

I went away to my study and stood for a moment gazing at my table. My wife had given up all attempts at tidying up my room, and it had lapsed into natural state of my hostel days. Once again all Milton and Shakespeare and Bradley jostled each other in a struggle for existence. There were four library books on my table which had been overdue, accumulating fines and bringing me fierce reminders from the librarian, but which I had not opened even once. There were the latest books on Plato, Swinburne, modern poetry, and others which the librarian had forced on me in one of his hospitable moods. I realized that I used to read better when I was in the hostel and had not become the head of a family. Nor were my hours spent in chatting with my wife or watching the child play or in running about on shopping errands. My conscience troubled me whenever I thought of it. 'I will not waste half an hour, but will get through this stuff on Plato.' I picked up the book and lounged in my canvas chair. 'Plato's idealism . . .' I read. 'Sickening fellows. Why won't they leave Plato alone? For the thousandth time someone restating Plato—I don't like this book. I shall return it.' I put it away. The other book too I found unreadable.

I found that I had spent half an hour in these attempted

studies. I put away the books. I leaned back in my chair, hoping I should be called. There was no sound in the house. I got up and went to the hall. I saw the mother and the child fast asleep where they lay. My first impulse was to waken Susila. I watched her for a moment. 'Too tired, let her sleep for a while,' I reflected. 'I will dine first, she may wake up and join me.' I went to the dining room and sat down before the leaf. The old cook served me. 'Where is . . .' she began in her croaking voice. 'Hush, not so loudly. She's asleep,' I said. 'She will wake up presently.' I went through my meal, and tiptoed out to the bathroom, washed my hands, and while I dried them, stood near her and watched. Her lips were slightly parted. 'Is she still reluctant to bring her lips together?' I asked myself. I sat by her side, and gently touched her eyelids with the tip of my finger. She opened her eyes, at once saw the child asleep by her side, clutching her toys, and disengaged herself gently and sat up. I said: 'I've had my food; I felt hungry. Won't you come and eat?'

I led her to the bathroom, and gently splashed a little cold water on her face. I took her to the kitchen, seated her before her leaf, and sat by her side. She obeyed implicitly without saying a word. The old lady muttered, 'You should never delay your food so long. An empty stomach makes poison.' She served some vegetables and dal. Susila murmured, 'None of these. Only a little rice and buttermilk for me.' After due protests she was allowed to have her choice. She sat gazing at her leaf. After a considerable amount of coaxing, she picked up a tiny quantity of rice between her fingers, put it in her mouth, and retched. 'Biliousness,' I remarked. 'Bring those lime pickles. Now be a good girl and finish off that rice with the help of the pickles. Go on—you can do it.' She sat staring at the leaf. She took another mouthful after a good deal of persuasion and sickened. It was impossible. She rose to her feet declaring, 'I can't. I won't eat any food now. I'll eat at night.' She washed her hands, and went back to the hall, and lay down. I sat beside her worrying myself. She confessed: 'Don't worry, it is nothing, I'll be all right.'

'What is wrong?'

'Shall I say?' she whispered. 'Don't be angry with me. That closet, and those, oh, oh,' she shuddered, 'flies and other things come before me and I can't eat. And that fly which sat here,' she pointed at her lip and finished the rest of the sentence with a shiver.

Three days, four, five, and six days passed and still she did not leave her bed. It was difficult for her to swallow any food or medicine, although she was doing everything in her power to forget the picture of that closet. Luckily for me, the college was closed and I could spend much of my time with the child, who looked forlorn ever since her mother took to bed. Susila lay on her bed, spread on the floor in her room. The grey, vine-patterned bedspread, green shawl, and that girl lying with her face to the wall, hardly awake for two hours in a day—it shattered my peace.

The old cook was very unhappy. 'Please call a doctor,' she suggested. It hadn't seemed to me necessary; moreover my wife was definitely against showing herself to a doctor. I told the cook, 'She won't allow any doctor to see her.' The cook made a gesture of despair: 'Oh, you young man! Is this the time to consult her wishes!' Her question stirred vague fears in me. So I asked haughtily: 'What is wrong with the time? It is quite a good time, take it from me . . .' She ignored my petulance and said: 'She has been in bed for five or six days, what have you done?'

'I have given her medicine.'

'That's not enough, you must ask a doctor to see her.'

'I know my duty,' I replied and went away. I sat by my wife and watched her. It was morning, and she looked fairly well.

'Can you take any solid food today?' I asked solicitously.

'No, no, some milk and gruel will do for me . . .'

'I will call a doctor to see you,' I said.

'No, no, please. I don't like doctors,' she pleaded. 'They press the stomach, and here and there, and it hurts. The press given by the doctor before Leela was born still pains.'

'Don't be absurd. You talk like a baby.' She merely looked at me. Her lips were dry. 'Where is the child?' she asked. She was playing in the next house. 'Bring her down. I will comb her hair and change her dress.'

'Don't exert yourself.'

'No, no, I can do it. If I don't, who will do it?' she asked. I went over to the next house. Leela was heaping wet sand on their front step and sticking twigs and flowers on its top. 'This is our temple,' she said. The god was a piece of stone embedded in the mud. She reverently prostrated herself before it. 'She is the temple man,' she pointed to her friend. 'She does the *puja*.' Her friend came up with a piece of coconut (a castor seed) and flowers (grass tufts) and offered them to me. I said to Leela: 'Your mother wants you.' She brightened. 'Has her fever gone?' she asked, and clutched my hand and ran down with me, leaving the temple and the priest behind.

Her mother sat up. Her hair was dishevelled, and seemed to be all in a knotted mass. Her lips were dry. She still wore the saree she had put on the day she came out with me. All the same I felt joyous. She was able to sit up—after all these days. 'Try and change your dress today,' I said. She sent out the child to fetch the coconut oil bottle and the comb from the cupboard in the dining hall. The child returned hugging the bottle, put it down, and ran out a second time to bring the comb; and sat down before her mother. Susila remarked: 'The poor child looks an orphan without proper attention.' She uncoiled her hair, oiled and combed it, and plaited it; and then said, 'Bring that blue silk frock and shirt.'

'Mother, Mother, I hate that blue silk . . .'

'You mustn't keep it in the box and outgrow it. It is nice, wear it out.'

'Mother, Mother.'

'Which is it?' I asked.

'The one your brother sent from Hyderabad last Deepavali,' Susila replied. All my affection for my brother returned immediately. Good fellow—I remembered the bullying he practised on me in that cart whenever we went out together, the wild claims he would make in the afternoon that he had trained a frog (living under a stone near the well) to come out at his call and follow him: remember him helplessly pacing up and down the house when his wife and mother had heated arguments over trifles, and now auditing, henpecked, and with ten children—a life of worry—so good of him to have thought of me in all this stress . . . All this flashed before my mind and I ordered, 'Little one, you must learn to obey your mother in all these matters, without a word . . .' The child threw a pained look at me, and went away. I heard her opening the box in the next room—the wicker trunk in which her clothes were kept. My wife said: 'Don't be so harsh with her, poor girl!' The child returned with the blue frock and shirt. I took it in my hand and said: 'How lovely!' The child replied swiftly: 'It is not lovely,' and submitted herself to her mother's handling. Halfway through it her mother said: 'Go and get a little water in a vessel—don't drop it on your toes. I will wash your face . . .'

'Here!' I cried. 'You mustn't touch cold water. You may catch a cold.' My wife said, 'I won't catch a cold. Her face is covered with mud.' The child hesitated, and then ran over to the bathroom and fetched a vessel of water and a towel. Her mother rubbed off the mud patches with a wet towel, put a vermilion dot on her forehead, powdered her cheeks, and dressed her in new clothes. Leela looked resplendent. 'Am I all right, Father?' she asked. I took her in my arms. 'You are beautiful,' I cried.

My wife changed her dress, combed her hair, and ate a little food, though she said it tasted bitter. She looked refreshed. She remade her bed. I was elated. The gloom which had hung on me for these four days lifted, and I hummed a little tune to myself as I went to my room. These exertions, however, tired her, and she lay down and slept. She woke up at five in the evening, and complained of headache. I felt her pulse, and found that she had a temperature. I said, 'Just wait. I will fetch the doctor.'

'Yes,' she agreed. 'Do something and stop this headache.'

'I will give you some Horlicks and go,' I said. I called for boiling water. The Horlicks, and a spoon and tumbler, were on a small table in the hall. I made the Horlicks and took it in to her. I found her crying. This was the first day I saw her broken and crying. 'Oh you are hungry!' I cried. I tried to make her drink the Horlicks, but it was at boiling point and wouldn't cool down easily. She lay with her face towards the wall and tears made a wet track all over her face. I lost my head. The cook stood by and advised: 'Give her food first, she is hungry, that is all, that is all.'

'But this damned thing is scalding, you can't bring a thing at bearable temperature. I have half a mind to fling away this rubbish.' The child had meanwhile come in and was quietly leaning against the wall and watching us. The cook was averse to seeing her there, and kept muttering: 'Come away, baby,' till I, trying to cool the milk with one hand, and comforting my wife with the other, shouted at her to leave the child alone. Meanwhile my wife's sobbing increased. 'Control yourself, child,' I said. 'Take this, you will be all right.' After all the drink cooled, and she drank it, and smiled at me, I felt relieved. I sat down and caressed her forehead and asked: 'Do you feel all right now? I will fetch the doctor.'

Dr Shankar of Krishna Medical Hall had been introduced to me by Rangappa who swore by him. 'The greatest physician on earth,' he used to say, 'easily the most successful practitioner in the town.'

Krishna Medical Hall was in Market Road, and it was a mile's walk from my house. I enjoyed this outing. It suddenly relieved the stress and gloom of the last few days. I met one or two people, and spent a little time in conversation on the way, purchased a packet of cigarettes and smoked. All this seemed to restore the old glow of life—its peace and tranquillity.

The doctor was away. His seat at the central table was vacant, but all around the benches and chairs were filled with patients and patients' relatives waiting for the doctor. An accountant and a clerk sat next to each other at the entrance poring over leather-bound ledgers and making entries.

'Be seated please, the doctor will be in presently,' said the clerk. I felt gratified by the warmth of his welcome and the smile he bestowed on me. I sat in a chair and looked about. The walls were lined with glass shelves loaded with the panacea that drug manufacturers invent—attractive boxes, cellophane wrappings. The days of bitter drugs were gone. All medicines were good to the taste and even to see. Piles and piles of sterilized cotton in blue packing reached the ceiling. 'How do these people know where they've got the things they want, and when do they take it?' I wondered. The walls were decorated with placards containing coloured pictures of beauties and beasts and skeletons and rosy-cheeked children, benefited by one cellophane covered nectar or another.

From an ante-chamber issued voices of women and cries of children. Somewhere else a dispenser was jingling his glasses. He came out presently, a businesslike man wearing silk trousers, in shirtsleeves and apron. He held up a bottle wrapped in brown. 'Who is Kesav?'

'It is for me,' said a feeble man wrapped in a shawl with a woollen muffler over his ears. The dispenser handed him the bottle with the brief remark: 'Three doses before meals,' and went in. This sufferer had some further question to ask, and opened his mouth to say something, but the dispenser was gone. The man clutched his bottle and looked about helplessly, turned to the clerk and asked: 'Can I take buttermilk?'

'Yes,' replied the clerk.

'Should I take this immediately after or a few minutes before food?'

'Say five minutes before food,' replied the clerk and added: 'Six annas, please.' The patient put down the change with a sad look, still feeling that he hadn't received his money's worth of doctor's advice. He hesitated, looked about and said, 'I would like to ask the doctor himself . . .'

'You need not see him till you have taken this mixture for three more days. I will tell him how you are.' The patient felt grateful. 'Please don't forget to say that the pain on the left side still persists.'

'Yes, yes,' replied the clerk, who seemed to be half a doctor. He scattered advice and suggestions liberally. He even examined throats, and suggested remedies for headache.

A car stopped, and there was an agitation in the gathering. The doctor had arrived. Everybody pressed forward to receive him. He looked like a film star being mobbed by admirers. He waved his hand, smiled, and gently pressed all admirers back to their seats.

His assistant placed some slips of papers and bottles before him and the doctor got down to work. He read out the names on the slips and bottles one by one, examined a throat here, tapped a chest there, listened in to the murmurs of hearts through a tube, and wrote prescriptions at feverish speed. Here he whispered into an ear something private, and there pushed someone into a private room and came out wiping his hands on a towel. He might have been a great machine dispensing health, welfare and happiness. I felt a great admiration for him. At last my turn came: 'What can I do for you, Professor?' he asked, mechanically picking up my wrist. For some reason he always called me professor. 'I'm not the patient, doctor,' I said.

I explained to him my wife's symptoms. He asked a few questions, wrote down a prescription, and put it away. He passed on to the next slip and called the next in order. A man from the village stood before him and began: 'Last night . . .' The doctor turned to me and asked: 'Have you brought a bottle?'

'No, I didn't expect . . .' I began apologetically.

'It is all right,' he said, and on my prescription made a mark, and turned to his next patient. 'Last night . . .' the other began and gave a long-winded account of a pain in the back of the head, which travelled all the way down to his ankle and went up again. He might have been a witness deposing before a magistrate. The doctor tapped his back, tingled his ear, looked into the pupils of his eyes and pinched his knee. He cracked a couple of jokes at the expense of this patient, prescribed the treatment, and disposed of him. In a quarter of an hour the smart dispenser who had swept in the prescriptions a few minutes ago, came out with a few paper-wrapped bottles and called: 'Mrs Krishna . . .' I stood up and took my bottle, and looked at the doctor, who was busy writing. The clerk said: 'It is your bottle?' and held his hand out for it. He looked at the label and read: 'A third every four hours before food, and five minutes before each dose one pill. Repeat the mixture for two days and then see the doctor. Diet—rice and buttermilk. Ten annas please.' I was disappointed with the mechanical, red-tape method I found here. I looked at the doctor, he was still busy. I paid down the cash, but returned to my seat. I waited for ten minutes in the hope of catching the doctor's eye. But he was far too busy.

'Doctor,' I butted in.

'Half a moment, please.' He finished the prescription he was writing, leaned back, and said: 'Yes, got your mixture and pills?'

'Yes.' Now that I had his attention I was at a loss to know what to ask. 'When is this to be given?' I asked, guiltily looking at the clerk.

'Didn't he tell you?' he asked pointing at the clerk. 'Yes, yes. he did,' I replied hastily. I now realized the need for this red-tape arrangement—everyone wanted to ask the same set of questions.

'But what I want to know is . . . Don't you have to see the patient?'

'Oh, no, it is just malaria. I have fifty cases like this on hand, no need to see her. I'll tell you if it is necessary. You can bring her down sometime if necessary.'

'But she can't move, she is rather weak . . .'

'Put her in a *jutka* and bring her along, nothing will happen . . . Just peep into that room and see how many persons with fever have come here. It is usually more convenient for me than calling on them.' I really felt it was absurd to have ever thought of asking this great man to visit me.

'No, no, I understand,' I said awkwardly.

'Really no need. She will be all right in a couple of days. She will be all right, don't worry.' He smiled confidently and it cheered me.

'Diet? What can I give her?'

'Buttermilk and rice, anything you like. Don't make it too heavy.' Clutching my bottle I went out.

At the door my daughter met me. 'Mother is very cross, Father.

She won't look at me at all, but keeps her hand over her eyes and . . .'

'Oh, she will be all right. I've brought her the medicines.' My wife looked at me and asked: 'Why've you taken such a long time to get back?' She was still moaning with headache. 'The old lady is cooking and the baby has no one to be with . . .'

On hearing my voice the old lady came out of the kitchen. She was overjoyed to see the medicine. 'I pray to the Lord of the Seven Hills that this medicine may put her on her feet again. I am longing to see her moving about the house. What food is to be given?'

'Buttemilk and rice.' She threw up her hands in horror: 'I have never heard of buttermilk being given for fever!'

'Never mind. The doctor knows better. The days are gone when buttermilk was dreaded,' I said haughtily.

Next day I went to the doctor, reported the patient's condition, and took home the mixture and pills, and then again the next day, and the next. It was becoming difficult to make Susila swallow the pills. It agitated her poor heart so much that she felt suffocated and perspiration left her prostrate. One night she perspired so much that she lay in a faint, and could communicate only by feeble signs. I gave her something hot to drink, and nursed her, but this condition frightened me. It was two o'clock at night. Her feet were cold.

I told the doctor about it when I met him next at his dispensary. He muttered something about idiosyncrasy and declared: 'But we can't stop this pill now. It is the latest anti-malarial compound; it must be effective. It's bound to depress the heart a bit, but don't worry about it. She will be very well again. Don't stop the pills on any account.'

She swallowed the medicine and pills for about a week more. The temperature did not go down.

I went to the doctor's house, and begged him to visit us. He dressed and came along. 'Usually it is unnecessary. All these cases are alike. But I'll do it for your sake, Professor . . .' He drove down with me by his side to our house. He was most amiable and leisurely—an entirely different man outside the dispensary. He played with my child and gave her a ride on his shoulder, examined all the books on my table, proved to be a great book-lover and a student of philosophy, and was delighted that we had similar tastes. He was overjoyed to hear that I also wrote. He had great reverence, he said, for authors as a class. He appreciated one or two pictures I had hung on the wall. All this established such a harmony between us that when he came to examine my wife he seemed an old friend rather than the medical automaton of Krishna Dispensary.

He took half an hour to examine the patient and declared at the end of it: 'Nothing to worry about . . .'

My wife asked him: 'When can I move about again?'

'Very soon. But all your life you will be moving about the house doing this and that, why should you grumble at staying a little while in bed now? Many people take it as an opportunity for a holiday . . .' He then narrated his experience at a house (he did not mention names) where a daughter-in-law fell ill and was in bed for two weeks or so, and put on weight. Her husband came to him privately and said: 'Doctor, please keep her in bed for a fortnight more. It is almost her only chance of being free from the harassment of her mother-in-law.' On hearing this story Susila laughed so much that her face became red and she broke into a sweat. He took her pulse and said: 'She is already shaking off her temperature . . . That is a good sign. She will be absolutely well again, in a couple of days unless she wishes to stay in bed like that daughter-in-law,' and he winked at me. 'Take the medicine and pills, madam,' he said and went away. He radiated health and cheer. Susila and I felt more confident and happy after this visit. So that when the child came from the next house she asked: 'Is Mother all right?'

The doctor's presence was so beneficial that I requested him to visit her at least once a day. He was very obliging; it was quite a thrill for us to hear the sound of his car every day. We gave him coffee and he stayed for over half an hour talking to us on various matters. In the evening I went to his shop to fetch the medicine. It went on for nearly a week more. Although his visit cheered us it did not help the temperature to go down. It remained unaffected by all the drugs so far administered.

One afternoon the doctor came in, removed his coat briskly, opened his bag, and took out his sterilizer, a syringe and other things. We had never seen him getting down to business in this manner before. 'Will you allow me to take just a little blood, please?' he asked. At this my wife started crying. I pacified her.

'It won't hurt, I assure you,' said the doctor. 'Give me a little blood and I will see what sort of fellow the mischief maker is and throw him out . . .'

'That's good, good,' he said, drawing up and sealing. 'Now we will know what stick to beat him with . . .'

I was asked to see him next morning at his dispensary. All night I kept awake. 'What is the blood test going to reveal?' I kept asking myself over and over again. My wife asked: 'Why is he taking the blood? Anything serious?'

'Don't be absurd, it is nothing more than malaria. He has taken it only to see what kind of malaria it is. Anyway, why do you worry? He is a good doctor, he will cure you whatever it may be . . .'

I sat next to the doctor at his dispensary. He passed me a brown piece of paper with the stamp of the govermnent hospital on it. 'I sent the blood for clinical test. This is the report.' I looked at the brown sheet. 'Widol test positive—Typhoid . . .' My throat went dry on reading it. 'Doctor, doctor . . .' I cried. He was once again in his official seat, and so was an automaton. He said merely: 'Don't worry. It is a mild attack. Take home a tin of glucose, barley and a bottle of Lentol—it is a good disinfectant. . . I will drop in on my way home in the afternoon.' I blabbered questions. He merely said: 'Don't get so nervous. I attend a dozen typhoid cases every day: nothing to worry. Here, give this gentleman . . .' he gave directions to the dispenser and passed on to other patients.

I entered my house clutching a tin of glucose, some barley, a bottle of Lentol, and broke the news. I said with affected cheerfulness: 'It is a very mild attack; perhaps it is only paratyphoid. If it is, you will be up and about again in two days.' She merely replied: 'Keep the child away. Write to my father. You must also take something to protect yourself . . .'

The doctor came at midday. He seemed cheered that it was typhoid. He beamed on all of us and joked continuously. 'I like typhoid,' he said. 'It is the one fever which goes strictly by its own convention and rules. It follows a time-table and shows a great regard for those who understand its ways! Don't look so miserable, lady. Like a good daughter-in-law, make up your mind to make the most of your stay in bed for the next few weeks . . .' Ever since she heard the word typhoid, Susila had become very silent. It was heartrending to see her in this state. I tried to speak to her and put a little courage into her, but it was a futile effort. She lay listening to my words with grim unresponsiveness. She felt now that the doctor deserved a remark and muttered: 'I thought it was malaria . . .' 'Malaria!' the doctor said. 'I was only dreading lest it should be malaria—the most erratic and temperamental thing on earth. I wouldn't trust it. But typhoid is the king among fevers—it is an aristocrat who observes the rules of the game. I'd rather trust a cobra than a green snake; you can depend upon the cobra to go its way if you understand its habits and moods . . .'

My wife's little room was converted into a sick ward.

All the furniture and odds and ends in the room were removed to the hall, where they were dumped in a heap on the floor. I had the room neatly swept. I dragged in an old wooden cot which had been put away somewhere and spread on it the thickest mattress and bedclothes, neatly folded the shawl and kept it at the foot of the bed. I fetched a small table which I used for writing and put it in a corner of the room, spread a white cloth on it and arranged all the bottles and tins on it—the yellow label of the glucose tin, the green of the barley, the pleasing violet-coloured label of Lentol— they were ranged artistically and formed a striking pattern. I looked about me proudly. The doctor nodded his head with approval. And then I brought in another stool and put on it a basin of water with a few drops of Lentol in it. It became a whitish solution and imparted a hospital aroma to the whole house. 'Whenever you touch the patient or her clothes you must dip your hand in it, the best disinfectant on the market . . .' There was a slight twinge at my heart at the new designation my wife was given: 'patient'. She would no longer be known as a wife or mother or Susila, but only as a patient! And all this precaution—was she an untouchable? It was a painful line of thinking, but I curbed it by much scientific argument within myself.

Now I gently lifted her and helped her to reach her new bed. 'See how nice,' I said with great pride. 'You will come out of it with a new life . . . All your old ailments will be gone. Even the pain at the waist you have been complaining of for so many days . . .' The doctor was tremendously pleased with the arrangement: 'It is the most attractive sickroom I've ever come across. You won't get this comfort even in a special ward . . .' I brought in a chair, put it beside the cot, and said: 'See, this is where I shall be rooted.'

'Plenty of glucose, barley water and mixture. (And gentle lady, don't ask for lime pickles please.) Temperature once in four hours, and note it down somewhere . . . It'll be nice to put up a chart on the wall—you have made it look so perfectly like a special ward . . .' I seized on this suggestion with fervour and brought out a piece of paper, and stuck it on the wall. I marked the date on it and her name. There was a morbid pleasure in this thoroughness . . . We

were setting the stage for a royal illness from which she was going
to emerge fresher, stronger . . .

The doctor said before he left: 'If my reckoning is correct she is
running her second week. So you have to spend less time in bed than
you've already done.' It was an exhilarating revelation. I stretched
my mind further and further back in order to know if she had been
ill longer than we counted.

'For practical purposes let us count it from the day I attended—
it leaves us with an outside limit of eleven or twelve days,' said the
doctor.

'No, doctor, it can't be so much . . .' I pleaded. I wanted it to be
all my own way. The doctor ignored me and said: 'I will see that her
fever comes down in eleven days, and it is up to you to see that she
doesn't have a relapse . . .'

'Oh, I will take great care. You may depend upon us . . .'

The following were days of iron routine. I had very little sleep
all night. I got up at six o'clock in the morning and took her
temperature. It was recorded once in four hours—starting with
six a.m. and ending with ten at night. It duly recorded 102 at the
first count. As the day progressed the mercury column rose step by
step till it reached and passed 104. I watched the mercury column
with a beating heart . . . When I pulled the thermometer out of its
shining case, it was always with a fine hope that the fever was going
to be mild. When I stuck it under her tongue and waited, it was
like waiting for a verdict—with prayer and trembling. And then
taking it against the light and straining to catch its growth from
102 and 104 and the fractions it touched! I began to dread this
instrument—it had something irrevocable, stern, like a judge on the
bench. I always commented to myself: 'Something wrong with this
thermometer. Must break it and get another one.' My wife asked:
'What does it show?' And she was always told a degree or two less.
And then the entry on the chart. When I had nothing else to do I
watched the total entries on this chart, always ranging between 102
and 104. My vision of a paradise was where all the entries would
be confined between normal and 100.

This was a world by itself—this sickroom. The aspirations in
this chamber were of a novel kind, different from what they were
outside. The chief ambition here was to see a fall in the chart. The
height of contentment was reached in observing perfect bodily

functions, which at other times would pass unnoticed. 'The patient is hungry!' Ah, very good. 'The patient likes her food.' 'Excellent. . .' 'The patient gives sensible answers.' Marvellous. And so on and on. The depth of misery was touched when there was any deviation from these standards. The doctor came in twice a day and radiated good cheer: 'Absolutely normal course. No complications. A perfect typhoid run . . .' he used to declare, make a few routine observations, and go away. I sat in that chair watching her sleep, every hour or so pouring into her throat medicine or barley water or glucose. I hardly stirred from the place, and got up only at nine in the evening when my father-in-law or mother-in-law (both of whom had arrived a few days before) took charge of the patient. After ablutions with Lentol, I went in, bathed, changed, and ate my dinner, and took charge of the child, who would not go to bed till she had me to sleep by her side in a corner of the hall.

The child exhibited model behaviour. She came and stood twice or thrice in the course of a day outside the threshold and watched her mother. Susila's eyes lit up when the child came to the door. She would ask if the little one had had her food, and put to her numerous other questions in her feeble voice, to none of which the child would reply. A sort of shyness had seized her. She conducted herself before her mother as if she were a stranger. But though she would speak no word, she liked to stand there and watch. She occasionally put a foot into the room and felt thrilled, as if it were an adventure. She went away and her mother shut her eyes and listened to her footfalls. The child spent all her time with her grandparents and her friend next door. Her grandfather took her out shopping and bought her sweets and toys. At night she waited for me to get free of sickroom duties. The moment I had sufficiently cleansed myself and warded off the poison, she hugged and clung to me, sat on my lap while I ate my dinner, and prattled away about all her day's activities. From the corner where I lay at night, I watched the sickroom, its shaded light, the low voices asking or answering; every time there was a movement in that room I woke up with a start. Once or twice when she snored, I got into a panic and ran to her door, only to see her sleeping peacefully with one of her parents sitting up in the chair.

My parents were unable to come. My father was down with his annual rheumatic attack, and my mother was unable to leave his side. They wrote me frantic letters every day, and it was my duty to drop them a card every day. I wrote a number of cards to others too. My brother at Hyderabad, my sister at Vellore, and the other sister at Delhi, wrote me very encouraging letters, and expected me to drop them postcards every day. They wrote, 'Nothing to fear in typhoid. It is only a question of nursing.' Everybody who met me repeated this like a formula, till I began to listen to it mechanically without following its meaning. Numerous people—my friends and colleagues—dropped in all day, some standing aloof fearing infection, and some coming quite close, reckless and indifferent.

I lost touch with the calendar. In doing the same set of things in the same place, I lost count of days. Hours flew with rapidity. The mixture once in three hours, food every two hours, but two hours and three hours passed with such rapidity that you never felt there was any appreciable gap between doses.

But I liked it immensely. It kept me so close to my wife that it produced an immense satisfaction in my mind. Throughout I acted as her nurse. This sickness seemed to bind us together more strongly than ever. I sat in the chair and spoke to her of interesting things I saw in the paper. She spoke in whispers as the weeks advanced. She said: 'My father said he would give me five hundred rupees when I got well again . . .'

'Very good, very good. Hurry up and claim your reward.'

'Even without it I want to be well again.' There was a deep stillness reigning in the house but for the voice of the child as she argued with her grandparents or sang to herself.

There was an interlude. The contractor and Sastri knocked on my door one day. 'Oh, come in,' I said and took them to my room, but there was no chair or table there. I said apologetically: 'No chair. It is in the other room and also the table, because my wife is down with typhoid.' Sastri said promptly, 'Oh, we will sit on the floor.' They squatted down on the floor.

And then after the preliminaries, Sastri said: 'It is about that house—they are keeping it in abeyance. There is another demand for it . . .' I remembered my decision was due long ago. 'I'm afraid I can't think of it. Wait a moment please.' I went up to my wife's bedside and asked: 'Susila, what shall I say about that house?' She took time to understand. 'Do you like it?' she asked.

'Yes, it is a fine house—if we are buying a house.'

'Why not think of it when all this is over?' she said.

'Yes, yes,' I agreed. I ran out and told them: 'I have no time to bother about it now. If it is a loss to you waiting for me . . .' As I spoke I disliked the house. I remembered the shock Susila had received in the back yard. They went away. Before going, they said: 'Nursing is everything.'

'Yes, yes. I know,' I said.

The contractor said: 'May I say a word about it?'

'Go on, by all means.'

'Never trust these English doctors. My son had typhoid. The doctors tried to give this and that and forbade him to eat anything; but he never got well though he was in bed for thirty days. Afterwards somebody gave him a herb, and I gave him whatever he wanted to eat, and he got well within two days. The last thing you must heed is their advice. The English doctors always try to starve one to death. Give the patient plenty of things to eat and any fever will go down. That is my principle . . .'

Susila's parents suffered quietly. There was a deep attachment between them and their daughter. My mother-in-law was brought up in a social condition where she had to show extreme respect for a son-in-law, and so she never came before me or spoke to me. My father-in-law was more sociable. He was an important landholder in his village, and beside that, he was on the directorate of a number of industrial concerns in Madras. He constantly travelled to and fro and met numerous people and had a very cosmopolitan outlook. So in spite of his age—he was past sixty (my wife being his last issue)—he was rather unorthodox in his speech and habits. He constantly admonished me to be careful not to have a large family: 'One grandchild from this quarter is quite adequate. We are quite satisfied.' He was an extraordinarily merry person for his age. But now he looked intimidated. He was full of anxiety for his daughter's welfare and recovery, but he concealed it under a mask of lightheartedness, for fear that it might frighten me. He sat up with his daughter all night, reading a novel and speaking to her very kindly, but without betraying any excessive sentimentality in his voice. 'Don't trouble me, Susila. The world is a bad enough place without your adding to it by refusing the medicine.' He told me: 'Your mother-in-law is definite that if you hadn't allowed her to go into that lavatory, Susila would not have fallen ill.'

All day he spent unobtrusively in the company of his

granddaughter, teaching her lessons, telling her stories, or taking her out shopping. He spoilt her a great deal: 'I believe in spoiling children; who should be spoilt if not children?' he often asked. He undid in a couple of weeks all the elaborate cultivation of character which we imagined we had been practising on the child for over three years now. As a result of his handling, Leela spoke like an infant-in-arms (if it could speak) and constantly insisted upon being carried on her grandfather's shoulder, or grandmother's arm. Her grandmother gave her plenty to eat, defeating all our regulated dieting. And I was not in a position to protest very effectively.

She was convinced that the evil eye had fallen on her daughter and that at the new house a malignant spirit had attacked her. She admonished me: 'You should never step into an unknown house in this manner. You can never be sure. How do you know what happened to the previous tenants or why they left?' She went out in the evening and visited a nearby temple and prayed to the god for her daughter's recovery. She brought in sacred ash and vermilion regularly every evening and smeared it on her daughter's forehead. She helped us run the house and got on well with the cook, who found her a willing help. All through the day, one heard their low voices going on in the kitchen, narrating each other's life and philosophy. My mother-in-law arranged with the help of the cook for an exorcist to visit us. One fine afternoon a man came and knocked on the door. My daughter was the first to see him. My father-in-law was having his afternoon nap in my room, and my mother-in-law was in the kitchen. The little girl had been playing on the front veranda with a doll when she looked up and saw a stranger entering the gate. She let out a cry of fear on seeing him, and she came running in and stood in the doorway of the sickroom, bubbling with excitement. I was just caressing the patient's forehead, because it was the hour when the temperature mounted and she complained of headache.

'What is it, Leela?'

'There is a bad man, a fearful man there!'

I rose and followed her. I saw a man with his forehead ablaze with sacred ash, and a thick rosary around his neck and matted hair, standing at the door. 'Go away,' I said, taking him to be a beggar.

'I am not come to beg,' he said, 'I have been asked to come.'

Meanwhile my mother-in-law came out, saw him, and with great respect brought him in. 'He's come for Susila,' she said, and conducted him to the bedside. He sat in the chair and watched the patient, while Susila who had never seen a bearded man at such close quarters gazed on him in panic. Her mother said: 'This Swamiji has come for your sake.' I watched it all from the doorway in fury, but I had to be silent because I couldn't argue with my mother-in-law, and I was uncertain how it would be viewed by the Swamiji. He felt her pulse. He uttered some mantras with closed eyes, took a pinch of sacred ash and rubbed it on her forehead, and tied to her arm a talisman strung in yellow thread. When he came out of the room, my mother-in-law seated him on a mat in the hall, gave him a tumbler of milk to drink and placed before him a tray containing a coconut, betel leaves, and a rupee. Meanwhile, the doctor's car stopped before the house, and I heard his steps approaching. I felt ashamed and wished I could spirit away this mystic. The doctor came in, and saw him and smiled to himself. The mystic sat without noticing him, though looking at him. 'My mother-in-law's idea of treatment,' I said apologetically. 'Ah, no, don't belittle these people,' said the doctor. 'There is a lot in him too, we don't know. When we understand it fully I am sure we doctors will be able to give more complete cures.' He said this with a wink at me. My mother-in-law was greatly pleased and said to the doctor: 'You must allow us old people to have our way now and then.' As I went in with the doctor, the Swamiji got up and took his leave, muttering: 'May God help you to see the end of your anxieties.'

The doctor stood at the bedside. He lifted her arm, saw the talisman, and said: 'Now how do you feel after this, lady?' My wife made an effort to smile. She indicated her abdomen and said, 'A lot of pain here.' The doctor pressed his fingers on it. He went over to the temperature chart and scrutinized it: 'You haven't taken the four o'clock temperature yet?' he said.

'No.' He inserted the thermometer, took it out, and washed it. 'How much?' my father-in-law asked, standing at the door, having been disturbed out of his nap by the visitors. 'The usual run,' the doctor answered. My father-in-law asked one or two questions about the patient and moved on. The doctor closely observed the patient and her movements and left the room. I followed him to his car, listening to instructions. At the car he told me, 'Have you an ice bag?'

'No.'

'I will send one. Get some ice and apply it constantly, whenever the temperature is above 102.'

'What is the temperature, doctor?'

'Rather high today, but don't get into a fright. A hundred and five, but that is common in this fever. Apply ice.' He went away.

All day I sat pressing down the ice bag on her forehead. The Bombay Anand Bhavan, where we had our morning tiffin on that Sunday, and perhaps where she had caught her typhoid, had a refrigerator and sold us ice. I purchased a block of ten pounds at a time, covered with sawdust and wrapped in gunny. My father-in-law obliged me by keeping an eye on the ice position and going out and getting it. I loved the smooth crystal appearance as I opened the gunny sack covering and wiped away the sawdust particles; the cool gust which emanated from it; and then the hammer blow which split it up into lumps just the size to be put into the ice bag. I always took a pride in the fact that the blow I gave was so well calculated that the pieces were neither too large nor too small but of the correct size and slipped into the mouth of the bag . . . It was a queer delight for me to see the bag bulging, I liked the feel of it as it acquired the correct weight. I carried it in, sat down, with a towel in hand, and pressed it down to form a cap on her head; when it fitted her head nicely it gave me a profound satisfaction. I sat pressing it down with one hand, while with the towel I wiped off the trickling drops of water condensing on it. My palm froze by this constant contact with ice and her forehead felt like a marble surface on a winter morning. And as the ice inside melted, it made a peculiar gurgling when the bag was shaken, so that by practice and intuition I learnt to gauge how much of the ice inside had melted, without opening the lid. Everything in this sickroom seemed to me profoundly ingenious and full of technical points and pleasures and triumphs. This impressed me so much that one day I wrote a poem about it. With my left hand I was applying the ice on her forehead. She slept and spoke a little in her sleep; I watched her for a while; a coloured bee had drifted in and was droning near the rafters. I had nothing else to do. I left the ice bag balanced on her head, ran in and returned with my writing pad and a pencil. I placed the pad on my lap and wrote, while she slept and talked in sleep:

The Great Kailas is one mound of ice
Where Shiva and Parvathi sport, which catch the
        Gleam of ethereal lights, heavenly rainbows.

Here for us God has sent a piece of Kailas down
      To subdue the Mercury column . . .
And here out of its wood dust it comes,
      Cold mist cloud rises on its crystal face,
And it reflects not mountain light
      But my face . . .
And here it is a great battleground,
      The great fight goes on
On either side of this red bag.
      But so far it is not the fever which cools,
But ice that melts.

It was a fact. Ice turned into water with great rapidity. I had to hammer out blocks into pieces every twenty minutes.

It was not necessary to keep the ice on at night but in a couple of days it became indispensable even then. The temperature declined only after midnight. She spoke less clearly now, took time to understand what was being said to her, and she constantly agitated her arms up down. 'Why do you do it?' I asked.

'Something is running up and down. I won't sleep here unless you make a new bed.' With elaborate difficulty, my father-in-law, mother-in-law and everybody assisting, we rolled her to one side and made a new bed for her. It took us nearly an hour. Changing the sheets was a daily adventure, but now we had to make an entirely new bed for her from top to bottom. But the labour was worth it, because she remained quiet, but only for an hour. Again she began to toss her arms and legs. 'You can't do it, child,' I said. 'You will put up your fever.' She merely glared at me and said: 'Don't tell me all that. I know how to look after myself.' I sat down and applied the ice. She tried to seize the ice bag and push it away. 'Oh, I don't want this, please. I am tired of it.' I had to cajole and admonish and keep the bag. She went on grumbling and muttering something. I had to beg her to keep quiet: and when she persisted, I called in her father.

'Do you think I am a child to be frightened?' she asked when her father stood in the doorway.

'Come in, come in, please,' I said to her father. He came over and stood at her bedside. She said: 'Father!' She implored weakly, 'He is worrying me too much. I don't want the ice bag.'

'All right, all right, child, it is good for you. I will apply it.' He sat down in the chair. He took up the ice bag and said to me: 'Why don't you go to your room and rest for a while? It will do you good. You have been sitting up without a break since six a.m. I will look after her.'

'No, it will be a bother for you. Not your hour. You'll have to sit up at night too.'

'Oh, it doesn't matter. I do not really mind a little overtime work,' he said. I dipped my hand in Lentol and left the room.

The child was delighted to see me out of the room so early. She clapped her hands in joy and ran towards me. 'Not yet, not yet. Don't touch me. You can speak to me from a distance, that is all. I have not had a wash yet. I'll have it only at night.' She made a wry face: 'All right. I'll go to grandfather.'

'He is with Mother.'

She became angry on hearing this. 'Everybody goes into that room. Who is to be with me?'

'Why don't you go to the next house and play with your friend?'

'I don't like her. She beats me whenever she sees me.' This amused me. I knew they were the thickest of friends a second ago. And they would be playing together next minute. So I asked: 'All right, then. Come to my room and see a picture book. You must not sit on my bed but a little way off.'

She agreed to this condition and came to my room. My room served as a guest room for my father-in-law. In a corner there was his canvas hold-all and a trunk, and his coats and clothes hung on the peg. My table was dusty and confused, the books lying in a chaotic jumble, untouched for days and days now. All my waking hours were spent at the bedside, and I seldom visited this room. 'In my happy days this table was a jumble. In my days of anxiety it was no less a jumble. Perhaps a table is meant to be so. No use wasting thought over it . . .' I remarked to myself. The habit of wishing to do something or other with the table top, whenever I saw it, had persisted with me for many years now. I kicked up a roll of matting and threw myself down, deciding to relax while the chance was there. 'Let the father and daughter settle it between themselves. I won't go till I am called.' My daughter, who had been standing in the doorway, asked: 'Can I come in, Father?'

'Yes, yes, this is not a sickroom,' I said. I had forgotten for a moment I had asked her to follow me in.

She sat down on the edge of the mat, and asked: 'Is this far enough?'

'Yes, you mustn't touch me, that is all, till I have a thorough wash at night.'

'Does Mother's fever climb on your hands and stick there?'

'Yes.'

'Won't it get into you?'

'No.'

'Why?'

'Because I am an elder,' I said with a touch of pride in my voice. She was gradually edging nearer to my mat, and now only an inch of space separated us. 'No, no. You are too near me,' I said.

'I'm not touching you,' she argued. I was too fatigued to argue with her, and left her alone, turned over to the other side, and shut my eyes, muttering: 'You are a fine girl. Don't disturb me. I am sleeping.' She agreed to this proposal. But the moment I shut my eyes, she stretched her leg and gently poked my back with her toe.

'Ah, why do you do it?'

'You must not turn away from me. It makes me afraid to be alone.' I turned over to face her and tried to sleep. She called: 'Father.'

'You mustn't disturb me.'

'You said you would give me a picture book.' I groaned, 'Leave me alone, baby. Take the book.' She went over to the table, but could not reach any part of its top. 'It is too high up, Father.' I got up and searched among the books on the table. There was not one fit for her perusal—all of them were heavy, academic, and unillustrated. Underneath all these was a catalogue of miscellaneous articles from a mail order firm in Calcutta. It was a stout enough volume. I gave it to her. She was delighted. It was full of small smudgy representations of all kinds of household articles. She kept it on her knee and was soon lost in it, turning the pages. Soothed by the rustling of the pages, I snatched a little sleep, although she constantly tried to get me to explain the pictures.

When I woke up it was about five o'clock. The catalogue was sprawling on the floor. The child was not there. Her voice came from the kitchen. I went in and asked for some coffee. The child was sitting there on her grandmother's lap, learning a song. On seeing me she stopped her song and asked: 'Can I touch you now?'

'Not yet.'

'You didn't know it when I got up and ran away!' she said with a great triumph in her voice, as if I had kept her in detention and she had managed to escape.

'No, I didn't. You are very cunning,' I replied and it pleased her greatly.

The patient was asleep. My father-in-law rose from his seat on seeing me, dipped his hand in the basin, and came out and whispered: 'Will you take the watch now?'

'Yes.'

'She has managed to sleep after all. Let her sleep quietly. Rather restless today . . .' he said and went away.

I resumed my seat, pressing down the ice bag. She woke up. She looked up at me and said: 'Oh, you have come!' She gripped my arms gratefully.

'I am always here. Don't worry, dear.'

'Yes, yes, I'm glad. Do you know what that man did?'

'Who?' I said.

'He was here when you were away.'

'Your father?' I said.

'Know what he did? He tried to remove this necklace,' she lifted her gold chain between her fingers and showed it to me. 'But I snatched it back. He wrenched my hand. Bad man. You must never leave my side hereafter.'

I agreed. Her fingers ran over the bedclothes as if searching for something, and tugged the edges. She tried to kick away the blanket. She attempted to roll out of bed. When I checked her, she was furious. 'Why do you stop me? I want to go away.'

She held up her arms and asked: 'Where is the baby?'

'In the kitchen,' I explained.

'Oh, who took her there?'

'Your mother,' I said.

'All right. Let them be careful. They must not take away a small baby without telling me. They may drop it.' I understood what she meant. She was imagining herself in childbed. Those memories were confusing her. She still held up her arms for the baby. I gently put them down. After that she started singing. Her faint voice choked with the strain. I couldn't make out the words or the tune. I said: 'Hush, stop it, please. You must not sing. You will not get well if you exert yourself.' But she would not stop. I protested, and she said: 'I want to sing, and I will sing. Why should it offend you?'

At night she ceased to sleep peacefully. She talked or sang all night. The doctor examined her more closely every time now. He examined her heart and said: 'She must sleep. It is imperative. This continuous temperature is very taxing. She must rest. I will watch how it goes, and then give a mild hypnotic.'

The ice was melting, we were wearing ourselves out, nursing, but the fever would not subside. It never went below 103 in the mornings and rose and hovered about 105 every day. The doctor said: 'The patient is very restless, that's why she has a temperature. If only she could sleep for six hours, you would see a wonderful change.'

The doctor was losing his cheerfulness, and looked harrowed and helpless. Next morning he brought in his car another doctor, a famous Madras physician. Even in our wildest dreams we could never have hoped to get this great physician. His reputation was all over the Presidency and his monthly income was in the neighbourhood of ten thousand. Dr Sankar came in advance and said: 'It's your luck, Doctor came here for another case. I begged him to see your wife. You are lucky he has agreed. Please ask him in. He is a very good man.' I and my father-in-law rushed out and greeted the great physician effusively, opened the door of the car, and led him in. Dr Sankar looked very nervous in his presence.

The great man spent an hour examining the patient. He tapped her abdomen, scratched a key on it and watched, lifted her arm, flashed a torch into her eyes, and examined the temperature chart. We waited in great suspense. He asked numerous questions. 'Mixture?' he said and held his hand out for it without turning. Dr Sankar jumped up, clutched the medicine bottle, and put it in his hand. The great doctor shook the contents and watched it for a moment: 'If I were you, I'd stop all this and go so far as to administer glucose and brandy every two hours, if possible with five minims of solomine. It is the best stimulant I can think of at the moment.'

'How do you find the patient, sir?' I asked.

'Well . . .' the expert drawled. 'Her vitality is not very good, though there are no complications.'

'What can we do? What can we do?' my father-in-law asked in consternation. My mother-in-law stood in the doorway, and behind her the child, looking with wonder on this scene. The doctor did not answer. But my father-in-law writhed: 'Is there anything wanting in our attention? Should we take her to the hospital?'

'Not at all. Everything is quite well done here,' said the physician, and we were greatly pleased with the compliment. 'Is there anything special we ought to do now?'

'I will speak to your doctor,' said the big man, with an air of snubbing us.

We poured out our gratitude as he moved to his car, and asked: 'Won't you have a cup of coffee?'

'Thank you, I never drink coffee,' he said.

Our doctor said: 'I'll see you again,' and went away.

The next morning I was jubilant. For the first time the temperature remained at 101. For weeks it had never gone below 102. Now it showed 101. What a joy! We were all jubilant. A ray of sun was breaking through the overcast sky. As soon as our doctor's car drove up at our gate, I ran out to announce, 'Doctor, the temperature has come down.'

'Splendid,' he cried. 'Didn't I tell you it would . . .'

'And the patient slept grandly,' I said. 'In fact she is still sleeping . . .'

The doctor examined her, but it didn't wake her up. 'Continue the mixture, and diet as usual. No ice bag . . . Have a hot water bottle ready. I will come again,' he said and went away. For the first time these weeks my hand did not have to perform the duty of pressing down the ice bag. It lay on a stool untouched. It was a happy sight for me. And also there were still five pounds of ice in the sack. 'Use it for ice cream, if you like,' I told my father-in-law. The atmosphere had suddenly relaxed. The patient had gone into a profound sleep. I had nothing to do in the sickroom. I sat there till afternoon. I disinfected my hands and requested my father-in-law to keep an eye on the patient. I bathed, changed, and took the child upon my shoulder. She was astonished: 'Has Mother got well?' she asked. 'Can I go in now?'

'Very soon you will be going in . . . but wait. I will take you out for a walk . . .' She was elated. She put on her small green coat, clung to my hand and came out. I took her down the road. Her friend was standing at the gate. Leela said: 'Let her also come with us, Father. She is so poor!'

'Is she very poor?'

'Yes.'

'What is meant by poor?' I asked.

'Nobody buys her peppermints . . .' the child exclaimed.

'Who taught you this?'

'Grandmother,' she replied promptly. So her friend joined us. We then paced down the road. They didn't speak much, but constantly looked at each other and giggled. I took them to a shop at the end of the street, and allowed them to buy whatever they wanted. They chose a few lozenges, and some bright bamboo whistles pasted over with green coloured paper. We returned, both of them blowing through their whistles. All this had taken about an hour, and I had lived in a great peace. Ahead, at our gate I saw the doctor's car standing. 'Let us hurry up,' I said walking fast, and the children trotted behind. At our door the child said: 'I will go and play in the next house, Father,' and ran off. I went in. The doctor and my father-in-law were in earnest discussion; the patient was sleeping, breathing noisily.

'The child, the child,' the old man said in a shaking voice the moment he saw me. 'Where is she?'

I didn't understand. 'She has gone to play in the next house,' I said.

'Very well, very well,' he replied. 'Take care of her. You must mind her and keep her.'

I looked at the patient. She had grown a shade whiter, and breathed noisily. There were drops of perspiration on her forehead. I touched it, and found it very cold. 'Doctor, the temperature is coming down.'

'Yes, yes, I knew it would . . .' he said, biting his nails. Nothing seemed to be right anywhere. 'Doctor . . . tell me . . .'

'For heaven's sake, don't ask questions,' he said. He felt the pulse; drew aside the blanket and ran his fingers over her abdomen which appeared slightly distended. He tapped it gently, and said: 'Run to the car and fetch the other bag please, which you will find in the back seat . . .'

The doctor opened it. 'Hot water, hot water, please.' He poured turpentine into the boiling water, and applied fomentations to her abdomen. He took out a hypodermic syringe, heated the needle, and pushed it into her arm: at the pressure of the needle she winced. 'Perhaps it hurts her,' I muttered. The doctor looked at me without an answer. He continued the fomentation.

An hour later, he drew up the blanket and packed his bag. I

stood and watched in silence. All through this, he wouldn't speak a word to me. I stood like a statue. The only movement the patient showed was the heaving of her bosom. The whole house was silent. The doctor held his bag in one hand, patted my back and pursed his lips. My throat had gone dry and smarted. I croaked through this dryness: 'Don't you have to remain, doctor?' He shook his head: 'What can we do? We have done our best . . .' He stood looking at the floor for a few moments, heaved a sigh, patted my back once again, and whispered: 'You may expect a change in about two and a half hours.' He turned and walked off. I stood stock still, listening to his shoe creaks going away, the starting of his car; after the car had gone, a stony silence closed in on the house, punctuated by the stentorian breathing, which appeared to me the creaking of the hinges of a prison gate, opening at the command of a soul going into freedom.

Here is an extract from my diary:

The child has been cajoled to sleep in the next house. The cook has been sent there to keep her company. Two hours past midnight. We have all exhausted ourselves, so a deep quiet has descended on us (moreover a great restraint is being observed by all of us for the sake of the child in the next house, whom we don't wish to scare). Susila lies there under the window, laid out on the floor. For there is the law that, the body, even if it is an emperor's, must rest only on the floor, on Mother Earth.

We squat on the bare floor around her, her father, mother, and I. We mutter, talk among ourselves, and wail between convulsions of grief, but our bodies are worn out with fatigue. An unearthly chill makes our teeth chatter as we gaze on the inert form and talk about it. Gradually, unknown to ourselves, we recline against the wall and sink into sleep. The dawn finds us all huddled on the cold floor.

The first thing we do is to send for the priest and the bearers . . . And then the child's voice is heard in the next house. She is persuaded to have her milk there, dress, and go out with a boy in the house, who promises to keep her engaged and out of our way for at least four hours. She is surprised at the extraordinary enthusiasm with which people are sending her out today. I catch a glimpse of her as she passes on the road in front of our house, wearing her green velvet coat, bright and sparkling.

Neighbours, relations and friends arrive, tears and lamentations, more tears and lamentations, and more and more of it. The priest roams over the house, asking for one thing or other for performing the rites . . . The corpse-bearers, grim and sub-human, have arrived with their equipment—bamboo and coir ropes. Near the front step they raise a small fire with cinders and faggots—this is the fire which is to follow us to the cremation ground.

A bamboo stretcher is ready on the ground in front of the house. Some friends are hanging about with red eyes. I am blind, dumb, and dazed.

The parting moment has come. The bearers, after brief and curt preliminaries, walk in, lift her casually without fuss, as if she were an empty sack or a box, lay her on the stretcher, and tie her up with ropes. Her face looks at the sky, bright with the saffron touched on her face, and the vermilion on the forehead, and a string of jasmine somewhere about her head.

The downward curve of her lips gives her face a repressed smile . . . Everyone gathers a handful of rice and puts it between her lips—our last offering.

They shoulder the stretcher. I'm given a pot containing the fire and we march out, down our street, Ellaman Street. Passers-by stand and look for a while. But every face looks blurred to me. The heat of the sun is intense. We cut across the sands, ford the river at Nallappa's Grove, and on to the other bank of the river, and enter the cremation ground by a small door on its southern wall.

The sun is beating down mercilessly, but I don't feel it. I feel nothing, and see nothing. All sensations are blurred and vague.

They find it necessary to put down the stretcher a couple of times on the roadside. Half a dozen flies are dotting her face. Passers-by stand and look on sadly at the smiling face. A madman living in Ellaman Street comes by, looks at her face and breaks down, and follows us on, muttering vile and obscure curses on fate and its ways.

Stretcher on the ground. A deep grove of tamarind trees and mangoes, full of shade and quiet—an extremely tranquil place. Two or three smouldering pyres are ranged about and bamboos and coirs lie scattered, and another funeral group is at the other end of this grove. 'This is a sort of cloakroom, a place where you leave your body behind,' I reflect as we sit down and wait. Somebody appears carrying a large notebook, and writes down name, age, and disease; collects a fee, issues a receipt, and goes away.

The half-a-dozen flies are still having their ride. After weeks, I see her face in daylight, in the open, and note the devastation of the weeks of fever—this shrivelling heat has baked her face into a peculiar tinge of pale yellow. The purple cotton saree which I bought her on another day is wound round her and going to burn with her.

The priest and the carriers are ceaselessly shouting for someone or other. Basket after basket of dry cowdung fuel is brought and dumped . . . Lively discussion over prices and quality goes on. The trappings of trade do not leave us even here. Some hairy man sits under a tree and asks for alms. I am unable to do anything but quietly watch in numbness . . . I'm an imbecile, incapable of doing anything or answering any questions. I'm incapable of doing anything except what our priest orders me to do. Presently I go over, plunge in the river, return, and perform a great many rites and mutter a lot of things which the priest asks me to repeat.

They build up a pyre, place her on it, cover her up with layers of fuel . . . Leaving only the face and a part of her chest out, four layers deep down. I pour ghee on and drop the fire.

We are on our homeward march, a silent and benumbed gang. As we cross Nallappa's Grove once again, I cannot resist the impulse to turn and look back. Flames appear over the wall . . . It leaves a curiously dull pain at heart. There are no more surprises and shocks in life, so that I watch the flame without agitation. For me the greatest reality is this and nothing else . . . Nothing else will worry or interest me in life hereafter.

4

THE DAYS HAD acquired a peculiar blankness and emptiness. The only relief was my child, spick and span and fresh, and mocking by her very carriage the world of elders. I dared not contemplate where I should have been but for her. So much so that I refused to allow her to be taken away by her grandparents and decided to keep her with me. It was a wonder to them how I was going to look after the girl—but our nature adapts itself to circumstances with wonderful speed. In three or four months I could give her a bath with expert hands, braid her hair passably, and wash and look after her clothes, and keep correct count of her jackets and skirts. I slipped into my double role with great expertness. It kept me very much alive to play both father and mother to her at the same time. My one aim in life now was to see that she did not feel the absence of her mother. To this end I concentrated my whole being. From morning till night this kept me busy. I had to keep her cheerful and keep myself cheerful too lest she should feel unhappy.

My mother could come and stay with me only for a couple of weeks occasionally, and whenever she was here, I could well imagine what it meant to my father, who could not get on for a day without her help. Of late he had become utterly helpless, nearly starved, and could not look after himself even for an hour if she was away. He did not know where his clothes were, when to go in for dinner, or what to ask for at dinner. When she came and stayed with me for a week or two at a time, it took months to bring him and his health under control again. My mother was very good and helped me ungrudgingly. But I could not accept her service indefinitely. 'God has given me some novel situations in life. I shall live it out alone, face the problems alone, never drag in another to do the job for me . . .' I found a peculiar satisfaction in making this resolve. And next time when my mother had to leave, I did not remonstrate with her as I used to do. She suggested: 'Kittu, send the child with me. Why are you so stubborn?' I was. She grew angry with me when I went to see her off. She sat in the bus. I and the little child stood by waiting for the bus to start. I made it a point to take the child wherever I went, except the college. 'You are unpractical and stubborn,' my mother persisted. 'How are you going to look after her?' 'As if it were a big feat!' I replied with bravado. 'God intends me to learn these things and do them efficiently. I can't shirk it . . .' Tears gathered in my mother's eyes. 'That I should be destined to see these scenes in our life—I have never known such things in our family.' I let her quietly have her cry. I was used to such situations and treated them with businesslike indifference. Condolences, words of courage, lamentations, or assurances, were all the same. I had become a sort of professional receptacle of condolence and sympathy, and I had received them in such quantity these months that they had ceased to move me or mean anything. Death and its associates, after the initial shock, produce callousness . . .

My mother averted her face in order that the child might not observe the tears in her eyes. The child asked: 'When will you be

back, Mother?' She controlled her voice and gave some vague reply.
I didn't want the child to have any illusions about things and be
misled. Living without illusions seemed to be the greatest task for
me in life now. So I explained, 'She can't come again for a long time,
child; she has to look after grandfather. . .' That was the stuff to give
humanity, nurtured in illusions from beginning to end! The twists
and turns of fate would cease to shock if we knew, and expected
nothing more than, the barest truths and facts of life. The child
accepted my answer with calmness. 'How long will she be away?'
This was a point about which I could not be very clear. But it moved
my mother and she said, 'I shall try to be back as soon as possible.
I only wish your grandfather was more helpful.'

The bus conductor blew his whistle. The driver sat on his seat.
An old village woman, with a basket on her knee, sitting next to my
mother asked, 'Where are you going?'

'Kamalapuram . . . My son is employed here. There you see
him with his child . . .' she whispered, 'A motherless child—and so
I come here often.' At which the village woman clapped her hands
and wailed, 'Oh, the poor child! Oh, the poor child!' She insisted
upon having the child lifted up and shown to her. She touched the
child's cheeks and cracked her Fingers on her temple as an antidote
for the evil eye. She cried: 'What a beauty! And a girl!' She sighed
deeply, and my mother was once again affected. I wished the bus
would move. But the conductor would not allow it to go, he was
deeply involved in a controversy with another villager who refused
to pay the regular fare but wanted some concession . . . The village
woman now said: 'When is he marrying again?' I was shocked to
hear it, and my mother felt confused. She knew how much such
talk upset me . . . She did not wish me to overhear it. But the old
woman stared at me and said: 'You must marry again, you are so
young!' My mother was agitated, and desperately tried to suppress
her. . . 'Oh, don't speak of all that now.' The old woman could not
be suppressed so easily. She said: 'Why not? He is so young! How
can he manage the child?'

'That is what I also say,' my mother echoed indiscreetly.

'Men are spoilt if they are without a wife at home,' added the
old woman. I looked desperately at the conductor who showed no
signs of relenting. I said: 'Conductor, isn't it time to start?'

'Yes, sir, look at this man . . .'

'He wants four annas for . . .' began the controversialist.

The old woman was saying: 'A man must marry within fifteen days of losing his wife. Otherwise he will be ruined. I was the fourth wife to my husband and he always married within three weeks. All the fourteen children are happy. What is wrong?' she asked in an argumentative manner. The bus roared and started and jerked forward. My daughter sat in my arms, watching the whole scene spellbound. As the bus moved my mother said: 'Don't fail to give her an oil anointment and bath every Friday. Otherwise she will lose all her hair . . .'

I was never a sound sleeper at any time in life, but now more than ever I lay awake most of the night, sleeping by fits and starts. My mind kept buzzing with thoughts and memories. In the darkness I often felt an echo of her voice and speech or sometimes her moaning and delirious talk in sickbed. The child lay next to me sleeping soundly. We both slept in my little study on the front veranda. The door of the room in which my wife passed away remained shut. It was opened once a week for sweeping, and then closed again and locked. This had been going on for months now. It was expected that I should leave the house and move to another. It seemed at first a most natural and inevitable thing to do. But after the initial shock had worn out, it seemed unnecessary and then impossible. At first I put it down to a general disinclination for change and shifting. To remove that chair, and that chaotic table with its contents . . . and then another and another . . . We had created a few favourite corners in the house, and it seemed impossible to change and settle in a new house. My daughter had played on the edge of that veranda ever since she came to me as a seven-month baby. Yes, at first I put it down to a general disinclination for change, but gradually I recalled the experience of life in that house was too precious and that I wouldn't exchange it for anything. There were subtle links with a happy past; they were not merely links but blood channels, which fed the stuff of memory . . . Even sad and harrowing memories were cherished by me; for in the contemplation of those sad scenes and hapless hours, I seemed to acquire a new peace, a new outlook; a view of life with a place for everything.

The room which was kept shut had an irresistible fascination for my daughter. She looked at the door with a great deal of puzzlement. On that unhappy day when we had returned from the cremation ground, the child had also just come home. 'Father, why is that door shut?' It threw us into a frenzy. We did not know what to reply. The house at that time was full of guests, all adults—all looking on, suffering, and bewildered by death. Death was puzzling enough, but this question we felt was a maddening conundrum. We looked at each other and stood speechless. My daughter would not allow us to rest there. She repeated authoritatively: 'Why is that door closed?' My father-in-law was deeply moved by this. He tried to change her mind by asking: 'Would you like to have a nice celluloid doll?'

'Yes, where is it?' she asked.

'In the shop. Let us go and buy one.' She picked up her green coat, which she had just discarded, and said: 'All right, let us go, Grandfather.' It had been a strenuous morning and we had eaten our food late in the day and were about to rest. He looked forlorn. 'Come on,' she said, and he looked at me pathetically. I told my daughter, 'You are a good girl, let your grandfather rest for a little while and then he will take you out . . .' She said: 'Why have you had your meal so late?' Another inconvenient question under which we smirked. We were all too fatigued to invent new answers to beguile her mind. She waited for a moment and returned to her original charge. 'Doll—come on Grandfather.' He had by this time thrown himself on the floor and was half sunk in sleep. I said: 'Child, you are a nice child. Allow your grandfather to rest. He will take you out and buy two dolls.' She was displeased at this, removed her coat and flung it down. I couldn't check her, as I would have done at other times. She looked at me fixedly and asked: 'Why is that door closed?' At which everyone was once again convulsed and confused and dismayed. She seemed to look on this with a lot of secret pleasure. She waited for an answer with ruthless determination. 'Mother is being given a bath, that is why the door is closed . . .' She accepted the explanation with a nod of her head, and then went up to her wooden trunk containing toys, rummaged and picked out a rag book. I went away to my room and reclined on my easy chair. As I closed my eyes, I heard her footfalls approaching. She thrust the rag book under my nose and demanded: 'Read this story.' I had read that 'story' two hundred times already. The book was dirty with handling. And she always kept it with all the junk in her trunk. It had illustrations in green, and a running commentary of a couple of lines under each. It was really not a story, there was not one in it, but a series of illustrations of tiger, lion, apple, and Sam—each nothing to do with the other. But Leela would never accept the fact that they were disconnected. She maintained that the whole book was one story—and always commanded me to read it; so I fused them all into a whole and gave her a 'story'—'Sam ate the apple, but the lion and tiger wanted some of it . . .' and so on. And she always listened with interest, completely accepting the version. But unfortunately I never repeated the same version and always mystified her! 'No, Father, Sam didn't hit the tiger,' she would correct. So when this book was pressed into my hand today my heart parched at the thought of having to narrate a story . . . 'Once upon a time . . .' I said, and somehow went on animating the pictures in the book with my narration. She said: 'You are wrong, Father, it didn't happen that way. Your story is very wrong . . .'

Towards the evening she came up once again and asked: 'The door is still closed, Father. Is she bathing still?'

'H'm. If the door is open, she may catch a cold . . .'

'Don't you have to go to her?'

'No . . .'

'Is she all alone?'

'There is a nurse who looks after her.'

'What is a nurse?'

'A person who tends sick people.'

'You don't have to go and stay with Mother any more, ever?'

'No, I will always be with you.' She let out a yell of joy and threw herself on me.

Four days later, she stole into my room one evening, and whispered, with hardly suppressed glee: 'Father, say what I have done?'

'What is it?'

'There was no one there and it wasn't locked; so I pushed the door open and went in. Mother is not there!' She shook with suppressed glee, at the thought of her own escapade.

'God, give me a sensible answer for this child,' I prayed.

'Oh,' I said casually and added, 'the nurse must have taken her away to the hospital.'

'When will she be back?'

'As soon as she is all right again,' I replied.

The first thing that woke me in the morning was the cold hands of my daughter placed on my forehead and the shout 'Appa' (father), or sometimes she just sat, with her elbows on the ground and her chin between her palms, gazing into my face as I lay asleep. Whenever I opened my eyes in the morning, I saw her face close to mine, and her eyes scrutinizing my face. I do not know what she found so fascinating there. Her eyes looked like a pair of dark butterflies dancing with independent life, at such close quarters.

'Oh, Father has woken up!' she cried happily. I looked at her with suspicion and asked: 'What have you been trying to do so close to me?'

'I only wanted to watch, that is all. I didn't wake you up.'

'Watch what?'

'I wanted to watch if any ant or fly was going to get into you through your nose, that is all . . .'

'Did any get in?'

'No. Because I was watching.' There was a hint in her tone as if a sentry had mounted guard against a formidable enemy.

'What do you do when you sleep, Father?' Once again a question that could not be answered by an adult; perhaps only another child could find an answer for it. 'I was saying something close to you and yet you didn't reply.'

'What were you saying?'

'I said: "There is a peppermint, open your mouth!"'

After these preambles we left the bed. I rolled her about a little on the mattress and then she sat up and picked a book from my table and commanded: 'Read this story.' I had no story book on my table. She usually picked up some heavy critical work and brought it to me. When I put it back on the table, she brought out her usual catalogue of the Calcutta mail order firm, and asked me to read out of it. This happened almost every morning. I had to put away the book gently and say to her: 'Not now. We must first wash.'

'Why?'

'That is how it must be done.'

'No. We must first read stories,' she corrected me.

'We must first wash, and then read stories,' I persisted.

'Why?'

'Because it is Goddess Saraswathi and we must never touch her without washing.'

'What will she do if we touch her without washing?'

'She will be very unhappy, and she is the goddess of learning, you see, and if you please her by washing and being clean, she will make you very learned.'

'Why should I be learned?'

'You can read a lot of stories yourself without my help.'

'Oh! What will you do then?' she asked, as if pitying a man who would lose his only employment in life.

It was as a matter of fact my chief occupation in life. I cared for little else. I felt a thrill of pride whenever I had to work and look after the child. It seemed a noble and exciting occupation—the sole responsibility for a growing creature.

5

THE DAY HAD been unusually heavy. I had more or less continuous work till three in the afternoon. And at three, when I was looking at the clock, hoping to drop things and go home, I received a note from Gajapathy to say that I was to take Fourth Hons. Class, because George of the language section was absent. Some teachers were absent this week, exhausting their leave, and those who were present were saddled with extra work. I implored Gajapathy to spare me this pain since as a student I had found language a torture, and as a teacher I still found it a torture. But he said: 'Just keep the boys engaged. The Principal doesn't want to let the boys off when they have not a teacher for a particular period. In the English department everybody ought to be able to handle any part of it; and I agree with him.' And I had no option but to sit down in the Fourth Hons. Class and engage their young minds in tittle-tattle for an hour. Our chief believed in keeping them well-read, and when they had spare time, in spending it over a library book of some consequence. I sent a boy to the library to fetch any book from the English section he liked. He brought down a book of nineteenth-century essays and I sat down to read mechanically through the pages aloud: the boys were busy, with a lot of conversation among themselves. In harmony with this din I read on. Some boys in the front listened. But they found it difficult to hear and complained: 'Can't hear, sir.'

'Ask your friends to shut up and you will hear better,' I said. They turned and stared helplessly at the noise-makers behind them. It was a small class and I could have easily established law and order, but I was too weary to exert myself. I was past that stage of exertion. A terrible fatigue and inertia had come over me these days and it seemed to me all the same whether they listened or made a noise or whether they understood what I said or felt baffled, or even whether they heard it at all or not. My business was to sit in that chair and keep my tongue active—that I did. My mind itself could only vaguely comprehend what was being read . . . 'This influence became so marked towards the later part of the century that those writers seized on it with avidity. It was a newfound treasure for the literary craftsman, a new weapon for his arsenal, shall we say . . .' My voice fell dully on my ears, but my mind refused to maintain pace with its sense. I caught myself constantly reflecting: 'What is it all about? What influence? On whom? Oh, good author, why not say arsenal or whatever you like if you choose?'

Into this pandemonium the most welcome sound impinged— the college bell. It was the end of the hour and of the day. I felt like a schoolboy, genuinely happy that I could go home now to the child waiting for me there, all ready and bubbling with joy; ready to be taken out and ready with a hundred questions on her lips . . .

I made my way into the common room, to put away the books in my locker, pick up my umbrella, and go out. As I was closing my locker, the servant came up and said, 'There is someone asking for you, master.' I looked out. He was a stranger, a young boy about fifteen years old. He was standing on the path below the veranda, a thin young man with a tuft behind, and wearing a small cap—a poor boy, I felt, by the look of him; out to ask for a donation for his school fee or something of the kind. 'Father seriously ill, money for his medicines.' One or other of the numerous sad excuses for begging. Of late they were on the increase . . . Formerly I used to investigate and preach to them and so on, but now I felt too weary to exert myself and paid out change as far as possible. I saw his hand, bringing out an envelope, and I put my hand in my pocket for my purse. 'The usual typewritten petition addressed to all whom it may concern,' I said to myself.

'What is it?' I asked.

'Are you Krishna of the English section?'

'Yes.'

'Here is a letter for you.'

'From whom?'

'My father has sent it . . .'

'Who is your father?'

'You'll find it all in that letter,' he replied. It was a bulky envelope. I tore it open. There was a long sheet of paper, wrapped around which was a small note on which was written:

Dear Sir,

I received this message last evening, while I was busy writing something else. I didn't understand what it meant. But the directions, address and name given in it are clear and so I have sent my son to find out if the address and name are of a real person, and to deliver it. If this letter reaches you (that is, if you are a real person) please read it, and if it means anything to you, keep it. Otherwise you may just tear it up and throw it away; and forgive this intrusion.

He had given his name and address. I opened the other large sheet. The handwriting on it seemed to be different. It began: 'This is a message for Krishna from his wife Susila who recently passed over. . . She has been seeking all these months some means of expressing herself to her husband, but the opportunity has occurred only today, when she found the present gentleman a very suitable medium of expression. Through him she is happy to communicate. She wants her husband to know that she is quite happy in another region, and wants him also to eradicate the grief in his mind. We are nearer each other than you understand. And I'm always watching him and the child . . .'

It was very baffling. I stared at the boy. I made nothing of it. 'Boy, what is this?' 'I don't know, sir. My father has been trying to send that for a week and could do it only today. I was searching everywhere; and I couldn't get away from my class . . .'

'Oh, stop, stop all that, boy. Why has your father sent this letter to me?'

'I don't know, sir.' I stood there and read it again and again and as my head cooled I was seized with elation.

'Take me to your house,' I cried.

'It's far off, sir. In the village Tayur. . .' It was on the other side of the river, a couple of miles off.

'No matter, I will come with you. What is your father?'

'He looks after his garden and lands in the village, sir. I read in the Board High School. I had leave today in the last period and so could bring you this letter.'

'Good boy, good boy, take me to your father.' I walked beside him. The child would be waiting at home. 'One minute, will you come with me to my house? I will give you coffee and sweets. We will go . . .'

'No, no, sir. I have to go away soon. I have to do some work at . . .' I tried to persuade him. But he was adamant. So was I. Finally we agreed upon a compromise. He gave me directions to reach his house. He'd go ahead and wait for me at the crossing and take me to his place. As I saw him go off towards the river, a sudden fear and doubt seized me. Suppose I should never meet him again. It was a horrible thought. 'Boy,' I had to beg him, 'are you sure to wait?'

'Yes, yes. I will stand on the Trunk Road.'

'If you will wait here a moment, I'll run home, get back and join you,' I said. If it had been any work other than seeing the child . . . The boy said: 'I will wait for you at the Trunk Road positively, even if you are very late.' 'Good boy, good boy,' I cried and raced home. The child was dressed and ready, waiting for me at the door.

As we left the kitchen and came to the hall, I told her: 'Today the little dear will go out with Granny—because Father has to go out on business . . .' She remained thoughtful and asked: 'What business! Have you to go to college again?'

'No. I've to go and see someone, very important business.'

'When will you come back?'

'As usual. But if you feel sleepy before I come, you just sleep . . .'

'I won't do that,' she replied. 'I will go with Granny. She has promised to show me a small doll's house which has electric light. Won't you buy one for me?'

'Well, see it first, we will buy it later.'

'Buy me a small house—this size,' she showed me her thumbnail size, 'with dolls so small.'

'Where can you buy it?'

The old lady answered, it is not for sale; it is a small house kept in that medicine shop for decoration . . .' I remembered seeing a small plywood doll's house kept in a small medicine seller's shop front. He sold some homemade pills; it was more or less a quack shop which gave medicine under no known system, but the shop was always crowded. In the centre of his shop he had mounted on a stand a plywood house with electric light . . . It was hard to understand what purpose it served there. But perhaps its real purpose was to interest a person like Leela . . .

I put on a shirt and an upper cloth and rushed out—along Ellaman Street, down the river, crossing at Nallappa's Grove. As I passed it I could not help looking at the southern wall of the cremation ground far off. Smoke was climbing over its walls. Jingling bullock carts, talkative villagers returning home from the town, and a miscellaneous crowd on the dusty path leading to the Tayur Road on the other side. The sun inclined to the west. If I did not reach the crossroad before dusk I'd never be able to spot the boy. I almost ran up the road, and I reached the crossroad, where the boy had promised to wait for me. There I was. The west was ablaze with the sun below the horizon. Dusk would soon fall on us. But there was no sign of the boy. 'Boy, Boy,' I cried; not having asked him his name. Birds twittered on the trees, passers-by moved about, and my voice cried to the evening 'Boy, Boy'. What a fool I was not to have asked his name or precise directions!

'Boy, Boy,' I shouted like a madman and passers-by looked at me curiously. I searched about frantically, and in the end saw the fellow coming up a path across the fields. 'Sorry to be late, excuse me, sir.'

'Good boy,' I cried. 'You are very kind to come.' I liked him. I said to myself that I would do him all the kindness possible when he came my way again. He would get a lot of marks from me when he came to college. I asked him about his school, books, teachers and all sorts of other things as we walked on.

'That's our house.' He pointed at the sloping tiles visible through the dense cluster of trees. A mongrel came and jumped at the boy. 'Oh, keep quiet, Tiger. Go and tell Father that a gentleman has come to see him.' Tiger listened with his head tilted and at the mention of Father bounced off in the direction of the house, vaulting over the gate of thorns and brambles. By the time we reached the gate, it was opened from the other side and a chubby and cheerful-looking person came towards me extending his hand. He had such good cheer in his face that it melted all the strangeness of the situation. He gripped my hand and said: 'You must forgive the trouble I have given you. You must have thought it was a call from a lunatic asylum!' He laughed. 'Oh, not at all, not at all,' I muttered idiotically. I was too confused. My feelings were all in a mess. I didn't know whether I was happy or unhappy. I was excited and muddled.

He said: 'You see, I would have searched you out, but it seemed too wild, and I thought it was all a fool's errand. I was most surprised to hear there was such a person. I hope you are the person . . .'

'I'm the person, name, initials, and address and in regard to the other things . . . Have you known my name before . . .?'

'Good God, no! You mustn't think so! I sent the letter as a test with the boy. I sent it out just as I got it, including the address. . . I sent it out with the boy . . . and you could have blown me over with a breath, in spite of my size, when the boy came and told me that he had delivered the letter. I thought the boy was playing a practical joke, but he said you were coming. Are you sure you are yourself?' he asked with a rich quiet laugh. It'd be wrong to say that he laughed . . . He hardly made any special sound or noise, but it was there all the time, a permanent background against which all his speech and gestures occurred, something like the melody of a veena string from which music arises and ends. 'Come in, come in, we have a lot of things to say to each other,' he said, and took me in through his small gate. The dog followed. He patted its back and said: 'Nice animal, isn't it? I'm very fond of him. I don't much fancy the sentimental cynicism of some dog lovers who say that they prefer dog to man! It's nonsense. A dog is a nice fellow to have around. Though an animate creature, when you don't like him you can put him away, out of sight and hearing. He will obey you cheerfully. He never talks back.'

I looked about. It looked like a green haven. Acres and acres of trees, shrubs and orchards. Far off, casuarina leaves murmured. 'Beyond that casuarina, would you believe it, I have a lotus pond, and on its bank a temple, the most lovely ruin that you ever saw! I was in ecstasy when I found that these delightful things were included in the lot.'

'I'd love to see that temple, what temple is it?'

'The goddess. It is said that Sankara when he passed this way built it at night, by merely chanting her name over the earth, and it stood up, because the villagers hereabouts asked for it. The goddess is known as *Vak Matha*, the mother who came out of a syllable. Would you like to see it? But first rest and refreshment and then the other things of life. This has always been my motto. Shall we sit down here?' We sat down on a stone bench under a spreading mango tree. He pointed at the cottage and said: 'You must also come in and see my home. I've a little library too. Here comes my wife.' He introduced me to her as the unknown man for whom a letter was sent. She looked at me and said: 'We wouldn't believe you really existed. I thought it was some joke of my husband's— won't you have some coffee and fruits?' She went in and brought a tray-load of good things. My host ate heartily, talking all the time; he told me numerous things about himself and the farm. How he purchased these acres eight years ago, and had worked on them night and day. He liked the pond, the temple and the trees, he wanted to be out of town, but near enough to be able to run into it. 'My views have always been that it must be a quiet retreat, but a railway line must be visible from your veranda or at least a trunk road. Now we have both. If you sit here for a while longer, you will see the Madras mail passing over that ridge. I came here, so near the town, but you know for eight years I've hardly moved out of this estate. I'm quite happy where I am. By the way, my wife thinks if I moved up and down a little more into the town, I could occupy less space in my house. As if town-going were a sort of slimming exercise!' I listened to it all with only partial interest. I was very anxious to hear more about that letter and other matters connected with it.

'Shall we go round and see things?' He fetched two staves from a cluster strung on the fork of the mango tree, and gave one to me. He explained: 'When an odd twig catches my eye I cut it off and make a stick. Tree twigs have a sense of humour and adopt funny shapes. I think it is one of nature's expressions of humour. If only we can see them that way . . .' He pointed at his collection: crooked, piked, stunted, awry, all shapes and kinds were there. 'It is better to carry a staff, there are a lot of cobras about. Though I've never killed one in my life. When I see a snake I usually cry for help.'

We wandered about the garden. He spoke incessantly, bursting with mirth, and explaining his garden. All the time he was talking my mind was elsewhere, in a hopeless tension, waiting to hear about the letter. I hoped he would open the subject himself. But he spoke on about all sorts of other things. I tried once or twice to ask him but checked myself and remained quiet. Somehow, I felt too shy to open the topic—like a newly-wed blushing at the mention of his wife.

It was nearly dark when we came to the northern edge of the

estate. It was ineffably lovely—a small pond with blue lotus; a row of stone steps leading down to the water. Tall casuarina trees swayed and murmured over the banks. A crescent moon peeped behind the foliage. On the bank on our side stood a small shrine, its concrete walls green with age, and its little dome showing cracks; it had a small portal, and a flagstaff at the entrance.

There was a small platform on the threshold of the temple. The temple was locked. We washed our feet and sat on the platform; it appeared an enchanting place. We squatted on the platform. 'Shall I have the temple opened?' he asked.

'No, don't worry about it now,' I said.

'There is an old priest who occasionally comes here once a month or so . . . A very fine man, with whom it is a pleasure to talk. A very learned man. I'm really afraid of him. He is too good for this place; but comes here only out of piety, and he is running some charity institution in the town. He treats this as an opportunity to worship the goddess . . .' He talked, and I listened to him in silence. My mind was trembling with eagerness. I listened in tense silence. He asked with a smile: 'You think I'm a bore?'

'Oh, no.'

'Doubtless, you want to know all about that letter . . .'

'Of course I'm very eager,' I said, and added with a pathetic foolishness: 'It was so long ago . . .' I stopped abruptly not knowing how to finish the sentence.

'Now listen,' he said. 'Of late I have got into the habit of spending more and more of my evenings all alone here on this *pyol*. This casuarina and the setting sun and the river create a sort of peace to which I've become more and more addicted. I spend long hours here, and desire nothing better than to be left here to this peace. It gives one the feeling that it is a place which belongs to eternity, and that it will not be touched by time or disease or decay. One day before starting for this place I felt a great urge to bring writing materials with me. Since the morning it had hung on my mind. I felt that an old sin of my undergraduate days of writing prose-poems was returning, but there was no harm in succumbing to it. I slipped a pad and a pencil into my pocket when I started out in the evening on my rounds. I sat down on this *pyol* with the pencil and pad. For some time I could write nothing; it seemed that a hundred ideas were clamouring to express themselves, crowding into my head. It was a lovely sky. I felt I must write something of this great beauty in my lines. Let me assure you that I'm by no means a poetical-minded fellow. I'm a dead sober farmer . . . but what was this thing within? I felt a queer change taking place within me.

'It was dusk when I sat down with the pad and pencil. Before the light should be fully gone I wanted to write down my verse or drama or whatever it was that was troubling me.

'I poised the pencil over the paper. Presently the pencil moved . . . I was struck with the ease with which it moved. I was pleased. All the fuction my fingers had was to hold the pencil, nothing more . . . "Thank you," began the page. "Here we are, a band of spirits who've been working to bridge the gulf between life and afterlife. We have been looking about for a medium through whom we could communicate. There is hardly any personality on earth who does not obstruct our effort. But we're glad we've found you . . . Please help us, by literally lending us a hand—your hand, and we will do the rest." I replied, "I'm honoured, I will do whatever I can."

' "You need do nothing more than sit here one or two evenings of the week, relax your mind, and think of us." "The pleasure is mine," I said. And then my hand wrote: "Here is Susila, wife of Krishna, but as yet she is unable to communicate by herself. But by and by she will be an adept in it. Will you kindly send the following as coming from her to her husband." And then I received the message I sent you—and they also gave me your name and address!'

Our next meeting was a week later; on the following Wednesday. He brought with him a pad of paper, and a couple of pencils, and a pencil sharpener. 'I don't want to risk a broken pencil,' he remarked. 'There must be no complaint of any omission on my part,' he explained.

The casuarina looked more enchanting than ever. Purple lotus bloomed on the pond surface. Gentle ripples splashed against the bank. The murmur of the casuarina provided the music for the great occasion. We took our seats on *the pyol* of the little shrine. My friend shut his eyes and prayed: 'Great souls, here we are. You have vouchsafed to us a vision for peace and understanding. Here we are ready to serve in the cause of illumination.' He sat with his eyes shut, and as the dusk gathered around us, utter silence reigned. I too sat, not knowing what we waited for. The casuarina murmured and hushed, the ripples splashed on the shore. A bright star appeared in the sky. I almost held my breath as I waited. There was such a peace in the air that I felt that even if nothing happened this was a rich experience—a glimpse of eternal peace. We sat in silence, not speaking a word to each other. I felt we could spend the rest of our life sitting there thus. He poised his pencil over the pad and waited. Suddenly the pencil began to move. Letters appeared on the paper. The pencil quivered as if with life. It moved at a terrific speed across the paper; it looked as though my friend could not hold it in check. It scratched the paper and tore the lines up into shreds and came through. The scratching it made drowned all other sounds. It seemed to be possessed of tremendous power. My friend said with a smile: 'I think my wrist will be dislocated at this rate, unless I have my wits about me . . .' Sheet after sheet was covered thus with scribbling, hardly clear or legible—not a word of it could be deciphered. It looked like the work of a very young child with paper and pencil. By the light of a lantern he tried to make it out and burst into a laugh: 'This writing does me no credit. If I leave it behind, it will be a headache for future epigraphists!' He looked at it again and again and laughed very happily. 'I remember that for writing precisely this sort of thing, my teacher broke my knuckles once.'

He put it away. After a few minutes interval he took his pencil to the paper again. His hand wrote: 'We are here, trying to express ourselves. Sorry if you find our force too much for you. It is because you are not accustomed to this pressure. Please steady yourself and slow down. You will have better results . . .'

'I have the feeling of a crow flying in a storm,' my friend muttered to me. 'But I . . . I suppose I must control myself. I am fat enough . . .'

He gripped the pencil as in a vice and steadied himself. 'No, no,' his hand wrote, 'you must relax, you must not set your teeth and get down to it so resolutely.' His hand wrote: 'Relax, slow down, control yourself, even if you feel like rushing off.'

'Rather a difficult combination of things. This relaxed control; till this moment I never imagined such a combination existed,' he muttered. He put away the pencil for a minute, stretched his arm, cracked his arm, cracked his fingers and picked up the pencil again and turned over a clean sheet. He said: 'Great souls, I'm ready.' Scrawled-up sheets of paper lay on one side. 'This is better. Go on slowly. Check yourself whenever you feel agitated.' As his hand steadied, his handwriting improved. The blank sheet was filling up. Letters and words danced their way into existence.

'We are sorry to put you to this trouble. But please understand that this work may revolutionize human ideas, and that you are playing a vital part in it. This is an attempt to turn the other side of the medal of existence, which is called Death . . . Please go on for just half an hour today and then stop, or if there are unfinished messages, a maximum of forty minutes. And don't attempt it again for a week more, that is, exactly this same hour, next week this day. We have to warn you that it will take some more sittings before your friend here gets accurate results, but for a start what you are going to receive today will be quite good. Now put away your pencil and then start after five minutes. Your nerves are too much in a tremble, and they must subside . . .' My friend put away the pencil, and said to me: 'Are you happy? The next batch of messages may be from your wife.' 'I don't know how to thank you,' I said. We watched the stars on their course for a few minutes; and gazed idly at the pond. Five minutes passed. He picked up his pencil and placed it over the paper. 'Your condition is better. Remember our instructions. Stop in half an hour.' 'I will remember,' he replied and asked aloud, 'Is my friend's wife here?' 'Yes. She is here,' his hand wrote, and the words covered half a page. My friend exercised control over his fingers, checked himself and presently the writing assumed normal form. His hand wrote: 'Your friend's wife has been here all along. In fact we are at this task mainly for her sake. She is so eager to communicate with her husband.' I looked about. The semi-dark air seemed to glisten with radiant presences—like myriad dewdrops sparkling on the grass on a sunny morning. I strained my eyes and mind to catch a glimpse of these presences.

I told my friend: 'Please ask if my wife will be able to communicate now directly . . .' In answer his hand wrote: 'She is very much excited and she is also not able to collect her thoughts easily. At the moment, she finds it easier to tell us . . .' I visualized her all a-tremble with excitement as on that day when I went to her place to see and approve the future bride. As I waited in the hall I caught a glimpse of her in another room through a looking-glass, agitated and trembling! I had never again seen her so excited. There fell a pause, as my friend's pencil waited. There did not seem to be any need to ask or answer. This was enough. The

greatest abiding rapture which could always stay, and not recede or
fall into an anti-climax like most mortal joys. After a few moments, I
asked, 'Do you remember the name of our child?' The pencil wrote:
'Yes, Radha.' This was disappointing. My child was Leela. I was
seized with a hopeless feeling of disappointment. To be unable to
recollect the name of the child! What was wrong? Where? My mind
buzzed with questions. 'The lady is smiling at the agitation which
this name is causing her husband, but assures him that he need
not feel so miserable over it. We've warned you that results will
not be very accurate today. There are difficulties. We will do our
best and gradually all these handicaps will be removed. Meanwhile
understand that this is as good as it can be.'

I asked: 'But our child's name? Could this ever escape your mind?'

'No. It can't and it has not. You commit the mistake of thinking
that she is responsible for giving that name. As a matter of fact it
is a piece of your friend's own mind. You see there are particular
difficulties in regard to proper names. We try to get through a
particular name, for instance your daughter's . . . but since we use
the mechanism of your friend's writing, more often than not his
mind interferes, bringing up its own selections. This is how you got
Radha now.'

'But how is this difficulty to be surmounted?' I asked. 'Is there
no hope at all?'

'Yes, yes, by and by. Even now you may remember we could
get through your name and address the other day and he was
able to send for you. But it was an exception: he was ideally un-
selfconscious and his mind was very passive. It will all depend upon
our friend's ability to remain passive, and keep his own thoughts
out of the field. That's why we have asked him to stop in half
an hour, which is the maximum time he can hold his ideas in the
background.' My friend said: 'No. I can manage a little longer.'
'No. Half an hour will do . . . But by and by you may go on even
longer . . . Please stop after this. The lady wants to say that she is as
deeply devoted to her husband and child and the family as ever. She
watches over them and prays for their welfare—only she is able to
see things far more clearly than when she was on Earth, although
you are not aware of my presence at times . . . God's blessing be
upon you and the child!' The pencil ceased. My friend looked at
me as if to say: 'Go on. Get up. It is over.' But I was reluctant. So
many questions to ask. My heart choked with the questions still

unasked: 'Just a second more,' I pleaded. 'I have just one more question.' I paused. It was not clear to me what the question was. I pondered. 'Can't we have it sooner than next week?. . . Please . . . Does she remember? . . .' It was no use. The pencil stood unmoving. We waited for a moment. And then my friend said: 'They are gone. We will try again next week.'

On the following week we sat there just at the same hour, with the dusk falling about us. They wrote: 'We are here. Conditions are favourable. But remember our instructions and go slowly. Susila, wife of Krishna, is here and will now go on by herself.'

'I have watched you since we met last and seen your mind. I saw the doubts crossing and recrossing your mind regarding identity. Naturally. How can you believe what you can't see? It might be me or someone else; was that not the line of thought going on in your mind? Correct me if I am wrong.'

'You are right, absolutely right,' I answered.

'It did not require much self-scrutiny to see it. And so I decided to clear this doubt first. And all this interval I have been trying to master the art of communication, and our helpers here have been very good to teach me. This is the first step. I hope you like this. I hope I do well for a start.'

'Very well, very well, for a start . . .' I replied in Tamil.

'I had not learnt very grammatical Tamil in my days, and if there are any mistakes, don't laugh at me.'

'Oh, you are very good. You wrote beautiful letters,' I said.

'And yet you have destroyed every one of them!' she said. 'You found it possible to destroy every one of them!' she repeated. I was startled. No one knew about it. In the secrecy of night, on that day her condition was declared to be hopeless, I sat in my room, bolted the door, took out of my drawer several bundles of letters she had written to me, tore them up into minute bits and burnt them, and I also did the same with a few diary pages I had kept in the first years of our married life. I remembered saying to myself, gritting my teeth: 'Let life do its worst, this is my answer. Every shed of memory will be destroyed, I will avoid torment thus . . .'

'How have you come to know of it?' I asked.

'By watching your mind. I saw you yesterday as you pulled out your table drawer and reflected. I might not have known it at all if you hadn't reflected on it every day. For on the occasion you were performing the deed, I was, you remember, passing over, and in that transition stage one is not aware of things. It takes some time before we are able to know things. You have destroyed not only all that I wrote, but also all the letters you wrote to me. Was that the reason why you demanded them back from me every time I came back to you from my parents?' It was an unwritten law existing between us: whenever we were parted we wrote to each other on alternate days, and when we met again, I took back from her all the letters, bundled them up, and offered to destroy them, but she always protested and I just kept them with me.

'Why did you do it?' she persisted.

'I am very sorry. I thought I might abolish memory!'

'Have you been able to forget? Wasn't it childish to work your temper on those letters?'

'It seemed that memory would torment me.'

'That's how it may appear at first sight; but later, let me tell you that you will have a desire to be surrounded by everything belonging to the departed. Just a turn of the wheel. A man takes to drink to forget sad thoughts, but after a while they return with gathered force. I understand your feelings but can only laugh at the remedy.' I felt really like a child who had misbehaved. 'Please forgive me if I appear to be speaking more than I ought. But I felt very unhappy about it. So this. I hope you will forgive this outburst,' she said.

'You are perfectly right, and entitled to it,' I said. 'God bless you. I felt so vacant yesterday, when I had a longing to see your handwriting and could not find a single letter anywhere,' I confessed.

'The lady is laughing,' the Helpers said. 'She is shaking with laughter. She says don't take anything too tragically—not even this!'

'I accept your advice . . .' I said.

'You need not be unduly docile,' she said, 'and strain yourself to be agreeable, just because I'm speaking from this side. Don't hesitate to correct me if I appear silly.'

'Oh, no, no, you are very sensible,' I said.

'You used to be so considerate on the first two days whenever we met after a visit to my parents. You would not contradict anything I said. Here is a piece of news for you. There are about fourteen letters which have been spared . . . I don't remember whether they were yours or mine, but I remember tying them up in a bundle; you will find them either in my trunk, or in one of the boxes in my father's place.'

I thought over this and said: 'I'm afraid you are wrong. There is not one letter left. I destroyed every bit that we wrote to each other.'

'I'm sure of these fourteen: I remember the number precisely. I counted them, I tied them up and did not give them to you because you were very busy with something or the other. I can't say how long ago; I put them away and then I remember coming across the bundle again and again. What I can't recollect is whether it was in my father's house or in ours. I am certain that the letters are there.' She insisted: 'Will you please make a thorough search once again?— and if you find them please don't repeat your previous act.'

'No, no. I will be very careful,' I said.

'Also, I want you to keep for my sake a sandalwood casket. I have put into it all my knick-knacks.' I cast my mind about. I had looked through all her possessions and I had a knowledge of everything she had.

'I don't think you ever had such a box,' I said. 'Where is it?'

'It is not a very big box, about eight or ten inches long, three inches high and about four inches wide; the lid of the box is not flat but slightly elevated. I kept all my knick-knacks in it. It was given to me by my mother-in-law. Box of ivory and sandalwood. Please find it and keep it. I was fond of it. You may throw away all my other things. They are of no particular value to me.'

'I can't throw out the tiniest speck that belonged to you. I will keep everything, including this box if I find it. But I'm not sure there is such a box.'

At the next meeting she remarked, 'You fret too much about the child. Have no kind of worry about her. When you are away at college, you hardly do your work with a free mind, all the time saying to yourself: "What is Leela doing? What is she doing?" Remember that she is perfectly happy all the afternoon, playing with that friend of hers in the next house, and listening to the stories of the old lady. Just about the time you return, she stands at the door and looks down the street for you. And when you see her you think that she has been there the whole day and feel miserable about it. How you can help it, you never pause to consider. Do you know that she sometimes insists upon being taken to the little children's school, which is nearby? And the old lady, whenever she is free, takes her there and she has become quite a favourite there? Why don't you put her in that school? She will be quite happy there.'

Immediately I contradicted: 'I don't think she is going to a school. She would have told me about it . . .'

'She went in casually once or twice, and perhaps forgot it later among other interests. I think she'll tell you when she remembers it. Anyway, if she likes it she may go there . . .'

'All right, but is she not too young to be put to school?'

'She'll find it interesting, and it is not regular study. She can go and see other children and come home when she likes . . .'

'I have no objection, but the teacher may have some other system.'

'No . . . It is a school meant for very small children.'

'How much of the child do you see?' I asked.

'As much as anyone else, perhaps a little more. I have direct access to her heart now: I am always watching her.'

'Does she see you?'

'Perhaps she does. Children are keener sighted by nature. She sees me, and perhaps takes it naturally, since children spontaneously see only the souls of persons. Children see spirit forms so often that it is natural to their condition and state of mind.'

'If she sees you why doesn't she cry out?'

'It is a natural state to them, and in the depth of their soul they have certain reservations. Perhaps she doesn't speak out as much as she would like because she observes and understands the reserve you are all exercising in her presence about me. She merely saves your feelings by not speaking of me. You must have observed how little she refers to me. Did you think that it was out of forgetfulness? And don't you agree that there is a certain peace about her, which elders lack, although I was no less important to her than to anyone else?'

Nowadays I went about my work with a light heart. I felt as if a dead load had been lifted. The day seemed full of possibilities of surprise and joy. At home I devoted myself to my studies more energetically. The sense of futility was leaving me. I attended to my work earnestly. All the morning I sat preparing my day's lectures. My little daughter watched me curiously. 'Father is reading!' she exclaimed. She drew a chair close to mine and sat up with a book, with any book that caught her fancy, till she saw a squirrel or a sparrow alighting on the roof of the opposite house, and exclaimed: 'Father, the sparrow is come. Do they also read? Do they also go to school?'

'Little girl, just go out near the gate and ask,' I said, with the idea of getting on with my work. Once she had gone out, she slowly got interested in something or the other and forgot to come back. When she mentioned school, I pricked up my ears and was on the point of asking her a question, but I restrained myself, because I wanted to watch if the answer would come from her first or from the old lady. That very evening I heard the subject mentioned. When I returned home the child was out. There was only the old lady in the kitchen. I asked: 'Where is Leela?'

'Oh, she has gone to the school,' the old lady replied.

'Which school?' I asked with feigned ignorance.

'That baby's school, in the next street. I took her there once or twice in the afternoon, because she liked to see the other children, and they all like her very much there. Today the teacher said he would bring her back in the evening. She wouldn't come away either: because she is making some animals and other things with clay. They have also given her scissors and coloured paper to cut. She is so happy!'

'Why didn't you tell me before that you had taken her there?'

'I took her out on two days just for a few minutes. When the child in the next house came home in the afternoon and went back to school, Leela also went with her one day,' she said and added, 'Poor thing, it was some way of engaging her mind and keeping her from longing for her mother!'

The child came home half an hour later. Her teacher left her at the gate and went away. 'Father,' she screamed at the gate, 'I've been to school like you.' I went out and picked her up in my arms. The teacher had moved off a few yards.

'Is that your teacher?' I asked.

'Yes.'

'Call him,' I said. At which she shouted: 'Schoolmaster!' and the teacher turned back. 'Come back and speak to my father.'

'You are the Headmaster of the school?' I asked.

'Yes.'

'Is there any class to which this girl can be admitted?'

'Oh, yes. She will be happy. We shall be very glad to admit her.'

'Any long hours?' I asked.

'Oh, no, she can come any time and go away when she likes. No restrictions. Please send her. She will be happy with us.'

'May I know your name?'

'Just Headmaster will do . . .' he said.

The child was dancing with joy. She was full of descriptions of her school. 'Father, do you know I have made a clay brinjal? The teacher said it was nice.' 'All right, all right,' I said, and sat by her side and made her take some tiffin which the old lady had prepared. She was too excited to relish anything. I coaxed her to eat. And then took her to the bathroom. Her face was streaked with the clay she had been handling. I soaked a towel in water and rubbed her cheeks till they glowed. And then I sent her in to the old lady and had her hair combed.

I took her out on her usual walk. I took her through the busy thoroughfare of Market Road. She loved the bustle of Market Road and kept asking questions and I found her view of life enchanting. I bought her some sweets at the stores. She mainly talked about her school. 'Father, at our school, I have a friend. You know her father gives her lots of sweets every day. Why do you always give me only one or two?'

'Children must not eat more than two at a time,' I replied.

'She is a good girl, always plays with me at school,' the child said. 'Shall I also grow tall when I go to school?'

'Yes, certainly.'

'Why do you go to that far-off school, and not to our school, Father?' she said. She saw some villagers moving about with turbans on their heads. She asked: 'Do they wear those things on their heads, even when they sleep?' I don't know what idea crossed her mind at such times. I took her to the river bank. She ran about on the sand. She watched the other children playing. She whispered: 'That girl is in our school.'

'What is her name?'

'Kamala,' she said.

'Is she your friend?'

'She is a very good girl.'

'Go and play with her if you like.' The girl was playing with another group around a circle on the sand. At my suggestion Leela blinked and said with great seriousness: 'She will be very angry if I ask to be taken also.'

'Call her, let me see,' I said.

'Kamala, Kamala,' she called faintly, and then added: 'That is her school name, she doesn't like to be called so when she is not in school.' We passed on. She stood near other girls also and pointed them out to me as her school friends, but she would not go near anyone or call aloud. She seemed to identify her friends in a general way, whatever might be their names and their schools; as far as she was concerned they were all her friends and schoolmates. She was endowing each of them with any character she chose.

Next morning there was great activity. She was to be put to school. I was as excited as if I myself were to be put to school. I did little work at my table that day. I ran about the house in great excitement. I opened her trunk and picked out a shirt and skirt, fresh ones, printed cotton. When she saw them my daughter put them back and insisted upon wearing something in lace and silk. 'Baby, you must not go to school wearing laced clothes. Have you ever seen me going with any lace on?'

'It's because you have no lace skirts, that is all,' she said. 'No, Father, I want that for school. Otherwise they will not allow me in.' She threw her clothes about and picked up a deep green, with a resplendent lace three inches wide, and a red skirt studded with stars: the whole thing was too gorgeous for a school. Her mother had selected them for her on a birthday, at the Bombay Cloth Emporium. Two evenings before the birthday we had gone there, and after an hour's search she picked up these bits for the child, who was delighted with the selection. I protested against it and was told, 'Gaudy! There is nothing gaudy where children are concerned, particularly if they are girls. Whom are these for if they are not meant to be worn by children?'

'Go on, go on,' I said cynically. 'Buy yourself two of the same pattern if you are so fond of it.' But the cynicism was lost on her. She disarmed me by taking it literally and said: 'No, no. I don't think they weave sarees of this pattern? Do they?' she asked turning to the shopman.

The child was excessively fond of this piece and on every occasion attempted to wear it. Today she was so adamant that I had to yield to her. She tried to wear them immediately, but I said: 'After your hair is combed and you have bathed . . .' And now as I put her clothes back in the box she grew very impatient and demanded: 'Bathe me, Father, bathe me, Father.' I turned her over to the old lady's care and arranged the box, carefully folded and kept away her clothes. She had over forty skirts and shirts. Her mother believed in stitching clothes for her whenever she had no other work to do, and all the child's grandparents and uncles and aunts constantly sent her silk pieces and clothes ever since the day she was born. The result was she had accumulated an unmanageable quantity of costly clothes, and it was one of my important occupations in life to keep count of them.

She was ready, dressed in regalia, and stood before me, a miniature version of her mother. 'Let us go,' she said, and for a moment I was unaware whether the mother or the daughter was speaking—the turn of the head and lips!

'I must carry books,' she insisted.

'No, no, not today . . .'

'My teacher will be angry if I don't take my books,' she said, and picked up her usual catalogue. She clasped it to her little bosom, and walked out with me, bubbling with anticipation and joy. The school was in the next street. A small compound and a few trees and a small brick-red building. The noise those children made reached me as I turned the street. The schoolmaster received us at the gate. As soon as we entered the gate, a few other children surrounded Leela and took her away. She left me without a thought. She behaved as if she had been in that school for years and years.

The Headmaster was in raptures over the new arrival. He said: 'Won't you come and have a look round?'

He had partitioned the main hall into a number of rooms. The partition screens could all be seen, filled with glittering alphabets and pictures drawn by children—a look at it seemed to explain the created universe. You could find everything you wanted—men, trees, animals, skies and rivers. 'All these—work of our children . . .' he explained proudly. 'Wonderful creatures! It is wonderful how much they can see and do! I tell you, sir, live in their midst and you will want nothing else in life.' He took me round. In that narrow space he had crammed every conceivable plaything for children, see-saws, swings, sand heaps and ladders. 'These are the classrooms,' he said. 'Not for them. For us elders to learn. Just watch them for a while.' They were digging into the sand, running up the ladder, swinging, sliding down slopes—all so happy. 'This is the meaning of the word joy—in its purest sense. We can learn a great deal watching them and playing with them. When we are qualified we can enter their life . . .' he said. The place was dotted with the coloured dresses of these children, bundles of joy and play. 'When I watch them, I get a glimpse of some purpose in existence and creation.' He struck me as an extraordinary man.

'If they are always playing when do they study?'

'Just as they play—I gather them together and talk to them and take them in and show them writing on boards. They learn more that way. Everybody speaks of the game-way in studies but nobody really practises it. It becomes more the subject of a paper in some pompous conference and brings a title or preference to the educational administrator. Oh, don't allow me to speak too much on this subject as you will find me a terrible bore. . . .' He was a slight man who looked scraggy; evidently he didn't care for himself sufficiently. His hair fell on his nape, not because he wanted it to grow that way, but, I was sure, because he neglected to get it cut. His coat was frayed and unpressed. I liked him immensely. I was sure there were many things about him which would fascinate me. I was seized with a desire to know more of him. I asked him: 'Please visit me some day.'

'I will certainly drop in one day when I take a holiday. You see I hate holidays. It is ten or fifteen years since I began this work, and I have not felt the need for a holiday at all. Holidays bore me. And I spend even my Sundays here looking about. This is a nice place; there is a garden too, entirely made by children.' He took me through a bamboo stile to a small plot with tiny lots. He was continually enthusiastic. 'Does he ever sleep?' I asked myself. 'Come to my house on a Sunday instead of coming here,' I said and he agreed. I had a feeling that I was about to make a profound contact in life.

The next sitting was a complete disappointment to me. But perhaps my own frame of mind was somewhat to blame. After the first thrill of discovery subsided, I fell into a questioning mood and asked, the moment my friend was ready with the pencil: 'Do you remember the last day we went out together?'

'Yes, I remember.'

'Can you say where we went and a few incidents of the day and so on?' I asked.

'I remember going out on the last day with you. I feel we

visited a temple, bought something for the child, and also visited a painted house. We went out followed by the servant and did a little marketing on the way.'

'Oh!' I said. 'What else do you remember?' The pencil paused for a while and then scratched off. 'We met a scorpion on the way and you nearly put your foot on it. We bought a brass lamp used for worship, and a toy engine.'

'Do you remember what happened in the house we visited?' I asked.

'No,' she replied.

'Absolutely nothing happened?' I asked. In answer to it the Helper wrote: 'The low roof of the kitchen knocked her head, and she is laughing because her husband slipped in the back yard . . .'

'To be frank this did not happen. I don't know why she is saying these things,' I said.

'She promises to do better next time,' the Helpers wrote. 'There are some difficulties both in expressing and picking out of memory the exact items. We would advise you to stop now. The lady sends her love and prayers for her husband and child . . .' And they were gone. The hand stopped. 'Half an hour over I suppose,' said my friend. I rose to go home very unhappily. Except one or two references, the rest was all too wild . . . I grumbled and went home in a most unhappy state of mind. 'To be in this state till next Wednesday.'

But a week passed. I was back there on the following Wednesday. Meanwhile I had scrutinized the pages again and again, and came to the conclusion that after all they were not so wild. Each detail was correct, temple, painted house, buying for the child and the lamps. Every time she went to her parents she purchased brass lamps and knick-knacks for someone or other; a toy engine was bought on the last day for the child. As for knocking her head against the kitchen roof, she was rather tall and was very proud of the fact that most doorways were too short for her and that they knocked her on the head, and she always spoke about it. I could not recollect when I had slipped in the back yard, but otherwise each individual item seemed to be after all correct, though chronologically mixed up in utter confusion. I mentioned it to my friend when I met him next and his explanation seemed to be plausible: 'I will ask you a question now at short notice. When did you buy the cloth for this shirt?' I looked at my blue shirt helplessly. 'Was it before or after you purchased the coat you are wearing over it? And on your way home from the shop that day what else did you buy and for how much? You see how difficult it is to place these exactly, while you are still living in the midst of these experiences. I can't say for instance what exactly I had for dinner this day last week . . . While chronological order and precision in details are so difficult for us, they must be more so to other beings whose surroundings are timeless and entirely different. If my speculation is right their vision of things embrace an experience as a whole rather than events in an order. All memories merge and telescope when the time element between them is removed. I think this is the reason for the apparent confusion. Add to this the possibility of their memory being finer and more selective; there may be a natural law operating by which unpleasant memories and impressions are filtered and left behind with the physical body. If you take all this into consideration, you may view their inaccuracies more charitably.'

At every sitting she urged me on to look for her sandalwood casket and the fourteen letters. I couldn't search very thoroughly because I found it impossible to enter her room and open her trunks. On a holiday afternoon I steeled myself to it. I opened the door and felt a pang at heart when I cast a look around at her trunks, her clothes and possessions. 'For all of us our possessions turn to mementos. Is there any one in the whole world who can say his lot is different?' I reflected, as I sat down amidst her trunks. My daughter was thrilled to see me there, and cancelled an appointment she had with her friend and joined me in my search.

I opened Susila's yellow trunk, in which she kept all kinds of toilet seats she had acquired in her lifetime. Three or four different coloured vulcanite cases with mirrors and small bottles. She used to be very fond of these boxes and asked for one whenever she saw them in the shop—green, orange, red, of all colours. I took them out one by one. And then all kinds of cardboard boxes and fancy tin containers stuffed with embroidery thread and woollen bits. The small sweater in yellow—she had been reading about knitting and had become very enthusiastic suddenly. She behaved like a child in her enthusiasm. Every day as I left for college she gave me a commission for a purchase on my way back. It was rarely I was able to pick up the correct colour that she wanted, and I had the task of exchanging it for the correct shade next evening. Finally, exasperated, I arbitrarily forced her to begin work on the yellow sweater for me. She sat down on the veranda step and plied her needles by the evening light, refusing to go out on a walk or do anything else. Night and day she thought and spoke of nothing else. At the end of the day the two shining needles were stuck into the ball and kept on a shelf in the hall. I made all kinds of jokes about it, saying that the sweater seemed to be promised for my hundredth birthday and so on. The back of the sweater was nearly ready and she looked triumphant. The ball of wool was satisfactorily going down in bulk. She proclaimed that the complete sweater would be on my back in eight days; and then our child caught a cold, and she lost all peace of mind and could not knit; thereafter one thing and another intervened and she never took it up again at all. In that condition it was still lying in the box, with the yellow back ready, the needles stuck, as they were on that day, into the ball of wool. 'What is this, Father?' the child asked picking it up. I shook my head and said: 'Put it away, girl, you may hurt yourself with the needles.' And then there were fancy borders meant to be stitched into some dress. I had always protested against the purchase of these things and she always waived my protest away with: 'You just see how they they look when they are stitched into my jackets and the baby's frocks! You will yourself ransack all the shops for more of them.' But they were still where they had been put the day she bought them. This box contained a couple of fancy lacquer caskets of Burmese origin, which her sister from Rangoon had sent; they were filled with small bottles of scent, which I had given her during the first two years of our married life. I opened their corks one by one and smelt them. Their delicate perfume brought immediately around me other days. Evenings when we went out, and spoke of nothing in particular, first years of married life when I used to be very vehement about my plans for the future. These tiny phials had compressed in them the essence of her personality, the rustle of her dress, her footfalls, laughter, her voice, and the light in her eyes, the perfume of her presence. The bottles were empty now but the lingering scent in them covered for a brief moment the gulf between the present and the past. I shut my eyes and dwelt in that ecstasy. I reflected: 'Of all the senses it is smell which is the subtlest; it takes you back to the core of your experience. Why have they not studied its laws and processes, while they have studied all the other senses? Do these scents mean anything to her in her present state?'

'What are you smelling, Father?' asked the child and brought me back to the earth. 'Why are you closing your eyes, Father?'

I drew down the lid. There was no trace of the fourteen letters and the sandalwood casket. I opened another trunk in which she had kept her clothes—dozens of sarees and a hundred and one jackets of all colours and shades; and above all else that glittering gold-woven purple saree, in which she was presented to me as a bride on the all-important day. Many of these clothes had not been taken out more than once because she had a dread of spoiling their sheen.

She picked up like a child every soap-box carton and empty container and preserved them in her cupboard and put into them coins and knick-knacks. In a cardboard box I found stuffed a few sheets of paper. I pulled them out. They were embroidery designs copied in pencil, and some recipe for a toothpowder. There was a sheet on which she had even begun a story with child-like simplicity of two brothers, woodcutters, one of whom was good and industrious and the other was lazy and bad. There were my corrections in between the lines. I remembered how on a certain day she sat for hours at table stroking her lips with the pencil, lost in thought. I do not know what made her want to write a story at all . . . But she was filled with shame when I found her out, and was so nervous when I read through it and corrected the grammar; she never proceeded beyond the first page of the story, where the brothers differ and separate . . . This seemed to me a precious document now crumpled and stuffed into the box. I carefully smoothed it out, and took it with me to my own table.

The child sat very quietly watching me and derived a great deal of pleasure in arranging the empty tins side by side . . . There was still powder in one of the tins, three quarters full, bought a month before she fell ill. I opened the lid and smelt it. 'You are once again shutting your eyes,' remarked my daughter.

At the next meeting, the moment my friend was ready with the pencil, she asked: 'Do you know what a wonderful perfume I have put on! I wish you could smell it . . . On second thoughts I had better not mention it because you will want to smell it and feel disappointed. Perhaps it may look like selfishness for me to be so happy here when there you are so sorrow-filled and unhappy . . . It would hardly be right if I produced that impression. If I succeed in making you feel that I am quite happy over here and that you must not be sorry for me, I will be satisfied. Your sorrow hurts us. I hope our joy and happiness will please and soothe you . . .'

'Undoubtedly,' I replied. 'But what makes you mention the perfume?' I asked.

'Just to enable you to have the most complete idea of our state of existence, that is all. Moreover, did you not speculate somewhat on those lines a few days ago?'

'How do you spend your time usually?' I asked.

'Time in your sense does not exist for us,' she replied. 'Our life is one of thought and experience. Thought is something which has solidity and power, and as in all existence ours is also a life of aspiration, striving, and joy. A considerable portion of our state is taken up in meditation, and our greatest ecstasy is in feeling the Divine Light flooding us . . . We've ample leisure. We are not constrained to spend it in any particular manner. We have no need for exercise as we have no physical bodies. Music is ever with us here, and it transports us to higher planes . . . Things here are far more intense than on earth; that means our efforts are far more efficient than yours. If by good fortune we are able to establish a contact with our dear ones who are receptive to our influence, then you say that that person is inspired. And a song or melody can establish a link between our minds, for instance, how sad that you should have neglected your veena. If you could take it up once again our minds could more easily join. Why don't you try it?'

It was years since I had put it away. I had a gift for it when I was young. 'I don't know scientific music. I have been after all a self-taught amateur . . .'

'Do not worry what anyone will think of your veena. For me it will be the most welcome music. I promise that you will feel my presence as you have never felt it yet. It will surely make your heart easier.

'You might have thought I did not very much care for music when on earth, but as a matter of fact I was really intensely interested in it . . .' she said. I remembered how quietly she liked music. She never took great pains to learn it although she could sing well. She could never be persuaded to sing; but sometimes unaware of my watching, she would sing to herself while combing her hair or putting the child to sleep. If I showed any signs of listening she would stop. She always listened to music wherever it came from—a gramophone in a house on the way, or a beggar singing; she listened with a silent rapture.

'You think I have become a very learned sort of person and all that kind of stuff?'

'Yes,' I replied. Ever since these communications began I felt, now and then, that she showed a greater wisdom than I had known her to possess. 'You would much rather that I was the same prattling person I was on earth, but let me tell you that the change that takes place when one comes over here is so great and the vision is so cleared that even I, your wife, whose nonsense pleased you so much more, am changed. I'm essentially the same person as far as you and my dear ones are concerned, but the only difference is that I'm without the encumbrance of the physical body and everything is finer and quicker than on earth.

'Between thought and fulfilment there is no interval. Thought is fulfilment, motion and everything. That is the main difference between our physical state and yours. In your state a thought to be realized must always be followed by effort directed towards conquering obstructions and inertia—that is the nature of the material world. But in our condition no such obstruction exists. When I think of you or you of me I am at your side. Music directly transports us. When I think of a garment, it is on me. In our world there is such a fine response for thought. When I come to you I prepare myself every time as befits the occasion. I come to meet my lord and I dress myself as befits the occasion. I think of the subtlest perfume and it already pervades my being; and I think of the garment that will most please you: the wedding saree, shimmering purple woven with gold, I have on me at this very moment. You think you saw it in that trunk, how can it be here? What you have seen is its counterpart, the real part of the thing is that which is in thought, and it can never be lost or destroyed or put away.'

Thereafter she mentioned at the close of every evening her appearance. 'Have no shadow of doubt that I'm here. I am wearing a pale orange dress with a clasp of brilliants to hold it in position.'

'What a gorgeous dress!' I exclaimed.

'If only you saw the colour you would not say how gorgeous, you would be speechless. Not even the colours of sunset give you such tints as we have here; to call it pale orange is to give you an idea as inadequate as the idea that a child forms when . . .'

I cast a look around. She at once said: 'You look round. I can see you. What a pity you can't see me! Some day let us hope you will see my form. I am at the moment sitting to your left on the floor with my arm resting on your lap, and directing your friend's hand by my thought.' I looked down at my lap. 'No use yet, even if you open your eyes so wide. But by and by, you will hear my bangles clanking and feast your eyes on my dress and form.

'I think I look the same person as on earth. Only free from all ailments, ills, and cares. You remember I used to have a sort of pain at the waist, even that I do not have now.

'My dress tonight is a shimmering blue interwoven with light and stars. I have done my hair parted on the left. (And what a load of jasmine and other rare flowers I have in my hair for your sake!) I wish a painter could sense me and do a picture for you . . .

'Rest assured that I shall always sit in the same place whenever I am here; when you lift your arm you touch me. At the close of this evening when you go home, I will accompany you, stay up with you till you go to bed and fall asleep thinking of me . . .

'If you want any evidence of my presence, pluck about ten jasmine buds and keep them near your pillow tonight. Before I go away I will take their scent with me: that I can do. You will see the difference when you smell the flowers in the morning.'

On my way home, through the dark night, across Nallappa's Grove my feet felt lighter, because I knew she was accompanying me. Her presence was unmistakably there. I could sense it. The darkness of the night was not felt by me. The distance and loneliness were nothing to me. She was with me. I quietly enjoyed the fact without stirring the slightest thought. Far off I saw the dark night lit with the fire of a cremation. But it did not disturb me! 'I know more than this . . .' I remarked.

6

SUNDAY. I DECIDED to spend the entire day in the company of the child. Of late my college work and the extra activities and the weekly visits to my friend took up so much of my time that I spent less than two hours a day with the child. It was a painful realization. 'Oh God,' went up my prayer, 'save me from becoming too absorbed in anything to look after the child properly.' And I felt very sorry and guilty when I returned home at nights and found the child asleep.

She had her own plans for the day. As soon as she got up and was ready for the road, she insisted upon being taken to the school.

'This is Sunday, you don't have to go,' I pleaded.

But it was no use. 'You don't know about our school. We have school.' She put on her coat and stepped out. I went out with her. 'Why do you follow me, Father?' she asked.

'I too want to see your school today,' I said.

'But my friends are filled with fear if they see you. Don't come with me, Father,' she pleaded.

'No, I will take good care not to frighten them,' I assured her. She stood for a moment undecided, looking at me and said to herself: 'Poor Father, let him come too,' and smiled patronizingly.

There was no sign at the school to show that it was a Sunday. It was alive with the shouts of children—about twenty of them had already gathered and were running about and playing: the swings and see-saw were all in full use. The Headmaster was with them.

'You don't rest even on a Sunday?' I asked the Headmaster.

'Rest? This is all right for a rest, what else should I do? They just come in, play, throw the sand about, and go away, and we also do it with them. It is quite good, you know. I feel quite happy. What else should I do on a Sunday?'

'Something to differentiate it from other days . . .'

'Quite. We don't do sums today. We just sing, hear stories, and play . . .' His eyes were red. He coughed. He did not look as if he had had sleep at night.

'What is the matter with you?' I could not help asking.

'I suffer from sleeplessness, my friend,' he said. 'It is some years since I had anything like sleep. I sleep about an hour. I used to make myself very miserable about it at first. But now I am used to it. I make up stories for children and I hardly feel the time passing. Come in and see.' He took me into his room. It was thatch-roofed. Its floor was covered with clay, and the walls were of bamboo splinters filled in with mud. The floor was uneven and cool, and the whole place smelt of Mother Earth. It was a pleasing smell, and seemed to take us back to some primeval simplicity, intimately bound up with earth and mud and dust. Along the wall was a sort of running ledge covered with a crazy variety of objects:

cardboard houses, paper flowers, clumsy drawings and head work. 'These are the work of children who have studied here, and some of them have a special significance: presented to me by the outgoing children or the very special effort of a child. They are the trophies of this school. I consider them a real source of joy. For instance, the very first work of a child has some peculiar value. I don't know if others understand that there is anything in it at all . . . you will understand it better if I say look at that green paper boat. Can you guess who has made it? Your daughter on the very first day she came here, she finished it within an hour.' I felt thrilled. Beside a parrot cut out of a cardboard picture and an inkpot made of paper, this green boat stood. I went over and picked it up. My little Leela in relation to an outside world, making her own mark on it: I was filled with pride and satisfaction. 'It is a whaler with a knife-edge at the keel!' I cried in joy. He jumped out of his seat: 'That's what I say. See how lovely it is!' The sight of it filled him with a mystic ecstasy. 'She is a grand child. So are the other children. The first work of almost every child is here and the other works go into the general hall.' The walls were hung with different pictures, tigers and lions and trees drawn with childish hands. He swept his hands about and declared: 'Every one of these is children's work. They are the real gods on earth.' He stopped before each picture and enjoyed the thrill of it anew. He had done away with table and chair. In a corner he had seat for visitors. 'This will do for a school. We are a poor country, and we can do without luxuries. Why do we want anything more than a shed and a few mats and open air? This is not a cold country for all the heavy furniture and elaborate buildings. This has cost me just fifty rupees, and I had three such built. But we have not much use for them, most of our time being spent outside, under the tree . . .'

'Many people think,' I said, 'that you can't have a school unless you have invested a few thousands in building and furniture.'

'It is all mere copying,' he replied. 'Multiply your expenses, and look to the government for support, and sell your soul to the government for the grant. This is the history of our educational movement. And another thing. What a fuss they have learnt to make of sports! As if colleges and schools were gymnasia, the main business of which is to turn out sturdy idiots. When I think of all the pampering and sentimentality of sports and games!' He shuddered. 'The mean business of an educational institution is to shape the mind and character and of course games have their value. Why worship sports, and the eleven stalwart idiots who bring in a shield or a cup? It is all a curse, copying, copying, copying. We could as well have been born monkeys to justify our powers of imitation.'

'Yes,' I said. 'In our college Brown forgoes even his club to see a match; loses himself in excitement, congratulates the team and shakes hands, and gives no end of liberties to the tournament players and even sends them on tour,' I said, catching the infection of his mood.

'And do you know, they not only get a lot more touring and tiffin than the others. They are even made to pass examinations! And this sort of thing is supposed to make our people modern and vigorous . . .' He laughed, but the excitement was too much for him, and he subsided into a fit of coughing.

'I'm sorry,' he said. 'Sit down, sit down. I wanted to show you the stories I've made . . .' He pulled out a box and brought out a big bundle of brown paper: huge pages covered with letters as well as figures cut out and pasted. 'This is a new method which I find fascinating,' he said. 'I invent a story, write it down in words, and illustrate it with pictures cut out of illustrated books and papers and pasted, at the appropriate places; for instance this,' he threw down ten volumes, 'is a pretty long story of a bison and a tiger in the forest . . . just glance through it.' Every page had a figure or two; the illustrations ran along with the story.

'They are almost real you know,' he said as I gazed on the pictures. 'Just watch, I'll show you how it works.' He stood in the doorway and announced: 'Story! Story!' The children who had been playing about, stopped, looked at him and came running in, uttering shrieks of joy.

They sat around their master. When they subsided into silence he opened the large album and said looking at it: 'This is the story of a tiger and his friend the jungle buffalo, called Bison. It happened in Mempi Forest. Who can tell me where Mempi Forest is?' There followed a discussion among the children and one girl said pointing at the doorway: 'There, near those mountains, am I right?'

'Right, right,' he said. 'There are a lot of jungles there. See here.' All the children leaned over each other's shoulders and fixed their eyes on the top of the album where a perfect jungle had been made with the help of dry tinted grass pasted together. 'These are all bamboo jungles, full of tigers, but we are only concerned with one tiger. His name is Raja. See this. There he is, a young cub.'

'He is very young.' said the children, looking at him. The album was passed round for the benefit of those sitting far off. 'What a fearful fellow!' commented a few. My daughter, sitting between two friends older than herself, refused to touch the album because of the tiger, but was quite prepared to see it if held by her neighbour. 'This little tiger was quite lonely, you know, because her mother had been taken away by hunters—bad fellows.' Thus the story of the tiger went on. The tiger came across a friend in the shape of a young bison, who protected him from a bear and other enemies. They both lived in a cave at the tail end of Mempi Hills—great friends. The bison grew up into a thick rock-like animal, and the tiger also grew up and went out in search of prey at nights. One night a party of hunters shot at the bison and carried him off to the town. And the tiger missed his friend and his cry rang through the Mempi Forest the whole night. The tiger soon adjusted himself to a lonely existence.

The children listened in dead silence and were greatly moved when this portion was read out. They all came over to have a look at the tiger in his loneliness, and our friend, rightly guessing that they would ask for it, had procured a picture. The tiger was standing forlorn before his cave. The children uttered many cries of regret and unhappiness. 'Master, how can he live without his friend any more? I hope he is not killed by the bear!'

'No. No, that bear was disposed of by the friend before he was caught.'

'Poor bear! Let me have a look at him,' said a girl. The pages were turned back and there he was, dark and shaggy. 'He could have fought with the bison. He looks so strong,' said the girl. She was, somehow, unaccountably, on the side of the bear. 'You should not like the bear,' said another girl. 'The teacher will be angry if you like the bear . . .'

'No, no, I won't be. You may like what you like,' said the teacher. This was an inducement for another child to join the ranks of bear-lovers. She said: 'I always like a bear. It has such a lot of hair. Who will comb her hair, teacher?' 'Of course, her mother,' said another child.

'Has she a mother? Poor thing, yet she was allowed to be killed by the bison. I don't like bisons. They should have more hair!'

'If you are so fond of bears, why do you listen to this story?'

'Because it's the story of a bear, of course,' replied the child.

'It isn't.'

'It is. You see the picture.'

'Master, she is looking too long at the bear. I want to see the tiger.' The teacher interfered at this stage and restored order. He whispered to me: 'The most enchanting thing among children is their quarrels. How they carry it on for its own sake, without the slightest bitterness or any memory of it later. This is how we were once, God help us: this too is what we have turned out to be!' He resumed the story. My daughter, who felt she had left me alone too long, came over and sat with her elbows resting on my lap. She whispered: 'Father, I want a tiger.'

'A real one?'

'Yes. Isn't it like a cat?' I nudged the teacher, and told him of her demand. He became very serious and said: 'You must not think of a tiger as a pet, darling. It is a very big and bad animal. I will show you a tiger when a circus comes to the town next. Meanwhile you may have a picture of a tiger. I will give you one.'

'All right, master, I will take it.'

'And you can have a real cat. I will give you a small kitten I have at home.'

She screamed with joy. 'Is it in your house?'

'Yes, yes. I will give it to you and also the picture of a tiger.'

'Father, let us go with him . . .'

'Surely, surely,' the teacher looked delighted. 'Come with me . . .' He went on for a few minutes more and ceased. The story would run on for a full week. He stopped because the clock struck twelve. The children wouldn't get up. The tiger had just been caught by a circus man for training. The children wanted to know more and more. 'Master, you mustn't stop. What happens to the tiger? Is he happy?' He would answer none of their questions. He ruthlessly shut his books and got up.

'We are hungry, teacher. We will go home.'

'That's why I stopped the story. Go home and come and listen to it tomorrow,' he said.

'Do they kill the tiger?' asked the child.

'No, no, he is quite safe. He will be quite all right, trust me,' said the teacher. The children, greatly pleased, ran out of the school. My daughter asked: 'Is it the same circus you promised to take me to?'

'Ah, something like it. Here too you will see a tiger,' he replied and we got up. He locked the shed and the gate and walked down with us. When we reached our house, my daughter insisted upon going with him though she was hungry. He cajoled and coaxed her to go in. But she was adamant. At which he offered to come in and wait for the girl to finish her food and then take her with him. I seated him in my study.

'This is the book I read,' the girl said placing the big catalogue in his hand. He turned over its leaves and was lost in its pictures. I took her in to dine. I told the old lady: 'There is another person for dinner today. Can you manage?'

'Oh, yes,' she said, although I knew she'd give her share of food or cook again. I invited the Headmaster to sit down with me. He looked happy and at the same time uncomfortable: 'My wife at home, she will be waiting . . .'

'Won't she guess you won't be in?' I asked. 'Come on.' He yielded.

It was a most delightful party. I found him more and more fascinating. He took off his coat, folded up his sleeves, and asked: 'Where is the bathroom? I should like to have a wash.' He came out of the bathroom and said (his face wet with water and hands dripping): 'Don't offer me a towel please . . .'

'Then how do you dry it?'

'I just leave it alone, and it will evaporate. I never use a towel.'

'Why, fear of infection?'

'I don't know. I have never liked a towel, not even my own. Even after a bath I just keep standing till the water evaporates, and then put on my dress with the result that every day my wife creates a most fearful row outside the bathroom, because you know it takes a little time for a wholesale drying like that.'

My daughter was delighted that her teacher was dining with us. She was sitting down in her place with her silver plate in front of her, and was halfway through her rice. But when she saw her teacher she exclaimed with joy: 'I will also eat with teacher,' and tried to get up. She was, however, pressed back into her seat. She was very unhappy. 'Eat slowly, but don't get up. Eat slowly till your teacher joins us,' I said. The teacher would want some more time for himself. 'Please grant me fifteen minutes. I usually pray and meditate for fifteen minutes before dinner, the only time that I can spare. Just fifteen minutes . . . Another thing that seems to upset my wife.' His wife seemed to be weighing on his mind. He muttered: 'I could have managed well as a bachelor, but they wouldn't let me alone.' There was something very appealing in the way he spoke. He spoke of himself as if it were someone else. His own life seemed to give him as much amusement as he found the company of children inspiring. I found a place for him to sit and meditate, left him alone and came away. He preferred the back courtyard facing the east. He squatted on the floor and closed his eyes and was lost in it. He was completely wrapped in his own vision for quite a long while, and then came and joined me. He did not seem to have the slightest feeling of being in a stranger's house. He conducted himself as if he were in his own house. As he came into the dining room and took his seat on the plank next to mine he asked: 'What have you done for dinner? I hope I have not put you to great difficulty or extra trouble?'

'Oh, no. Some simple fare. I hope you won't find it too bad . . .' The usual courtesies were going on in the usual manner, and he said suddenly: 'Don't you think we have evolved some silly social customs? For instance . . .' Now as the old lady served us on the leaf the first course, fried brinjals, 'I am not very fond of this. But can I say so?' He gently pushed it away to a corner of the leaf. 'Please forgive me if I don't touch it. I would sooner swallow poison than eat brinjal . . .' A most eccentric man. But we had almost arrived at a tacit understanding to be strictly truthful rather than formal. So I replied: 'Well, I won't apologize for it, you know. If you don't like it, it is a pity. I hope you will like something else presently . . .'

'That's right. I like to speak and hear only on these lines. This is the simplicity to which all human conduct must be reduced. This is what the company of children has taught me. A fact which makes it very difficult for me to manage in an adult society. But then why should I ever try to get on with adults?' My daughter remarked: 'Our master doesn't look like himself without his coat.' He usually wore a loose, colourless coat, buttoned up to his neck. Now without it he certainly looked different. He looked rather young and slight. He seemed to put away ten years when he took off his coat. Indistinct features, greying at the temples, pouches under the red eyes. With all this there was a touch of freshness about him. My daughter asked: 'Tell me a story, teacher.'

'No, no, we must never tell stories while eating. Only at school.

What should we do at school, if we had spent all the stories at home while eating?'

After food he reclined on the mat in the hall. My daughter placed before him a plate of betel leaves and arecanut. He chewed them with contentment. His lips became as red as his eyes. He looked very happy. The child sat nestling close to him and exhibited to him all her toys: the scores of coloured utensils, and brass miniature vessels, the rubber balls and her big doll. She carried the doll on her arm and said: 'This girl wants to come with me every day to school. She cries and shouts every day. What shall I do, master?'

He looked at the doll and said: 'Not a bad girl.' He pretended to pinch its cheeks and said: 'See how soft she is . . .' My daughter was greatly pleased. She looked at the doll affectionately and said: 'She is a most lovely girl, master. But she does want to go with me to school, what shall I do?'

'Do you want to bring her or not?' She shook her head sadly. 'No, master. She is a bad baby and will give a lot of trouble at the school. She will not allow me to study there. She will quarrel with everyone.' Certain inescapable anti-social characteristics of this doll seemed to sadden Leela, but she had steeled herself to a sort of resignation. So her teacher said: 'Well, why don't you lock her up in a box when you come to school?' Leela shook her head: 'That I can't do because she will die. I will lock her up in a room.'

The teacher asked: 'Do you mind if I lie down and rest a while?' He lay down and shut his eyes. My daughter insisted upon lying down beside him. Soon she was fast asleep. So was he. I went away to my room, picked up a book, lay on my camp easy chair, and dozed.

We were all ready to start out at four in the afternoon, my daughter persistently asking for a cat.

We walked down the road. His house was in Anderson Lane, which was a furlong east of my house—a locality we had never visited. It was a street within a street, and a lane tucked away into a lane. There was every sign that the municipality had forgotten the existence of this part of the town. Yet it seemed to maintain a certain degree of sanitation, mainly with the help of the sun, wind and rain. The sun burned so severely most months that bacteria and infection turned to ashes. The place had a general clean up when the high winds rose before the monsoon set in, and whirled into a column the paper scraps, garbage, egg-shells, and leaves; the column precipitated itself into the adjoining street, and thence to the next and so on, till, perhaps, it reached a main thoroughfare where the municipal sanitary staff worked, if they worked anywhere at all. And it was followed by a good wash down, when the rains descended in November and December and flushed the streets, and water flowed along the roadway and joined the river.

Malgudi had earned notoriety for its municipal affairs. The management was in the hands of a council with a president, a vice-president, and ten elected members; they met on the last Saturday of every month and battled against each other. One constantly read of disputed elections, walk-outs, and no-confidence motions. Otherwise they seemed to do little by way of municipal work. However, when a distinguished visitor came to the town, the president and the members led him up the stairs of a tower in the municipal building and from there pointed out to him with great pride the Sarayu cutting across the northern boundary of the town, glistening like a scimitar in moonlight.

Carpenters, tinsmiths, egg-sellers and a miscellaneous lot of artisans and traders seemed gathered in this place. The street was littered with all kinds of things—wood shavings, egg shells, tin pieces and drying leaves. Dust was ankle deep. I wondered why my friend had selected this of all places. I was afraid to allow my daughter to walk here. I felt she would catch all kinds of dreadful diseases. Unkempt and wild-looking children rolled about in the dust, mangy dogs growled at us, donkeys stood at attention here and there. I offered to carry my daughter on my arm but she refused to be lifted. Her teacher said: 'Don't worry, leave her alone. This is really a healthy place for all its appearance. She will be all right, don't worry about her too much . . . No harm will come to her . . .' I left her alone, rather abashed, and feeling rather that I had been found out.

'Who is the Anderson of this lane?' I asked, looking at the impressive nameplate nailed on to the wall of a house.

'God knows. At least to honour the name I hope they do something for this place . . . I have often tried to find out who Anderson was. But nobody seems to know. Perhaps some gentleman of the East India Company's days!'

He suddenly stopped and said: 'Now this is my house.' The

tiles of the roof jutted into the street, a gutter gurgled and ran down in front of the house.

'Come on carefully, don't fall off into the gutter,' he said.

As soon as we had crossed the gutter, three children of ages between seven and ten stood in the doorway and hugged him. 'Is your mother at home?' he asked.

'No,' they replied.

'Excellent,' he said and went in. He looked relieved to hear it.

'Now, young fellows, here is a new friend, see what a fine girl she is.' The children looked at Leela with interest. Somehow this attention seemed to puzzle her. She gripped my hands tight and tried to get behind me. The children adjusted their positions so that she might still be within range. Finally she could stand it no longer. 'Let us go, Father. Where is the cat?'

'Wait, wait,' I whispered. 'You must not ask for it at once. See how nice those children are.' They weren't. They looked too wild. Their hair full of mud almost matted, their dress torn and dirty, an abnormal liveliness about them. They stood relentlessly staring at my child. Their father had slipped in and now came out with a roll of mat. He spread it in the passage, between the front door and the central hall, a large part of which was an open courtyard with a well in the middle; the whole place was unspeakably wet. The hall was choked with old furniture, clothes and vessels. Beyond was a narrow kitchen, black with soot. The mat was an old, tattered, Japanese one with a girl holding a parasol painted in the centre. I and my child sat down. The three children stood around gazing. He asked: 'Where is your mother gone?'

'We don't know. We couldn't ask because she was angry you hadn't come. Why didn't you come home, Father?' 'I had somewhere else to go to,' he replied lightly and tried to dismiss it from their minds. But they insisted until he said: 'You mustn't keep asking the same question.'

The eldest asked: 'Have you had your food?'

'Yes.'

They looked at each other and said: 'Mother went away thinking that you wouldn't have eaten, and that you would come and ask for it.'

'Not I,' he said. 'I know your mother—well, children you may all go away now . . . or take this baby with you and play with her.' There was consternation in my daughter's face and she muttered:

'Father, don't let them call me.' He saw this and said: 'You don't want to go with them? Then don't. Now you may all leave us.' With a great shout they ran towards the street and vanished. I couldn't help asking: 'Where are they going?'

'I don't know. I can't say—perhaps to the gutter, or to some low-class den in the neighbourhood. I've no control over them. They are their mother's special care, you know.' There was a hint of a terrible domestic condition. I did not wish to pursue it. But I blundered into it. 'Don't they attend your school?'

'They!' he repeated. 'I could sooner get the Emperor's children. My school is for all the children in the world except my own.'

'Where do they study?'

'You may know better . . .' At this point a fat woman of about thirty-five, with sparse hair tied into a knot at the back of her head, her face shining with oil and perspiration, strode up the steps of the house. She threw a look at him and did not seem in the least to notice me sitting in the passage, though striding past us. She walked into the house, muttering: 'So you have found the way home after all!' gritting her teeth. He didn't reply but merely looked at me sadly. She stood in the doorway of the house and said, 'How long must I keep dinner waiting? Do you think I'm made of stone?'

'Nobody asked you to wait.'

'You are not to decide who should wait and who should not. You and your school! You don't know the way back from your school, I suppose.'

'Don't speak rubbish. Here is a cultured visitor, who will laugh at us.'

'Let him, what do I care? If he is big, he is a big man to you. He is not a big man to me. What do I care? Answer me first. Where were you all the time? Do you think I'm a paid watch-keeper for this house?'

I could not watch this scene any longer. I got up and said: 'We will be going.' He looked at his wife and said: 'I can't bring a gentleman to visit me without your driving him away with your fine behaviour.'

'Oh, no, it is not . . .' I began.

She replied: 'Ah, what a fine sermon. I'm not going to be another woman than myself even if the king is here. What did I do to him?'

'Don't take it . . .' I began, starting up. My daughter said: 'The cat. He hasn't given me the cat.' He said: 'Right. I never meant to forget.' He looked at his wife and asked: 'Where is that kitten? Is it inside?'

'I don't know,' the wife said, 'I have too much to do to be keeping count of the cats and dogs that pass this way.' He smiled at me weakly and said: 'Can't get a straight answer from her, at any time of the day! There are people in this world who have rough tongues but who are soft at heart—but this lady! I look ridiculous, speaking of my wife in this manner. But why should I not? Children have taught me to speak plainly, without the varnish of the adult world. I don't care if it strikes anyone as odd.' My daughter punctuated his narration with 'Where is the cat?' I had the feeling that I ought to run away. So I said: 'Perhaps it has gone out, he will bring it when it comes back home.' He said, 'Wait,' and went in and looked about and returned shaking his head. 'It used to be in the store behind that tin. Forgive me, baby. I will positively get you a cat soon.' My daughter looked very disappointed. So I cheered her up with a joke or two and walked out. He followed us back to our house. He seemed to feel more at home in my house than in his. He reclined in the easy chair, pulled out a book and was soon lost in study. I looked at him in surprise. The book was a criticism of the Elizabethan dramatists, Beaumont and Fletcher. 'This is the dullest work I've read in the English language. How is it that it interests you so much?'

He lowered the book, removed his silver spectacles and said, 'I'm not reading it. If I open a book like this and allow my eyes to rest on the lines, it helps me to do a lot of private thinking. I read very few books for any other purpose. This book for instance, has helped me to reflect deeply and earnestly on the question of family, marriage, and such other institutions.' My daughter came in and showed him a house she had made out of a matchbox. He seemed to forget all his troubles in an instant. 'Oh, what a house, what a house. The only house worth having in this world,' he added turning to me, as she went out, carrying it away with her. Her friends were at the gate calling for her, and she shouted, 'Father, I'm going to play,' and ran away and joined them. 'She seems to have had enough of adults' company since this morning,' he remarked, putting away Beaumont and Fletcher. He looked at the book and said with a smile, 'Not a line in the whole book to distract

your thought—an ideal book for a contemplative turn of mind . . .
Not a line in it . . .' He put away the book, remained silent for a
moment and said: 'Did you notice how quickly that child dropped us
and joined her fellows? Adult company is unfit for angels. Adults who
can't even keep a promise in regard to a kitten. Helpless fools we must
appear to her. What wishy-washiness!'

It was nearing six. I looked over the wall of our next house, and
saw my child playing with half a dozen children. I asked: 'Come on,
child, are you coming out with us for a walk?' She hesitated. Her
friend suggested: 'Let us play here. Let Father go out and return.'
She accepted the advice and said: 'I am not coming, Father, you may
go.'

I and the Headmaster walked down to the river bank, sat on
the sand, and watched the sunset. He told me: 'Some twenty years
ago when I passed my BA at the university, they wanted me to
take law; and then wanted to rush me into an office chair, but I
resisted. I loved children and wanted to start the school. How can
anyone prevent me from doing what I want? I had been hustled
into a marriage which did not interest me, and I was not going to
be hustled into a profession I did not care for.

'I was the only son of my father, but he said such bitter things
that I left home. We had a fine house in Lawley Extension, you
wouldn't believe it. I was brought up there, it is the memory of
those days which is rankling in my wife's heart and has made her so
bad and mad. I walked out over the question of employment; and
went back home only on the day he died. And then my wife thought
I would occupy that house after his death, but not I. I don't know
what he has done with it. He had married a second time after my
mother died and I think she and her children or his brothers must
be fighting for it. I don't want that house, I have no use for it, I don't
want any of his money either. But my wife expects me to be fighting
for these rights. I can't enjoy these rights even if I get them, and I
think it is a waste of one's precious hours of living to be engaged
in a contest.'

'But your wife and children could be in better circumstances . . .'

'You think so? No chance of it, my friend. She will create just
those surroundings for herself even in a palace.'

'But you have not put her in a very happy locality . . .'

'Perhaps not. But I chose it deliberately. It is where God
resides. It is where we should live. And if we have any worth in us

the place will change through our presence. But my wife does not believe in anything like it. She thinks my school a fool's idea; won't send the children there. I did my best. But it is no use. She has a right to send them where she likes. I think she sends them to the gutter and pigsty: you saw what they are like. She is an impossible type. But my only hope is that there may be a miraculous transformation some day and that she may change. We should not despair for even the worst on earth.'

'Till then don't you think you should concede to her wishes and move to a better place?'

'No. First because it is a duty for me, and secondly because she will carry the same surroundings wherever she goes. You see, the trouble is not external.'

The river flowed on against the night. I listened to him; he appeared to me a man who had strayed into a wrong world.

'How did you get this idea of a school for children?' I asked.

'The memory of my own young days. Most of us forget that grand period. But with me it has always been there. A time at which the colours of things are different, their depths greater, their magnitude greater, a most balanced and joyous condition of life; there was a natural state of joy over nothing in particular. And then our own schooling which put blinkers on to us; which persistently ruined this vision of things and made us into adults. It has always seemed to me that our teachers helped us to take a wrong turn. And I have always felt that for the future of mankind we should retain the original vision, and I'm trying a system of children's education. Just leave them alone and they will be all right. The Leave Alone System, which will make them wholesome human beings, and also help us, those who work along with them, to work off the curse of adulthood.' He was seized with a fit of coughing. He recovered from it, paused, and said: 'I will tell you a secret now. I strictly want to live according to my own plan of living and not subordinate it for anybody's sake, because the time at my disposal is very short. I know exactly when I am going to die. An astrologer, who has noted down every minute detail of my life, has fixed that for me. I know the exact hour when I shall die . . . that lady will have the surprise of her life,' he said and chuckled. 'That's why I'm so patient with her.'

We walked back home. I invited him in: 'No, no, not fair. But be assured I shall make myself completely at home whenever I like.

I hope you won't mind.'

'Not at all, I replied. 'Treat this as your own home.'

'Good Lord! No. Let it always be your home,' he said with a smile and bade me good night.

7

I MISSED MY friend's sittings continuously for three or four weeks. He was ill for a few days, and then he had some work or other on hand, and then guests, all of which prevented his giving me a sitting. I went there and turned back with a feeling of disappointment, and on the fourth Wednesday I went there hoping again. There was only a garden servant to answer me. My friend had left a note behind: 'Awfully sorry. Have had to start for Trichinopoly on some urgent business, at an hour's notice. Can't say when I shall be returning, but I will write to you.' He had gone with his entire family. I asked: 'May I go and rest a while near the pond?' The servant gave me permission. I sat there on the *pyol* of the shrine as the evening declined. The still surface of the pond, the lotus, the evening breeze, all had a reviving effect, but the sense of disappointment was very keen within me. I shut my eyes and visualized the form of my wife. The casuarina murmured. I said aloud: 'Are you all here, can't you devise some means of communicating with me, O great spirits?' I felt ridiculous talking to myself thus. My words fell on a deep silence and died without a response—the faintest would have made me happy, but it was not there. I repeated my appeal in a low tone and felt ashamed of myself for appearing to be talking to myself. For the first time in months, I felt desolate. The awful irresponsiveness of Death overwhelmed me again. It unnerved me. All the old moods returned now. It looked as though they had been in bondage all these days and were now suddenly unleashed. I was overwhelmed.

I went home and slept badly that night. I kept asking myself: 'I have been clinging to the veriest straw, thinking that I was on land. Now the straw has snapped and I know my position. I can only drown. I'm drowned, and did not know it all these days. I was clinging to a grass blade at the brink of a well.' I went about my business next day with a heavy heart. As soon as she saw me in the morning my daughter was seized with a doubt and asked: 'Father,

you are angry!' 'No, no,' I said, and with a great effort of will played
with her and saw her off to school. I hated my food, I hated my
work, I loathed my friends. That day I continuously lost my temper
with the boys. A student in the BA class rose in his seat to have a
doubt cleared. He was a first-class student, always serious and well-
behaved: but I snapped: 'Will you sit down? I can't stand all these
interruptions . . .'

'But, sir . . .'

'That'll do. Because you obtain more marks than your
neighbours, you needn't . . .' He looked crushed, and sat down. I
could never forget the expression on his face, nor forgive myself for
it. At the end of the period I called him aside and said: 'Well, what
did you want?'

He at once mentioned his difficulty. I cleared it and added:
'Don't worry so much about these things—they are trash, we are
obliged to go through and pretend that we like them, but all the
time the problem of living and dying is crushing us . . .' 'Yes, sir, but
for the examination . . .' he added. And I said: 'I'm sorry, my dear
fellow, if I have been rude to you. A lot of things are weighing on
my mind . . .' 'I understand, sir,' he said and went away. I showed
less tolerance to Gajapathy. At the quadrangle when we passed each
other at the end of a day he said: 'Krishna, I must have a word with
you.' I stopped without a word and waited for him to speak. He
said: 'Can I speak to you now?' I said sharply: 'Yes, why not now?'
'Here?' he asked. 'Yes, what's wrong with here?' 'You seem to be
upset over something.' 'Nothing. All is perfect in the world. I'm all
attention.' He took me to his room, seated me in a chair and said:
'First, I want to tell you that Brown feels we have been neglecting
the history of literature. He saw the test papers of the fourth year
and is disappointed. He thinks the boys will ruin themselves in the
public exam.'

'Well, what are we to do?'

'He wants you to take a special period for them in the history
of literature.'

'Why do they make so much of the history of literature? They
have to make a history of every damned thing on earth—as if
literature could not survive without some fool compiling a bogus
history. If he won't mind my saying this to the boys, I will accept
the special classes . . .'

'Don't be frivolous,' Gajapathy said. 'Your college habits have not left you yet . . .'

'Far from it. I see more clearly now between fatuities and serious work.'

He had grown more tolerant with me these days. He waited for me to finish my lecture and gave me his own advice and orders. 'All right,' I said. 'I cannot but obey you. But I will tell the boys what's sense and what is nonsense. I will tell them that they are being fed on literary garbage and that we are all the paid servants of the garbage department.'

As I was standing at the door of my house, Leela's teacher passed along the street. I saw him at a distance and tried to pretend I had not seen him and turned in. It vexed me to see people and talk to them. It was a tremendous strain. I sat in my room waiting for him to pass. But he stopped and cried 'Krishna'. I was bound to meet him. I went to the gate and greeted him. I didn't like to call him in. So I rushed out to dispose of him in the doorway. He asked: 'Not well?'

'Quite well. I have never been in better health.'

'Coming out for a walk in the evening?'

'Sorry, I have another engagement.'

'Where is your daughter?'

'Gone out to play.' We carried on thus for a few minutes, for my part brief sentences and monosyllables.

Till late in the evening I sat alone at a corner of the river. 'A long dip in this river, or a finger poked into a snake hole—there are two thousand ways of ending this misery. But the child, the child . . . she will be looked after by God, and by everyone. She is an entity. She was able to go on without her mother, and she could equally well carry on without her father. I have put by a little money for her . . . Well, she will be looked after quite well—God bless her.' Far off I saw the glow of a funeral pyre over the walls of the cremation ground, and I sighed for it. It seemed to be the greatest aspiration one could have. 'Exactly where she was placed and burnt . . .' I recollected her pale face, with the flies on it, and the mole on her lips, and broke down at the memory. I recovered and said to myself: 'This is also my end. Oh God, send me to those flames at once.' I saw a picture of myself being carried there and the funeral ceremonies. And this vision seemed to give me a little peace.

Thus days followed, bleak, dreary, and unhappy days, with a load on the mind. I felt as though I had been filled with molten lead.

And then came a letter one morning from my friend, 'I'm sorry to have remained silent so long. I have been up to my ears in litigation and it looks as though all these affairs are going to take more and more of my time. But anyway, I will arrange these things and return in a few weeks. My house here is in the extension with a fine small compound, and a room all to myself, where I spend the larger part of my day in reading when I don't talk over matters with lawyers and witnesses. You see, I had to come away suddenly because an uncle of mine passed away, and there are all kinds of arrangements to be made in regard to property. He married three times and has numerous children, and you know how many complications can arise out of that!

'Anyway, my purpose in writing to you today is not to trouble you with my affairs, but a different one. I have a feeling that we might attempt an experiment while we are out of each other's reach. I want to see if we can manage a sitting—a sort of *in absentia* business. For spirit matters, space is of no account, and so there is no reason why we should not succeed. On Sunday at four o'clock in the evening I propose to try the experiment. So please keep yourself in your room and link up with me mentally with a request to your wife to communicate. As far as possible keep all other business from your mind. At precisely 4.30, you may consider it closed. I will send you the result of this sitting by post immediately.'

This offered me a new lease of life. Two days before me. All the weariness melted.

On Sunday I cajoled my daughter into spending her time at the school with the old lady and then shut myself in my room and lay down in my chair and closed my eyes. The clock showed two minutes to four. I stilled myself. My heart was palpitating with excitement. I had to hold my breath for a moment before it could be stilled. I opened my eyes and saw that it was four and said: 'Oh, dear wife, my friend at the other end and I have linked up. Please communicate.' I visualized my friend sitting in his room, and I fancied myself occupying a chair beside him, and my wife communicating through him. I shut my eyes and remained in a sort of half-sleep till 4.35.

Two days later the postman brought me a long envelope, as I

was just starting for the college. With the books under my arm, I tore open the letter, and pulled out two long sheets of paper covered over with pencil writing. There was a covering letter from my friend.

The message read: 'It is a long time since I spoke to you through your friend. I have a feeling as if I were sitting on a wall. On one side I see your big friend. On the other I see you, lying in your green canvas easy chair and also trying to be present here at the same time . . . Seeing you now in your old chair, as you shut your eyes and try to keep your mind still, I forget for a moment that we are in two totally different mediums of existence . . .

'The most important thing I wish to warn you about is not to allow your mind to be disturbed by anything. For some days now you have allowed your mind to become gloomy and unsettled. You are not keeping very strong either. You must keep yourself in better frame . . .

'We must thank your friend who has yielded to our suggestion, to try these absent sittings. I'm sure you will benefit by them. Please think yourself as being able to establish communication with us direct. You will have to prepare yourself for it. There will be a change in your state. Moreover you should not expect your friend to be troubled by you all your life. You must make yourself fit for it, and this communication will restore to you health and better nerves because of the greater harmony that comes into your life; but you must also do your bit to utilize this harmony. You must keep your body and mind in perfect condition, before you aspire to become sensitive and receptive; I have learnt a great deal after coming here; believe me if it is peace of mind you want, you cannot have it better than from us . . .'

'How do I become sensitive?' I asked.

The following Sunday we again linked up at the same hour. On Monday morning the postman brought me the message: 'Don't feel sorry. It hurts me more than you can imagine. So please keep your mind free from choking thoughts. I wish to give you a picture in words.

'A weary and thirsty traveller was returning home from a long day's march. The setting sun had touched all the objects around him with a rosy magic. The birds were returning to their nests. A rumbling brook rolled along. He sat down and quenched his thirst with water. He saw a black bird sit on a thorn and whistle. A batch of white cranes flew across, tinted by the sunset. Their rhythm and their colour filled the traveller's heart with an indescribable joy. He said to himself, "Worshipping and wondering, how much life's journey is made easier for one who can see nature and God every moment!" He returned home fatigued in body, but his soul was in the rapture of a song.

'I don't know what you are going to make of this. Somehow, this picture has been haunting my soul all along: and a great inexplicable satisfaction reigns in my heart because I have communicated it to you. I have set a song to sing this to me. When I sit down and sing it, a most heavenly sunset, birds of wonderful colours, and the serenity of the brook, everything comes up palpably and we can even converse with the traveller. And the melody. It is just created out of thought, in a manner which you cannot grasp. The responses of our world are immediate and fine; you have a glimpse of it only in your striving; there your deeper mind impels you, there it is a striving; here it is an achievement. Your striving itself is proof of its reality here; to be realized when the obstructions of your state are cleared. . . .

'I don't know if you think I'm becoming a poet as well. I have given you many thoughts lately for writing by impressing them on your mind; you might have caught them if you had continued your old habit of occasionally writing verse. Some day I hope we sat together produce a great epic. I'm not joking. I'm in earnest. Nobody may think much of these efforts. They may appear, just as the picture of the weary traveller does, obvious or obscure to others, but certainly you will like them because they are your dear wife's efforts.'

In about ten days my friend returned to his garden and we were able to have a sitting as before. I was very happy to be back at the old seat beside the lotus pond.

After the preliminary remarks and suggestions my wife asked abruptly: 'When are you starting an attempt at your own psychic development?'

'How can I say?' I replied.

'Oh! if you do not know what you are going to do or not do, who else can?'

I felt snubbed and explained: 'I didn't mean that. I should like to be told when and what to do. I look to you for guidance!'

'Why not make a start tomorrow? Tomorrow is a day that never comes. Why not begin today as soon as you go home? Just ten minutes will be sufficient. Keep your mind free for impressions just for ten minutes. Just ten minutes of communion and relaxation. Please make the attempt and do not postpone it. You think of me by fits and starts. Sometimes for long periods you do not let your mind do anything else. I can only tell you that I am very happy here. I shall be very happy to meet you when you come over here. Don't doubt me, but it is not right for you to think of passing over before the appointed time. So do not let your thoughts go in that direction. It is to prevent it that I want you regularly to bring me to your side at a stated time.'

'So you want me to think of you only at stated hours?'

'Yes, for the purpose of your complete communion with me or with anyone a degree of concentration is necessary and this can be done only with some order and plan. At other moments when you are despondent, woebegone and hopelessly in grief and think of me, I can hardly come to you, because the grief creates a barrier, and this should be avoided for both our sakes.'

'But look here,' I pleaded. 'How can I help having you as the permanent background to my thoughts? I can't help thinking of you . . .'

'Just as I am thinking of you, I know you will also be thinking of me. But I want this thought to be coupled with the desire to commune with me. It is this aspect that I want to impress upon you as necessary for psychic development and free communion between us.'

'So do you wish me to check thoughts of you at all other times?'

'No, no, no. At stated hours sit for psychic development, that is, to enable me to get into touch with you directly without the intervention of the medium; this I will make possible.'

'Should I sit down with pencil and paper?'

'It is a secondary matter, pencil, paper and the rest. The most important thing is to get the mind ready and receptive, the actual form will follow automatically. Prepare your mind for this adventure. You will then know and feel my real presence. You now keep looking round to get a glimpse of me; then by and by, you will feel that I'm by your side, and it will bring real peace to your heart. Relax, be passive and think of me, and be receptive. Just ten minutes. Try.'

'Tonight?'

'Yes, tonight.'

'It may be eleven before I'm ready.'

'The time is immaterial.'

I went home singing. I felt I had picked up the key to a new world. I had never known such joy before. I felt that my duty was now to conserve all the force of my mind for this communion.

At home, the child lay awake in bed. I went in to dine, and she came over and sat on my lap as I ate. I went to bed, stroked her forehead and she soon fell asleep. I put out the light, sat down and prayed: 'I am ready.'

I looked at the clock—ten to eleven. 'My wife,' I called. I had made it all too easy in my imagination. I thought I had only to say 'be passive' to make the mind passive, 'still' to be stilled, and I would see her standing radiantly—foolish expectation. I had to struggle with my mind. I desperately cried for her. My mind seethed with ideas—irrelevant things came rushing in, college, work, evening friends, my wife's voice—in the midst of it all I struggled to keep the mind receptive. It was a desperate fight. It nearly reduced me to tears. I tried to improve matters by picking up a pencil and poising it over the paper. Beyond the scratch that I inadvertently made, there was no result. I looked at the clock. Eleven-thirty nearly. I felt exhausted. I lay down to sleep, and slept badly.

The little peace and joy I had seemed to grasp suddenly once again receded, and I became hopelessly miserable. It was as if a person lost in an abyss found a ladder, and the ladder crumbled. When I went to my friend next Wednesday, I was all anxiety for further guidance. I hoped somehow that there was a magic password which would be imparted to me, whereby I would be able to walk hand in hand with my wife. But as soon as we were ready for it, she said: 'At the last sitting I gave you advice about psychic development. Since then, I have been observing the struggle going on within you and your utter helplessness. To receive impressions from our side, the mind must be calm and unruffled. In your case, I find that thoughts of me produce just the opposite effect. I feel that it is too early and that the wound is still very raw. I think therefore you ought to postpone your attempts for some time, until you are less agitated than you are now. As it is, it does not serve the purpose I thought it would. So please do not bother now. Am I clear?' This made me more desperate. Even the ladder that I saw was removed and I was forbidden to go near it. I could almost hear her voice as she said this, slightly quivering with excitement, and with a touch of reprimand. I was in despair for a moment—but only for a moment. I became indignant. She couldn't deny me my right to attempt. I said: 'I won't stop this attempt on any account. I feel quite confident I can go on.' This had the desired effect, and she replied, 'Oh, if you are feeling confident, it is another matter. But as I watch you, I find that your mind is very unprepared. This makes communication more difficult. So I suggest that you wait for some more time. Possibly there may be a change in your outlook. Then you will derive greater benefit. I'm not saying stop it at all costs. If you feel confident, go ahead. I am only indicating the circumstances that stand in the way.' I felt very happy. And a regret seized me, as it always did, that I had perhaps been too sharp in my expression. So I felt I ought to be more considerate, and asked: 'Oh, I'm glad, so may I continue my efforts, and will you do your best still?'

'Yes, continue then. If I can give you any further assistance, I will.'

I asked testingly: 'Just to know that you are aware of my efforts, can you tell me what you saw me do on these nights?'

'I am aware and I am present, but I cannot make myself known better because of the difficulty. I have seen you every night wanting contact with me and praying for it. You had a few sheets of paper and a green-handled pencil . . .'

I had over a dozen pencils in my drawer; I hadn't noticed which one I had picked up that day.

She continued: 'You put pencil to paper and hardly made a dot . . . And this after trying without paper and pencil, at first. I am keen on impressing on you the fact that it will be possible for you to appreciate my presence even more than my physical presence in course of time, if the development takes place properly, that is, the necessary mental atmosphere is made available for me.'

'Can you give me some details of where you saw me sit for communions?' I asked.

'I saw you sitting on your bed. You sat up with your eyes closed. You had just begun to concentrate when a carriage passed along the street, wheels rattling and the driver singing lustily—and you gnashed your teeth and said something very rough about him.'

'I am so happy you feel the attempts I made at communication.'

'I tell you I can feel your thoughts even when you are not exactly sitting for development. Even when you just think of me anywhere and everywhere, on the road, at home, or on the river-bank when a streak of moonlight lights the water surface, and you think of me, I feel it and know your thoughts. But development is necessary for the reverse process to take place, that is, for you to feel my thoughts.'

This restored my peace of mind. 'Calm, calm,' I repeated to myself like a mantra. I blamed myself for not being aware of so simple a remedy. I think I sang lightly as I returned home that night. 'Be calm, my dear fellow,' I said.

Suddenly there dawned on me the meaning of her statement: 'When you see the moonlight lighting up the water surface.' Weeks ago, in my period of desolation, as I sat on the sands of the Sarayu, a late moon rose in the east, and the flowing water shimmered with it. It only added to my desolation. Again, it reminded me of my wife. How often had she expressed a wish to walk along the river in moonlight, and for all the years of married life I had not been able to give her that fulfilment even once; some pointless thing postponed it every time; we never went out in moonlight at all. And this regret tormented me when I saw moonlight on water, that night . . .

At our next meeting she said: 'I still feel you have not done well. Why can't you postpone your attempt for a while?' I had been dreading this suggestion all along. Now it had come. I was not going to accept it. I said stubbornly: 'No, I feel I can still try. I find these very attempts very beneficial. I want to continue them. Will you help me as much as you can?'

'I'm very happy to hear it. Why don't you change the time from night to morning and see if it will improve matters? Not more than ten minutes. I think after a night's sleep, such sleep as you can get, the attempts in the morning will be more successful.'

'Early morning?' I asked apprehensively.

'No. After you get up and have your coffee, shut yourself in a room for ten minutes. At night your mind is not very receptive. All the day's affairs are there boiling up again and again. Sleep lulls your thoughts, and it may be you will succeed if you try then.' I shook my head. She said: 'Just try for ten days.' I was somehow very reluctant to try in daylight—there was all the hurry for school and college, the attention to the child, the shutting the door on her (she was sure to bang on it), the visitors or tradesmen who might call on me, and above all the daylight. The softness of night was essentially psychic, I felt. So I said: 'I don't usually feel very fresh in the mornings. I still think night is the best . . .'

'Well, get on with your attempts at night then,' she said. I was seized with a sudden fear. Suppose she said this out of despair, unable to coax me out of my obstinacy. So I asked with trepidation: 'Will you be present whatever the time?'

'I shall be present morning, noon or night. Don't worry. Just go on as usual, but with greater relaxation and ease. No harm in trying with paper and pencil too; when you feel an urge, please relax and let your hand move. If you keep a pencil, it helps concentration.'

'How will you make me feel your presence?'

'At first it will be a matter of belief—a belief in the possibility of my presence. Later on as you progress, you will know I'm there by your side. I have high hopes of making myself heard or seen, but certainly known; I shall be with you very soon.'

'I shall continue my attempts whatever happens,' I said gratefully.

'I'm trying to make matters easier and more rapid for your development. I know you sense my presence, but I feared that you might give up all attempts at communication if you did not get messages from me sufficiently early. I feared that you might then feel that your awareness of my presence was imaginary and give up the attempt for ever. That's why I wanted you to postpone rather than run the risk of losing faith . . .'

I was greatly moved at hearing this: 'It is enough that I feel you are there. Don't trouble yourself to give me any sort of proof. It is not necessary.'

For a fortnight I tried to follow her instructions rigidly. I relaxed with a vengeance. I kept my mind open. I posted a sentry at the threshold of my mind to stop and run away any intruder who might try to gain entrance. I rigorously educated my whole being, including the subconscious (where still perhaps lurked unsuspected raw grief), with the assurance that my wife was everywhere, happy and well, and I was to think of her only with the greatest joy in mind; no cause for any sort of grief. I lay down on my bed, and then pictured her as I had known her in her best days, and centred my mind on this image without the slightest wavering for ten minutes. I felt very satisfied with my effort till on a subsequent evening she said: 'I must tell you now that your sittings for development must be even more relaxed than they are at present. Why don't you allow your mind to move round about me? Now you just picture me in your mind and do not allow your thoughts to move an inch this side or that. This rigid exercise does not help our contact. By your intense and severe thought you make almost a stone image of me in your brain. Your thoughts must give me greater scope for movement within an orbit of feelings. Your mind may now be compared to the body of a yogi who sits motionless. This is not what you seek to achieve, do you? I want you to keep your mind at these times open for my impression. What happens now is that your mind is full of your thoughts of me, which are unrelated, and I find it difficult to move about in your head and heart.

'The only trouble now is that your mind is rigid. Till lately I had even greater difficulty because of your poignant sorrow. This barrier is now lifted more or less. What is still required is that you should be able to receive my thoughts. It can be done only if you do not make a stone image of me. I want you to behave just as you would if I were conversing with you. You would pay attention. Now it borders on worship. This rigidity must go and you will have better results. It takes time, but it is worth attempting.'

I had a visit from the Headmaster at an unusual hour one night. I was in bed. My child had just gone to sleep. And I was preparing to sit up and attempt my daily experiment. I was about to put out the light, when there was a call for me at the gate, 'Krishna, Krishna.' I didn't like to be disturbed. So I kept quiet for a moment hoping that the caller might go away and I regretted I had not put out the light a minute earlier. But the call was repeated. I had to get up and go to the gate. There I saw the Headmaster. 'Krishna,' he cried on seeing me, 'forgive my intrusion at this hour. May I come in and talk to you?'

'Yes, yes,' I said, opening the gate. We sat down on the veranda steps. A ray of light fell on him from our sleeping room, and I noticed that he looked very agitated. He sat without speaking for a few minutes. A donkey brayed in a neighbouring lane; wind rustled the avenue trees. I waited for him to open his mouth and tell me his business. I felt he might be wanting a loan of money; he must be in terrible straits.

'I want to ask you . . .' he began. It was at this point that the donkey brayed into the night. 'It is a good omen they say, the braying of a donkey. So my request is well-timed.'

'Go on,' I said, wondering how much he was going to want. 'Tell me what you want,' I said.

'I want you to take charge of my school, and see that it does not go to ruin,' he said. Worry seemed to have done its work on this poor man, I thought. 'All right,' I said, but added, 'but I have my college . . .'

'I know it,' he said. 'But do you think you are happy in your work there?' he asked. I did not reply. It needed no reply. 'But who cares for happiness in work? One works for the money . . .' said I in my sober cynicism.

'True, true,' he said. 'I cannot compel you. Please at least keep an eye on the school, and see that these children are not thrown into a hostile world . . .'

'All right, all right,' I said, not wishing to offend a man mentally unsound. The light from our bedroom illuminated a part of his face. I looked at it. He had the abstraction of a mystic rather than of a maniac. I could not contain myself any longer, and so I cried, 'Tell me, what is the matter?' He smiled and said: 'This is perhaps my last day. Tomorrow, I may be no more.' His voice fluttered. 'You may remember that I had an astrologer's report with me, and I have also mentioned that my wife would get a big surprise in life; this is it. I never wanted to speak to anyone about it. But I felt I owed it to the children, not to leave the school without any arrangement for it. I hesitated the whole day, and a dozen times came up to your gate and turned away . . .' I looked at him greatly puzzled: the man was talking as if he were moving to the next street. . . This was too disturbing—even for me who had been educated to accept and accommodate the idea of death. He spoke on quietly: 'My astrologer has written a month-to-month report, and my life has been going on in its details like a time-table. I see it so clearly that nothing ever worries me. I give things just their value—never unduly disturb my mind over affairs; which include also my wife, who, I find, conducts herself according to the time-table.' 'What is to happen to her?' I asked, almost involuntarily.

'God knows. I only hope she won't start a litigation against my brother, over their house and property.' I sat up, thinking it over . . . It seemed absurd to be talking thus. 'No, no, no,' I cried. 'It can't be.'

'It is,' he persisted.

'Astrologers are not allowed to mention these things . . .'

'Not my astrologer. He is not a professional predictor, but a hermit, who can see past, present and future as one, and give everything its true value. He doesn't want you to put your head under the sand, thinking that you are unseen. Man must essentially be a creature of strength and truth. You would love him if you met him, but I don't know where he is. He came one day for alms, took a fancy to me, and sat down and dictated my life to me after a glance at my palm, and took the road again in the evening. I have never seen him since. But the few hours he was with me he charged my mind with new visions, ideas and strength. My life underwent a revolution. It was after that I left my family and home and set up the school. They jeered at us and made fun of me, but I don't mind. My life has gone on precisely as he predicted.'

'You have a duty to your wife and children,' I persisted.

'Yes, but what can I do? I shall bequeath to them the school, but would she care for it? Not she.'

'What can she do with the school? Will it give her food and shelter?'

'It ought to mean more than that if she had trained herself to view things properly,' he replied. 'I could have done so much more, if she taken an interest. But she wouldn't even send the children. So independent a person as that, I believe, will get on whatever may happen.' I felt he could not be made to see my point, however much I might argue about it. 'Don't bother about it all,' he added. 'Leave us alone. Will you look after the school? See that it goes on at least till the present set of children leave there? Please promise.'

'I will do my best, but I have to mind my college,' I added again.

'I think my time is nearing. It is midnight, isn't it? I may not see the sunrise tomorrow.' I was greatly moved to hear him say it. I implored him: 'Don't believe all this, my friend. You will be back in the morning. Or will you sleep here in my house?' I suggested apprehensively. He shook his head: 'It's my last night. I should like to spend it with my wife and children.'

'Shall I see you home?' I asked, hoping he wouldn't agree. I had forgotten the child when I made the offer. He brushed it aside: 'No, don't trouble yourself. I can go home quite safely. I am quite sober and sound in mind, I assure you. If you have still any doubt about me, see this paper . . .' He took out of his pocket a folded piece of paper, and spread it out on his knee. He tilted it towards the light, 'Go on, read it. I took it out of the file. It is nearly the last sheet, you know,' he said with a forced laugh. 'Go on, read it aloud.' I read out with difficulty: 'This person's earthly duties over, he will pass over on this day, surrounded by his wife and children at his last moment . . .' I read it, and did not know what to say about it. What does one say on such occasions?

'You are looking quite well?' I said testingly.

'I'm in perfect condition,' he said. 'But what is there to prevent anyone dying in perfect health as well as in ill-health?' he said. This was the strangest man I had ever come across. I had never known this side of the man. I felt foolish and fatuous. I had never thought that he viewed death in this manner, even theoretically. On the one or two occasions he had condoled with me on the loss of my wife, he was casual and offhand; but I put it down to the delicacy which he might have felt. I never discussed with him my psychic efforts or experiences, thinking that it would not interest him; but now I felt like telling him about them and said: 'Do you know, I don't believe in death myself. My wife communicated with me so often, and has given me directions for self-development.' I went on and on. He listened in silence, his head looking large in a shadow on the ground in front of us. He answered: 'Don't mistake me. It is all a matter of personal faith and conviction. But I am not interested in the life after death. I have no opinion either way. There may be a continuation in other spheres, under other conditions, or there may not be. It is immaterial to me. The only reality I recognize is death. To me it is nothing more than a full-stop. I have trained myself to view it with calm. Beyond it . . .' he shook his head. 'In fact in my prediction, if you will turn over the page, he says something about my next birth too. I'm to be born in a Cochin village to Brahmin parents and so on . . . but I don't really care for that part . . .'

'When you trust so much in these predictions, you must trust in that too . . .'

'But my trust is only in regard to matters of this life, not an inch beyond . . . I've never looked at that page more than once. My knowledge of past, present and future strictly pertain to this life.

Beyond that I have nothing to say, because I believe I shall once again be resolved into the five elements of which I'm composed: and my intelligence and memory may not be more than what we see in air and water!'

I felt very unhappy to hear all this. I thought of my wife—all that I heard from her. Were they all self-deceptions? Was she nothing more than the mute elements, the funeral fire resolving her into vapour, unseen air, and dust? I felt sad and shaken. He said: 'This is my view. But don't let it disturb you . . .' My daughter stirred in her sleep and moaned. I started up. He rose, gripped my hand, and said: 'Good-bye. If we meet once, again tomorrow, don't laugh at me.' 'Oh, no,' I said. 'I shall celebrate it with a feast. I shall think you have a new life.'

I saw him off at the gate. He went away without turning his head.

I awoke earlier than usual. I was very anxious about my friend. My child was still asleep. I had a wash, drank my coffee, requested the old lady to mind the child, and went out.

At Anderson Lane my heart thumped with excitement. I gazed towards the Headmaster's house. It was still half dark. A few artisans were moving about, and a few more were sleeping in front of their houses. Even this street looked soft in the morning light.

In a dozen bounds I reached the Headmaster's house. The door was shut. I strained my ears to catch any sound of weeping inside. But I heard nothing except the clanging of vessels. The housewife was apparently up, and nothing untoward had happened. I took this as an encouraging sign and decided to turn back. But I changed my mind. I couldn't resist the desire to go in and see. Only the sight of him safe and talking to me would satisfy me. I knocked. His wife opened the door, and scowled on seeing me.

'What do you want?' she asked.

'Is the Headmaster in?'

'No.'

'Where is he?'

'He doesn't tell me,' she said. 'Does he keep all those courtesies? Not he. He went out after dinner, and has not been in since . . . Not for him such things as wife, children, home, and so on. These boys are fatherless . . .' she said bitterly. I was irritated to see her in this mood, so early in the morning. I felt an admiration for the man who had stood her company for so many years. She turned to go. I felt like wringing her neck—it seemed co offer an ideal grip with her hair knotted high up. 'Why do men marry such wives?' I reflected. 'A moment, lady,' I said. 'There is a very important thing I want to tell you. Was he not here last night?'

'No. I have told you that,' she replied.

'Perhaps you will never see him again. I hope it pleases you,' I said. She could not make out what I meant. She turned, threw at me a puzzled look, and asked, with her throat going dry: 'Why?'

'Do you care enough to know?' I asked. 'It was in your hands to have made his life happier, while he lived. But now he is gone, and I hope you have a free and happy life before you now . . .' She let out a shrill cry, 'What has happened? What has happened?' By this time her children, dishevelled and in rags as usual, more so because just out of bed, came up rubbing their eyes and stood beside their mother. She embraced them sentimentally and sobbed. 'Oh, these are orphans today, who will feed them? They are in the streets, from this moment.' She wrung her hands and cried, 'Tell me sir, tell me, what is happening?' I told her of the prediction and his visit. 'Ah, couldn't he have confided this in me, his wife?' She broke down utterly. She collapsed on the floor and her lamentation filled the whole street, and the whole street crowded into the house. I slipped out. I began to wonder what had happened to him. I walked back home, and then saw that my child was still sleeping. My purpose was to search for him by the river, and then tell the police. I stepped out of my house and was going down the road. As I passed the school I saw him standing at the school gate. 'Ghost, ghost,' I muttered to myself. 'I never heard of a ghost being seen by morning light . . .' He grinned, came towards me, and shook my hands. 'I'm not my ghost, be assured,' he said. An unusual cheerfulness had seized him. He looked rejuvenated. 'Don't look so full of questions. I can't answer them any more than you can. It simply didn't happen, that is all . . . I don't know why that sadhu thought fit to put my last date thus. One mistake in an otherwise perfect prediction. The first error in it, and the most agreeable . . .'

'Didn't I say that it might be wrong . . .' I gripped his hand and jumped about in glee. 'I am so happy . . .'

'So am I,' he said. 'You have no idea how it has been weighing me down all these years, in spite of what I might have felt and said; it was like having cancer and knowing fully when you would be finished. It was a terrible agony stretching over years. I rejoice it is over. I have no more pages to watch in my notebook. I can live free and happy.'

'But there is that thing about your next birth . . .'

'Rubbish, I don't care. This life is good enough for me . . .'

'You shouldn't have put such faith in that thing . . . They are after all . . .'

'But see here, my friend. For all these years it has been so accurate that I had no reason to doubt its soundness; but this is the first mistake, and the last you know, for the reading stops with this, except for the next birth. I don't know what made that great hermit say this. It might be after all a test,' he said. He sighed: 'I don't know where he is. No chance of ever clearing this point with his help . . .' He looked radiant.

'Didn't you go home last night?' I asked.

'No. I went up to my door, and turned back. If I had to die, I'd prefer to wait for it at the school, rather than at home.'

'But you said you wished to be with your wife and children.'

'Yes. But I felt they did not deserve it on second thoughts.'

'Go home, go home,' I said. 'The whole street is in your house. Poor lady! Her lamentations can be heard over the whole town!'

'Oh, is that so!' he cried in joy. 'What a happy piece of information! I don't care. Let her cry till she brings down the sky. I am going to treat myself as dead and my life as a new birth. You will see—I don't know if that hermit might not have meant my death, after all, in that sense . . .' I implored him to go and relieve his wife and end the confusion in his street.

'Not I,' he said. 'I'm dead, I wish I could change my face somehow, so that I should not be recognized.'

'Even by your schoolchildren?' I asked.

'Oh, no', he said. I tried to hustle him into returning home. But he stubbornly refused. 'I have ceased to be my old self, and so don't belong to that home in Anderson Lane . . . It is all over. This school is my house hereafter. I will settle here . . .'

'But what about them? . . .'

'They can come and see me here if they like, that is all. I give them a monthly allowance for their upkeep. That is all I am prepared to do, but not behave as a father and a husband hereafter. I didn't sleep a wink the whole night. It is a novel feeling sitting up and waiting for death . . . I was wondering how it'd take me. I felt so fit and well. When I felt a little drowsy with sleep, I thought the end had come!'

After all I persuaded him to pay a visit (at least the last one) to his house. He agreed, adding: 'After all it is not given to every man to watch his own death scene . . .' We walked there together. People in the street looked at him in wonder and cried: 'Here he is.' 'Yes,' he said. 'What of it?' Soon the news spread, and a great crowd poured out of his house and surged towards us. The whole of Anderson Lane was there—very few tinsmiths were at their foundry, very few blacksmiths and tailors at their work. People surrounded him and fired questions at him. But he refused to answer anyone. 'I cannot tell you why I am alive,' he said. 'There is no explanation for it, as there is no explanation for death.' The crowd gaped at him and pressed us on all sides. 'I never imagined that I had such a large public!' he said. 'I thought I was fairly obscure!'

His wife, whom news of his arrival reached, picked herself up, her hair all over her face, swollen and tear-drenched. She looked at him, and let out a cry of relief: 'Oh, my lord, you are here! What demon thought fit to tell me . . .?' She fell down and clung to his feet. His children came up and, with cries of rapture, hung on to his arms. He tried to shake himself free, but found it difficult. The crowd looked at him expectantly. He faced them and said: 'Why don't you all go away now?' They murmured something and waited for an explanation. He looked at them helplessly, with his family clinging to his feet. The crowd looked at him. He put his hand into his pocket, and took out the slip of paper, jerked it open and held it to the crowd. 'Who can read this?' A man came forward, received the slip and read it. 'Read it aloud,' the Headmaster commanded; at which he read out the prophesy to the gathering, and the Headmaster added, 'This is the prediction and it has not proved false. I tell you, friends, no more of this wife and family for me. You may treat me as dead or as one who has taken *Sanyasa Ashrama.*'

His wife protested and cried hoarsely. But he was adamant. He announced his decision grandly. 'She will get her money for her monthly expenses, but that is all. They will never see me here again . . .' She clung to him and pleaded: 'Whatever wrong I have committed forgive me. I will be careful hereafter . . .' He shook her off without a word. The children came after him. 'You may all come and see me in school later. But remember you have no father any more . . .' He pushed his way through the crowd, and walked away.

I followed him sheepishly. The whole business was too confusing. I didn't know what to make of it. His wife ran after us and appealed to me. I looked at her helplessly. I felt a tremendous pity for this creature now. I said: 'Headmaster, just think . . .'

'Krishna, leave me alone,' he said. 'I have a far greater work to do, and I'm going to do it. I feel such a freedom now . . .' He set his face and walked off resolutely. The crowd followed us for a while, and then dissipated. His wife and children followed. 'Go back,' he said, 'create a scene if you like, it is none of my business to stop you, but don't put me in that scene, that is all, do you understand?'

Months rolled on. Life falls into ruts of routine, one day following another, expended in set activities: child, school, college, boys, walks, and self-development. This last was the most enchanting item of my life's programme. It was a perpetual excitement, ever promising some new riches in the realm of experience and understanding. I sat up at nights faithfully following the instructions she had given, keeping my mind open, and I was beginning to be aware of a slight improvement in my sensibilities. There was a real cheerfulness growing within me, memory hurt less, and I was more and more aware of vague perceptions, like a three-quarter deaf man catching the rustle of a dress of someone he loves . . . That this was not a vain presumption on my part was borne out at a sitting we had about this time. Our regular Wednesday meetings were gradually given up, and we met now at unspecified intervals, once in six or seven weeks or so. Nor did I feel these days the hopeless longing for a regular sitting. My nightly contacts gave me peace. 'At first it will be a matter of nightly belief,' I remember her saying. I clung to it fast; 'Belief, belief.' Above reason, scepticism, and even immediate failures, I clung to it. 'I do meet her when I sit down, and she is with me when I sit with my mind passive, calling her,' I repeated to myself night and day, and it wrought a curious success. Any other thought was impossible.

After a long time my friend gave me a sitting one dusk beside the lotus pond. The hour was as beautiful as ever. She started by saying: 'Have you observed one effect of your development? I can say now that you are developing quite satisfactorily. Think of about four days ago—the small hours of the night. I tried to appear and make my presence felt by you. I purposely wore the garb which you called on a former occasion "gorgeous"—the blue, shimmering with light interwoven. I appeared, and I tried to make my presence felt. We went out together into the garden. We walked for a while, indeed for a considerable time, and then the experience ended. You returned to bed, and went to sleep again . . . You turned over and resumed your sleep, thinking that you had had a slight disturbance. If there is any chance that you remember this experience, let me assure you that it was I myself who was there with you and if you remember it, it is a sign that you are developing quite well . . .'

It required no great effort to recollect this. I was overcome with great joy. I seized my friend's hand and cried: 'It is true, absolutely true. I thought it was a private dream. It wasn't. How little do we know what a dream is, how little do we understand! Yes, friend, every word of it is true. I don't remember it clearly, but I dreamt of her as standing before me with some gorgeous dress on. I greeted her, and I held her hand. We went out into the garden. That is all the dream I remember. It was not a shadow cast and created by a troubled mind, but the substance . . . It was she, it was herself,' I cried.

'Ask her,' I said. 'After the dream we parted. How long did she stay with me? How often does she meet me?' It was a series of incoherent questions. I myself had no clear notion what I wanted to ask or how to ask it. I only felt the urge to ask questions . . . She evidently understood whatever it was that was in my mind, and replied: 'I shall try to answer these questions of yours, but I have to do it unsatisfactorily, because of their nature. You have been in this garden house today for over two hours. Can you say you have been in the company of your friend just once, twice or thrice? The moment you call someone who is in the next room, he answers you and comes to your side if need be. I am present at your side when you sit for development and communion. At other times it is as if I were in the next room, aware of the fact of your presence, easily accessible and ready to come at your slightest behest. You may even think of the walls separating us as walls of glass.'

It was a delightful surprise for me one day, returning home from college, to receive a card from my mother, saying she was coming by the eleven o'clock bus on the following morning. I told the child immediately. But she asked: 'Who is coming with her? Is she bringing dolls?'

'Oh, yes, yes,' I said. I cancelled the walk that evening. The house needed a lot of tidying up, otherwise mother would spend her entire stay doing it. I took off my shirt, tucked up my *dhoti*, and wrapped a towel round my head, as a preparation. In the kitchen I told the old lady, 'Please polish all the vessels. My mother will be here tomorrow. You know how she views these things!' The old lady pulled down all the vessels, and the swish of her broom, sweeping the store, resounded through the house. I took a duster and a long-handled broom, and cleaned up the cornices and dusted everything, dragged the trunks about, pulled down all the books, sneezed and caught a cold which lasted a day or two. The child followed me about. She had caught the fever of activity and followed me about whining and imploring for work. I said: 'Your toy box, you have stuffed it in such a way that we cannot close it. It looks ugly in the hall with its lid thrown back agape; do something about it. Throw away all the unimportant things, and clean and arrange the things in the box. What will your grandmother say if she sees your box?'

Leela at first grumbled and demanded to be alloted some worthwhile work. But I persuaded her by dinning into her over and over again: 'What will your grandmother say if she sees your box!' Finally she realized the seriousness of the position and said: 'Yes.' She went over to her box, and as usual held it by the handle on one side and tipped the entire contents on the floor. They came down with a terrific clatter and crash—a dozen cardboard boxes, her slate, books, wooden toys and engines and motors and dolls, all crashed down in a heap on the floor. She squatted in their midst and said, 'Shall I throw away the things I don't want?'

'Yes.' She started this operation. She picked up and looked at each, and said: 'This thing is not wanted, and flung it off to another corner of the hall. This mood had caught her and cardboard boxes and all kinds of things which she cherished seemed to vex her suddenly by their very presence. In a short time in another corner of the hall were heaped the bulk of her possessions. Except her schoolbooks and five wooden vessels, and a large doll, all the other things were there. I had to go on with my work in another part of the house. But when I saw what she had done, I protested, 'I tidied up this hall.' 'I will throw them in the street now,' she explained. She came over, picked up a handful, looked wistfully at the heap and appealed: 'Father, I must put them all back in the box.'

'Why?'

'They are all important . . .' she said very earnestly, looking at me fixedly. And forthwith all the toys returned to the box in the same manner as they came out—in a clattering rush.

I applied for leave in order to meet my mother. I waited at the bus stand, beyond the market-square. The glare was blinding; the dust unbearable. The bus from Trichinopoly due to arrive at eleven was not showing any signs even half an hour later. I was growing impatient. The bus service people had made no provision for waiting. There was a miserable tamarind tree with sparse leaves, under which were gathered three women waiting to catch the bus, a coolie waiting for fares, an ass in the neighbourhood who could not stand the heat of the day—and a *jutka* with horse strapped to it; the *jutka* man had just brought it in so that there should be a patch of shade on the horse's snout; he seemed to feel satisfied that he had saved the horse from the heat of the sun. The *jutka* man was also waiting for the bus to arrive and provide him a fare. He waited for the bus, felt drowsy, curled up in his seat and was soon asleep. The donkey moved nearer and put his mouth into the bunch of grass thrown down on the ground for the horse to munch while the master slept. The donkey pulled out a mouthful, at which the horse stamped and neighed. The cart driver woke up and flourished his whip at the donkey. And we enjoyed the whole show, although the sun baked us.

After all the bus arrived at twelve precisely. Parched and dusty, my mother wriggled herself out from among her fellow passengers. 'How is the child?' she asked getting down. It was her very first question. We put her luggage into the *jutka*, haggled with the driver, and started home. Over the rattling of the wheels she spoke—complaining about my correspondence, enquiring about the child, if the old cook was well, and how I was managing to look after the child. I was tremendously pleased: as I looked at her, warm and throbbing with life and enquiries, it seemed to restore for a moment one's sense of security, the solid factors of life, and its warmth and interests.

My child as usual was waiting at the door, and hardly had the old lady got down from the carriage when she ran to her and was, in a moment, in her arms. I could hardly comprehend—there were so many excited changes between the grandmother and daughter. 'Granny, open your trunk, open your trunk, what have you brought for me? . . .' she went on pestering even before the trunk and bed were brought in. They went in. I paid off the carriage, received the change, and followed. By that time I found there was a great argument going on between them—the little one standing on my mother's ancient trunk, and insisting upon having it opened immediately. My mother, mildly protesting, requesting to be allowed to rest for a few minutes: 'Oh, child, there're no shops in our little place. What should I bring you?' There were tears in her eyes. She cast a slight look at the room on our right in the hall, my wife's room, now empty, and touched away the tears with the tip of her fingers.

My daughter stamped on the steel trunk, and made such a row that I felt it was time for me to interfere: 'Hush, you must learn. . .' I began. But my mother stopped: 'Don't be harsh; poor child, jump down. I'll open the trunk for you.' She muttered as she fumbled with the key and the lock: 'You used to be exactly the same: you'd cling to your father, and wouldn't let him remove even his sandals before giving you your presents.' She opened the trunk. My daughter sat on her lap and gazed into the trunk expectantly. My mother pulled out a few sarees, a couple of towels, jackets, a horn comb, and lastly a little casket, out of which she produced a gold chain. 'I had this made for the child at the town shop when your father went there last time. He is the only goldsmith we have near at hand, though fifteen miles away . . .' She slipped the chain over the child's head. 'Three sovereigns weight. How do you like it?' Leela looked down at her chest with great satisfaction. The gold chain glistened, but I was absorbed elsewhere. I was staring at the casket from which mother had taken out the chain. 'Mother, give it here!' I cried.

I examined it, measured it with my finger, held it off and scrutinized it—an ivory-worked sandalwood casket. 'Wait a minute!' I said and ran into my room. I pulled out the table-drawer, turned over the pages containing my wife's messages. She had written: 'It is not a very big box—about eight or ten inches long, three inches high, and about four inches wide . . . the lid of the box is not flat but slightly elevated . . . It was given to me by my mother-in-law. Box of ivory and sandalwood . . .' I took out a little scale and measured the box. The measurements she had given were slightly more or less by about half an inch all round. I put away the scale and read over the message again. I couldn't yet decide whether her reference was to this casket or some other. And presently I came upon a sentence, which had nearly escaped me all these days. 'The casket is mounted on short ivory legs, resembling tiger-paws.' I lifted the casket and examined its legs. The tiger-paws were there. I grew red with excitement. I clutched the pages and was about to run out to read them to my mother. But I checked myself. I had never spoken of these to anyone so far. She might not see it as I did, she might doubt, cross-examine, feel on the whole disturbed. It meant a new habit of thinking in regard to death, all too difficult at her age, or she might think I was mad. In any case this information was too precious to part with, to make public even to a mother. I put the papers into the drawer, went back, and sat down beside my mother. I said, 'I like this box, Mother, what do you keep in it?' 'All your,' she lowered her voice and muttered in my ear, so that the child should not hear, 'wife's jewels. I got this from my sister years ago. Susila used to be fond of it and had once or twice even made bold to ask for it. But somehow I didn't give it to her . . . Now I keep her jewels in it. I'll give it to the child . . .'

'Can I keep it with me?' I asked.

'Why do you want it? It's a jewel box . . .'

'I like it, Mother. I'll keep some of the child's knick-knacks in it,' I said. She gave it to me.

This discovery made me write to my father-in-law next day for the bundle of fourteen letters, which Susila had often mentioned. Four days later I received a reply. 'I have searched every nook and corner in the house and every box, but not a single letter is to be found. Perhaps they were in that lot which I saw her and her brother destroying in the fire one day when she was here last. I hope you will forgive this disappointment and not feel dejected.' In his last paragraph he wrote: 'I don't know if you are already aware of it. I have written to your father about it. I intend to make an endowment for my dear grandchild Leela to benefit her when she comes of a marriageable age.'

I went to my mother. She was sitting in the hall, combing the child's hair. She did everything with her own hands nowadays, often complaining that my neglect had made the child's tresses shorter.

'I have a letter from my father-in-law,' I began.

'Oh, has he written to you about this matter?' she said slyly pointing at the child.

'Yes—he has.'

'He wrote to your father,' she said. 'He proposes to set apart,' she indicated with her fingers six, 'for this person, to be given to her on the day of her marriage.'

'Whose marriage, Mother?' the child asked.

'Somebody's marriage, child, don't listen to our talk,' she said, and continued. 'And your father also proposes to set apart a similar sum for the same purposes.'

'Oh,' I said, not knowing what to say. 'She is very lucky!'

My mother smiled cynically, 'Of course you must admire her luck.' She added, with a sigh, 'What are these? Can these things ever compensate for the absence of that one person?'

'Who is to be married, Mother?' the child asked again.

'A girl in our place,' said her grandmother.

'How big is she?' asked the child. For some unknown reason she seemed to be concerned with the bulk of this bride. My mother said: 'Even if she has proved unlucky in other matters, let her at least have a well-provided future.'

My mother stayed with us for four weeks. My father's condition had improved and she could stay with us—happy days; the child bloomed with a new life, under her handling. She ceased to approach me for company or help. She stuck to her grandmother morning to night and slept on her bed at night. She bloomed in this warmth. Children need above all else the warmth of a mother's touch. Watching her now I realized with a pang that the very best I could provide was still hopelessly inadequate. And if the child had looked happy under my handling it was more out of tolerance than anything else.

On the eve of her departure Mother was packing up. The child stood beside her watching and asked: 'Mother, are you going?'

'Yes, dear, yes.'

'Don't go,' she said and looked so miserable that Mother said, 'Will you come with me?' Leela jumped at this suggestion. She cried: 'Give me a box, Father, I want to put my things into it.' I said soothingly: 'There is time, there is time.' At which she became uncontrollable. My mother said: 'Seriously, why don't you let me take her with me?' I said: 'She will not go. She will want me too . . .' Granny said: 'Your father will not come with us.'

'Oh!' said the child, 'Why not?'

'He has his school to attend . . .'

'But I have also my school,' Leela replied irrelevantly.

'So, you must stay and let Grandmother go,' I said.

'Why will she not stay here?' the child asked. I saw that she had made up her mind to go with her grandmother. She was thrilled to hear that there were other children in the house. My sister's two children and a few others, numbering in all seven. Leela could not understand what it meant. How could there be children at home? Children were to be seen only in schools. So she asked: 'Is it a school?'

Next afternoon she was ready to start with her grandmother. I felt acute anxiety about sending her by bus. I had never been separated from her; the thought appalled me. But as I saw her bubbling over with enthusiasm I told myself, 'Don't be selfish. She must have her own life.' Her trunk of toys and her bed of clothes were there, perched upon the bus next afternoon. I had been dinning into my mother's ears instructions regarding the child. Even as the conductor blew his whistle I shouted instructions. 'Don't allow her to lean out. See that she doesn't eat too many sweets. She gets a racking cough at nights. Oil and bath every Friday, but the water must not be too hot . . . She must be immediately wrapped up . . . Milk, only half a tumbler . . .' My mother merely smiled.

The child said: 'Father, I will write you a letter.'

The bus groaned and moved, and was soon lost in a screen of dust of its own kicking.

A few weeks later a letter arrived from my father, enclosing a scrap of paper with a scrawl on it. My father wrote: 'The enclosed letter is from your Leela I just mentioned today that I was going to write to you, and at once she declared she had much to write to you too. I gave her my pencil and the paper, and she has written this letter.' I looked at a small slip of paper: the familiar memo pad of my father's neatly torn in half. I saw huge scrawls looking like trees or clouds and a few letters of the alphabet and at the bottom the huge word: LEELA. It was folded and on the flap was written 'To my beloved father', which was in my father's handwriting, though he tried to disguise it by writing rounded capital letters. Moreover there was his favourite ink. I looked at this communication from my daughter and felt very happy. I folded it and put it in my purse as if it were a rare document. My father's letter explained: 'You may want to know what she has written. Here is the paraphrase. She is always surrounded by a dozen children, always playing, building a castle on the *pyol* on which her grandfather is resting. He is spending all his time watching her and what a great joy it is. It has made him forget his illness, watching her. In the evening she goes out with her granny to the tank or the garden. She is in splendid health, eating and digesting everything that her granny gives her. A teacher comes to teach her in the afternoon. She sleeps beside her granny. I asked her if she wants her father. 'Yes,' she says, 'let him come here,' which is a very profound suggestion. I would ask you to come and spend your weekend holidays with her. After all she is only four hours off from your place. So I hope you will not allow any feeling of loneliness to oppress you . . .'

I boarded the bus for the village next weekend.

I returned from the village. The house seemed unbearably dull. But I bore it. 'There is no escape from loneliness and separation . . .' I told myself often. 'Wife, child, brothers, parents, friends . . . We come together only to go apart again. It is one continuous movement. They move away from us as we move away from them. The law of life can't be avoided. The law comes into operation the moment we detach ourselves from our mother's wornb. All struggle and misery in life is due to our attempt to arrest this law or get away from it or in allowing ourselves to be hurt by it. The fact must be recognized. A profound unmitigated loneliness is the only truth of life. All else is false. My mother got away from her parents, my sisters from our house, I and my brother away from each other, my wife was torn away from me, my daughter is going away with my mother, my father has gone away from his father, my earliest friends—where are they? They scatter apart like the droplets of a water-spray. The law of life. No sense in battling against it . . .' Thus I reconciled myself to this separation with less struggle than before. I read a lot, I wrote a lot, I reflected as much as I could. I saw pictures, went out for walks, and frequently met my friend the Headmaster. I spent a great deal of my time watching the children at play or hearing him narrate his stories for the children as they sat under the mango tree in the school compound. When I sat there at the threshold of his hut and watched the children, all sense of loneliness ceased to oppress, and I felt a deep joy and contentment stirring within me. I felt there was nothing more for me to demand of life. The Headmaster's presence was always most soothing. He was a very happy man nowadays. His school had over two hundred pupils studying in it and he was able to spend as much as he wanted in staffing and equipping the school.

His wife and children visited him often, at least thrice in a day. He treated them kindly, although he still refused to visit them at home, and strictly forbade them to call him father or husband. His wife, a greatly chastened person now, often implored him to let her bring him his food. He firmly declined the offer, declaring: 'No, it is there that all the trouble starts. The kitchen is the deadliest arsenal a woman possesses.'

8

MY MIND WAS made up. I was in search of a harmonious existence and everything that disturbed that harmony was to be rigorously excluded, even my college work. One whole night I sat up in the loneliness of my house thinking it over, and before the night was out my mind was made up. I could not go on with that work; nor did I need the one hundred rupees they gave me. At first I had thought of sending in my resignation by letter to Brown, and making an end of it. I would avoid all the personal contacts, persuasions, and all the possible sentimentalities inevitable in the act of snapping familiar roots. I would send in a letter which would be a classic in its own way, and which would singe the fingers of whoever touched it. In it I was going to attack a whole century of false education. I was going to explain why I could no longer stuff Shakespeare and Elizabethan metre and Romantic poetry for the hundredth time into young minds and feed them on the dead mutton of literary analysis and theories and histories, while what they needed were lessons in the fullest use of the mind. This education had reduced us to a nation of morons; we were strangers to our own culture and camp followers of another culture, feeding on leavings and garbage.

After coffee I sat down at my table with several sheets of large paper before me. I began, 'Dear Mr Brown: This is my letter of resignation. You will doubtless want to know the reasons. Here they are . . .' I didn't like this. It was too breezy. I scored it out and began again. I filled three sheets, and reading it over, felt ashamed of myself. It was coo theatrical and pompous for my taste. I was entangled too much in theories and platitudes and holding forth to all whom it might concern. It was like a rabid attack on all English writers, which was hardly my purpose. 'What fool could be insensible to Shakespeare's sonnets or the "Ode to the West Wind" or "A thing of beauty is a joy forever"?' I reflected. 'But what about examinations and critical notes? Didn't these largely take the place of literature? What about our own roots?' I thought over it deeply and felt very puzzled. I added: 'I am up against the system, the whole method and approach of a system of education which makes us morons, cultural morons, but efficient clerks for all your business and administrative offices. You must not think that I am opposed to my particular studies of authors . . .' The repetition of ideas uttered a hundred times before. It looked like a rehash of an article entitled 'Problems of Higher Education', which appeared again and again in a weekend educational supplement—the yarn some 'educationist' was spinning out for ten rupees a column.

'This is not what I want to say,' I muttered to myself and tore up the letter and stuffed it into the waste paper basket. 'There is something far deeper that I wish to say.'

I took out a small sheet of paper and wrote: 'Dear Sir, I beg to tender my resignation for personal reasons. I request you to relieve me immediately . . .' I put it in an envelope.

I walked into Brown's room that afternoon with this envelope in my hand. He was in a leisurely mood sitting back in his swivel chair, reading a book. I placed the envelope before him.

'What is this? Applying for leave?' he said, a smile spreading on his aged handsome face. 'Be seated . . .' He read the letter. His face turned slightly red. He looked at me and said: 'What is the matter?' He lit a cigarette, blew out a ring of smoke and waited for my answer, looking at me with his greenish eyes. I merely replied: 'I can't go on with this work any longer, sir . . .'

'Any special reason?' I remained silent. I didn't know what to say. I replied: 'I am taking up work in a children's school.' 'Oh!' he said. 'But I didn't know you had primary school training . . .' he replied. I looked at him in despair; his western mind, classifying, labelling, departmentalizing . . . I merely replied: 'I am beginning a new experiment in education, with another friend.' 'Oh, that is interesting,' he replied. 'But look here, must you resign? Couldn't you keep it on as an extra interest . . . We do want a lot of experimenting in education, but you could always . . .' He went on suggesting it as a hobby. I replied: 'Sir, what I am doing in the college hardly seems to me work. I mug up and repeat and they mug up and repeat in examinations . . . This hardly seems to me work, Mr Brown. It is a fraud I am practising for a consideration of a hundred rupees a month . . . It doesn't please my innermost self . . .' Thus I rambled on.

'I do not know,' he said, scratching his head, 'It seems to me unfortunate. However, I wouldn't make up my mind in a hurry if I were you . . .'

'I have thought it over deeply, sir.' I replied. 'My mind is made up.'

He asked: 'What does it mean to you financially?'

'About twenty-five rupees a month . . .' I replied.

'That means a cutting down . . .'

'That is so. I have no use for money. I have no family. My child is being looked after by others and they have provided for her future too. I have a few savings. I have no use for a hundred rupees a month . . .' Brown looked quite baffled. I added: 'Of all persons on earth, I can afford to do what seems to me work, something which satisfies my innermost aspiration. I will write poetry and live and work with children and watch their minds unfold . . .'

'Quite,' he replied. 'A man like you ought to derive equal delight in teaching literature. You have done admirably as a teacher of literature . . .'

I shook my head, 'I don't feel I have done anything of the kind . . .'

'Do you mean to say that all those poets and dramatists have meant nothing to you?'

I was in danger of repeating the letter I had torn up. 'It is not that. I revere them. And I hope to give them to these children for their delight and enlightenment, but in a different measure and in a different manner.' I rambled on thus. I could not speak clearly. Brown bore with me patiently. Our interview lasted an hour. At the end of it he said: 'Take another week, if you like, to consider. I do wish you wouldn't leave us.' He held out his hand. I gripped his large warm palm, and walked out of the room.

They arranged a grand send-off for me. The function was timed to begin at six. I arrived five minutes earlier and was at once seized on by Sastri and Rangappa, the moving spirits of the occasion. They waited at the porch and the moment they sighted me, they dashed forward, and gripped my hand and dragged me on to the quadrangle, where they had made spectacular arrangements. The hotel man had risen to the occasion; he had tied up coloured buntings and streamers, spread his embroidered tablecloth on a dozen tables, and placed his usual gold mohur bunches in nickel vases. Porcelain cups and plates clanked somewhere. White-shirted serving boys stood respectfully on the edge of the scene. They looked at me with respectful interest. In fact everyone looked on me as a sort of awe-inspiring personality. What was there in this to make a sudden hero of me? It was very embarrasing. On the air was borne a gentle suggestion of jasmine and rose. I knew a garland was waiting for me somewhere.

I was pressed into a high-backed chair. Next to mine was another chair for Brown. On my left sat Gajapathy. All around were gathered a miscellaneous crowd of teachers and boys. Everybody kept staring at me. I felt very unhappy. I had never felt more self-conscious in all my life. Gajapathy was highly nervous and excited, and wriggled in his chair. He kept muttering, 'Why is not Brown here yet?' And constantly looked at his watch.

There was the sound of a car stopping outside. 'The Principal,' everyone muttered. The creaking of fast footsteps and Brown arrived in an evening suit. 'Even he is dressed for the occasion,' I said to myself. 'Why, why all this ceremony?' Gajapathy shot up in his seat. Sastri and Rangappa went forward to receive him. Now we were all ready. Brown bent over to me and whispered: 'I was afraid the weather wouldn't let us use the quadrangle today.' I looked at the sky and mumbled something about the weather. Gajapathy, uninvited, joined us in this conversation. 'Rain is very unusual at this season, but strangely enough we have had it for the past two days. But today our luck is good . . .'

'Yes,' Brown echoed, 'rather unusual . . .' Perspiring and puffing, Rangappa moved about, and passed a signal on to the servers. There were nearly ten courses. Brown lightly touched each one of them; withdrew with quick caution from items which were over-spiced (experience born of thirty years' stay in India), put small bits of sweets into his mouth and sent them on without moving his lips. Gajapathy sat back with his fingers locked into each other, sadly looking at the plates. The other guests were talking among themselves; a merry hum pervaded the place. I asked

Gajapathy: 'Why?' He shook his head sadly: 'I am a sick man, can't afford these luxuries . . .' Brown looked at him without comment. He wanted to change the subject from personal ailments. He held up between his thumb and forefinger a gold coloured sweet and said: 'This is also a variant of *jalebi*, isn't it?'

'I suppose so, sir,' replied Gajapathy. 'I think it is the stuff made of American flour, while the real *jalebi* . . .'

'Ah, I'm right. I know my *jalebi* when I see it.' A smile spread round his eyes. We laughed. Rangappa, who had been observing us from his chair far off, looked at us enquiringly, and also smiled out of politeness . . .

When coffee was served, Brown clutched his cup and stood up. A silence fell on the gathering. 'To the health of our guest of this evening,' he said in his deep sonorous voice. 'I don't know if it would be right to toast with coffee but we won't bother about these proprieties now . . .' On behalf of the assembly he wished me all prosperity and happiness. He continued, 'I have known him, I have lost count now for how many years. I remember the day he came to my room with an application for a seat in English Honours. I've seen him grow under my eyes; he has shown himself an able teacher. The boys have loved him. And I'm sure they have had reason to dread him very much as an examiner.' Some boys looked at me with a grin. 'Everywhere, under every condition, he has proved himself to be an uncompromising idealist. His constant anxiety has been to find the world good enough for his own principles of life and letters. Few men would have the courage to throw up a lucrative income and adopt one very much lower. But he has done it. Success must be measured by its profitlessness, said a French philosopher. Our college can look upon this idealist with justifiable pride. And . . .' looking at me he said: 'when your institution has developed and made a mark in the world, I do hope you will allow us a small share of the gratification that you yourself may feel . . . Gentlemen, I'm sure you will all join me in wishing our friend all success.' He raised his cup.

I felt too disturbed to look up. My hands trembled. I sat looking down. Brown sat down. I was too moved. 'Many thanks,' I murmured. Three more speeches followed: one by Rangappa who traced our friendship to the hostel days, one by Sastri and one by an Honours boy. 'Our country needs more men like our beloved teacher who is going out today,' he said in his high-pitched tender voice. 'The national regeneration is in his hands . . .' Goodwill and adulation enveloped me like a thick mist. In the end I got up and said: 'Gentlemen, permit me to thank you all for your kind words. Let me assure you I'm retiring not with a feeling of sacrifice for a national cause, but with a very selfish purpose. I'm seeking a great inner peace. I find I can't attain it unless I withdraw from the adult world and adult work into the world of children. And there, let me assure you, is a vast store-house of peace and harmony. I have not had in mind anything more than that, and I hope you will correct your estimates accordingly. I am deeply grateful to you and to our chief for your great kindness . . .' I sat down because I found my voice quivering.

Rangappa brought a heavy rose and jasmine garland and slipped it over my neck. He brought another and put it on the Principal. Applause. 'Three cheers for our guest of the evening,' somebody screamed. 'Hip! Hip . . .' burst like an explosion. And then 'Three cheers for our Principal . . .' On this thunderous note our evening concluded.

I was walking down our lone street late at night, enveloped in the fragrance of the jasmine and rose garland slung on my arm. 'For whom am I carrying this jasmine home?' I asked myself. Susila would treasure a garland for two whole days, cutting up and sticking masses of it in her hair morning and evening. 'Carrying a garland to a lonely house—a dreadful job,' I told myself.

I fumbled with the key in the dark, opened the door and switched on the light. I hung up the garland on a nail and kicked up the roll of bedding. The fragrance permeated the whole house. I sprinkled a little water on the flowers to keep them fresh, put out the light and lay down to sleep.

The garland hung by the nail right over my head. The few drops of water which I sprinkled on the flowers seemed to have quickened in them a new life. Their essences came forth into the dark night as I lay in bed, bringing a new vigour with them. The atmosphere became surcharged with strange spiritual forces. Their delicate aroma filled every particle of the air, and as I let my mind float in the ecstasy, gradually perceptions and senses deepened. Oblivion crept over me like a cloud. The past, present and the future welded into one.

I had been thinking of the day's activities and meetings and associations. But they seemed to have no place now. I checked my mind. Bits of memory came floating—a gesture of Brown's, the toy house in the dentist's front room, Rangappa with a garland, and the ring of many speeches and voice—all this was gently overwhelmed and swept aside, till one's mind became clean and bare and a mere chamber of fragrance. It was a superb, noble intoxication. And I had no choice but to let my mind and memories drown in it. I softly called 'Susila! Susila, my wife . . .' with all my being. It sounded as if it were a hypnotic melody. 'My wife . . . my wife, my wife . . .' My mind trembled with this rhythm, I forgot myself and my own existence. I fell into a drowse, whispering, 'My wife, wife.' How long? How could I say? When I opened my eyes again she was sitting on my bed looking at me with an extraordinary smile in her eyes.

'Susila! Susila!' I cried. 'You're here!' 'Yes, I'm here, have always been here.' I sat up leaning on my pillow. 'Why do you disturb yourself?' she asked.

'I am making a place for you,' I said, edging away a little. I looked her up and down and said: 'How well you look!' Her complexion had a golden glow, her eyes sparkled with a new light, her saree shimmered with blue interwoven with 'light' as she had termed it . . . 'How beautiful!' I said looking at it. 'Yes, I always wear this when I come to you. I know you like it very much,' she said. I gazed on her face. There was an overwhelming fragrance of jasmine surrounding her. 'Still jasmine-scented!' I commented.

'Oh wait,' I said and got up. I picked up the garland from the nail and returned to bed. I held it out to her. 'For you as ever. I somehow feared you wouldn't take it . . .' She received it with a smile, cut off a piece of it and stuck it in a curve on the back of her head. She turned her head and asked: 'Is this all right?'

'Wonderful,' I said, smelling it.

A cock crew. The first purple of the dawn came through our window, and faintly touched the walls of our room. 'Dawn!' she whispered and rose to her feet.

We stood at the window, gazing on a slender, red streak, over the eastern rim of the earth. A cool breeze lapped our faces. The boundaries of our personalities suddenly dissolved. It was a moment of rare, immutable joy—a moment for which one feels grateful to Life and Death.

Waiting for the Mahatma

1

HIS MOTHER, WHO died delivering him, and his father, who was killed in Mesopotamia, might have been figures in a legend as far as Sriram was concerned. He had, however, concrete evidence of his mother in a framed photograph which for years hung too high on the wall for him to see; when he grew tall enough to study the dim picture, he didn't feel pleased with her appearance; he wished she looked like that portrait of a European queen with apple cheeks and wavy coiffure hanging in the little shop opposite his house, where he often went to buy peppermints, with the daily money given him by his granny. Of his father, at least, there were recurring reminders. On the first of every month the postman brought a brown, oblong envelope, addressed to his granny. Invariably Granny wept when it came to her hand, and his childish mind wondered what it could contain to sting the tears out of her eyes. Only years later he understood that his granny had been receiving a military pension meant for him. When the envelope came she invariably remarked: 'I don't have to spend your pension in order to maintain us. God has left us enough to live on.' Then she took it to the fourth house in their row, which was known as the 'Fund Office' (what the name meant, he never understood) and came back to say: 'There is nothing so fleeting as untethered cash. You can do what you like with it when you are old enough.'

That portrait in the opposite shop fascinated his adolescent mind. The shopman was known as Kanni, a parched, cantankerous, formidable man, who sat on his haunches all day briskly handing out goods to his customers. Until eleven at night, when he closed the shop, his hollow voice could be heard haranguing someone, or arguing, or cowing his credit-demanding clientèle: 'What do you think I am! How dare you come again without cash? You think you can do me in? You are mistaken. I can swallow ten of you at the same time, remember.' The only softening influence in this shop of cigars, beedis, explosive aerated drinks, and hard words was the portrait of the lady with apple cheeks, curls falling down the brim of her coronet, and large, dark eyes. 'Those eyes look at me,' Sriram often thought. For the pleasure of returning the look, he went again and again, to buy something or the other at the shop.

'Whose is that picture?' he asked once, pausing between sips of a coloured drink.

'How should I know?' Kanni said. 'It's probably some queen, probably Queen Victoria,' although he might with equal justification have claimed her to be Maria Theresa or Ann Boleyn.

'What did you pay for it?'

'Why do you want to know all that?' said Kanni, mildly irritated. If it had been anyone else, he would have shouted, 'If you have finished your business, be gone. Don't stand there and ask a dozen questions.'

But Sriram occupied a unique position. He was a good customer, paid down a lot of cash every day, and deserved respect for his bank balance. He asked, 'Where did you get the picture?'

Kanni was in a jovial mood and answered, 'You know that man, the Revenue Inspector in Pillaiah Street. He owed me a lot of money. I had waited long enough, so one day I walked in and brought away this picture hanging in his room. Something at least for my dues.'

'If there is any chance,' said Sriram with timid hesitation, 'of your giving it away, tell me its price.'

'Oh, oh!' said Kanni, laughing. He was in a fine mood. 'I know you can buy up the queen herself, master *zamindar*. But I won't part with it. It has brought me luck. Ever since I hung the picture there, my business has multiplied tenfold.'

One evening his grandmother asked: 'Do you know what star it will be tomorrow?'

'No. How should I?' he asked, comfortably reclining on the cold cement window sill, and watching the street. He had sat there, morning to night, ever since he could remember. When he was a year old his grandmother put him down there and showed him the traffic passing outside; bullock-carts, horse-carriages, and the first few motor cars of the age, honking away and rattling down the road. He would not be fed unless he was allowed to watch what went on in the street. She held a spoonful of rice and curd to his lips and exclaimed: 'Oh, see that great motor car. Shall our little Ram travel in it?' And when he blinked at the mention of his name and opened his mouth, she thrust in the rice. This window became such a habit with him that when he grew up he sought no other diversion except to sit there, sometimes with a book, and watch the street. His grandmother often reproached him for it. She asked: 'Why don't you go and mix with others of your age?'

'I am quite happy where I am,' he answered briefly.

'If you left that seat, you would have many things to see and learn,' said the old lady sharply. 'Do you know at your age your father could read the almanac upside down, and could say at a moment's notice what star was reigning over which particular day?'

'He was probably a very wise man,' ventured Sriram.

'He *was* very wise. Don't say "probably",' corrected his grandmother. 'And your grandfather, you know how clever he was! They say that the grandfather's reincarnation is in his grandson. You have the same shaped nose as he had and the same eyebrows. His fingers were also long just like yours. But there it stops. I very much wish you had not inherited any of it, but only his brain.'

'I wish you had kept a portrait of him for me to see, Granny,' Sriram said. 'Then I could have worshipped it and become just as clever as he.'

The old lady was pleased with this, and said: 'I'll teach you how you could improve yourself.' Dragging him by the hand to the little circle of light under the hall lamp, she took the brown paper-covered almanac from under a tile of their sloping roof. Then she sat down on the floor, clamoured for her glasses till they were fetched, and forced Sriram to open the almanac and go through it to a particular page. It was full of minute, bewildering symbols in intricate columns. She pushed his face close to the page.

'What is it you are trying to do?' he pleaded pathetically.

She put her finger on a letter and asked: 'What is this?'

'Sa . . .' he read.

'It means *Sadhaya*. That's your star.' She drew her finger along the line and pointed at the morrow's date. 'Tomorrow is this date, which means it's your birth star. It's going to be your twentieth birthday, although you behave as if you are half of that. I am going to celebrate it. Would you like to invite any of your friends?'

'No, never,' said Sriram positively.

So all alone next day he celebrated his twentieth birthday. His guest as well as hostess was his grandmother. No one outside could have guessed what an important occasion was being celebrated in that house in Kabir Street numbered '14'. The house was over two hundred years old and looked it. It was the last house in the street, or 'the first house' as his great-grandfather used to say at the time he built it. From here one saw the backs of market buildings and heard night and day the babble of the big crowd moving on the market road. Next door to Sriram's house was a small printing press which groaned away all day and next to it another two-hundred-year-old house in which six noisy families lived, and beyond that was the Fund Office, where Granny kept her grandson's money. A crooked street ran in front of these houses; their closeness to the market and to a Higher Elementary Town School, the Local Fund Dispensary, and above all to the half-dozen benches around the market fountain, was said to give these houses in Kabir Street a unique value.

The houses were all alike—a large single roof sloping down to the slender rosewood pillars with carvings and brass decorations on them, and a *pyol*, an open brick platform under the windows, on which the household slept in summer. The walls were two feet thick, the doors were made of century-old teak planks with bronze knobs, and the tiles were of burnt mud which had weathered the storms and rains of centuries. All these houses were alike; you could see end to end the slender pillars and tiles sloping down as if all of them belonged to a single house. Many changes had occurred since they were built two centuries ago. Many of them had changed hands, the original owners having been lost in the toils of litigation; some were rented out to tradesmen, such as the Sun Press, the Butter Factory, or the Fund Office, while their owners retired to villages or built themselves modern villas in Lawley Extension. But there were still one or two houses which maintained a continuity, a link with the past. Number 14 was such a one. There the family lineage began centuries ago and continued still, though reduced to just two members—Sriram and his grandmother.

Granny had somewhere secured a yard-long sugar cane for the celebration, although it was not the season. She said: 'No birthday is truly celebrated unless and until a sugar cane is seen in the house. It's auspicious.' She strung mango leaves across the doorway, and decorated the threshold with coloured rice-powder. A neighbour passing down the road stopped to ask: 'What's the celebration? Shall we blow out the oven fires in our houses and come for the feast in yours?'

'Yes, by all means. Most welcome,' said the old lady courteously, and added, as if to neutralize the invitation, 'You are always welcome.' She felt sorry at not being able to call in the neighbours, but that recluse grandson of hers had forbidden her to invite anyone. Left to herself she would have engaged pipes and drums and processions, for this particular birthday was a thing she had been planning all along, this twentieth birthday when she would hand over the savings passbook to her grandson and relinquish the trust.

It was an adventure accompanying Granny to the Fund Office, four doors off. She seemed to shrink under an open sky—she who dominated the landscape under the roof of Number 14 lost her stature completely in the open. Sriram couldn't help remarking, 'You look like a baby, Granny.' Granny half-closed her eyes in the glare and whispered, 'Hush! Don't talk aloud, others may hear.'

'Hear what?'

'Whatever it may be. What happens behind one's door must be known only to the folk concerned. Others had better shut up.'

As if confirming her worst suspicion, Kanni cried breezily from his shop: 'Oho, grandmother and her pet on an outing! A fine sight! The young gentleman is shooting up, madam!'

Sriram felt proud of this compliment; he was seized with a feeling of towering height, and he pursed his lips in a determined manner. He gripped in his right hand the brown calico-bound passbook presented to him with a somewhat dramatic gesture by his grandmother a moment ago.

'Oh, the young *subedar* is going to the right school with the right book,' Kanni remarked. 'He must live to be as great as his father and grandfather put together.'

Granny muttered, quickening her steps, 'Don't stand and talk to that man; he will plague us with his remarks; that's why I never wanted your grandfather to sell that site opposite, but he was an obstinate man—such an obstinate man! He was also fond of this Kanni, who was then a young fellow.'

'Did Grandfather also buy plantains?'

'Not only plantains,' she muttered, with a shudder, recollecting his habit of buying cheroots in Kanni's shop. She had thought it degrading for any person to be seen smoking a cheroot. 'Like a baby sucking a candy stick!' she was wont to remark, disturbing the even tenor of their married life. She had always blamed Kanni for encouraging her husband to smoke and never got over a slight grudge on that account.

Before reaching the Fund Office they had interruptions from other neighbours who peeped out of their doorways and demanded to be told what extraordinary thing made the old lady go out in the company of her grandson. They could understand her going out all alone on the first of the month in the direction of the Fund Office—that was understandable. But what made the lady go out in the company of the young fellow, who was—an unusual sight— holding on to a bank book?

'What!' cried a lady who was a privileged friend of Granny's, 'Does it mean that this urchin is going to have an independent account?'

'He is no longer an urchin,' cried the old woman. 'He's old enough to take charge of his own affairs. How long should I look after him! I'm not immortal. Each responsibility should be shaken off as and when occasion arises to push off each responsibility.' This was a somewhat involved sentiment expressed in a roundabout manner, but her friend seemed to understand it at once, and cried, coming down the steps of her house, 'How wisely you speak! The girls of these days should learn from you how to conduct themselves,' which pleased Granny so much that she stopped to whisper in her ear: 'I was only a trustee of his money. From today he will take care of his own.'

'Wisely done, wisely done,' the other cried and asked, 'how much in all?'

'That you will never know,' said Granny and walked off. Sriram, who had gone ahead, asked: 'How is it, Granny, you stop and talk to everyone! What were you telling her?'

'Nothing,' she replied. 'You follow the same rule and you will be a happier man. Your grandfather ruined himself by talking. Anything that happened to him, good or bad, was bound to be known to everyone in the town within ten minutes; otherwise his soul felt restless.'

'Why should anything be concealed from anyone?' asked the boy.

'Because it's better so, that's all,' said the old lady.

All these interruptions on the way delayed her arrival at the bank. The clock struck four as she showed her face at the counter.

'Must you be on the last second, madam?' the manager asked.

'Is there any reason why you could not come a little earlier?'

'No, none,' she said, 'except that I'm not a young creature who can frisk along.' The manager, used to her ways, got down from his high seat, opened a side door, and without a word, let her in.

Sriram was being initiated into the mysteries of banking. The bank manager opened the last page of his passbook and said: 'What figure do you see here?' Sriram wondered for a moment if he was testing him in arithmetic, a terrible memory of his early school days. He became wary and ventured to say: 'Thirty-eight thousand, five hundred rupees, seven annas, and six pies.'

'Quite right!' cried Granny. She appeared surprised at the intelligence he exhibited.

Sriram asked petulantly, 'What did you take me for, Granny? Did you think I would not be good enough even for this?'

'Yes,' she said quietly. 'How should I think otherwise, considering how well you have fared in your studies!'

The manager, a suave and peaceloving man, steered them out of these dangerous zones by changing the subject: 'You see, this is your savings deposit. You may draw two hundred and fifty rupees a week, not more than that. Here is the withdrawal form. See that you don't lose it, and that nobody gets at it.'

'Why? Would it be possible for anyone else to get at my money with that form?'

'Probably not, but it's our duty to take all possible precautions in money matters,' said the manager.

Granny for some reason felt upset at Sriram's questions. 'Why do you ask so many things? If the manager says, "Do this," or "Do that," it's your duty to obey, that is all.'

'I always like to know what I am doing,' said Sriram, and added, 'there's nothing wrong in that.'

Granny turned to the manager and said with pride, 'You see the present generation! They are not like us. How many years have you been seeing me here? Have you ever heard me asking why or how and why not at any time?'

The manager made indistinct noises, not wishing to displease either his old customer or the new one. He placed a letter before the old lady, tapped the bottom of the page with his finger, and said, 'May I have your signature here? It's the new authorization, and you won't be bothered to come here often as before.'

'After twenty years, relief!' Granny cried. She had the triumphant expression of one who had run hard and reached the winning post. Sriram did not fully realize what it all meant, but took it quite casually. He simply said, 'If I had been you I wouldn't have taken all this trouble to accumulate the money.'

'You are not me, and that's just as well. Don't say such things before this man who has watched and guarded your property all these years!'

Sriram wanted to test how far the magic toy put into his hands would work. He seized the pen-holder, stabbed it into the ink-well, wrote off a withdrawal for two hundred and fifty rupees, tore off the page and pushed it before the manager with an air of challenge. 'Let us see if I am really the owner of this money!'

The manager was taken aback by the speed of his activity. He smiled and said: 'But my dear fellow, you know we close at four, and cash closes at two every day. If you want cash, you must be here before two on any working day. Change the date, and you can come and collect it the first thing tomorrow. Are you sure that you want all that sum urgently for the first draw?'

'Yes, I am positive,' said Sriram. 'I would have taken more if you had permitted more than two hundred and fifty at a time.'

'May I know why you need all this amount?' asked Granny.

'Is it or is it not my money?' asked Sriram.

'It is and it is not,' said Granny in a mystifying manner. 'Remember, I don't have to ask you what you do with your own funds. It's your own business. You are old enough to know what you do. I don't have to bother myself at all about it. It's purely your own business. But I want to ask you—just to know things, that is all—why you want two hundred and fifty rupees now. It's your business, I know, but remember one thing. One is always better off with money unspent. It's always safer to have one's bank balance undamaged.'

'Quite right, quite right,' echoed the bank manager. 'Great words of wisdom. I tell you, young man, come tomorrow morning,' he said, picking up the form.

Granny cried: 'Give it here,' and, snatching the paper from his hand, said, 'Correct it to fifty. You need only fifty rupees now and not two hundred and fifty. I'd have torn this up, but for the fact that it is your first withdrawal form and I don't want to commit any inauspicious act.'

'Ah! That's a good idea,' said the manager, 'It's better if you carry less cash about you nowadays with pickpockets about.'

He dipped the pen in the ink and passed it to Sriram: 'Write your signature in full on all the corrections.'

Sriram obeyed, muttering, 'See! This is just what I suspected! I'm supposed to be the master of this money, but I cannot draw what I want! A nice situation!'

The manager took the form back and said: 'Come at ten-thirty tomorrow morning for your cash.'

'I hope you won't expect me to come again with my grandmother!' Sriram said with heavy cynicism.

Next day Sriram stood at Kanni's shop and ordered coloured drinks and plantains. 'How much?' he asked after he was satisfied.

'Four annas,' said Kanni.

Sriram drew from his pocket several rolls of notes, and pulled one out for Kanni. It was a veritable display of wealth. Kanni was duly impressed. He immediately became deferential.

'Have you examined your pockets to see if there may not be some small change lying somewhere there?'

'If I had small change, would I be holding this out to you?' asked Sriram grandly.

'All right, all right.'

Kanni received the amount and transferred it immediately to his cash chest. Sriram waited for change. Kanni attended to other customers.

Sriram said, 'Where is my change?'

Kanni said: 'Please wait. I have something to tell you. You see—'

An itinerant tea vendor just then came up with his stove and kettle to ask for a packet of cigarettes. And then there were four other customers. The place was crowded and Kanni's customers had to stand on the road below his platform and hold out their hands like supplicants. All the while Sriram stood gazing on the portrait of the rosy-cheeked queen who stared out at the world through the plantain bunches suspended from the ceiling. School children came in and clamoured for peppermints in bottles. Kanni served everyone like a machine.

When everybody had gone Sriram asked, 'How long do you want me to wait for my change?'

'Don't be angry, master,' Kanni said. He pulled out a long notebook, blew the dust off its cover, turned an ancient page, and pointed at a figure and asked, 'Do you see this?'

'Yes,' said Sriram, wondering why everybody was asking him to read figures these days. He read out: 'Nine rupees, twelve annas.'

'It's a debt from your grandfather which is several years old. I'm sure he'd have paid it if he had lived—but one doesn't know when death comes: I used to get him special cheroots from Singapore, you know.'

'Why didn't you ask Granny?'

'Granny! Not I. He wouldn't have liked it at all. I knew some day you would come and pay.'

'Oh,' Sriram said generously. 'Take it, by all means,' and turned to go.

'That's a worthy grandson,' muttered Kanni. 'Now the old man's soul will rest in peace.'

'But where will the soul be waiting? Don't you think he will have been reborn somewhere?' said Sriram.

Kanni did not wish to be involved in speculations on postmortem existence, and turned his attention to the other customers.

Before going away Sriram said, 'I can buy that picture off you whenever you can sell it, remember.'

'Surely, surely. When I wind up this shop, I will remember to give it to you, not till then: it's a talisman for me.'

'If the lady's husband turns up and demands the picture, what will you do?' Sriram asked, which made Kanni pause and reflect for a moment what his line of action should be.

Sriram walked down the street, not having any definite aim. He felt like a man with a high-powered talisman in his pocket, something that would enable him to fly or go anywhere he pleased. He thrust his fingers into his *jibba* pocket and went on twirling the notes. He wished he had asked the manager to give him new ones: he had given him what appeared to be second-hand notes: probably the Fund-Office Manager reserved the good notes for big men. Who was a big man anyway? Anyone was a big man. Himself not excluded. He had money, but people still seemed to think he was a little boy tied to the apron strings of his grandmother. His grandmother was very good no doubt, but she ought to leave him alone. She did not treat him as a grown-up person. It was exasperating to be treated like a kid all the time. Why wouldn't she let him draw two hundred and fifty instead of fifty, if he wanted it? It would be his business in future, and she ought to allow him to do what he pleased. Anyway it was a good thing he had only fifty to display before Kanni. If he had shown two hundred he might have claimed half of it as his grandfather's debt. Sriram was for a moment seized with the problem of life on earth: was one born and tended and brought up to the twentieth year just in order to pay off a cheroot bill? This philosophical trend he immediately checked with the thought: 'I shall probably know all this philosophy when I grow a little older, not now . . .' He dismissed his thought with: 'I am an adult with my own money, going home just when I please. Granny can't ask me what I have been doing . . .'

He walked round and round the Market Road, gazing into shops, and wondering if there was anything he could buy. The money in his pocket clamoured to be spent. But yet there seemed to be nothing worth buying in the shops. He halted for a moment, reflecting how hard it was to relieve oneself of one's cash. A man who wore a cotton vest and a tucked-in *dhoti* held up to him a canvas folding chair.

'Going cheap, do you want it?'

Sriram examined it. This seemed to be something worth having in one's house. It had a red striped canvas seat and could be folded up. There was not a single piece of furniture at home.

'Ten rupees sir, best teakwood.'

Sriram examined it keenly, although he could not see the difference between rosewood and teak or any other wood.

'Is this real teak?' he asked.

'Guaranteed Mempi Hill teak, sir, that is why it costs ten rupees: if it were ordinary jungle wood, you could have got it for four.'

'I will give seven rupees,' said Sriram with an air of finality, looking away. He pretended to have no further interest in the transaction. The man came down to eight rupees. Sriram offered him an extra half rupee if he would carry it to his door.

Granny opened the door and asked in surprise, 'What is this?'

Sriram set up the canvas chair right in the middle of the hall and said, 'This is a present for you, Granny.'

'What! For me!' She examined the canvas and said, 'It's no use for me. This is some kind of leather, probably cowhide, and I can't pollute myself by sitting on it. I wish you had told me before going out to buy.'

Sriram examined the seat keenly, dusted it, tapped it with his palm and said, 'This is not leather, Granny, it is only canvas.'

'What is canvas made of?' she asked.

Sriram said, 'I have no idea,' and she completed the answer with, 'Canvas is only another name for leather. I don't want it. You sleep on it if you like.'

He followed this advice to the letter. All day he lounged on this canvas seat and looked at the ceiling or read a tattered novel borrowed from the municipal library. When evening came he visited the Bombay Anand Bhavan and ordered a lot of sweets and delicacies, and washed them down with coffee. After that he picked up a paan covered with coloured coconut gratings, chewed it with great contentment, and went for a stroll along the river or saw the latest Tamil film in the Regal Picture Palace.

It was an unruffled, quiet existence, which went on without a break for the next four years, the passing of time being hardly noticed in this scheme—except when one or the other of the festivals of the season turned up and his granny wanted him to bring something from the market. 'Another Dussera!' or 'Another Deepavali! It looks as though I lighted crackers only yesterday!' he would cry, surprised at the passage of time.

It was April. The summer sun shone like a ruthless arc lamp—and all the water in the well evaporated and the road-dust became bleached and weightless and flew about like flour spraying off the grinding wheels. Granny said as Sriram was starting out for the evening, 'Why don't you fetch some good jaggery for tomorrow, and some jasmine for the *puja?*' He had planned to go towards Lawley Extension today and not to the market, and he felt reluctant to oblige her. But she was insistent. She said, 'Tomorrow is New Year's Day.'

'Already another New Year!' he cried. 'It seems as though we celebrated one yesterday.'

'Whether yesterday or the day before, it's a New Year's Day. I want certain things for its celebration. If you are not going, I'll go myself. It's not for me! It's only to make some sweet stuff for you.'

Grumbling a great deal, he got up, dressed himself, and started out. When he arrived at the market he was pleased that his granny had forced him to go there.

As he approached the Market Fountain a pretty girl came up

and stopped him.

'Your contribution?' she asked, shaking a sealed tin collecting box.

Sriram's throat went dry and no sound came. He had never been spoken to by any girl before; she was slender and young, with eyes that sparkled with happiness. He wanted to ask, 'How old are you? What caste are you? Where is your horoscope? Are you free to marry me?' She looked so different from the beauty in Kanni's shop; his critical faculties were at once alert, and he realized how shallow was the other beauty, the European queen, and wondered that he had ever given her a thought. He wouldn't look at the picture again even if Kanni should give it to him free.

The girl rattled the money-box. The sound brought him back from his reverie, and he said, 'Yes, Yes'; he fumbled in his *jibba* side-pocket for loose change and brought out an eight-anna silver coin and dropped it into the slot. The girl smiled at him in return and went away, seeming to move with the lightest of steps like a dancer. Sriram had a wild hope that she would let him touch her hand, but she moved off and disappeared into the market crowd.

'What a dangerous thing for such a beauty to be about!' he thought. It was a busy hour with cycles, horse carriages and motor cars passing down the road, and a jostling crowd was moving in and out of the arched gateway of the market. People were carrying vegetables, rolls of banana leaves and all kinds of New Year purchases. Young urchins were hanging about with baskets on their heads soliciting, 'Coolie, sir, coolie?' She had disappeared into the market like a bird gliding on wings. He felt that he wanted to sing a song for her. But she was gone. He realized he hadn't even asked what the contribution was for. He wished he hadn't given just a nickel but thrust a ten rupee note into her collection box (he could afford it), and that would have given her a better impression of him, and possibly have made her stand and talk to him. He should have asked her where she lived. What a fool not to have held her up. He ought to have emptied all his money into her money-box. She had vanished through the market arch.

He vaguely followed this trail, hoping that he would be able to catch another glimpse of her. If ever he saw her again he would take charge of the money-box and make the collection for her, whatever it might be for. He looked over the crowd for a glimpse again of the white saree, over the shoulders of the jostling crowd, around the vegetable stalls . . . But it was a hopeless quest, not a chance of seeing her again. Who could she be and where did she come from? Could it be that she was the daughter of a judge or might she be an other-worldly creature who had come suddenly to meet him and whom he did not know how to treat? What a fool he was. He felt how sadly he lacked the necessary polish for such encounters. That was why it was urged on him to go to a college and pass his BA. Those who went to colleges and passed their BA were certainly people who knew how to conduct themselves before girls.

He passed into the market arch in the direction she took. At the fly-ridden jaggery-shop he said tentatively: 'A lot of people are about collecting money for all sorts of things.'

The jaggery merchant said sourly, 'Who will not collect money if there are people to give?'

'I saw a girl jingling a money-box. Even girls have taken to it,' Sriram said, holding his breath, hoping to hear something.

'Oh, that,' the other said. 'I too had to give some cash. We have to. We can't refuse.'

'Who is she?' Sriram asked, unable to carry on diplomatically any further.

The jaggery merchant threw a swift look at him which seemed slightly sneering, and said: 'She has something to do with Mahatma Gandhi and is collecting a fund. You know the Mahatma is coming.'

Sriram suddenly woke from an age-old somnolence to the fact that Malgudi was about to have the honour of receiving Mahatma Gandhi.

In that huge gathering sitting on the sands of the Sarayu, awaiting the arrival of Mahatma Gandhi, Sriram was a tiny speck. There were a lot of volunteers clad in white *khaddar* moving around the dais. The chromium stand of the microphone gleamed in the sun. Police stood about here and there. Busybodies were going round asking people to remain calm and silent. People obeyed them. Sriram envied these volunteers and busybodies their importance, and wondered if he could do anything to attain the same status. The sands were warm, the sun was severe. The crowd sat on the ground uncomplainingly.

The river flowed, the leaves of the huge banyan and peepul trees on the banks rustled; the waiting crowd kept up a steady babble, constantly punctuated by the pop of soda-water bottles; longitudinal cucumber slices, crescent-shaped, and brushed up with the peel of a lime dipped in salt, were disappearing from the wooden tray of a vendor who was announcing in a subdued tone (as a concession to the coming of a great man), 'Cucumber for thirst, the best for thirst.' He had wound a green Turkish towel around his head as a protection from the sun.

Sriram felt parched, and looked at the tray longingly. He wished he could go up and buy a crescent. The thought of biting into its cool succulence was tantalizing. He was at a distance and if he left his seat he'd have no chance of getting back to it. He watched a lot of others giving their cash and working their teeth into the crescent. 'Waiting for the Mahatma makes one very thirsty,' he thought.

Every ten minutes someone started a canard that the great man had arrived, and it created a stir in the crowd. It became a joke, something to relieve the tedium of waiting. Any person, a microphone-fitter or a volunteer, who dared to cross the dais was greeted with laughter and booing from a hundred thousand throats. A lot of familiar characters, such as an old teacher of his and the pawnbroker in Market Road, made themselves unrecognizable by wearing white *khaddar* caps. They felt it was the right dress to wear on this occasion. 'That *khaddar* store off the Market Fountain must have done a roaring business in white caps today,' Sriram thought. Far off, pulled obscurely to one side, was a police van with a number of men peering through the safety grill.

There was a sudden lull when Gandhi arrived on the platform and took his seat.

'That's Mahadev Desai,' someone whispered into Sriram's ears.

'Who is the man behind Gandhiji?'

'That's Mr Natesh, our Municipal Chairman.'

Someone sneered at the mention of his name. 'Some people conveniently adopt patriotism when Mahatmaji arrives.'

'Otherwise how can they have a ride in the big procession and a seat on the dais?'

Over the talk the amplifiers burst out: 'Please, please be silent.'

Mahatma Gandhi stood on the dais, with his palms brought together in a salute. A mighty cry rang out, '*Mahatma Gandhi ki jai!*' Then he raised his arm, and instantly a silence fell on the gathering. He clapped his hands rhythmically and said: 'I want you all to keep this up, this beating for a while.' People were half-hearted. And the voice in the amplifier boomed, 'No good. Not enough. I like to see more vigour in your arms, more rhythm, more spirit. It must be like the drumbeats of the non-violent soldiers marching on to cut the chains that bind Mother India. I want to hear the great beat. I like to see all arms upraised, and clapping. There is nothing to be ashamed of in it. I want to see unity in it. I want you all to do it with a single mind.' And at once, every man, woman, and child, raised their arms and clapped over their heads.

Sriram wondered for a moment if it would be necessary for him to add his quota to this voluminous noise. He was hesitant.

'I see someone in that corner not quite willing to join us. Come on, you will be proud of this preparation.'

And Sriram felt he had been found out, and followed the lead.

Now a mighty choral chant began: '*Raghupati Raghava Raja Ram, Pathita Pavana Sita Ram*', to a simple tune, led by a girl at the microphone. It went on and on, and ceased when Mahatmaji began his speech. Natesh interpreted in Tamil what Gandhi said in Hindi. At the outset Mahatma Gandhi explained that he'd speak only in Hindi as a matter of principle. 'I will not address you in English. It's the language of our rulers. It has enslaved us. I very much wish I could speak to you in your own sweet language, Tamil; but alas, I am too hard-pressed for time to master it now, although I hope if God in His infinite mercy grants me the longevity due to me, that is one hundred and twenty-five years, I shall be able next time to speak to you in Tamil without troubling our friend Natesh.'

'Natesh has a knack of acquiring good certificates,' someone murmured in an aggrieved tone.

'Runs with the hare and hunts with the hounds,' said a schoolmaster.

'He knows all of them inside out. Don't imagine the old gentleman does not know whom he is dealing with.'

'I notice two men there talking,' boomed Gandhiji's voice. 'It's not good to talk now, when perhaps the one next to you is anxious to listen. If you disturb his hearing, it is one form of *himsa*.' And at once the commentators lowered their heads and became silent. People were afraid to stir or speak.

Mahatma Gandhi said: 'I see before me a vast army. Every one of you has certain good points and certain defects, and you must all strive to discipline yourselves before we can hope to attain freedom for our country. An army is always in training and keeps itself in good shape by regular drill and discipline. We, the citizens of this country, are all soldiers of a non-violent army, but even such an army has to practise a few things daily in order to keep itself in proper condition: we do not have to bask in the sun and cry "Left" or "Right". But we have a system of our own to follow: that's *Ram Dhun*, spinning on the *charka* and the practice of absolute Truth and Non-violence.'

At the next evening's meeting Sriram secured a nearer seat. He now understood the technique of attending these gatherings. If he hesitated and looked timid, people pushed him back and down. But if he looked like someone who owned the place, everyone stood aside to let him pass. He wore a pair of large dark glasses which gave him, he felt, an authoritative look. He strode through the crowd. The place was cut up into sectors with stockades of bamboo, so that people were penned in groups. He assumed a tone of bluster which carried him through the various obstacles and brought him to the first row right below the dais. It took him farther away from the sellers of cucumber and aerated water who operated on the fringe of the vast crowd. But there was another advantage in this place: he found himself beside the enclosure where the women were assembled. Most of them were without ornaments, knowing Gandhiji's aversion to all show and luxury. Even then they were an attractive lot, in their sarees of varied colours, and Sriram sat unashamedly staring at the gathering for his favourite hobby at the moment was to speculate on what type he would prefer for a wife.

He fancied himself the centre of attraction if any women happened to look in his direction. 'Oh, she is impressed with my glasses—takes me to be a big fellow, I suppose.' He recollected Gandhiji's suggestion on the previous day: 'All women are your sisters and mothers. Never look at them with thoughts of lust. If you are troubled by such thoughts, this is the remedy: walk with your head down, looking at the ground during the day, and with your eyes up, looking at the stars at night.' He had said this in answering a question that someone from the audience had put to him. Sriram felt uncomfortable at the recollection: 'He will probably read my thoughts.' It seemed to be a risky business sitting so near the dais.

Gandhi seemed to be a man who spotted disturbers and cross-thinkers however far away they sat. He was sure to catch him the moment he arrived on the platform., and say, 'You there! Come up and make a clean breast of it. Tell this assembly what your thoughts were. Don't look in the direction of the girls at all if you cannot control your thoughts.' Sriram resolutely looked away in another direction, where men were seated. 'A most uninteresting and boring collection of human faces; wherever I turn I see only some shopkeeper or a schoolmaster. What is the use of spending one's life looking at them?' Very soon, unconsciously, he turned again towards the women, telling himself, 'So many sisters and mothers. I wish they would let me speak to them. Of course I have no evil thoughts in my mind at the moment.'

Presently Mahatmaji ascended the platform and Sriram hastily took his eyes off the ladies and joined in the hand clapping with well-timed devotion and then in the singing of *Raghupati Raghava Raja Ram*. After that Gandhi spoke on non-violence, and explained how it could be practised in daily life. 'It is a perfectly simple procedure provided you have faith in it. If you watch yourself you will avoid all actions, big or small, and all thoughts, however obscure, which may cause pain to another. If you are watchful, it will come to you naturally,' he said. 'When someone has wronged you or has done something which appears to you to be evil, just pray for the destruction of that evil. Cultivate an extra affection for the person and you will find that you are able to bring about a change in him. Two thousand years ago, Jesus Christ meant the same thing when he said, 'Turn the other cheek'.

Thus he went on. Sometimes Sriram found it impossible to follow his words. He could not grasp what he was saying, but he looked rapt, he tried to concentrate and understand. This was the first time he felt the need to try and follow something, the first time that he found himself at a disadvantage. Until now he had had a conviction, especially after he began to operate his own bank account, that he understood everything in life. This was the first time he was assailed by doubts of his own prowess and understanding. When Mahatmaji spoke of untouchability and caste, Sriram reflected, 'There must be a great deal in what he says. We always think we are superior people. How Granny bullies that ragged scavenger who comes to our house every day to sweep the back yard!' Granny was so orthodox that she would not let the scavenger approach nearer than ten yards, and habitually adopted a bullying tone while addressing him. Sriram also took a devilish pleasure in joining the baiting and finding fault with the scavenger's work, although he never paid the slightest attention to their comments. He simply went about his business, driving his broom vigorously and interrupting himself only to ask, 'When will master give me an old shirt he promised so long ago?'

He suddenly noticed on the dais the girl who had jingled a money-box in his face a few days ago, at the market. She was clad in a saree of *khaddar*, white home-spun, and he noticed how well it suited her. Before, he had felt that the wearing of *khaddar* was a fad, that it was apparel fit only for cranks, but now he realized how lovely it could be. He paused for a moment to consider whether it was the wearer who was enriching the cloth or whether the material was good in itself. But he had to postpone the whole problem. It was no time for abstract considerations. There she stood like a vision beside the microphone, on the high dais, commanding the whole scene, a person who was worthy of standing beside Mahatmaji's microphone. How confidently she faced the crowd! He wished he could go about announcing, 'I know who that is beside the microphone into which Mahatmaji is speaking.' The only trouble was that if they turned and asked him, 'What is her name?' he would feel lost. It would be awkward to say, 'I don't know, she came jingling a collection box the other day in the market. I wish I could say where she lives. I should be grateful for any information.'

At this moment applause rang out, and he joined in it. Gandhiji held up his hand to say, 'It is not enough for you to clap your hands and show your appreciation of me. I am not prepared to accept it all so easily. I want you really to make sure of a change in your hearts before you ever think of asking the British to leave the shores of India. It's all very well for you to take up the cry and create an uproar. But that's not enough. I want you to clear your hearts and minds and make certain that only love resides there, and there is no residue of bitterness for past history. Only then can you say to the British, "Please leave this country to be managed or mismanaged by us, that's purely our own business, and come back any time you like as our friends and distinguished guests, not as our rulers," and you will find John Bull packing his suitcase. But be sure you have in your heart love and not bitterness.'

Sriram told himself, looking at the vision beside the microphone, 'Definitely it's not bitterness. I love her.'

'But,' Mahatmaji was saying, 'if I have the slightest suspicion that your heart is not pure or that there is bitterness there, I'd rather have the British stay on. It's the lesser of two evils.'

Sriram thought: 'Oh, revered Mahatmaji, have no doubt that my heart is pure and without bitterness. How can I have any bitterness in my heart for a creature who looks so divine?'

She was at a great height on the platform, and her features were not very clear in the afternoon sun which seemed to set her face ablaze. She might be quite dark and yet wear a temporarily fair face illumined by the sun or she might really be fair. If she were dark, without a doubt his grandmother would not approve of his marrying her. In any case it was unlikely that they would have her blessing, since she had other plans for his marriage: a brother's granddaughter brought up in Kumbum, a most horrible, countrified girl who would guard his cash. If Granny was so solicitous of his money she was welcome to take it all and hand it to the Kumbum girl. That would be the lesser of two evils, but he would not marry the Kumbum girl, an unsightly creature with a tight oily braid falling on her nape and dressed in a gaudy village saree, when the thing to do was to wear *khaddar*. He would refuse to look at anyone who did not wear *khadi, khadi* alone was going to save the nation from ruin and get the English out of India, as that venerable saint Mahatmaji explained untiringly. He felt sad and depressed at the thought that in the twentieth century there were still people like the Kumbum girl, whom he had seen many many years ago when his uncle came down to engage a lawyer for a civil suit in the village.

Sriram wanted to go and assure the girl on the grandstand that he fully and without the slightest reservation approved of her outlook and habits. It was imperative that he should approach her and tell her that. He seized the chance at the end of the meeting.

Mahatmaji started to descend from the platform. There was a general rush forward, and a number of volunteers began pushing back the crowd, imploring people not to choke the space around the platform. Mahatmaji himself seemed to be oblivious of all the turmoil going on around him. Sriram found a gap in the cordon made by the volunteers and slipped through. The heat of the sun hit him on the nape, the huge trees on the river's edge rustled above the din of the crowd, birds were creating a furore in the branches, being unaccustomed to so much noise below. The crowd was so great that Sriram for a moment forgot where he was, which part of the town he was in, and but for the noise of the birds would not have remembered he was on the banks of the Sarayu. 'If that girl can be with Mahatmaji I can also be there,' he told himself indignantly as he threaded his way through the crowd. There was a plethora of white-capped young men, volunteers who cleared a way for Mahatmaji to move in. Sriram felt that it would have been much better if he had not made himself so conspicuously different with his half-arm shirt and *mull-dhoti*, probably products of the hated mills. He feared that any moment someone might discover him and put him out. If they challenged him and asked, 'Who are you?' he felt he wouldn't be able to answer coherently, or he might just retort, 'Who do you think you are talking to, that girl supporting the Mahatma is familiar to me. I am going to know her, but don't ask me her name. She came with a collection box one day in the market . . .'

But no such occasion arose. No one questioned him and he was soon mixed up with a group of people walking behind Mahatmaji in the lane made by the volunteers, as crowds lined the sides. He decided to keep going till he was stopped. If someone stopped him he could always turn round and go home. They would not kill him for it anyway. Killing! He was amused at the word: no word could be more incongruous in the vicinity of one who would not hurt even the British. One could be confident he would not let a would-be follower be slaughtered by his volunteers.

Presently Sriram found himself in such a position of vantage that he lost all fear of being taken for an intruder and walked along with a jaunty and familar air, so that people lining the route looked on him with interest. He heard his name called. 'Sriram!' An old man who used to be his teacher years before was calling him. Even in his present situation Sriram could not easily break away from the call of a teacher; it was almost a reflex: he hesitated for a moment wondering whether he would not do well to run away without appearing to notice the call, but almost as if reading his mind, his teacher called again, 'A moment! Sriram.' He stopped to have a word with his master, an old man who had wrapped himself in a coloured shawl and looked like an apostle with a slight beard growing on his chin. He gripped Sriram's elbow eagerly and asked, 'Have you joined them?'

'Whom?'

'Them—' said the teacher, pointing.

Sriram hesitated for a moment, wondering what he should

reply, and mumbled, 'I mean to . . .'

'Very good, very good,' said the master. 'In spite of your marks I always knew that you would go far, smart fellow. You are not dull but only lazy. If you worked well you could always score first-class marks like anyone else, but you were always lazy; I remember how you stammered when asked which was the capital of England. Ho! Ho!' he laughed at the memory. Sriram became restive and wriggled in his grip.

The teacher said, 'I am proud to see you here, my boy. Join the Congress, work for the country, you will go far, God bless you . . .'

'I am glad you think so, sir,' said Sriram and turned to dash away.

The teacher put his face close to his and asked in a whisper, 'What will Mahatmaji do now after going in there?'

'Where?' Sriram asked, not knowing where Gandhi was going, although he was following him.

'Into his hut,' replied the teacher.

'He will probably rest,' answered Sriram, resolutely preparing to dash off. If he allowed too great a distance to develop between himself and the group they might not admit him.

A little boy thrust himself forward and asked, 'Can you get me Mahatma's autograph?'

'Certainly not,' replied Sriram, gently struggling to release himself from his teacher's hold.

His teacher whispered in his ear, 'Whatever happens, don't let down our country.'

'No, sir, never, I promise,' replied Sriram, gently pushing away his old master and running after the group, who were fast disappearing from his view.

They were approaching a wicket gate made of thorns and bamboo. He saw the girl going ahead to open the gate. He sprinted forward as the crowd watched. He had an added assurance in his steps now he felt that he belonged to the Congress. The teacher had put a new idea into his head and he almost felt he was a veteran of the party. He soon joined the group and he had mustered enough pluck to step up beside the girl. It was a proud moment for him. He looked at her. She did not seem to notice his presence. He sweated all over with excitement and panted for breath, but could not make out the details of her personality, complexion or features. However, he noted with satisfaction that she was not very tall, himself being of medium height. Gandhi was saying something to her and she was nodding and smiling. He did not understand what they were saying, but he also smiled out of sympathetic respect. He wanted to look as much like them as possible, and cursed himself for the hundredth time that day for being dressed in mill cloth.

The Mahatma entered his hut. This was one of the dozen huts belonging to the city sweepers who lived on the banks of the river. It was probably the worst area in the town, and it was an exaggeration even to call them huts; they were just hovels, put together with rags, tin sheets, and shreds of coconut matting, all crowded in anyhow, with scratchy fowls cackling about and children growing in the street dust. The municipal services were neither extended here nor missed, although the people living in the hovels were employed by the municipality for scavenging work in the town. They were paid ten rupees a month per head, and since they worked in families of four or five, each had a considerable income by Malgudi standards. They hardly ever lived in their huts, spending all their time around the municipal building or at the toddy shop run by the government nearby, which absorbed all their earnings. These men spent less than a tenth of their income on food or clothing, always depending upon mendicancy in their off hours for survival. Deep into the night their voices could be heard clamouring for alms, in all the semi-dark streets of Malgudi. Troublesome children were silenced at the sound of their approach. Their possessions were few; if a cow or a calf died in the city they were called in to carry off the carcass and then the colony at the river's edge brightened up, for they held a feast on the flesh of the dead animal and made money out of its hide. Reformers looked on with wrath and horror, but did little else, since as an untouchable class they lived outside the town limits, beyond Nallappa's Grove, where nobody went, and they used only a part of the river on its downward course.

This was the background to the life of the people in whose camp Gandhi had elected to stay during his visit to Malgudi. It had come as a thunderbolt on the Municipal Chairman, Mr Natesh, who had been for weeks preparing his palatial house, Neel Bagh in the aristocratic Lawley Extension, to receive Gandhi. His arguments as to why he alone should be Mahatmaji's host seemed unassailable: 'I have spent two lakhs on the building, my garden and lawns alone have cost me twenty-five thousand rupees so far. What do you think I have done it for? I am a simple man, sir, my needs are very simple.

I don't need any luxury. I can live in a hut, but the reason I have built it on this scale is so that I should be able for at least once in my lifetime to receive a great soul like Mahatmaji. This is the only house in which he can stay comfortably when he comes to this town. Let me say without appearing to be boastful that it is the biggest and the best furnished house in Malgudi, and we as the people of Malgudi have a responsibility to give him our very best, so how can we house him in any lesser place?'

The Reception Committee applauded his speech. The District Collector, who was the head of the district, and the District Superintendent of Police, who was next to him in authority, attended the meeting as *ex officio* members.

A dissenting voice said, 'Why not give the Circuit House for Mahatmaji?'

The Circuit House on the edge of the town was an old East India Company building standing on an acre of land, on the Trunk Road. Robert Clive was supposed to have halted there while marching to relieve the siege of Trichinopoly. The citizens of Malgudi were very proud of this building and never missed an opportunity to show it off to anyone visiting the town, and it always housed the distinguished visitors who came this way. It was a matter of prestige for Governors to be put up there. Even in this remote spot they had arranged to have all their conveniences undiminished, with resplendent sanitary fittings in the bathrooms. It was also known as the Glass House, by virtue of a glass-fronted bay room from which the distinguished guests could watch the wild animals that were supposed to stray near the building at night in those days.

The dissenting voice in the Reception Committee said. 'Is it the privilege of the ruling race alone to be given the Circuit House? Is our Mahatmaji unworthy of it?'

The Collector, who was the custodian of British prestige, rose to a point of order and administered a gentle reproof to the man who spoke: 'It is not good to go beyond the relevant facts at the moment: if we have considered the Circuit House as unsuitable it is because we have no time to rig it up for receiving Mr Gandhi.'

It was a point of professional honour for him to say *Mr* Gandhi and not *Mahatma*, and but for the fact that as the Collector he could close the entire meeting and put all the members behind bars under the Defence of India Act, many would have protested and walked out, but they held their peace and he drove home the point.

'Since Mr Gandhi's arrival has been a sudden decision, we are naturally unable to get the building ready for him; if I may say so, our chairman's house seems to suit the purpose and we must be grateful to him for so kindly obliging us.'

'And I am arranging to move to the Glass House leaving my house for Mahatmaji's occupation.'

That seemed to decide it, and his partisans cheered loudly. It was resolved by ten votes to one that Mahatmaji should stay in Neel Bagh, and the chairman left the meeting with a heavy, serious look. He wrote to Gandhiji's secretary, receiving a reply which he read at the next meeting: 'Mahatma Gandhi wishes that no particular trouble should be taken about his lodging; and that the matter may be conveniently left over till he is actually there.'

The council debated the meaning of the communication and finally concluded that it only meant that though the Mahatma was unwilling to be committed to anything he would not refuse to occupy Neel Bagh.

The dissenting voice said, 'How do you know that he does not mean something else?'

But he was soon overwhelmed by the gentle reprimand of the Collector. The communication was finally understood to mean, 'I know Mahatmaji's mind, he does not want to trouble anyone if it is a trouble.'

'He probably does not know that it is no trouble for us at all.'

'Quite so, quite so,' said another soothsayer. And they were all pleased at this interpretation.

A further flattering comparison was raised by someone who wanted to create a pleasant impression on the Chairman: 'Let us not forget that Mahatmaji takes up his residence at Birla House in Delhi and Calcutta; I am sure he will have no objection to staying in a palatial building like the one our Chairman has built.'

The dissenting voice said, 'Had we better not write and ask if we have understood him right, and get his confirmation?'

He was not allowed to complete his sentence but was hissed down, and the District Superintendent of Police added slowly, 'Even for security arrangements any other place would present difficulties.'

For this sentiment he received an appreciative nod from his superior, the District Collector.

When Gandhi arrived, he was ceremoniously received, all the bigwigs of Malgudi and the local gentry being introduced to him one by one by the Chairman of the municipality. The police attempted to control the crowd, which was constantly shouting, '*Mahatma Gandhi ki jai.*' When the Chairman read his address of welcome at the elaborately constructed archway outside the railway station, he could hardly be heard, much to his chagrin. He had spent a whole week composing the text of the address with the help of a local journalist, adding whatever would show off either his patriotism or the eminent position Malgudi occupied in the country's life. The Collector had taken the trouble to go through the address before it was sent for printing in order to make sure that it contained no insult to the British Empire, that it did not hinder the war effort, and that it in no way betrayed military secrets. He had to censor it in several places: where the Chairman compared Malgudi to Switzerland (the Collector scored this out because he felt it might embarrass a neutral state); a reference to the hosiery trade (since the Censor felt this was a blatant advertisement for the Chairman's goods and in any case he did not want enemy planes to come looking for this institution thinking it was a camouflage for the manufacture of war material); and all those passages which hinted at the work done by Gandhiji in the political field. The picture of him as a social reformer was left intact and even enlarged; anyone who read the address would conclude that politics was the last thing that Mahatmaji was interested in. In any case, in view of the reception, the Collector might well have left the whole thing alone since cries of '*Mahatmaji ki jai*' and 'Down with the Municipal Chairman' made the speech inaudible. The crowd was so noisy that Mahatmaji had to remonstrate once or twice. When he held up his hand the crowd subsided and waited to listen to him. He said quietly, 'This is sheer lack of order, which I cannot commend. Your Chairman is reading something and I am in courtesy bound to know what he is saying. You must all keep quiet. Let him proceed.'

'No,' cried the crowd. 'We want to hear Mahatmaji and not the Municipal Chairman.'

'Yes,' replied Mahatmaji. 'You will soon hear me, in about an hour on the banks of your Sarayu river. That is the programme as framed.'

'By whom?'

'Never mind by whom. It has my approval. That is how it

stands. On the sands of the Sarayu in about an hour. Your Chairman has agreed to let me off without a reply to his very kind address. You will have to listen to what he has to say because I very much wish to . . .'

This quietened the mob somewhat and the Chairman continued his reading of the address, although he looked intimidated by the exchanges. The Collector looked displeased and fidgety, feeling he ought to have taken into custody the dissenting member, who had perhaps started all this trouble in the crowd. He leaned over and whispered to the Chairman, 'Don't bother, read on leisurely. You don't have to rush through,' but the Chairman only wished to come to the end of his reading; he was anxious to be done with the address before the crowd burst out again. He did not complete his message a second too soon, as presently the crowd broke into a tremendous uproar, which forced the Police Superintendent hastily to go and see what was the matter, an action which had to be taken with a lot of discretion since Gandhi disliked all police arrangements.

Through archways and ringing cries of '*Gandhi ki jai*', Gandhi drove in the huge Bentley which the Chairman had left at his disposal. People sat on trees and house-tops all along the way and cheered Gandhiji as he passed. The police had cordoned off various side streets that led off from the Market Road, so the passage was clear from the little Malgudi station to Lawley Extension. There were policemen everywhere, although the District Superintendent of Police felt that the security arrangements had not been satisfactory. All shops had been closed and all schools, and the whole town was celebrating. Schoolchildren felt delighted at the thought of Gandhi. Office-goers were happy, and even banks were closed. They waited in the sun for hours, saw him pass in his Bentley, a white-clad figure, fair-skinned and radiant, with his palms pressed together in a salute.

When they entered Neel Bagh, whose massive gates were of cast iron patterned after the gates of Buckingham Palace, the Chairman, who was seated in the front seat, waited to be asked: 'Whose house is this?' But Gandhiji did not seem to notice anything. They passed through the drive with hedges trimmed, flower pots putting forth exotic blooms, and lawns stretching away on either side, and he kept his ears alert to catch any remark that Gandhiji might let fall, but still he said nothing. He was busy looking through some papers which his secretary had passed to him.

The thought that Gandhiji was actually within his gates sent a thrill of joy up and down the Chairman's spine. He had arranged everything nicely. All his own things for a few days had been sent off to the Circuit House (which the Collector had given him on condition that he limewash its walls and repaint its wooden doors and shutters). He felt a thrill at the thought of his own sacrifice. Some years before he would never have thought of forsaking his own air-conditioned suite and choosing to reside at the Circuit House, for anybody's sake. The Chairman had now surrendered his whole house to Gandhiji. No doubt it was big enough to accommodate his own family without interfering with his venerable guest and his party (a miscellaneous gathering of men and women, dressed in white *khaddar*, who attended on Mahatmaji in various capacities, who all looked alike and whose names he could never clearly grasp); but he did not like to stay on because it seemed impossible to live under the same roof with such a distinguished man and to take away a little from the sense of patriotic sacrifice that his action entailed. So he decided to transfer himself to the Circuit House.

He had effected a few alterations in his house, such as substituting *khaddar* hangings for the gaudy chintz that had adorned his doorways and windows, and had taken down the pictures of hunting gentry, vague gods and kings. He had even the temerity to remove the picture of George V's wedding and substitute pictures of Maulana Azad, Jawaharlal Nehru, Sarojini Naidu, Motilal Nehru, C. Rajagopalachari and Annie Besant. He had ordered his works manager to secure within a given time 'all the available portraits of our national leaders', a wholesale order which was satisfactorily executed; and all the other pictures were taken down and sent off to the basement room. He had also discreetly managed to get a picture of Krishna discoursing to Arjuna on the Bhagavad-Gita, knowing well Gandhi's bias towards the Bhagavad-Gita. He had kept on the window sill and in a few other places a few specimens of the *charka* (spinning wheel).

No film decorator sought to create atmosphere with greater deliberation. He worked all the previous night to attain this effect, and had also secured for himself a *khaddar jibba* and a white Gandhi cap, for his wife a white *khaddar* saree, and for his son a complete outfit in *khaddar*. His car drove nearly a hundred miles within the city in order to search for a white *khaddar* cap to fit his six-year-old son's dolicho-cephalic head, and on his shirt front he had embroidered the tricolour and a spinning wheel.

Now he hoped as he approached the main building that his wife and son would emerge in their proper make-up to meet Gandhi: he hoped his wife would have had the good sense to take away the diamond studs not only in her ears but also in their son's. He had forgotten to caution them about it. The moment the car stopped in the decorated porch of the house, the Chairman jumped down, held the door open and helped Mahatmaji to alight.

'You are most welcome to this humble abode of mine, great sire,' he said in confusion, unable to talk coherently. Mahatmaji got down from the car and looked at the house.

'Is this your house?' he asked.

'Yes, sir, by the grace of God, I built it four years ago,' the Chairman said, his throat going dry.

He led Gandhi up the veranda steps. He had placed a divan in the veranda covered with *khaddar* printed cloth. He seated Gandhi on it and asked his secretary in a whisper: 'May I give Mahatmaji a glassful of orange juice? The oranges are from my own estates in Mempi.' A number of visitors and a miscellaneous crowd of people were passing in and out. It seemed to the Chairman that Mahatmaji's presence had the effect of knocking down the walls of a house, and converting it into a public place—but that was the price one had to pay for having the great man there. People were squatting on the lawns and the Chairman saw helplessly that some were plucking flowers in his annual bed, which had been tended by his municipal overseers.

Gandhi turned in his direction and asked: 'What were you saying?' His secretary communicated the offer of oranges.

Gandhi said: 'Yes, most welcome. I shall be happy to look at the oranges grown in your own gardens.'

The Chairman ran excitedly about and returned bearing a large tray filled with uniform golden oranges. He was panting with the effort. He had gone so far in self-abnegation that he would not accept the services of his usual attendants. He placed the tray in front of Mahatmaji.

'My humble offering to a great man; these are from my own orchards on the Mempi hills,' he said. 'They were plucked this morning.'

Then he asked, 'May I have the honour of giving you a glass

of orange juice? You must have had a tiring day.'

The Mahatma declined, explaining that it was not his hour for taking anything. He picked up one fruit and examined it with appreciative comments, turning it slowly between his fingers. The Chairman felt as happy as if he himself were being scrutinized and approved. On the edge of the crowd, standing below on the drive, Mahatmaji noticed a little boy and beckoned to him to come nearer. The boy hesitated. Mahatmaji said: '*Ao, Ao*—' in Hindi. When it made no impression on the boy, he said in the little Tamil he had picked up for this part of the country, '*Inge va*.' Others pushed the boy forward; he came haltingly. Gandhi offered him a seat on his divan, and gave him an orange. This acted as a signal. Presently the divan was swarming with children. When the tray was empty, the Mahatma asked the Chairman: 'Have you some more?' The Chairman went in and brought a further supply in a basket; and all the children threw off their reserve, became clamorous and soon the basket was empty. 'There are some flowers and garlands in the car,' Gandhi whispered to his secretary—these had been presented to him on his arrival and all along the way by various associations. The place was fragrant with roses and jasmine. These he distributed to all the little girls he saw in the gathering. The Chairman felt chagrined at the thought that the event was developing into a children's party. After the oranges and flowers he hoped that the children would leave, but he found them still there. 'They are probably waiting for apples now, I suppose!' he reflected bitterly. Gandhi had completely relaxed. His secretary was telling him: 'In fifteen minutes the deputation from—will be here, and after that—' He was reading from an engagement pad.

The Chairman regretted that both the District Superintendent of Police and the Collector had turned away at his Buckingham Palace gate after escorting the procession that far as an act of official courtesy: if they had been here now, they would have managed the crowd. For a moment he wondered with real anxiety whether the crowd proposed to stay all night. But his problem was unexpectedly solved for him. Mahatmaji saw one child standing apart from the rest—a small dark fellow with a protruding belly and wearing nothing over his body except a cast-off knitted vest, adult size, full of holes, which reached down to his ankles. The boy stood aloof from the rest, on the very edge of the crowd. His face was covered with mud, his feet were dirty, he had stuck his fingers into his mouth and was watching the proceedings on the veranda keenly, his eyes bulging with wonder and desire. He had not dared to come up the steps, though attracted by the oranges. He was trying to edge his way through.

The Mahatma's eyes travelled over the crowd and rested on this boy—following his gaze the Chairman was bewildered. He had a feeling of uneasiness. Mahatmaji beckoned to the young fellow. One of his men went and fetched him. The Chairman's blood boiled. Of course people must like poor people and so on, but why bring in such a dirty boy, an untouchable, up the steps and make him so important? For a moment he felt a little annoyance with Mahatmaji himself, but soon suppressed it as a sinful emotion. He felt the need to detach himself sufficiently from his surroundings to watch without perturbation the happenings around him. Mahatmaji had the young urchin hoisted beside him on the divan. 'Oh, Lord, all the world's gutters are on this boy, and he is going to leave a permanent stain on that Kashmir counterpane.' The boy was making himself comfortable on the divan, having accepted the hospitality offered him by the Mahatma. He nestled close to the Mahatma, who was smoothing out his matted hair with his fingers, and was engaged in an earnest conversation with him.

The Chairman was unable to catch the trend of their talk. He stepped nearer, trying to listen with all reverence. The reward he got for it was a smile from the Mahatma himself. The boy was saying: 'My father sweeps the streets.'

'With a long broom or a short broom?' the Mahatma asked.

The boy explained, 'He has both a long broom and a short broom.' He was spitting out the seeds of an orange.

The Mahatma turned to someone and explained: 'It means that he is both a municipal sweeper and that he has scavenging work to do in private houses also. The long broom ought to be the municipal emblem.'

'Where is your father at the moment?'

'He is working at the market. He will take me home when he has finished his work.'

'And how have you managed to come here?'

'I was sitting on the road waiting for my father and I came along with the crowd. No one stopped me when I entered the gates.'

'That's a very clever boy,' Mahatmaji said. 'I'm very happy to see you. But you must not spit those pips all over the place, in fact you must never spit at all. It's very unclean to do so, and may cause others a lot of trouble. When you eat an orange, others must not notice it at all. The place must be absolutely tidy even if you have polished off six at a time.'

He laughed happily at his own quip, and then taught the boy what to do with the pips, how to hide the skin, and what to do with all the superfluous bits packed within an orange. The boy laughed with joy. All the men around watched the proceedings with respectful attention. And then Gandhi asked:

'Where do you live?'

The boy threw up his arm to indicate a far distance: 'There at the end of the river . . .'

'Will you let me come to your house?'

The boy hesitated and said, 'Not now—because, because it's so far away.'

'Don't bother about that. I've a motor car here given to me, you see, by this very rich man. I can be there in a moment. I'll take you along in the motor car too if you will show me your house.'

'It is not a house like this,' said the boy, 'but made of bamboo or something.'

'Is that so!' said the Mahatma. 'Then I'll like it all the more. I'll be very happy there.'

He had a brief session with a delegation which had come to see him by appointment; when it left, he dictated some notes, wrote something, and then, picking up his staff, said to the Chairman, 'Let us go to this young man's house. I'm sure you will also like it.'

'Now?' asked the Chairman in great consternation. He mumbled, 'Shall we not go there tomorrow?'

'No, I've offered to take this child home. I must not disappoint him. I'd like to see his father too, if he can be met anywhere on the way.'

Mahatmaji gave his forefinger to the young boy to clutch and allowed himself to be led down the veranda steps. The Chairman asked dolefully, 'Won't you come in and have a look round my humble home?'

'I know how it will be. It must be very grand. But would you not rather spare an old man like me the bother of walking through those vast spaces? I'm a tired old man. You are very hospitable. Anyway, come along with us to this little man's home. If I feel like it, you will let me stay there.'

The Chairman mumbled, 'I hoped—' But Gandhiji swept him aside with a smile:

'You will come along with me too. Let me invite you to come and stay with me in a hut.'

Unable to say anything more, the Chairman merely replied, 'All right, sir, I obey.'

The warmth of the Mahatma's invitation made him forget his problems as a Chairman and his own responsibilities. Otherwise he would not have become oblivious of the fact that the sweepers' colony was anything but a showpiece. Not till the Collector later sought him out and arraigned him for his lapse did it occur to him what a blunder he had committed.

The Collector said, 'Have you so little sense, Chairman, that you could not have delayed Mr Gandhi's visit at least by two hours, time to give the people a chance to sweep and clean up that awful place? You know as well as I do, what it is like!' All of which the Chairman took in without a word.

He was gloating over the words spoken to him by Mahatmaji. Not till his wife later attacked him did he remember his omission in another direction. She said in a tone full of wrath, 'There I was waiting, dressed as you wanted, with the boy, and you simply went away without even calling us!'

'Why couldn't you have come out?' he asked idiotically.

'How could I, when you had said I must wait for your call?' she sobbed. 'With the great man at our house, I had not the good fortune even to appear before him. And the child—what a disappointment for him!'

When they got over their initial surprise, the authorities did everything to transform the place. All the stench mysteriously vanished; all the garbage and offal that lay about, and flesh and hide put out to sun-dry on the roofs, disappeared. All that night municipal and other employees kept working, with the aid of petrol lamps: light there was such a rarity that the children kept dancing all night around the lamps. Gandhiji noticed the hectic activity, but out of a sense of charity refrained from commenting on it. Only when it was all over did he say, 'Now one can believe that the true cleansers of the city live here.' The men of the colony tied round their beads their whitest turbans and the women wore their best sarees, dragged their children to the river and scrubbed them till they yelled, and decorated their coiffures with yellow chrysanthemum flowers. The men left off fighting, did their best to keep away from the drink shops, and even the few confirmed topers had their drinks on the sly, and suppressed their impulse to beat their wives or break their household pots. The whole place looked bright with lamps and green mango leaves tied across lamp-posts and tree branches.

Gandhi occupied a hut which had a low entrance. He didn't like to oust anyone from his hut, but chose one facing the river sand, after making certain that it had been vacant, the occupant of the hut having gone elsewhere. The Chairman brought in a low divan and covered the floor with a coarse rush mat for Gandhi's visitors to sit on. Sriram lowered himself unobtrusively on the mat. Gandhi sat on his divan, and dictated to one of his secretaries. They wrote voluminously. Mahatmaji performed a number of things simultaneously. He spoke to visitors. He dictated. He wrote. He prayed. He had his sparse dinner of nuts and milk, and presently he even laid himself down on the divan and went off to sleep. It was then that someone turned off the lamp, and people walked out of the hut.

Sriram now felt that he could not continue to sit there. Although no one bothered to ask him what he was doing, he could not stay any more. When he saw the girl was preparing to leave the hut, he thought he had better get up and go; otherwise someone might say something unpleasant to him.

The girl lifted Gandhi's spinning wheel, put it away noiselessly, and tip-toed out of the room. She passed without noticing him at first, but the fixed stare with which he followed her movements seemed to affect her. She went past him, but suddenly stopped and whispered: 'You will have to go now,' and Sriram sprang up and found himself outside the hut in one bound.

She said rather grimly: 'Don't you know that when Bapuji sleeps, we have to leave him?'

He felt like asking, 'Who is Bapuji?' but using his judgement for a second, he understood it must refer to the Mahatma, and not wanting to risk being chased out by the resolute girl said, 'Of course, I knew it. I was only waiting for you to come out.'

'Who are you? I don't think I have seen you before.'

This was the question he had been waiting to be asked all along, but now when it came he found himself tongue-tied. He felt so confused and muddled that she took pity on him and said, 'What is your name?'

He answered, 'Sriram.'

'What are you doing here?' she asked.

'Don't you remember me?' he said irrelevantly. 'I saw you when you came with a money-box in the market, the other day . . .'

'Oh, I see,' she said out of politeness. 'But I might not remember you since quite a lot of people put money into my box that day. Anyway, I asked you what you are doing here now?'

'Perhaps I'm one of the volunteers,' Sriram said.

'Why "perhaps"?' she asked.

'Because I'm not yet one,' he replied.

'Anybody cannot be a volunteer,' she said. 'Don't you know that?' she asked.

'Don't I know that? I think I know that and more.'

'What more?' she asked.

'That I am not an anybody,' he replied and was amazed at his own foolhardiness in talking to the girl in that fashion; she could put him out of the camp in a moment.

'You are a somebody, I suppose?' the girl asked laughing.

'Well, you will help me to become somebody, I hope,' he said, feeling surprised at his own powers of rash and reckless speech.

She seemed a match for him, for presently she asked, with a little irritation, 'Are we going to stand here and talk the whole night?'

'Yes, unless you show me where we can go.'

'I know where I ought to go,' she said. 'You see that hut there,' she pointed to a small hut four doors off Gandhi's, 'that's where all the women of this camp are quartered.'

'How many of them are there?' Sriram asked just to keep up the conversation.

She answered sharply, 'More than you see before you now,' and added, 'why are you interested?'

Sriram felt a little piqued. 'You seem to be a very ill-tempered and sharp-tongued girl. You can't answer a single question without a challenge.'

'Hush! You will wake up Bapuji standing and talking here,' she said.

'Well, if he is going to be awakened by anyone's talk, it will be yours, because no one else is doing the talking,' he replied.

'I have a right to ask you what you are doing here and report to our *chalak* if I don't like you,' she said with a sudden tone of authority.

'Why should you not like me?' he asked.

'No one except close associates and people with appointments is allowed to enter Bapuji's presence.'

'I will tell them I am your friend and that you took me in,' he replied.

'Would you utter a falsehood?' she asked.

'Why not?'

'None except absolute truth-speakers are allowed to come into Mahatma's camp. People who come here must take an oath of absolute truth before going into Mahatma's presence.'

'I will take the vow when I become a member of the camp. Till then I will pass off something that looks like truth,' he said.

'When Mahatma hears about this he will be very pained and he will talk to you about it.'

Sriram was now genuinely scared and asked pathetically, 'What have I done that you should threaten and menace me?'

This softened her, and for the first time he noticed a little tenderness had crept into her tone.

'Do you mind moving off and waiting there? We should not be talking like this near Mahatmaji's hut. I will go to my hut and then join you there.'

She turned and disappeared; she had the lightning like motion of a dancer, again the sort of pirouetting movement that she had adopted while carrying off other people's coins in a jingling box. She passed down the lane. He moved off slowly. He was tired of standing. He sat on a boulder at the edge of the river, kicking up the sand with his toes, and ruminating on his good fortune. He had never hoped for anything like it. It might have been a dream. This time yesterday he could not have thought he would talk on these terms to the money-box girl. He realized he had not yet asked her her name. He remembered that he had felt hungry and thirsty long ago. 'I wish they would give us all something to eat in Mahatmaji's camp.' He remembered that Mahatma ate only groundnuts and dates. He looked about hoping there would be vendors of these things. The Taluk Office gong sounded nine. He counted it deliberately, and wondered what his granny would make of his absence now. 'She will fret and report to the police, I suppose!' he reflected cynically. He wished he had asked his teacher to go and tell Granny not to expect him home till Gandhiji left the town. On second thoughts it struck him that it was just as well that he had not spoken to the teacher, who would probably have gone and spread the rumour that his interest in Gandhi was only a show and that he was really going after a girl. What was her name? Amazing how he had not yet asked her it, and the moment she came back he said, 'What is your name?'

'Bharati,' she answered. 'Why?'

'Just to know, that's all. Have I told you my name is Sriram?'

'Yes, you have told me that more than once,' she said. 'I have heard again and again that you are Sriram.'

'You are too sharp-tongued,' he replied. 'It is a wonder they tolerate you here, where peace and kindness must be practised.'

'I am practising kindness, otherwise I should not be speaking to you at all. If I didn't want to be kind to you I wouldn't have gone in and taken my *chalak's* permission and come here right away. We must have permission to talk to people at this hour. There is such a thing as discipline in every camp. Don't imagine that because it is Mahatmaji's camp it is without any discipline. He would be the first to tell you about it if you raised the question with him.'

'You have the same style of talk as my grandmother. She is as sharp-tongued as you are,' Sriram said pathetically.

She ignored the comparison and asked, 'What about your mother?'

'I have never seen her, my grandmother has always been father and mother to me. Why don't you meet her? You will like her, both of you speak so much alike!'

'Yes, yes,' said the girl soothingly, 'some day I will come and meet her as soon as this is all over. You see how busy I am now.'

She became tender when she found that she was talking to someone without a mother, and Sriram noticing this felt it was worthwhile being motherless and grandmother-tended. She sat on the same step, with her legs dangling in the river leaving a gap of a couple of feet between them. The river rumbled into the dark starlit night, the leaves of the huge tree over the ancient steps rustled and sighed. Far off bullock carts and pedestrians were fording the river at Nallappa's Grove. Distant voices came through the night. Mahatmaji's camp was asleep. It was so quiet that Sriram felt like taking the girl in his arms, but he resisted the idea. He feared that if he touched her she might push him into the river. The girl was a termagant, she would surely develop into the same type as his grandmother with that sharp tongue of hers. Her proximity pricked his blood and set it coursing.

'There is no one about. What can she do?' he reflected. 'Let her try and push me into the river, and she will know with whom she is dealing,' and the next moment he blamed himself for his own crude thoughts. 'It is not safe with the Mahatma there. He may already have read my thoughts and be coming here.' He was a Mahatma because awake or asleep he was fully aware of what was going on all round him. God alone could say what the Mahatma would do to someone who did not possess absolute purity of thought where girls were concerned. It meant hardship, no doubt, but if one was to live in this camp one had to follow the orders that emanated from the great soul. He struggled against evil thoughts and said, 'Bharati!' She looked startled at being called so familiarly and he himself felt startled by the music of her name.

'What a nice name!' he remarked.

'I am glad you like it,' she said. 'The name was given by Bapuji himself.'

'Oh, how grand!' he cried.

She added, 'You know my father died during the 1920 movement. Just when I was born. When he learnt of it Bapuji, who had come down South, made himself my godfather and named me Bharati, which means—I hope you know what.'

'Yes, Bharat is India, and Bharati is the daughter of India, I suppose.'

'Right,' she said, and he was pleased at her commendation.

'After my mother died, I was practically adopted by the local Sevak Sangh, and I have not known any other home since,' she said.

'Do you mean to say you are all the time with these people?'

'What is wrong in it?' she asked. 'It has been my home.'

'Not that, I was only envying you. I too wish I could be with you all and do something instead of wasting my life.'

This appealed to her and she asked, 'What do you want to do?'

'The same as what you are doing. What are you doing?' he asked.

'I do whatever I am asked to do by the Sevak Sangh. Sometimes they ask me to go and teach people spinning and tell them about Mahatmaji's ideas. Sometimes they send me to villages and poor quarters. I meet them and talk to them and do a few things. I attend to Mahatmaji's needs.'

'Please let me also do something along with you,' he pleaded.

'Why don't you take me as your pupil? I want to do something good. I want to talk to poor people.'

'What will you tell them?' she asked ruthlessly.

He made some indistinct sounds. 'I will tell them whatever you ask me to tell them,' he said, and this homage to her superior intelligence pleased her.

'H'm! But why?' she asked.

He summoned all his courage and answered, 'Because I like you, and I like to be with you.'

She burst into a laugh and said, 'That won't be sufficient . . . They . . .' she indicated a vast army of hostile folk behind her back. 'They may chase you away if you speak like that.'

He became sullen and unhappy. He rallied and said presently, 'Well, I too would willingly do something.'

'What?' she taunted him again.

He looked at her face helplessly, desperately, and asked, 'Are you making fun of me?'

'No, but I wish to understand what you are saying.'

She relented a little, presently, and said, 'I will take you to Bapu, will you come?'

He was panic-stricken. 'No, no. I can't.'

'You have been there already.'

He could give no reasonable explanation and now he realized the enormity of his rashness. He said, 'No, no, I would be at a loss to know how to talk to him, how to reply to him and what to tell him.'

'But you sat there before him like someone always known to him!' she said. 'Like his best friend.'

She laughed and enjoyed teasing him.

'Somehow I did it, but I won't do it again,' he declared. 'He may find me out if I go before him again.'

Suddenly she became very serious and said, 'You will have to face Bapuji if you want to work with us.'

Sriram became speechless. His heart palpitated with excitement. He wished he could get up and run away, flee once and for all the place, be done with it, and turn his back on the whole business for ever. This was too much. The gods seemed to be out to punish him for his hardihood and presumption.

He cried, 'Bharati, tell me if I can meet you anywhere else, otherwise please let me go.' He was in a cold sweat. 'What should

I say when I speak to him? I would blabber like an idiot.'

'You are already doing it,' she said, unable to restrain her laughter.

He said pathetically, 'You seem to enjoy bothering me. I am sorry I ever came here.'

'Why are you so cowardly?' she asked.

Sriram said resolutely, 'I can't talk to Mahatmaji. I wouldn't know how to conduct myself before him.'

'Just be yourself. It will be all right.'

'I wouldn't be able to answer his questions properly.'

'He is not going to examine you like an inspector of schools. You don't have to talk to him unless you have something to say. You may keep your mouth shut and he won't mind. You may just be yourself, say anything you feel like saying. He will not mind anything at all, but you will have to speak the truth if you speak at all.'

'Truth! In everything!' he looked scared.

'Yes, in everything. You may speak as bluntly as you like, and he will not take it amiss, provided it is just truth.'

Sriram looked more crushed than ever. In this dark night he seemed to have a terrible problem ahead of him. After brooding over it for a while he said, 'Bharati, tell me if I may meet you anywhere else. Otherwise let me go.'

She replied with equal resolution, 'If you wish to meet me come to Bapuji, the only place where you may see me. Of course, if you don't want to see me any more, go away.'

This placed him in a dilemma. 'Where? How?' he asked.

'Come to the door of Bapu's hut and wait for me.'

'When? Where?'

'At three a.m. tomorrow morning. I'll take you to him.'

Saying this, she jumped to her feet and ran off towards her hut.

Granny had slept fitfully. She had gone up to Kanni's shop five times during the evening to enquire if anyone had seen Sriram, and sent a boy who had come to make a purchase there to look for Sriram everywhere. At last the schoolmaster who lived up the street told her as he passed her house, 'Your pet is in Mahatma's camp. I saw him.'

'Ah! What was he doing there?' asked Granny alarmed. For her the Mahatma was one who preached dangerously, who tried to bring untouchables into the temples, and who involved people in difficulties with the police. She didn't like the idea. She wailed, 'Oh, master, why did you allow him to stay on there? You should have brought him away. It is so late and he has not come home. As his old teacher you should have weaned him away.'

'Don't worry, madam, he is perfectly safe. How many of us could have the privilege of being so near the Mahatma? You must be happy that he is doing so well! Our country needs more young men like him.'

Granny replied, 'It is teachers like you who have ruined our boys and this country,' and turned in, slamming the door.

When Sriram arrived and knocked she was half asleep and in the worst possible mood. She opened the door, let him in, bolted the door again, and went back to her bed saying, 'I have kept some rice in that bowl mixed with curd and the other one is without curd. Put out the lamp after you have eaten.' Lying in bed, she listened to the sound of Sriram putting away his plate and leaving the kitchen. And then she turned her face to the wall and pretended to be asleep. She hoped that her grandson would understand her mood, come over, and assure her that he would not get into bad ways: but the young man was otherwise engaged. He was in a state of semi-enchantment. Bharati's presence and talk still echoed in his mind, and he recollected the thrill of her touch. He liked to think that when he was not noticing she had touched his arm and patted his shoulder. He thought how he would prefer the rest of his life listening to her banter, but that meant—here was the conflict—he would have to go into the Presence. All else seemed to him insignificant beside this great worry. If it had been any other day he would have pulled his granny out of her sleep and narrated to her all the day's events. If she happened to be in a bad mood he would have pulled her out of it. He knew now that she was not in a proper temper; he could sense it the moment he stepped on the threshold, but he preferred to leave her alone; he felt he had a far greater problem to tackle than appeasing the mood of a mere granny.

He went to bed and slept in all less than an hour. Bharati wanted him there at three a.m., and he needed an hour to reach the place. He got up before one, washed and bathed and put on special clothes, bent over his granny's bed to whisper, 'I have to be going now, bolt the door.'

She tried to ask, 'What! At this hour, what has come over you?' but he was gone on soft footsteps, closing the door behind him.

He stood at the entrance to Mahatmaji's hut, holding his breath. It was very difficult to decide what he should do now. She had asked him to be present at the portals of the Great Presence, but perhaps she had been fooling him. He feared that any sound he made might rouse the Mahatma and bring the entire camp about his ears. He stood ruefully looking at the camp. Street dogs were barking somewhere. Occasionally the branches of trees over the river rustled and creaked. He stood looking ruefully towards the women's quarters. There a lantern was burning, people seemed to be awake and moving about. He thought, 'What if the lantern is burning? They may be sleeping with lights on. Women are cowardly anyway.' The stirring he heard might be them rolling in their beds, noisy creatures! Unaccountably he was feeling irritated at the thought of women, the species to which Bharati belonged. He saw a light in Mahatmaji's camp. The door was shut. He heard soft footsteps moving in there. Long ago the Taluk Office gong had struck some small hour. He could hardly believe he had actually sacrificed his sleep and was standing here in the cold wind, at an unearthly hour. Even the scavengers, the earliest to rise in the town, were still asleep. He felt suddenly afraid that he might be attacked by thieves or ghosts. Or if a policeman saw him and took him to be a prowler, how should he explain himself? He couldn't very well say, 'Bharati asked me to wait at Mahatmaji's hut at about three a.m.' He wanted to turn and go away: he could at least go home and make up to his grandmother instead of hanging around here and wondering what to do. He could tell her: 'I went to see the Mahatma, but changed my mind and came away. Why should I get to know him and then get into all sorts of difficulties? Don't you think so, Granny?' And she was sure to revive and look happy again.

He gave one forlorn look at the women's quarters and turned away, his mind completely made up to earn the concrete goodwill of a granny rather than the doubtful and strange favours of bigwigs like the Mahatma and snobs like Bharati. Heaven knew who else would be there. But still the pull of Bharati was strong and he could not get away from the place so easily as he had imagined. He wanted to make just one more attempt to see her and bid her goodbye. Perhaps she was in a situation in which he could help her:

people might have tied her up to her cot and gagged her mouth. Anything might happen to a beautiful girl like her. Otherwise there could be no explanation for her absence. Anyway, he felt it would be his duty to go and find out what was wrong and where. He'd have willingly gone near the women's quarters, but he lacked the necessary courage and did the next best thing: once again repeating a rash act he tip-toed towards Mahatmaji's hut: his idea was to peep in unobtrusively, and see if Bharati was there or anywhere else safe and sound and then move off. But in his befuddled state it did not occur to him that possibly he might be seen before he saw anyone. And it happened so. The door of Mahatmaji's hut was half open. Light streamed out through the gap. Sriram went towards it like a charmed moth. If he had paused to reflect he would not have believed himself to be capable of repeating a foolhardy act a second time. But through lack of sleep, and tension of nerves, a general recklessness had come over him, the same innocent charge that had taken him tumbling into the hut the previous evening took him there again now. He peeped in like a clown. The door was half open; he had overestimated its width from a distance, for he could not peep in without thrusting his head through.

'Oh, there he is!' cried Bharati, with laughter in her voice. 'You may open the door if you wish to come in,' she said. Sriram felt again that the girl was making fun of him. Even in the great presence, she didn't seem to care. Here at least Sriram had hoped she would speak without the undertone of mischief. He felt so irritated at the thought that he replied with all the pungency he could muster in his tone: 'You have—I waited for you there—'

'Come in, come in,' said the Mahatma. 'Why should you be standing there? You could have come straight in.'

'But she asked me to wait outside,' said Sriram, stepping in gingerly. From the door to where the Mahatma sat the distance was less than ten feet, but he felt he was taking hours to cover it. His legs felt weak and seemed to intertwine, he seemed to be walking like a drunkard, a particularly dangerous impression to create in the Mahatma, who was out to persuade even the scavengers to give up drinking. In a flash it occurred to him that he ought to have a sensible answer ready if the Mahatma should suddenly turn round and ask, 'Have you been drinking toddy or whisky?'

But his trial came to an end, when Gandhi said, 'Bharati has just been mentioning you.' He spoke while his hands were busy turning a spinning wheel, drawing out a fine thread. A man sitting in a corner, with a pad resting on his knee, was writing. Mahatmaji himself as always was doing several things at the same time. While his hands were spinning, his eyes perused a letter held before him by another, and he found it possible too to put in a word of welcome to Sriram. Through the back door of the hut many others were coming in and passing out. For each one of them Mahatmaji had something to say.

He looked up at Sriram and said: 'Sit down, young man. Come and sit as near me as you like.' There was so much unaffected graciousness in his tone that Sriram lost all fear and hesitation. He moved briskly up. He sat on the floor near Mahatmaji and watched with fascination the smooth turning of the spinning wheel. Bharati went to an inner part of the hut, threw a swift look at Sriram, which he understood to mean, 'Remember not to make a fool of yourself.'

The Mahatma said, 'Nowadays I generally get up an hour earlier in order to be able to do this: spinning a certain length is my most important work: even my prayer comes only after that. I'd very much like you to take a vow to wear only cloth made out of your own hands each day.'

'Yes, I will do so,' promised Sriram.

When the gong in the Taluk Office struck four, the Mahatma invited Sriram to go out with him for a walk. He seized his staff in one hand and with the other supported himself on the shoulder of Bharati, and strode out of the hut—a tall figure in white. He had tucked his watch at his waist into a fold of his white *dhoti*. He pulled it out and said: 'Half an hour I have to walk, come with me, Sriram. You can talk to me undisturbed.' A few others joined them. Sriram felt he was walking through some unreal dream world. The Mahatma was in between him and Bharati, and it was difficult to snatch a look at her as often as he wanted. He had to step back a quarter of an inch now and then, in order to catch a glimpse of her laughing face. They walked along the river bank. The sky was rosy in the east. Gandhi turned and spoke some business to those behind him. He suddenly addressed himself to Sriram: 'Your town is very beautiful. Have you ever noticed it before?' Sriram felt unhappy and gasped for breath. The morning air blew on his face, birds were chirping, the city was quiet: it was all well known, but why did the Mahatma mention it especially now? Should he say 'Yes' or 'No'? If he said 'Yes' he would be lying, which would be detected at once; if he said

'No', God knew what the Mahatma would think of him. He looked about. A couple of scavengers of the colony who had joined the group were waiting eagerly to know what he would say: they were evidently enjoying his predicament, and he dared not look in the direction of Bharati. The Mahatma said: 'God is everywhere, and if you want to feel his presence you will see him in a place like this with a beautiful river flowing, the sunrise with all its colours, and the air so fresh. Feeling a beautiful hour or a beautiful scene or a beautiful object is itself a form of prayer.' Sriram listened in reverential silence, glad to be let off so lightly. When Gandhiji spoke of beauty, it sounded unreal as applied to the sun and the air, but the word acquired a practical significance when he thought of it in terms of Bharati. Gandhi said: 'By the time we meet again next, you must give me a very good account of yourself.'

He laughed in a kindly manner, and Sriram said, 'Yes, Bapuji, I will be a different man.'

'Why do you say "different"? You will be all right if you are fully yourself.'

'I don't think that is enough, Bapu,' said Bharati. 'He should change from being himself, if he is to come to any good. I think he is very lazy. He gets up at eight o'clock, and idles away the day.'

'How do you know?' Sriram asked indignantly.

'It's only a guess,' said the girl. Sriram felt angry with her for her irresponsible talk. Everyone laughed.

The Mahatma said: 'You must not say such things, Bharati, unless you mean to take charge of him and help him.'

During the last fifteen minutes of this walk the Mahatma said nothing; he walked in silence, looking at the ground before him. When the Mahatma was silent the others were even more so, the only movement they performed was putting one foot before another on the sand, keeping pace with him: some were panting hard and trying hard to suppress the sound. The Mahatma's silence was heavy and pervasive, and Sriram was afraid even to gulp or cough, although he very much wanted to clear his throat, cough, sneeze, swing his arms about. The only sound at the moment was the flowing of the river and the twitter of birds. Somewhere a cow was mooing. Even Bharati, the embodiment of frivolity, seemed to have become sombre. The Mahatma pulled out his watch, looked at it briefly and said, 'We will go back, that is all the walk I can afford today.' Sriram wanted to ask, 'Why?' but he held his tongue. The

Mahatma turned to him as they were walking back, 'You have a grandmother, I hear, but no parents.'

'Yes. My grandmother is very old.'

'Yes, she must be, otherwise how can you call her a grandmother?' People laughed; Sriram too joined in this laughter out of politeness.

'Does she not miss you very much when you are away from her so long?'

'Yes, very much. She gets very angry with me. I don't know what to do about it,' said Sriram courageously rushing ahead. He felt pleased at having said something of his own accord; his only fear was that Bharati might step in and say something nasty and embarrassing, but he was happy to note that Bharati held her peace.

Mahatmaji said: 'You must look after your granny too, she must have devoted herself to bringing you up.'

'Yes, but when I am away like this she is very upset.'

'Is it necessary for you to be away from her so much?'

'Yes, Bapu, otherwise how can I do anything in this world?'

'What exactly do you want to do?'

It was now that Sriram became incoherent. He was seized with a rush of ideas and with all the confusion that too many ideas create. He said something, and the Mahatma watched him patiently, the others too held their breath and watched, and after a few moments of struggle for self-expression, Sriram was able to form a cogent sentence. It was the unrelenting pressure of his subconscious desires that jerked the sentence out of his lips, and he said, 'I like to be where Bharati is.' The Mahatma said, 'Oh, is that so!' He patted Bharati's back and said, 'What a fine friend you have! You must be pleased to have such a devoted friend. How long have you known him?'

Bharati said like a shot, 'Since yesterday. I saw him for the first time sitting in your hut and I asked him who he was.'

Sriram interposed and added, 'But I knew her before, although I spoke to her only yesterday.'

The Mahatma passed into his hut, and went on to attend to other things. Many people were waiting for him. Bharati disappeared into the Mahatma's hut the moment they arrived. Sriram fell back and got mixed up with a crowd waiting outside. He felt jealous of Bharati's position. She sought him out later and said, 'You are probably unused to it, but in Bapu's presence we speak only the absolute truth and nothing less than that, and nothing more than that either.'

He took her to task: 'What will he think of me now when he knows that I have not known you long enough and yet—'

'Well, what?' she twitted him.

'And yet I wish to be with you and so on.'

'Why don't you go in and tell him you have been speaking nonsense and that you were blurting out things without forethought or self-control? Why couldn't you have told him that you want to serve the country, that you are a patriot, that you want to shed your blood in order to see that the British leave the country? That is what most people say when they come near the Mahatma. I have seen hundreds of people come to him, and say the same thing.'

'And he believes all that?' asked Sriram.

'Perhaps not, but he thinks it is not right to disbelieve anyone.'

'But you say we must only speak the truth in his presence.'

'If you can, of course, but if you can't, the best thing to do is to maintain silence.'

'Why are you so angry with me, is it not a part of your duty not to be angry with others?' asked Sriram pathetically.

'I don't care,' said Bharati, 'this is enough to irritate even the Mahatma. Now what will he think of me if he realizes I am encouraging a fellow like you to hang about the place, a fellow whom I have not known even for a full day yet!'

Sriram became reckless, and said breezily, 'What does it matter how long I have known you? Did you think I was going to lie to him if you had not spoken before I spoke?'

These bickerings were brought to an end by someone calling 'Bharati' from another hut. Bharati abandoned him and disappeared from the spot.

Bharati's words gave him an idea. He realized his own omission, and proposed to remedy it next time he walked with the Mahatma. Sriram's anxiety lest he fall asleep when the Mahatma was up kept him awake the whole night. He shared the space on the floor with one of the men in the camp. It was a strange feeling to lie down in a hut, and he felt he was becoming a citizen of an entirely new world. He missed the cosy room of his house in Kabir Lane, he missed the two pillows and the soft mattress and the carpet under it; even the street noises of Kabir Street added much to the domestic quality of life, and he missed it badly now. He had to adopt an entirely new mode of life. He had to live, of his own choice, in a narrow hut, with thatch above, with a dingy, sooty smell hanging about everything. The floor had been swept with cow dung and covered with a thin layer of sand. He had to snuggle his head on the crook of his arm for a pillow. He had to share this place with another volunteer in the camp, a cadaverous serious young man wearing *khadi* shorts, a *khadi* vest, and a white cap on his closely shaved head. He had a fiery look and an unsmiling face. He was from north India, he could only speak broken English and he was totally ignorant of Tamil words. This man had already stretched himself on the floor with a small bag stuffed with clothes under his head.

Bharati had told Sriram, 'You had better stick on here, around the camp, if you want to be with Mahatmaji. You won't have any comforts here, remember. We are all trained to live like this.'

Sriram sniffed and said, 'Oh, who wants any comforts? I don't care for them myself. You think I am a fellow who cares for luxuries in life?'

There was a class of society where luxuries gave one a status, and now here was the opposite. The more one asserted one cared for no luxury, the more one showed an inclination for hardship and discomfort, the greater was one's chance of being admitted into the fold. Sriram had understood it the moment he stepped into the camp. Here the currency was suffering and self-mortification. Everyone seemed to excel his neighbour in managing in uncomfortable situations, and Sriram caught the spirit, though it took him time to grasp the detail and get accustomed to it.

There had been a meeting in the evening and after that the Mahatma retired at his usual hour of seven-thirty, and it was a signal for the entire camp to retire. Bharati sought out Sriram and gave him a plateful of rice and buttermilk and an orange, and she also held out to him a small jasmine out of a bouquet which had earlier been presented to the Mahatma by some children's deputation. He received the flower gratefully, smelt it, and asked, 'How did you know I liked jasmine?'

'It is not so difficult a thing to know,' she said and dismissed the subject immediately.

She said, 'I have found a place for you to sleep, with a volunteer named Gorpad.'

Gorpad was half asleep when Sriram entered his hut. Bharati

peeped and said, '*Bhai* . . .' and something in Hindi and turned and disappeared from the spot. The other lifted his head slightly and said, 'You can come in and sleep.'

'Only on the floor?' Sriram asked.

'Of course, of course,' said the other.

'Why?' asked Sriram.

'Why? Because Mahatmaji says so.'

'Oh,' said Sriram, feeling that he was treading on dangerous ground. 'I see that otherwise there is no reason why we should sleep on the floor.'

'What do you mean by otherwise?' said the other argumentatively.

Sriram settled himself beside Gorpad, and said, 'I didn't mean it.'

'Mean what?' said the other. He seemed to be a pugnacious fellow. Sriram felt afraid of him. What did the girl mean by putting him in with this fighter? Could it be that she disliked him, and wanted him to be beaten? If she disliked him, she would not have given him a jasmine flower. It was well known that jasmine was exchanged only between persons who liked each other, and yet the girl gave him a jasmine with one hand and with the other led him into the company of this terrible man. The other might sit on his chest while he slept and try to choke him.

Gorpad said, 'You are new, I suppose?'

'Yes,' said Sriram. 'I am new to this place. It is through Mahatmaji's kindness I am now here, otherwise I should have gone home and slept.'

'Yes,' Gorpad said, seeming to understand the situation in a fresh light. 'You are welcome here. We are all persons who have to live like soldiers in a camp. We are indeed soldiers in our fight to eject the British from our land. We are all prepared to sacrifice our lives for the task. We sleep here on the bare floor because the major part of our lives we shall have to spend in jail, where we won't be given such a comfortable bed unless we are A or B class prisoners. We are not important enough to be classified as A or B, and you had better get used to it all; and we are always prepared to be beaten by the police, *lathi*-charged, dragged to the jail, or even shot: my father died ten years ago facing a policeman's gun.'

Sriram said, not to be outdone in the matter of political reminiscences, 'I know Bharati's father also died in the same way, when he was beaten by the police.'

'That was during the first non-cooperation days in 1920; her father led the first batch of *Satyagrahis* who were going to take down the Union Jack from the Secretariat at Madras. He was beaten with a police *lathi*, and a blow fell on his chest and he dropped dead, but my father was shot. Do you know he was actually shot by a policeman's rifle? I was also in the crowd watching him. He was picketing a shop where they were selling toddy and other alcoholic drinks, and a police company came and asked him to go away, but he refused. A crowd gathered, and there was a lot of mess and in the end the police shot him point blank.' He wiped away tears at the memory of it. 'I will not rest till the British are sent out of India,' his voice was thick with sorrow. 'My brother became a terrorist and shot dead many English officials, nobody knows his whereabouts. I should also have joined him and shot many more Englishmen, but our Mahatma will not let me be violent even in thought,' he said ruefully.

Sriram, wishing to sound very sympathetic, said, 'All Englishmen deserve to be shot. They have been very cruel.'

'You should not even think on those lines, if you are going to be a true *Satyagrahi*,' said the other.

'No, no, I am not really thinking on those lines,' Sriram amended immediately. 'I was only feeling so sorry. Of course we should not talk of shooting anyone, and where is the gun? We have no guns. My grandmother used to say that there was a gun in our house belonging to my father. Do you know that he died in Mesopotamia? He was also shot point blank.'

'He died in the war, the last war?'

'Yes,' said Sriram.

'Then he must have been a soldier in the British Army,' Gorpad said with a touch of contempt in his voice.

Sriram noted it, but accepted it with resignation. He added as a sort of compensation, 'They say he was a great soldier.'

'Possibly, possibly,' said the other with patronage in his voice. Sriram bore it as a trial.

That night he picked up a great deal of political knowledge. Gorpad went on speaking till two a.m. and afterwards both of them left for the river, performed their ablutions there, and by the time the camp was awake Sriram had returned fresh and tidy, so that Bharati said, 'You are coming through your first day with us quite

well.' Through diligently listening to Gorpad he had picked up
many political idioms, and felt himself equipped to walk with the
Mahatma without embarrassment.

He told the Mahatma, 'It is my greatest desire in life to take a
vow to oust the British from India.'

The Mahatma looked at him with a smile and asked, 'How do
you propose to do it?'

Sriram could not find a ready answer; it was one of the many
occasions when he felt that he had spoken unnecessarily. He caught a
glimpse of Bharati on the other side, her mischievous face sparkling
with delight at his confusion. He felt piqued by her look. He said
haughtily, 'With your blessing, sir, I shall make myself good enough
for the task. I shall be with you as long as possible, and if you will
kindly guide me you can make me a soldier fit to take up the fight
to make the British leave our country.'

The Mahatma took his resolve with every sign of pleasure.
He remained silent for a while as their footsteps pit-patted on the
sands, a sombre silence fell on the gathering. 'Well, young friend, if
God wills it, you will do great things, trust in him and you will be
all right.'

To Sriram this seemed a rather tame preparation for a soldierly
existence. If it had been possible, he would have strutted before
Bharati in khaki and a decorated chest, though the world was
having a surfeit of decorations just then.

Presently the Mahatma himself spoke dispelling his notions:
'Before you aspire to drive the British from this country, you must
drive every vestige of violence from your system. Remember that it
is not going to be a fight with sticks and knives or guns but only
with love. Until you are sure you have an overpowering love at heart
for your enemy, don't think of driving him out. You must gradually
forget the term "enemy". You must think of him as a friend who
must leave you. You must train yourself to become a hundred per
cent *ahimsa* soldier. You must become so sensitive that it is not
possible for you to wear sandals made of the hide of slaughtered
animals; you should prefer to go barefoot rather than wear the hide
of an animal killed for your sake, that is if you are unable to secure
the skin of an animal that has died a natural death.'

Sriram said, 'Yes, I promise,' but while saying it his eyes were
fixed on Mahatmaji's feet; he struggled to suppress the questions
that were welling up in his mind.

The Mahatma read his thoughts and said, 'Yes, these are sandals made of just such leather. In our tannery at Wardha we specialize in it. No one in our Ashram wears anything else.'

Sriram wanted to ask, 'How do you know when an animal is dying, and how do you watch for it?' but ruthlessly suppressed the question as an unworthy one, which might betray him.

Sriram was told that he could accompany Mahatmaji in his tour of the villages on condition that he went home, and secured Granny's approval. Sriram tried to slur the matter over, he said it would not be necessary, he hinted he was an independent man used to such outings from home. The Mahatma's memory was better than that. He said with a smile, 'I remember you said that she didn't like to see you mixing with us.'

Sriram thought it over and said, 'Yes, master, but how can I for ever remain tied to her? It is not possible.'

'Are you quite sure that you want to change your style of life?' asked the Mahatma.

'I can think of nothing else,' Sriram said. 'How can I live as I have lived all these years?' He threw a quick glance at Bharati as she came in with some letters for the Mahatma. Her look prevented him from completing the sentence, which would have run, 'And I always wish to be with Bharati and not with my grandmother.'

The Mahatma said, 'I shall be happy to have you with us as long as you like, but you must first go home and tell your grandmother and receive her blessing. You must tell her frankly what you wish to do, but you must cause her no pain.'

Sriram hesitated. The prospect of facing Granny was unnerving. The thought of her was like the thought of an unreal troublesome world, one which he hoped he had left behind for ever: the real world for him now was the one of Bharati, Gorpad, unslaughtered naturally dying animals, the Mahatma, spinning wheels. He wanted to be here all the time: it seemed impossible for him to go back to Kabir Street, that *pyol*, and that shop, and those people there who treated him as if he were only eight years old. He stood before the Mahatma as if to appeal to him not to press him to go and face his grandmother, but the master was unrelenting. 'Go and speak to her. I don't think she is so unreasonable as to deny you your ambitions. Tell her that I like to have you with me. If you tour with me the next two weeks, you will observe and learn much that may be useful to you later in life. Tell her she will feel glad that she let you go. Assure her that I will look after you safely.' Every word filled him with dread when he remembered the terms in which Granny referred to the Mahatma. He dared not even give the slightest indication as to how she would react. He felt a great pity for the Mahatma, so innocent that he could not dream of anyone talking ill of him. He felt angry at the thought of Granny, such an ill-informed, ignorant and bigoted personality! What business had she to complicate his existence in this way? If he could have had his will he would have ignored his grandmother, but he had to obey the Mahatma now.

He said, 'All right, sir. I will go and get my granny's blessing. I'll be back early tomorrow.'

Half a dozen times on the way he resolved to turn back and tell Mahatma Gandhi that he had seen Granny. How could he find out the truth, anyway? But he dismissed the thought as unpractical, though perhaps not so unworthy under the circumstances. Suppose Granny created a row, went into a faint or threatened to kill herself, and made enough noise to attract the neighbours who might come and lock him up in his house, refusing to let him out? Should he face this risk in order to tell Gandhiji that he had seen the obstinate old lady as ordered? Would it not be prudent like a sensible man to say that it had been done? Probably Granny would guess there was Bharati behind all this and disbelieve anything he might say about Mahatmaji. Or if she spoke insultingly about Mahatmaji, he couldn't trust himself to listen patiently. He might do something for which he might feel sorry afterwards. He visualized himself suppressing his granny's words with force and violence, but he remembered that it would not be right to act like that where the Mahatma was concerned. He would be upset to hear about it.

The thing to do was to turn the *jutka* back and tell the Mahatma that he had Granny's blessings. But then, being a Mahatma, he might read his thoughts and send him back to Granny or he might cancel all his programme until he was assured that Granny had been seen or begin a fast until it was done. What made the Mahatma attach so much importance to Granny when he had so many things to mind? When he had the all-important task of driving the British out he ought to leave simple matters like Granny to be handled by himself. His thoughts were in a welter of confusion while he was in the *jutka*, but soon the horse turned into Kabir Street. He paid the fare without haggling and sent away the *jutka* quietly. He didn't want his movements to become noticeable in the neighbourhood.

He found his granny in a semi-agreeable frame of mind. His prolonged absence seemed to have made her nervous, and she tried to be nice to him. She probably feared he would flounce out of the house if she attempted to talk to him in the manner of yesterday.

She merely said: 'What a long time you have been away, my boy,' attempting to keep out all trace of reproach from her tone. He pretended to settle down. He drew up the canvas chair he had bought for her and sat down under the hall lamp. His granny fussed about as if she had recovered someone long lost. She set before him a plateful of food fried in ghee, saying, 'They sent this down from the lawyer's house: the first birthday of his eighth son. They don't seem to miss anything for any child.'

Sriram put a piece into his mouth, munched it, nodded his approval and said: 'Yes, they have made it of pure ghee. Good people.' He crunched it noisily.

Granny said: 'I kept it for you, I knew you would like it. I was wondering how long I should keep it. You know I have no teeth. Who would want stuff like that when you are not here? Don't eat all of it, you will not be able to eat your dinner.'

'Oh, dinner! I've had my dinner, Granny.'

'So soon!'

'Yes, in the Ashram camp, we have to dine before seven usually. It's the rule.'

'What sort of a dinner can it be at seven!' she cried in disappointment. 'Come and eat again, you ought to be fit for a real dinner now.'

'No, Granny. It is all regulated very strictly. We can't do anything as we like. We have got to observe the rules in all matters. We get quite good food there.'

'Have you got to pay for it?' asked Granny.

'Of course not,' said Sriram. 'What do you think, do you think Mahatmaji is running a hotel?'

'Then why should they feed you?'

'It's because we belong there.'

'Do they provide a lot of public feeding?'

Sriram lost his temper at this. He was appalled at Granny's denseness. 'I said they feed all of us who belong there, don't you follow?'

'Why should they feed you?'

'It is because we are volunteers.'

'Nice volunteers!' cried Granny, threatening to return to her yesterday's mood any second. 'And what do they give you to eat?'

'Chappatis, curd, and buttermilk and vegetables.'

'I'm glad. I was afraid they might force you to eat egg and fowl.'

Sriram was horrified. 'What do you take the Mahatma for! Do you know, he won't even wear sandals made of the hide of slaughtered animals!'

Granny was seized with a fit of laughter. Tears rolled down her cheeks. 'Won't wear sandals!' she cried in uncontrollable laughter. 'Never heard of such a thing before! How do they manage it? By peeling off the skin of animals before they are slaughtered, is that it?'

'Shut up, Granny!' cried Sriram in a great rage. 'What an irresponsible gossip you are! I never thought you could be so bad!'

Granny for the first time noticed a fiery earnestness in her grandson, and gathered herself up. She said. 'Oh! He is your God, is he?'

'Yes, he is, and I won't hear anyone speak lightly of him.'

'What else can I know, a poor ignorant hag like me! Do I read the newspapers? Do I listen to lectures? Am I told what is what by anyone? How should I know anything about that man Gandhi!'

'He is not a man; he is a Mahatma!' cried Sriram.

'What do you know about a Mahatma, anyway?' asked Granny.

Sriram fidgeted and rocked himself in his chair in great anger. He had not come prepared to face a situation of this kind. He had been only prepared to face a Granny who might show sullenness at his absence, create difficulties for him when he wanted to go away and exhibit more sorrow and rage than levity. But here she was absolutely reckless, frivolous, and without the slightest sense of responsibility or respect. This was a situation which he had not anticipated, and he had no technique to meet it. It was no use, he realized, showing righteous indignation: that would only tickle the old lady more and more, and when the time came for him to take her permission and go, she might become too intractable. She might call in the neighbours, and make fun of him. He decided that he must change his tactics. Suddenly springing up he asked: 'Granny, have you had your food? I am keeping you away from it, talking like this!'

'It doesn't matter,' she said, almost on the point of giggling. 'How many years is it since I had a mouthful of food at night— must be nearly twenty years. You couldn't have seen me in your lifetime eating at night.' There was such a ring of pride in her voice that Sriram felt impelled to say: 'There is nothing extraordinary in it. Anybody might be without food.' He wanted to add, 'The Mahatma has fasted for so many days on end, and so often,' but suppressed it. The old lady however had no need of being told anything. She added at once, 'No! When Mahatma Gandhi fasts, everybody talks about it.'

'And when you fast at nights only, nobody notices it, and that is all the difference between you and Gandhiji?' She was struck by the sharp manner in which he spoke.

She asked: 'Do you want your dinner?'

'Yes, just to please you, that is all. I am not hungry, I told you that. And this stuff is good, made of good ghee. You may tell them so. I've eaten a great quantity of it and I'm not hungry.'

Granny came back to her original mood after all these unexpected transitions. She said: 'You must eat your dinner, my boy,' very earnestly. She bustled about again as if for a distinguished visitor. She pulled a dining leaf out of a bundle in the kitchen rack, spread it on the floor, sprinkled a little water on it, and drew the bronze rice pot nearer, and sat down in order to be able to serve him without getting up again. The little lamp wavered in its holder. He ate in silence, took a drink of water out of the good old brass tumbler that was by his side; he cast a glance at the old bronze vessel out of which rice had been served to him for years. He suddenly felt depressed at the sight of it all. He was oppressed with the thought that he was leaving these old associations, that this was really a farewell party. He was going into an unknown life right from here. God knew what was in store for him. He felt very gloomy at the thought of it all. He knew it would be no good ever talking to his granny about his plans, or the Mahatma or Bharati. All that was completely beyond her comprehension. She would understand only edibles and dinner and fasting at night in order to impress a neighbour with her austerity. No use talking to her about anything. Best to leave in the morning, without any fuss. He had obeyed Mahatmaji's mandate to the extent of seeing her and speaking to her. The Mahatma should be satisfied and not expect him to be able to bring about a conversion in the old lady's outlook, enough to earn her blessing.

Granny was very old, probably eighty, ninety, or a hundred. He had never tried to ascertain her age correctly. And she would not understand new things. At dead of night, after assuring himself that Granny was fast asleep, he got up, scribbled a note to her by the night lamp, and placed it under the brass pot containing water on the window sill, which she was bound to lift first thing in the morning. She could carry it to a neighbour and have it read to her if she had any difficulty in finding her glasses. Perhaps she might not like to have it read by the neighbours. She would always cry: 'Sriram, my glasses, where are the wretched glasses gone?' whenever anything came to her hand for reading, and it would be his duty to go to the cupboard, and fetch them. Now he performed the same duty in anticipation. He tip-toed to the almirah, took the glasses out of their case silently, and returned to the hall, leaving the spectacle case open, because it had a tendency to close with a loud clap. He placed the glasses beside his letter of farewell, silently opened the door, and stepped into the night.

2

HE WAS AN accredited member of the group, and in many villages he was glad to find himself fussed over and treated with respect by the villagers. They looked on him with wonder. He formed a trio with Bharati and Gorpad; and whenever the villagers wanted to know anything about the Mahatma, they came and spoke to him reverentially, and that gave him an opportunity to work off all the knowledge he had gathered in his contacts with Gorpad and Bharati. It was a way of learning the job while being on it. Till then he had no notion of village life. He had been born and bred in the township of Malgudi, and even there his idea of the bounds of the universe were confined to Kabir Street, Market Road, and one or two other spots. Whenever he heard the word 'villages', his mental picture was always one of green coconut groves, long and numerous steps leading down to the large tank, with elegant village women coming up bearing pitchers, and the temple spire showing beyond the tank bund, low-roofed houses with broad *pyols*, and mat-covered wagons moving about dragged by bulls with tinkling bells around their necks, the cartmen singing all the time. He owed his idea to the various Tamil films, which he had frequently seen at the Regal. But he saw nothing of the kind here. The reality was different. Some villages were hardly more than a cluster of huts. For the first time he was seeing actual villages, and on the first day at a village ten miles from Malgudi, he felt so bewildered that he asked Bharati secretly: 'Where is the village?'

'Which village?'

'Why, any village,' he said.

'Doesn't this look like a village to you?' she asked.

'No,' he replied. They had found time for a chat, after the Mahatma had retired for the evening.

'What a pity,' she said, 'that it's so. But learn, young man, this is really a village. I'm not lying. There are seven hundred thousand other villages more or less like this in our country.'

'How do you know?' he asked to prolong the conversation.

'I learn from wise men,' she said.

'How wise?' he asked.

She ignored his frivolity and started talking of their mission. They were out to survey the villages which had recently been affected by famine. It was a mission of mercy; Mahatmaji had set out to study the famine conditions at first hand, and to put courage and hope into the sufferers. It was a grim, melancholy undertaking. The Mahatma attached so much value to this tour that he had set aside all his other engagements. A distant war being fought in Europe, and probably about to start in the Far East, had their repercussions here. Though not bombed, they still suffered from the war; one did not see ARP signs or even a war poster, but small wayside stations acted as a vital link, a feeding channel, to a vast war reservoir in western Europe. The wagons at the sidings carried away night and day timber cut in the Mempi forests, the corn grown here, and the able-bodied men who might have been working on their land.

However grim the surroundings might be, Sriram and Bharati seemed to notice nothing. They had a delight in each other's company which mitigated the gloom of the surroundings. Gorpad alone looked oppressed with a sense of tragedy. He spoke less, retired early, mortified himself more and more. He said: 'See what the British have done to our country: this famine is their manoeuvring to keep us in enslavement. They are plundering the forests and fields to keep their war machinery going, and the actual sufferer is this child,' pointing at any village child who might chance to come that way, showing its ribs, naked and pot-bellied.

'There is no food left in these villages,' he cried passionately. 'There is no one to look after them; who cares for them? Who is there to help them out of their difficulties? Everyone is engaged in this war. The profiteer has hoarded all the grain beyond the reach of these growers. The war machine buys it at any price. It's too big a competitor for these poor folk.'

'Why does he say all that to me?' Sriram reflected while impatiently waiting to be left alone with Bharati. 'I'm not responsible for it.' Gorpad was an iron man and could be trusted to leave them alone because he had something else to do; and when his back was turned, their eyes met and they giggled at the memory of all the sad, bad matters they had just heard or noticed.

Sriram's idea of a village was nowhere to be seen. Hungry, parched men and women with skin stretched over their bones, bare earth, dry ponds, and miserable tattered thatched roofing over crumbling mud walls, streets full of pits and loose sand, unattractive dry fields—that was a village. Sriram could hardly believe he was within twenty miles of Malgudi and civilization. Here pigs and dogs lounged in dry gutters. Everything in these parts had the appearance of a dry gutter. Sriram wondered how people ever managed to go on living in such places. He wanted to stop and ask everyone: 'How long are you going to be here? Won't you return to Malgudi or somewhere else? Have you got to be here for ever?'

The Mahatma defeated the calculation of officials by refusing to give a programme of his tour, and by visiting unexpected places. The officials politely asked him to tell them where he wished to go. He merely replied: 'Everywhere if I can' or 'I wish I knew'.

'But we'd like to make proper arrangements.'

'For me? Don't trouble yourself. I can sleep in any hut. I can live where others are living. I don't think I shall demand many luxuries. Don't worry. We can look after ourselves. I'm not a guest here; I'm a host. Why don't you join us, as our guest?' He said this to the District Collector. 'We will promise to look after you, giving you all the comforts that you may want.'

Quite a band of officials followed him about on his tour. Mahatma Gandhi toured the villages mostly on foot. He halted wherever he liked. He stationed himself at the lowliest hut in the village if it was available, or in a temple corridor, or in the open air. For hours he walked silently, holding his staff and supporting his arm on one or other of his disciples. Often he stopped on the way to speak to a peasant cutting a tree or digging a field.

Sriram felt it unnecessary to know which village they were passing at a particular time. All were alike: it was the same routine. Gandhiji's personal life went on as if he had been stationary in one place; the others adjusted themselves to it. He met the local village men and women, spoke to them about God, comforted the ailing, advised those who sought his guidance. He spoke to them about spinning, the war, Britain, and religion. He met them in their huts, spoke to them under the village banyan tree (no village was so bare yet that it was without its banyan tree). He trudged his way through ploughed fields, he climbed hard rocky places, through mud and slush, but always with the happiest look, and no place seemed too small for his attention.

Gandhiji's tour was drawing to an end. He was to board a train at Koppal, a tiny station at the foot of the Mempi Hills. The Mahatma wanted his arrival and departure to be kept a secret, and except a couple of officials deputed to see him off, there were no outsiders on the platform. The station master, a small man with a Kaiser-like moustache, who wore a green lace-edged turban and *dhoti*, had, with the help of his porter, dragged a huge antique chair on to the platform. He had tidied up his children, six of them in a row, and made them stand quietly aside in the shade of a gold mohur tree in bloom. He had to act as Mahatmaji's host in between tapping various messages. He had begged Mahatmaji to occupy the chair on the platform. 'I can stand as well as anyone else,' said the Mahatma, looking around at his followers. Sriram noted the sadness in the other's face, and urged him, 'Please take your seat, Bapuji,' and the Mahatma sat down, his followers standing around. The little station master was excited and agitated and beads of perspiration ran down to his eyelids. Beyond the railway line there was a row of hills, standing against purple skies. The station master panted for breath, and constantly nudged and instructed his children to behave themselves although they were all the time standing stiffly as if on a drill parade.

Mahatmaji said: 'Station Masterji, why don't you let them run about and play as they like? Why do you constrain them?'

'I'm not constraining them, master. It's their habit,' he said with the hope of impressing the visitor with the training of his children.

The Mahatma said: 'Friend, I fear you are trying to put them on good behaviour before me. I would love it better if they ran about and played normally, and picked up those flowers dropping on the ground, which they want to do. I'm very keen that children should be free and happy.'

True to his custom the Mahatma took out the garlands and fruits given to him on the way, called up the children, and distributed them. Their father fidgeted, his nerves on edge lest someone should suddenly misbehave. The sky was turning red beyond the railway line. A bell sounded inside his little office. He ran to it, and came back with more dew drops clouding his face: 'The 7 Down has left Periapur. It'll be here in fifteen minutes. At the stroke of eighteen forty-two.' He looked anxious in case the train might defeat his promise.

The Mahatma said: 'You may attend to your work in your cabin, don't bother about us.'

'May I?' he asked desperately. 'I have to write the fare records, sir, and prepare the line to receive the train.'

'Certainly, go on,' said the Mahatma.

For the first time during all these weeks Sriram felt depressed and unhappy. The thought of having to live a mundane existence without Mahatmaji appalled him. Not even the proximity of Bharati seemed to mitigate his misery. As the sound of the approaching train was heard, he looked so stunned that Mahatmaji said: 'Be happy. Bharati will look after you.' Sriram looked at Bharati hopefully. Mahatmaji added: 'Remember that she is your guru, and think of her with reverence and respect, and you will be all right and she will be all right.' Sriram took time to digest this sentence. The train steamed in. Mahatmaji entered a third-class compartment.

Gorpad, a cold-headed stoic whom no parting moved, told Sriram: 'Now you know what your duties are, and how to do them. Sister, you will receive our instructions. *Namaste*,' and climbed into Gandhiji's compartment. His party followed him in.

The first bell rang, and then the second. The station master came out, and said: 'The 7 Down generally halts here only two minutes, but today we have detained it for three-and-a-half minutes, sir.' He looked despairingly at the crowd of passengers from other carriages gathered before Mahatmaji's window. The engine was humming. The engine driver from one end and the guard from the other had left their stations in order to see the Mahatma, who returned their greetings and asked: 'How can the train move sir, when its heart and soul are here?' The engine driver withdrew with a grin on his face. The Mahatma said to the other people, 'Now, you will all have to go back to your places.' The crowd dispersed and the station master waved his flag.

Gandhiji told Sriram: 'Write to me often. I'll also promise you a fairly regular correspondence. In the future you know where your work lies. Become a master-spinner, soon. Don't be despondent.'

'Yes, master,' said Sriram; the parting affected him too much.

Bharati merely said in a clear voice: '*Namaste*, Bapu.'

Bapu smiled and put out his hand and patted her shoulder. 'You will of course keep up your programme and write to me often.'

'Yes, of course, Bapu.'

'Be prepared for any sacrifice.'

'Yes, Bapu,' she said earnestly. 'Let nothing worry you.'

'Yes, Bapu.'

The sky became redder and darker, and the 7 Down moved away, taking the Mahatma to Trichy, and then to Madras, Bombay, Delhi and out into the universe. Night fell on the small station, and the little station master proceeded to light his gas lamps and signals.

Though the Mahatma's physical presence was no longer with him, Sriram had a feeling that his movements were being guided. His home now was a deserted shrine on a slope of the Mempi Hill, overlooking the valley. Down below, the road zigzagged and joined the highway which ended a mile off at Koppal station. He often saw the mail runner trudging up a curve, with a bag on his shoulder, a staff on one arm (the staff had little bells tied to its end, heralding his arrival even a mile away). Sriram expected no mail but he loved to watch the runner till he stepped on a rock, and took a diverging cross-cut, leading him to various estates and villages on the higher reaches of the Mempi Hills.

This place seemed to have been destined for him, built thousands and thousands of years ago by someone who must have anticipated that Sriram would find a use for an abandoned building. It was a ruin, a few sculptures showed along the wall, the masonry was crumbling here and there. There was an image of some god with four hands in an inner sanctum overgrown with weed. But it was the most comfortable ruin a man could possess. There were stately pillars in a central hall, with bricks showing; there were walls without a ceiling, but from which exotic creepers streamed down; one of the stubborn, undisturbed pieces of sculpture was a bull-and-peacock over the large portal, which had very large knobbed wooden doors that could not be moved at all on their immense hinges. This was no great disadvantage for Sriram since no one came this way, and even if they did, he did not have anything to lock up. If he wished to be out of sight, he had only to slip away beyond a curtain of weeds, into a cellar. He could hear the train arrive and depart far away. He could hear the voices of villagers as they moved up in groups from the villages down below to the estates above. His possessions were a spinning wheel, a blanket on which to sleep, and a couple of vessels, some foodstuff, and a box of matches. He lit the wick of a small lantern whenever he wanted to work at night. He had set duties to perform every day when he woke up with the cries of birds. 'Oh, God, it's much better in Kabir Street,' he used to think. 'The birds make so much uproar here that they won't allow a man to sleep in peace.' In spite of this he got up from bed. He was going through a process of self-tempering, a rather hard task, for he often found on checking his thoughts that they were still as undesirable as ever. He had thought that by practising all the austerities that he had picked up in Gorpad's company, he could become suddenly different. Mahatmaji had blessed his idea of self-development. He had said: 'Spin and read the Bhagavad Gita, and utter *Ram nam* continuously, and then you will know what to do in life.'

Sriram carried a change of dress and went downhill to a brook and bathed. He felt so invigorated after the cold bath that he sang aloud all alone in his wilderness. He went on repeating: '*Raghupati Raghava Raja Ram, Pathita Pavana Sita Ram*'—Mahatmaji's litany. When he sang it, he had a feeling of being near him and doing something on his orders. He was overcome with such a sense of holiness that he nearly danced with joy when he went back to his retreat. He carried the two pieces of dress he had washed in the brook and put them out to dry on the green fence surrounding the shrine. He was very proud of wearing cloth made with his own hand. Bharati had taught him how to insert the cotton thread, how

to turn the wheel, and how to spin. Gandhiji had presented him
with a spinning wheel in one of the villages with the explanation:
'This is the key to your future.' Sriram had felt too respectful to ask
what he meant. But he took the wheel with proper reverence and
literally put it close to his heart, although it was a heavy cumbrous
apparatus.

Bharati tried to teach him how to use it during their sojourn in
one of the villages. He tried his hand at spinning and made countless
blunders while learning. He never managed to produce more than
a couple of inches of yarn at a time, without snapping—it looked
more like bits of twisted cotton wool than yarn. Bharati could not
restrain her laughter when she saw his handiwork. She remarked:
'You will waste all the cotton in India and Egypt before you make
yourself a yard of yarn.' After this she held his fingers down at the
correct pressure at the spinning point, but when she took away her
hand, Sriram let his fingers go too, and the cotton fell down and
became worthless for any purpose.

All through the tour he had worked at it, his lessons starting
the moment they came to a halt for the day. Every day Mahatmaji
enquired: 'Well, what is the progress?'

And before he could answer Bharati generally broke in and
said: 'Two more inches Bapuji; in all he has produced six inches
today, but the count must be specially measured. It must be a five-
count yarn, probably the same count as a lamp-wick!'

The Mahatma said: 'Well, there will be a time soon when he
will give you a hundred-count, don't be too proud, little daughter.'

'I'm not,' Bharati said. 'I'm merely mentioning the facts.'

'How proud she is! Do you know she won her prize in a *khadi*
competition some years ago? Her yarn is kept in an exhibition.'

'She scores one over me in everything,' Sriram reflected. 'It's
because of the excessive support she gets. She is being spoilt. That is
what is wrong with her. She thinks no end of herself.'

'I'm sure Bharati will teach you how to excel her,' said the
Mahatma, and Bharati lived up to this promise. She allowed Sriram
no rest, night or day, Whenever there was the slightest respite from
travel, she came up with, 'Now, what is the programme of the great
pupil?' And Sriram dragged the wheel out, took the little packets
of cotton, and started nervously. He dreaded making a mistake
and provoking the girl's mirth. He hated her for her levity, and for
making him feel like a fool so often. But he kept up a desperate

effort. He slipped, he made her laugh, he struggled in the grips of unholy thoughts when she stooped over him, held his hand, and taught him the tricks. He concentrated until his mind was benumbed with the half-whispering movement of the spinning wheel. His fingers ached with holding a vibrant ever-growing thread, and his eyes smarted.

Finally he did emerge a victor, nearly twelve weeks after Mahatmaji had left. Sriram had stationed himself for his novitiate at one of the spinning centres, about fifty miles from Malgudi. Bharati was perfectly at home there and proved herself to be a task-mistress of no mean order; she did not let go her grip on Sriram until he had spun enough yarn free from entanglement for a *dhoti* and a short shirt. It was a result of continuous work over weeks. But it was worth it. She became very excited at the success of his efforts. She tore off the blank edge of a newspaper and wrote on it in minute letters: 'This is to say that Sri Sriram is henceforth to be called a master spinner, and he must be respected wherever he goes.' She helped him to bundle off the yarn to a central depot at Madras and secure in exchange woven cloth of the same count. Sriram suddenly felt that he was the inhabitant of a magic world where you created all the things you needed with your own hands. His regret was that he still could not make the hundred-count, and that his yarn was somewhat rugged. But Bharati said: 'The forty-count is the real cloth that can be used: hundreds are merely for show and prizes, don't worry about it.'

On the day he got his *khadi* clothes, a simple *dhoti* and a *jibba* (cut and stitched on the spot by the village tailor), he took off the clothes he had been wearing (mill manufactured), heaped them in the middle of the street, poured half a bottle of kerosene over the lot, and applied a match; his old clothes caught fire and burned brightly. A few members of the spinning centre stood around the fire and watched. Some of the villagers looked on with interest.

Sriram explained to the gathering, fascinated by the leaping flames: 'I will never again wear clothes spun by machinery.' The *dhoti* and *jibba* were heavy, it was as if a piece of lead were interwoven with the texture. But he felt it was something to be proud of. He felt he had seen and reached a new plane of existence. He sat down and wrote to the Mahatma, 'Burnt my old clothes today. Spun forty-count. Bharati satisfied.'

Mahatmaji immediately wrote back to him: 'Very pleased. Keep it up. God bless you.'

Bharati came uphill at dusk. Sriram became fussy: 'How can you walk barefoot in all these places?'

'Why not? We are not born with sandals on our feet. I have not yet got the leather from Wardha, and I shall have to manage with this until we get it. But—' she said with a sigh, 'there is probably no one there who can attend to our wants. We don't even know how many of them are in prison. The government have stopped giving even that information.'

They were sitting on the cool mud floor, with a lamp between them. Sriram studied her face, so full of lines nowadays as if the burden of the country were on her back, with Mahatmaji in prison since the August of 1942. Bharati (along with Sriram) was a little cog in a vast complicated machinery working, in spite of the police hunting down politics everywhere, to eject the British from the land.

Sriram said again: 'You should not walk barefoot.'

'Why not? India's three hundred and sixty million walk barefoot.'

Her national statistics bored him. He said sharply: 'They may, but it doesn't mean you should also walk barefoot. There may be cobras about, this place is full of such things.'

'Bah, as if cobras would not bite if trodden upon with sandalled feet!'

'You are too argumentative.'

'I tell you I am not able to get the usual leather from Wardha,' she complained, and then added: 'I am not afraid of you, and I don't have to explain to you why I am like this or like that. I am not afraid of cobras either, or the lonely road. Otherwise I should not be here.'

'Of course, you need not be afraid of me,' said Sriram. 'Only you expect others to be afraid of you.'

'Yes, because I am your guru.'

Sriram felt, 'The whole thing is extremely false. She ought to be my wife and come to my arms.' He wondered for a moment, 'What is it that prevents me from touching her? What can she do? She is all alone in this place. Even if she shouts nobody will hear her for ten miles around.' He revelled in this terrific possibility. But it was only a dream.

She explained her mission: 'I am leaving for Madras tomorrow, and you won't see me for some time.'

'When? Where are you going?'

'I have been summoned for instructions. The police are watchful, no doubt, but I can manage to go and return without any trouble.' She started to leave.

He wondered, 'Why has she come to tell me this? What is the matter? Can I interpret it as her love for me? No one would come two miles barefoot just to say there would be nothing to do for the next three days. She must have come with some other motive. Probably she likes me very much, waits for me to take her hand and tell her what I have in mind; and then she would yield to me.' Absurd to think that she was just his 'guru'. Guru indeed! Absurd that a comely young woman should be set to educate a man! Educate him in what? He chuckled at the thought. She said: 'You have become suddenly very thoughtful. Why?' He touched her arm; the lonely atmosphere was very encouraging, but she pushed his hand down gently, remarking, 'You rest here till I am back with instructions,' and she turned and was off down the road saying, 'Don't show yourself too much outside.'

He said: 'I will escort you halfway.'

'It's not necessary,' she said and was off.

Sriram watched her go downhill. 'Some day, someone is going to abduct her; she doesn't seem to feel she is a woman,' he thought and turned in. He stood brooding over the ruins around him. Far away a train halted and proceeded on its journey, its shaded ARP lights crawling along the landscape. He hoped that the girl would reach her village safely, without any mishap.

Three days later she turned up bringing instructions, and from that moment Sriram's activities took a new turn. Bharati came to him bearing a can of paint and a brush. She handed them over to him with the air of an ordnance chief distributing weapons from the armoury. She said: 'They have assigned to you all the plantations above. It means a lot of walking. You must not miss any of the dozen villages on the way. The villagers will help you everywhere. We shall be at work in Malgudi and the surroundings. Be careful, I will see you again sometime. With Mahatmaji in prison, we have to carry on the work in our own manner. We must spread his message everywhere.'

The Mahatma had in his famous resolution of August 1942 said: 'Britain must quit India', and the phrase had the potency of a mantra or a magic formula. Throughout the length and breadth of the land, people cried 'Quit India'. The Home Secretary grew uneasy at the sound of it. It became a prohibited phrase in polite society. After the Mahatma uttered the phrase, he was put in prison; but the phrase took life and flourished, and did ultimately produce enough power to send the British away. There was not a blank wall in the whole country which did not carry the message. Wherever one turned one saw 'Quit India'.

On the following day Sriram trudged up the mountain path carrying his little tin can, brush and a rag, in a satchel slung over his shoulder. He stopped at the first village on the way, selected the most suitable wall, which happened to be the outer wall of a new house, on whose *pyol* the village children were learning the alphabet. Their lips had been reciting the letters of the alphabet in a chorus, which incidentally lulled their teacher into a slight doze, but their eyes were following the bullock carts rattling down the road in a caravan, buses flying past and disappearing in a cloud of churned up dust, and people passing to and fro. The day was bright and the glare on green trees and boughs and hedge creepers was enticing; their eyes wandered, their minds wandered. And so when Sriram came up to write on the wall they slipped out of their class with a feeling of profound relief. The elders of the village too suspended their normal occupations and stood around to watch.

Sriram dipped the brush in paint and fashioned 'Quit India' carefully on the wall. He wished that he didn't have to write the letter 'Q', which consumed a lot of black paint. It was no use wasting all the available paint on a single letter. He wondered if, for economy's sake, he could manage without drawing its tail. They were launching on a war with a first-rate, war-equipped nation like England, all their armament being this brush and black paint and blank walls. They could not afford to squander their war resources in writing just a single letter. It also seemed to him possible that Britain had imported the letter 'Q' into India so that there might be a national drain on black paint. He was so obsessed with this thought that he began to write a modified 'Q', expending the very minimum of paint on its tail so that it read, until one scrutinized it closely, 'Quit India'. The villagers asked: 'How long ought this to be on our wall, sir?'

'Till it takes effect.'

'What does it say, sir?'

'It is "Quit"—meaning that the British must leave our country.'
'What will happen, sir, if they leave? Who will rule the country?'
'We will rule it ourselves.'

'Will Mahatmaji become our Emperor, sir?'

'Why not?' he said, shaping the letters, with his back turned to them. He taught the schoolchildren to cry, 'Quit India' in a chorus. They gleefully obeyed him. Their teacher came and expostulated: 'What is this you are doing, sir, you are spoiling them!'

'How?'

'By teaching them seditious behaviours. The police will be after us soon. Do you want us to end in jail?'

'Yes, why not? When more important persons than you are already there.' The crowd jeered at the teacher. The boys were ever ready to seize an opportunity to jeer him. But the old man was more tough than he looked. He put on his spectacles and looked Sriram up and down.

The boys cried: 'Oh, the master is looking through his spectacles, oh! oh!' They laughed and cried: 'Quit India.'

The teacher pushed his way through and cried: 'Add if possible one "e" before "t"; what we need in this country is not a "Quit" programme, but a "Quiet India". Why don't you write that?'

Sriram finished his job of writing. He had borrowed a ladder from someone. He turned round and said to the teacher: 'Please do something more useful than standing there and talking, master. Please see that this ladder is returned to its owner, I forget his name, and you will have done your bit to free our country.'

The teacher relented a little. He came forward and said: 'It's not that I don't want to see our country freed. I am as much a patriot as you, but honestly do you think we are ready to rule ourselves? We aren't. Don't delude yourself. We are not ready yet for anything. Let this war be over, and you will find me the first to fight for *Swaraj*. Patriotism is not your monopoly.' The boys stood around and cried slogans.

Sriram said: 'Be careful, you will be beheaded when Britain leaves India. We have a list of everybody who has to be beheaded.'

The teacher lost his temper completely and said: 'How dare you say that! I don't want to see Britain go. I am not one of those who think that we'll be happier when Hitler comes, perhaps with the help of people like you. Let me tell you, you will be the first to be shot then.'

Part of the crowd was appreciative of the teacher's point of view, and said: 'The master is right, why should we irritate the *sircar*?'

Sriram turned on them with rage and said: 'You should not only irritate, you must not recognize the government. You don't have to pay taxes to it at all. They are ten thousand miles away from us, why do you give them your tax?'

'Fellows like this should not be allowed to go about as they like: that's why I've always asked for a police outpost here. If there had been a policeman here, would he have dared to come and lecture like this?'

'How far away is the police station?' asked Sriram.

'The Circle Station is beyond ten stones,' replied someone.

'See that,' said Sriram, 'your *sircar* have not given you even a police station! Is it because it is unnecessary when there is a person like this master in your midst?'

The boys raised a shout of appreciation and cried 'Quit India' in a singsong manner. It was a vociferous, happy gathering. Their shouts and general riotous behaviour frightened a pair of bullocks drawing a load of hay down the road. The bullocks lowered their heads and pulled the cart into a ditch, and it created a general mêlée, people running hither and thither, and shouting directions to each other. The carter, while pulling the animals back to the road, swore at them and at the disturbance. 'These politicians, Gandhi folk, they won't leave anyone in peace. Why do you come and trouble us here?'

Sriram said: 'Hey, pull up your cart and listen. Don't talk like a baby. You are old enough to know what you are talking about. What's your age?'

The carter pulled up his reins and said over the jingle of the bells round the necks of his animals, 'I think I'm twenty!'

'Twenty! More likely you are fifty.'

'Maybe, sir, a little this way and that. I used to be twenty.'

'How many children have you?'

'Five sons, sir, and a grandson.'

'You are fifty, my dear fellow, and you look it. Don't talk irresponsibly. Do you know Mahatma Gandhi is in jail?'

'Yes, master.'

'You know why he is there?' The man shook his head. 'So that you may be a free man in this country. You are not a free man in this country now.'

Sriram's orbit of operations lay in the mountain villages scattered here and there, connected by more or less self-formed roads, which wound their way through thick wooded vegetation and forests. Their connection with the outside world was through a postal runner, who passed through some of the better villages once or twice a week, bringing in the mails dumped at the railway station at Koppal. There were a few police outposts scattered over the whole area, with a petty officer and a handful of men in each, who kept in touch with their headquarters through the telephone lines which passed overhead and often vanished into the vegetation on the mountain slope. One would hardly have associated this remote green wilderness with politics, but it was as good a front line in the fight with Britain as any other.

He went into a part of the jungle where elephants were hauling timber. Huge logs were being cut and herds of elephants picked them up on their trunks and rolled them and piled them on trucks waiting in the heart of the jungle. Sriram penetrated here with his own message. He watched them at work and remarked: 'You are cutting down green unripe timber. You know where it is going?' The mahouts on the elephants paused in their tasks, and looked down at him with amusement. Sriram explained, 'They are going into the making of ships and rifles and bridges and what not, all of which are to be used for the destruction of this world. They are going into a war which we are forced to fight because Britain chose to drag us into it. We shouldn't have to strip our forests for this task. It's going far away, to far off countries, and the money you are getting is a puffed up, illusory currency, which will lose its value soon. Don't supply these materials for the war, it will take centuries for us to grow all this timber again. Refuse to do this job; it's in your hands. Don't strengthen the hand that is oppressing you.'

The timber-contractor who was observing him came up and pleaded, 'Don't trouble us please, after all we are businessmen. If tomorrow you place an order with us for a fair quantity at a good price—'

'This is not the time for acquiring wealth. This is the time to join in the fight for independence.'

The contractor merely said, 'Please leave us alone. We don't wish to get into all this bother.' He whispered, 'Please don't disturb our labour, please.'

'I'm not out to create labour trouble. You must not send that timber out of the country for this hellish purpose. All wars are against Mahatmaji's creed of *Ahimsa*. Do you accept it or not?'

'Ah, Mahatmaji. I gave five thousand rupees to the Harijan fund. I have a portrait of him in my house, the first face I see is his, as soon as I get up from bed.'

'Do you know what he means by non-violence?'

'Yes, yes, I never missed a day's lecture when he came to Malgudi.'

'You must also have attended an equal number of loyalist meetings, I suppose.'

The contractor bowed his head shyly. He muttered: 'After all, when the Collector comes and says, "Do this or that," we have to obey him. We cannot afford to displease government officials.'

'How much have you given to the War Fund?'

'Only five thousand. I'm very impartial; when the Governor himself comes and appeals how can we refuse? After all we are businessmen.'

The man had inveigled Sriram into entering his tent under a tree. It prevented the mahouts from wasting their time listening to their talk. The forest resounded with the sound of logs rolling down and mahouts goading the elephants, chaffing among themselves, and laughing. The air had a slight smell of eucalyptus and green leaf, and also of the tobacco that the mahouts had been smoking. The contractor seated Sriram on a chair, took out an aluminium kettle smoking on a stove and poured two cups of tea. Sriram felt depressed at the sight of him. He was a lank man with a clean shaven head wearing a knitted banian and a *dhoti*, and at his waist he had tucked in a leather purse and some rolls of paper. The man seemed prosperous, with a thin gold chain around his neck, and a wristwatch on his left hand, but he looked haggard with overwork.

Sriram said: 'You are no doubt making a lot of money, but it is worth nothing unless you develop some spirit of—of—' He fumbled for words. He wanted to say, 'national service', or 'patriotism', but he was tired of these expressions, they smacked of platform speeches. He said: 'If you have a photo of Mahatma Gandhi, pray that he may inspire you with reasonable thinking, that's all I can say.' He got up abruptly.

The man said: 'Drink your tea and go.'

Sriram said, 'I don't want it.' He walked out of the tent, slipped through a gap in the hedge, and was off.

He lost count of time. He went on doing things in a machinelike manner. He entered forests and villages and conveyed what he felt to be Mahatmaji's message. Wherever he went he wrote, 'Quit India'. And it was followed by loyalists amending it with: 'Don't' or an 'I' before 'Quit'. In one place a man asked Sriram: "What is the use of your writing "Quit India" in all these places? Do you want us to quit?'

'It does not mean that.'

'Then write it where it can be seen by those for whom it is meant.'

'They are everywhere, sometimes seen and sometimes unseen. It is better to have it written everywhere.'

'Waste of time and paint,' said the man.

'I'm merely carrying out an order, and I cannot afford to stop and listen to too much wisdom.'

There was a plantation 4,000 feet above sea level, whither Sriram carried his pot of paint and his brush. It meant nearly half a day's job for him. He arrived at the estate late one afternoon. He saw a picturesque gate-post with the sign, 'Mathieson Estates', over it. There wasn't a single human being to be seen for miles around. Sriram wondered for a moment: 'Is it worth writing any message here?' He looked about and hesitated, but dismissed the doubt as unworthy. He briskly dusted a portion of the gate-post and wrote in a beautiful round handwriting: 'Quit India', and turned to go.

An estate labourer who was passing, stopped to look at the message and asked: 'Are you writing a board?'

Sriram explained at length the import of the message. The man listened for a while and said: 'Go away. That *Dorai* is a bad fellow. Always with a gun. He may shoot you.'

Sriram hesitated for a moment, wondering whether it would be more worthwhile to get shot or to go away peacefully. He suddenly felt he need not have come up so far if it were only to go back safely. He hadn't climbed 4,000 feet above sea level for nothing. The labourer with the pickaxe went away after uttering his warning. Sriram walked forward towards an ancient bungalow that he saw in front. 'Hope he doesn't have bulldogs,' he reflected. He pictured the scene ahead in a somewhat gory way. He would approach the

steps and the *Dorai* would level his double-barrelled gun, and
Sriram would go up in smoke and blood. Probably that would fill
Bharati with remorse. She would tell herself: 'I wish I had shown my
love more definitely when he was alive.' Anyway why was he doing
this? The High Command had not instructed him to go and bare his
chest before a gunman.

A seven-foot figure with a red face and sandy hair accosted
him by the porch. He was smoking a pipe, and had one hand
comfortably tucked in his trouser pocket. For a second Sriram felt
a little reluctant to go forward.

'Hullo! Who may you be?'

Sriram felt dwarfed by his side. He went up and said in a shrill
voice: 'I have brought a message.'

'Oh, good. From where?'

'From Mahatmaji.'

The man took out his pipe and said: 'Oh! What?'

'From Mahatma Gandhi.'

'Well? What is it?'

'That you must quit India.'

The other looked abashed for a second. But he recovered his
composure in a moment. He said: 'Why do you say that?'

'I'm not saying it. I'm merely giving you the message.'

'Oh! Come in and have a drink, won't you?'

'No. I never drink.'

'Oh, yes, yes. I didn't mean spirits, but you can have anything
you want, sherbet, or coffee or tea.'

'I need nothing.'

'You look tired, come in, let us have a chat anyway. Boy!' he
shouted and his bearer appeared. 'Two glasses of orange juice,' he
ordered. 'Look sharp.'

'Yes, sir,' said the Boy, going away.

The servant wore a white uniform with a lot of buttons.
Sriram reflected, 'This man wants even a particular kind of dress
for Indians who act as his servants,' and felt an inexplicable rage.
The other watched his face for a while, then said, 'Come along,
let us go on the veranda.' He conducted him up the steps to the
veranda, which had been furnished with wicker chairs covered with
a beautiful chintz: there were also a few decorative plants in large
pots here and there. Sriram contrasted it with his own surroundings,
a ruined building built thousands of years ago, full of snakes and

scorpions and with only a mat to sleep on. He could not help asking, 'How do you manage to do all this? May I know?'

'Do what?' asked Mathieson.

'Manage so much decoration and luxury so far away?' said Sriram and pointed at all the things around.

Mathieson laughed gently and said, 'I wouldn't call this luxury, my friend.'

'And all this while millions of people here are going without food or shelter!' he said in a general way, the statistics he had picked up from Bharati deserting him for the moment.

'It is our prayer,' said Mathieson, 'that all of them may have not only enough to eat soon but also beautiful houses to live in, something, I hope, better than this, which is only a makeshift.'

Sriram put down this explanation to racial arrogance. 'It is his prosperity and the feeling of owning the country that makes him talk like this,' he reflected, and wanted to shout at the top of his voice, 'Quit, quit, we shall look after ourselves, we don't care for wicker furniture and gaudy coverings for them, we don't care even for food, what we care for—' He was not clear how to end his sentence. He merely said aloud, 'What we most care for is to do what Mahatmaji tells us to do.'

'And what has he advised you to do?'

'We will spin the *charka*, wear *khadi*, live without luxury, and we shall have India ruled by Indians.'

'But you have rejected the opportunity to try it. Don't you think it is a pity you should have turned down Cripps's offer?'

Sriram did not reply for a while. It seemed to him a technical point with which he was not concerned. Such intricate academic technicalities refused to enter his head, and so he merely said, 'Mahatmaji does not think so,' and there was an end to the discussion. He knew a jumble of phrases—Dominion Status, Reservation for Muslims, and this and that, but although he had gathered all these from the newspapers they seemed to him beside the point, the only thing that mattered was the Mahatmaji did not think the proposals had anything to do with the independence of India. 'It is just eyewash,' he said, remembering a newspaper comment. 'We don't want all that. We have no use for such proposals. We don't want charity.'

This last thought so worked him up that presently when the butler came bearing a tray with two glasses of orange juice he wanted to knock the tray down dramatically and say, 'I don't want it,' but it was a beautiful drink, yellow and fresh, in a long and almost invisible tumbler, and the climb and exertion had parched his throat. He hesitated.

Mathieson handed him a glass and, raising his own, said, 'Here's to your health and luck.'

Sriram could merely mumble, 'Thanks', and drained his glass. The passage of the juice down his throat was so pleasant that he felt he could not interrupt it under any circumstance. He shut his eyes in ecstasy. For a moment he forgot politics, Bharati, strife, and even Mahatmaji. Just for a second the bliss lasted. He put down his glass and sighed. The other had taken an invisible infinitesimal layer off the top level in his glass and was saying, 'Care to have another?'

'No,' said Sriram and started to leave. The other walked with him halfway down the drive. Sriram said, 'Don't rub off the message I have painted on your doorway.'

'Oh, no, I shan't. It is a souvenir and I shall keep it proudly.'

'But won't you be leaving this country, quitting, I mean?' asked Sriram.

'I don't think so. Do you wish to quit this country?'

'Why should I? I was born here,' said Sriram indignantly.

'I was unfortunately not born here, but I have been here very much longer than you. How old are you?'

'Twenty-seven, or thirty. What does it matter?'

'Well, I was your age when I came here and I am sixty-two today. You see, it is just possible I am as much attached to this country as you are.'

'But I am an Indian,' Sriram persisted.

'So am I,' said the other, 'and perhaps I am of some use to the people of this country, seeing that I employ five thousand field labourers and about two hundred factory hands and office workers.'

'You are doing it for your own profit. You think we can only be your servants and nothing else,' said Sriram, not being able to think of anything better, and then he asked, 'Aren't you afraid? You are all alone, if the Indians decide to throw you out, it may not be safe for you.'

Mathieson remained thoughtful for a moment and said, 'Well, I suppose I shall take my chance, that is all, but of one thing I feel pretty sure—I am not afraid of anything.'

'It is because Mahatmaji is your best friend. He wants this

struggle to be conducted on perfectly non-violent lines.'

'Of course that is also a point. Well, it was nice meeting you.' he said, extending his hand. 'Good-bye.'

Sriram went down the pathway, overhung with coffee shrubs, hedge plants, bamboo clusters, and pepper vine winding over everything else, with very dark green grass covering the ditches at the side. He felt so tired that he wondered why he did not lay himself down on the velvet turf and sleep, but he had other things to do. He had unremitting duties to perform.

It was the village named Solur three miles away that was his next destination. The place consisted of about fifty houses on a hill slope. Valleys and meadows stretched away below it. It was seven o'clock when Sriram arrived. The village was astir with activity. Men, women and children were enthusiastically gathered under the banyan tree of the village, in bright chattering groups. A gas light had been hung from the tree, and one or two people were arranging a couple of iron chairs brought in from one of the richer households in the village. The two iron chairs were meant for some distinguished men who were expected. Sriram went to the only shop in the village, purchased a couple of plantains, and washed them down with a bottle of soda-water. He felt refreshed. He asked the shopman, 'What time does the meeting begin?'

'Very soon, they are bringing someone to entertain us. It is going to be a nice function. Can't you stay on for it?'

'Yes, I will.'

'Where are you coming from?'

'From far away,' said Sriram.

'Where are you going?' the other asked.

'Far away again,' said Sriram, attempting to be as evasive as possible. The other laughed, treating it as a nice joke. The man supported himself lay clutching with one hand a rope dangling from the ceiling. It was a box-like little shop made entirely of old packing cases, with a seat cushioned with gunny sacks for the proprietor to sit on. Bottles containing aerated water in rainbow colours adorned his top shelf, bunches of green bananas hung down by nails in front of his shop, almost hitting one in the face, and he had several little boxes and shallow tins filled with parched rice, fried gram, peppermints, sugar candy, and so forth. He enjoyed Sriram's joke so much that he asked, 'I have some nice biscuits, won't you try them?'

'Are they English biscuits?' Sriram asked.

'The best English biscuits.'

'How can you be sure?'

'I got them through a friend in the army. They are supplied only to the army now. Purely English biscuits which you cannot get for miles around. In these days, no one else can get them.'

'Have you no sense of shame?' Sriram asked.

'Why, why, what is the matter?' the other said, taken aback, and then said, 'Hey, give me the money for what you took and get out of here. You are a fellow in *khadi*, are you? Oh! Oh! I didn't notice. And so you think you can do what you like, talk as you like, and behave like a rowdy.'

'You may say anything about me, but don't talk ill of this dress. It is—it is—too sacred to be spoken about in that way.'

The shopman felt cowed by his manner and said, 'All right, sir, please leave us alone and go your way. I don't want you lecturing here. Your bill is two annas and six pies . . . two bananas one anna each, and soda six pies . . .'

'Here it is,' Sriram said, taking out of his tiny purse two small coins and a six pie piece and passing them to him.

'You see,' the other said, softening, 'this is not the season for bananas and so they are not as cheap as they might be.'

'I am not questioning your price, but I want you to understand that you should not be selling foreign stuff. You should not sell English biscuits.'

'All right, sir, hereafter I will be careful, after I dispose of the present stock.'

'If you have any pride as an Indian you will throw the entire stock in the gutter and won't let even a crow peck at it. Do you understand?'

'Yes, sir,' said the shopman, not liking the little circle of watchful people who were gathering. At the end of the street the lecture platform was being set up with groups of people standing around watching. The villagers were very happy, some lively business was going on there as well starting here. The shopman saw an old enemy of his who liked to see him in trouble standing on the edge of the crowd with a grin on his face. As if to satisfy him, the gods had brought this man in *khadi* here, a born troublemaker. He appealed to Sriram, 'Now sir, please go away a little. I must close the shop.'

'You may close the shop if you like but I want you to destroy those biscuits,' said Sriram firmly.

'What biscuits?' asked the shopman alarmed. 'Please leave me alone, sir.'

'You have English biscuits, you said.'

'I have no English biscuits, where should I get them? Even in the black market they are not available.'

'If they are not English biscuits, so much the better. My esteem for you goes up, but may I have a look at one of them?'

'I have no biscuits at all,' pleaded the shopman. The crowd guffawed. Somebody shouted to someone else: 'Hey, here is Ranga in the soup, come on.'

'You have got them in that box,' Sriram said, pointing to one of the tin boxes. The shopman immediately lifted its lid and displayed its contents, white flour, luckily for him.

'But did you not say that you had biscuits a moment ago?'

'Who? I? I was merely joking. I am a poor shopkeeper, how could I afford to pay black market rates for biscuits and keep them for sale?'

'He has got them inside, sir. Let him show us the inside of his shop,' said one of the wags.

'Shut up and go your way,' shouted the shopman.

The situation was getting more complicated every moment.

'I am very sorry to note that you are a liar, in addition to being a seller of foreign black market stuff. I am prepared to lay my life at your threshold, if it will only make you truthful and patriotic. I will not leave this place until I see you empty all your stock in that drain, and give me an undertaking that you will never utter a falsehood again in your life. I am going to stay here till I drop dead at your door.'

'You are picking an unnecessary fight with me,' wailed the man.

'I am only fighting the evil in you, it is a non-violent fight.'

A woman came to buy half an anna's worth of salt. Sriram interposted and said, 'Please don't buy anything here.' When the woman tried to get past him he threw himself before her on the muddy ground: 'You can walk over me if you like, but I will not allow you to buy anything in his shop.'

The shopman looked miserable. What an evil day! What evil face did he set his eyes on when he awoke that morning! He pleaded, 'Sir, I will do anything you say, please don't create trouble for me.'

Sriram said: 'You are completely mistaking me, my friend. It's not my intention to create trouble for you. I only wish to help you.'

The woman who came to buy salt said: 'The sauce on the oven will evaporate if I wait for your argument to finish,' and, looking at the figure lying prone on the ground, she pleaded: 'May I buy my salt at the other shop over there, sir?'

Sriram with his head down could not help laughing. He said: 'Why should you not buy your salt wherever you like?'

She didn't understand his point of view and explained: 'I buy salt once a month, sir. After all, we are poor people. We cannot afford luxuries in life. Salt used to cost—'

Sriram, still on his belly, raised his head and said, 'It's for people like you that Mahatma Gandhi has been fighting. Do you know that he will not rest till the Salt Tax is repealed?'

'Why, sir?' she asked innocently.

'For every pinch of salt you consume, you have to pay a tax to the English government. That's why you have to pay so much for salt.'

Someone interposed to explain: 'And when the tax goes, you will get so much salt for an anna,' he indicated a large quantity with his hands.

The woman was properly impressed and said, opening her eyes wide: 'It used to be so cheap,' and added, throwing a hostile glance at the shopman standing on his toes, supporting himself by the dangling rope, with tears in his eyes, 'Our shopmen are putting up the prices of everything nowadays. They have become very avaricious,' a sentiment with which most people were in agreement. A general murmur of approval went round the gathering.

The shopman standing on his toes said, 'What can we do, we sell the salt at the price the government have fixed.'

'You might support those of us who are fighting the government on these questions,' said Sriram, 'if you cannot do anything else. Do you remember Mahatma's march to Dandi beach in 1930? He walked three hundred miles across the country, in order to boil the salt-water on the beach of Dandi and help anyone to boil salt water and make his own salt.'

The shopman was the very picture of misery. He said in an undertone, 'I'll do anything you want me to do, please get up and go away. Your clothes are getting so dirty lying in the dirt.'

'Don't bother about my clothes. I can look after them; I can wash them.'

'But this mud is clayey, sir, it is not easily removed,' said the shopman.

Someone in the crowd cried, 'What do you care? He will probably give it to a good *dhobi.*'

'If you can't find a *dhobi*, you can give it to our *dhobi* Shama, he will remove any stain. Even Europeans in those estates above call him for washing their clothes, sir.'

Someone else nudged him and murmured, 'Don't mention Europeans now; he doesn't like them.'

It seemed to Sriram that the people here liked to see him lying there on the ground, and were doing everything to keep him down. When this struck him, he raised himself on his hands and sat up. There was a smear of mud on his nose and forehead and sand on his hair. A little boy, wearing a short vest and a pair of trousers twice his size, came running, clutching tightly a six pie coin in his hand. He shouted: 'Give me good snuff for my grandfather, three pies, and coconut *barfi* for three.' He dashed past Sriram to the shop and held out his coin. The shopman snatched the coin from his hand in the twinkling of an eye. Sriram touched the feet of the young boy and importuned him: 'Don't buy anything in this shop.'

'Why not?'

Sriram started to explain, 'You see, our country—' when two or three people in the crowd pulled the young boy by the scruff, saying, 'Why do you ask questions? Why don't you just do what you are asked to do?' They tried to pull him away, but he clung to a short wooden railing and cried: 'He has taken my money. My money, my money.'

People shouted angrily at the shopman, 'Give the boy his money.'

The shopman cried: 'How can I? This is a Friday, and would it not be inauspicious to give back a coin? I'll be ruined for the rest of my life. I am prepared to give him what he wants for the coin, even a little more if he wants; but no, I can't give back the cash. Have pity on me, friends. I am a man with seven children.'

The little boy cried: 'My grandfather will beat me if I don't take him the snuff. His box is empty. He is waiting for me.'

'Go and buy it in that other shop,' someone said.

The boy answered, 'He'll throw it away if it is from any other shop.'

The shopman added with untimely pride, 'He has been my customer for the last ten years. He can't get this snuff from any other place. I challenge anyone.'

The boy clung to the railing and cried, 'I must have the snuff, otherwise—'

Someone from the crowd pounced upon him muttering imprecations and tore him away from the railing. The boy set up a howl. The crowd guffawed. The shopman wrung his hands in despair. Sriram sat in the dust like a statue, solemnly gazing at the ground before him. Someone pacified the boy, murmuring in his ears, 'Come and fetch your snuff after that fellow leaves.'

'When will he go?' whispered the boy.

'He will go away soon. He is not a man of this place,' another whispered.

'But my grandfather's snuff box must be filled at once.'

'I'll come and speak to your grandfather, don't worry.'

Sriram sat listening to everything, but he said nothing, without moving.

The crowd by the shop gradually melted away as the gathering at the other end started to form. A second lantern was being taken up the tree. The crowd looked up and said, 'Ramu is climbing the tree with the lantern.' They pointed at a youth wearing a striped banian over his bare body and khaki shorts. His mother watching from below cried, 'Hey, Ramu, don't go up the tree, someone pull that boy down, he's always climbing trees.'

'Why do you bother, what if boys do climb trees?' asked someone. A quarrel started, the mother retorting, 'You wouldn't talk like that if you had a son always endangering himself.'

The boy shouted from the treetop, 'If you are going to quarrel, I will jump down and make you all scream.' The crowd enjoyed the situation. For a moment the shopman lost sight of his own troubles, gazed at the treetop, and remarked, 'That's a terrible boy, always worrying his mother with his desperate antics. She knows no peace with him about.'

'Well, he looks old enough to look after himself,' said Sriram.

'Yes, but he has been spoilt by his mother, he is always climbing trees, or swimming or teasing people, a rowdy,' said the shopman.

'You people trouble him too much. He will not bother anyone if he is left alone,' said Sriram. 'Everyone is advising and worrying him.'

Now came a shout from the treetop: 'I have fixed the lantern. Who else could have done it?' The lantern swung in the air and threw moving shadows on the rocky hill slope behind. The crowd jeered and laughed at him. 'If anyone jeers at me, I'll cut the rope and throw the lamp on you all,' he challenged.

'Devil of a boy,' shouted his mother. It was pointless banter, it seemed to Sriram. He felt angry at the thought of all the aimless, light-hearted folk in this place. The shopman added, 'There is no peace in this village—those two are always bothering everyone in some way or other.'

'You are no better,' said Sriram angrily. The country was engaged in a struggle for survival; in a flash there passed before his mind Gandhi, his spinning wheel, the hours he spent in walking, thinking and mortifying himself in various ways, his imprisonment, and all this seemed suddenly pointless, seeing the kind of people for whom it was intended. He suddenly felt unhappy. All his own activity seemed to him meaningless. He might as well return to the cosy isolation of Kabir Street—that would at least make one old soul happy. What did it matter whether the shopman sold British biscuits or Scandinavian ones or Chinese crackers or French butter? It was only a matter of commerce between a conscienceless tradesman and a thick-skinned public. All this sitting in the mud and bothering and fighting was uncalled for. He felt suddenly weary. He asked the shopman, 'Can you give me a piece of paper and a pen and an envelope? I will pay for it.'

'No, sir,' said the shopman. 'There is no demand for paper and such things at this shop. People who come here are all simple folk, who want something to eat or drink.'

'And who ask only for English biscuits, I suppose?' said Sriram cynically.

'Forget it, sir. I'll never do it again,' assured the shopman, 'if you will only get up from that spot and forget me.'

Sriram felt pleased at the compliment and at the great importance his personality had acquired. It was very gratifying. 'You are not lying, I hope, about the paper and envelope?' he asked. 'Possibly you have only the costliest English paper and ink?'

'No, sir, I swear by the goddess in that temple. I have no stock, and I swear by all that is holy I will hereafter avoid all English goods. I will fling into the gutter any biscuit that I may ever see anywhere. I will kick anyone who asks for an English biscuit. At least in this village there will be no more English biscuits. Meanwhile, may I go to the schoolmaster and fetch you a sheet of paper and a pen? He is the only one who ever writes anything in this place.' The shopman added, 'Please move up a little, I can't leave the shop open, there are too many thieves about.'

Sriram said, 'I'll look after your shop while you are away,' and then, in a sinister manner, 'you know how well I can keep people off.' He seemed to enjoy it as a joke.

The shopman thought it best to join in and laughed nervously, preparing to close the doors of the shop. His nerves were taut lest Sriram should suddenly change his mind. He added, in order to safeguard himself against this possibility, 'You must write your letters, sir, without fail, however busy you may be. I'll be back in a moment.' He felt happy when he gave a tug to his brass lock and jumped down. He felt like a free man. This was his first taste of absolute freedom in all his life. 'I will be back, sir, I will be back, sir,' he cried, running away jingling his bunch of keys. It was an amusing sight to watch the portly man run.

Sriram enjoyed it for a while, leaned back on the door of the shop decorated with enamel plates advertising soaps and hair oil, and composed in his mind the letter he would write when the paper arrived. His eyes were watching the swaying lanterns dangling from the tree branch over the shrine, and the people assembled for the meeting under it. His mind was busy with the letter: 'Revered Mahatmaji, I don't know why we should bother about these folk. They don't seem to deserve anything we may do for them. They sell and eat foreign biscuits. They are all frivolous-minded, always bothering too much about a young scamp who has climbed a tree. I don't know if he has come down; I don't care if he falls down; it'll be a good riddance for all concerned. They will thank us for leaving them alone, rather than for telling them how to win *Swaraj*. They simply don't care. At this very moment I find them engrossed in preparing for a loyalists' meeting. What I want to know, my revered Mahatmaji, is—' He wondered what it was that he wanted to tell the Mahatmaji. What was really the problem?

He lost sight of the problem. He felt suddenly that he was too tired and unhappy. He was hungry and homesick. He wanted to go back to his Kabir Street home, preferably with Bharati, and forget all this. The banana and soda-water were hardly adequate for the strain he was undergoing. He wished he could ask the man for more if he came back and opened the shop door. He was seized with such inertia that he watched without stirring the proceedings of the meeting ahead of him. His conscience pricked him all the time. Something told him: 'You are here to counteract this meeting, but you are doing nothing about it.' He merely told himself, 'I can't do anything. I want to suspend everything till I have guidance from my leader. There is no use rushing along without a point.' He saw without emotion a set of people arrive in a jeep. A gramophone ground away, with amplifiers, producing some film songs to which the public marked time. And then someone came up with a harmonium, and accompanied it in a loud voice. Sriram shut his ears at the sound of the harmonium: 'Damned instrument,' he muttered to himself. His nerves were ajangle with its raucous cry. 'I hope when Mahatma Gandhi becomes the Emperor of India, he will make it a penal offence to make or play this instrument. This too is a British gift, I suppose,' he told himself.

After the music someone presented a scene from the *Ramayana*, with music and narration. The public enjoyed the show. Right in the midst of it all, the two officers occupying the iron chairs suddenly got up and delivered a speech in very bad Tamil. They explained the importance of the war, how Britain was winning, how it was India's duty to help, and how India should protect herself from enemies within and without. There were policemen in plain clothes, made less plain by their broad belts and khaki shirts, civil officers in tweed and bush-coats, with sleek hair; somebody was distributing toffee out of a tin to all the children in the assembly. Sriram said to himself, 'I'm here to stop it, but—but—let me first write to the Mahatma and get his advice—' He looked about him. He had an excuse to wait for the promised letter-paper. But he spotted the shopman in the crowd. 'Oh, liar!' Sriram commented. 'He is probably going to pretend that he is a child, ask for toffee and sell it at black market rates tomorrow at his shop.'

As if in answer to his unwritten letter he received a communication from Mahatmaji. It was enclosed in a note to Bharati and said: 'Your work should be a matter of inner faith. It cannot depend upon what you see or understand. Your conscience should be your guide in every action. Consult it and you won't go wrong. Don't guide yourself by what you see. You should do your duty because your inner voice drives you to do it. Look after Bharati as well as she looks after you, that's all. God bless you both in your endeavours.'

The message had given Bharati an occasion to come up and see him. It was one of his off-days, a day of soldier's leave, as he thought. He had sat at the portal of his ruined temple resigning himself to doing nothing for the day, going through an old issue of a paper he had picked up. It was full of dead news—of the Maginot Line and the like. But that was enough for him. The mail carrier had stepped off the boulder down below long ago on his return journey, and had gone back to the plains. The evening train had crawled in and out of the landscape. The sun stood poised over the western horizon.

Sriram brought out his rush mat, spread it out and threw himself on it, and was presently absorbed not only in reading all the stale news in the paper, but also in all those jokes, tit-bits, and syndicated cartoons which filled the bottom of its columns. He had picked up the paper on the highway, when returning from his expedition at Solur village. It had blown across the highway and hugged a tree trunk. He unwound the sheet from the tree trunk, flashed his torch on it and saw that it was an up-country paper which was well known for its reactionary views and carping references to Gandhiji, but still it contained some interesting Sunday reading. He felt irritated for a second at the thought that someone should have been scattering such an imperialistic paper in these parts, but he carefully folded it and put it into his bag. He had been the victim of certain moments of extreme boredom, when he felt that the huge teak trees and bamboo clumps and the estate trees covering slope upon slope would destroy his mind. They got on his nerves and made him want to shout aloud in protest. He once tried talking aloud to himself in order to get over the tedium. He asked himself, 'Hello, what are you doing here?' and told himself, 'I am fighting for my country.'

'What sort of fight is it? You look like a vagabond, with no uniform, no weapon, and no enemy in sight, what sort of fight is this? Are you joking?' and he laughed aloud, 'Oh, oh, oh!' He spoke at the top of his voice till the hills echoed with his voice, and one or two birds sitting on a tree nearby took off in fright. This exuberance had greatly relieved his mind. Now he hoped to be provided against boredom with this sheet of newspaper. Here at least was something to read instead of watching endlessly those treetops and valleys. It was his lot to be here. He could not kick against it.

He stretched himself on his mat. He had rolled a block of stone over to serve as a back-support for his couch. He had found it a couple of days before lying about in the grass and weeds, and had moved it up with difficulty. It had taken him nearly an hour. There were smoothed out lettering and ornamental carvings on the stone. He had speculated what they might signify, they were circular letters which looked familiar but eluded study; probably a message carved thousands of years ago by some king or emperor or tyrant one found pictured in history books. History books were full of ruffianly-looking characters, according to Sriram. He had often wondered what good purpose could possibly be served in reading and allowing oneself to be questioned about side-whiskered *goondas*? Reclining against his tablet he thought that if he had at least passed his examinations normally, he needn't have got into this present life. He might have settled as a good-natured clerk in an office, as his friend Prasanna had done. It was only yesterday he had been a champion street-footballer, but already he was in harness, slaving at the Treasury desk several hours a day.

Sriram reclined comfortably against the ancient tablet, and read a joke in which a 'He' and a 'She' indulged in a four line dialogue. 'When am I going to get my tie pressed?' To which she gave the smart reply: 'Exactly an hour after I get that gown.' Sriram read it over again and again, and felt irritated. What was the joke? Where lay its humour? He looked it over and examined it minutely, but failed to spot any sense in it. It was accompanied by a grotesque-looking couple, fat about the waist. Sriram thought: 'One can't tell what humour Englishmen will enjoy!' He put away the paper and its corners rustled in the wind. Now it was as if he heard the anklet-sound of his beloved, and there she was down below. Bharati was coming up the road half a mile away. She had never been more welcome. He got up and ran to her with a wild cry of joy. He saw her as an angel come to relieve him of his tedium. She carried a bag in her hand, as usual, and she strode on with such assurance and happiness. She was taken aback, when turning a bend, she was accosted by Sriram.

'Hello!' he cried at the top of his voice: 'Here is my *devata* come!'

She slowed down her pace and said: 'What has come over you? What will anyone seeing us think!'

'Who is there to see and think?' he asked haughtily. 'As if a big crowd were milling about!' he said, putting into his expression all the venom he felt at his lonely existence. She detected his tone of bitterness but preferred to overlook it.

'What do you want? A big fair around you all the time?' she asked light-heartedly, walking on.

He asked, 'Where are you going?'

'I'm going to meet you.'

'Here I am!'

'I won't take official notice of your presence here, but if you want me to state my business, I will say it and go back. I have come to you with excellent news.'

'What is it?' he cried anxiously, following her.

She went on, saying, 'Come and hear it at your own place.'

At his place, he ceremoniously showed her the mat, and begged her to recline with ease against the tablet. She obeyed him. She stretched her legs, leaned back on the tablet, and while her figure was rousing wild emotions in Sriram, she picked up the letter from her little bag and gave it to him. 'Here is a letter from Bapu for you. How do you like it?' He read it and remained thoughtful. Owls were hooting, the sky had darkened; crickets were making a noise in the dark bushes. He sat beside her on the mat. He could see her left breast moving under her white *khaddar* saree. She seemed to be unaware of the feelings she was rousing in him.

She said, 'Do you know what it means? Bapu wants you to stay on and do your work here. He feels your work here is worthwhile and that you will have to go on with it.'

'How do you know he means that and not something else?'

'I know it because I can read what he writes and understand it.'

'I can also read what he writes,' said Sriram with pointless haughtiness.

'Did you write anything to him?' she aked.

He didn't like the cross-examination. 'Perhaps or perhaps not,' he said with anger in his voice.

'Why should you be angry? I'll write to Bapu next time that you are a very angry man.'

In answer he suddenly threw himself on her, muttering, 'You will only write to him that we are married.' It was an assault conducted without any premeditation, and it nearly overwhelmed her.

He gave her no opportunity to struggle or free herself. He held her in an iron embrace in his madness. He lost sight of her features. The hour was dark. He felt her breath against his face when she said, 'No, this can't be, Sriram.'

Sriram muttered, 'Yes, this can be. No one can stop me and you from marrying now. This is how gods marry.'

Her braid laid its pleasant weight on his forearm. Her cheeks smelt of sandalwood soap. He kissed the pit of her throat. He revelled in the scent of sandalwood that her body exuded. 'You are sweet-smelling,' he said. 'I will be your slave. I will do anything you ask me to do for you. I will buy you all the things in the world.' He behaved like an idiot. She wriggled in his grasp for a moment and at the same time seemed to respond to his caresses. He rested his head on her bosom and remained silent. He felt that any speech at this moment would be sacrilege. It was a night of absolute darkness. The trees rustled, crickets and night insects carried on their unremitting drone. He wanted to say something about the stars and moonlight, but he felt tongue-tied. The only thing that seemed to be of any consequence now was her warm breathing body close to his.

He murmured: 'I always knew it. You are my wife.'

She gently released herself from his hold and said, 'Not yet. I must wait for Bapu's sanction.'

'How will you get it?'

'I shall write to him tomorrow.'

'If he doesn't sanction it?'

'You will marry someone else.'

'Don't you like me? Tell me—tell me—' he said in a fevered manner.

She felt the trembling of his body, and said: 'I shouldn't be coming here or meeting you if I didn't.'

'Wouldn't Mahatmaji have known?'

'No. His mind is too pure to think anything wrong—'

'What is wrong with what—?'

'This is very wrong—we—we should not have—I—I—' she sobbed. 'I don't know what Bapu will think of me now. I—must—write to him what has happened.'

He had never seen her so girlish and weak. He felt a momentary

satisfaction that he had quashed her pride, quelled her turbulence.
He said aggressively: 'Bapuji will say nothing. He will understand.
He knows human feelings, and so don't worry. There is nothing
wrong in loving. You and I are married.'

'When?'

'On the very first day I saw you.'

'That's not enough. I can't marry without Bapu's sanction.'

He became positive and dynamic. He swore. 'We shall marry
this very moment.' He dragged her by the hand into the inner
sanctum. He ran hither and thither doing things feverishly. He lit
the lamp and placed it before the image, whose nose and arms were
broken, but whose eyes still shed grace. He ran out and came back
with a few leaves and flowers, and placed them at the foot of the
pedestal. He took out a thread from his spinning wheel saying, 'You
cannot have a *thali* more sacred than this, nor a priest more holy
than this god.' When he attempted to place the thread round her
neck, she gently drew herself away from him.

A sudden firmness came in her voice, as she said: 'Know this,
Sriram. If I had not trusted you I'd not have come here again
and again.' He did not understand why she was saying it. He felt
bewildered. Why was she talking like this? Perhaps she suddenly
remembered that she ought to marry Gorpad or someone else. Yes,
now it flashed across his mind there used to be some significant
exchange of looks between her and Gorpad. What a fellow to
marry, rough as emery paper! A stab of jealousy shook him for a
moment and he said, 'Will you swear before this god that you will
marry only me?'

'Yes, if I marry at all, and mark this, if Bapu agrees to it.'

'Bapu! Bapu!' It filled him with despair. He wailed: 'He is too
big to bother about us. Don't trouble him with our affairs.'

She said, 'I won't marry if he doesn't sanction it. I can't do it.'

'If he asks you to marry someone else?' he asked pathetically,
checking at the last second the name 'Gorpad'.

'Bapu has better things to do than finding a husband for me,'
she said clearly, unequivocally.

He blinked for a moment. The excitement made his throat
parched. He wanted to ask something again. But even in his
confused state, he was aware that he was saying the same thing over
and over. He blinked pathetically. The broken-armed god looked
on. Sriram had never bargained for such an inconclusive love-

making. It had begun with such spirit that he had felt he would be shot into Elysium next moment, but here he was, standing before a god immobilized and listening to an obscure speech. The girl would probably take him for a fool to leave so much space between them. He tried to remedy it by approaching her again and attempting to storm her as he did a moment ago. The first time he had the advantage of a sudden impulse. But now it didn't work. She just beat down his outstretched arm: 'No. You will not touch me again.' She said it with such authority that he felt foolish.

'I didn't intend to if you don't want it. I know you hate me,' he said childishly.

She simply said, 'Why should I hate you?'

'Because I am bothering you.'

'How?' she asked.

'By, by—asking you to marry me. It's wrong, perhaps wrong.'

'It wouldn't be if Bapu agreed to it.'

He resigned himself. 'All right,' he said. 'As you please—'

'We shall marry,' she said, 'the very minute Bapu agrees.' She was very considerate.

He felt it was time for him to ask again: 'Do you—like me?'

'Yes, when you don't misbehave.'

Days of listlessness and suspense followed. Sriram lost sight of her for a considerable period. He thought he had lost her forever. It made him so paralysed that all day he did nothing but lounge in front of his cottage going over in mind again and again all that had happened that night. He had suspended his usual round of lecturing, agitation, and demonstrations; he didn't seem to think he owed any duty to the country. He ate and stayed in his den all day, he had read the joke about a 'He' and a 'She' two hundred times already. He saw the train arrive and depart. He saw the postman stop on the boulder and go away to the estates. He lounged against the corner tablet and brooded endlessly.

After all, one day she turned up. She came at noon. It seemed significant that she should avoid the dusk. The moment he sighted her on the bend, he gave a shout of joy and wanted to ask, 'Are you coming now, because it is a safe hour?' But he checked himself. He ran to meet her at the usual bend of the road. He asked: 'What news?' She didn't speak till they were back in their place. She sat down, leaned back on the tablet, took a letter out of her bag. Sriram snatched it hungrily and glanced through it:

'Blessed one: Not yet . . . I am going to ask all workers if they are underground to come out. I want you to give yourself up at the nearest police station. Take your disciple along too. God bless you both.'

Sriram felt stunned. He read the letter over and over trying to make out its significance. He tried to interpret it. '"Not yet," he says. What does he mean?'

'He just means that and nothing more,' she replied. 'It is never hard to understand what Bapuji says.'

Sriram felt amazed at the hardihood and calmness of the girl. She didn't seem to possess any feeling. She spoke of it with such indifference. He was appalled at her calmness. She was probably feeling relieved that Bapuji had vetoed their plans. It suited her very well—Gorpad. And of course, in his sick imagination he felt that probably Maliatmaji was also in favour of Gorpad, he'd naturally prefer to marry her to a grim and dry-as-dust worker like Gorpad. But why couldn't she be plain with him?

'Why can't you be plain?' he asked her all of a sudden.

'What do you mean?'

He felt tongue-tied, and asked: 'Why should Bapu not want us to marry?'

'He doesn't say so.'

He sighed: 'I thought he would send us his blessing, but he has only turned down our programme.' In his disappointment, he felt sore with the whole world, not excluding Bapu. He suddenly asked her: 'Don't you feel disappointed that we are not married?'

'I have other things to think of,' she said.

'Oh!' Sriram said significantly. 'What may they be?'

'I am going to jail . . .'

The full significance of the whole thing dawned upon him now. He cried, 'Bharati, you just can't do that, what do you mean?'

She replied, 'You will have to come too . . .' She opened the letter and glanced through it again. 'Bapu has also given instructions as to how I should occupy my time in jail. "This is an opportunity for you to learn some new language. I wish you could read *Tulasi Das Ramayana* without any assistance; you speak Hindi well, but your literary equipment will also have to be equally good. You may ask the jail superintendent to give you facilities if you are going to be classed as B to take your *charka* along. I would like to hear that

you are spinning your quota in jail. Don't for a moment ever feel
that you are wasting your time. Wherever you may be with a copy
of the *Ramayana* and Gita, and a spinning wheel, there you are
rightly occupied. Anyway look after your health. Very mild exercise
may be necessary, you may get it by walking around the compound
if you are permitted . . . If you would rather not be in B class but
would like to be an ordinary class prisoner like others, you will
have to ask for it. All that I am saying to you applies to your disciple
too." '

Sriram pleaded, 'Don't. Please tell Bapu . . .'

Bharati looked at him with wonder, 'After all these months of
association and work, how can you speak like this? How can we do
anything other than what Bapuji asks us to do?'

Sriram had no cogent answer to give. He hung down his head.
For the moment he seemed to have forgotten that he was a soldier
in the struggle for freedom.

She said resolutely, 'I ought to be there already. I am reporting
to the police station at . . .'

'How long will they keep you in jail?' he asked pathetically.

'How can I say?' she replied. 'Are you coming too?'

He said, 'Not now. I want to think it over. But I will readily
come if they will keep me in the same prison, preferably in the same
cell.'

'It won't be possible, the government won't keep us together,'
she said.

This enraged Sriram. The whole universe seemed to be
organized to defeat his purpose, even the government which
differed from the Mahatma on most matters seemed to be in
accord with him where it concerned him and Bharati. The worst
of it was that Bharati herself seemed to rejoice in the arrangement.
He became wild at the thought and said, 'Why is everyone opposed
to my loving you?'

She took pity on him and said tenderly, 'Poor fool. You have
lost your wits completely.'

'How dare you say that?' he shouted.

'There is no point in your shouting,' she said. 'Don't let us
quarrel. I will be gone in a moment . . . I want to report myself
before it strikes four. If they want to send me to the Central or some
other jail they must have time to catch the evening train.'

'What shall I do without you?' he wailed.

'That is why Bapu has asked you to report too.'

He shook his head. 'I have a lot of things to do outside . . . Bapu has given everyone freedom to carry on the *Satyagraha* in his own manner. He doesn't really mean me,' he said dolefully.

In answer Bharati seized the letter and held it open under his nose. '"This applies to your disciple also," he says.'

'But that doesn't mean me. It may mean anyone,' said Sriram.

'I thought you always understood whom he meant by "disciple",' she said grimly. 'Anyway the choice is yours. You may do what you think best. I am doing what seems to me the right thing to do.'

'How do you know it is the right thing to do?'

'I need not answer that question,' she said irritated. 'If I had known that you would treat Bapuji's word so lightly—'

Sriram felt crushed by her tone. 'Oh, Bharati, don't add to my troubles by mistaking me so completely. I revere the Mahatma, you know I do. Why do you suspect me? Have I not followed every word of what he has been saying? . . . Otherwise I should not have been here. I should not have left the comfort of my house. All that I want is some more time to think it over. I am . . .' he brought out his masterpiece on an inspiration, 'I am only thinking of my grandmother. I want to see her before I am finally jailed. That is why I asked you how long we should be in prison. She is very old, you know. I will surrender myself after I have seen her once. I must manage to see her.'

This idea seemed to soften the girl. She thought it over, leaning back on the tablet. She seemed to appreciate his tender feelings for his grandmother.

'That is all right, Sriram. I am sorry I mistook you.' He wanted to touch her arm, but he felt afraid to do so. She would surely say, 'Keep off, not until,' and that would irritate him again and make him speak nonsense.

She got up. He asked, 'Must you go?'

'Yes, it is late for me.'

He followed her sheepishly, 'When we meet again after the jail, and wherever we may meet . . . you will not forget me?'

'I will not forget you,' she said, catching her breath ever so lightly.

He loved her as she drew herself up, more than at any other time in his life, but he also felt afraid of her more than at any other time. He simply said, 'If you will not be angry with me, Bharati, I wish to ask one thing.'

'Yes?' she said, stopping and looking at him. He noticed beads of perspiration on her upper lip and wanted to wipe them off with his fingers. He was seized with desolation at the thought that he would not see her any more coming round the bend of the road. He wanted to seize her in his arms and take a stormy leave of her, but he had to content himself with asking, 'Will you marry me after we are out of all this, will you promise, if Bapuji permits?'

'Yes, I promise . . .' she said and hurried off before he could talk to her or follow her. He stood where he was and saw her raising her hands to her eyes once or twice in order to wipe off the tears gathering there.

3

A PERSON CALLED Jagadish dropped in one day very casually and introduced himself as a national worker. He said he was a photographer in Malgudi by profession, and claimed he had a formula for paralysing Britain in India. His studio in Malgudi with its dark interior served as a meeting ground for a group who were bent upon achieving immediate independence for the country. Jagadish came because he was in need of an out-of-town lair for his activities, and he was looking for a place where he could install a small radio set which could also transmit code messages.

He came trudging uphill while Sriram was reclining against his stone tablet. He came with a haversack on his back and wore a *khadi* dress. Sriram had been reading his old newspaper. Bharati's exit from his life had created a vacuum, which he found hard to fill. He felt somewhat confused as to what he should do with himself now.

Jagadish set down his haversack, sat beside Sriram and asked, 'You are Sriram?'

'Yes.'

'I am Jagadish. I used to know Bharati also. We are all doing more or less the same work.'

This was enough to stir Sriram out of his lethargy. He sat up and welcomed the other profusely with a great deal of warmth and asked, 'Where, where is she?'

'In detention . . . we don't know where, but one of our boys met her just before she surrendered herself to the police.'

Sriram asked, 'Where is this man?'

'He too has surrendered to the police; before that he came and saw me.'

'Are you going to court imprisonment?'

'No, I have other things to do. That is why I have come here.'

Sriram was happy to find a kindred soul and at once poured into his ears his own feelings. 'I told Bharati not to be a fool . . .'

'Don't say that. In this matter we all judge and act individually. Those who cannot follow Mahatmaji's orders are free to act as they think best.'

'How right you are,' Sriram cried, feeling he had blundered into the right set.

The other said, 'This is a war in which we are engaged, we are passing through abnormal times, and we do what we think best.'

He began to unpack his haversack. Sriram, always hungry and rather tired of the monotonous food he was eating, hoped childishly that something nice to eat would come out of it. He hoped it would be chocolate or fruit or biscuits. Oh, how long it was since he had eaten anything like *idli*, those white sensitive things made by his granny on most Sundays. Why Sunday and not on any other day, he had often asked. Now Jagadish took from his bag a small box, unwrapped the paper around it and brought out a tiny radio set.

'You will have to keep this,' he said. 'It can transmit as well as receive. I had it in my studio all these days . . . but the police have become very watchful nowadays.' He installed it behind the god's image, and camouflaged it with some bamboo leaves.

From then on the god with the eyeless sockets saw a great deal of Jagadish. He was of short stature with a brown wrap around his shoulders. He had a shaggy crop of minute, springy curls, which spread out parallel to the earth, projecting several inches beyond his ears. He parted his shaggy crop in the middle and applied a vast quantity of oil over his curls so that the top of his skull was always resplendent, and often Sriram saw the mid-day sun shining back from his head in a thousand colours. He was a very dark man with a large bulbous nose, but there was a fire in him that consumed everything before it, and Sriram felt afraid to oppose him. It seemed incredible that an elegant slender creature like Bharati should ever have spoken to this bear-like personality.

A stab of jealously passed through him. Could it be that she had

ever toyed with the notion of marrying him? God knew what he
did with himself when he was out of sight. How did he make a
living out of photography? Sometimes he didn't appear for days,
and when he turned up he explained, 'The wedding season,
you know. More fools getting married, and they drop in to get
themselves photographed. I can't afford to waive all the business.'
Or he explained, 'The jasmine season, and this is a heavy time
for a photographer. What a lot of young girls come with jasmine
buds knitted in their braids—the problem for the photographer is
to photograph a girl's face and the back of her jasmine-covered
head simultaneously, which is what they demand. Poor things,
they sit up all night when they have the jasmine in their hair, for
fear of crushing it on the pillows. They arrive at the rate of two
a minute. When they are in the darkness of a studio, I try to find
out their politics and give them our cyclostyled circulars and the
latest news. The studio is a help for us in this job. When anyone
comes there he is more responsive than he is anywhere else. People
generally come to a studio with a cheerful mind, ready to oblige the
photographer by being agreeable and responsive, and by listening
to all he has to say, the same as being with a barber. They have a
feeling that they are obliged to the photographer in some vague
way and readily listen to his talk, and I make use of this for our
national cause. That's why I keep the studio going, although it's so
difficult, without a proper supply of materials. When our country
gets independence, if I have anything to do with things, you will
see what I shall do to the beggars who are black-marketing spools
now!' He ground his teeth at the thought of them.

He was soon converting the temple into a fortress. He explained.
'The advantage of this place, do you know what it is? Except for
a few antiquarians, no one knows of its existence. And it is not
visible from outside. I've observed it from various points. It cannot
be seen from the road down below. I wonder why anyone built a
temple here at all. I believe it must have been used as a place for
conspirators a thousand years ago,' and he laughed grimly. Sriram
laughed. He began to like him.

'Don't think this is always going to be safe,' said the other.
'Sooner or later they will find it.'

'There is an underground chamber,' began Sriram.

'Yes, where I know aged cobras live, if you prefer them to the
police. But we have to manage somehow between the cobras and

the police.'

'Yes, yes, with so much to do—'

Jagadish handed him a small axe and told him to cut the bamboo foliage, large branches of it, and drag them up. Sriram went at it till the skin on his palm smarted and peeled off. Jagadish induced Sriram to climb the rampart of the old temple and stick the foliage here and there according to his directions. He was shouting energetically. Standing in the sun all day, his face shone like mahogany with sweat. He said, 'I can screen this whole mountain if it comes to that.' Sriram felt tired and indignant. He wondered, 'Why should I let this follow order me about, when he does nothing but stand around and instruct?' Probably it would have been more pleasant to have gone to jail. But Jagadish never gave him much opportunity to dwell on such thoughts. He said: 'We are waging a war, remember. Mahatmaji in his own way and we in our own. All our aims are the same.'

'But I thought we were all working out the Mahatma's orders.'

'We are, we are,' he said vaguely. 'I used to be a devoted follower too. I'm still one, but he is no longer there to guide us. What can we do? He permits us all to carry on our work to the best of our abilities.'

'But strictly non-violently,' said Sriram.

'Of course, this camouflaging is not violence. It doesn't hurt anybody. It's done only that we may be left alone to work out our plans without interference. I don't want even that postman to see too much of this place. After all, he is a member of the Imperial Govrnment.'

Sriram's next assignment was more complicated. He found he had become a blind slave of Jagadish, and a word of encouragement from him pleased him to the depths of his soul. He felt proud of his position. He thought that perhaps the other associates hardly ever got a good word from him. All day long, he sat up with the radio behind the god, with a writing pad on his lap, and a pencil between his finger, taking down the news and messages coming from Rangoon, Singapore and Germany, which purported to give the hour-to-hour progress of the war in Europe and the Far East. Sriram worked far into the night. His pencil wore out every three days. He had never worked so hard in his life. The only reward he got was Jagadish's 'Very good! Excellent job. More of our troops have joined the Indian National Army, they will soon be marching into

India.' He sat by the lamp and went over the reports with concentration as Sriram sat chasing out the gnats and beetles that were trooping in towards the light. Jagadish made several markings on the messages, and carried them off to be cyclostyled and distributed from his studio at Malgudi.

The radio said: 'This is Tokyo calling. Here is Subhas Chandra Bose, your own leader at the mike, addressing you on a special occasion.' A few seconds later the message said, 'This is Subhas Chandra Bose speaking.' Sriram sat up respectfully. 'What good fortune that I should hear his voice!' At the sound of it, Sriram felt reverence for this man who had abandoned his home, comfort, and security, and was going from country to country, seeking some means of liberating his motherland. With what skill he had managed to slip away from his home in Calcutta in spite of police vigilance, disguising himself as a sadhu! Sriram felt he was peculiarly fortunate to be hearing the hero's voice.

Subhas Chandra Bose's voice said, 'Men of the Indian Army, be patriots. Help us free our dear motherland. Many of your friends are here, having joined the Indian National Army which is poised for attack on your borders. We are ready. We shall soon be across, and then you can join the fight on our side. Till then don't aim your guns at us, but only at the heart of our enemy.' And then followed a ten-point programme of National Service that the men of the Indian Army should undertake. Sriram wrote at breakneck speed. He felt as if the commanding presence of Subhas Chandra Bose itself was at his elbow dictating. He filled up several sheets of the pad in respectful silence. He was overawed by the look of the radio now as its lamps burned red. Outside crickets chirped, a train rattled away somewhere, and the bamboo clumps rustled. The radio went on and on. Its red eyes glowed, and threw a red glare on the ankle of the god on the pedestal. Sriram lost count of time. He had never written so much in his life. That the broadcast came through in English was a great trial, for his spelling was none too good.

Subhas Chandra Bose was saying: 'And now stand by for a most important message. Be attentive.' Sriram wanted to catch it without fail, without any possibility of a mistake, but just at that moment a contrary noise began to emanate from the radio. It was as if a bee had started buzzing in time with the Great Message. Sriram felt distressed. If the thing went on undisturbed for a few seconds more, the message would be over. He strained his ears, but the

other noise was becoming too loud. He ground his teeth. His left
hand strayed towards the knob of the radio, and turned it. It only
seemed to irritate the radio further. He lifted his eyes from the
paper and glared at the radio. He saw on the dial on the outside
of the glass sheet, illuminated by a small light inside, a very small
cockroach, its pale body quivering with the battery of noise from
the radio. Sriram felt revulsion at the sight of its white belly pressed
against the glass dial. He could see but not reach it. He felt sick
and angry. He cried, 'You cursed creature, how dare you come and
interfere with this most important message! Get away.' He tapped
the glass with his finger. He felt indignant. 'Am I here to wear out
my pencil, taking down your stupid loathsome noises!' His tapping
was so furious that whether it affected the insect or not, he tapped
the light away, and all noise from the machine ceased. The radio
was dead. Sriram laid aside his pad and pencil and shook the radio,
but nothing happened. He turned the knobs, shook his fist at it
and cursed and cried, but nothing happened. He asked pathetically,
'Couldn't you have waited for five minutes more!' Why should this
have happened just when the most serious part of the message was
coming through? What would Jagadish say about him now? Sriram
looked at the radio and realized his utter helplessness. He had seen
youngsters who could take any mechanism to pieces and assemble
it again. He wasn't fit to turn even a screw. His own limitations
came back to him with a good deal of force, and he said, 'I am a
fool, I have been brought up as a fool by that granny of mine. It is
a wonder that a girl like Bharati cares for me at all!'

This note of self-reproach was fully endorsed when Jagadish
turned up at two a.m. After putting the radio out of commission,
Sriram sat for a while wondering what to do, blew out the lamp,
kicked open his mat and lay down on it. When Jagadish arrived
and struck a match to look for the lamp, Sriram woke up and cried
excitedly, 'Who are you?' A sleepy vision of the very dark man
illumined by a match-flare was unnerving.

'Hush, it is myself, get up.'

Sriram sat up, rubbing his eyes. The lamp was lit. Jagadish gave
him a slight shake in order to wake him fully; he sat beside him and
asked, 'What is special today?'

Sriram triumphantly held out his pad to him. He snatched it,
crying excitedly: 'Ah, a message from Subhas Babu! How lucky you
are to have heard him. Good boy! Good boy! You shall be a big man

when our country becomes free and independent.' He ran his eyes down it, muttering, 'These are men who arc gods on earth; whose deeds must be recited in odes to posterity. I'll have a *lavani* composed of Subhas Babu's life, his sacrifice, patriotism, courage, and make it compulsory to sing it every day in every school in this country.' He went on reading aloud, '"My countrymen, heroes of our Indian Army"—' in a singsong manner, interspersing it with appreciative comments of his own, such as 'Very good!' 'Precisely', 'It is a great mind speaking!' 'Listen and learn, all ye good folk,' and so on and so forth. Till he came down to:' "Now be attentive. In the first place all of you who"—' He turned the paper over in his hand and asked, 'Where is the continuation?'

'There is no continuation, the message stopped there. Someone has been tampering with the broadcast.'

'What do you mean? Let us see.' He dashed to where the radio was and turned the knob. There was no sign of life. He shook it and cried, 'What has happened to this blessed radio?'

'How can I say? Am I a radio engineer?'

'Don't get into an argument with me about it. It'll not take us anywhere. Subhas Babu must have said some very vital things, and you have chosen to choke the radio.'

'No. You are wrong. It choked itself. Probably a cockroach I saw there must have done it.'

Jagadish clenched his great fist and remained silent. Sriram feared he would hit him. If he did, he wouldn't go down without a fight. He looked at a corner where he kept a bamboo staff for cobras and scorpions. He wondered for a moment whether he should make an immediate dash to it. Would the other give him the necessary time?

After many moments of grim silence the man said, 'Well, let us not bother about it any more. As soldiers, we must learn not to brood over what is definitely past, mind you, what is definitely past.' He said, 'Give me that pencil.' Sriram passed the pencil to him. Jagadish adjusted the lamp, read the message carefully, and after spending one minute thinking, filled in the rest of the sheet briskly. 'You must, you must and you must.' He wrote with inspiration. It took him nearly an hour to complete the writing of the message, he looked over it and shook his head with satisfaction. He gave the pad to Sriram and commanded, 'Now read it, young man, this is exactly how he would have gone on if the cockroach had not stood there acting like a censor.' After this triumph a sudden sorrow assailed him. He was reminded of the radio. 'The last battery set—you could have spoken back to Subhas Babu, if you had only been careful. It was a two-way radio ... I suppose I'd better take it back with me and repair it. As a soldier I will not cry over split milk.'

'Is it *split* milk?' Sriram asked nervously.

'Of course it is,' asserted Jagadish. 'When milk goes bad, it splits into water, and solid, you know. It's no use crying over split milk,' he repeated.

Next afternoon, a little while after the train blew its whistle, Jagadish arrived with a bundle of papers hidden under his shirt. For the purpose of carrying that quantity of paper he wore an inner shirt with an enormous pocket and over it another large cloak-like shirt, and looked so big with all this literature hidden about his person that Sriram sometimes wondered if the impressiveness of his personality might not be due to excessive padding.

Jagadish unwound his robes and took out a bundle of papers, and once again Sriram childishly as ever expected him to produce some nice eatables. 'Come on, sit down,' said Jagadish. Jagadish first went to look up and down and assure himself that no one was watching. He dramatically attempted to close the large door which creaked on its mighty hinges, but could be moved only half an inch forward. Sriram watched him without a word. After these preparations, he pulled Sriram to a seat beside him on the mat. He pressed a sheet of cyclostyled messages into his hand, and said, 'Read it.' Sriram read aloud, 'Men of the Indian Army, etc. etc.', all that he had monitored on the previous day, but it continued for several paragraphs more. 'First, don't cooperate with our enemy government. Lay down your arms and lay down your lives, if necessary. You will be the heroes of the day when the Indian National Army marches into Delhi and flies its flag on the Red Fort, the very place where our men are now imprisoned.' And it went on and on, giving precise directions to the army as to what it should do for the liberation of the country. Sriram felt a profound admiration for the man. 'How did you manage to get the rest of the message?' he asked innocently.

'Don't bother how,' replied Jagadish, 'where there is a will there is a way. All out of this,' he said proudly touching his forehead. 'I could easily guess how the rest of the message would have run. It is just a matter of thought-reading, more or less,' he declared proudly. 'It is an extremely important message for our army at this moment. It is very vital to us. And it is to your honour that you got it first, although (never mind, let us not think of what is past) you couldn't get the full message; nothing is lost, and so don't bother about it. Furthermore, it should be your honour to see that the message reaches those for whom it is intended.'

Sriram was somewhat confounded. He asked, 'What should I do?'

'Listen to me carefully. I will give you fifty copies of this and you will take them to the army camp at Belliali. The poor fellows there cannot have any notion of what is happening in the world since they are not allowed to listen in to truth, but only to the cock-and-bull stories that the British War Department issues. Our boys must know the truth. They must know where Subhas Babu is, where the Indian National Army is stationed, and what is to be done. It is our duty to propagate truth wherever it may be. Has not Mahatmaji told us so?'

'Yes, yes,' agreed Sriram, to whom this argument appealed. 'What will you do with the rest of the copies? Why don't you let me carry some more?'

'No, I can spare only fifty. I have made one hundred and fifty copies in all. These are days of paper shortage, remember. I am going to send fifty copies to Lakshi camp, and take fifty myself to the third one at—. You will have to go up tonight and complete the task allotted to you.'

'Agreed,' said Sriram.

Before parting Jagadish said, 'We shall probably all three of us get shot in this enterprise. But don't bother. Our lives are not very important. Our work is more important.'

'I don't care whether I live or die,' said Sriram, remembering the frustrations he had experienced with Bharati. What was the use of dragging on one's existence with this girl always inaccessible? Probably this national fight would never be over, and if over, might probably involve her in further activities. She was bound to be pursuing something else all her life . . . This thought caused him so much weariness that he declared with all sincerity his readiness to die. He added, 'If I fail to return, will you tell Bharati what I think of her?'

'What do you think of her?' asked the other with amusement.

'That if she had married me I should probably not have died or something like that.'

'Well, I will tell her that. If I am shot, you can take charge of my studio. It is yours for the asking.'

Sriram felt too moved to speak. 'You are kind,' he murmured. 'How good you are.'

The other just twirled the end of his fancy scarf, 'But I am afraid you will find it hard to run it with the position of chemicals being what it is! Anyway, I wish you luck.'

The pamphlets were written in a convenient size which could easily be carried concealed on one's person. Sriram placed them neatly in a small bundle in a long strip of a towel, brought together its corners and tied them, put the towel around his waist and knotted it; over it he put on his *khadi* vest, and over it his *jibba*. The messages pressed his stomach uncomfortably, but he bore this with fortitude. He went down hill at nightfall. Jagadish had given him precise directions.

Sriram walked down the road and waited under a tree for a bus. There were one or two villagers sitting under the tree, waiting too. It was dark, and beyond the horizon there was the glow of Malgudi town. He sighed like an outcast. 'What a wretched hour it was when I set out to face life! Granny!' he addressed her mentally. 'I want to be back but I can't be, don't worry. All troubles must end. I wish they would release Mahatmaji. As long as he is in prison we will fight this devilish government. How dare they lay their hands on him? If they hadn't done that, Bharati would be out and happy, and Mahatmaji would have given his consent to her marriage.'

'Eh? What do you say, sir?' asked one of the villagers, peering at him curiously.

Sriram became cautious and asked, 'Who is there?' He looked closer, and asked, 'What are you waiting for?'

'The bus is late today,' they said by way of conversation, and Sriram agreed, 'It should have been here long ago, isn't that so?'

'How is the war going, sir?' asked one of them, the usual question that any villager would put to any man who looked informed.

Sriram suddenly became very cautious. He asked, 'Why?'

The other said, 'Because if it is over soon, we shall all be free from troubles.'

'I don't know,' Sriram drawled. In the darkness he could not make out the features of the man to whom he was talking. It might be a police spy or a constable.

'How is the war going, sir?' persisted the man.

'Well, the papers say this and that, and that is all I know,' replied Sriram.

'But someone says that it is all false! My brother knows a lot of people and he said that the English are being defeated everywhere. He said that the Germans are already in Madras. If they come, will they release our Mahatmaji from prison?'

Sriram wished to divert the question and asked, 'Have you seen Mahatma Gandhi?'

'Yes, sir, he passed through our village,' began the man, and the headlights of the bus became visible far off. The man picked up his bundle, ran to the middle of the road crying, 'Unless we stop the bus, he won't stop.' By the time the bus arrived he stood right in the middle of the road gesticulating wildly.

'You will be run over!' cried Sriram.

The driver jammed on his brakes and cursed: 'What are you doing? Do you want to kill yourself? Why don't you join the army and die, if you want to die?' he asked and laughter came from the bus.

The villager cried, 'I wish to go to—'

'Clear off and don't stand there talking. There's no place even for an ant in this chariot.'

'Let him in,' cried the conductor, to whom this meant extra income. Such passengers were unaccounted for at the end of the day.

'I will sit on the floor,' pleaded the villager.

'Five annas,' cried the conductor.

'Three annas,' cried the passenger. 'Last week you took me for three annas.'

'Last week is not this week,' cried the conductor.

Sriram, who had watched the proceedings with detachment till now, suddenly came forward. 'Take him for three annas if you did so last week.'

'Yes, sir,' said the conductor, awed by Sriram's manner.

'And drop me at—. How much?'

'Three annas, sir.'

'I will stand on the footboard if there is no space inside,' said Sriram.

The conductor became officious. He said, 'You may come in, sir. I'll make room.'

All the passengers craned their necks out of the bus; the engine was hissing like a serpent. 'No, I will stand on the footboard,' said Sriram and clutched the hand-rail when the bus moved. 'He probably thinks I am a bus inspector off duty', reflected Sriram, clutching the cold hand-rail as the night breeze blew on his face. Within the bus someone was snoring, someone was explaining the war and its progress on all fronts, someone was talking about God and Fate, a child was crying, a woman was yawning, the driver and conductor exchanged private jokes and giggled. 'They are probably enjoying the thought of their ill-gotten money,' thought Sriram. The bus ached and groaned under its load. He feared that its bottom might fall out. Unfortunately, he was not a bus inspector.

All the same, he assumed a voice of authority and asked, 'Conductor, what is your limit of loading?'

The conductor replied with humility, 'The government has set aside the rule, sir. We may take in as many as we can hold. This is wartime, sir, otherwise how many poor folk would get stranded on the highway.'

Many murmurs of approval came from the passengers. 'What with these air raids and troubles, it would be most dangerous to get stranded on the road,' someone ventured.

The bus rocked past sleeping villages. The lights were shaded according to the wartime rule, and the headlights threw a faint patch of light ahead. Someone was humming a tune; all these human sounds were welcome to Sriram's ears, which had grown atrophied through his lonely existence. He revelled in the music of human voices.

The bus slowed down and he jumped off at a village called Sangram. The time was about eleven at night and the entire village was asleep. He waited on the road till the bus was out of sight, and then patted his person to see if his material was intact: a wire-cutter in his inner pocket, and the precious message at his waist. When he stooped, a lump in the belly pained him. 'If only to be relieved of this pain, I must scatter the message,' he reflected. Turning down a road to his left, he walked on the extreme side of the road since one or two military lorries were passing, and he did not want to be noticed. He came up against a vast jungle of barbed wire entanglements, enclosing a group of bamboo and mud huts with a private road winding through. The main entrance was on the other side. This was a military depot and training centre, and from here all day the rattle of convoys agitated the silence.

Presently he found himself cutting a portion of the barbed wire fence. The snap resounded through the place; he feared somebody might machine-gun him. He heard the footsteps of the patrol sentry, and lay low. He thought, 'Well, this is my last moment. Suppose I am sent to hell?' He remembered all the details of hell that his grandmother had given him in childhood, and shuddered. 'There is no sense in getting shot by an unknown sentry,' he reflected. 'One unknown man shooting another unknown man, a ridiculous thing to happen.' On the strength of this, he put away the cutter. He took out a little glue, sat down and applied it neatly to the back of a few sheets, pasted the notices on the pillars supporting the wire and facing the inner barracks. The barb scratched the skin of his forearm. 'Blood is drawn, and this is the utmost I'm prepared to shed on Jagadish's orders.' After this, he rolled up his sheets into one mass, and flung them into the enclosure. He saw under the starlit heavens the notices fluttering down. 'The boys may pick up and read the messages at their leisure tomorrow morning,' he reflected, and turned back.

Jagadish said, 'Why that lacklustre and faraway look in your eyes, young man? You do a lot of service to the great cause. But your heart is not really in it. May I know why?' Sriram had nothing definite to reply. 'I should have said, "Look pleasant, please," or "Smile please," as becomes a photographer. You must put your heart into your job, my dear young man, otherwise you will not help our country. We are passing through crucial times, as our statesmen say, and we have to do something. I have a suspicion that you let your thoughts play too much around a certain person. Am I right?'

'Yes.'

'Well, that's a futile occupation, since it's the government who think it would be in your best interests to keep you two apart. You don't even know where they are keeping her.'

'That's true,' said Sriram dolefully.

'But I know where she is,' said Jagadish. 'I have my own agents. She is not actually in any regular prison, all jails being full now. She

is in a hurriedly made up one . . . You know the old slaughterhouse?
She is in it, along with a number of other women prisoners.'

'How do you know?'

'I know a guard who works there. He likes me because he is an
old customer, whose photograph in my stock helped him in some
family litigation. He will help you to meet your friend if you are
inclined that way.'

Sriram's heart palpitated. This was as if the dead had come to
life, or at least were promising to come to life.

'A nice fellow, he will help you, at the risk of his own life, to
meet and talk to Bharati for about half an hour.'

'When? When?' Sriram asked anxiously.

'As soon as you have done your job smartly. Some business
about chrome ore, and I need your assistance.'

'You mean I shall be rewarded for my services.'

'Yes, that's what I mean. One good turn deserves another.'

'Who is going to be benefited by my good turn?' Sriram asked.

'Well, the country. A train load of chrome ore is leaving a
certain railway station for England. It should not reach the port.
If it reaches the port, it will return to us in the form of triggers and
what not and plague us . . . I can't think of anyone but you to assist
me in this job.'

It was inevitable that soon the police should publish Sriram's
photograph and announce a reward for anyone giving information
of his whereabouts.

Sriram had a racking fear that Jagadish might be playing a practical
joke. 'If he is playing a joke, heaven help him,' he told himself. 'I
will crush his skull with a big stone,' and he revelled in visions of
extraordinary violence. He pulled his mind back sharply when he
realized how Bharati would react. The thought of Bharati softened
him. He told himself he would not hesitate to fall at the feet of any
villain if Bharati desired him to do so. Anything to please her and
earn her approval. His whole being acquired a meaning only when
he was doing something in relation to Bharati. He wondered how
he should conduct himself when she came out and the photographer
too was there. He hoped that his jealousy would not drive him to
do wild things. Anyway, he hoped that the photographer would
mind his business and leave him alone in order to pursue his life
as he liked, he hoped the fight with the British Government would

end soon, he hoped Britain would leave India, so that he might return to Kabir Street and live in peace with Bharati and Granny! Ah, that was the trouble. What would Granny do about it? She would probably nag Bharati night and day and compare her with her brother's granddaughter in looks and competence in household duties, but he hoped Bharati would turn round and challenge her to say whether that village niece of hers would have faced a charging police force or spoken to Mahatmaji. As he reclined on his couch at the entrance to his cave and looked at the top of the blue gum trees his mind roamed unchecked.

In a moment Jagadish had come up, and was standing by his side. He said, 'Very unsafe, young man. If it had been a policeman instead of myself, you would still have been sitting there, daydreaming, and he'd have put a nice collar round your neck and led you along to the jail.'

Sriram, rather irritated, asked, 'What's wrong with day-dreaming?'

'There is much that is not right. You must be more, watchful. Our cave is probably not visible from outside, but someone may think of exploring these parts. You are probably for ever. You should always watch, even through the camouflage. Be careful.'

'All right,' Sriram said, cowed by the other's manner, very much like a tiger in the circus ring which subsides on the spot indicated by the ring-master with a rolling growl.

Jagadish sat down beside him with the remark, 'And if you imagine that it's better the police come after you so that they may detain you at the old slaughterhouse, you are mistaken. They will do nothing of the kind: it's reserved for women prisoners.'

At the mention of the old slaughterhouse, Sriram softened. The associations of the old slaughterhouse might not be pleasant for everyone, but for Sriram the name produced the happiest associations and a very profound sense of peace.

'Old slaughterhouse? old slaughterhouse?' Sriram said, adopting a playful attitude for the first time these many days. 'Old slaughter, the sound is familiar! What has that to do with us?'

'It's virtue is that it is an old slaughterhouse, and not a new one,' said Jagadish. 'Many a goat trembles when it passes that building, but it makes you smile and joke. All the slaughter of the place is forgotten . . .

Yet it's still a place that attacks the heart, doesn't it?' he said.

Sriram felt completely happy. He would have gone on talking of the slaughterhouse for the rest of his days: it was an opiate which made him forget politics, history, the police, and his own loneliness.

'If you wish to visit the place, you will have to make certain alterations to your good self,' Jagadish said. He explained, 'First you must look unlike the photo the police have published. If someone wants to make money by informing, you should not help him to do so. I fear the police have published your photo far and wide, and any street urchin may denounce you. It shows the evil of leaving one's photos about. I have an advantage in this respect—there is no photo of me and they have only described me: having been so busy photographing others, I had no time for myself. You have been scattering your portraits about like a film star.'

'Yes, yes,' Sriram had to agree dolefully. He recollected the cheap four-for-one-rupee quick photos that he had indulged in some time after he came into his wealth. Often Sriram had seen his pictures displayed on the advertisement boards of the photographers; and the walls of his house were full of his own pictures. He remembered his grandmother saying: 'In our days people hung up portraits of gods and ancestors, you have nothing but your own! I wonder why you do it?'

'Does it mean the police have taken the photos from our house in Kabir Street?' Sriram asked, assailed by a sudden thought.

'Definitely. That's the first thing they will have done.'

'I wonder what Granny said.'

'She will repeat it all when she sees you next. Don't worry,' he replied. He studied Sriram closely and said: 'You will have to change your appearance. You will have to undertake some drastic changes. First and foremost grow a nice small moustache, a little one that droops at the ends will make you look slightly like a Mongol, but don't let that weigh on your mind, they are looking for you, nor for a Mongol. And then, do you think you could shave off your crop in order to complete the picture?'

Sriram's heart quailed ac the suggescion, remembering all the heartaches he had undergone in order to get rid of his old tuft and grow his present crop. His granny would not hear of it at first. She was certain that it would spoil his appearance, but one day he had just slipped away to the temple-tank on whose steps barbers sat and shaved their customers. He induced an old barber to cut off his tuft and run the machine over his ears, and on his lap he emptied all the pocket money he had purloined from his own sealed money-box. He had widened the slit of the money-box and shaken out the coins, when his granny was in the kitchen. To disguise the rattling he had muffled it with a piece of cloth and carried the operation on till it shed eight annas in small coppers. His granny kept shouting from the kitchen, 'What is that noise?' 'Which noise?' shouted back Sriram, and went on with his job. He had had no clear idea how much a barber would demand for a crop-cut. He put it down at six annas, and two annas extra for any unlooked-for expense. But the barber at the tank had demanded a rupee to cut off the thick curly tuft Sriram possessed. By haggling Sriram brought it down to six annas; and the barber went on muttering disappointed remarks to the tune of snapping scissors. Sriram saw himself in a small mirror produced out of the barber's tin box, and was delighted. He felt he had rid himself of a couple of pounds of tuft: it lay on the stone-steps of the tank; and Sriram remembered how he shivered at the sight of the appendage, for no known reason. They were long and curly tresses, and he said: 'Sell it and you will get ten rupees for it.' The barber lost his temper at the suggestion: 'You take me for a hawker of hair. Mind how you speak, young gentleman. I should have cut your throat if it hadn't been yourself but someone else. Look, I don't want anything, but give me the *dhoti* you are wearing: that's the usual custom under these circumstances.'

Sriram was aghast: 'And how shall I reach home?'

'Bathe in this tank and run before anyone notices. Anyway, haven't you got your piece cloth under your *dhoti*? That'll do for a young man of your age.' So saying he almost tugged the ends of Sriram's *dhoti*, and Sriram had to dodge him desperately. 'Oh!' cried the barber in great surprise. He made queer faces to indicate his feelings. 'Do you mean to say that you go about with—' He described vividly the underclothes of respectable and honest citizens, and the habits of the modern generation. The topic was so below-the-waist that Sriram blushed and finally, wrenching himself free, ran off.

All this flashed across his mind now. He put his hand to the top of his head, ran his fingers over it and said to Jagadish: 'I can't sacrifice this crop. I like it.'

Sriram spent a sleepless night wondering how he could change his appearance. He even thought that he might disguise himself as a *purdah* lady and not show his face at all. Jagadish laughed all his propositions away. He seemed intent on disfiguring him in his own manner; bent upon shaving him like an egg, and making him as ridiculous as possible. Perhaps he wanted to make him the laughing stock of the world and ruin his chance once and for all with Bharati. She would refuse to take a second look at his face for the rest of his life. He wondered why he did not refuse to do anything that Jagadish suggested. Even the slaughterhouse might be a huge practical joke or turn out to be a real slaughtering place after all! But his fears had no value. Whatever he might feel or fear the fact was always there that Jagadish was inescapable, and one had to do what he ordered.

Jagadish granted a period of three weeks for a respectable moustache to develop on Sriram's upper lip. He bought him a small bottle of coconut oil for massage to help a quick growth. 'How many things I have to do before I can see Bharati!' Sriram reflected. Jagadish checked the growth on the other's upper lip day after day. He nodded his head discouragingly each time. 'Very slow, very slow, too slow,' he said as if Sriram himself were responsible. Sriram clicked his tongue apologetically.

The period of three weeks was by no means wasted. In association with Jagadish and under his expert guidance, Sriram did a variety of jobs which he hoped would help the country in its struggle for freedom: he set fire to the records in half a dozen law courts in different villages; he derailed a couple of trains and paralysed the work in various schools; he exploded a crude bomb which tore off the main door of an agricultural research station, tarred out 'V' for victory and wrote 'Quit India' over the emblem. He became so seasoned in this activity that a certain recklessness developed in him. He had no fear of the police: they seemed to him a remote, theoretical body, unconnected with his affairs. He knew he could always slip through. They were looking for him everywhere, except where they could find him. Jagadish kept repeating: 'Britain will leave India with a *salaam*, if we crush the backbone of her administration.' He was always talking in terms of backbone. Sometimes he said: 'Britain's backbone is, you know where?'

'At her back, I suppose?' said Sriram facetiously.

'Do you know where her back is?'

'Behind her front, I suppose,' said Sriram, still facetiously. He was beginning to enjoy these bouts, which were a relief in his lonely, drab life, isolated from all human association.

Jagadish forgave him his tricks. He explained: 'The prospect of the slaughterhouse makes you sharp-witted, doesn't it?' He explained with a good deal of tolerance, 'Britain's backbone must be smashed, and it lies in the courts and schools and offices and railway lines, from these she draws the strength for her survival.'

It was an intricate logic which Sriram could not easily grasp. He asked pathetically, 'Why don't we smash her front also?'

'Because it's far away, and we can't reach so far.'

Jagadish dragged him about and made him his instrument and agent. Sriram was actually beginning to enjoy the excitement and novelty and above all the game of hide and seek with the police. It gave him a feeling of romantic importance. He felt that he was a character out of an epic, and on his activities depended future history. But now and then some kind of misgiving assailed his mind, when sitting concealed in a ditch in Jagadish's company, he saw the flames rising from a railway station or a government building and lighting up the night. Once he whispered, 'Do you think Britain will be affected by this fire?'

Jagadish declared unequivocally, 'Churchill will already know of it. It will make him groan. It will make him sit up. It must go on and on every hour of the day, all over the country, until Britain tells us, "We are bundling ourselves out tomorrow, do what you like with your country".'

Sriram asked next, 'I wonder what Mahatmaji will say about all this!'

'I don't know,' replied Jagadish. 'It is not his line. But when the results turn out satisfactorily, I am sure he'll say, "You did well, my boy".'

Sriram felt doubtful. He shook his head. 'I'm not sure. Only Bharati knows exactly what Mahatmaji will say or think . . .' And then his thoughts went off to the slaughterhouse.

Jagadish seemed to weaken slightly at this point: 'We have not wilfully caused anybody's death. I'm always careful to see that no life is lost, but if in spite of our precautions, some people are accidentally caught in a mess and killed, we can't help it.'

'A lot of people are also shot down by the police when they disperse the mobs that gather to help us.'

'But that is none of our concern,' said Jagadish, and added, 'in a war lives are bound to be lost. However, the job of the moment is more important than any amount of theoretical speculation. Mahatmaji taught me this philosophy when I was with him at Wardha. Anyway, don't bother too much about these questions. He has asked us to work for the movement according to our individual capacities.'

On a certain day Jagadish examined Sriram's face and declared, 'The most satisfactory moustache that I ever saw in my life.' With a razor and scissors he helped Sriram to give its end a downward turn. He produced also some old silver-rimmed spectacles, and mounted them on his nose. He provided him too with an ill-fitting, close-buttoned coat, and a white turban for covering his head. He ordered him to tie up his *dhoti* bifurcated, like all respectable men. After all this, Sriram looked into a mirror, the very tiny one which he used for his shaving; it did not reveal a full picture but it showed enough for him to remark: 'I look like a wholesale rice merchant.'

Jagadish nodded appreciatively and said with considerable delight in his tone, 'True, true . . . If I could only put a dark caste-mark on your forehead, that'd indeed complete the picture.'

Sriram, as he sallied forth at about seven, after sunset, felt so different that he wondered why he should expect Bharati to admit him at all. He chuckled at the thought, 'Bharati may wonder why a rice merchant has taken a fancy to call on her, all of a sudden.' The spectacles gave him a dull ache on the bridge of his nose, and kept constantly slipping down, pestering him with a dull, misty vision. 'This is what comes of not surrendering oneself to the police when Bharati advises one to do so!' he reflected. At the little station he climbed into the train going towards Malgudi. There were a few sleepy passengers in his compartment. He ignored the whole lot. 'It's no business of a self-respecting rice merchant to speak to these folk,' he reflected and sat looking at his fellow-passengers with indifference. Jagadish had proved himself a genius: the moustache was a tremendous asset; it was as if Sriram had worn a mask over his face, the transformation was so complete.

From Malgudi station it was an hour's walk southward through Market Road to the slaughterhouse. As he passed along the familiar roads, Sriram felt sentimental and unhappy. It seemed as if he had left this world ages ago. Beyond those rows of silent and darkened shops was the house of his grandmother.

Jagadish had given precise instructions. The rice merchant

crouched behind the eastern wall of the old slaughterhouse. Bharati would come to the lavatory at that corner, stand up on a large stone, rolled into position for the purpose, look down and talk to him. Sriram was wondering if Bharati would notice his moustache in the darkness; he wondered if he could reach up and touch her hand. He waited patiently. The Taluk Office gong sounded two in the morning. He felt sleepy. He remembered Bharati asking him to meet her at three a.m., when the Mahatma came to Malgudi. 'She seems fond of spoiling other people's sleep,' he reflected. He sat there on the ground. The Taluk Office gong struck the next hour. 'How long am I to stay here?' he reflected. 'Has someone been playing a prank?' Angry thoughts were rising in his heart.

'Hey,' cried a voice.

He looked up hopefully. Over the wall a head appeared, but it was not Bharati's. It was one of the wardresses.

'Where is . . .?' Sriram began, stretching himself up on his toes.

'Hush, listen. She won't come.'

'Is she not coming?'

'No. Catch this.' She dropped a letter. 'Read it,' said the head, 'and be off.'

The rice merchant moved away clutching the piece of paper in his hand, his head buzzing with a thousand speculations.

Under the first streetlamp, he spread out the note. It was a piece torn out of a memo pad. On it was a hurried pencil scribbling: 'I cannot bring myself to see you today. It seems degrading to have a meeting under these conditions. Bapu has always said that it is dishonourable to assume subterfuges. In a jail we must observe the rules, or change them by *Satyagraha* openly, if possible. Forgive me. We shall meet again. But before that, please go and see your granny. A detenue who came in here told me that she was very ill. It is your duty to risk your life to see her. Go before it is too late.'

Not many people were able to recognize him when he ascended the steps of 14 Kabir Street. He saw Kanni, the shopman, coming out of the house. He was softly closing the door behind him. He didn't recognize Sriram, who for a moment forgot that he could not be recognized, and called 'Kanni!' almost involuntarily. His voice betrayed him. Kanni halted and suddenly cried, 'Oh! It's our young master. O Ram, what is it you have been doing to yourself, deserting your house and the old lady who was your father, mother,

and cousin and everything. Have you no heart? Thank God you
have come now anyway. But you are too late.'

'Why? Why?' screamed Sriram. 'What has happened?'

'She is dead. She died at ten o'clock last night.'

Sriram ran past him into the house. There, in the old familiar
place, under the good old hall lamp, lay the old lady. A white sheet
was drawn over her. A couple of women from the neighbouring
houses were sitting beside her, keeping vigil.

Sriram was sorrow-stricken: the familiar household, the old
almanac still there under the roof tile: the copper vessel in which
she kept drinking water still on the window sill. The easy chair
which he had bought for her with his first money was still where he
had put it. He had a glimpse of a past life. He went up to the corner
of the house which used to be his and examined his books, pens,
clothes; he opened the lid and looked into his old tin trunk. All
the articles with which he had grown up were there, kept safe and
intact. The vigil-keepers followed his movements with dull, sleep-
filled eyes. Sriram wept. But he could not wipe away his tears; he
realized that his spectacles were a nuisance: he suddenly plucked
them off and flung them down, feeling: 'I'm answerable to Jagadish
for this. I'm betraying myself.'

Kanni stood in the doorway, respectfully watching. 'How
imperious she looks! Even now!' he cried. 'A great soul.'

'I can't believe she is dead. She looks asleep! How do you know
that she is dead?' Sriram asked.

Kanni merely laughed grimly. 'You had better telegraph to all
your relatives. I'm sure many would want to have a last look at her
face.'

Sriram sat down on the floor beside the old lady, quietly sobbing.
The women looked at him for a moment, and lapsed into mournful
silence. One of them turned to Kanni and asked, 'Is he the only
relative to arrive or should we wait for some more?' Kanni preferred
to ignore the question. The night was absolutely still and silent. Even
the street dogs were asleep. Except the low voices conversing under
the dim light, the entire world was asleep, following the example
of Granny herself. Sriram suddenly rose to his feet, went to Kanni,
put his arm round his shoulder, and whispered, 'Kanni, I am very
hungry. Can't you open your shop and give me something to eat?
There is nothing in the kitchen.'

'How can there be anything? She was ill so long; those ladies were bringing her milk and gruel.'

'I'm very hungry, Kanni,' Sriram said again pathetically.

Kanni jingled his keys and said, 'Come with me.'

They crossed the street. Kanni unlocked the door of his shop and lit a lamp. Sriram climbed the platform and went in, then bolted the door again from inside. The shop was hot and stuffy. Bananas hung down in bunches, buns and biscuits filled various glass containers; all, of course, were presided over by the European queen with apple cheeks. Sriram complained that it was stuffy. Kanni explained, 'I don't want anyone to suspect your presence. Though handing you over and collecting the reward might prove a better proposition than running a business in these difficult days!'

Sriram had not realized how hungry he was. He demanded and ate everything that he saw. Kanni took out a paper and calculated: 'That will be two rupees and four annas. I will put it down on your account.'

Now he was no longer hungry Sriram said: 'Tell me about my granny. What was wrong with her?'

Kanni paused for a while before answering. 'Ever since the police came asking for you in this house, she lost, if I may say so, her original spirit. She was always feeling that you had betrayed her. You may know all about the Mahatma and so on, but all she knew was what people told her, that you had run after a girl. The old lady was much hurt. She hardly ever came out after that, and when the police came to take away your photograph, she was very upset. She felt that she could not hold up her head in public again. She was always saying that you had betrayed her. The police came and questioned me too about you. I said, "You are merely wasting my shop time. I am not to be bothered about every scapegrace in the town because I have the ill-luck to have a shop opposite his house," and that satisfied them. I wish you had not gone away without telling her. It worried her too much. She kept saying, "What can a little cobra do even if you have brought it up on cow's milk? It can only do what its breeding tells it to do."'

Sriram was visibly annoyed at this comparison. 'She was a very bitter-tongued person, that's why I preferred to go away without telling her at all. What chance did one have of talking to such an unreasonable character?' He forgot for a moment that he was talking about someone dead.

'People came and told her hair-raising tales about you. She was alarmed by your activities. What was the matter with you? I never thought the young master I had known so long ago could ever grow up into a Zigomar.'

Sriram felt hurt by this comparison with an old classical bandit. He said with a lot of self-pity, 'I wouldn't have come if I wasn't eager to see my granny.'

'That's true,' said Kanni. 'The Market Road doctor attended her often; even last evening he was there with his tube and needle and stayed till she passed away.'

'Was she talking all the time?' asked Sriram.

'She wasn't, but she might have been. Why think of all that now?' Kanni said. 'Let us think of what we should do next.'

'Yes, what is to be done?'

'The funeral. Get through it quickly. Are you going to wait for relatives?'

These were tough and complex domestic questions to which he was unaccustomed. He brooded over them. The word 'relative' brought to his mind only his grand-uncle whose dark descendant he was expected to marry; and a batch of miscellaneous folk who dropped in for a meal or two occasionally from their village, and always spoke of lands and litigation. Granny used to find their talk fascinating and forgot to notice Sriram's arrivals and departures, while he generally sneaked out to a nearby cycle-shop and learnt to balance himself on the pedal of a bicycle taken on hire. Sriram had a sudden vision of being responsible for gathering that entire crowd again: they might stand around the corpse and lament over their lands and litigation. He was aghast at the thought. He said: 'I don't care for anyone.'

'Yes, I know. I too think you should not keep the body too long. Better hurry through the funeral. But at least let the lady have the satisfaction of having her pyre lit by her grandson. That may assuage her spirit.'

'I don't know what to do about such things,' Sriram wailed.

'I will help you,' said Kanni.

'One thing. I can't go with the funeral procession,' said Sriram. 'I will manage to come at the end if you will manage the other things.'

'Even the police may not interfere now. After all, they are also human,' said Kanni.

Sriram went back into his house and took another look at his granny. The two vigil-keepers were asleep. They sat hunched up with their heads on the floor, curled beside the body. 'They look more dead than Granny,' thought Sriram. A cock crowed somewhere. Sriram went out, softly closing the door behind him. Meanwhile Kanni had locked the shop, and had returned. 'She is in your charge,' said Sriram. 'Will you be there at eight? Do everything nicely. Don't bother about expense.'

'Yes, I know. I can always get my debts. I have kept your account in full detail. You should have no misgiving even about an anna. I have even put into the account what I have been paying the doctor from time to time. Are you sure her relatives will not be angry with us later?'

'What do you care whether they are angry or pleased? What have we to do with them? A set of useless rustics,' said Sriram with a certain amount of unnecessary bitterness in his voice.

At about eight Sriram was on the cremation ground beyond the Sarayu river. A couple of pyres which had been lit on the previous day were still smouldering. Bamboo and discarded pieces of shroud were scattered here and there. A funeral procession was crossing Nallappa's Grove. The bier was decorated with flowers and some men wearing white shirts and rings on their fingers were shouldering the corpse. 'Must be devoted relatives,' he thought. 'They are bearing the burden. But poor Granny has no one to carry her.' Once again he felt angry at the thought of those village relatives. The heat was intense although it was not even eight in the morning. 'This is a very hot place,' he reflected. Bullock carts were crossing the river, villagers on their way into the town with baskets on their heads chattered incessantly. He noticed people coming to the river for a wash. His mind made a dull note of all that his eyes saw. His main job now was to await the arrival of Granny. Why were they taking all this time? Probably priests were holding up the body so that they might get a higher fee for funeral citations. Or could the police have held up the procession? For a moment a fantastic fear seized him lest the police should have suspected foul play and held up the body for a post-mortem. The other, the pampered body carried by the devoted relatives, was now brought in through the gate and laid down on the ground. They were going through a lot of ceremonial activity . . . Granny's pyre was also being built up, with dried cow-dung cakes, on a small platform: all the arrangements were supervised by Kanni's shop assistant, who was haggling with fuel suppliers and ordering the graveyard assistants about. They obeyed him cheerfully, which made Sriram wonder why they obeyed him at all. 'It is in some people's blood to be respected by all kinds of people,' Sriram reflected, watching with a certain amount of envy all the fuss that the rich were making with the body in their hands.

Led by Kanni, who bore in his hand a pot of fire, a couple of neighbours, the manager of the Fund Office, and two priests, Granny arrived on a bier made of bamboo, carried by four grim subhuman professional carriers. Sriram rushed to the small wooden doorway to meet the procession. Kanni was the first to step through. He held the pot of fire to Sriram saying, 'Really it is your duty to carry it.' Sriram took charge.

Granny's face was uncovered and faced the sun. Sriram felt a pang of fresh sorrow at the sight. The bier was laid on the ground. 'Sriram, bathe in the river and come back soon with wet clothes on you. She is at least entitled to so much consideration.' The words came from the old family priest. Sriram realized that he was still in the garb of a wholesale rice merchant, and felt ridiculous. The old priest had officiated at festivals and domestic ceremonies ever since Sriram could remember, including the grand ceremony of his first birthday. The old man was several years Granny's senior, but remarkably wiry and alert, with his greenish eyes and hooked nose and greed for ceremonial fees.

He asked Sriram, 'Have you two rupees in coins?'

While Sriram fumbled for an answer, the ever watchful Kanni descended on him wrathfully. 'Why do you ask that? Haven't we agreed on a lump sum for everything?'

The priest who was squatting beside the body turned and said, 'Whoever said the lump sum included this? This can never go into that. This is a separate account. Our elders have decreed that the dear departed should have two silver coins on his or her chest from the hand of the nearest and dearest. It is said to smooth out the passage of the soul into further regions. I am only repeating what the *shastras* say. Our ancestors knew what was best for us, I am merely a mouthpiece.'

'And what happens to the coins?' asked the Fund Office manager. The priest pretended to ignore the question, but Kanni said, 'It goes the way of other coins, that is into a priest's money-box.'

'Yes, it does. Do you expect the soul to carry the silver with it? You must view it all in the proper light, you must take only its philosophical meaning. We carry nothing from this earth,' said the priest and quoted a Sanskrit verse. He suddenly looked across at the other part of the ground where the rich men were conducting their ceremonies. 'See there. They are devoted and very correct. They are not omitting a single rite.'

'We are not omitting anything either,' said Kanni angrily.

His tone cowed the priest, who mumbled, 'Don't think I am after money: I only do things in order to satisfy a great soul known to me for several decades now.' He looked up at Sriram and said, 'Now go and bathe quickly. Nothing can begin until after that.' He paused and added, 'You will find a barber there. You will have to shave off your moustache and the top of your head. Otherwise it would be very irregular. The *shastras* say . . .'

'I will not shave my moustache nor my head,' said Sriram emphatically.

'All right,' said the priest. 'It is my duty to suggest what the *shastras* say, and it is left to you to follow it or modify it in any manner. Of course modern life makes it difficult to follow all the rules, and people have to adjust themselves. There are even people who like to perform their funerals with European hats on, nowadays. What can one do about them? "It is wisdom to accept what has come to pass," say the *shastras*, and we bow our heads to that injunction.'

Sriram presently returned from his bathe in the river, dripping wet with his hair sticking on his head and his clothes stuck to his body. They had now laid the corpse on the pyre. The pyre beyond was already aflame and the party was leaving the ground. 'They are very businesslike,' said the priest. He seemed to admire everything they did. Sriram felt piqued, and Kanni said, 'Don't go on talking unnecessarily.'

The rites before the lighting of the pyre started. The old lady lay stretched out on the cow-dung fuel. The priest placed a small vessel in Sriram's hand and asked him to pour the milk in it over the lips of the dead. Sriram poured the milk, chanted some mantras, and finally dropped the fire over Granny's heart, which was actually below a layer of fuel. The fire smouldered and crackled. 'Now it is all over with her,' Sriram said.

The Fund Office manager suddenly cried, 'See there, see

there.' He was excited. They looked where he pointed. The big toe
on the left foot of the lady was seen to move. 'Pull off the fire, pull
off the fire . . .' Someone thrust his hand in and snatched off the
burning piece. The old lady's saree was already burning at one end.
Sriram flung a pail of water on it and put it out. Now with the fire
out, they stood around and watched. The toe was wagging.

'She is not dead, take her out,' cried Sriram.

'I've never heard of such a thing, you can't do that,' the priest
cried. People seemed to have suddenly lost all common sense.

'You want us to burn Granny alive, do you? Get out of our
way, priest,' cried Sriram. He kicked away the pile of fuel, lifted the
body and placed it down again on the ground. 'I knew something
was wrong. I knew Granny wouldn't die,' said Sriram. He sprinkled
water on her face, forced some milk down her throat, and fanned
her face. The priest stood aside with a doleful expression. Kanni
seemed too stunned to speak. The shop-assistant was running in
circles announcing the glad tidings and collecting a crowd.

The Fund Office manager cried, 'Let us not waste time. I will
fetch the doctor.' He started running towards the city.

Kanni cried, 'Oh, what doctors, these days! They don't even
know whether someone is alive or dead! If we had failed to notice
in time . . . oh, what doctors.' Under their nursing, the movement
in the toe gradually spread. All the toes showed signs of revival,
then her leg, then her arms. The old lady seemed to be coming back
to life, inch by inch. Her eyes were still shut. Sriram murmured,
'Granny, Granny, open your eyes. I am here.' At this moment all
politics were forgotten, all disputes and wars, Britain, even Bharati.
'Get up Granny, you are all right.' Now her heart began to throb,
her breathing returned, ever so faintly. Sriram let out a cry of
tremendous relief. He called the shop-assistant, 'My Granny will
not die, she is not dead. God bless her.' He dragged Kanni by his
hand and said, 'Kanni, Granny is alive.' He nursed his granny with
one hand and put the other around Kanni's shoulder and sobbed.
His face was wet with tears.

Kanni patted his back and said, 'Don't, don't. Be brave. You
must not break down. She may open her eyes and she must see a
happy face.'

The rattle of an old car was heard far off. Everyone cried,
'Doctor's car.' Presently a little car with a flapping hood was
struggling over the sand and pebbles at the Nallappa's Grove

crossing, and on through the rough sandy track leading to the southern door of the crematorium. The doctor was a puny man wearing an enormous white overall, with a straggling crop of hair resembling Einstein's; a small man above whom everyone seemed to tower. He jumped out of his car, followed by the Fund Office manager. 'Is this true, is this true?' cried the doctor running forward. He stopped suddenly and said, 'Someone go and fetch that bag from the car.' Presently he knelt above the old lady, took her wrist in his hand, pulled out his watch, held his fingers under her nostrils, and smiled at Kanni. 'Yes, she is not dead.'

'Oh, doctor, can't you even say whether a person is dead or alive?' asked Kanni.

'Why go into all that now? Let us be happy that she is back from the other world.' The doctor brooded. This was the first situation of the kind in his experience. Previously he had known only one-way traffic. He rubbed his chin thoughtfully.

'How is she, doctor?' asked Kanni.

'Her pulse is good. She is all right. She will need some rest and recuperation.' He took several things out of his bag. He sterilized a syringe needle, picked up a phial, and injected Granny's forearm. She twitched at the touch of the needle and groaned slightly. The doctor looked at her with approbation. 'Well, freaks like this just happen. We can't say why or how. Last night she was practically dead. I don't know. This is enough to make one believe in the soul, *karma*, and all that.' He stood looking at her and biting his lips. 'I read about a similar thing in a medical journal years ago but never thought it would come within my view.'

Granny was reviving little by little. Her breathing was becoming normal. The doctor said, 'It is not right to keep her here when she becomes fully conscious. She must be moved. Why not take her back home? Take her in my car.'

The priest interrupted, 'How can you suggest such a thing? No one who has been carried here can ever step into the town bounds again. Don't you know that it will . . . it will . . .'

'What will happen?'

'Happen! The whole town will be wiped out by fire or plague. It is very inauspicious. Do anything you like, but she can't come back into the town.'

This point of view gathered a lot of support. The news spread to the town. People began to throng into the cremation ground.

Everyone who came said, 'This is a big problem. What are you going to do with her?'

In deference to this view she had to be carried to one of the small abandoned buildings on the river bank, which had once been used as a toll-gate station, and since the river was between her and the town, she was out of bounds. She was kept at the toll office, and nursed by the doctor. Her world hummed round her, Kanni, the Fund Office manager, Sriram, the old hook-nosed priest, and the two mournful women who had kept vigil. They nursed and fed the old lady as she lay on a bed in the old building. The doctor's little car drove up half a dozen times a day and Kanni practically abandoned his shop in order to conduct the operations. A vast concourse began to arrive in order to witness the miracle. Some close relatives of Granny who had not seen her for years came and cried, 'Oh, sister, how good to see you. No one sent word to us that you were dead.'

'Word was not sent because there was nothing to send.'

'But when a close relation is dead, is it not . . .?'

'But she was not dead, so why send word?'

'How did you know that she was not dead?' asked the relatives, and the conversation flowed on in rather bewildering channels. Sriram feared all along that this crowd and publicity would ultimately lead to trouble. He tried to keep himself aloof. When too many people arrived he went away to the back of the building, while Kanni and the others managed the visitors. He overheard people ask, 'Where is that grandson of hers?'

'Oh, that ne'er-do-well adventurer is probably in Burma,' said Kanni.

But none of this helped. A police inspector in plain clothes and two constables arrived on the third afternoon as Sriram, having fed his granny and eaten a meal brought in a vessel by the Fund Office manager, was enjoying a siesta in the shade of a tree behind the toll-gate building. Granny and her attendants were peacefully sleeping. The inspector looked down at Sriram and said, 'Get up.'

'Why?' asked Sriram, rising. 'What do you want?'

'You are under arrest,' said the inspector. 'We have been looking for you for a long time now.'

'Who gets the reward?' asked Sriram with heavy cynicism.

The inspector did not reply. He said, 'We know the special occasion which has brought you here, and we don't want to make any fuss, provided you make none. That is why we have stationed our jeep over there. I have some more men in it. You may come with us as soon as you are ready. Don't be too long.'

Sriram said, 'Yes, give me a little time.'

'I am armed and will shoot if you try to escape,' the inspector said.

Sriram went to take a look at Granny. He found her sitting up and conversing with the two people near her. The moment she saw Sriram she cried, 'Oh, boy, when did you come back? They told me that you were here, but with a moustache. Whatever made you grow one, my boy? Take it off, don't come before me with that, whatever else you may do.'

'Yes, Granny,' he said obediently. He was so happy to find her old spirit revived. One could not doubt that it was Granny speaking. There was the genuine ring in her tone. Her personality seemed to have returned from the other world unscathed by the contacts there. He sat down on the edge of her bed, took her arm into his hands, and stroked it. She looked at him closely and said, 'You are down and out, no doubt about it.' She shook her head dolefully. 'Whatever induced you to get mixed up with all those people, I can't say. I tried to bring you up as a respectable citizen. If you didn't go up for your BA, it wasn't my fault. No one can blame me for it. But is it all true, all the things people say about you?'

Sriram thought and replied slowly, 'Don't believe a word of anything you hear. People talk falsehoods, remember.'

Granny's face puckered in a happy smile. 'Vile-tongued folk,' she cried. 'May all those that talk ill, think ill, slander you, or mislead you, or tempt you out of your way . . .'

At this point Sriram had a slight misgiving that the old lady might mean Bharati. He tried to divert her attention. 'Don't exert yourself, Granny, lie down.'

'Why should I? There is nothing wrong with me. You believe that doctor! Let him come before me. I will tell him what I think of him. He would have burnt me alive if he had had his way!' She laughed grimly. Presently she recollected the interrupted curse she had intended to hurl on someone. 'Whoever has been responsible for taking you away, whether it be man, woman, or whatever, may they perish and suffer in the worst hell!' After uttering her imprecation she felt both relieved and happy. Sriram thought of the police waiting outside, and said, 'Don't exert yourself, Granny, you must not talk too much.'

'Why not? And who says that?' she asked, 'I will speak as much as I like and no one shall stop me.'

At this point one of the policemen peeped in at the doorway and Granny asked, 'Who are you?' so authoritatively that he withdrew his head immediately.

'Who is he?' asked Granny.

'Someone to see me,' said Sriram.

He went on stroking her arm so soothingly that she presently felt drowsy. He gave her a few ounces of milk. She said, 'I am glad to see you. Good boy, don't let people tempt you out of your way. Be with me. Don't leave me again.' Sriram helped her to stretch herself on her bed, and she was soon asleep. He walked over to the police officer and said, 'Let us go.' Kanni followed him to the jeep. Sriram said, 'Kanni, look after Granny till I am back. I don't know how long they will keep me. Try to see me and tell me how she is. I think the Collector will let you see us in jail. I don't know what you are going to do about her.' He stood with bowed head for a moment, and then as though the problem was beyond any solution, he stepped into the jeep.

Kanni said, 'Don't be anxious. She is like a mother to us. We shall take care of her.'

4

HE WAS IN detention at the Central Jail. He occupied a cell with a few others and slept on the hard cement floor. They woke him up at five in the morning. This irked him most. He sometimes wished that they wouldn't pull him out of his retreat in a soft dream into the harsh reality of the prison world. And then the hurried getting up and washing at the dribbling water tap, and the public toilet; this sickened him at first. He prayed that they might let him wait at least till the others had gone, but that could not be; the warder stood over him and the others and hustled them.

Sriram once attempted to approach the Most High of this world, in regard to it, when he came to inspect the prison. The superintendent of the prison lagged behind the Most High respectfully, with all the other officials trooping after them. Sriram had been in a file awaiting inspection at the central yard which was surrounded by the horrible slate coloured barracks; the great man was marching by throwing a haughty glance at the file. The prisoners had been advised to stand stock-still, and not to utter a word or move a muscle when the man passed; they were not to speak unless spoken to. But when Sriram saw the great god approach his part of the file, he could not resist the impulse to step forward and begin: 'I have a complaint and a request to make, sir.' At once several people seized him and pulled him out of the way; and the great man passed on, pretending not to have noticed anything. After he was gone, Sriram was summoned to the superintendent's office. The guards held his biceps and kept him standing at attention before the superintendent's table. The superintendent looked up and said: 'You have violated jail discipline and you are liable to receive punishment.'

'What punishment?' Sriram asked.

The man, who had trailed like a meek puppy behind the visitor an hour ago, stamped his foot under the table and shouted, 'I will not have you talk to me in that manner, understand?'

Sriram felt cowed. He feared the other might go mad and kick him: he was the overlord here and was entitled to kill people if he chose. People might talk of monarchy being abolished, but here was absolute monarchy. This was his world, ruled by his authority, and no one could do anything about it, so Sriram said meekly, 'Yes, sir,' the very first time in his life he had adopted a tone of meekness.

The other was pleased with his submission and asked, 'Why did you step out of the line? What did you want to say?'

Sriram felt it would be better to speak plainly. 'I wanted to ask if something might not be done to provide us some privacy for our toilet.'

The superintendent sniggered, 'So you thought you might get things done over my head? Eh?'

'Not that, sir, but it hadn't occurred to me earlier, that's all.' Sriram said.

The other said, 'You saved yourself by not talking more, understand? If you had spoken to him, you would have been put in chains. Remember, we don't want indiscipline in this prison, understand?'

'Yes, sir,' Sriram said, completely crushed by his manner.

The other softened a little at this and said, 'Ask me for anything you may want.'

'Yes, sir.' Sriram found that this was the best way of talking to the man; the only idiom that didn't upset him.

The superintendent asked, 'What did you say you wanted to tell the IG?'

'I wanted to ask about the privy arrangements,' he said, feeling tired of all the repetition and publicity.

'Oh, is that so?' the other asked, and added, 'Here is the reply to your representation.'

'What, sir?'

'You will not be getting any arrangements other than what you have already got, understand?'

'Yes, sir,' said Sriram, uttering the soothing word. 'But may I know why?'

The guards pinched his biceps, alarmed at his impudence. But the superintendent did not seem to mind. He merely replied, 'If it had been any other time you would have been shot without a word, remember. You are not our guest, but our prisoner. You are not a classified prisoner, but one in custody under the Defence of India Rules, remember.'

'But there has been no trial. How long am I to be here?'

'There is no need for a trial in cases such as yours. The whole world knows why you are here.'

'I was only trying to do my duty,' Sriram said.

The superintendent kicked the table and said, 'I'll not have you fellows talking politics here.' The word 'politics' seemed to sting him.

'Yes, sir,' Sriram said, and this again soothed the man's temper.

He said as a concession, 'You are neither Gandhi's man nor an ordinary criminal, but more dangerous than either.'

Sriram could express no opinion in the matter himself. The word 'Gandhi' brought to his mind the memory of Bharati and he heartily wished that he had surrendered himself to the police with her. They would probably have treated him as an honourable political prisoner. 'Where is Bharati? Is she by any chance in this jail? If so won't you let me see her? Is she keeping well?' Questions by the score buzzed in his head, as he stood staring at the wall.

The superintendent said, 'I'm glad you are paying close attention to my words. But let me say at once, it won't pay you to be troublesome within these walls. What are you thinking?' he demanded suddenly.

'I was only wondering how long I shall be kept here. It's already several months. I have lost count of the months.'

'It is unnecessary for you to keep count of anything, it's not going to be of any use to you. Your stay here will be as long as His Majesty wishes you to be here, that is all. We're instructed to keep you not very differently from your other friends here, under sentence of various terms of rigorous imprisonment. That's all, dismiss.'

The guards clicked their heels, saluted, and turned Sriram round. As he was going the superintendent threw after him the remark, 'You will ask me for anything you want.'

'Yes, sir.'

'That's all, dismiss.' And the guards marched him off. The days, weeks, and months that followed were similar, one day following another without much distinction. Sriram began to feel at home: he looked forward to the little excitements that came to him in the course of his existence. When he was taken to break stones in the quarry behind the jail, he welcomed it as a change: the rocks that he hewed were hot under his seat, the sun scorched his body, the iron hammer with which he broke the stones peeled his skin, but still he liked the job because it took him, though under surveillance, outside the jail. He was with a gang of men, miscellaneous criminals, who were there for anything from murder down to confirmed pocket-picking. Most of them were planning what they would do at the end of their term. Some of them were planning to return again and again, and spend the rest of their lives here. Sriram felt uneasy in this rough company, who laughed at the soft-handed, soft-headed man. They simply could not make out why he should have courted all this trouble from the police because someone wanted him to do something, and not because such exploits as derailing a train brought him a share of profit. This was a fresh outlook that had not occurred to Sriram in his self-centred political existence. He had a feeling that he was running up against a new species of human being, speaking like monsters, but yet displaying sudden human qualities; they were solicitous that he should not undernourish himself; they pitied him for his inability to relish the food: a tough ball of boiled millet with very watery buttermilk. (The buttermilk was a recent addition because somebody had agitated for it in the Press and in the assemblies, and the buttermilk content was just enough to satisfy the technical needs of all agitators in general.) While he ate he thought of all the good things that his granny had made for him and remembered how even during his very last visit to her, at their house, she had offered him something that a neighbour had sent. He felt agony at the memory of the crunchy, ghee-flavoured rice; he could almost hear the music of his bite, while he held up his aluminium platter to receive his quota. The very manner in which he munched made his fellow-prisoners comment.

'You still think of *badam halwa*?' asked the culpable homicide not amounting to murder. They were sitting side by side during the break for food at midday.

'If ever I leave this place, I am going to spend a hundred rupees on *badam halwa* at the corner shop, you know Krishna Vilas, the shop is small but it is a wonderful place; he serves on clean banana leaves and not on plates. You know his *idlis* are almost as if made of the lightest . . .' Sriram was at a loss for a comparison, and his companion helped him with similes of jasmine, rose-petals, soft butter, and so forth. Sriram added passionately, 'And you know he gives free chutney to go with it, you can't see the like of it anywhere else on the globe. You must have known the corner hotel?'

'No,' his companion shook his head. 'I am from Bellary, I am not familiar with the town.'

'I know that hotel,' the guard added, joining in their conversation. 'It's a good place, but I go there rarely. I haven't much chance of getting out of this place.'

'You are like us?' said one of the prisoners and all of them laughed happily at the joke.

Meal times were the best. Sriram's neighbour, a veteran forger, whispered to him, 'Don't tell anyone. I am getting some good things to eat and drink next Thursday. I will give you some when I get them.'

'What are you getting?' asked Sriram, unable to control his curiosity.

'Some *vadai*, and the nicest chicken *pulav*.'

Sriram retched at the mention of the chicken. He made a wry face: 'Chicken! Chicken! Oh! I can't stand the thought of it!' he said, his face twisting with disgust. 'I don't eat those things!' he cried. 'I have not even eaten cakes because they contain eggs.'

The forger was amused. He rolled with laughter till the guard, who had been friendly hitherto, objected: 'Stop that, where do you think you are!'

The central tower threw a welcome shade. The afternoon was languid, though warm. The superintendent would be snoring in his quarters, enjoying his afternoon siesta: there was really no one to object to anything, and this was the only hour when the prison ceased to be a prison for a while and gained a human and habitable atmosphere; the wardens themselves acquired a friendly mellowness, and all conversation flowed on the human level. This was the hour at which it was impossible to continue the rigours of the jail atmosphere—it was almost like the midday recess at Albert Mission School of Sriram's younger days.

The forger pleaded with the warder: 'Don't bother us for a while, please. A man needs some rest after all the labour of the day. Please leave us alone for a while.' And then he turned his attention to Sriram: 'I know they will use the purest ghee and nutmeg leaf and cinnamon bark for the *pulav*. If you scoop a handful of it, ghee will drip down your finger; it's so rich. Don't say that you won't have it. You must accept it. It will do you good. Once you taste it, you will keep demanding it every day. That's the worst of it. It'll be impossible to get it into the place every day, though once in a way we can do anything. Our friend here and his friends will not mind what we do. He knows he will get his share.'

A gong struck the hour. The warder jumped to his feet and said: 'Get up and march', and he led them back to their quarry at the back of the jail.

At night, Sriram had companions in his cell. Before lying down on their cement beds, wrapped in their blankets, they sat up talking. The sentry at the corridor cried, 'Hush! Don't talk.' One fellow, the one who had committed house-breaking and murder, took it into his head to sing a hymn and insisted upon all the others joining him. '*Rama Rama, Sita Rama*', he sang musically, and urged all the others to follow the chorus. He said, 'This is the only thing which is real,' in a very philosophical manner. 'You must know what is real and what is unreal. You must know the nature of the world in which we live. You must repeat the name of the Lord ceaselessly.' And he began a singsong devotional recitation of the Lord's name. Others followed. If they stopped, he shouted in the dark, 'What Satan's offspring is in this room with me? I will cast him out.'

Sriram could not help asking, 'If you were so religious, why couldn't you have remained outside and led your followers?'

'It's because the police would not let me be, that's all,' he said.

'Of course, but for the police we would all be happier men,' someone said.

After this they all started their chant again. The sentry came and peeped at them. They guffawed. He muttered something and went away. The leader said in the dark, 'I am not afraid of anyone, I am not afraid of any jailer.'

'It's because you are so experienced,' said another admiringly.

'I would have been swinging in that shed long ago, but the judge understood I didn't kill because I wanted to. I only wanted to break the bones of that ill-fated fool.'

'Which ill-fated fool?' asked Sriram, unable to check his curiosity. Here were men who formed a new species. He might have to spend the rest of his life as a member of this family.

The other answered: 'I only wanted him to give me the keys, as so many others had done, but he suddenly ran to the window, shouted for the police, and when I tried to run away he jumped on me and held me down. What could I do? I had to do something. I thought I might crack his legs and—but he pushed me, and that didn't work. These people force us to do unhappy, unpleasant things.' He ruminated for a while and sighed, 'No use thinking of it, but the magistrate understood, and when I leave the jail I shall take him some fruits, oranges, plantains, things like that. Let us not waste our time.' And he began his chant with the others joining in. Sriram wanted to speak to them about politics, Mahatmaji and nonviolence, and the British rule. He began to speak, but he was cut short by the man saying, 'Who cares who rules? We don't belong to that world. I've seen all those Gandhi followers in prison, and they think they are honoured guests! If you had been careful you could have enjoyed that too. They'd have put you in a bungalow with a cook and pocket money and they would have given you books to read and sherbet to drink.'

Sriram's blood boiled at his words. 'How dare you speak like that of those who are suffering for the country's cause? You are mistaken. You are completely mistaken.' He wanted to get up and hit him, but he remembered that Bharati would have labelled him a traitor to the non-violence creed of Mahatmaji. Perhaps she would have said, 'I don't want to look at your face again. Get out of here.' And so he merely mumbled, 'Don't talk in that utterly ignorant manner of our patriots.'

The other growled. 'Who are you, to talk to me in that tone?'

There was a pause. The forger at his side nudged him and said, 'Say you regret it. Don't rouse him. He is very strong.'

Sriram heard heavy steps approaching him from the other end of the cell. The man stood over Sriram and growled: 'I insist upon saying that your political prisoners are no true prisoners, do you understand? I've been in ten jails so far. I have seen a lot of them. They feel they are in their father-in-law's house, visiting for Deepavali. I know what I'm talking about. I won't have you correcting me, do you hear?'

'I don't agree with you,' said Sriram. 'They are great patriots. They put themselves through much suffering.'

'I will knock your teeth out if you contradict me. Am I clear?'

'I will say what I please,' said Sriram defiantly. 'Even the British Government could not make me do what I didn't want to do!'

The other sneered: 'H'm, this is what comes of reading and writing. You don't know obedience of any sort, let me tell you. People should never go to school. They talk too much.'

'If I had been out, I'd have made you prostrate yourself before Mahatmaji, and confess your crimes,' said Sriram with passion.

At the mention of the Mahatma, the other brought his palms together and said, 'Don't drag his name in here; that great saint.'

'He is also in prison, I suppose you know that,' said Sriram.

'He may be, but what is that to you? Do you think you are also Mahatmaji because you are here?'

'Go back to your bed, man,' commanded Sriram. 'You don't know what you are talking about.'

'You call yourself the Mahatma's disciple, and you have derived no good from it. What business have you to come in our midst?'

Sriram said in disgust, 'Go back to your bed, man, I won't talk to you.'

The gangster swung his arm to hit Sriram. Sriram felt the rush of air in the dark, and ducked his head, and the other went back to his bed. Sriram felt happy and relieved only after he heard him stretch himself out and utter a long noisy yawn, which he prolonged into a song, till the sentry cried through the bars, 'Hush! Silence. No more talk.'

During the day the various duties he had to perform and the variety of derelict humanity he watched in the prison kept his mind from too much gloom. But when the last of the prisoners in his cell fell asleep and snored, loneliness came down on him and he became a prey to introspection. He was seized with a desire to meet and talk to Bharati. Where was she? Dead? Married to someone else? Or hanged in the prison? There was no way for him to know. He was amazed at the isolation that had been devised—inhabiting the same planet people were completely cut off from one another. States and their police minions seemed capable of devising any torture for human beings. Bharati had probably married Gorpad and gone to north India. It was months and years since they had met. He had lost count of time. The only reckoning they had was morning, midday and night punctuated by meal hours, drudgery, and occasional excitements such as that caused by the bully in his cell. He wondered if Bharati would ask, 'Who are you?' if he appeared before her. He was seized with the obsession that day by day he was deteriorating so much that he wouldn't be fit to be seen by her. He was losing his identity. He had lost his patriotic aim. He wondered what he had done to warrant anyone calling him a political sufferer. But for Jagadish he would not have done things that he wouldn't wish to enumerate before any decent person now. If it had not been for Jagadish he would probably have gone on living in his ruined temple until the police forgot him. And then he might have been worthy of associating with Bharati.

The thought of her produced in him a certain uneasiness: he heartily wished that she had not been such an uncompromising zealot. Everything that she thought or said or expected was set in grooves and hard to practise. For all practical purposes he was a back-number now, nothing better than the associate of forgers and homicides: their world was his world. Why should he be thought of differently? The longer he stayed here the more likely he was to drift away from Bharati. It was imperative that he should get away. How? He revolved in his mind all the things he had read in story books—of files and hacksaws being smuggled into prisons and people working their way out. The more he thought of it, the more unhappy he became. The sheer helplessness of the whole business weighed him down. He became silent and glum. All night he was racked with dreams of being caught while escaping, taken out and shot, the shooting party being directed by Bharati. He woke up in a cold sweat and was greatly relieved to find that after all he was still in the solid and homely prison. Why was Bharati causing him worry even in his dreams? Why couldn't she make herself agreeable and amenable like any other normal sweetheart?

The Fund Office manager sought special permission to meet him. The call came to him when he was at work in the weaving shed. A warder came to say, 'You are allowed to see a visitor today, between three and four in the afternoon.'

Sriram felt excited. 'What visitor?' he cried. 'Man or woman?' He had a wild hope that his visitor might be Bharati. Could it be? What would he say to her? How was he going to talk to her? How could he tell her all that he wanted to within the time? Perhaps she would spurn him when she saw him. Better not see her. Could he send word back that he would not see anyone? All this passed through his mind in a flash. He asked: 'What sort of a person?'

But the warder said, 'See for yourself. The interview is in the Chief's room. If you don't waste too much time asking questions, you can have a few minutes with the visitor.'

Sriram followed the other meekly, dropping his job. His neighbours muttered: 'Your mother-in-law has probably come to see you with sweets!'

At the entrance to the Chief's office, the warder halted for just a second to look him up and down, flick off a cake of dirt from his jacket, and pull up his dress in general; he murmured: 'Remember how you should behave before the Chief. If you make any trouble, he will have you whipped.'

Sriram answered, 'I don't like whipping,' to which the other retorted, 'Don't talk back. It is enough if you do what you are told.'

It was only after Sriram had mumbled an unqualified affirmative that he would behave properly that the warder pushed him in. He saw the Fund Office manager waiting for him. He looked intimidated by his surroundings; he sat on a stool, his legs dangling, afraid to cross them.

The Chief looked up briefly and said, 'Prisoner, you have special permission to meet a visitor today.'

Sriram felt abashed to stand there in that uniform and face the Fund Office manager. He stared at the manager, who stared back at him. The Chief was busy looking through the papers on his table.

'You may speak,' he ordered. 'I can't allow this interview to be prolonged beyond four p.m. If you have anything to say to each other, go ahead, and don't waste time.'

Sriram felt like a fool. He thought that the manager should break the ice and begin the conversation. But the man seemed bereft of speech.

The Chief tried to ease the situation again by interrupting his study of the papers to order, 'Guards wait outside.'

Two men who had mounted guard over Sriram saluted, clicked their heels, and went out. This brought a slight improvement, but still the interview did not proceed beyond the stage of mutual staring. The Fund Office man seemed to be stunned by the sight of the Sriram he saw before him now. He seemed to doubt whether this lank, sallow close-cropped man in striped knickers and jacket could be the one he had come to see. Sriram noted his surprise and hesitation and said to himself: 'When even the manager is so reluctant to admit my identity, what will Bharati do? Perhaps she will say, "Get out, you *badmash*. Who do you think you are?"'

The Chief looked at his watch and fretted. He said: 'You may talk about anything except politics and other banned subjects.'

Sriram suddenly found his voice to say, 'How is everybody, manager?'

'Very well, very well,' the man said swinging his short legs, still afraid to cross them.

'Tell me about Granny,' said Sriram.

'That is why I have come here,' said the manager. 'We had a communication from her today.'

'Communication! Where from?'

'Don't you know? She is in Banaras now.'

'When did she go there?'

'Don't you know the story? When she revived at the cremation ground, some orthodox people said that she could not come back into the town because it was inauspicious and might blight the city. She respected their wishes and stayed in the toll-gate house for some days, and then said she would go to Banaras. We helped her to take the train at Talapur.'

'Banaras! What is she doing at Banaras?'

'She is with a number of others, who spend their last years there, old persons who are waiting to die. They cheerfully await their death, and look forward to the final fire and the final ablution in the sacred Ganges.'

'Did she ask for me?'

'Oh, she was so—' the manager began, and at this point the

Chief said, without looking up from his papers, 'Not allowed. Talk of something else.'

'But it is not politics,' began Sriram.

'Don't argue. Talk of something else,' ordered the Chief.

Sriram helplessly glared at him and said to the manager: 'And then what happened?'

'She is quite well in Banaras. There is a whole street of them, old people who have retired there to the banks of the great Ganges, awaiting their end. Some have been there for years. That's as it is enjoined upon old people in the *shastras*. No one could wait for a happier end.'

The man from the Fund Office seemed to be so repressed with this that he became very eloquent, and Sriram could not help asking, 'You too want to retire there?'

'Yes, in good time. If God wills it. Everyone can't be as fortunate as your granny!' He paused to reflect, gently swinging his short legs. He had respectfully left his sandals outside the office and Sriram noted how dirty his feet were, and blackened with dust and wear. When he came back to the sordid world again, the manager said, 'She has given instructions regarding the disposal of the rent of her house. She wants the amount to be sent to her.'

'Is someone living in the house?'

'Of course, of course. Didn't you know?'

Sriram seemed to be hopelessly out of date, he knew nothing of what had happened anywhere. 'It was her instruction that a tenant should be found for the house, and accordingly we found one to pay a rent of forty rupees only, which they are crediting to the old lady's account in the bank.'

It was an appalling thought for Sriram that someone else should be living in the old house, shutting and opening its doors.

'Who are they?'

'Some yarn merchant.'

'Yarn merchant! I never thought we would have to surrender our old house to a yarn merchant!' he said with disgust.

'It's no surrender, they will vacate at a month's notice.'

This information filled Sriram with uneasiness. 'Where am I to live?' he thought. 'Where am I to accommodate Bharati, when I marry her?'

Although he had lived away from the old house for so many years, he still had a feeling that everything was all right so long as

Granny lived there and so long as he could think of it as a home. He was filled with nostalgia for its brass-bonded, slender pillars, the *pyol* over the gutter, and the coconut-treetops beyond the row of buildings.

'This is the point,' said the manager. 'She wanted me to tell you about it, and if you didn't want this money—it's been accumulating, as I have already told you, into a considerable amount—she said it might be sent to her. She seems to have exhausted all the cash she had taken with her. This can be done, I suppose?'

'Of course, why not?'

'I am merely carrying out her instructions. She wants me to consult your wishes in the matter.'

'Do anything she asks you to do. If she needs more money, don't hesitate to take it out of my funds. Poor Granny! I wish I had more time to give to her affairs. She has done so much for me. How is she? Does she feel very lonely?'

'Far from it. A friend came from Banaras today. She is keeping very well; bathes thrice in the Ganges, and prays in the temple, cooks her food, has good company. A sublime life; it's this friend who has brought the letter.'

Sriram thought of his house again and felt unhappy.

'They are probably driving nails in all the walls, and what has happened to all my books and other things?' He gave a list of articles he possessed, and the manager said soothingly, 'Don't worry about all that. They are all safely kept in that end room, which we have reserved for your own use.'

'What others news? How is the war?'

'Don't talk of that,' said the Chief.

'How is everything else?'

The man got up to say something, but Sriram interrupted with: 'I don't even know what year or month it is.'

'Nothing on those lines,' said the Chief. 'No politics, no war.'

Sriram in the solitude of midnight in his cell developed the notion of escape. He revolved in his mind all the techniques of escape that he had read or heard about. Smuggled files and rope formed, of course, the staple points in the whole business. Scaling the walls and crawling through ventilators were an inevitable feature. He dwelt on reminiscences of Monte Cristo's escapades; it was all very interesting and kept his mind busy planning. His admiration for the old prisoners became genuine; his sympathies were really widening. He realized how impossible it was to do anything within the walls of a prison except what the jailer permitted. The warders seemed to take a personal pleasure in carrying out their duties, they were incorruptible and could not in any way be influenced. And yet how did people smuggle in hacksaws and things like that? While his hands were busy digging the earth or turning a wheel, his mind revelled in dreams of filed bars and nimble ascents up dangling ropes, escapes which story and film writers presented so slickly. This dream became so troublesome that he could not contain himself any longer. Lying on his cement bed at night he was busy weaving a rope that would go up to the ventilator in the ceiling, through which the night sky was visible, the only glimpse of a shining free world.

His only consoling thought, perversely enough, was that perhaps Bharati herself was languishing similarly within the bounds of the old slaughterhouse. It was not that he wanted to see her suffer, but the idea of her suffering established a community of interest. If he succeeded in escaping from the jail, he would smuggle the tip to Bharati, wherever she might be, so that she might climb out of her prison, meet him outside its formidable walls, and hug him as her hero. But she might insist upon going back to her cell, refusing to walk out of it unless they opened the gates for her in a right royal manner. She might spurn him for his labour. She was incalculable in her behaviour. She would want the sanction of Bapuji, perhaps. Bapuji would probably applaud the proposal, if it could be proved that-Sriram's technique would enable all prisoners to climb out of jails; they would at once understand its national implications: how the British could be driven to despair if they were made to realize that their prisons could hold no one. It might drive them mad and make them decide, 'Well, we will quit. We can't hold India any longer.'

It was wishful thinking on a very big scale, but that could not be helped. It was the only excitement that he could ever conjure up. In his desperation he consulted the bully in his cell when an opportunity occurred. One evening he was unusually friendly, and Sriram slipped over to his cement bed and sat there. He whispered: 'Why don't we all escape from this hell?'

The other laid a clammy sympathetic hand on Sriram and said,

'It's usual to get that feeling. But nowadays I don't get it. I just do my *bhajan* and feel all right. You must also join us in our *bhajan*.'

'Well, we will speak about that later. But now let us discuss how we should escape.'

'How?' asked the other.

'You must help us. You are experienced. Have you never escaped from a prison?'

'Yes, twice, that's why I'm doing my seven years now.'

'You should not have allowed yourself to be caught.'

'Well, these things just happen, we can't help it,' said the other philosophically.

Sriram was interested in the method, and asked, 'How did you escape?'

'Easy,' said the other, looking up at the ventilator. 'We were just six in a cell. We spun out the blanket strands, raised ourselves on each other's shoulders, tied up the rope, and climbed out: it didn't take much time. We were crossing the *cholam* fields in about an hour. No one would have found us again, but a fellow who had come out with us broke the lock of a house on the way and was caught.'

'Shall we do something like that and get out of here?'

The other thought it over and said, 'Why should I? What have I to do outside?'

'But I wish to get out. I can't stand this place any more,' said Sriram.

'If you didn't like this place, you should not have done things to bring you here, that's all,' said the other. 'Even if you manage to get out, they will bring you back in no time, it's not worth all the trouble. You can't hide your face.'

'I will grow a beard.'

'They will pluck out your beard just to see how you look. That is how you bring dishonour on even holy sadhus, who have beards.'

'I promise I will keep out of the way of the police.'

The other shook his head. 'What is the use of going out if you can't move about freely?' He seemed to take pleasure in teasing him and to disapprove of people who didn't appreciate their life in jail.

Finally, Sriram took out his trump card and said, 'I want to escape because a girl I want to marry is out there.'

'Where?' asked the man ruthlessly.

Sriram was afraid to give the reply, but he blurted it out before he could hold it back. 'She is in jail too.'

'Oh! Oh!' the other cried amused. 'Do you mean to say you are going to slip into her jail and ask the jailer to officiate at your nuptials?' he asked coarsely.

Sriram felt angry and regretted that he had ever mentioned his angel to this coarse man. God knew what terrible things he would say now. He remained silent, afraid to open his mouth. And the other said: 'If she is the kind to go to jail, listen to my advice, leave her alone. You can't bring up your children in jail. There must be someone to look after the house. It's not at all right that both a man and his wife should be the jail-going sort.'

'How is it with you?' Sriram asked.

'I have three wives, here and there, and they run the homes in my absence: if they didn't I wouldn't hesitate to put sense into them. That's the way. You are not going to be here all your life. When you are let out, go and marry a good girl, I tell you. This jailbird will be no good for you.'

'She is not a criminal, she has gone to prison on Mahatmaji's command.'

'Oh! Oh! Oh!' the other sneered. 'Why do you drag in that great man's name here?'

Sriram grew annoyed. Somehow the mention of Bharati seemed to rouse in the other the worst ideas. Sriram abruptly rose to his feet and went to his bed muttering, 'Go on and sleep. Let us not talk any more.'

'You are afraid I shall tell the Chief, aren't you?' the other sneered. 'If you don't join me with gusto in our *bhajans*, I will report you to the Chief.'

'I'm not afraid,' said Sriram defiantly.

'Well, we will see, don't be surprised if they lock you up in a solitary cell. You will have only the walls to talk to,' said the other. He took a fiendish pleasure in promising hell to Sriram.

Sriram paused for a moment and said, 'I have not wronged you. Why do you hate me?'

The other said sulkily, 'I have no sympathy for those who don't believe in God. I don't like fellows who speak ill of God.'

'I have not said a word against God,' Sriram said, wondering at the turn the subject was taking. 'What have I said?'

'I won't repeat it,' the other replied. 'If you don't respect God, you will be whipped in jail, remember. That's my experience. You should listen to a man with experience, that's all.'

'I am in need of no advice from anyone', said Sriram haughtily.

The forger turned in his sleep and swore, 'Are you going to sleep or keep on talking all night? A wretched place, it's becoming worse than the marketplace. No peace for a man who wants to sleep. I will call the guard if you fellows don't shut up at once.'

In answer the bully let out a loud, challenging song in a stentorian voice enough to wake the whole town. There was a sound of running feet outside. Sriram sneaked back to his bed. The guard asked through the bars: 'What's going on here?'

'People are chattering and chattering. This has become worse than the marketplace,' said the bully from his bed.

A friendly warder brought them the news of the outside world: 'Mahatma Gandhi is becoming the Emperor of India,' he said one day. 'I heard it today from a person who knows these things. Some men have come by plane from England with the proposal.'

'Don't be silly. How can they want the Mahatma to become the king of India when they have put him in prison for fear that he may become one?'

'Didn't you know? It seems he is out of prison.'

'I don't believe it.'

'I swear he is. They released him long ago because he was ill and his wife died. A woman who comes here to cut grass told me so.'

'It is not safe to have any transaction with grass-cutting women. They will get you into trouble,' said a veteran prisoner.

'How do you know?'

'It is because I have suffered. They are sirens. They will seduce you before you know where you are. And then you will have trouble everywhere. They don't like such goings-on in a jail.'

'But this is an old woman who cannot seduce anyone. She is a grandmother, so don't fear.'

'Then it is all right. Go on.'

'Her son is in the army. Her grandson sells newspapers in the market and he tells her what goes on in the world.'

Every one of the prisoners and their guards as well eagerly crowded round him to ask, 'What is happening? What is happening? Tell us.'

'It seems that some men have come from England and they want to make the Mahatma a king.'

They clapped their hands in glee. 'Oh, how good to hear this!'

'Why does it make you so happy?'

'Because if Mahatmaji becomes the king of our country he will not allow anyone to be kept in prison. He doesn't like it. It's because he is a very good man. It seems the British don't like him because he says such things.'

'They like him now, all right.'

The indulgent warder looked on as the prisoners discussed these matters among themselves, while going through their various duties. The warder didn't however like the idea of a prisonless state. He said: 'How can there be no prisons? There will always be prisons whoever may become the king.' This was a ticklish technical point. The best thing was to consult the political expert in their midst. They turned to Sriram for guidance.

Sriram was breaking the stones unmindful of what they were saying. He was listening to their discussions, but he chose not to display any enthusiasm. He said, 'I don't know anything about anything.'

They plied him with questions: 'Is it a fact or is it not a fact?'

'How should I know? I am in your midst.'

'Will they release us all from prison?'

'All? I don't think so; they are likely to release only political prisoners.'

The warder seemed relieved to hear it. 'Ah, you say so. Political prisoners are different. There are some in the other block. I have heard that some of them are leaving every day. That is a different thing altogether. But you are not all political prisoners.'

They all said, 'What if we aren't? We are also human beings. Why should we not be treated well too? Whatever you may say, Mahatma Gandhi will help us. Do you mean to say that Mahatmaji will not care for us? He is a kind man.'

Their curiosity could not be contained. Night and day they worried about it, until one day a newspaper was smuggled in through the good offices of the friendly warder, and put into Sriram's hand for perusal and explanation. While his audience sat round him, and the guard watched over them, at the quarry outside the jail, Sriram read out to them the *Daily News* from the first line to the last. It was as if he had been given a sudden vision of a broad and active world. He read of the impending political changes, of the proposed division of India into Hindustan and Pakistan, of Mahatmaji's firm refusal to countenance the proposal, of the Cabinet Mission, and the endless amount of talking that was going on at Delhi, of death, disaster, and convulsive changes. The greatest triumph for Sriram was that the British were definitely quitting India. He said proudly: 'I myself wrote on all the walls "Quit India", and you see it has taken effect.'

People looked at him with wonder. He became a hero in their midst. 'Will they give you some reward for all your work now?'

He read, and this was heartening, of the release of political prisoners from all the jails in the country; but he could not hope to come under this category. He was not classified as a political prisoner.

The Chief sent for Sriram. His tone was suddenly friendly. 'I don't know what the government order will be about you. But we have received a number of names for release this week. I am glad to do it, because it will reduce our pressure of work. However,' he said, looking through the list, 'your name is not on it.'

Sriram's heart sank. He had a feeling that he was being kept in a cage when all the others were roaming the wide earth freely. He thought unhappily that someone was discriminating against him. It was a cruel and sadistic world. The Chief noted the pain in his face and said, 'Evidently you have not been classified as a political prisoner. All those who have done what you have done are under the consideration of the government. If you like, you may send in a representation, with an undertaking, and I will forward it.'

'What representation and what undertaking?' asked Sriram.

'You will have to give an undertaking to report your movements to the police for some time till all the papers are scrutinized and your classification is settled.'

Sriram thought it over. 'Is this a New India or are the British still here?'

The Chief answered, 'I cannot tell you anything about it. That is politics. I am merely carrying on as per the rules.'

In a moment it flashed across Sriram's mind that all the difficult, hazardous things he had done would be set at naught by this undertaking. If he met Bharati she'd probably say, 'You sneak out of prison, do you? You have degraded yourself beyond description. Get out of my sight.' He told the Chief: 'No. I can't give any such undertaking.'

'All right, please yourself. Right, dismiss.' The warders tugged his biceps and he turned and walked out of the room, more depressed than ever.

After all there came a day when he went into the office adjoining his Chief's room, a spacious office in which there were a number of racks. He was led in there by his usual warders without much ado; he handed a slip of paper to a uniformed man sitting at the table; there were a number of others standing around him, to each of whom he was passing bundles of clothes. Sriram waited patiently till his turn came; the man took the slip from his hand, looked him up and down, and cried, 'Number six seven,' at which one of the attendants ran up a ladder and brought out a bundle, and placed it on the table. The man scrutinized the bundle, looked at Sriram and asked, 'Are these yours?' Sriram looked at the clothes; he had been made to take them off long, long ago and change into jail uniform. He was thrilled at the sight. He hugged them close to his breast and said, 'Yes, these are mine.'

'Wait,' said the other, snatching them back from his hand, 'sign here.' He held a sheet of paper; there were numerous sheets of papers to be signed. Sriram was irked by the number of hurdles he had to cross before going out of this hateful place. At last the man was satisfied. He handed him the bundle, his old close-collared coat, shirt, and *dhoti*, in which he had been arrested ages ago at the cremation ground.

'Change into your own clothes now. You are no longer a prisoner.'

Sriram proceeded to strip his jail dress before everybody. Life here had toughened him. The man said, 'You can go behind that shelf and undress.'

When Sriram emerged from behind a shelf loaded with old discoloured bundles of papers and documents, he felt he was back in his old shape. He rolled up his striped shorts and jacket, and shoved them into a corner. The man said, 'You are free, you are discharged.' Sriram stood still unable to decide which direction to take. 'Go this way, the door opens out,' said the man. Sriram saluted him vaguely, and muttered, 'I am going,' and opened the door; it gave on to a small yard which was closed with a barred gate at the other end; an armed sentry paced in front of it. Sriram's first instinct was to turn back at the sight of him, but he told himself, 'I am no longer a prisoner,' and walked on haughtily. The man opened the door at his approach. He said as Sriram passed, 'Going out! Very good, try not to come back, unless you like this place very much.'

'I hate it,' said Sriram with feeling. 'I never wish to see a prison again.'

'That is the right spirit,' said the man, 'keep it up.' He was evidently used to uttering this formula to every outgoing prisoner. It was a sort of convocation address.

When the barred gate closed behind him Sriram could hardly believe that he was free. He felt weak and faint, and inexplicably unhappy. The memory of his cellmates who had become sullen and gloomy when it became known that he would be leaving was painful.

The bully had said, 'You are a selfish sort. I don't like your type.'

The forger said, 'If you can be released, why not we? Tell Mahatmaji that we want to come out.'

Another one said, 'If you become a big minister or some such thing, don't forget me.'

The bully had added, 'When I am released I will break into your house some night, and teach you good sense. I don't like selfish fellows like you.'

The warders had trooped behind him for tips. There was a little money that had accumulated as his wages, which the Jail Accountant had handed over to him, and his old warders followed him muttering, 'We have been together so long. I would like you to remember us.' 'This is my child's birthday. Give me something to remember you by.' 'We cannot come beyond this block—please give anything you like.' 'We have looked after you all these months.'

Sriram gave a rupee to each of the crowd that followed him importuning, and that took away fifty per cent of his earnings.

5

HE WALKED ON as in a dream. It was difficult for him to move about without a guard following him, and without being told where he should go. He found the evening light dazzled his eyes, the wide open spaces were oppressive. He turned back to cast a look at the building which he had occupied for years now. It looked in its slate-grey colour innocent enough, but what a tyrannical world it had contained: a fellow there could not do anything he wanted, even the calls of nature had to be answered as per regulations! The jail was outside the town limits at the Trunk Road end. He had never gone so far before; he had been living all along on the Trichy Trunk Road, not knowing where he was.

He walked down the road towards the town, wondering where he should go now. A few buses passed him. He hoped people would not recognize him. There was a policeman sitting in one of the buses and Sriram turned instinctively away from the direct line of his vision. He walked on along the edge of the road. 'This is an independent India into which I am walking now,' he reflected. What was the sign that it was independent? He looked about him. The trees were as usual, the road was not in the least improved, and policemen still rode on the footboard of highway buses. He felt tired and hungry. He had not more than a few rupees left after the warders had had their claim. He wished that some sort of transport was provided for prisoners let out of jail: it was very inconsiderate, even in a free India to have to face this! He hoped that some day they would make him a minister and then he would open a canteen, and place station-wagons at the disposal of prisoners at the jail gate so that those that came out might not feel so lost.

It was dusk when he got into the Market Road. Nobody seemed to notice him. Here and there he saw buildings hung with the tricolour flags, the *charka* in the middle. He saw that there was less traffic than formerly. Shops were lit and crowded as ever. He felt a pang of disappointment. He had a gnawing hunger inside him. There were still a few rupees in his pocket, hard-earned, literally earned by the sweat of his brow. He put his hand into his pocket and jingled the coins, and remembered the axe he had wielded, and all the undreamt-of tasks that he had performed. He had a feeling of pride at the thought of all he had earned by his hard labour: no one could say that he was one who lived off the fat of the land. Even his granny could feel proud of his achievement and ability. He sat on the bench of a small park that had been formed at the traffic junction of New Extension and the Market Road. He sat there in order to think clearly how he ought to manage. There was no use trying to settle things while walking. This was a free country and no one was going to demand why he sat there and not somewhere else. It was difficult to get used to the idea, it was a luxurious idea worth brooding over. But he felt startled again and again as he thought from habit that he was exposing himself to the public gaze too much, and that he might have to slip swiftly into a hiding place. Sitting there on the cement bench beside a potted fern, he told himself: 'I'm free. No one can come after me now. No one will bother whether I have a clean-shaven face or a hairy one.' He felt hurt at first that the pedestrians went by without noticing him and the traffic without pausing to say, 'Hello, hero!' But he soon realized the blessedness of being left alone after all the years of being hunted and looked for everywhere.

He realized that his first business was to eat something. He could do the clear thinking while sitting on a hotel chair instead of a park bench. He got up and moved briskly off down the road; the first hotel that showed itself in sparkling bulbs was 'Sri Krishna Vilas'. He turned in. Most of the tables were empty. It was long past the rush hour. He sat at a marble-topped table and waited for someone to come and ask what he wanted. A man sat at the exit on a raised seat with a cash box. The waiting-boys were all in a group chattering among themselves. 'They don't care,' Sriram told himself. 'I suppose I look like a gutter-rat. They will drive me out.' He looked around him. He recognized one of the waiters: he used to come here often in other days.

'Hey, Mani!' he called and the waiter turned. 'Come here,' he commanded.

The other came up. He recognized Sriram, and cried, 'Why, it's you! Where have you been all these years, sir? It's a long time since we saw you.'

'I was away on business. Give me something good to eat.'

At the word 'good' the boy puckered his face in worry.

'There is nothing very good now, sir, what with the present difficulty of getting rice and any pure food. Our government does not do anything about it yet. Do you know how hard it is to get any frying oil? Most of it's adulterated stuff, I tell you.' He started on a long narrative about the situation in the country, the food shortage, the post-war confusion, and the various difficulties and hardships that people experienced. All this was a revelation: it was the first report that Sriram was getting of the contemporary world. But he had no patience to listen to much of it.

'What have you?'

The boy cast a brief look at the shelf on which trays of edibles were on display and started, '*Kara sev, vadai,* and potato *bonda* . . .'

Sriram said sharply, 'I can see all that from here. I want to know if you have anything fresh inside, on the oven, something more solid.' The thought of *idli,* soft and light, and of *dosai,* was alluring. It seemed as if he had tasted them in a previous birth. While he spoke he was racked with the thought that he had probably lost the necessary idiom to get on with ordinary folk. Perhaps he only had the ability to talk to jailmates. He said, 'Something very g—' He avoided the word 'good' lest it should start the other off again analysing the world situation. He said, 'I want something heavy, just made, I am very hungry.'

'There's nothing inside, sir. This is closing hour, and the kitchen department is the first to shut up. While our proprietor wants *us* to work till ten, those who sit at the fireside—'

Sriram lost his patience. He didn't want to spend the rest of the evening listening to shop-talk. He said sharply, 'All right, all right, get me something, anything to eat, now run and get me coffee, *good* coffee,' and he felt sorry that he had again blundered into the word, for the boy began to say something about the difficulties of making good coffee: milk-supply difficulties, the sugar racket, and the general avarice of black marketeers of various kinds. Sriram didn't know what to do. He lost his patience completely, 'Why do you tell me all that?'

'Because it is so.'

'All right,' he said callously. 'I'm hungry. If you are going to give me anything look sharp. If you stand here and talk, I shall get up and go away.'

'What shall I give you, sir?' the boy asked officially, for the first time giving an impression that he was on duty.

'Two sweets, one savoury and a large quantity of hot coffee,' commanded Sriram. This was the first time in many months he was able to order anyone about. He was surprised at his own voice, almost fearing that someone would say that he was to be put in solitary confinement. But it worked. The boy ran off with alacrity and interest.

He felt elated after his tiffin, and after chewing a betel leaf and nut he felt as if he were back in the times when there was no war, no political struggle of any kind. He was himself, grandson of a grand old lady, with no worries in life, shuttling between a free reading room, the marketplace and Kanni's shop, living in a world with well-defined boundaries, with set activities, no surprises or worries, everything calculable and capable of anticipation.

He hurried on to Kabir Street. It was a fine homecoming. It was seven o'clock, but as usual children were playing in the streets, and the space in front of every house was washed and decorated with white flour. Why could he not have lived like these folk without worries of any kind or any extra adventures; there seemed to be a quiet charm in a life verging on stagnation and no change of any kind. The lights were on in most of the houses. He ran down the street with his eyes wide open. He stopped in front of his house. He looked through the doorway. Some strangers were moving about. He felt angry and cheated. What right had they to usurp his place? Some unknown children were chasing each other in the front hall under the lamp—that old lamp where Granny had taught him so many things in life! He wanted to run up the steps and tell the children: 'You can't run around here, I can stop you if I want to.' They were probably knocking holes in the wall, banging the doors and shutters, only leaving wreckage behind for him to occupy when the time came.

He turned round to see Kanni and talk to him. But the shop had gone: the portrait of Maria Theresa was no longer there to brighten up the surroundings. In Kanni's place, a new cement structure rose without windows, probably a godown. He felt pained and cheated again. He walked up and down the road. None of his neighbours noticed him. He saw a few of them in their houses, sitting by the window reading an evening paper—comfortable folk. He felt like going up and talking to them, but they'd probably reprimand him for various lapses and he felt diffident about his ability to talk to anyone! He was obsessed with the thought that he had lost the idiom of communication with these people. The street remained very much unchanged since he saw it last—only Kanni's shop was gone, and there was no one of whom he could enquire.

Suddenly he felt that he had nowhere to go that night. In the prison at least, one had been assured of a place of retirement for the night.

The photographer's establishment was brightly lit, and threw its illumination on the road. It was a low-roofed shop with the usual glass front displaying a variety of enlarged portraits of children, pretty girls, and important men.

There was no one in the front parlour with its coir carpet and a small stool with a decorative potted plant on it. There was no sign of anyone living there. Sriram stepped into the next room, which was also empty. He cleared his throat and made sounds with his feet in order to indicate his presence.

'Who is there?' came the call. It was the photographer's voice. Sriram replied: 'A jail-bird.'

He felt happy that after all there was someone he knew to meet him in this world. The other came out of the innermost chamber and advanced, trying to find out the identity of the visitor. He had evidently been working close to a light and could not see clearly. When he came near enough, he cried, 'You! When were you released? What a pity I didn't know. I was wondering what you had done with yourself. Where were you? They would not tell us where you were. If I had known you were coming out today, I'd have arranged a grand reception for you at the jail gate with flowers and garlands. The trouble is that things are still disorganized. But I blame no one. Ours is an infant State, still a baby, many things have still to be done, we must be happy that we are our own rulers and no foreign nation rules over us. We must be happy that things are being done and not spend the time finding fault with anyone.'

'We ought to rejoice that it's our own people that are blundering, isn't that so?' Sriram asked, some of his irresponsible spirit returning.

'Fancy Nehru and Patel and the rest sitting there where there were haughty Viceroys before. Didn't Churchill call Mahatmaji "the Naked Fakir"? The "Naked Fakir" is everything now, think of it . . .' He was excited. 'There are bound to be mistakes, bound to be blunders everywhere, but we must not make much of them.' He was wildly incoherent and happy. 'If you had been out of jail, you would have been garlanded and carried in a procession on Independence Day. What a pity you missed it. It was a grand affair.'

Jagadish seated Sriram on a large sofa, put a great album on his lap, took a seat by his side and turned its leaves. He remarked, 'As a photographer, I am proud of this. Future generations can never blame me for being neglectful. I have done my best. Here is a complete history of our struggle and the final Independence Day celebration.' He had put various pictures of himself into the album, subscribing himself as a humble soldier. There were even photographs of the ruined temple, where Sriram had lived and worked. The photographer had titled it: 'One of the secret headquarters of the Independence Army'. Sriram looked through the album which in effect was a documentary of the independence movement.

Jagadish had even stuck in photographs of jails and their exteriors. He had pictures of barbed wire entanglements. It was a completely romantic picture. Nor could he be said to suffer from modesty in any way. He was the chief architect of independent India, the chief operator in ejecting the British. He had included several pictures of Malgudi street scenes. Flags flew from every doorway and shop, crowds were moving in procession with people singing and playing musical instruments. Flowers everywhere. Great masses of men moving down the roads. Jagadish looked at the scenes with great pride. He felt he had striven to give people a good time and had succeeded. He said, 'After all, what do I get for all the trouble I took and the risks I ran? Are they going to make me the minister of this and that? Not a chance, sir, there are others waiting for the privilege. Even if I stand for election, who will know who I am? Will the parliamentary board choose me as their candidate? Not a chance, sir, that is the reason why I have held fast to my camera and studio all through my various activities. Nobody can take it away.' There was a tone of regret in his voice which Sriram did not understand.

'After all, as you said now, we are an infant nation.' The word was very convincing, it had a homely and agreeable sound, nobody need worry what it meant or why it was mentioned.

'True, true,' said the photographer, 'I'm not complaining or grumbling. What I have done, I have done with the utmost satisfaction. I am not worried about it at all. What I say is I have got these photographs to record all that we have done, that's all.'

There were hundreds of pictures to wade through. Sriram began to turn the leaves fast. He felt bored. They were monotonous to see. More and more processions. More and more people. Flags. Pictures carried in the procession of national leaders and others, and more and more people. There was a sameness about the whole thing; he simply could not stand any more. He briskly turned the leaves of the album and came to the last page of the sequence in which Jagadish was seen hoisting the flag at some public gathering. Sriram put away the album and asked, 'How did you manage to photograph yourself?'

'Ah, a pertinent question, who could photograph the photographer? Guess how it was done. Do you imagine I attached a camera to my back to follow me and take the pictures?'

'Possibly, possibly,' said Sriram, losing interest in the whole question. He didn't want to look at any more pictures or hear about them. The sight of the Independence Day celebrations irritated him. He almost said, 'If only I had known that people would reduce it all to this. I didn't go about inscribing "Quit" and overturning trains just to provide a photographer with material for his album.' He decided that he wouldn't look at any more pictures.

The photographer said, 'I have three more albums. They present another phase of our struggle.' He attempted to reach them down from a shelf.

Sriram held his hand, saying, 'No, not now. I have a headache. I won't look at any more pictures.' He was terrified at the prospect of having to look through more crowds, flags, and assemblies.

The photographer said: 'Good photographs are a sure remedy for headache. That's what an American scientist has recently found out.'

Sriram said defensively, 'I will examine them again tomorrow.'

'Very well. You know what my greatest regret is?' He paused to give him time to guess, and added, 'That I haven't a cine camera. If only I had had one I'd have shown you all the scenes you have missed as if you were seeing them before your eyes. That's the stuff. If I had charged as much as other photographers, I'd have had the biggest movie camera there is. But oh, this troublesome conscience with which some of us are burdened!'

Sriram felt disappointed with the man: he had looked so imposing as an underground worker: so precise and clear-headed and purposeful. Now he seemed woolly-headed and vague. The atmosphere of peace did not suit his nature. Sriram wondered for a moment why he had ever carried out his orders at all. He was disappointed that the other showed so little interest in his own jail existence. Sriram asked, 'Did the police get you?'

'Me! Oh, no! How could they? They didn't know my whereabouts. It was possible for me to evade them completely. I lived in that temple after you left; didn't you see it in the first picture? Didn't you notice how I labelled it?' He again tried to reach out for the album.

Sriram said hastily, 'Yes, yes, quite right. It was very apt,' although he could not clearly recollect what it was.

'Moreover,' concluded the photographer, 'there was no occasion for the police to get me. My grandmother did not start dying at a wrong moment. If it hadn't been for your grandmother, you would not have gone to jail at all.'

Sriram said nothing in reply. This was a subject which he did not wish to brood over. He had a hope they might have something to talk about in common, some diversion from the photographs. He asked point blank, 'Where is Bharati? Did she come out of jail?'

'Oh, yes, I was wondering why you hadn't asked anything about her. I thought perhaps you had forgotten her!'

'No, never! Not even for a moment!' cried Sriram passionately. 'Have you seen her?'

'Of course,' said the photographer in a tone which made Sriram anxious and jealous. While he had been having social intercourse with homicides, she seemed to have come out of prison, been received and garlanded by the photographer and his friends, and probably they had all had a good time. She must have wondered why he was not there! He hoped that the others had had at least the goodness to remind her that he was still in jail.

'Did you receive her at the prison?' he asked suddenly.

'We should have, but it was impossible to meet her. She was in one of the earliest batches to be released and she immediately took the train that very evening for Noakhali.'

'Noakhali; what is her business there? Where is it?' His geography was poor.

The photographer ignored the geographical question and said, 'Are you aware of what has been going on in East Bengal? Hindus versus Muslims. They are killing each other. Are you not aware of anything?'

'No. How could I be?' said Sriram. 'I was not kept in a municipal reading room or the public library. I'm not aware of anything or of what you are talking about.'

'Whole villages have been burnt in inter-communal fights. Thousands of people have been killed, bereaved, dispossessed, demented, crushed.'

'Who is doing that and why?'

'Don't ask all that. I am a man without any communal notions and I don't like to talk about it. Somebody is killing somebody else. That is all I care to know. Life is at a standstill and Mahatmaji is there on a mission of peace. He is walking through villages, telling people not to run away, to be brave, to do this and that. He is actually making the lion and the lamb eat off the same plate. And Bharati seems to have had a call.'

Sriram was seized with cold fear. This was a new turn of events for which he had not bargained at all. Noakhali, Calcutta, Bengal, what was the meaning of it? What did she mean by going so far away from him? Did she do it by design? Did she try to make good her escape before he could come out of prison?

'What did she mean by going away?'

The photographer simply laughed at the question.

'Couldn't she have come and seen me in prison? She must have known I was in prison?'

'How?' asked the photographer.

'By enquiring, that is all, it is simple,' said Sriram with feeling. He said, 'Probably she has no thought of me. Perhaps she has forgotten me completely!'

Jagadish became serious on seeing his gloom. 'Don't let all that disturb you so much. Did you think of her often?'

Sriram began to say something in reply, but could not find the words, spluttered, remained silent and began to sob. The photographer patted his back and said, 'What has happened now that you feel so bad about it?' Sriram had nothing much to say in reply. He merely kept on sobbing. The photographer said, 'You are a fool! What have you done to keep in touch with her?'

'What do you mean? What could I do, chained and caged?'

'Now, I mean. What are you going to do about it now? Now you are not chained or caged. What are you going to do about it?'

'She is so far away, thousands of miles from me,' Sriram wailed. The thought of Noakhali was very disturbing.

'But there is such a thing as a postal service. You don't have to employ a special runner to carry your mails. Why don't you write to her?'

'Will you see the letter addressed and despatched properly?'

'I promise. Give it to me. I will send it off.'

This brought a ray of hope to Sriram. He suddenly asked, 'What shall I write to her?'

'H'm, that is a thing I can't tell you. Each man has his own style in these matters.'

It was clear that his mind was in a complete fog. To think or plan clearly was beyond him. Prison-life showed its damage only now.

The photographer took pity on him. He said, 'Please rest a while. Close your eyes and relax.' He went to a small table and took out a pen and a sheet of paper, and started writing. The traffic on the road outside had ceased.

'Don't you wish to close your shop?' Sriram asked.

'Don't let that bother you. I can look after myself. I'm not much good at writing this sort of stuff. Anyway, I will try. Meanwhile, shut your eyes and switch off your thoughts, if you can.'

He sat and faithfully wrote a long letter which began:

'my darling—who keeps slipping away like this! I might as well be in jail. But in jail or out of it—there is only one thought in my mind, that's you. I have been thinking of you night and day, and not all the jail regulations could prevent me from thinking of you. And today I came out of the prison and my good friend Jagadish (he is a very fine man, let me say) told me about you. The prison bars kept me away from you so long, and now all the miles between here and there, but that is of no consequence. This distance is no distance for me. May I come and join you, because I will gasp and die like a stranded fish unless I see you and talk to you? Give me your answer in the quickest time possible.'

Jagadish got so lost in writing the letter that he forgot how long he was taking, and Sriram began dozing in his seat and snoring gently. Jagadish looked at him and hesitated for a moment. He put the letter under a paperweight and wrote a covering note: 'If approved, this letter may be signed and sent first thing in the morning, though preferably it should be copied in your own hand.' He got up and shut the front door of the shop. He switched off the light, and went into his living apartments, softly closing the door behind him.

Ten days of anxious, desperate waiting, and then Sriram received a letter:

'Happy to hear from you. Come to Delhi. Birla House at New Delhi, if you can. Our programme is unsettled. We are going to Bihar with Bapu, where there is trouble. There is much to tell you. We shall be in Delhi on fourteenth January. After that come any time you like. We shall be happy to meet you.

BHARATI'

The Grand Trunk Express finally arrived at New Delhi station. Sriram struggled to reach a window in order to have the first glimpse of Bharati. The men near the window would not let him near it. It was no use speaking to them: they seemed to live in a different world. He spoke Tamil and English, and they understood Hindi, Hindustani, Urdu or whatever it might be. He could now realize the significance of Bharati's insistence that he should learn Hindi. Just to please her he had looked through readers and primers, but that took him nowhere. He had been isolated for the last thirty-six hours. He had sat brooding, jail life had trained him to keep his own company. His greatest trial had been when two men appeared suddenly from somewhere when the train was in motion, and scrutinized all the people in the compartment; when they came to him, they stopped in front of him and asked him a question. He could catch only the words 'Mister' and 'Hindu' with a lot of other things thrown in. They were rowdy-looking men. He said something in his broken Hindi, and Tamil and English, which seemed to make no impression on them. They came menacingly close to him, peering at his face; Sriram was getting ready to fight in self-defence. He sprang up and demanded in the language that came uppermost, 'What do you mean, all of you staring at me like this?' As he rose, one of the two pulled his earlobe for a close scrutiny, saw the puncture in it made in childhood, and let go, muttering, 'Hindu'. They lost interest and moved off. After they were gone, a great tension relaxed in the compartment. Someone started explaining, and after a good deal of effort in a variety of languages, Sriram understood that the intruders were men looking for Muslims in the compartment: if Muslims were found they would be thrown out of the moving train: an echo of the fighting going on in other parts of the country. Sriram lapsed into silence for the rest of the journey.

It was a most uncomfortable journey: he was crushed, could not find the space even to stretch his length or swing his arm: people came crowding in and sat on him. Sometimes he could not even extricate his legs. When he felt sleepy, he leaned his head back on the window or on the shoulder of a total stranger. When he felt hungry, he called to someone selling tea outside, and drank it. He could not get coffee. The people here seemed strange men who could swallow the very sweet *jalebi* and wash it down with bitter tea the very first thing in the day: this only confirmed his feeling that he was in a strange, fantastic world. He yearned for coffee, his favourite, like a true South Indian, but coffee could not be had here. He had to content himself by dreaming of it as he used to do in jail. In fact this seemed only an extension of prison life: this life in a crowded, congested compartment, with a lot of strangers. He felt more uncomfortable here than he had felt in the prison. There at least he could say something or hear something from others' lips, but here the human voice conveyed nothing but jabber. The compartment was full of people who smoked *beedis* and filled the air with it, spat on the floor without a second thought, and the closet was nearly always inaccessible. He managed by jumping out of the train when the train halted and rushing back to the train when it whistled.

At ten-thirty or eleven on some day or other the train came to New Delhi. '*Nai Dheheli*,' people in the compartment cried and bustled about. He tried to run to the window or door to catch a glimpse of Bharati. She had written promising to meet him at the station. He felt ashamed of his appearance: he combed back his hair with his fingers: it was dishevelled and standing on end. He knew he was grimy, grisly, and unsightly. He wished he could tidy himself up before Bharati set eyes on him after all these years. He caught a glimpse of her through a number of heads and shoulders jammed at the window, and, in his anxiety he pushed and bumped into people rudely, and the train moved past before coming to a halt. He saw her standing, gazing earnestly at the window. For a brief second he caught a glimpse of her figure, and his heart sank. He wished he could improve his appearance before facing her. He wished he could skulk away with the crowd and see her later. He had great misgivings as to what she might think of him if she saw him in his present state. But even in that desperate state, he knew, by his experience in the train itself, that he could never ask his way again and go in search of her. She might be lost to him for ever.

When he got down from the train, carrying a roll of bedding and a trunk, Bharati's searching eye picked him out in the crowd. She waved her arms and came running to him. She gripped his hands and said, 'Oh, how good to see you again!' and in that tone of spontaneous affection Sriram lost himself, forgot his own appearance and griminess, and acquired self-confidence. He looked her up and down, and cried, 'You look like a North Indian, yourself. You look like a Punjabi. I hope you understand our language.'

She took charge of him immediately. She picked up his bedding and said, 'You carry your trunk.' He snatched the bedding from her hand, and took the load on his own shoulder. She said, 'Don't be silly. You haven't four arms, remember.' And she snatched back the bed from his hands. Sriram lost his bewilderment. The proximity of Bharati gave him a sense of homeliness. It was as if he were back in Malgudi with her. He didn't notice the strange surroundings, the strange avenues, and buildings, the too broad roads, the exotic men and women, and the strange shops they were passing. He had no time to notice anything. His attention was concentrated on Bharati. She looked darker, and more tired, but her tresses were as black as ever. She looked tired, as if she had undernourished herself. He could not get over the novelty of meeting her again. He was always on the point of disbelieving what he saw and felt. Perhaps he was going through a fantastic dream. Perhaps he was dead. Or dreaming from his confinement. For the first time these many months and years he had a free and happy mind, a mind without friction and sorrow of any kind. No hankering for a future or regret for a past. This was the first time in his life that he was completely at peace with himself, satisfied profoundly with existence itself. The very fact that one was breathing, feeling, and seeing, seemed sufficient matter for satisfaction now. She kept looking at him, and asked, 'When did they release you?'

He gave a summary of his jail existence and a resumé of all that had happened to him since she saw him last. The *tonga* ran smoothly. The extreme sympathy with which she listened to his story pleased him greatly. It gave it a touch of importance. As he spoke, he was impressed with his own doings. He was on the point of asking himself: 'Am I the one who has done all this or is it someone else?' He was filled with a sense of extreme heroism. 'I never thought I could put up with all this sort of trouble. I was very keen that the man in the street—' he began, and puffed with his own importance. The listener, Bharati, gave his whole life a new meaning and a new dimension. When they arrived at a colony of huts somewhere in New Delhi, he was completely satisfied with all the things he had done in his life.

'This is my present headquarters,' Bharati explained. She had taken him to her own hut. 'Yes, this is my home.' There was a spinning wheel in one corner, and her clothes hung on a rope tied across the doorway.

'After all, she is going to be my wife, that's why she doesn't mind my staying with her,' he reflected.

She said, 'You will have your "room" ready in about an hour, till then you may rest here. There is another block, where you may wash yourself. Make yourself comfortable.' As she was speaking a group of children came running in crying, '*Moi, Moi*—' and they said something that Sriram could not make out. They came and surrounded Bharati and dragged her by her hand. She stopped and said something to them in their own language. They left her and went away.

'Who are they?' asked Sriram with a touch of jealousy.

'Children, that's all we know about them,' she said.

'Where do they belong?'

'Here at the moment,' she said, and added, 'they are refugee children, we don't know anything more about them. I will be back in about an hour. Make yourself comfortable.' And she went out.

She was gone a long while. By the time she returned he had explored his surroundings. He had discovered the bathroom and the tap, and washed and tidied himself. He went back to her hut and spent a long time combing back his hair and studying himself in the mirror in order to decide whether he was worthy of Bharati. Bharati's kindness had restored his confidence in himself. He had never hoped that she would treat him with such warmth and kindness. The years that had separated them did not seem to make the slightest difference. It was as if they had separated only an hour ago: all the moments of loneliness and hankering and boredom that had made life a hell for him within the last few years were gone as if they had not existed.

He saw one of her sarees hanging up, a white one with yellow spots. It was of course made of *khadi*, hand spun; the rope sank under its weight. He pulled it down to take it in his hands and gauge its weight, reflecting, 'She ought to wear finery, poor girl. I will give her everything.' He took it in his hand and weighed it: 'It seems to weigh twenty pounds.' He stretched it and held it before his eyes. 'It's like a metal sheet. She must feel stuffy under it. I can't see any light through it.' He rolled it up and pressed it to his breast. It had a faint aroma of sandalwood which pleased him. 'It has the fragrance of her own body,' he reflected, closing his eyes. As he sat there the door opened and Bharati stood before him.

'What are you doing with my saree?' she asked in surprise. 'One would think that you were trying to wear it,' she said with a laugh. Sriram reddened, and put it hastily away.

'It does not try to ward me off,' he said, 'when I take it to my heart.'

'Hush!' she cried. 'Don't try to be silly. We are all very serious people, here, remember. I see you have tidied yourself up. If you have any clothes for washing, give them to me.'

Sriram handed her a small roll that he had brought back from his bathroom. 'They are terribly soiled,' he murmured apologetically.

She snatched the bundle from his hands and went out. He reflected, 'She is almost my wife, she is doing what a wife would do, good girl! God bless her. If I tie a *thali* around her neck somehow, when she is asleep, things will be all right.'

She returned in a moment saying, 'Your clothes will come to you in the evening. Here in this camp everyone is expected to wash his or her own clothes and not employ others to do the job, but you are new and I have got a *dhobi* to wash for you as an exception. Are you hungry?'

'Extremely,' he said. 'I am longing for something to eat.'

'I don't know what you mean by something,' she said. 'You can't expect all our South Indian stuff. It is months and months since I tasted anything like that. You will have to learn to eat chappati, and vegetable and curd and fruit, and not ask for rice or *sambar*.' She led him to a shack where some people were eating and children were sitting with plates before them. There were two platters laid for her and Sriram, side by side. 'This is how husbands and wives sit together,' Sriram reflected as he sat beside her and tried to work his way through wheat chappati. He longed for the taste of the pungent South Indian food and its sauces and vegetables, but he suppressed the thought. Jail life had trained him to eat anything offered him. 'I am really still in a jail,' he reflected.

She was extremely busy all through the day. She seemed to have numerous things to do. She was always attending on children, changing one's dress, combing another's hair, engaging another group in dance or play, and continuously talking to them; besides this she had a great deal to say to a lot of miscellaneous men and women who came in search of her. Hers was a full-time occupation. She gave the children a wash, fed them, put them to sleep on mats in various sheds, drew their blankets over them, said something to each one of them, and finally came back to her own room, sat down on her cot, and stretched her arms. Sriram followed her about for hours but could not get in a word of his own. He tried to smile at the children, thinking that that might please Bharati, but she hardly noticed his presence when she was with them. It infuriated him. After a time, he turned on his heels, and went back to his hut. It was furnished with a rope cot and a mat and had no door. There was a common bath at the end of the alley which he shared with a number of others. He had felt indignant when he was transferred here. It seemed to dash his hopes to the ground. 'Did she put me in here in order to get rid of me?' he reflected. 'Was it because I picked up her spotted saree? If I had not done so, she would probably have let me sleep in the same room. I have probably destroyed her trust,' he reflected ruefully. 'Trust! Who wants her trust! I only want *her*.'

He had switched on the light and was sitting on bed. The entrance darkened. The low roof of the hut made it stuffy, although it kept the place warm in winter. She came in bearing his clothes which he had given her for washing. Sitting in his hut, Sriram had been seized again with the feeling that he was still cooped up in a cell. 'My jail seems to be on my back, all the time,' he reflected. The fatigue of the journey had begun to affect him, the intense cold air, and the gloomy and novel surroundings depressed him and made him feel unhappy—a gloom and unhappiness without any cause. The brief spurt of happiness he had experienced seemed chimerial.

Bharati put his clothes on his bed and said, 'Are you comfortable?'

'Yes and no. I feel happy when you are with me, and miserable when you go away.' She looked at him, startled. He continued, 'Won't you sit down here?' and he made a space for her. She sat down. He moved close to her, and laid his arm on her shoulder.

She said, 'Not yet,' and gently pushed away his arm. 'What a strange man!' she cried. 'You have not changed at all.'

He sat away from her and asked, 'Am I still an untouchable?'

She said, 'Bapuji alone can decide.'

'Have you spoken to him about it?'

'Yes, more than once, but he has not given an answer yet.' She sat with bowed head when she said it, her voice was low. She looked subdued.

There was an uneasy silence for a while, then he asked, 'Why?

Doesn't he want us to marry?'

'It may not be that,' she said. 'But he really did not have the time to give it a thought, there were other things to do.'

It was a relief for him to know that Bapuji was not against the notion of their marrying, but it was not enough. He held his breath and listened without speaking. He had a fear that his slightest word might spoil everything. This was an occasion for speech in the most delicate of whispers. Anything more harsh might destroy the whole fabric. He wanted to be on his guard. He wanted to do nothing that might scare her and take her away from him, nothing that might make fruitless all the thousands of miles he had come. So he refrained from speaking. He wanted to shout at her and demand if it was only for this that she had wanted him to come all that way, he wanted to tell her that he regretted ever having set eyes on her. He wanted to threaten her that he would seize her by force and carry her back to south India.

'More than anything else,' she said, 'the thing that pains Mahatmaji now is the suffering of women. So many of them have been ruined, so many of them have lost their honour, their home, their children, and the number of women who are missing cannot be counted. They have been abducted, carried away by ruffians, ravished or killed, or perhaps have even destroyed themselves.' She appeared to be on the point of breaking down at the thought.

Sriram felt he must say something in sympathy. 'Why do these things happen?' And he felt ashamed of the utter inanity of his question. She didn't notice his question, but just went on speaking.

'On the fifteenth of August when the whole country was jubilant, and gathered here to take part in the Independence Day festivities, do you know where Bapu was? In Calcutta where fresh riots had started. Bapu said his place was where people were suffering and not where they were celebrating. He said that if a country cannot give security to women and children, it's not worth living in. He said it would be worth dying if that would make his philosophy better understood. He walked through villages barefoot on his mission. We followed him. Each day we walked five miles through floods and fields, silently. He walked with bowed head, all through those swamps of East Bengal. We stopped for a day or two in each village, and he spoke to those who had lost their homes, property, wives, and children. He spoke kindly to those who had perpetrated crimes—he wept for them, and they swore never to do

such things again. I have seen with my own eyes aggressive rowdy-
looking men taking a vow of non-violence and a vow to protect the
opposite faction—don't ask what community they were: what one
community did in one part of the country brought suffering on the
same community in another part of the country. I have seen what
has happened both at Noakhali and Bihar, and then at Delhi. How
can one choose? Human beings have done impossible things to
other human beings. It's no use discussing whether this community
committed greater horrors or the other one. Bapuji forbade us to
refer to anyone in terms of religion as Muslims, Hindu, or Sikh,
but just as human beings. He said one day that he sometimes pitied
those who committed acts of violence—he advised some women
in a village that they should sooner take their lives with their own
hands than surrender their honour . . .'

'You must have gone to many places,' said Sriram, not having
anything else to say.

'Yes, for about a year I have been with Mahatmaji. He was at
first unwilling to take me to all those places but I bothered him
again and again after I was released from jail. I don't know how
many villages I have seen. We followed the Master through burning
villages. Of course, anything might have happened to us anywhere.
There were a few places where they showed their anger even against
Mahatmaji. They held up placards threatening Bapu's life unless he
turned back and left them. But in such places he stayed longer than
in other places. And ultimately he held his ground.'

'Were you at any time in danger?'

'Of what? Of being assaulted? Yes, sometimes, but Mahatmaji
had advised women as a last resort to take their lives with their own
hands rather than surrender their honour. There was no sense of fear
where Mahatmaji was. But . . . if any unexpected thing happened, I
was always prepared to end my life.'

'No, no,' said Sriram horrified.

'It seemed quite a natural thing to do in those places, where
one saw burning homes, children orphaned, men killed, and women
carried away. I felt we were in some other country. My special
charges were children wherever I saw them. I gathered them and
brought them here. All those children you saw here, we don't know
anything about them. They escaped death, somehow, that's where
providence has shown its presence. They are all gathered from
various villages in Bengal and Bihar. We had more, but some were

reclaimed in Calcutta itself. But the ones we have now with us, we don't know anything about them. If their parents are alive, they will know they are here and come for them: otherwise we will bring them up. We have collected toys and clothes for them. Don't ask whether they are Muslim children or Hindu children or who they are. It is no use asking that; we don't know. We have given them only the names of flowers and birds. Bapuji said once that even a number would be better than a name, if a name meant branding a man as of this religion or that. You see one child was called Malkaus, that's a melody: a girl is known as Gulab, that is a rose. These children must grow up only as human beings.'

Sriram shivered a little, and Bharati said, 'I'll give you some warm clothes and blankets out of what we have collected for refugees. For this purpose, we'll count you as a refugee, no harm in that.' She laughed slightly. He was frightened of her. She seemed too magnificent to be his wife. 'You now understand why I could not talk to Mahatmaji about our own affairs. It would have been sacrilegious. Even so, I mentioned you to him one day in a village in Bengal. He was about to say something, when someone dashed in crying that he had been stabbed, and then another time in Calcutta I was telling him about you, and he asked when you were coming out of jail; it was late at night. I had waited for our opportunity when there would be no one about, and suddenly some big men, ministers of the place and others, arrived for urgent consultations. I never got a chance again.'

'Will he remember me?'

'He never forgets anyone. I felt that the time was not yet . . . Tomorrow, let us go together and see him at Birla House, and if there is an opportunity, we shall ask him together.'

'If he says no?' asked the anxious lover, with a shudder.

Bharati rose saying: 'I will send you the blankets in a minute.'

Next afternoon, Sriram, before setting out for Birla House, tidied himself, looked into a mirror, and suddenly decided that he was probably looking too smart for the occasion. He rumpled his hair a little. His mind was buzzing with numerous doubts. Bharati had gone ahead to arrange an interview with the Mahatma. She had left a guide behind to conduct him to Birla House. He picked out a *khaddar* shirt and vest, wrapped a shawl round his shoulder, and satisfied himself that he looked unostentatious. His greatest fear was that Mahatmaji would be reduced to saying, 'Marry you? Bharati marrying you! Begone, you presumptuous worm!'

Bharati took charge of him at the gate of Birla House. She said: 'He is terribly busy, but he will see us both for a moment. He knows we wish to see him urgently.' A lot of people were going in and out, people in *khadi* and white caps, foreign correspondents in European dress, and motor cars passed on the drive. Sriram was blind to his surroundings. He asked Bharati: 'If he asks me about anything, what shall I say?'

'Say anything, he will not mind it, as long as you speak the truth.'

Sriram was amazed at the ease with which she moved about the place. He was confirmed in his view that she was too good for him, that he had no right to expect her to become his wife. All kinds of people stopped to have a word with her. She spoke English, Tamil, Hindi, Urdu, and God knew what else. She spoke with great ease to men, women, young boys, and old men of all nationalities. She had a smile or a word for everyone.

'What a lot of people you know!' Sriram said with admiration. She acknowledged the compliment with a smile that charmed him.

'Yes, but I don't know the names of most of them,' she said. They went through the drive and the garden.

'What a mansion!' he cried. They had to speak mechanical trifles: both of them were preoccupied with one thought: the impending interview with the Mahatma. If he said 'Yes', what should they do next? To Sriram it was entirely unbelievable. It meant that he needn't dwell in a separate hut, that he could touch her, take her, he would have rights over her person, and he could always be with her. He took her aside on the lawn.

'Just a moment, Bharati,' he whispered, 'if Bapu permits us to marry, shall we go through it immediately?'

Her breath blew on him warmly as she whispered: 'Yes, without doubt.'

'How could we do it immediately? How could we make the necessary arrangements?' he asked.

'What arrangements? Are we going to have pipes and drums and a dowry and feasts?' she asked.

'Don't we have to buy flowers at least? Where am I to buy them in this place? I don't know anyone. I don't know my way about. How can I ask my bride to undertake all this for me? If only it were Malgudi, instead of Delhi, you would have seen what I would do.'

'Don't worry about all that. Bapu himself will tell us what to do.'

They crossed a small stretch of ground on which already some people were sitting. There was a dais at one end.

'This is where Bapu holds his evening prayers every day,' she said.

She entered the main building through the back. They reached a small veranda, crossed a passage, and stopped just ten yards from a window. She hushed her voice and pointed through the window. 'There he is!' There he sat with spectacles on his nose, with his legs folded under him. He was earnestly listening to the talk of two people sitting with him. 'That's Nehru, that's Patel,' the girl whispered. There were a number of others also in the room—very busy men. 'We must not disturb them,' she whispered, and flattened herself against the wall. Sriram followed her example. The men inside were talking in low whispers. Someone came out of the room and smiled at Bharati. Bharati told her something in Hindi.

'She is Bapu's grand-niece, she looks after him.'

'Won't they mind our being here?' Sriram asked. 'They seem to be talking over important things.'

'But Bapu has asked me to wait here for him and take a chance. I'll peep in at the right moment and show my face at the window. He will call me in, or he may come out for a moment.'

'I tremble at the thought of his coming out!' Sriram confided to her.

'This is the only way we can have a word with Bapu. He is always busy and surrounded by people.'

'He is looking somewhat weak,' Sriram ventured, peeping through the window for a moment.

'Yes, his last fast has completely fatigued him. Sometimes, he lay there without moving, unconscious.' She stopped talking as a couple of girls passed. Someone with a shorthand notebook and pencil hurried off. A liveried government-house servant went in bearing a glass of water.

Seeing all this, Sriram wanted to postpone his meeting with Gandhi. 'Should we disturb him today? He may not be free.'

'He is always busy. This is the way. He has told me to wait for him and meet him today. I just told him that you were here and he said, "Bring him along *today*." "Sometime tomorrow, Bapuji, you are busy today," I said, knowing that he was going to have important conferences with the prime minister and others. "I *mean* today," he emphasized. He even indicated the spot where we should wait. He said when he had a moment to spare he would see us.'

'I know you are waiting there, come in, come in with your friend,' came Mahatmaji's voice. 'You may come now, all the dreadfully serious business in life is over. Come, come my daughter.'

'That is Bapu,' said Bharati, clutching Sriram's hand and leading him. His heart palpitated. Just before stepping into the room, she whispered, 'Be natural and truthful. And tell him about the marriage.'

'Yes, yes,' Sriram gulped. They stepped in.

The Mahatma was seated on the floor. He looked up from a paper. Bharati brought her palms together and saluted. Sriram said, '*Namaste*, oh revered master!' The Mahatma returned their salutations with a smile. He indicated a place near him and said, 'Come and be seated here. I have postponed meeting you too long. Now tell me about yourself. Bharati, I hope your children are flourishing: you are a mother to thirty already, what a blessing!'

'Yes, Bapu,' she said. 'They are all fine. There was a little one who was down with a cold, that little girl whom you named Anar.'

'Oh, yes, I remember her, you know what Anar means, pomegranate bud; what a beauty! God reveals himself to us in the shape of children. I have collected a lot of fruit today, you know the fuss people make when I fast: they always seem to think that it must always be followed by a feast! Well, I have kept them for you: take them to the little ones and let them enjoy the feast.' He indicated in a corner a heap of bright oranges and apples.

'Yes, Bapu.'

'And don't forget to take for them the flowers too.' The Mahatma now turned to Sriram: 'Now tell me about yourself.' Sriram hesitated for a moment. 'What have you been doing in your part of the world?'

'They kept me in prison till a week ago,' he said.

'Why didn't they release you earlier?' Gandhi said.

'I was awarded an ordinary sentence,' he replied, putting into it all the poignancy he felt at the thought.

'That's very good. What did you do?'

Sriram hesitated for a moment and remembered Bharati's injunction to be truthful. He said, 'For some time I preached "Quit

India", but later I was overturning trains and—'

Mahatmaji looked grave. 'You have done many wrong things. It's no comfort to think that worse things have happened since.'

'Bharati went away to jail, and there was no one who could tell me what to do: no one who could show me the right way.'

'That is an excellent confession,' Mahatmaji said with a smile. 'Yes, the mistake was hers in leaving you behind.'

'No,' said Sriram. 'The mistake was mine. I refused to go with her to the jail, when she told me about it.'

'Indeed, is that so, Bharati?'

'Yes, Bapu, he said he was—'

'Very well, when all this stress is over, you will tell me in detail all you have done as a political worker, and we will decide what we should do.' He laughed. 'We will hear if there has been anything so serious as to warrant my going on a fast again. Do you know how well a fast can purify?'

'I will fast if you order me to,' Sriram said.

'I hope you have done nothing to warrant it. We will go into the question later.'

'If it is decided, I'll be prepared to go through a fast myself,' Bharati added, her face all flushed and red.

'You!' said Mahatmaji, 'for your friend!'

At this point, at the farthest end of the hall someone was moving. The Mahatma said: 'There is my conscience-keeper dangling a watch, telling me it is time to get up.' He held up five fingers and said, 'Give us five minutes more.' He turned to his visitors: 'I'm sorry I have to leave you in five minutes. Already people must have assembled on the prayer ground. Don't you hear their voices?' Sriram was seized with anxiety at the thought of time running out. Every minute counted. Already, even as he was thinking, he was losing precious moments. Only three-and-a-half minutes more. He must speak before the watch was dangled again. He threw a side-glance at Bharati in the hope that she might at least seize the precious hour. But she turned on him what seemed to him a look of silent appeal. The Mahatma kept looking at them with an amused look. Sriram suddenly heard himself saying, 'We are waiting for your blessed permission to marry.'

Mahatmaji looked from one to the other with joy. 'Do you like each other so much?'

Sriram burst out, 'I've waited for five years thinking of nothing else.'

'What about you, Bharati, you are saying nothing.'

Bharati bowed her head and flushed and fidgeted.

'Ah, that is a sign of a dutiful bride,' said the Mahatma and asked, 'Does this silence mean yes?' Sriram looked at her with bated breath. Mahatmaji observed her for a moment and said, 'She'd be a very unbecoming bride, who spoke her mind aloud! Good, good, God bless you. When is the happy occasion, tomorrow?'

'Yes, if you bless us so.'

'Very well. Tomorrow morning, the first thing I do will be that. I will be your priest, if you don't mind. I've been a very neglectful father; I'll come and present the bride. Tomorrow, the very first thing; other engagements only after that. I already have here all the fruits and flowers ready, and so after all you can't say I have been very neglectful.'

When the man with the watch appeared again, the Mahatma said, 'I'm ready for you.' He rose to his feet. Sriram and Bharati also got up. The Mahatma said, 'You have already a home with thirty children. May you be their father and mother!' He went into an ante-chamber and came out after a minute. Bharati waited at the door for him. He passed her with his eyes on the floor. Bharati followed him out with Sriram trailing behind her.

Mahatmaji suddenly stopped, turned round and said: 'Bharati, I have a feeling that I may not attend your wedding tomorrow morning.'

'Why? Why, Bapu?' she asked.

'I don't know.' His voice trailed away: 'I seem to have been too rash in promising to officiate as your priest.'

'Bapu, without you—'

'Tut, tut,' said Gandhi. 'You don't have to say all that. I want to be there very much, but I don't know. If God wills it I shall come. Otherwise, know my blessing is always on you both. Anyway you are not to put off your marriage for any reason, remember,' he said, with a new command in his voice, and Bharati replied, 'Yes, Bapu.'

The Mahatma patted her back, threw a smile at Sriram, and hurried down the passage. He walked leaning on the shoulder of his granddaughters. Sriram and Bharati followed, their heads full of their plans. Mahatmaji took out his watch and said, 'I hate to be late . . .'

As they stepped on to the lawn, Bharati said to Sriram, 'Let us attend the prayer today. There is a place for the two of us.' They stepped aside.

As the Mahatmaji approached the dais, the entire assembly got up. At this moment a man pushed himself ahead of the assembly, brushing against Bharati, and Sriram cried petulantly, 'Why do you push like that?' Unheeding, the man went forward.

'I'm sorry to be late today,' murmured the Mahatma. The man stood before the Mahatma and brought his palms together in a reverential salute. Mahatma Gandhi returned it. The man tried to step forward again. Mahatmaji's granddaughter said, 'Take your seat,' and tried to push him into line. The man nearly knocked the girl down, and took a revolver out of his pocket. As the Mahatma was about to step on the dais, the man took aim and fired. Two more shots rang out. The Mahatma fell on the dais. He was dead in a few seconds.

The Guide

1

RAJU WELCOMED THE intrusion—something to relieve the loneliness of the place. Th e man stood gazing reverentially on his face. Raju felt amused and embarrassed. 'Sit down if you like,' Raju said, to break the spell. The other accepted the suggestion with a grateful nod and went down the river steps to wash his feet and face, came up wiping himself dry with the end of a chequered yellow towel on his shoulder, and took his seat two steps below the granite slab on which Raju was sitting cross-legged as if it were a throne, beside an ancient shrine. The branches of the trees canopying the river course rustled and trembled with the agitation of birds and monkeys settling down for the night. Upstream beyond the hills the sun was setting. Raju waited for the other to say something. But he was too polite to open a conversation.

Raju asked, 'Where are you from?' dreading lest the other should turn round and ask the same question.

The man replied, 'I'm from Mangal.'

'Where is Mangal?'

The other waved his arm, indicating a direction across the river, beyond the high steep bank. 'Not far from here,' he added. The man volunteered further information about himself. 'My daughter lives nearby. I had gone to visit her; I am now on my way home. I left her after food. She insisted that I should stay on to dinner, but I refused. It'd have meant walking home at nearly midnight. I'm not afraid of anything, but why should we walk when we ought to be sleeping in bed?'

'You are very sensible,' Raju said.

They listened for a while to the chatter of monkeys, and the man added as an afterthought, 'My daughter's married to my own sister's son, and so there is no problem. I often visit my sister and also my daughter; and so no one minds it.'

'Why should anyone mind in any case if you visit a daughter?'

'It's not considered proper form to pay too many visits to a son-in-law,' explained the villager.

Raju liked this rambling talk. He had been all alone in this place for over a day. It was good to hear the human voice again. After this the villager resumed the study of his face with intense respect. And Raju stroked his chin thoughtfully to make sure that an apostolic beard had not suddenly grown there. It was still smooth. He had had his last shave only two days before and paid for it with the hard-earned coins of his jail life.

Loquacious as usual and with the sharp blade scraping the soap, the barber had asked, 'Coming out, I suppose?' Raju rolled his eyes and remained silent. He felt irritated at the question, but did not like to show it with the fellow holding the knife. 'Just coming out?' repeated the barber obstinately.

Raju felt it would be no use being angry with such a man. Here he was in the presence of experience. He asked, 'How do you know?'

'I have spent twenty years shaving people here. Didn't you observe that this was the first shop as you left the jail gate? Half the trick is to have your business in the right place. But that raises other people's jealousies!' he said, waving off an army of jealous barbers.

'Don't you attend to the inmates?'

'Not until they come out. It is my brother's son who is on duty there. I don't want to compete with him and I don't want to enter the jail gates every day.'

'Not a bad place,' said Raju through the soap.

'Go back then,' said the barber and asked, 'What was it? What did the police say?'

'Don't talk of it,' snapped Raju and tried to maintain a sullen, forbidding silence for the rest of the shave.

But the barber was not to be cowed so easily. His lifelong contact with tough men had hardened him. He said, 'Eighteen months or twenty-four? I can bet it's one or the other.'

Raju felt admiration for the man. He was a master. It was no use losing one's temper. 'You are so wise and knowing. Why do you ask questions?'

The barber was pleased with the compliment. His fingers paused in their operations; he bent round to face Raju and say, 'Just to get it out of you, that is all. It's written on your face that you are a two-year sort, which means you are not a murderer.'

'How can you tell?' Raju said.

'You would look different if you had been in for seven years, which is what one gets for murder only half-proved.'

'What else have I not done?' Raju asked.

'You have not cheated in any big way; but perhaps only in a small, petty manner.'

'Go on. What next?'

'You have not abducted or raped anyone, or set fire to a house.'

'Why don't you say exactly why I was sent to jail for two years? I'll give you four annas for a guess.'

'No time now for a game,' said the barber and went on, 'What do you do next?'

'I don't know. Must go somewhere, I suppose,' said Raju thoughtfully.

'In case you like to go back to your old company, why don't you put your hand in someone's pocket at the market, or walk through an open door and pick out some trash and let the people howl for the police? They'll see you back where you want to be.'

'Not a bad place,' Raju repeated, nodding slightly in the direction of the jail wall. 'Friendly people there, but I hate to be awakened every morning at five.'

'An hour at which a night-prowler likes to return home to bed, I suppose,' said the barber with heavy insinuation. 'Well, that's all. You may get up,' he said, putting away the razor. 'You look like a maharaja now'—surveying Raju at a distance from his chair.

The villager on the lower step looked up at his face with devotion, which irked Raju. 'Why do you look at me like that?' he asked brusquely.

The man replied, 'I don't know. I don't mean to offend you, sir.' Raju wanted to blurt out, 'I am here because I have nowhere else to go. I want to be away from people who may recognize me.' But he hesitated, wondering how he should say it. It looked as though he would be hurting the other's deepest sentiment if he so much as whispered the word 'jail'. He tried at least to say, 'I am not so great as you imagine. I am just ordinary.' Before he could fumble and reach the words, the other said, 'I have a problem, sir.'

'Tell me about it,' Raju said, the old, old habit of affording guidance to others asserting itself. Tourists who recommended him to one another would say at one time, 'If you are lucky enough to be guided by Raju, you will know everything. He will not only show you all the worthwhile places, but also help you in every way.' It was in his nature to get involved in other people's interests and activities. 'Otherwise,' Raju often reflected, 'I should have grown up like a thousand other normal persons, without worries in life.'

My troubles would not have started (Raju said in the course of narrating his life-story to this man who was called Velan at a later stage) but for Rosie. Why did she call herself Rosie? She did not come from a foreign land. She was just an Indian, who should have done well with Devi, Meena, Lalitha, or any one of the thousand names we have in our country. She chose to call herself Rosie. Don't imagine on hearing her name that she wore a short skirt or cropped her hair. She looked just the orthodox dancer that she was. She wore sarees of bright hues and gold lace, had curly hair which she braided and beflowered, wore diamond earrings and a heavy gold necklace. I told her at the first opportunity what a great dancer she was and how she fostered our cultural traditions, and it pleased her.

Thousands of persons must have said the same thing to her since, but I happened to be the first in the line. Anyone likes to hear flattering sentiments, and more than others, I suppose, dancers. They like to be told every hour of the day how well they keep their steps. I praised her art whenever I could snatch a moment alone with her and whisper in her ear, out of range of that husband of hers. Oh, what a man! I have not met a more grotesque creature in my life. Instead of calling herself Rosie, she could more logically have called him Marco Polo. He dressed like a man about to undertake an expedition, with his thick coloured glasses, thick jacket, and a thick helmet over which was perpetually stretched a green, shiny, waterproof cover, giving him the appearance of a space-traveller. I have, of course, no idea of the original Marco Polo's appearance, but I wanted to call this man Marco at first sight, and I have not bothered to associate him with any other name since.

The moment I set eyes on him, on that memorable day at our railway station, I knew that here was a lifelong customer for me. A man who preferred to dress like a permanent tourist was just what a guide passionately looked for all his life.

You may want to ask why I became a guide or when. I was a guide for the same reason as someone else is a signaller, porter, or guard. It is fated thus. Don't laugh at my railway associations. The railways got into my blood very early in life. Engines, with their tremendous clanging and smoke, ensnared my senses. I felt at home on the railway platform, and considered the station master and porter the best company for man, and their railway talk the most enlightened. I grew up in their midst. Ours was a small house opposite the Malgudi station. The house had been built by my father with his own hands long before trains were thought of. He chose this spot because it was outside the town and he could have it cheap. He had dug the earth, kneaded the mud with water from the well, and built the walls, and roofed them with coconut thatch. He planted papaya trees around, which yielded fruit, which he cut up and sold in slices: a single fruit brought him eight annas if he carved it with dexterity. My father had a small shop built of dealwood planks and gunny sack; and all day he sat there selling peppermint, fruit, tobacco, betel leaf, parched gram (which he measured out in tiny bamboo cylinders), and whatever else the wayfarers on the Trunk Road demanded. It was known as the 'hut shop'. A crowd of peasants and drivers of bullock-wagons were always gathered in front of his shop. A very busy man indeed. At midday he called me when he went in for his lunch and made a routine statement at the same hour. 'Raju, take my seat. Be sure to receive the money for whatever you give. Don't eat off all that eating stuff, it's kept for sale; call me if you have doubts.'

And I kept calling aloud, 'Father, green peppermints, how many for half an anna?' while the customer waited patiently.

'Three,' he shouted from the house, with his mouth stuffed with food. 'But if he is buying for three-quarters of an anna, give him . . .' He mentioned some complicated concession, which I could never apply.

I appealed to the customer, 'Give me only half an anna,' and gave him three peppermints in return. If by chance I had happened to take four greens out of the big bottle, I swallowed the fourth in order to minimize complications.

An eccentric cockerel in the neighbourhood announced the daybreak when probably it felt that we had slept long enough. It let out a shattering cry which made my father jump from his bed and wake me up.

I washed myself at the wall, smeared holy ash on my forehead, stood before the framed pictures of gods hanging high up on the wall, and recited all kinds of sacred verse in a loud, ringing tone. After watching my performance for a while, my father slipped away to the back yard to milk the buffalo. Later, coming in with the pail, he always remarked, 'Something really wrong with that animal this time. She wouldn't yield even half a measure today.'

My mother invariably answered, 'I know, I know. She is getting wrong-headed, that is all. I know what she will respond to,' she said in a mysterious, sinister manner, receiving the pail and carrying it into the kitchen. She came out in a moment with a tumblerful of hot milk for me.

The sugar was kept in an old tin can, which looked rusty but contained excellent sugar. It was kept on a wooden ledge on the smoke-stained wall of the kitchen, out of my reach. I fear that its position was shifted up and up as I grew older, because I remember that I could never get at that rusty can at any time except with the co-operation of my elders.

When the sky lightened, my father was ready for me on the *pyol*. There he sat with a thin broken twig at his side. The modern notions of child psychology were unknown then; the stick was an educator's indispensable equipment. 'The unbeaten brat will remain unlearned,' said my father, quoting an old proverb. He taught me the Tamil alphabet. He wrote the first two letters on each side of my slate at a time. I had to go over the contours of the letters with my pencil endlessly until they became bloated and distorted beyond recognition. From time to time my father snatched the slate from my hand, looked at it, glared at me, and said, 'What a mess! You will never prosper in life if you disfigure the sacred letters of the alphabet.' Then he cleaned the slate with his damp towel, wrote the letters again, and gave it to me with the injunction, 'If you spoil this, you will make me wild. Trace them exactly as I have written. Don't try any of your tricks on them,' and he flourished his twig menacingly.

I said meekly, 'Yes, Father,' and started to write again. I can well picture myself, sticking my tongue out, screwing my head to one side, and putting my entire body weight on the pencil; the slate pencil screeched as I tried to drive it through and my father ordered, 'Don't make all that noise with that horrible pencil of yours. What has come over you?'

Then followed arithmetic. Two and two, four; four and three, something else. Something into something, more; some more into less. Oh God, numbers did give me a headache. While the birds were out chirping and flying in the cool air, I cursed the fate that confined me to my father's company. His temper was rising every second. As if in answer to my silent prayer, an early customer was noticed at the door of the hut shop and my lessons came to an abrupt end. My father left me with the remark, 'I have better things to do of a morning than make a genius out of a clay-head.'

Although the lessons had seemed interminable to me, my mother said the moment she saw me, 'So you have been let off! I wonder what you can learn in half an hour!'

I told her, 'I'll go out and play and won't trouble you. But no more lessons for the day, please.' With that I was off to the shade of a tamarind tree across the road. It was an ancient, spreading tree, dense with leaves, amidst which monkeys and birds lived, bred, and chattered incessantly, feeding on the tender leaves and fruits. Pigs and piglets came from somewhere and nosed about the ground, thick with fallen leaves, and I played there all day. I think I involved the pigs in some imaginary game and even fancied myself carried on their backs. My father's customers greeted me as they passed that way. I had marbles, an iron hoop to roll, and a rubber ball, with which I occupied myself. I hardly knew what time of the day it was or what was happening around me.

Sometimes my father took me along to the town when he went shopping. He stopped a passing bullock-cart for the trip. I hung about anxiously with an appealing look in my eyes (I had been taught not to *ask* to be taken along) until my father said, 'Climb in, little man.' I clambered in before his sentence was completed. The bells around the bull's neck jingled, the wooden wheels grated and ground the dust off the rough road; I clung to the staves on the sides and felt my bones shaken. Still, I enjoyed the smell of the straw in the cart and all the scenes we passed. Men and vehicles, hogs and boys—the panorama of life enchanted me.

At the market my father made me sit on a wooden platform within sight of a shopman known to him, and went about to do his shopping. My pockets would be filled with fried nuts and sweets; munching, I watched the activities of the market—people buying and selling, arguing and laughing, swearing and shouting. While my father was gone on his shopping expedition, I remember, a question kept drumming in my head: 'Father, you are a shopkeeper yourself. Why do you go about buying in other shops?' I never got an answer. As I sat gazing on the afternoon haze, the continuous din of the marketplace lulled my senses, the dusty glare suddenly made me drowsy, and I fell asleep, leaning on the wall of that unknown place where my father had chosen to put me.

'I have a problem, sir,' said the man.

Raju nodded his head and said, 'So has everyone,' in a sudden access of pontificality. Ever since the moment this man had come and sat before him, gazing on his face, he had experienced a feeling of importance. He felt like an actor who was always expected to utter the right sentence. Now the appropriate sentence was, 'If you show me a person without a problem, then I'll show you the perfect world. Do you know what the great Buddha said?' The other edged nearer. 'A woman once went wailing to the great Buddha, clasping her dead baby to her bosom. The Buddha said, "Go into every home in this city and find one where death is unknown; if you find such a place, fetch me a handful of mustard from there, and then I'll teach you how to conquer death"'

The man clicked his tongue in appreciation and asked, 'And what happened to the dead baby, sir?'

'She had to bury it, of course,' said Raju. 'So also,' he concluded, while doubting in his mind the relevance of the comparison, 'if you show me a single home without a problem, I shall show you the way to attain a universal solution to all problems.'

The man was overwhelmed by the weightiness of this statement. He performed a deep obeisance and said, 'I have not told you my name, sir. I am Velan. My father in his lifetime married thrice. I am the first son of his first wife. The youngest daughter of his last wife is also with us. As the head of the family, I have given her every comfort at home, provided her with all the jewellery and clothes a girl needs, but . . .' He paused slightly before bringing out the big surprise. But Raju completed the sentence for him, 'The girl shows no gratitude.'

'Absolutely, sir!' said the man.

'And she will not accept your plans for her marriage?'

'Oh, too true, sir,' Velan said, wonderstruck. 'My cousin's son is a fine boy. Even the date of the wedding was fixed, but do you know, sir, what the girl did?'

'Ran away from the whole thing,' said Raju, and asked, 'How did you bring her back?'

'I searched for her three days and nights and spotted her in a festival crowd in a distant village. They were pulling the temple chariot around the streets and the population of fifty villages was crowded into one. I searched every face in the crowd and at last caught her while she was watching a puppet show. Now, do you know what she does?' Raju decided to let the other have the satisfaction of saying things himself, and Velan ended his story with, 'She sulks in a room all day. I do not know what to do. It is possible that she is possessed. If I could know what to do with her, it'd be such a help, sir.'

Raju said with a philosophic weariness, 'Such things are common in life. One should not let oneself be bothered unduly by anything.'

'What am I to do with her, sir?'

'Bring her over; let me speak to her,' Raju said grandly.

Velan rose, bowed low, and tried to touch Raju's feet. Raju recoiled at the attempt. 'I'll not permit anyone to do this. God alone is entitled to such a prostration. He will destroy us if we attempt to usurp His rights.' He felt he was attaining the stature of a saint. Velan went down the steps meekly, crossed the river, climbed the opposite bank, and was soon out of sight. Raju ruminated. 'I wish I had asked him what the age of the girl was. Hope she is uninteresting. I have had enough trouble in life.'

He sat there for a long time, watching the river flow into the night; the rustle of the peepul and banyan trees around was sometimes loud and frightening. The sky was clear. Having nothing else to do, he started counting the stars. He said to himself, 'I shall be rewarded for this profound service to humanity. People will say, "Here is the man who knows the exact number of stars in the sky. If you have any trouble on that account, you had better consult him. He will be your night guide for the skies."' He told himself, 'The thing to do is to start from a corner and go on patch by patch. Never work from the top to the horizon, but always the other way.' He was evolving a theory. He started the count from above a fringe of palmyra-trees on his left-hand side, up the course of the river, over to the other side. 'One . . . two . . . fifty-five . . .' He suddenly realized that if he looked deeper a new cluster of stars came into view; by the time he assimilated it into his reckoning, he realized he had lost sight of his starting point and found himself entangled in hopeless figures. He felt exhausted. He stretched himself on the stone slab and fell asleep under the open sky.

The eight o'clock sun shone fully on his face. He opened his eyes and saw Velan standing respectfully away on a lower step. 'I have brought my sister,' he said and thrust up a young girl of fourteen, who had tightly braided her hair and decorated herself with jewellery. Velan explained, 'These jewels were given by me, bought out of my own money, for she is after all my sister.'

Raju sat up, rubbing his eyes. He was as yet unprepared to take charge of the world's affairs. His immediate need was privacy for his morning ablutions. He said to them, 'You may go in there and wait for me.'

He found them waiting for him in the ancient, pillared hall. Raju sat himself down on a slightly elevated platform in the middle of the hall. Velan placed before him a basket filled with bananas, cucumbers, pieces of sugar cane, fried nuts, and a copper vessel brimming with milk.

Raju asked, 'What is all this for?'

'It will please us very much if you will accept them, sir.'

Raju sat looking at the hamper. It was not unwelcome. He could eat anything and digest it now. He had learned not to be fussy. Formerly he would have said, 'Who will eat this? Give me coffee and *idli*, please, first thing in the day. These are good enough for munching later.' But prison life had trained him to swallow anything at any time. Sometimes a colleague in the cell, managing to smuggle in, through the kindness of a warder, something unpalatable like mutton-puff made six days ago, with its oil going rancid, shared it with Raju, and Raju remembered how he ate it with gusto at three in the morning—a time chosen before the others could wake up and claim a share. Anything was welcome now. He asked, 'Why do you do all this for me?'

'They are grown in our fields and we are proud to offer them to you.'

Raju did not have to ask further questions. He had gradually come to view himself as a master of these occasions. He had already begun to feel that the adulation directed to him was inevitable. He sat in silence, eyeing the gift for a while. Suddenly he picked up the basket and went into an inner sanctum. The others followed. Raju stopped before a stone image in the dark recess. It was a tall god with four hands, bearing a mace and wheel, with a beautifully chiselled head, but abandoned a century ago. Raju ceremoniously placed the basket of edibles at the feet of the image and said, 'It's *His* first. Let the offering go to Him, first; and we will eat the remnants. By giving to God, do you know how it multiplies, rather than divides? Do you know the story?' He began narrating the story of Devaka, a man of ancient times who begged for alms at the temple gate every day and would not use any of his collections without first putting them at the feet of the god. Halfway through the story he realized that he could not remember either its course or its purport. He lapsed into silence. Velan patiently waited for the continuation. He was of the stuff disciples are made of; an unfinished story or an incomplete moral never bothered him; it was all in the scheme of life. When Raju turned and strode majestically back to the river step, Velan and his sister followed him mutely.

How could I recollect the story heard from my mother so long ago? She told me a story every evening while we waited for Father to close the shop and come home. The shop remained open till midnight. Bullock-carts in long caravans arrived late in the evening from distant villages, loaded with coconut, rice, and other commodities for the market. The animals were unyoked under the big tamarind tree for the night, and the cartmen drifted in twos and threes to the shop, for a chat or to ask for things to eat or smoke. How my father loved to discuss with them the price of grain, rainfall, harvest, and the state of irrigation channels. Or they talked about old litigations. One heard repeated references to magistrates, affidavits, witnesses in the case, and appeals, punctuated with roars of laughter—possibly the memory of some absurd legality or loophole tickled them.

My father ignored food and sleep when he had company. My mother sent me out several times to see if he could be made to turn in. He was a man of uncertain temper and one could not really guess how he would react to interruptions, and so my mother coached me to go up, watch his mood, and gently remind him of food and home. I stood under the shop awning, coughing and clearing my throat, hoping to catch his eye. But the talk was all-absorbing and he would not glance in my direction, and I got absorbed in their talk, although I did not understand a word of it.

After a while my mother's voice came gently on the night air, calling, 'Raju, Raju,' and my father interrupted his activities to look at me and say, 'Tell your mother not to wait for me. Tell her to place a handful of rice and buttermilk in a bowl, with just one piece of lime pickle, and keep it in the oven for me. I'll come in later.' It was almost a formula with him five days in a week. He always added, 'Not that I'm really hungry tonight.' And then I believe he went on to discuss health problems with his cronies.

But I didn't stop to hear further. I made a swift dash back home. There was a dark patch between the light from the shop and the dim lantern shedding its light on our threshold, a matter of about ten yards, I suppose, but the passage through it gave me a cold sweat. I expected wild animals and supernatural creatures to emerge and grab me. My mother waited on the doorstep to receive me and said, 'Not hungry, I suppose! That'll give him an excuse to talk to the village folk all night, and then come in for an hour's sleep and get up with the crowing of that foolish cock somewhere. He will spoil his health.'

I followed her into the kitchen. She placed my plate and hers side by side on the floor, drew the rice-pot within reach, and served me and herself simultaneously, and we finished our dinner by the sooty tin lamp, stuck on a nail in the wall. She unrolled a mat for me in the front room, and I lay down to sleep. She sat at my side, awaiting Father's return. Her presence gave me a feeling of inexplicable cosiness. I felt I ought to put her proximity to good use, and complained, 'Something is bothering my hair,' and she ran her fingers through my hair and scratched the nape of my neck. And then I commanded, 'A story.'

Immediately she began, 'Once upon a time there was a man called Devaka . . .' I heard his name mentioned almost every night. He was a hero, saint, or something of the kind. I never learned fully what he did or why, sleep overcoming me before my mother was through even the preamble.

Raju sat on the step and watched the river dazzling in the morning sun. The air was cool, and he wished he were alone. His visitors sat patiently on a lower step, waiting for him to attend to them, like patients in a doctor's room. Raju had many problems of his own to think of. He suddenly felt irritated at the responsibility that Velan was thrusting on him, and said frankly, 'I am not going to think of your problems, Velan; not now.'

'May I know why?' he asked humbly.

'It is so,' Raju said with an air of finality.

'When may I trouble you, sir?' he asked.

Raju replied grandly, 'When the time is ripe for it.' This took the matter from the realms of time into eternity. Velan accepted his answer with resignation and rose to go. It was rather touching. Raju felt indebted to him for the edibles he had brought, so he said pacifyingly, 'Is this the sister you told me about?'

'Yes, sir; it is.'

'I know what your problem is, but I wish to give the matter some thought. We cannot force vital solutions. Every question must bide its time. Do you understand?'

'Yes, sir,' Velan said. He drew his fingers across his brow and said, 'Whatever is written here will happen. How can we ever help it?'

'We may not change it, but we may understand it,' Raju replied grandly. 'And to arrive at a proper understanding, time is needed.' Raju felt he was growing wings. Shortly, he felt, he might float in the air and perch himself on the tower of the ancient temple. Nothing was going to surprise him. He suddenly found himself asking, 'Have I been in a prison or in some sort of transmigration?'

Velan looked relieved and proud to hear so much from his master. He looked significantly at his difficult sister, and she bowed her head in shame. Raju declared, looking fixedly at the girl, 'What must happen must happen; no power on earth or in heaven can change its course, just as no one can change the course of that river.' They gazed on the river, as if the clue to their problems lay there, and turned to go. Raju watched them cross the river and climb the opposite bank. Soon they were out of sight.

2

WE NOTICED MUCH activity in the field in front of our house. A set of men arrived from the town every morning and were busy in the field all day. We learned that they were building a railway track. They came to my father's shop for refreshments. My father inquired anxiously, 'When shall we have the trains coming in here?'

If they were in a good mood, they answered, 'About six or eight months, who can say.' Or if they were in a black mood, 'Don't ask us. Next you will tell us to drive a locomotive to your shop!' And they laughed grimly.

Work was going on briskly. I lost to some extent my freedom under the tamarind tree, because trucks were parked there. I climbed into them and played. No one minded me. All day I was climbing in and out of the trucks, and my clothes became red with mud. Most of the trucks brought red earth which was banked up on the field. In a short while, a small mountain was raised in front of our house. It was enchanting. When I stood on the top of this mound I could see far-off places, the hazy outlines of Mempi Hills. I became as busy as the men. I spent all my time in the company of those working on the track, listening to their talk and sharing their jokes. More trucks came, bringing timber and iron. A variety of goods was piling up on every side. Presently I began to collect sawn-off metal bits, nuts and bolts, and I treasured them in my mother's big trunk, where a space was allotted to me amidst her ancient silk sarees, which she never wore.

A boy grazing his cows approached the spot just below the mound on which I was playing a game by myself. His cows were munching the grass right below the mound on which the men were working, and the little fellow had dared to step on the slope where I played. I was beginning to have a sense of ownership of the railway, and I didn't want trespassers there. I frowned at the boy and barked, 'Get out.'

'Why?' he asked. 'My cows are here, I'm watching them.'

'Begone with your cows,' I said. 'Otherwise they will be run over by the train, which will be here shortly.'

'Let them be. What do you care?' he said, which irritated me so much that I let out a yell and pounced on him with 'You son of a . . .' and a variety of other expressions recently picked up. The boy, instead of knocking me down, ran screaming to my father, 'Your son is using bad language.'

My father sprang up on hearing this. Just my misfortune. He came rushing toward me as I was resuming my game and asked, 'What did you call this boy?' I had the good sense not to repeat it. I blinked, wordlessly, at which the boy repeated exactly what I had said. This produced an unexpectedly violent effect on my father. He grabbed my neck within the hollow of his hand, and asked, 'Where did you pick that up?' I pointed at the men working on the track. He looked up, remained silent for a second, and said, 'Oh, that is so, is it? You will not idle about picking up bad words any more. I will see to it. You will go to a school tomorrow and every day.'

'Father!' I cried. He was passing a harsh sentence on me. To be removed from a place I loved, to a place I loathed!

A tremendous fuss was made before I started for my school each day. My mother fed me early and filled up a little aluminium vessel with refreshment for the afternoon. She carefully put my books and slate into a bag and slung it across my shoulder. I was dressed in clean shorts and shirt; my hair was combed back from the forehead, with all the curls falling on my nape. For the first few days I enjoyed all this attention, but soon developed a normal aversion; I preferred to be neglected and stay at home to being fussed over and sent to a school. But my father was a stern disciplinarian; perhaps he was a snob who wanted to brag before others that his son was going to a school. He kept an eye on my movements till I was safely on the road each morning. He sat in his shop and kept calling every few minutes, 'Boy, have you left?'

I walked endlessly to reach my school. No other boy went in my direction. I talked to myself on the way, paused to observe the passers-by or a country cart lumbering along, or a grasshopper going under a culvert. My progress was so halting and slow that when I turned into the Market Street I could hear my classmates shouting their lessons in unison, for the old man, our master, who taught us, believed in getting the maximum noise out of his pupils.

I don't know on whose advice my father chose to send me here for my education, while the fashionable Albert Mission School was quite close by. I'd have felt proud to call myself an Albert Mission boy. But I often heard my father declare, 'I don't want to send my boy there; it seems they try to convert our boys into Christians and are all the time insulting our gods.' I don't know how he got the notion; anyway, he was firmly convinced that the school where I was sent was the best under the sun. He was known to boast, 'Many students who have passed through the hands of this ancient master are now big officials at Madras, collectors and men like that . . .' It was purely his own imagining or the invention of the old man who taught me. No one could dream that this was in any sense a school, let alone an outstanding school. It was what was called a *pyol* school, because the classes were held on the *pyol* of the gentleman's house. He lived in Kabir Lane, in a narrow old house with a cement *pyol* in front, with the street drain running right below it. He gathered a score of young boys of my age every morning on the *pyol*, reclined on a cushion in a corner, and shouted at the little fellows, flourishing a rattan cane all the time. All the classes were held there at the same time, and he bestowed attention on each group in turn. I belonged to the youngest and most elementary set, just learning the alphabet and numbers. He made us read aloud from our books and copy down the letters on our slates, and looked through each and gave corrections and flicks from the cane for those who repeated their follies. He was a very abusive man. My father, who wanted to save me from the language of the railway trackmen, had certainly not made a safer choice in sending me to this old man, who habitually addressed his pupils as donkeys and traced their genealogies on either side with thoroughness.

The thing that irritated him was not merely the mistakes that we made but our very presence. Seeing us, such short, clumsy youngsters, always fumbling and shuffling, I think got on his nerves. Of course, we made a lot of noise on his *pyol*. When he went into his house for a moment's nap or for his food or for any of a dozen domestic calls, we rolled over each other, fought, scratched, bleated, yelled. Or we tried to invade his privacy and peep in. Once we slipped in and passed from room to room until we came to the kitchen and saw him sitting before the oven, baking something. We stood at the doorway and said, 'Oh, master, you know how to cook also!' and giggled, and a lady who was standing nearby also giggled at our remark.

He turned on us fiercely and ordered, 'Get out, boys; don't come here; this is not your classroom,' and we scampered back to our place, where he found us later and twisted our ears until we screamed. He said, 'I am admitting you devils here because I want you to become civilized, but what you do is . . .' and he catalogued our sins and misdeeds.

We were contrite, and he softened and said, 'Hereafter let me not catch you anywhere beyond that threshold. I will hand you over to the police if you come in.' That settled it. We never peeped again, but when his back was turned confined our attention to the drain that flowed beneath the *pyol*. We tore off loose leaves from our notebooks, made boats, and floated them down the drain, and in a short while it became established practice, and a kind of boat-racing developed out of it; we lay on our bellies and watched the boats float away on the drainwater. He warned us, 'If you fall off into the gutter, you will find yourselves in the Sarayu river, remember, and I shall have to tell your father to go out and look for you there, I suppose!' and he laughed at the grim prospect.

His interest in us was one rupee a month and anything else in kind we cared to carry. My father sent him every month two cubes of jaggery, others brought in rice and vegetables and anything else he might demand from time to time. Whenever his store at home ran out, he called one or another to his side and said, 'Now if you are a good boy, you will run to your house and fetch me just a little, only so much, mind you, of sugar. Come, let me see if you are smart!' He adopted a kindly, canvassing tone on such occasions, and we felt honoured to be able to serve him, and pestered our parents to give us the gifts and fought for the honour of serving him. Our parents showed an excessive readiness to oblige this master, grateful probably because he kept us in his charge for the major part of the day, from morning till four in the afternoon, when he dismissed us and we sprinted homeward.

In spite of all the apparent violence and purposelessness, I suppose we did make good under our master, for within a year I proved good enough for the first standard in the Board High School; I could read heavier books, and do multiplication up to twenty in my head. The old master himself escorted me to the Board School, which had just established itself, and admitted me there; he saw me off in my new class, seated me and two others, and blessed us before taking leave of us. It was a pleasant surprise for us that he could be so kind.

Velan was bursting with news of a miracle. He stood before Raju with folded hands, and said, 'Sir, things have turned out well.'

'I'm so happy. How?'

'My sister came before our family gathering and admitted her follies. She has agreed . . .' He went on to explain. The girl had all of a sudden appeared before the assembled family that morning. She faced everyone straight and said, 'I have behaved foolishly all these days. I will do what my brother and the other elders at home tell me to do. They know what is best for us.'

'I could hardly believe my ears,' explained Velan. 'I pinched myself to see whether I was dreaming or awake. This girl's affair had cast a gloom on our home. If you left out our partition suit and all the complications arising from it, we had no worry to equal this. You see, we are fond of the girl, and it pained us to watch her sulk in a dark room, without minding her appearance or dress or caring for food. We did our best to make her cheerful and then had to leave her alone. We had all been very miserable on account of her, and so we were surprised this morning when she came before us with her hair oiled and braided, with flowers in it. Looking bright, she said, "I have been a bother to you all these days. Forgive me, all of you. I shall do whatever my elders order me to do." Naturally, after we got over the surprise, we asked, "Are you prepared to marry your cousin?" She did not answer at once, but stood with bowed head. My wife took her aside and asked whether we might send word to the other family, and she agreed. We have sent the happy message around, and there will soon be a marriage in our house. I have money, jewellery, and everything ready. I will call the pipers and drummers tomorrow morning and get through it all quickly. I have consulted the astrologer already, and he says that this is an auspicious time. I do not want to delay even for a second the happy event.'

'For fear that she may change her mind once again?' Raju asked. He knew why Velan was rushing it through at this pace. It was easy to guess why. But the remark threw the other into a fit of admiration, and he asked, 'How did you know what I had in mind, sir?'

Raju remained silent. He could not open his lips without provoking admiration. This was a dangerous state of affairs. He was in a mood to debunk himself a little. He told Velan sharply, 'There is nothing extraordinary in my guess,' and promptly came the reply, 'Not for you to say that, sir. Things may look easy enough for a giant, but ordinary poor mortals like us can never know what goes on in other people's minds.'

To divert his attention, Raju simply asked, 'Have you any idea of the views of the bridegroom? Is he ready for you? What does he think of her refusal?'

'After the girl came round, I sent our priest to discuss it with him, and he has come back to say that the boy is willing. He prefers not to think of what is past. What is gone is gone.'

'True, true,' Raju said, having nothing else to say and not wishing to utter anything that might seem too brilliant. He was beginning to dread his own smartness nowadays. He was afraid to open his lips. A vow of silence was indicated, but there was greater danger in silence.

All this prudence did not save him. Velan's affairs were satisfactorily ended. One day he came to invite Raju to his sister's marriage, and Raju had to plead long and hard before he could make him leave him alone. However, Velan brought him fruit on huge trays covered with silk cloth, the sort of offering which Raju would conjure up for the edification of his tourists when he took them through an ancient palace or hall. He accepted the gift gracefully.

He avoided the girl's marriage. He did not want, to be seen in a crowd, and he did not want to gather a crowd around him as a man who had worked a change in an obstinate girl. But his aloofness did not save him. If he would not go to the wedding, the wedding was bound to come to him. At the earliest possible moment Velan brought the girl and her husband and a huge concourse of relatives to the temple. The girl herself seemed to have spoken of Raju as her saviour. She had told everyone, 'He doesn't speak to anyone, but if he looks at you, you are changed.'

His circle was gradually widening. Velan, at the end of his day's agricultural toil, came and sat on the lower step. If Raju spoke, he listened; otherwise he accepted the silence with equal gratitude, got up without a word when darkness fell, and moved away. Gradually, unnoticed, a few others began to arrive very regularly. Raju could not very well question who they were; the river bank was a public place, and he himself was an intruder. They just sat there on the lower step and looked at Raju, and kept looking at him. He didn't have to say a word to anyone; he just sat there at the same place, looking away at the river, at the other bank, and tried hard to think where he should go next and what to do. They did not so much as whisper a word for fear that it might disturb him. Raju was beginning to feel uncomfortable on these occasions; and wondered if he could devise some means of escape from their company. Throughout the day he was practically left alone, but late in the evening, after doing their day's work, the villagers would come.

One evening before the company arrived, he moved himself to the back yard of the temple and hid himself behind a gigantic hibiscus bush full of red flowers. He heard them arrive, heard their voices on the river step. They were talking in low, hushed voices. They went round the building and passed by the hibiscus bush. Raju's heart palpitated as he crouched there like an animal at bay. He held his breath and waited. He was already planning to offer an explanation if they should discover his presence there. He would say that he was in deep thought and that the hibiscus shade was congenial for such contemplation. But fortunately they did not look for him there. They stood near the bush talking in a hushed, awed whisper. Said one, 'Where could he have gone?'

'He is a big man, he may go anywhere; he may have a thousand things to do.'

'Oh, you don't know. He has renounced the world; he does nothing but meditate. What a pity he is not here today!'

'Just sitting there for a few minutes with him—ah, what a change it has brought about in our household! Do you know, that cousin of mine came round last night and gave me back the promissory note. As long as he held it, I felt as if I had put a knife in his hand for stabbing us.'

'We won't have to fear anything more; it is our good fortune that this great soul should have come to life in our midst.'

'But he has disappeared today. Wonder if he has left us for good.'

'It would be our misfortune if he went away.'

'His clothes are still all there in the hall.'

'He has no fears.'

'The food I brought yesterday has been eaten.'

'Leave there what you have brought now; he is sure to come back from his outing and feel hungry.' Raju felt grateful to this man for his sentiment.

'Do you know sometimes these yogis can travel to the Himalayas just by a thought?'

'I don't think he is that kind of yogi,' said another.

'Who can say? Appearances are sometimes misleading,' said someone. They then moved off to their usual seat and sat there. For a long time Raju could hear them talking among themselves. After a while they left. Raju could hear them splashing the water with their feet. 'Let us go before it gets too dark. They say that there is an old crocodile in this part of the river.'

'A boy known to me was held up by his ankle once, at this very spot.'

'What happened, then?'

'He was dragged down, next day . . .'

Raju could hear their voices far off. He cautiously peeped out of his hiding. He could see their shadowy figures on the other bank. He waited till they vanished altogether from sight. He went in and lit a lamp. He was hungry. They had left his food wrapped in a banana leaf on the pedestal of the old stone image. Raju was filled with gratitude and prayed that Velan might never come to the stage of thinking that he was too good for food and that he subsisted on atoms from the air.

Next morning he rose early and went through his ablutions, washed his clothes in the river, lit the stove, made himself coffee, and felt completely at ease with the world. He had to decide on his future today. He should either go back to the town of his birth, bear the giggles and stares for a few days, or go somewhere else. Where could he go? He had not trained himself to make a living out of hard work. Food was coming to him unasked now. If he went away somewhere else certainly nobody was going to take the trouble to bring him food in return for just waiting for it. The only other place where it could happen was the prison. Where could he go now? Nowhere. Cows grazing on the slopes far off gave the place an air of sublime stillness. He realized that he had no alternative: he must play the role that Velan had given him.

With his mind made up he prepared himself to meet Velan and his friends in the evening. He sat as usual on the stone slab with beatitude and calm in his face. The thing that had really bothered him was that he might sound too brilliant in everything he said. He had observed silence as a precaution. But that fear was now gone. He decided to look as brilliant as he could manage, let drop gems of thought from his lips, assume all the radiance available, and afford them all the guidance they required without stint. He decided to arrange the stage for the display with more thoroughness. With this view he transferred his seat to the inner hall of the temple. It gave one a better background. He sat there at about the time he expected Velan and others to arrive. He anticipated their arrival with a certain excitement. He composed his features and pose to receive them.

The sun was setting. Its tint touched the wall with pink. The tops of the coconut trees around were aflame. The bird-cries went up in a crescendo before dying down for the night. Darkness fell. Still there was no sign of Velan or anyone. They did not come that night. He was left foodless; that was not the main worry, he still had a few bananas. Suppose they never came again? What was to happen? He became panicky. All night he lay worrying. All his old fears came back. If he returned to the town he would have to get his house back from the man to whom he had mortgaged it. He would have to fight for a living space in his own home or find the cash to redeem it.

He debated whether to step across the river, walk into the village, and search for Velan. It didn't seem a dignified thing to do. It might make him look cheap, and they might ignore him altogether.

He saw a boy grazing his sheep on the opposite bank. He clapped his hands and cried, 'Come here.' He went down the steps and cried across the water, 'I am the new priest of this temple, boy, come here. I have a plantain for you. Come and take it.' He flourished it, feeling that this was perhaps a gamble; it was the last piece of fruit in his store and might presently be gone, as might the boy, and Velan might never know how badly he was wanted, while he, Raju, lay starving there until they found his bleached bones in the temple and gadded them to the ruins around. With these thoughts he flourished the banana. The boy was attracted by it and soon came across the water. He was short and was wet up to his ears. Raju said, 'Take off your turban and dry yourself, boy.'

'I am not afraid of water,' he said.

'You should not be so wet.'

The boy held out his hand for the plantain and said, 'I can swim. I always swim.'

'But I have never seen you here before,' Raju said.

'I don't come here. I go farther down and swim.'

'Why don't you come here?'

'This is a crocodile place,' he said.

'But I have never seen any crocodile.'

'You will sometime,' the boy said. 'My sheep generally graze over there. I came to see if a man was here.'

'Why?'

'My uncle asked me to watch. He said, "Drive your sheep before that temple and see if a man is there." That is why I came here today.'

Raju gave the boy the banana and said, 'Tell your uncle that the man is back here and tell him to come here this evening.'

He did not wait to ask who the uncle was. Whoever he might be, he was welcome. The boy peeled the plantain, swallowed it whole, and started munching the peel also. 'Why do you eat the peel? It will make you sick,' Raju said.

'No, it won't,' the boy replied. He seemed to be a resolute boy who knew his mind.

Raju vaguely advised, 'You must be a good boy. Now be off. Tell your uncle—'

The boy was off, after cautioning him, 'Keep an eye on those till I get back.' He indicated his flock on the opposite slope.

3

ONE FINE DAY, beyond the tamarind tree, the station building was ready. The steel tracks gleamed in the sun; the signal posts stood with their red and green stripes and their colourful lamps; and our world was neatly divided into this side of the railway line and that side. Everything was ready. All our spare hours were spent in walking along the railway track up to the culvert half a mile away. We paced up and down our platform. A gold mohur sapling was planted in the railway yard. We passed through the corridor, peeping into the room meant for the station master.

One day we were all given a holiday. 'The train comes to our town today,' people said excitedly. The station was decorated with festoons and bunting. A piper was playing, bands were banging away. Coconuts were broken on the railway track, and an engine steamed in, pulling a couple of cars. Many of the important folk of the town were there. The Collector and the Police Superintendent and the Municipal Chairman, and many of the local tradesmen, who flourished green invitation cards in their hands, were assembled at the station. The police guarded the platform and did not allow the crowds in. I felt cheated by this. I felt indignant that anyone should probibit my entry to the platform. I squeezed myself through the railings at the farthest end, and by the time the engine arrived I was there to receive it. I was probably so small that no one noticed my presence.

Tables were laid and official gentlemen sat around refreshing themselves, and then several men got up and lectured. I was aware only of the word 'Malgudi' recurring in their speeches. There was a clapping of hands. The band struck up, the engine whistled, the bell rang, the guard blew his whistle, and the men who had been consuming refreshments climbed into the train. I was half inclined to follow their example, but there were many policemen to stop me. The train moved and was soon out of sight. A big crowd was now allowed to come on to the platform. My father's shop had record sales that day.

By the time a station master and a porter were installed in their little stone house at the back of the station, facing our house, my father had become so prosperous that he acquired a *jutka* and a horse in order to go to the town and do his shopping.

My mother had been apathetic. 'Why should you have all this additional bother in this household, horse and horse-gram and all that, while the buffalo pair is a sufficient bother?'

He did not answer her in any detail, just swept off her objections with, 'You know nothing about these things, I have so much to do every day in the town. I have to visit the bank so often.' He uttered the word 'bank' with a proud emphasis, but it did not impress my mother.

And so there was an addition of a thatch-roofed shed to our yard, in which a brown pony was tied up, and my father had picked up a groom to look after it. We became the folk of the town with this horse and carriage, but my mother never reconciled herself to it. She viewed it as an extraordinary vanity on my father's part and no amount of explanation from him ever convinced her otherwise. Her view was that my father had overestimated his business, and she nagged him whenever he was found at home and the horse and carriage were not put to proper use. She expected him to be always going round the streets in his vehicle. He had not more than an hour's job any day in the town and he always came back in time to attend to his shop, which he was now leaving in charge of a friend for a few hours in the day. My mother was developing into a successful nagger, I suppose, for my father was losing much of his aggressiveness and was becoming very apologetic about his return home whenever the horse and the carriage were left unused under the tamarind tree. 'You take it and go to the market, if you like,' he often said, but my mother spurned the offer, explaining, 'Where should I go every day? Some day it may be useful for going to the temple on a Friday. But ought you to maintain an extravagant turnout all through the year, just for a possible visit to the temple? Horse-gram and grass, do you know what they cost?' Fortunately, it did not prove such a liability after all. Worn out by Mother's persistent or position, my father seriously considered disposing of the horse and (a fantastic proposal) converting the carriage into a single bullock-cart with a 'bow spring' mounted over the wheel, which a blacksmith of his acquaintance at the market gate had promised to do for him.

The groom who minded the horse laughed at the idea and said that it was an impossible proposition, convincing my father that the blacksmith would reduce the carriage to a piece of furniture fit for lounging under the tamarind tree. 'You could as well listen to a promise to turn the horse into a bullock!' he said, and then he made a proposal which appealed to my father's business instinct. 'Let me ply it for hire in the market. All gram and grass my charge—only let me use your shed. I will hand you two rupees a day and one rupee a month for the use of the shed, and anything I earn over two rupees should be mine.'

This was a delightful solution. My father had the use of the carriage whenever he wanted it, and earned a sum for it each day, and no liabilities. As the days passed, the driver came along and pleaded lack of engagements. A great deal of argument went on in the front part of my house, in semi-darkness, between my father and the driver as my father tried to exact his two rupees. Finally my mother too joined in, saying, 'Don't trust these fellows. Today with all that festival crowd, he says he has not made any money. How can we believe him?'

My mother was convinced that the cart-driver drank his earnings. My father retorted, 'What if he drinks? It is none of our business.'

Every day this went on. Every night the man stood under the tree and cringed and begged for remission. It was evident that he was misappropriating our funds. For within a few weeks the man came and said, 'This horse is growing bony and will not run properly, and is becoming wrong-headed. It is better we sell it off soon and take another, because all the passengers who get into this *jutka* complain and pay less at the end because of the discomfort suffered. And the springs over the wheels must also be changed.' The man was constantly suggesting that the turnout had better be sold off and a new one taken. Whenever he said it within my mother's hearing she lost her temper and shouted at him, saying that one horse and carriage were sufficient expense. This reduced my father to viewing the whole arrangement as a hopeless liability, until the man hinted that he had an offer of seventy rupees for both horse and carriage. My father managed to raise this to seventy-five and finally the man brought the cash and drove off the turnout himself. Evidently he had saved a lot of our own money for this enterprise. Anyway, we were glad to be rid of the thing. This was a nicely calculated transaction for as soon as the trains began to arrive regularly at our station we found our *jutka* doing a brisk business carrying passengers to the town.

My father was given the privilege of running a shop at the railway station. What a shop it was! It was paved with cement, with shelves built in. It was so spacious that when my father had transferred all the articles from the hut-shop, the place was only one-quarter filled; there were so many blank spaces all along the wall that he felt depressed at the sight of it. For the first time he was beginning to feel that he had not been running a very big business after all.

My mother had come out to watch the operation and taunted him, 'With this stock you think of buying motor cars and what not.' He had not at any time proposed buying a motor car but she liked to nag him.

Father said, rather weakly, 'Why drag in all that now?' He was ruminating. 'I shall need at least another five hundred rupees' worth of articles to fill up all this space.'

The station master, an old man wearing a green turban round his head and silver-rimmed spectacles, came along to survey the shop. My father became extremely deferential at the sight of him. Behind him stood Karia the porter in in his blue shirt and turban. My mother withdrew unobtrusively and went back home. The station master viewed the shop from a distance with his head on one side as if he were an artist viewing a handiwork. The porter, ever faithful, followed his example, keeping himself in readiness to agree with whatever he might say. The station master said, 'Fill up all that space, otherwise the ATS might come round and ask questions, poking his nose into all our affairs. It has not been easy to give you this shop.'

My father sat me in the shop and went over to the town to make the purchases. 'Don't display too much rice and other stuff—keep the other shop for such things,' advised the station master. 'Railway passengers won't be asking for tamarind and lentils during the journey.' My father implicitly accepted his directions. The station master was his palpable God now and he cheerfully obeyed all his commands. And so, presently there hung down from nails in my father's other shop bigger bunches of bananas, stacks of Mempu oranges, huge troughs of fried stuff, and colourful peppermints and sweets in glass containers, loaves of bread, and buns. The display was most appetizing, and he had loaded several racks with packets of cigarettes. He had to anticipate the demand of every kind of traveller and provide for it.

He left me in charge of his hut-shop. His old customers came down to gossip and shop, as had been their habit. But they found me unequal to it. I found it tedious to listen to their talk of litigation and irrigation. I was not old enough to appreciate all their problems and the subtleties of their transactions. I listened to them without response, and soon they discovered that I was no good as companion for them. They left me in peace and wandered off to the other shop, seeking my father's company. But they found it untenable. They felt strange there. It was too sophisticated a surrounding for them. Very soon, unobtrusively, my father was back in his seat at the hut-shop, leaving me to handle the business in the new shop. As soon as a certain bridge off Malgudi was ready, regular service began on our rails; it was thrilling to watch the activities of the station master and the blue-shirted porter as they 'received' and 'line-cleared' two whole trains each day, the noon train from Madras and the evening one from Trichy. I became very active indeed in the shop. As you might have guessed, all this business expansion in our family helped me achieve a very desirable end—the dropping off from my school unobtrusively.

4

THE BANANA WORKED a miracle. The boy went from house to house, announcing that the saint was back at his post. Men, women and children arrived in a great mass. All that they wanted was to be allowed to look at him and watch the radiance on his face. The children stood around and gazed in awe. Raju tried to manage the situation by pinching a few cheeks and saying some inanities, or even indulging in baby-talk in order to soften the awkwardness of the situation. He went up to young boys and asked, 'What are you studying?' in the manner of big men he had seen in cities. But it was stupid to imitate that question here, because the boys giggled, looked at one another, and said, 'No school for us.'

'What do you do all day?' he asked, without any real interest in their problems.

One of the elders interposed to say, 'We cannot send our boys to the school as you do in towns; they have to take the cattle out for grazing.'

Raju clicked his tongue in disapproval. He shook his head. The gathering looked pained and anxious. Raju explained grandly, 'Boys must read, first. They must, of course, help their parents, but they must also find the time to study.' He added on an inspiration, 'If they cannot find the time to read during the day, why should they not gather in the evenings and learn?'

'Where?' asked someone.

'Maybe here.' Raju added, pointing at the vast hall, 'Maybe you could ask one of your masters. Is there no schoolmaster in your midst?'

'Yes, yes,' several voices cried in unison.

'Ask him to see me,' Raju commanded authoritatively, with the air of a president summoning a defaulting assistant master. Next afternoon a timid man, who wore a short tuft with a turban over it, turned up at the temple hall. Raju had just finished his repast and was enjoying a siesta in the hall, stretching himself on its cool, granite floor. The timid man stood beside an ancient pillar and cleared his throat. Raju opened his eyes and looked at him blankly. It was not the custom there, in that society, to ask who or why, when so many came and went. Raju flourished an arm to indicate to the other to sit down and resumed his sleep. When he awoke later, he saw the man sitting close to him.

'I'm the teacher,' the man said, and in the muddled state of half-sleep Raju's old fears of schoolteachers returned: he forgot for a split second that he had left all those behind years ago. He sat up.

The master was rather surprised. He said, 'Don't disturb yourself. I can wait.'

'That's all right,' said Raju, recovering his composure and understanding his surroundings better. 'You are the schoolmaster?' he asked patronizingly. He brooded for a moment, then asked in a general way, 'How is everything?'

The other merely replied, 'No different from what it used to be.'

'How do you like it?'

'What does it matter?' the other said. 'I only try to do my best and do it sincerely.'

'Otherwise, what's the use of doing anything at all?' asked Raju. He was marking time. He was not very clear-headed yet after the deep sleep, and the problem of boys' education was not uppermost in his mind at the moment. He said tentatively, 'After all, one's duty—'

'I do my utmost,' said the other defensively, not wishing to give way. After these parleys, which lasted for half an hour, the village master himself clarified the position. 'It seems you suggested that the boys should be assembled here and taught at nights.'

'Oh! eh!' Raju said. 'Yes, I did, of course, but it's a matter in which the decision should be purely yours. After all, self-help is the best help; I may be here today and gone tomorrow. It's up to you to arrange it. I meant that if you want a place—you can have it.' He swept his arm about with the air of one conferring a gift on a whole community.

The teacher looked thoughtful for a moment and began, 'I'm not sure, however—'

But Raju suddenly became argumentative and definite. He said with a lot of authority, 'I like to see young boys become literate and intelligent.' He added with fervour because it sounded nice, 'It's our duty to make everyone happy and wise.'

This overwhelming altruism was too much for the teacher. 'I'll do anything,' he said, 'under your guidance.' Raju admitted the position with, 'I'm but an instrument accepting guidance myself.'

The result was that the teacher went back to the village a changed man. Next day he was back at the pillared hall with a dozen children of the village. They had their foreheads smeared with sacred ash, and their slates creaked in the silent night, while the teacher lectured to them, and Raju, seated on his platform, looked on benignly. The teacher was apologetic about the numbers: he could muster only about a dozen boys. 'They are afraid of crossing the river in the dark; they have heard of a crocodile hereabouts.'

'What can a crocodile do to you if your mind is clear and your conscience is untroubled?' Raju said grandly. It was a wonderful sentiment to express. He was surprised at the amount of wisdom welling from the depths of his being. He said to the teacher, 'Don't be dispirited that there are only a dozen. If you do your work sincerely by a dozen, it'll be equivalent, really, to serving a hundred times that number.'

The teacher suggested, 'Do not mistake me, but will you speak to these boys whenever you can?' This gave Raju a chance to air his views on life and eternity before the boys. He spoke to them on godliness, cleanliness, spoke on the *Ramayana*, the characters in the epics; he addressed them on all kinds of things. He was hypnotized

by his own voice; he felt himself growing in stature as he saw the
upturned faces of the children shining in the half-light when he
spoke. No one was more impressed with the grandeur of the whole
thing than Raju himself.

Now that I reflect upon it, I am convinced I was not such a dud after
all. It seems to me that we generally do not have a correct measure
of our own wisdom. I remember how I was equipping my mind
all the time. I read a certain amount of good stuff in my railway-
shopkeeping days. I sat in that shop, selling loaves of bread and
aerated water. Sometimes schoolboys left their books with me for
sale. Though my father thought very highly of our shop, I could not
share his view. Selling bread and biscuits and accepting money in
exchange seemed to me a tame occupation. I always felt that I was
too good for the task.

My father died during the rainy part of that year. His end was
sudden. He had been selling and talking to his cronies in his hut-
shop till late at night; then he counted the cash, came into the house,
consumed his rice and buttermilk, laid himself down to sleep, and
never woke again.

My mother adjusted herself to the status of a widow. My father
left her enough to live on comfortably. I gave her as much of my
time as possible. With her consent, I closed down my father's shop
and set up at the railway station. It was then that I began to develop
new lines. I stocked old magazines and newspapers, and bought
and sold schoolbooks. Of course my customers were not many, but
the train brought in more and more school-going population, and
the 10.30 local was full of young men going off to Albert Mission
College, which had just been started at Malgudi. I liked to talk to
people. I liked to hear people talk. I liked customers who would
not open their mouths merely to put a plantain in, and would say
something on any subject other than the state of crops, price of
commodities, and litigation. I am afraid, after my father's death,
his old friends wilted away and disappeared one by one, chiefly for
want of an audience.

Students gathered at my shop while they waited for the trains.
Gradually books appeared where there were coconuts before.
People dumped old books and stolen books and all kinds of printed
stuff on me. I bargained hard, showed indifference while buying and
solicitude while selling. Strictly speaking, it was an irregular thing

to do. But the station master was a friendly man who not only obtained unlimited credit for anything he and his children took from my shop, but also enjoyed the privilege of drawing his reading material from the stack growing in front of my shop.

My bookselling business was an unexpected offshoot of my search for old wrapping-paper. When people bought something I hated to see them carry it off in their hands. I liked to wrap it up nicely, as well as I could, but as long as my father was in control he said, 'If anyone brings a piece of paper, he is welcome to wrap up anything; but I can't do it for him. Profit being what it is, we can't afford to spend it on wrapping-paper. If a man buys oil, let him bring a pot to carry it in. Do we provide him with that?' While he practised this philosophy it was impossible for anyone to find even a scrap of paper in our shop. After his death I adopted a new policy. I made it known far and wide that I was looking for old paper and books, and soon gathered a big dump. In my off-hours I sat sorting it out. During the interval between trains, when the platform became quiet, there was nothing more pleasing than picking up a bundle of assorted books and lounging in my seat and reading, occasionally breaking off to watch through the doorway the immense tamarind tree in the field. I read stuff that interested me, bored me, baffled me, and dozed off in my seat. I read stuff that pricked up a noble thought, a philosophy that appealed, I gazed on pictures of old temples and ruins and new buildings and battleships, and soldiers, and pretty girls around whom my thoughts lingered. I learned much from scrap.

The children were enchanted by the talk they had had in their class from Raju (even their master sat absorbed in open-mouthed wonder). They went home and described the wonders they had been told about. They were impatient to be back on the following evening and listen to more. Very soon the parents joined their children. They explained apologetically, 'Children come home rather late, you see, master, and are afraid to return home, especially crossing the river at night.'

'Excellent, excellent,' Raju said. 'I wanted to suggest it myself. I'm glad you have thought of it. There is no harm. In fact, you may also benefit by keeping your ears open. Keep your ears open and mouth shut, that'll take you far,' he said, hitting upon a brilliant aphorism.

A circle formed around him. They sat there looking on. The children sat there looking on. The master sat there looking on. The pillared hall was bright with the lanterns the villagers had brought with them. It looked like a place where a great assembly was about to begin. Raju felt like an actor who had come on the stage, and, while the audience waited, had no lines to utter or gestures to make. He said to the master, 'I think you may take the children away to their corner for their usual lessons; take one of the lamps with you.'

Even as he said it he could not help thinking how he was issuing an order about the boys who were not his, to the teacher who need not obey him, pointing to a lamp which again was not his. The teacher started to obey him, but the boys lingered on. He said, 'You must read your lessons first and then I will come and speak to you. Now I will first speak to your elders; what I say to them will not interest you.' And the children got up and went away with the teacher to a farther corner of the pillared hall.

Velan ventured to suggest, 'Give us a discourse, sir.' And as Raju listened without showing any emotion, but looking as if he were in deep contemplation, Velan added, 'So that we may have the benefit of your wisdom.' The others murmured a general approval.

Raju felt cornered. 'I have to play the part expected of me; there is no escape.' He racked his head secretly, wondering where to start. Could he speak about tourists' attractions in Malgudi, or should it be moral lessons? How once upon a time there was a so-and-so, so good or bad that when he came to do such-and-such a thing he felt so utterly lost that he prayed, and so on and so forth? He felt bored. The only subject on which he could speak with any authority now seemed to be jail life and its benefits, especially for one mistaken for a saint. They waited respectfully for his inspiration. 'Oh, fools,' he felt like crying out, 'why don't you leave me alone? If you bring me food, leave it there and leave me in peace, thank you.'

After a long, brooding silence, he brought out the following words: 'All things have to wait their hour.' Velan and his friends who were in the front row looked worried for a moment; they were deferential, no doubt, but they did not quite realize what he was driving at. After a further pause, he added grandiosely, 'I will speak to you, when another day comes.'

Someone asked, 'Why another day, sir?'

'Because it is so,' said Raju mysteriously. 'While you wait for the children to finish their lessons, I'd advise you to pass the hour brooding over all your speech and actions from morning till now.'

'What speech and actions?' someone asked, genuinely puzzled by the advice.

'Your own,' said Raju. 'Recollect and reflect upon every word you have uttered since daybreak—'

'I don't remember exactly . . .'

'Well, that is why I say reflect, recollect. When you don't remember your own words properly, how are you going to remember other people's words?' This quip amused his audience. There were bursts of subdued laughter. When the laughter subsided Raju said, 'I want you all to think independently, of your own accord, and not allow yourselves to be led about by the nose as if you were cattle.'

There were murmurs of polite disagreement over this advice. Velan asked, 'How can we do that, sir? We dig the land and mind the cattle—so far so good, but how can we think philosophies? Not our line, master. It is not possible. It is wise persons like your good self who should think for us.'

'And why do you ask us to recollect all that we have said since daybreak?'

Raju himself was not certain why he had advised that, and so he added, 'If you do it you will know why.' The essence of sainthood seemed to lie in one's ability to utter mystifying statements. 'Until you try, how can you know what you can or cannot do?' he asked. He was dragging those innocent men deeper and deeper into the bog of unclear thoughts.

'I can't remember what I said a few moments ago; so many other things come into one's head,' wailed one of his victims.

'Precisely. That is what I wish to see you get over,' said Raju. 'Until you do it, you will not know the pleasure of it.' He picked out three men from the gathering. 'When you come to me tomorrow or another day, you must each repeat to me at least six words that you have been speaking since the morning. I am asking you to remember only six words,' he said pleadingly as a man who was making a great concession, 'not six hundred.'

'Six hundred! Is there anyone who can remember six hundred, sir?' asked someone with wonder.

'Well, I can,' said Raju. And he got the appreciative clicking of tongues which he expected as his legitimate due. Soon the children were there, a great boon to Raju, who rose from his seat as if to say, 'That is all for the day,' and walked towards the river, the others following. 'These children must be feeling sleepy. Take them safely home, and come again.'

When the assembly met next, he provided it with a specific programme. He beat a soft rhythm with his hands and chanted a holy song with a refrain that could be repeated by his audience. The ancient ceiling echoed with the voices of men, women, and children repeating sacred texts in unison. Someone had brought in tall bronze lamps and lit them. Others fed them with oil; others had spent a whole day twisting bits of cotton into wicks for the lamps. People brought of their own accord little framed pictures of gods and hung them on the pillars. Very soon women started to come in batches during the day to wash the floor and decorate it with patterns in coloured flour; they hung up flowers and greenery and festoons everywhere. The pillared hall was transformed. Someone had also covered the platform in the middle of the hall with a soft, coloured carpet; mats were rolled out for the assembly to sit on.

Raju soon realized that his spiritual status would be enhanced if he grew a beard and long hair to fall on his nape. A clean-shaven, close-haired saint was an anomaly. He bore the various stages of his make-up with fortitude, not minding the prickly phase he had to pass through before a well-authenticated beard could cover his face and come down to his chest. By the time he arrived at the stage of stroking his beard thoughtfully, his prestige had grown beyond his wildest dreams. His life had lost its personal limitations; his gatherings had become so large that they overflowed into the outer corridors and people sat right up to the river's edge.

With the exception of Velan and a few others, Raju never bothered to remember faces or names or even to know to whom he was talking. He seemed to belong to the world now. His influence was unlimited. He not only chanted holy verses and discoursed on philosophy, he even came to the stage of prescribing medicine; children who would not sleep peacefully at night were brought to him by their mothers; he pressed their bellies and prescribed a herb, adding, 'If he still gets no relief, bring him again to me.' It was believed that when he stroked the head of a child, the child improved in various ways. Of course, people brought him their disputes and quarrels over the division of ancestral property. He had to set apart several hours of his afternoon for these activities. He could hardly afford a private life now. There came a stage when he had to be up early and rush through all his own personal routine before his visitors should arrive. It was a strain. He sighed a deep sigh of relief and longed to be himself, eat like an ordinary human being, shout and sleep like a normal man, after the voices on the river had ceased for the night.

5

I CAME TO be called Railway Raju. Perfect strangers, having heard of my name, began to ask for me when their train arrived at the Malgudi railway station. It is written on the brow of some that they shall not be left alone. I am one such, I think. Although I never looked for acquaintances, they somehow came looking for me. Men who had just arrived always stopped at my shop for a soda or cigarettes and to go through the book stack, and almost always they asked, 'How far is . . .?' or 'Are there many historical spots here?' or 'I heard that your River Sarayu has its source somewhere on those hills and that it is a beauty spot.' This sort of inquiry soon led me to think that I had not given sufficient thought to the subject. I never said, 'I don't know.' Not in my nature, I suppose. If I had had the inclination to say, 'I don't know what you are talking about,' my life would have taken a different turn. Instead, I said, 'Oh, yes, a fascinating place. Haven't you seen it? You must find the time to visit it, otherwise your whole trip here would be a waste.' I am sorry I said it, an utter piece of falsehood. It was not because I wanted to utter a falsehood, but only because I wanted to be pleasant.

Naturally, they asked me the way. I said, 'If you just go that way down to the Market Square and ask one of those taxi-drivers This was not a very satisfactory direction. Soon a man wanted me to show him the way to the Market Square and the taxi. There was a young son of the porter doing points-signalling duty whenever a train was about to arrive, who had no specified work to do at other times. I asked the young fellow to mind the shop while I helped the traveller to find a taxi.

At the market fountain stood the old shark Gaffur, looking for a victim. He made a speciality of collecting all the derelict vehicles in the country and rigging them up; he breathed new life into them and ran them on the mountain roads and into the forests. His usual seat was on the parapet of the fountain, while his car basked on the roadside beside the gutter. 'Gaffur,' I called out. 'Here is a very good gentleman, a friend of mine. He wants to see . . . You must take him out and bring him back safely—that is why I have brought him to you personally, although this is not an hour when I should be away from my shop.' We haggled over the prices; I allowed the customer to mention his figure and always tried to beat Gaffur down to it. When he demurred at the sight of the vehicle, I took up Gaffur's brief and explained, 'Gaffur is no fool to have this kind of car. He searched far and wide to find this particular model; this is the only car which can go up to all those places where in some parts there are no roads at all, but Gaffur will take you there and bring you back in time for dinner tonight. Can't you, Gaffur?'

'Well,' he drawled, 'it is seventy miles each way; it is one o'clock now. If we leave at once and if there are no punctures on the way . . .' But I hustled him so much that Gaffur never really completed his sentence. When they returned it could not exactly be called dinner-time, unless you stretched it to include midnight, but Gaffur did bring him back intact, honked his car to wake me up, took his cash, and departed. The next train for the man would be at eight on the following morning. He had to stretch himself under the awning on the platform of my shop and spend the night thus. If he felt hungry, I opened my store and sold him fruits and such things.

Travellers are an enthusiastic lot. They do not mind any inconvenience as long as they have something to see. Why anyone should want to forgo food and comfort and jolt a hundred-odd miles to see some place, I could never understand, but it was not my business to ask for reasons; just as I did not mind what people ate or smoked in my shop, my business being only to provide the supply and nothing more. It seemed to me silly to go a hundred miles to see the source of the Sarayu when it had taken the trouble to tumble down the mountain and come to our door. I had not even heard of its source till that moment; but the man who had gone was all praise for the spot. He said, 'I am only sorry I did not bring my wife and mother to see the place.' Later in life I found that everyone who saw an interesting spot always regretted that he hadn't come with his wife or daughter, and spoke as if he had cheated someone out of a nice thing in life. Later, when I had become a full-blown tourist guide, I often succeeded in inducing a sort of melancholia in my customer by remarking, 'This is something that should be enjoyed by the whole family,' and the man would swear that he would be back with his entire brood in the coming season.

The man who had gone to the source of the river spoke all night about it: how there was a small shrine on the peak right at the basin. 'It must be the source of the Sarayu mentioned in the mythological stories of goddess Parvathi jumping into the fire; the carving on one of the pillars of the shrine actually shows the goddess plunging into the fire and water arising from the spot,' et cetera. Sometimes someone with a scholarly turn of mind would come and make a few additions to the facts, such as that the dome of the shrine must have been built in the third century before Christ or that the style of drapery indicated the third century after Christ. Rut it was all the same to me, and the age I ascribed to any particular place depended upon my mood at that hour and the type of person I was escorting. If he was the academic type I was careful to avoid all mention of facts and figures and to confine myself to general descriptions, letting the man himself do the talking. You may be sure he enjoyed the opportunity. On the other hand, if an innocent man happened to be at hand, I let myself go freely. I pointed out to him something as the greatest, the highest, the only one in the world. I gave statistics out of my head. I mentioned a relic as belonging to the thirteenth century before Christ or the thirteenth century after Christ, according to the mood of the hour. If I felt fatigued or bored with the person I was conducting. I sometimes knocked the whole glamour out by saying, 'Must be something built within the last twenty years and allowed to go to rack and ruin. There are scores of such spots all over the place.' Hut it was years before I could arrive at that stage of confidence and nonchalance.

The porter's son sat in the shop all day. I spent a little time each night to check the cash and stock. There was no definite arrangement about what he should be paid for his trouble. I gave him a little money now and then. Only my mother protested. 'Why do you want him to work for you, Raju? Either give him a definite commission or do it yourself instead of all this wandering in the country. What good does it do you, anyway?'

'You don't know, Mother,' I said, eating my late dinner. 'This is a far better job I am doing than the other one. I am seeing a lot of places and getting paid for it; I go with them in their car or bus, talk to them, I am treated to their food sometimes, and I get paid for it. Do you know how well known I am? People come asking for me from Bombay, Madras, and other places, hundreds of miles away. They call me Railway Raju and have told me that even in Lucknow there are persons who are familiar with my name. It is something to become so famous, isn't it, instead of handing out matches and tobacco?'

'Well, wasn't it good enough for your father?'

'I don't say anything against it. I will look after the shop also.'

This pleased the old lady. Occasionally she threw in a word about her brother's daughter in the village before blowing out the lamp. She was always hoping that some day I would consent to marry the girl, though she never directly said so. 'Do you know Lalitha has got a prize in her school? I had a letter from my brother today about it.'

Even as the train steamed in at the outer signal, I could scent a customer. I had a kind of water-diviner's instinct. If I felt the pull of good business I drifted in the direction of the coming train; I could stand exactly where a prospective tourist would alight and look for me: it was not only the camera or binoculars slung on a shoulder that indicated to me the presence of a customer; even without any of that I could spot him. If you found me straying away in the direction of the barrier while the engine was still running through the lines onto the platform you might be sure that there was no customer for me on the train. In a few months I was a seasoned guide. I had viewed myself as an amateur guide and a professional shopman, but now gradually I began to think of myself as a part-time shopkeeper and a full-time tourist guide. Even when I had no tourist to guide I did not go back to my shop, but to Gaffur on the fountain parapet, and listened to his talk about derelict automobiles.

I had classified all my patrons. They were very varied, I can tell you. Some were passionate photographers; these men could never look at any object except through their viewfinders. The moment they got down from the train, even before lifting their baggage, they asked, 'Is there a place where they develop films?'

'Of course, Malgudi Photo Bureau. One of the biggest . . .'

'And if I want roll-films? I have, of course, enough stock with me, but if I run out . . . Do you think super-panchro three-colour something-or-other is available there?'

'Of course. That's his special line.'

'Will he develop and show me a print while I wait?'

'Of course, before you count twenty. He is a wizard.'

'That is nice. Now, where are you going to take me first?'

These were routine questions from a routine type. I had all the satisfactory answers ready. I generally took time to answer the latter question as to where I was going to take him first. It depended. I awaited the receipt of certain data before venturing to answer. The data were how much time and money he was going to spend. Malgudi and its surroundings were my special show. I could let a man have a peep at it or a whole panorama. It was adjustable. I could give them a glimpse of a few hours or soak them in mountain and river scenery or archaeology for a whole week. I could not really decide how much to give or withhold until I knew how much cash the man carried or, if he carried a cheque-book, how good it was. This was another delicate point. Sometimes a traveller offered to write a cheque for this man or that, and, of course, our Gaffur or the photo store or the keeper of the forest bungalow on top of Mempi Hills would not trust a stranger enough to accept his cheque. I had to put off such an offer with the utmost delicacy by saying, 'Oh, the banking system in our town is probably the worst you can think of. Sometimes they take twenty days to realize a cheque, but these poor fellows, how can they wait?'—rather a startling thing to say, but I didn't care if the banking reputation of our town suffered.

As soon as a tourist arrived, I observed how he dealt with his baggage, whether he engaged a porter at all or preferred to hook a finger to each piece. I had to note all this within a split second, and then, outside, whether he walked to the hotel or called a taxi or haggled with the one-horse *jutka*. Of course, I undertook all this on his behalf, but always with detachment. I did all this for him simply for the reason that he asked for Railway Raju the moment he stepped down on the platform and I knew he came with good references, whether he came from north or south or far or near. And at the hotel it was my business to provide him with the best room or the worst room, just' as he might prefer. Those who took the cheapest dormitory said, 'After all, it's only for sleeping, I am going to be out the whole day. Why waste money on a room which is anyway going to be locked up all day? Don't you agree?'

'Surely, yes, yes,' I nodded, still without giving an answer to 'Where are you going to take me first?' I might still be said to be keeping the man under probation, under careful scrutiny. I never made any suggestion yet. No use expecting a man to be clearheaded who is fresh from a train journey. He must wash, change his clothes, refresh himself with *idli* and coffee, and only then can we expect anyone in south India to think clearly on all matters of this world and the next. If he offered me any refreshment, I understood that he was a comparatively liberal sort, but did not accept it until we were a little further gone in friendship. In due course, I asked him point blank, 'How much time do you hope to spend in this town?'

'Three days at the most. Could we manage everything within the time?'

'Certainly, although it all depends upon what you most wish to see.' And then I put him in the confessional, so to speak. I tried to draw out his interests. Malgudi, I said, had many things to offer, historically, scenically, from the point of view of modern developments, and so on and so forth; or if one came as a pilgrim I could take him to a dozen temples all over the district within a radius of fifty miles; I could find holy waters for him to bathe in all along the course of the Sarayu, starting, of course, with its source on Mempi Peaks.

One thing I learned in my career as a tourist guide was that no two persons were interested in the same thing. Tastes, as in food, differ also in sightseeing. Some people want to be seeing a waterfall, some want a ruin (oh, they grow ecstatic when they see cracked plaster, broken idols, and crumbling bricks), some want a god to worship, some look for a hydro-electric plant, and some want just a nice place, such as the bungalow on top of Mempi with all-glass sides, from where you could see a hundred miles and observe wild game prowling around. Of those again there were two types, one the poet who was content to watch and return, and the other who wanted to admire nature and also get drunk there. I don't know why it is so: a fine poetic spot like the Mempi Peak House excites in certain natures unexpected reactions. I know some who brought women there; a quiet, wooded spot looking over a valley one would think fit for contemplation or poetry, but it only acted as an aphrodisiac. Well, it was not my business to comment. My business stopped with taking them there, and to see that Gaffur went back to pick them up at the right time.

I was sort of scared of the man who acted as my examiner, who had a complete list of all the sights and insisted on his money's worth. 'What is the population of this town?' 'What is the area?' 'Don't bluff. I know when exactly that was built—it is not second-century but the twelfth.' Or he told me the correct pronunciation of words. 'R-o-u-t is not . . .' I was meek, self-effacing in his presence and accepted his corrections with gratitude, and he always ended up by asking, 'What is the use of your calling yourself a guide if you do not know . . . ?' et cetera, et cetera.

You may well ask what I made out of all this? Well, there is no fixed answer to it. It depended upon the circumstances and the types of people I was escorting. I generally specified ten rupees as the minimum for the pleasure of my company, and a little more if I had to escort them far; over all this Gaffur, the photo store, the hotel manager, and whoever I introduced a customer to expressed their appreciation, according to a certain schedule. I learned while I taught and earned while I learned, and the whole thing was most enjoyable.

There were special occasions, such as the trapping of an elephant herd. During the winter months the men of the Forest Department put through an elaborate scheme for trapping elephants. They watched, encircled, and drove a whole herd into stockades, and people turned up in great numbers to watch the operation. On the day fixed for the drive, people poured in from all over the country and applied to me for a ringside seat in the spacious bamboo jungles of Mempi. I was supposed to have special influence with the men who were in charge of the drive: it meant several advance trips to the forest camp, and doing little services for the officials by fetching whatever they required from the town, and when the time came to arrange for the viewing of the elephant-drive only those who came with me were allowed to pass through the gates of the special enclosures. It kept all of us happy and busy and well-paid. I escorted visitors in bunches and went hoarse repeating, 'You see, the wild herd is watched for months . . .' and so forth. Don't imagine that I cared for elephants personally; anything that interested my tourists was also my interest. The question of my own preferences was secondary. If someone wanted to see a tiger or shoot one, I knew where to arrange it: I arranged for the lamb to bait the tiger, and had high platforms built so that the brave hunters might pop off the poor beast when it came to eat the lamb, although I never liked to see either the lamb or the tiger die. If someone wanted to see a king cobra spread out its immense hood, I knew the man who could provide the show.

There was a girl who had come all the way from Madras and who asked the moment she set foot in Malgudi, 'Can you show me a cobra—a king cobra it must be—which can dance to the music of a flute?'

'Why?' I asked.

'I'd like to see one. That's all,' she said.

Her husband said, 'We have other things to think of, Rosie. This can wait.'

'I'm not asking this gentleman to produce it at once. I am not demanding it. I'm just mentioning it, that's all.'

'If it interests you, you can make your own arrangements. Don't expect me to go with you. I can't stand the sight of a snake; your interests are morbid.'

I disliked this man. He was taunting such a divine creature. My sympathies were all for the girl; she was so lovely and elegant. After she arrived I discarded my khaki bush-coat and *dhoti* and took the trouble to make myself presentable. I wore a silk *jibba* and lace *dhoti* and groomed myself so well that my mother remarked when she saw me leave the house, 'Ah, like a bridegroom!' and Gaffur winked and said many an insinuating thing when I went to meet them at the hotel.

Her arrival had been a sort of surprise for me. The man was the first to appeal. I had put him up at the Anand Bhavan Hotel. After a day of sightseeing he suddenly said one afternoon, 'I must meet the Madras train. Another person is coming.'

He didn't even stop to ask me what time the train would arrive. He seemed to know everything beforehand. He was a very strange man, who did not always care to explain what he was doing. If he had warned me that he was going to meet such an elegant creature at our station I should perhaps have decorated myself appropriately. As it was, I wore my usual khaki bush-coat and *dhoti*, a horrible unprepossessing combination at any time, but the most sensible and convenient for my type of work. The moment she got down from the train I wished I had hidden myself somewhere. She was not very glamorous, if that is what you expect, but she did have a figure, a slight and slender one, beautifully fashioned, eyes that sparkled, a complexion not white, but dusky, which made her only half visible—as if you saw her through a film of tender coconut juice. Forgive me if you find me waxing poetic. I gave some excuse and sent them off to the hotel, and stayed back to run home and tidy up my appearance.

I conducted a brief research with the help of Gaffur. He took me to a man in Ellaman Street, who had a cousin working in the municipal office said to know a charmer with a king cobra. I carried on the investigation while I left the visitor to decipher episodes from the *Ramayana* carved on the stone wall in Iswara Temple in North Extension—there were hundreds of minute carvings all along the wall. They kept the man fully occupied as he stooped and tried to study each bit. I knew all those panels and could repeat their order blindfolded, but he spared me the labour, he knew all about it.

When I returned from my brief investigation, I found the girl standing apart with every sign of boredom in her face. I suggested, 'If you can come out for an hour, I can show you a cobra.'

She looked delighted. She tapped the man on the shoulder as he was stooping over the frieze and asked, 'How long do you want to be here?'

'At least two hours,' he said without turning.

'I'll go out for a while,' she said.

'Please yourself,' he said. Then to me, 'Go to the hotel direct. I'll find my way back.'

We picked up our guide at the municipal office. The car rolled along the sand, crossed the stretch at Nallappa's Grove, and climbed the opposite bank, the entire route carved by the wheels of wooden bullock-carts. Gaffur looked sourly at the man sitting by his side. 'Do you want me to reduce this to a bullock cart, dragging us about these places? Where are we going? I see no other place than the cremation ground there,' he said, pointing at the smoke above a forlorn, walled area on the other side of the river. I didn't like such inauspicious words to be uttered before the angel in the back seat. I tried to cover them up hastily by saying something else aloud.

We arrived at a group of huts on the other side of the river. Many heads peeped out of the huts as soon as our car stopped, and a few bare-bodied children came and stood around the car, gaping at the occupants. Our guide jumped out and went at a trot to the

farthest end of the village street and returned with a man who had
a red turban around his head, his only other piece of clothing being
a pair of drawers.

'This man has a king cobra?' I looked him up and down and
said hesitantly, 'Let me see it.'

At which the young boys said, 'He has a very big one in his
house; it is true.' And I asked the lady, 'Shall we go and see it?'

We set off. Gaffur said, 'I'll stay here, otherwise these monkeys
will make short work of this automobile.'

I let the other two go forward and whispered to Gaffur, 'Why
are you in such a bad mood today, Gaffur? After all, you have gone
over worse roads and never complained!'

'I have new springs and shock-absorbers. You know what they
cost?'

'Oh, you will recover their cost soon; be cheerful.'

'What some of our passengers need is a tractor and not a motor
car. That fellow!' He was vaguely discontented. I knew his wrath
was not against us, but against our guide, because he said, 'I think
it will be good to make him walk back to the town. Why should
anyone want to come so far to see a reptile?' I left him alone; it was
no use trying to make him cheerful. Perhaps his wife had nagged
him when he started out.

The girl stood under the shade of a tree while the man prodded
a snake to make it come out of its basket. It was fairly large, and
hissed and spread out its hood, while the boys screamed and ran
off and returned. The man shouted at them, 'If you excite it, it will
chase you all!'

I told the boys to keep quiet, and asked the man, 'You are sure
you will not let it slip through?'

The girl suggested, 'You must play on the flute, make it rear its
head and dance.' The man pulled out his gourd flute and played on
it shrilly, and the cobra raised itself and darted hither and thither
and swayed. The whole thing repelled me, but it seemed to fascinate
the girl. She watched it swaying with the raptest attention. She
stretched out her arm slightly and swayed it in imitation of the
movement; she swayed her whole body to the rhythm—for just a
second, but that was sufficient to tell me what she was, the greatest
dancer of the century.

It was nearly seven in the evening when we got back to the
hotel. As soon as she got down, she paused to murmur a 'Thanks'

to no one in particular and went up the staircase. Her husband, waiting at the porch, said, 'That's all for the day. You could give me a consolidated account, I suppose, later. I shall want the car at ten o'clock tomorrow.' He turned and went back to his room.

I felt annoyed with him at this stage. What did he take me for? This fellow, telling me that he wanted the car at this hour or that hour. Did he think that I was a tout? It made me very angry, but the fact was that I really was a tout, having no better business than hanging around between Gaffur and a snake-charmer and a tourist and doing all kinds of things. The man did not even care to tell me anything about himself, or where he wanted to go on the following morning; an extraordinary fellow!

A hateful fellow. I had never hated any customer so much before. I told Gaffur as we were driving back, 'Tomorrow morning! He asks for the car as if it were his grandfather's property! Any idea where he wants to go?'

'Why should I bother about it? If he wants the car he can have it if he pays for it. That is all. I don't care who pays for a thing as long as they engage me . . .' He rambled on into a personal philosophy which I didn't care to follow.

My mother waited for me as usual. While serving me food she said, 'Where have you been today? What are the things you have done today?'

I told her about the visit to the snake-charmer. She said, 'They are probably from Burma, people who worship snakes.' She said, 'I had a cousin living in Burma once and he told me about the snake women there.'

'Don't talk nonsense, Mother. She is a good girl, not a snake-worshipper. She is a dancer, I think.'

'Oh, dancer! Maybe, but don't have anything to do with these dancing women. They are all a bad sort.' I ate my food in silence, trying to revive in my mind the girl's scent-filled presence.

At ten next day I was at the hotel. Gaffur's car was already at the porch; he cried, 'Aha! again,' at the sight of me. 'Big man! Hm, trying improvements!' His idiom was still as if he spoke of automobiles. He winked at me.

I ignored everything and asked in a businesslike manner, 'Are they in?'

'I suppose so. They have not come out yet, that's all I know,' said Gaffur. Twenty words where one would do. Something was wrong with him. He was becoming loquacious. And then I felt a sudden stab of jealousy as I realized that perhaps he too had been affected by the presence of the damsel and was desirous of showing off in her presence. I grew jealous and unhappy and said to myself, 'If this is how Gaffur is going to conduct himself in the future, I shall get rid of him and find someone else, that's all.' I had no use for a loquacious, nosepoking taxi-driver.

I went upstairs to Room 28 on the second floor of the hotel and knocked authoritatively. 'Wait,' said the voice from inside. It was the man's, not the girl's as I had hoped. I waited for a few minutes and fretted. I looked at my watch. Ten o'clock. And this man said, 'Wait.' Was he still in bed with her? It was a fit occasion, as it seemed to me, to tear the door down and go in. The door opened, and he came out, dressed and ready. He shut the door behind him. I was aghast. I was on the point of demanding, 'What about her?' But I checked my impulse. I went sheepishly down with him.

He gave me a look of approval, as if I had dressed to please *him*. Before getting into the car he said, 'Today I want to study those friezes again for a short while.'

'All right, all right,' I thought, 'study the friezes or whatever else you like. Why do you want me for that?' As if in answer to my thoughts, he said, 'After that—' He took out of his pocket a piece of paper and read.

This man would go on wall-gazing all his life and leave her to languish in her hotel room. Strange man! Why did he not bring her along with him? Probably he was absentminded. I asked, 'Is no one else coming?'

'No,' he replied curtly, as if understanding my mind. He looked at the paper in his hand and asked, 'Are you aware of the existence of cave-paintings in these parts?'

I laughed off the question. 'Of course, everyone does not have the taste to visit places like that, but there have been a few discriminating visitors who insisted on seeing them. But—but—it will take a whole day, and we may not be able to get back tonight.'

He went back to his room, returned after a few minutes with a downcast face. Meanwhile I, with Gaffur's help, calculated the expense involved in the trip. We knew that the path lay past the Peak House forest bungalow. One would have to halt there for the night and walk down a couple of miles. I knew where the caves were, but this was the first time I was going to set eyes on them.

Malgudi seemed to unroll a new sightseeing place each time.

The man sat back in the car and said, 'You have probably no notion how to deal with women, have you?'

I was pleased that he was becoming more human in his approach. I said, 'I have no idea,' and laughed, thinking it might please him if I seemed to enjoy his joke. Then I made bold to ask, 'What is the trouble?' My new dress and deportment gave me a new courage. In my khaki bush-coat I would not have dared to take a seat beside him or talk to him in this way.

He looked at me with what seemed a friendly smile. He leaned over and said, 'If a man has to have peace of mind it is best that he forget the fair sex.' This was the first time in our association of three days that he had talked to me so freely. He had always been curt and taciturn. I judged that the situation must be pretty grave if it loosened his tongue to this extent.

Gaffur sat in his seat with his chin in his hand. He was looking away from us. His whole attitude said, 'I am sorry to be wasting my morning with such time-killers as you two.' A courageous idea was developing in my head. If it succeeded it would lead to a triumphant end, if it failed the man might kick me out of his sight or call the police. I said, 'Shall I go and try on your behalf?'

'Would you?' he asked, brightening up. 'Go ahead, if you are bold enough.'

I didn't wait to hear further. I jumped out of the car and went up the steps four at a time. I paused at Number 28 to regain normal breath, and knocked.

'Don't trouble me, I don't want to come with you. Leave me alone,' came the girl's voice from within.

I hesitated, wondering how to speak. This was my first independent speech with the divine creature. I might either make a fool of myself or win the heavens. How should I announce myself? Would she know my famous name? I said, 'It's not he, but me.'

'What?' asked the sweet voice, puzzled and irritated.

I repeated, 'It is not him, but me. Don't you know my voice? Didn't I come with you yesterday to that cobra man? All night I didn't sleep,' I added, lowering my voice, and whispered through a chink in the door, 'The way you danced, your form and figure haunted me all night.'

Hardly had I finished my sentence when the door half opened

and she looked at me. 'Oh, you!' she said, her eyes lighting up with understanding.

'My name is Raju,' I said.

She scrutinized me thoroughly. 'Of course, I know you.' I smiled affably, my best smile, as if I had been asked for it by a photographer. She said, 'Where is he?'

'Waiting in the car for you. Won't you get ready and come out?' She looked dishevelled, her eyes were red with recent tears, and she wore a faded cotton saree; no paint or perfume, but I was prepared to accept her as she was. I told her, 'You may come out as you are and no one will mind it.' And I added, 'Who would decorate a rainbow?'

She said, 'You think you can please me by all this? You think you can persuade me to change my mind?'

'Yes,' I said. 'Why not?'

'Why do you want me to go out with him? Leave me in peace,' she said, opening her eyes wide, which gave me another opportunity to whisper close to her face, 'Because life is so blank without your presence.'

She could have pushed my face back, crying, 'How dare you talk like this!' and shut the door on me. But she didn't. She merely said, 'I never knew you would be such a troublesome man. Wait a minute, then.' She withdrew into her room. I wanted to cry with all my being, 'Let me in,' and bang on the door, but I had the good sense to restrain myself. I heard footsteps and saw that her husband had come to see the results.

'Well, is she coming or not? I am not prepared to waste all—'

'Hush,' I said. 'She will be out in a moment. Please go back to the car.'

'Really!' he muttered in amazement. 'You are a wizard!' He noiselessly turned and went back to his car. Presently the lady did come out like a vision, and said, 'Let us go. But for you I would have given you all a few surprises.'

'What?'

'I would have taken the next train home.'

'We are going to a wonderful spot. Please be your usual sweet self, for my sake.'

'All right,' she said and went down the steps; I followed. She opened the door of the car, went straight in, and took her seat, as her husband edged away to make space for her. I came over to the other side and sat down beside him. I was not prepared to go and sit down beside Gaffur at this stage.

Gaffur now turned his head to ask whether we might go. 'We cannot return tonight if we are going to the Peak House.'

'Let us try and come back,' the man pleaded.

'We will try, but there is no harm in being prepared to stay over if necessary. Take a change of clothing. No harm in it. I am asking Gaffur to stop at my house.'

The lady said, 'Just a minute, please.' She dashed upstairs and returned with a small suitcase. She said to the man, 'I have your clothes too in this.'

The man said, 'Very good,' and smiled, and she smiled and in the laughter the tension of the morning partly disappeared. Still, there was some uneasiness in the air.

I asked Gaffur to pull up at the railway station for a moment, the car facing away from my house. I didn't want them to see my house. 'Just a moment, please.' I dashed out. Directly the shop-boy sighted me he opened his mouth to say something. I ignored him, dashed up to my house, picked up a bag, and ran out, saying, 'I may stay out tonight. Don't wait,' to my mother in the kitchen.

We reached the Peak House at about four in the afternoon. The caretaker was delighted to see us. He was often rewarded by me unstintingly with my clients' money. I always made it a point to tell my clients beforehand, 'Keep that caretaker in good humour and he'll look after you and procure for you even the most impossible articles.' I repeated the formula now and the husband—he shall be referred to as Marco henceforth—said, 'Go ahead and do it. I look to you to help us through. You know I have only one principle in life. I don't want to be bothered with small things. I don't mind the expense.'

I told Joseph, the caretaker, to get us food and foodstuffs from his village, two miles away. I asked Marco, 'Will you leave some cash with me? I'll render accounts later. I need not worry you again and again for small payments.'

One could not foresee how he would react to such a request. He was unsteady—sometimes he announced aloud his indifference to money, the next minute he'd suddenly show every symptom of miserliness and behave like an auditor, but ultimately he'd pay for everything if, as I discovered, he got a voucher for payments. He would not yield an anna without a voucher, whereas if you gave him a slip of paper you could probably get him to write off his entire fortune.

Now I knew the trick. As I found him stumbling for words, I said, 'I'll see that you get proper receipts for every payment.' It pleased him; he opened his purse.

I had to dispose of the taxi. Gaffur would come back on the following afternoon. I made Gaffur sign a receipt, and gave some money to Joseph to fetch us food from a hotel in the village. Now that I was in charge of the arrangements, I had not much time to gaze on my beloved's face, although I was darting glances in her direction.

'The caves are a mile off, down that way,' Joseph said. 'We can't go there now. Tomorrow morning. If you leave after breakfast, you can come back for lunch.'

The Peak House was perched on the topmost cliff on Mempi Hills—the road ended with the house; there was a glass wall covering the north veranda, through which you could view the horizon a hundred miles away. Below us the jungle stretched away down to the valley, and on a clear day you might see also the Sarayu sparkling in the sun and pursuing its own course far away. This was like heaven to those who loved wild surroundings and to watch the game, which prowled outside the glass wall at nights. The girl was in ecstasy. Our house was surrounded with rich vegetation. She ran like a child from plant to plant with cries of joy, while the man looked on with no emotion. Anything that interested her seemed to irritate him.

She suddenly halted, gazing on the sun-bathed plains thousands of feet below. I feared that when night came on she might get scared. We heard the jackals howling, and all kinds of grunts and roars. Joseph brought a hamper of food for us and left it on a table. He brought milk, coffee, and sugar, for the morning, and showed me where the coal stove was.

The lady cried, 'Nobody should get up till I call. I'll have coffee ready for everyone.'

Joseph said, 'Please lock the door inside,' and added, 'if you sit up on that veranda, you can watch tigers and other animals prowling about. But you must not make any noise; that's the secret of it.' We watched Joseph pick up a lantern and go down the steps; we could see his lantern faintly light the foliage on the way and disappear.

'Poor Joseph, how bold of him to go down alone!' the girl said, at which the husband replied casually, 'Nothing surprising. He has probably been born and bred here. Do you know him?' he asked, turning to me.

'Yes; he was born in that village and came to mind this place as a boy. He must be at least sixty years old.'

'How has he come to be a Christian?'

'There was a mission somewhere here; missionaries go and settle down in all sorts of places, you know,' I said.

Joseph had given us two lamps, brass ones filled with kerosene. One I kept on the kitchen table, and the other I gave the man for his room, leaving the rest of the building in darkness. Outside through the glass we could see the stars in the sky. We sat around the table. I knew where the plates were. I set them on the table and served food—or, rather, attempted to serve food. It was about seven-thirty in the evening. We had seen a gorgeous sunset. We had seen the purple play of colour in the northern skies after that, and admired it; we saw the tops of the trees lit up by stray red rays even after the sun was out of view, and had found a common idiom to express our admiration.

The man just followed us about. I had become so lyrical that he suddenly said, 'Hey, Raju, so you are a poet too!' a compliment I accepted with becoming modesty.

At dinner, I picked up a dish and tried to serve. She said, 'No, no. Let me serve you both, and I will be the last to eat, like a good housewife.'

'Aha, that's a good idea,' the man said jocularly. She extended her hand for me to pass the dish to her. But I insisted on doing it myself. She suddenly darted forward and forcibly snatched it away from my hand. Oh, that touch made my head reel for a moment. I didn't see anything clearly. Everything disappeared into a sweet, dark haze, as under chloroform. My memory dwelt on the touch all through the dinner: I was not aware what we were eating or what they were saying. I sat with head bowed. I was nervous to see her face and meet her looks. I don't recollect when we finished eating and when she took away the dishes. I was only conscious of her soft movements. My thoughts dwelt on her golden touch. A part of my mind went an saying, 'No, no. It is not right. Marco is her husband, remember. It's not to be thought of.' But it was impossible to pull the thoughts back. 'He may shoot you,' said my wary conscience.

'Has he a gun?' commented another part of my mind.

After dinner she said, 'Let us go to the glass veranda. I must watch the game. Do you think they will come out at this hour?'

'Yes; if we are patient and lucky,' I said. 'But won't you be afraid? One has to wait in the dark.'

She laughed at my fears and invited Marco to go with her. But he said he wanted to be left alone. He pulled a chair to the lamp, took out his portfolio, and was soon lost in his papers. She said, 'Shield your lamp. I don't want my animals to be scared off.' She moved with light steps to the veranda, pulled up a chair, and sat down. On the way she had said to me, 'Have *you* documents to see to?'

'No, no,' I said, hesitating midway between my room and hers.

'Come along, then. Surely you aren't going to leave me to the mercy of prowling beasts?' I looked at the man to know what he would have to say, but he was absorbed in his papers. I asked, 'Do you want anything?'

'No.'

'I'll be on the veranda.'

'Go ahead,' he said without looking up from his papers.

She sat close to the glass pane, intently looking out. I softly placed a chair beside her, and sat down. After a while she said, 'Not a soul. Do animals come here at all, I wonder, or is it one of the usual stories?'

'No, lots of people have seen them—'

'What animals?'

'Lions . . .'

'Lions here?' she said and began laughing. 'I have read they were only in Africa. But this is really—'

'No, excuse me.' I had slipped. 'I meant tigers, and panthers, and bears, and sometimes elephants too are to be seen crossing the valley or coming for a drink of water at the pool.'

'I'm prepared to spend the whole night here,' she said. 'He will, of course, be glad to be left alone. Here at least we have silence and darkness, welcome things, and something to wait for out of that darkness.'

I couldn't find anything to say in reply. I was overwhelmed by her perfume. The stars beyond the glass shone in the sky.

'Can't an elephant break through the glass?' she asked, yawning.

'No; there is a moat on the other side. They can't approach us.'

Bright eyes shone amidst the foliage. She pulled my sleeve and whispered excitedly, 'Something—what can it be?'

'Probably a panther,' I said to keep up the conversation. Oh, the whispers, the stars, and the darkness—I began to breathe heavily with excitement.

'Have you caught a cold?' she asked.

I said, 'No.'

'Why are you breathing so noisily?'

I wanted to put my face close to her and whisper, 'Your dance was marvellous. You are gifted. Do it again sometime. God bless you. Won't you be my sweetheart?' But fortunately I restrained myself. Turning back, I saw that Marco had come with soft steps. 'What luck?' he asked in a whisper.

'Something came, but it's gone. Sit down, won't you?' I said, giving him the chair. He sat down, peering through the glass.

Next morning I found the atmosphere once again black and tense—all the vivacity of the previous evening was gone. When their room opened, only he came out, fully dressed and ready. I had made the coffee on the charcoal stove. He came over and mechanically held his hand out as if I were the man on the other side of a coffee bar. I poured him a cup of coffee. 'Joseph has brought tiffin. Will you not taste it?'

'No; let us be going. I'm keen on reaching the caves.'

'What about the lady?' I asked.

'Leave her alone,' he said petulantly. 'I can't afford to be fooling around, wasting my time.' In the same condition as yesterday! This seemed to be the spirit of their morning every day. How cordially he had come over and sat beside her last night on the veranda! How cordially they had gone into the hotel on that night! What exactly happened at night that made them want to tear at each other in the morning? Did they sit up in bed and fight, or did she fatigue him with a curtain lecture? I wanted to cry out, 'Oh, monster, what do you do to her that makes her sulk like this on rising? What a treasure you have in your hand, without realizing its worth—like a monkey picking up a rose garland!' Then a thrilling thought occurred to me—probably she was feigning anger again, so that I might intercede.

He put down his cup and said, 'Now let us go.' I was afraid to ask him again about his wife. He was swinging a small cane impatiently. Could it be that he had been using it on her at night?

Even in my wild state, I did not make the mistake of asking again, 'Shall I call her?' as that might have led to a very serious situation. I only asked, 'Does she know about coffee?'

'Yes, yes,' he cried impatiently. 'Leave it there; she'll take it. She has enough sense to look after herself.' He waved the switch, and we started out. Only once did I turn my head to look back, in the hope that she might appear at the window and call us back. 'Did I come all the way for this monster's company?' I asked myself as I followed him down the hill slope. How appropriate it would be if he should stumble and roll downhill! Bad thought, bad thought. He walked ahead of me. We were like a couple of African hunters—in fact, his dress, with his helmet and thick jacket, as I have already mentioned, was that of a wild African *shikari*.

Our path through grass and shrub led to the valley. The cave was halfway across it. I felt suddenly irritated at the speed of his walk, as if he knew the way, swinging his cane and hugging his portfolio. If he could show half the warmth of that hug elsewhere! I suddenly asked, 'Do you know the way?'

'Oh no,' he said.

'You are leading me!' I said, putting into it all the irony I was capable of.

He cried, 'Oh!', looked confused, and said, stepping aside, 'Well, lead us,' and through an irrelevant association added, 'kindly light.'

The entrance to the cave was beyond a thicket of lantana. A huge door on its rusty hinges stood open. And, of course, all the crumbling brick and plaster was there. It was a cave with a single rock covering its entire roof; why any man should have taken the trouble to build a thing like this in a remote spot was more than I could understand.

He stood outside and surveyed the entrance. 'You see, this entrance must have been a later improvisation; the cave itself, I know, must have been about first century AD. The entrance and the door are of a later date. You see, that kind of tall entrance and the carved doorway became a current fashion in the seventh or eighth century, when the South Indian rulers became fond of . . .' He went on talking. Dead and decaying things seemed to loosen his tongue and fire his imagination, rather than things that lived and moved and swung their limbs. I had little to do as a guide; he knew so much more of everything!

When he passed in, he completely forgot the world outside and its inhabitants. The roof was low, but every inch of the wall space was covered with painted figures. He flashed a torch on the walls. He took out of his pocket a mirror and placed it outside to catch the sunlight and throw a beam on the paintings. Bats were whirring about; the floor was broken and full of holes. But he minded nothing. He became busy measuring, writing down, photographing, all the time keeping up a chatter, not bothered in the least whether I listened or not.

I was bored with his ruin-collecting activities. The wall-painting represented episodes from the epics and mythology, and all kinds of patterns and motifs, with men, women, and kings and animals, in a curious perspective and proportion of their own, and ancient like the rocks. I had seen hundreds like them, and I saw no point in seeing more. I had no taste for them, just as he had no taste for other things.

'Be careful,' I said. 'There may be reptiles in those cracks.'

'Oh, no,' he said indifferently, 'reptiles don't generally come to such interesting places; moreover, I have this.' He flourished his stick. 'I can manage. I'm not afraid.'

I suddenly said, 'I seem to hear the sound of a car. If it's Gaffur, I'd like to be there at the bungalow, so do you mind if I go? I'll be back.'

He said, 'Keep him. Don't let him go away.'

'When you return, come the same way—so that we may not get lost.' He didn't answer, but resumed his studies.

I reached the house at a run and rested a while in the back yard to regain my breath. I went in, brushing back my hair with my hand and composing my features. As I entered, I heard her voice. 'Looking for me?' She was sitting on a boulder in the shade of a tree. She must have seen me come up. 'I saw you even half a mile away, but you couldn't see me,' she said like one who had discovered a fault.

'You were on the peak and I was in the valley,' I said. I went up to her and made some polite inquiries about her coffee. She looked both sad and profound. I sat down on a stone near her.

'You have returned alone. I suppose he is wall-gazing?' she said.

'Yes,' I replied briefly.

'He does that everywhere.'

'Well, I suppose he is interested, that's all.'

'What about me, interested in something else?'

'What is your interest?'

'Anything except cold, old stone walls,' she said.

I looked at my watch. I had already been away from him for nearly an hour. I was wasting time. Time was slipping through my fingers. If I were to make good, I should utilize this chance. 'Every night you generally sit up and quarrel, do you?' I asked boldly.

'When we are alone and start talking, we argue and quarrel over everything. We don't agree on most matters, and then he leaves me alone and comes back and we are all right, that's all.'

'Until it is night again,' I said.

'Yes, yes.'

'It's unthinkable that anyone should find it possible to quarrel or argue with you—being with you must be such bliss.'

She asked sharply, 'What do you mean?'

I explained myself plainly. I was prepared to ruin myself today if need be, but I was going to talk and tell her. If she wanted to kick me out, she could do it after listening to me. I spoke my mind. I praised her dancing. I spoke out my love, but sandwiched it conveniently between my appreciations of her art. I spoke of her as an artist in one breath, and continued in the next as a sweetheart. Something like, 'What a glorious snake dance! Oh, I keep thinking of you all night. World's artist number one! Don't you see how I am pining for you every hour!'

It worked. She said, 'You are a brother to me ('Oh, no,' I wanted to cry) and I'll tell you what happens.' She gave me an account of their daily quarrels.

'Why did you marry at all?' I asked recklessly.

She remained moody and said, 'I don't know. It just happened.'

'You married him because of his wealth,' I said, 'and you were advised by your uncle and the rest.'

'You see,' she began, plucking my sleeve. 'Can you guess to what class I belong?'

I looked her up and down and ventured, 'The finest, whatever it may be, and I don't believe in class or caste. You are an honour to your caste, whatever it may be.'

'I belong to a family traditionally dedicated to the temples as dancers; my mother, grandmother, and, before her, her mother. Even as a young girl I danced in our village temple. You know how our caste is viewed?'

'It's the noblest caste on earth,' I said.

'We are viewed as public women,' she said plainly, and I was thrilled to hear the words. 'We are not considered respectable; we are not considered civilized.'

'All that narrow notion may be true of old days, but it's different now. Things have changed. There is no caste or class today.'

'A different life was planned for me by my mother. She put me to school early in life; I studied well. I took my master's degree in economics. But after college, the question was whether I should become a dancer or do something else. One day I saw in our paper an advertisement—the usual kind you may have seen: "Wanted: an educated, good-looking girl to marry a rich bachelor of academic interests. *No caste restrictions*; good looks and university degree essential." I asked myself, "Have I looks?"'

'Oh, who could doubt it?'

'I had myself photographed clutching the scroll of the university citation in one hand, and sent it to the advertiser. Well, we met, he examined me and my certificate, we went to a registrar and got married.'

'Did you like him the moment you saw him?'

'Don't ask all that now,' she snubbed me. 'We had had many discussions before coming to a decision. The question was, whether it would be good to marry so much above our wealth and class. But all the women in my family were impressed, excited that a man like him was coming to marry one of our class, and it was decided that if it was necessary to give up our traditional art, it was worth the sacrifice. He had a big house, a motor car, he was a man of high social standing; he had a house outside Madras, he was living in it all alone, no family at all; he lived with his books and papers.'

'So you have no mother-in-law!' I said.

'I'd have preferred any kind of mother-in-law, if it had meant one real, live husband,' she said. I looked up at her to divine her meaning, but she lowered her eyes. I could only guess. She said, 'He is interested in painting and old art and things like that.'

'But not one which can move its limbs, I suppose,' I said.

I sighed deeply, overcome with the sadness of her life. I placed my hand on her shoulder and gently stroked it. 'I am really very unhappy to think of you, such a gem lost to the world. In his place I would have made you a queen of the world.' She didn't push away my hand. I let it travel and felt the softness of her ear and pushed my fingers through the locks of her hair.

Gaffur's car did not turn up. A passing truck-driver brought the message that it had had a breakdown and would be coming on the following day. No one in the party minded really. Joseph looked after us quite well. Marco said it gave him more time to study the walls. I did not mind. It gave me an occasion to watch the game beyond the sheet glass every night, holding her hand, while Marco sat in his room, poring over his notes.

When Gaffur's car did turn up Marco said, 'I want to stay on here; it is going to take more time than I thought. Could you fetch from my room in the hotel my black trunk? I have some papers in it. I'd prefer to have you here also, if it is all the same to you.'

I seemed to hesitate, and then looked up at the girl for a moment. There was a mute appeal in her eyes. I said yes.

'You may treat it as a part of your professional work,' he said, 'unless you feel it's going to hurt your general business.'

'All right,' I said, hesitantly. 'It's true, but I'd also like to be of service to you. Once I take charge of anyone, I always feel that they are my responsibility till I see them off again safely.'

As I was getting into the car she said to her husband, 'I'll also go back to the town; I want a few things from my box.'

I added, 'We may not be able to return tonight.'

He asked his wife, 'Can you manage?'

'Yes,' she said.

As we were going down the mountain road I often caught Gaffur, looking at us through the mirror, and we moved away from the range of his vision. We reached our hotel in the evening. I followed her to her room. 'Should we go back this evening?' I asked her.

'Why?' she asked. 'Suppose Gaffur's car stops on the way? Better not risk it on that road. I'll stay here tonight.'

I went home to change. My mother was full of information the moment she saw me, and full of inquiries. I brushed everything aside. I rushed through my washing and grooming and took out another set of special clothes. I gave my old clothes in a bundle to my mother. 'Will you tell that shop-boy to take them to the *dhobi* and have them washed and ironed neatly? I may want them tomorrow.'

'Becoming a dandy?' she said, surveying me. 'Why are you

always on the run now?' I gave her some excuse and started out again.

I engaged Gaffur for my own rounds that day. I was a true guide. Never had I shown anyone the town with greater zest. I took Rosie all over the place, showed her the town hall tower; showed her the Sarayu, and we sat on the sands and munched a large packet of salted nuts. She behaved like a baby—excited, thrilled, appreciative of everything. I took her through the Suburban Stores and told her to buy anything she liked. This was probably the first time that she was seeing the world. She was in ecstasies. Gaffur warned me when he got me alone for a moment outside the store, 'She is a married woman, remember.'

'What of it?' I said. 'Why do you tell me this?'

'Don't be angry, sir,' he said. 'Go slow; that is all I can say.'

'You are unhealthy-minded, Gaffur. She is like a sister to me,' I said, and tried to shut him up.

All he said was, 'You are right. What is it to me? After all, that man is here, who has really married her. And I've my own wife to bother about.'

I left him and went back to the store. She had picked up a silver brooch, painted over and patterned like a peacock. I paid for it and pinned it on her saree. We dined on the terrace of the Taj, from where she could have a view of the River Sarayu winding away. When I pointed it out to her she said, 'It's good. But I have had views of valleys, trees, and brooks to last me a lifetime.' We laughed. We were getting into a state of perpetual giggling.

She liked to loaf in the market, eat in a crowded hotel, wander about, see a cinema—these common pleasures seemed to have been beyond her reach all these days. I had dismissed the car at the cinema. I did not want Gaffur to watch my movements. We walked to the hotel after the picture. We had hardly noticed what it was. I had taken a box. She wore a light-yellow crêpe saree which made her so attractive that people kept looking at her.

Her eyes sparkled with vivacity and gratitude. I knew I had placed her in my debt.

It was nearing midnight. The man at the hotel desk watched us pass without showing any interest. Deskmen at hotels learn not to be inquisitive. At the door of Number 28 I hesitated. She opened the door, passed in, and hesitated, leaving the door half open. She stood looking at me for a moment, as on the first day.

'Shall I go away?' I asked in a whisper.

'Yes. Good night,' she said feebly.

'May I not come in?' I asked, trying to look my saddest.

'No, no. Go away,' she said. But on an impulse I gently pushed her out of the way, and stepped in and locked the door on the world.

6

RAJU LOST COUNT of the time that passed in these activities, one day being like another and always crowded. Several months (or perhaps years) had passed. He counted the seasons by the special points that jutted out, such as the harvest in January, when his disciples brought him sugar cane and jaggery cooked with rice; when they brought him sweets and fruits, he knew that the Tamil New Year was on; when Dussera came they brought in extra lamps and lit them, and the women were busy all through the nine days, decorating the pillared hall with coloured paper and tinsel; and for Deepavali they brought him new clothes and crackers and he invited the children to a special session and fired the crackers. He kept a rough count of time thus, from the beginning of the year to its end, through its seasons of sun, rain, and mist. He kept count of three cycles and then lost count. He realized that it was unnecessary to maintain a calendar.

His beard now caressed his chest, his hair covered his back, and around his neck he wore a necklace of prayer-beads. His eyes shone with softness and compassion, the light of wisdom emanated from them. The villagers kept bringing in so many things for him that he lost interest in accumulation. He distributed whatever he had to the gathering at the end of the day. They brought him huge chrysanthemum garlands, jasmine and rose petals in baskets. He gave them all back to the women and children.

He protested to Velan one day, 'I'm a poor man and you are poor men; why do you give me all this? You must stop it.' But it was not possible to stop the practice; they loved to bring him gifts. He came to be called Swami by his congregation, and where he lived was called the Temple. It was passing into common parlance. 'The Swami said this or that', or 'I am on my way to the Temple'. People loved this place so much that they lime-washed its walls and drew red bands on them.

In the first half of the year they had evening rains, which poured
down fussily for a couple of hours to the tune of tremendous thunder;
later in the year they had a quieter sort of rain, steadily pattering
down. But no rain affected the assembly. People came shielding
themselves with huge bamboo mats or umbrellas or coconut
thatch. The hall became more packed during the wet season, since
the people could not overflow into the outer courtyard. But it made
the gathering cosy, interesting, and cool; and the swish of rain and
wind in the trees and the swelling river (which made them carry
their children aloft on their shoulders and cross the river only at
certain shallow points) lent a peculiar charm to the proceedings.
Raju loved this season, for its greenness everywhere, for the
variety of cloud-play in the sky, which he could watch through the
columned halls.

But he suddenly noticed at the end of the year that the skies
never dimmed with cloud. The summer seemed to continue. Raju
inquired, 'Where are the rains?'

Velan pulled a long face. 'The first rains have totally kept off,
Swamiji, and the millet crop, which we should have harvested by
now, is all scorched on the stalks. It's a big worry.'

'A thousand banana seedlings are dead,' said another. 'If it
continues, who knows?' They looked anxious.

Raju, ever a soothsayer, said consolingly, 'Such things are
common; don't worry too much about them. Let us hope for the
best.'

They became argumentative. 'Do you know, Swamiji, our cattle
which go out to graze nose about the mud and dirt and come back,
having no grass to eat?'

Raju had some soothing remark for every complaint. They went
home satisfied. 'You know best, master,' they said and left. Raju
recollected that for his bath nowadays he had to go down three more
steps to reach the water. He went down and stood looking along
the river course. He looked away to his left, where the river seemed
to wind back to the mountain ranges of the Mempi, to its source,
where he had often conducted tourists. Such a small basin, hardly a
hundred square feet with its little shrine—what had happened there
to make this river shrink so much here? He noticed that the borders
were wide, more rocks were showing, and the slope on the other
side seemed to have become higher.

Other signs too were presently to be noticed. At the Harvest Festival, the usual jubilation was absent. 'Sugar canes have completely wilted; with difficulty we have brought in this bit. Please accept it.'

'Give it to the children,' Raju said. Their gifts were shrinking in size and volume.

'The astrologer says that we shall have very early rains in the coming year,' someone said. The talk was always about the rains. People listened to discourses and philosophy with only half-interest. They sat around, expressing their fears and hopes. 'Is it true, Swami, that the movement of aeroplanes disturbs the clouds and so the rains don't fall? Too many aeroplanes in the sky.' 'Is it true, Swami, that the atom bombs are responsible for the drying up of the clouds?' Science, mythology, weather reports, good and evil, and all kinds of possibilities were connected with the rain. Raju gave an explanation for each in the best manner he could manage, but he found his answers never diverted their minds.

He decreed, 'You must not think too much of it. The rain-god sometimes teases those who are obsessed with thoughts of him. How would you feel if someone went on mentioning and repeating your name all hours of the day and night for days and days on end?' They enjoyed the humour of the analogy, and went their ways. But a situation was developing which no comforting word or discipline of thinking could help. Something was happening on a different plane over which one had no control or choice, and where a philosophical attitude made no difference. Cattle were unable to yield milk; they lacked the energy to drag the plough through the furrows; flocks of sheep were beginning to look scurvy and piebald, with their pelvic bones sticking out.

The wells in the villages were drying up. Huge concourses of women with pitchers arrived at the river, which was fast narrowing. From morning to night they came in waves and took the water. Raju watched their arrival and departure as they passed in files on the high ground opposite, looking picturesque, but without the tranquillity inherent in a picture. They quarrelled at the water-hole for priorities, and there was fear, desperation, and lamentation in their voices.

The earth was fast drying up. A buffalo was found dead on a foot-track. The news was brought to the Swami early one morning by Velan. He stood above him as he slept and said, 'Swami, I want you to come with us.'

'Why?'

'Cattle have begun to die,' he said with quiet resignation.

'What can I do about it?' Raju felt like asking, sitting up in his bed. But he could not say such a thing. He said soothingly, 'Oh, no; it can't be.'

'A buffalo was found dead on the forest path beyond our village.'

'Did you see it yourself?'

'Yes, Swami, I come from there.'

'Can't be as bad as that, Velan. It must have died of some other disease.'

'Please come along and see it, and if you can tell us why it is dead, it will relieve our minds. A learned man like you should see and tell.'

They were clearly losing their heads. They were entering a nightmare phase. The Swami knew so little of cattle, dead or alive, that it was of no practical use his going to see this one, but since they wanted it, he asked Velan to be seated for a few moments, and went down with him. The village street looked deserted. Children played about in the road dust, because the master had gone to town with a petition for relief addressed to the revenue authorities, and so the day-school was closed. Women were moving about with water-pots on their heads. In passing, 'Could hardly get half a pot today,' said some. 'What's the world coming to? You must show us the way, Swami.'

Raju merely raised a hand and waved it as if to say, 'Be peaceful; everything will be all right; I will fix it with the gods.' A small crowd followed him and Velan to the forest path, saying the same thing over and over again. Someone reported worse happenings in the next village; cholera was breaking out and thousands were dying, and so forth; he was snubbed by the rest as a scaremonger. Raju paid little attention to the jabber around him.

There it was outside the village, on a rough foot-track that led into the forest, a buffalo with bones sticking out. Crows and kites, already hovering about, flew off at the approach of men. There was a sickening odour, and henceforth Raju began to associate the season with it. It could not be mitigated with soothsaying. He held his upper cloth to his nostrils and gazed at the carcass for a while. 'Whose was this?' he asked.

They looked at one another. 'Not ours,' someone said. 'It belonged to the next village.' There was some relief at this thought. If it was one from the next village, it was far removed. Anything, any explanation, any excuse served to console people now.

'It belonged to no one,' said another. 'It looks like a wild buffalo.'

This was even better. Raju felt relieved at the possibility of there being other solutions and explanations. He added, peering at it again, 'It must have been bitten by a poisonous insect.' This was a comforting explanation, and he turned back without letting his eye dwell on the barren branches of trees, and the ground covered with bleached mud without a sign of green.

The piece of interpretations by the Swamiji pleased the public. It brought them untold comfort. The air of tension suddenly relaxed. When the cattle were penned for the night, they looked on them without anxiety. 'There is enough about for the cattle to feed on,' they said. 'Swami says that the buffalo died of a poisonous bite. He knows.' In support of it, many anecdotes were told of the death of animals from mysterious causes. 'There are snakes which bite into their hooves.' 'There are certain kinds of ants whose bite is fatal to animals.'

More cattle were found dead here and there. When the earth was scratched it produced only a cloud of fine dust. The granary of the previous year, in most of the houses, remained unreplenished and the level was going down. The village shopman was holding out for bigger prices. When people asked for a measure of rice he demanded fourteen annas for it. The man who wanted the rice lost his temper and slapped his face. The shopman came out with a chopper and attacked the customer; and those who sympathized with the man gathered in front of the shop and invaded it. The shopman's relatives and sympathizers came at night with crowbars and knives and started attacking the other group.

Velan and his men also picked up axes and knives and started out for the battle. Shrieks and cries and imprecations filled the air. The little hay that was left was set on fire, and the dark night was ablaze. Raju heard the cries, coming on the night air, and then he saw the blaze lighting up the landscape beyond the mound. Only a few hours before, everything had seemed peaceful and quiet. He shook his head, saying to himself, 'The village people do not know how to remain peaceful. They are becoming more and more agitated. At this rate, I think I'll look for a new place.' He went back to sleep, unable to take any further interest in their activities.

But news was brought to him early in the morning. Velan's brother told him while he was still half asleep that Velan was down with an injured skull and burns, and he gave a list of women and children hurt in the fight. They were mustering themselves to attack the other group tonight.

Raju was amazed at the way things were moving. He did not know what he was expected to do now, whether to bless their expedition or prevent it. Personally, he felt that the best thing for them would be to blow one another's brains out. That'd keep them from bothering too much about the drought. He felt a pity for Velan's condition. 'Is he seriously hurt?' he asked.

Velan's brother said, 'Oh, no. Just cut up here and there,' as though he wasn't satisfied with the marks.

Raju wondered for a while whether he should visit Velan, but he felt a tremendous reluctance to move. If Velan was hurt, he'd get healed; that was all. And now the brother's description of the injuries, whether false or true, suited his programme. There was no urgency to go and see Velan. He feared that if he made it a habit he would not be left in peace, as the villagers would always have a reason to call him out. He asked Velan's brother, 'How did you yourself manage to remain intact?'

'Oh, I was also there, but they didn't hit me. If they had I would have laid ten of them low. But my brother, he was careless.'

'Thin as a broomstick, but talks like a giant,' thought Raju, and advised, 'Tell your brother to apply turmeric to his wounds.' From the casual tone with which this man was speaking, Raju wondered if it was possible that he himself had dealt a blow to Velan from behind; anything seemed possible in this village. All the brothers in the place were involved in litigation against one another; and anyone might do anything in view of the present sensational developments. Velan's brother rose to go. Raju said, 'Tell Velan to rest in bed completely.'

'Oh, no, master. How can he rest? He is joining the party tonight and he will not rest till he burns their houses.'

'It is not right,' Raju said, somewhat irritated by all this pugnacity.

Velan's brother was one of the lesser intelligences of the village. He was about twenty-one, a semi-moron who had grown up as a dependent in Velan's house, yet another of Velan's trials in life. He spent his days taking the village cattle out to the mountains for grazing: he collected them from various houses early in the day, and drove them to the mountainside, watched over them, and brought them back in the evening. All day he lounged under a tree's shade, eating a ball of boiled millet when the sun came overhead, and watching for the sun to slant westward to drive the cattle homeward. He had hardly anyone to speak to except his cattle the whole day and he spoke to them on equal terms and abused them and their genealogy unreservedly. Any afternoon in the stillness of the forest, if one had the occasion to observe, one could hear the hills echoing to the choice, abusive words that he hurled at the animals as he followed them with his stick. He was considered well-equipped for this single task, and from each house was given four annas a month. They did not trust him with any more responsible tasks. He was one of those rare men in the village who never visited the Swamiji, but preferred to sleep at home at the end of the day. But now he had come, almost for the first time. The others were preoccupied and busy with their preparations for the coming fight, and he was one of those whose employment was affected by the drought; no one saw any sense in sending the cattle out to nose about the dry sand and paying the idiot four annas a month.

He had come here this morning, not because anyone had sent him to carry a message for the Swamiji, but because he was at a loose end and had suddenly felt that he might as well pay a visit to the temple and receive the Swami's blessing. The fight was the last thing the villagers would have liked to bring to the Swami's attention, although after finishing it they might have given him a mild version. But this boy brought the news on his own initiative and defended their action. 'But, Swami, why did they cut my brother's face?' He added sullenly, 'Should they be left free to do all this?'

Raju argued with him patiently. 'You beat the shopman first, didn't you?'

The boy took it literally and said, 'I didn't beat the shopman. The man who beat him was . . .' He gave a number of local names.

Raju felt too weary to correct him and improve his understanding. He simply said, 'It is no good; nobody should fight.' He felt it impossible to lecture him on the ethics of peace, and so merely said, 'No one should fight.'

'But they fight!' the boy argued. 'They come and beat us.' He paused, ruminating upon the words, and added, 'And they will kill us soon.'

Raju felt bothered. He did not like the idea of so much commotion. It might affect the isolation of the place and bring the police on the scene. He did not want anyone to come to the village. Raju suddenly began to think positively on these matters. He gripped the other's arm above his elbow and said, 'Go and tell Velan and the rest that I don't want them to fight like this. I'll tell them what to do later.' The boy prepared himself to repeat his usual arguments. But Raju said impatiently, 'Don't talk. Listen to what I say.'

'Yes, master,' the boy said, rather frightened at this sudden vehemence.

'Tell your brother, immediately, wherever he may be, that unless they are good I'll never eat.'

'Eat what?' asked the boy, rather puzzled.

'Say that I'll not eat. Don't ask what. I'll not eat till they are good.'

'Good? Where?'

This was frankly beyond the comprehension of the boy. He wanted to ask again, 'Eat what?' but refrained out of fear. His eyes opened wide. He could not connect the fight and this man's food. He wanted only to be released from the terrific grip over his left elbow. He felt he had made a mistake in coming to this man all alone—the bearded face, pushed so close to him, frightened him. This man might perhaps eat him up. He became desperately anxious to get out of the place. He said, 'All right, sir. I'll do it,' and the moment Raju let his hold go he shot out of the place, was across the sands and out of sight in a moment.

He was panting when he ran into the assembly of his village elders. They were sitting solemnly around a platform in the centre of the village, discussing the rains. There was a brick platform built around an ancient peepul tree, at whose root a number of stone figures were embedded, which were often anointed with oil and worshipped. This was a sort of town hall platform for Mangala. It was shady and cool and spacious; there was always a gathering of men on one side conferring on local problems, and on the other women who carried loaded baskets on their heads and rested; children chased each other; and the village dogs slumbered.

Here were sitting the elders of the village, discussing the rain, the fight tonight, and all the strategies connected with it. They had still many misgivings about the expedition. How the Swami would view the whole thing was a thing that could be understood only later. He might not approve. It would be best not to go to him until they themselves were clear in their heads about what to do. That the other group deserved punishment was beyond question. Among those talking were quite a number with bruises and cuts. But they had a fear of the police; they remembered a former occasion when there had been a faction fight, and the government posted a police force almost permanently and made the villagers feed them and pay for their keep.

Into this council of war burst Velan's brother. The atmosphere became tense. 'What is it, brother?' asked Velan.

The boy stopped to recover breath before speaking. They took him by the shoulder and shook him, at which he became more confused and blabbered and finally said, 'The Swami, the Swami, doesn't want food any more. Don't take any food to him.'

'Why? Why?'

'Because, because—it doesn't rain.' He added also, suddenly, recollecting the fight, 'No fight, he says.'

'Who asked you to go there?' asked his brother authoritatively.

'I—I didn't, but when I—found myself there he asked me and I told him—'

'What did you tell him?'

The boy became suddenly wary. He knew he would be thrashed if he said he had mentioned the fight. He didn't like to be gripped by the shoulder—in fact, he was averse to being gripped in any manner at all; but there the Swami squeezed his elbow and brushed his beard on his face, and here these men were tearing at his shoulder. He felt sorry he had ever got involved. It was best not to have anything to do with them.

They would wrench his shoulder off if they knew he had been telling the master about the fight. So he covered up the entire business in the best manner he could think of. He blinked. They demanded of him again, 'What did you tell him?'

'That there is no rain,' he said, mentioning the easiest subject that occurred to him.

They patted him on the head and said contemptuously, 'Big prophet to carry the news! He didn't know about it till then, I suppose.' A laugh followed. The boy also simpered and tried to get over it.

Then he remembered the message he had been entrusted with, and thought it safer to say something about it, otherwise the great man might come to know of it and lay a curse on him. And so he said, coming back to the original starting point, 'He wants no food until it is all right.'

He uttered it with such solemnity and emphasis that they asked, 'What did he say? Tell us exactly.'

The boy deliberated for a moment and said, 'Tell your brother not to bring me any more food. I won't eat. If I don't eat, it'll be all right; and then everything will be all right.' They stared at him, puzzled. He smiled, rather pleased at the importance he was receiving. They remained in thought for a moment.

And then one of them said, 'This Mangala is a blessed country to have a man like the Swami in our midst. No bad thing will come to us as long as he is with us. He is like a Mahatma. When Mahatma Gandhi went without food, how many things happened in India! This is a man like that. If he fasts there will be rain. Out of his love for us he is undertaking it. This will surely bring rain and help us. Once upon a time a man fasted for twenty-one days and brought down the deluge. Only great souls that take upon themselves tasks such as this—' The atmosphere became electrified. They forgot the fight and all their troubles and bickerings.

The village was astir. Everything else seemed inconsequential now. Someone brought the news that upstream a crocodile had been found dead on the sand, having no watery shelter and being scorched by the sun. Someone else came with the news that the fast-drying lake bed in a nearby village was showing up an old temple which had been submerged a century ago, when the lake was formed. The image of the god was still intact in the inner shrine, none the worse for having lain under water so long; the four coconut trees around the temple were still there . . . And so on and so forth. More and more details were coming in every hour. Hundreds of people were now walking across the lake bed to visit the temple, and some careless ones lost their lives, sucked in by loose mud. All this now produced a lot of public interest, but no fear. They were now even able to take a more lenient view of the shopman who had assaulted his customer. 'After all, so and so should not have called him a whoreson; not a proper word.'

'Of course, one's kith and kin are bound to support one. What are they worth otherwise?' Velan brooded over the cut on his forehead, and a few others suddenly recollected their various injuries. They could not decide how far this could be forgiven. They consoled themselves with the thought that a good number in the other group must also be nursing injuries at that moment; it was a very satisfying thought. They suddenly decided that they should have a third party to come and arbitrate, so that the fight could be forgotten, provided the other group paid for the burned-down haystacks and entertained the chief men of this group at a feast. And they spent their time discussing the conditions of peace and rose in a body, declaring, 'Let us all go and pay our respects to Swami, our saviour.'

Raju was waiting for his usual gifts and food. He had, no doubt, fruits and other edible stuff left in his hamper, but he hoped they would bring him other fare. He had suggested to them that they should try to get him wheat flour, and rice flour, and spices. He wanted to try some new recipes, for a change. He had a subtle way of mentioning his special requirements. He generally began by taking Velan aside and saying, 'You see, if a little rice flour and chili powder could be got, along with some other things, I can do something new. On Wednesdays . . .' He enunciated some principle of living such as that on a special Wednesday he always liked to make his food with rice flour and such-and-such spice, and he mentioned it with an air of seriousness so that his listeners took it as a spiritual need, something of the man's inner discipline to keep his soul in shape and his understanding with the heavens in order. He had a craving for *bonda*, which he used to eat in the railway station stall when a man came there to vend his edibles on a wooden tray to the travellers. It was composed of flour, potato, a slice of onion, a coriander leaf, and a green chili—and oh! how it tasted—although he probably fried it in anything; he was the sort of vendor who would not hesitate to fry a thing in kerosene, if it worked out cheaper. With all that, he made delicious stuff, and when Raju used to ask the vendor how he made it, he gave him a recipe starting with, 'Just a small piece of ginger,' and then it went on to this and that. While discoursing on the Bhagavad-Gita to his audience the other evening, Raju had had a sudden craving to try this out himself—he was now equipped with a charcoal stove and frying pan, and what could be more musical than well-kneaded dough dropping into boiling oil? He had enumerated his wants to Velan as delicately as possible.

When he heard voices beyond the mound, he felt relieved. He composed his features for his professional role and smoothed out his beard and hair, and sat down in his seat with a book in his hand. As the voices approached, he looked up and found that a bigger crowd than usual was crossing the sands. He was puzzled for a second, but felt that perhaps they were jubilant over the fact that he had prevented a fight. He felt happy that he had after all achieved something, and saved the village. That idiot brother of Velan did not seem so bad after all. He hoped that they had the flour in a bag. It'd be improper to ask for it at once; they were bound to leave it in the kitchen.

They softened their steps and voices as they came nearer the pillared hall. Even the children hushed their voices when they approached the august presence.

They sat around in a silent semicircle as before, each in his place. The women got busy at once sweeping the floor and filling the mud lamps with oil. For ten minutes Raju neither looked at them nor spoke, but turned the leaves of his book. He felt curious to see how much of Velan's person was intact. He stole a glance across, and saw the scars on his forehead, and threw a swift look around and found that actually there was less damage than he had pictured in his mind. He resumed his studies, and only after he had gone through ten minutes of reading did he look up as usual and survey the gathering. He looked at his flock, fixed his eyes on Velan in particular, and said, 'Lord Krishna says here—' He adjusted his page to the light and read a passage. 'Do you know what it means?' He entered into a semi-philosophical discourse on a set of rambling themes, starting with the eating of good food and going on to absolute trust in God's goodness.

They listened to him without interrupting him, and only when he paused for breath at the end of nearly an hour did Velan say, 'Your prayers will surely be answered and save our village. Every one of us in the village prays night and day that you come through it safely.'

Raju was puzzled by what he heard. But he thought that such high and bombastic well-wishing was their habit and idiom and that they were only thanking him for putting enough sense into their heads not to go on with their fight. The assembly grew very loquacious and showered praise on him from all directions. A woman came up and touched his feet. Another followed. Raju cried, 'Have I not told you that I'll never permit this? No human being should ever prostrate before another human being.'

Two or three men came up, one of them saying, 'You are not another human being. You are a Mahatma. We should consider ourselves blessed indeed to be able to touch the dust of your feet.'

'Oh, no. Don't say that—' Raju tried to withdraw his feet. But they crowded round him. He tried to cover his feet. He felt ridiculous playing this hide-and-seek with his feet. He could find no place to put them. They tugged at various sides and they seemed ready to tickle his sides, if it would only give them his feet. He realized that there was really no escape from this demonstration and that it would be best to let them do what they liked. Almost everyone in the crowd had touched his feet and withdrawn, but not too far away; they surrounded him and showed no signs of moving. They gazed on his face and kept looking up in a new manner; there was a greater solemnity in the air than he had ever known before.

Velan said, 'Your penance is similar to Mahatma Gandhi's. He has left us a disciple in you to save us.' In their own rugged idiom, in the best words they could muster, they were thanking him. Sometimes they all spoke together and made a confused noise. Sometimes they began a sentence and could not get through with it. He understood that they spoke with feeling. They spoke gratefully, although their speech sounded bombastic. The babble was confusing. But their devotion to him was unquestionable. There was so much warmth in their approach that he began to feel it was but right they should touch his feet; as a matter of fact, it seemed possible that he himself might bow low, take the dust of his own feet, and press it to his eyes. He began to think that his personality radiated a glory . . . The crowd did not leave at the usual hour, but lingered on.

Velan had assumed that he was on a fast today and for the first time these months had failed to bring in any food. Just as well. When they attached so much value to his fasting he could not very well ask, 'Where is the stuff for my *bonda*?' It would be unseemly. No harm in attending to it later. They had assumed that he was fasting in order to stop their fight, and he was not going to announce to them that he had already had two meals during the day. He would just leave it at that, and even if his eyes should droop a little out of seeming fatigue, it would be quite in order. Now that it was all over, why couldn't they go away? He signalled to Velan to come nearer, 'Why not send away the women and children? Isn't it getting late?'

The crowd left at nearly midnight, but Velan remained where he had sat all the evening, leaning against a pillar. 'Don't you feel sleepy?' Raju asked.

'No, sir. Keeping awake is no big sacrifice, considering what you are doing for us.'

'Don't attach too much value to it. It's just a duty, that is all, and I'm not doing anything more than I ought to do. You can go home if you like.'

'No, sir. I'll go home tomorrow when the headman comes to relieve me. He will come here at five o'clock and stay on till the afternoon. I'll go home, attend to my work, and come back, sir.'

'Oh, it's not at all necessary that someone should always be here. I can manage quite well.'

'You will graciously leave that to us, sir. We are only doing our duty. You are undertaking a great sacrifice, sir, and the least we can do is to be at your side. We derive merit from watching your face, sir.'

Raju felt really touched by this attitude. But he decided that the time had come to get to the bottom of it. So he said, 'You are right. "One who serves the performer of a sacrifice derives the same merit", says our scripture, and you are not wrong. I thank God that my effort has succeeded, and you are all at peace with one another; that's my main concern. Now that's over, things are all right. You may go home. Tomorrow I'll take my usual food, and then I shall be all right. You will remember to fetch me rice flour, green chili, and—'

Velan was too respectful to express his surprise loudly. But he couldn't check himself any more. 'Do you expect it to rain tomorrow, sir?'

'Well . . .' Raju thought for a moment. What was this new subject that had crept into the agenda? 'Who can say? It's God's will. It may.' It was then that Velan moved nearer and gave an account of what his brother had told them, and its effect on the population around. Velan gave a very clear account of what the saviour was expected to do—stand in knee-deep water, look to the skies, and utter the prayer lines for two weeks, completely fasting during the period—and lo, the rains would come down, provided the man who performed it was a pure soul, was a great soul. The whole countryside was now in a happy ferment, because a great soul had agreed to go through the trial.

The earnestness with which he spoke brought tears to Raju's eyes. He remembered that not long ago he had spoken to them of such a penance, its value and technique. He had described it partly out of his head and partly out of traditional accounts he had heard his mother narrate. It had filled an evening's programme and helped him divert his audience's mind from the drought. He had told them, 'When the time comes, everything will be all right. Even the man who would bring you the rain will appear, all of a sudden.' They interpreted his words and applied them now to the present situation. He felt that he had worked himself into a position from which he could not get out. He could not betray his surprise. He felt that after all the time had come for him to be serious—to attach value to his own words. He needed time—and solitude to think over the whole matter. He got down from his pedestal; that was the first step to take. That seat had acquired a glamour, and as long as he occupied it people would not listen to him as to an ordinary mortal. He now saw the enormity of his own creation. He had created a giant with his puny self, a throne of authority with that slab of stone. He left his seat abruptly, as if he had been stung by a wasp, and approached Velan. His tone hushed with real humility and fear; his manner was earnest. Velan sat still as if he were a petrified sentry.

'Listen to me, Velan; it is essential that I should be alone tonight. It is essential that I should be alone through the day tomorrow too. And then come and see me tomorrow night. I'll speak to you tomorrow night. Until then neither you nor anyone else should see me.'

This sounded so mysterious and important that Velan got up without a word. 'I'll see you tomorrow night, sir. Alone?'

'Yes, yes; absolutely alone.'

'Very well, master; you have your own reasons. It is not for us to ask why or what. Big crowds will be arriving. I'll have men along the river to turn them back. It'll be difficult, but if it is your order it must be carried out.' He made a deep obeisance and went away. Raju stood looking after him for a while. He went into an inner room which he was using as a bedroom, and laid himself down. His body was aching from too much sitting up the whole day; and he felt exhausted by the numerous encounters. In that dark chamber, as the bats whirred about and the far-off sounds of the village ceased, a great silence descended. His mind was filled with tormenting problems. He tried to sleep. He had a fitful, nightmare-ridden, thought-choked three hours.

Did they expect him to starve for fifteen days and stand in knee-deep water eight hours? He sat up. He regretted having given them the idea. It had sounded picturesque. But if he had known that it would be applied to him, he might probably have given a different formula: that all villages should combine to help him eat *bonda* for fifteen days without a break. Up to them to see that the supply was kept up. And then the saintly man would stand in the river for two minutes a day, and it should bring down the rain sooner or later. His mother used to say, 'If there is one good man anywhere, the rains would descend for his sake and benefit the whole world,' quoting from a Tamil poem. It occurred to him that the best course for him would be to run away from the whole thing. He could walk across, catch a bus somewhere, and be off to the city, where they would not bother too much about him—just another bearded *sadhu* about, that was all. Velan and the rest would look for him and conclude that he had vanished to the Himalayas. But how to do it? How far could he go? Anyone might spot him within half an hour. It was not a practical solution. They might drag him back to the spot and punish him for fooling them. It was not even this fear; he was perhaps ready to take the risk, if there was half a chance of getting away. But he felt moved by the recollection of the big crowd of women and children touching his feet. He felt moved by the thought of their gratitude. He lit a fire and cooked his food, bathed in the river (at a spot where he had to scoop the sand and wait five minutes for the spring to fill his vessel), and gulped down a meal before anyone should arrive even accidentally. He kept a reserve of food, concealed in an inner sanctum, for a second meal at night. He thought suddenly that if they would at least leave him alone at night, he could make some arrangement and survive the ordeal. The ordeal then would be only standing knee-deep in water (if they could find it), muttering the litany for eight hours. (This he could suitably modify in actual practice.) It might give him cramps, but he'd have to bear it for a few days, and then be believed the rains would descend in their natural course sooner or later. He would not like to cheat them altogether about the fast if he could help it.

When Velan arrived at night, he took him into his confidence. He said, 'Velan, you have been a friend to me. You must listen to me now. What makes you think that I can bring the rain?'

'That boy told us so. Did you not tell him so?'

Raju hesitated without giving a direct reply. Perhaps even at this point he might have rectified the whole thing with a frank statement. Raju hesitated for a moment. By habit, his nature avoided the direct and bald truth even now. He replied dodgingly, 'It's not that that I am asking. I want to know what has made you think so about me.'

Velan blinked helplessly. He did not quite understand what the great man was implying. He felt that it must mean something very noble, of course, but he was unable to answer the question. He said, 'What else should we do?'

'Come nearer. Sit down and listen to me. You may sleep here. I'm prepared to fast for the sake of your people and do anything if I can help this country—but it is a task to be taken on only by a saint. I am no saint.' Velan uttered many sounds of protest. Raju felt really sorry to be shattering his faith; but it was the only way in which he could hope to escape the ordeal. It was a cool night. Raju asked Velan to go up with him to the river step. He took his seat on it, and Velan sat on a step below. Raju moved down to his side. 'You have to listen to me, and so don't go so far away, Velan. I must speak into your ears. You must pay attention to what I am going to say. I am not a saint, Velan, I'm just an ordinary human being like anyone else. Listen to my story. You will know it yourself.' The river trickling away in minute driblets made no noise. The dry leaves of the peepul tree rustled. Somewhere a jackal howled. And Raju's voice filled the night. Velan listened to him without uttering a word of surprise or interjection, in all humility. Only he looked a little more serious than usual, and there were lines of care on his face.

7

I WAS ACCEPTED by Marco as a member of the family. From guiding tourists I seemed to have come to a sort of concentrated guiding of a single family. Marco was just impractical, an absolutely helpless man. All that he could do was to copy ancient things and write about them. His mind was completely in it. All practical affairs of life seemed impossible to him; such a simple matter as finding food or shelter or buying a railway ticket seemed to him a monumental job. Perhaps he married out of a desire to have someone care for his practical life, but unfortunately his choice was wrong—this girl herself was a dreamer if ever there was one. She would have greatly benefited by a husband who could care for her career; it was here that a handy man like me proved invaluable. I nearly gave up all my routine jobs in order to be of service to them.

He stayed for over a month at Peak House and I was in entire charge of all his affairs. He never stinted any expense as long as a voucher was available. They still kept their room in the hotel. Gaffur's car was permanently engaged, almost as if Marco owned it. The car did at least one trip a day between the Peak House and the town. Joseph looked after Marco so well that it was unnecessary for anyone else to bother about him. It was understood that I should devote a lot of time to looking after him and his wife, without sacrificing any other job I might have. He paid me my daily rate and also let me look after my 'routine jobs'. My so-called routine jobs now sounded big, but actually reduced themselves to keeping Rosie company and amusing her. Once in two days she went up to see her husband. She was showing extra solicitude for him nowadays. She fussed a great deal over him. It was all the same to him. His table was littered with notes and dates, and he said, 'Rosie, don't go near it. I don't want you to mess it up. It is just coming to a little order.' I never cared to know what exactly he was doing. It was not my business. Nor did his wife seem to care for the task he was undertaking. She asked, 'How is your food?' She was trying a new technique on him, after the inauguration of our own intimacy. She arranged his room. She spoke to Joseph about his food. Sometimes she said, 'I'll stay on here and keep you company.' And Marco acknowledged it in an absentminded, casual manner. 'All right. If you like. Well, Raju, are you staying on or going back?'

I resisted my impulse to stay on, because I knew I was having her company fully downhill. It would be polite to leave her alone with him. So I said, without looking at him, 'I must go back. I have some others coming in today. You don't mind, I hope.'

'Not at all. You are a man of business. I should not monopolize you so much.'

'What time will you need the car tomorrow?'

He looked at his wife and she just said, 'Tomorrow, as early as you can.' He generally said, 'Bring me a few sheets of carbon, will you?'

As the car sped downhill, Gaffur kept throwing glances at me through the looking-glass. I was cultivating a lot of reserve with him nowadays. I didn't like him to gossip too much about anything. I was afraid of gossip. I was still sensitive to such things and I was nervous at being alone with Gaffur and felt relieved as long as his remarks were confined to automobiles; but it was not in his nature to stick to this subject. He would begin with automobiles but soon get mixed up. 'You must give me an hour for brake adjustments tomorrow. After all, mechanical brakes, you know; I still maintain they are better than hydraulic. Just as an old, uneducated wife is better than the new type of girl. Oh, modern girls are very bold. I wouldn't let my wife live in a hotel room all by herself if I had to remain on duty on a hilltop.'

It made me uncomfortable and I turned the topic deftly. 'Do you think car designers have less experience than you?'

'Oh, you think these engineers know more? A man like me who has to kick and prod a car to keep it on the road has, you may be sure . . .' I was safe; I had turned his mind from Rosie. I sat in suspense. I was in an abnormal state of mind. Even this did not escape Gaffur's attention. He mumbled often as he was driving me downhill, 'You are becoming rather stuck-up nowadays, Raju. You are not the old friend you used to be.' It was a fact. I was losing a great deal of my mental relaxation. I was obsessed with thoughts of Rosie. I revelled in memories of the hours I had spent with her last or in anticipation of what I'd be doing next. I had several problems to contend with. Her husband was the least of them. He was a good man, completely preoccupied, probably a man with an abnormal capacity for trust. But I was becoming nervous and sensitive and full of anxieties in various ways. Suppose, suppose—suppose? What? I myself could not specify. I was becoming fear-ridden. I couldn't even sort out my worries properly. I was in a jumble. I was suddenly seized with fears, sometimes with a feeling that I didn't look well enough for my sweetheart. I was obsessed with the thought that I hadn't perhaps shaved my chin smoothly enough, and that she would run her fingers over my upper lip and throw me out. Sometimes I felt I was in rags. The silk *jibba* and the lace-edged *dhoti* were being overdone or were old-fashioned. She was about to shut the door on me because I was not modern enough for her. This made me run to the tailor to have him make a few dashing bush-shirts and corduroys, and invest in hair- and face-lotions and perfumes of all kinds. My expenses were mounting. The shop was my main source of income, together with what Marco gave me as my daily wage. I knew that I ought to look into the accounts of the shop a little more closely. I was leaving it too much to the boy to manage. My mother often told me, whenever she was able to get at me, 'You will have to keep an eye on that boy. I see a lot of hangers-on there. Have you any idea what cash he is collecting and what is happening generally?'

I usually told her, 'I should certainly know how to manage these things. Don't think I'm so careless.' And she left me alone. And then I went over to the shop, assumed a tone of great aggressiveness, and checked the accounts. The boy produced some accounts, some cash, a statement of stock, something else that he needed for running the show, and some of his problems. I was in no mood to listen to his problems. I was busy and preoccupied, so I told him not to bother me with petty details and gave an impression (just an impression and nothing more) of being a devil for accounts.

He always said, 'Two passengers came asking for you, sir.'

Oh, bores, who wanted them, anyway? 'What did they want?' I asked with semi-interest.

'Three days' sightseeing, sir. They went away disappointed.'

They were always there. My reputation had survived my interest in the job. Railway Raju was an established name, and still pilgrims and travellers sought his help. The boy persisted. 'They wanted to know where you were.' This gave me food for thought. I didn't want this fool of a fellow to send them up to my Room 28 at the hotel. Fortunately, he did not know. Otherwise he might have done so. 'What shall I tell them, Raju-sir?' He always called me 'Raju-sir'. It was his idea of combining deference with familiarity.

I merely replied, 'Tell them I'm busy; that is all. I have no time. I'm very busy.'

'May I act as their guide, sir?' he asked eagerly. This fellow was acting as a successor in my jobs one by one. Next, probably, he would ask permission to keep the girl company! I felt annoyed with his question and asked him, 'Who will look after the shop?'

'I have a cousin. He can watch the shop for an hour or two, while I am away.'

I could not think of a reply. I could not decide. The whole thing was too bothersome. My old life, in which I was not in the least interested, was dogging my steps; my mother facing me with numerous problems: municipal tax, the kitchen tiles needing attention, the shop, accounts, letters from the village, my health, and so on and so forth; to me she was a figure out of a dream, mumbling vague sounds; and this boy had his own way of cornering and attacking me. Then Gaffur with his sly remarks and looks, ever on the brink of gossip—oh, I was tired of it all. I was in no mood for anything. My mind was on other matters. Even my finances were unreal to me, although if I cared to look at my savings-book I could know at a glance how the level of the reservoir was going down. But I did not want to examine it too closely as long as the man at the counter was able to give me the cash I wanted. Thanks to my father's parsimonious habits, I had a bank account. The only reality in my life and consciousness was Rosie. All my mental powers were now turned to keep her within my reach, and keep her smiling all the time, neither of which was at all easy. I would willingly have kept at her side all the time, as a sort of parasite; but in that hotel it was not easy, I was always racked with the thought that the man at the desk and the boys at the hotel were keeping an eye on me and were commenting behind my back.

I did not want to be observed going to Room 28. I was becoming self-conscious about it. I very much wished that the architecture of the place could be altered so that I might go up without having the desk-man watch me. I was sure he was noting down the hour of my arrival with Rosie, and of my departure. His morbid, inquisitive mind, I was sure, must have been working on all the details of my life behind the closed doors of Room 28. I didn't like the way he looked at me whenever I passed: I didn't like the curve of his lip—I knew he was smiling at an inward joke at my expense. I wished I could ignore him, but he was an early associate of mine, and I owed him a general remark or two. While passing him, I tried to look casual, and stopped to say, 'Did you see that Nehru is going to London?' or 'The new taxes will kill all initiative,' and he agreed with me and explained something, and that was enough. Or we discussed the Government of India's tourist plans or hotel arrangements, and I had to let him talk—the poor fellow never suspected how little I cared for tourism or taxes or anything now. I sometimes toyed with the thought of changing the hotel. But it was not easy. Both Rosie and her husband seemed to be deeply devoted to this hotel. He was somehow averse to changing, although he never came down from his heights, and the girl seemed to have got used to this room with its view of a coconut grove outside, and people irrigating it from a well. It was a fascination that I could not easily understand or explain.

In other ways too I found it difficult to understand the girl. I found as I went on that she was gradually losing the free and easy manner of her former days. She allowed me to make love to her, of course, but she was also beginning to show excessive consideration for her husband on the hill. In the midst of my caresses, she would suddenly free herself and say, 'Tell Gaffur to bring the car. I want to go and see him.'

I had not yet reached the stage of losing my temper or speaking sharply to her. So I calmly answered, 'Gaffur will not come till this time tomorrow. You were up only yesterday. Why do you want to go again? He expects you there only tomorrow.'

'Yes,' she would say and remain thoughtful. I didn't like to see her sit up like that on her bed and brood, her hair unattended, her dress all crinkled. She clasped her knees with her hands.

'What is troubling you?' I had to ask her. 'Won't you tell me? I will always help you.'

She would shake her head and say, 'After all, he is my husband. I have to respect him. I cannot leave him there.'

My knowledge of women being poor and restricted to one, I could not decide how to view her statements. I could not understand whether she was pretending, whether her present pose was pretence or whether her account of all her husband's shortcomings was false, just to entice me. It was complex and obscure. I had to tell her, 'Rosie, you know very well that even if Gaffur came, he couldn't drive uphill at this hour.'

'Yes, yes, I understand,' she would reply and lapse into a mysterious silence again.

'What is troubling you?'

She started crying. 'After all . . . after all . . . is this right what I am doing? After all, he has been so good to me, given me comfort and freedom. What husband in the world would let his wife go and live in a hotel room by herself, a hundred miles away?'

'It is not a hundred miles, but fifty-eight only,' I corrected. 'Shall I order you coffee or anything to eat?'

'No,' she would say point blank, but continue the train of her own thoughts. 'As a good man he may not mind, but is it not a wife's duty to guard and help her husband, whatever the way in which he deals with her?' This last phrase was to offset in advance any reminder I might make about his indifference to her.

It was a confusing situation. Naturally, I could take no part in this subject: there was nothing I could add to or subtract from what she was saying. Distance seemed to lend enchantment to her view now. But I knew that she would have to spend only a few hours with him to come downhill raging against him, saying the worst possible things. Sometimes I heartily wished that the man would descend from his heights, take her, and clear out of the place. That would at least end this whole uncertain business once and for all and help me to return to my platform duties. I could possibly try to do that even now. What prevented me from leaving the girl alone? The longer Marco went on with his work, the longer this agony was stretched. But he seemed to flourish in his solitude; that's probably what he had looked for all his life. But why could he not do something about his wife? A blind fellow. Sometimes I felt angry at the thought of him. He had placed me in a hopeless predicament. I was compelled to ask her, 'Why don't you stay up with him, then?'

She merely replied, 'He sits up all night writing, and—'

'If he sits up all night writing, during the day you should talk to him,' I would say with a look of innocence.

'But all day he is in the cave!'

'Well, you may go and see it too. Why not? It ought to interest you.'

'While he is copying, no one may talk to him.'

'Don't talk to him, but study the objects yourself. A good wife ought to be interested in all her husband's activities.'

'True,' she said, and merely sighed. This was a thoroughly inexperienced and wrong line for me to take; it led us nowhere, but only made her morose.

Her eyes lit up with a new hope when I spoke about the dance. It was after all her art that I first admired; of late, in our effort to live the lovers' life, that all-important question was pushed to the background. Her joy at finding shops, cinemas, and caresses made her forget for a while her primary obsession. But not for long. She asked me one evening, point blank, 'Are you also like him?'

'In what way?'

'Do you also hate to see me dance?'

'Not at all. What makes you think so?'

'At one time you spoke like a big lover of art, but now you never give it a thought.'

It was true. I said something in excuse, clasped her hands in mine, and swore earnestly, 'I will do anything for you. I will give my life to see you dance. Tell me what to do. I will do it for you.'

She brightened up. Her eyes lit up with a new fervour at the mention of dancing. So I sat up with her, helping her to day-dream. I found out the clue to her affection and utilized it to the utmost. Her art and her husband could not find a place in her thoughts at the same time; one drove the other out.

She was full of plans. At five in the morning she'd start her practice and continue for three hours. She would have a separate hall, long enough and wide enough for her to move in. It must have a heavy carpet, which would be neither too smooth under the feet nor too rough, and which would not fold while she practised her steps on it. At one corner of the room she'd have a bronze figure of Nataraja, the god of dancers, the god whose primal dance created the vibrations that set the worlds in motion. She would have incense sticks burning. After her morning practice, she would call up the chauffeur.

'Are you going to have a car?' I asked.

'Naturally, otherwise how can I move about? When I have so many engagements, it will be necessary for me to have a car. It'll be indispensable, don't you think?'

'Surely I'll remember it.'

She would then spend an hour or two in the forenoon studying the ancient works of the art, *Natya Shastra* of Bharat Muni, a thousand years old, and various other books, because without a proper study of the ancient methods it would be impossible to keep the purity of the classical forms. All the books were in her uncle's house, and she would write to him to send them on to her by and by. She would also want a pundit to come to her to help her to understand the texts, as they were all written in an old, terse style. 'Can you get me a Sanskrit pundit?' she asked.

'Of course I can. There are dozens of them.'

'I shall also want him to read for me episodes from *Ramayana* and *Mahabharata*, because they are a treasure house, and we can pick up so many ideas for new compositions from them.'

A little rest after lunch; and at three o'clock she would go out and do shopping, go for a drive and return home in evening or see a picture, unless, of course, there was a performance in the evening. If there was a performance, she would like to rest till three in the afternoon and reach the hall only half an hour before the show. 'That would be enough, because I shall do all the make-up and dressing before I leave the house.'

She thought of every detail, and dreamed of it night and day. Her immediate need would be a party of drummers and musicians to assist her morning practice. When she was ready to appear before the public, she would tell me and then I could fix her public engagements. I felt rather baffled by her fervour. I wished I could keep pace at least with her idiom. I felt that I ought immediately to pick up and cultivate the necessary jargon. I felt silly to be watching her and listening to her, absolutely tongue-tied. There were, of course, two ways open: to bluff one's way through and trust to luck, or to make a clean breast of it all. I listened to her talk for two days and finally confessed to her, 'I am a layman, not knowing much of the technicalities of the dance; I'd like you to teach me something of it.'

I didn't want her to interpret it as an aversion on my part to the art. That might drive her back into the arms of her husband, and so I took care to maintain the emphasis on my passion for the art. It gave us a fresh intimacy. This common interest brought us close together. Wherever we were she kept talking to me on the various subleties of the art, its technicalities, and explaining as to a child its idioms. She seemed to notice our surroundings less and less. In Gaffur's car as we sat she said, 'You know what a *pallavi* is? The time-scheme is all-important in it. It does not always run in the simple style of one-two, one-two; it gets various odds thrown in, and at a different tempo.' She uttered its syllables, 'Ta-ka-ta-ki-ta, ta-ka.' It amused me. 'You know, to get the footwork right within those five or seven beats requires real practice, and when the tempo is varied . . .' This was something that Gaffur could safely overhear, as we went up the hill, as we came out of a shop, as we sat in a cinema. While seeing a picture, she would suddenly exclaim, 'My uncle has with him a very old song written on a palm leaf. No one has seen it. My mother was the only person in the whole country who knew the song and could dance to it. I'll get that song too from my uncle. I'll show you how it goes. Shall we go back to our room? I don't want to see more of this picture. It looks silly.'

We immediately adjourned to Room 28, where she asked me to remain seated, and went into the ante-room and came back with her dress tucked in and tightened up for the performance. She said, 'I'll show you how it goes. Of course, I'm not doing it under the best of conditions. I need at least a drummer. . . Move off that chair, and sit on the bed. I want some space here.'

She stood at one end of the hall and sang the song lightly, in a soft undertone, a song from an ancient Sanskrit composition of a lover and lass on the banks of the Jamuna; and it began with such a verve, when she lightly raised her foot and let it down, allowing her anklets to jingle, I felt thrilled. Though I was an ignoramus, I felt moved by the movements, rhythm, and time, although I did not quite follow the meaning of the words. She stopped now and then to explain: '*Nari* means girl—and *mani* is a jewel . . . The whole line means: "It is impossible for me to bear this burden of love you have cast on me."' She panted while she explained. There were beads of perspiration on her forehead and lip. She danced a few steps, paused for a moment, and explained, 'Lover always means God,' and she took the trouble to explain further to me the intricacies of its rhythm. The floor resounded with the stamping of her feet. I felt nervous that those on the floor below might ask us to stop, but she never cared, never bothered about anything. I could see, through her effort, the magnificence of the composition, its symbolism, the boyhood of a very young god, and his fulfilment in marriage, the passage of years from youth to decay, but the heart remaining ever fresh like a lotus on a pond. When she indicated the lotus with her fingers, you could almost hear the ripple of water around it. She held the performance for nearly an hour; it filled me with the greatest pleasure on earth. I could honestly declare that, while I watched her perform, my mind was free, for once, from all carnal thoughts; I viewed her as a pure abstraction. She could make me forget my surroundings. I sat with open-mouthed wonder watching her. Suddenly she stopped and flung her whole weight on me with: 'What a darling. You are giving me a new lease of life.'

Next time we went up the hill our strategy was ready. I would drop her there and come back to town. She would stay behind for two days, bearing all the possible loneliness and irritation, and speak to her husband. It was imperative that before we proceeded any further we should clear up the entire matter with her husband. She would do the talking for two days. And then I would go up and meet them, and then we would plan further stages of work for her career. She had suddenly become very optimistic about her husband, and often leaned over to whisper, 'I think he will agree to our proposal,' so that Gaffur should not know, or revelled in further wishful thoughts. 'He is not bad. It's all a show, you know. He is merely posing to be uninterested. You don't talk to him at all. I'll do all the talking. I know how to tackle him. Leave him to me.' And so she spoke until we reached the top. 'Oh, see those birds! What colours! You know, there is a small piece about a parrot on a maiden's arm. I'll dance it for you sometime.'

He was in an unbelievably cheerful mood. He greeted his wife with greater warmth than ever before. 'Do you know there is a third cave; a sort of vault leads into it. I scraped the lime, and there you have a complete fresco of musical notations, in symbolic figures. The style is of the fifth century. I am puzzled how such a wide period-difference has come about,' he said, greeting us on the veranda itself. He had pulled up a chair and was watching the valley, with papers on his lap. He held up his latest discovery. His wife looked at it with due ecstasy and cried, 'Musical notations! What wonderful things! Do take me to see them, will you?'

'Yes; come with me tomorrow morning. I'll explain it to you.'

'Oh, wonderful!' And she cried, in a highly affected voice, 'I'll try and sing them to you.'

'I doubt if you can. It's more difficult than you imagine.'

She looked fevered and anxious about pleasing him. It seemed to bode no good. This all-round cheeriness somehow did not please me. He turned and asked, 'What about you, Raju? Would you like to see my discovery?'

'Of course, but I have to get back to town as soon as possible, I just came to leave the lady here, because she was so anxious; and to know if you want anything and if things are quite satisfactory.'

'Oh, perfect, perfect!' he cried. 'That Joseph is a wonderful man. I don't see him, I don't hear him, but he does everything for me at the right time. That's how I want things to be, you know. He moves on ball-bearings, I think.'

That's what I thought when I saw Rosie demonstrate to me in

her hotel room, her whole movement being so much against the fixed factors of bone and muscle, walls and floor.

Marco continued his rhapsody on Joseph. 'I can never thank you enough for finding me a place like this and a man like Joseph. He's really a wonder. What a pity he should be wasting his talent on this hilltop!'

'You are very appreciative,' I said. 'I'm sure he'll be elated to know your opinion.'

'Oh, I have told him that without any reserve. I have also invited him to join my household any time he wishes to come and settle in the plains.'

He was unusually loquacious and warm. His nature flourished on solitude, and cave-frescoes. How happy he'd have been, I thought, to have had Joseph for a wife! My mind was busy with these thoughts as he was talking. Rosie went on like a good wife, saying, 'I hope there is food to eat, and everything is okay. If there is milk may I give you all coffee?' She ran in and returned to say, 'Yes, there is milk. I'll make coffee for all of you. I won't take more than five minutes.'

I was somehow feeling not quite at ease today. There was a lot of suspense and anxiety at the back of my mind. I was nervous of what he would say to Rosie and really anxious that he should not hurt her. Also, at the same time, a fear that if he became too nice to her, she might not care for me. I wanted him to be good to her, listen to her proposals, and yet leave her to my care! What an impossible, fantastic combination of circumstances to expect!

While Rosie was fussing with the coffee inside, he brought out another chair for me. 'I always do my work here,' he said. I felt that he honoured the valley with his patronage. He took out a bundle of sheets in an album, and a few photographs. He had made voluminous notes on all the cave-paintings. He had filled sheet after sheet with their description, transcription, and what not. They were obscure, but still I went through them with a show of interest. I wished I could ask questions on their value, but again I found myself tongue-tied, because I lacked the idiom. I wished I had been schooled in a jargon-picking institution; that would have enabled me to move with various persons on equal terms. No one would listen to my plea of ignorance and take the trouble to teach me as Rosie did. I listened to him. He was flinging at me dates, evidence, generalizations, and descriptions of a variety of paintings

and carvings. I dared not ask what was the earthly use of all that
he was doing. When coffee arrived, brought on a tray by Rosie (she
had glided in softly, as if to show that she could rival Joseph's steps,
I was startled when she held the cups under my nose), he said to
me, 'When this is published, it'll change all our present ideas of the
history of civilization. I shall surely mention in the book my debt to
you in discovering this place.'

Two days later I was back there. I went there at noon, at a time
when I was sure that Marco would have gone down to the cave so
that I might possibly get Rosie alone for a few moments. They were
not in the bungalow. Joseph was there, arranging their midday meal
in the back room. He said, 'They have gone down and are not back
yet.'

I looked up at Joseph's face as if to get a sign of how things
were. But he seemed evasive. I asked cheerily, 'How is everything
Joseph?'

'Very well, sir.'

'That man thinks so well of you!' I said to flatter him.

But he took it indifferently. 'What if he does! I only do my duty.
In my profession, some may curse, and some may bless, but I don't
care who says what. Last month there was a group who wanted
to assault me because I said I could not procure girls for them, but
was I afraid? I ordered them to quit next morning. This is a spot
for people to live in. I give them all the comforts ungrudgingly. It
costs eight annas sometimes to get a pot of water, and I have to send
cans and pots with any bus or truck going downhill, and wait for
its return—but the guests will never know the difficulty. They are
not expected to. It's my business to provide, and it's their business
to pay the bill. Let there be no confusion about it. I do my duty and
others must do theirs. But if they think I'm a procurer, I get very
angry.'

'Naturally, no one would like it,' I said just to cut his monologue.
'I hope this man does not bother you in any way?'

'Oh, no, he is a gem. A good man; would be even better if his
wife left him alone. He was so happy without her. Why did you
bring her back? She seems to be a horrible nagger.'

'Very well, I'll take her downhill and leave the man in peace,'
I said, starting for the cave. The pathway on the grass had become
smooth and white with Marco's tread. I passed through the thicket
and was crossing the sandy stretch when I found him coming from

the opposite direction. He was dressed heavily as usual, the portfolio swung in his grip. A few yards behind him followed Rosie. I could not read anything from their faces.

'Hello!' I cried cheerily, facing him. He looked up, paused, opened his mouth to say something, swallowed his words, stepped aside to avoid encountering me, and resumed his forward march. Rosie followed as if she were walking in her sleep. She never even turned to give me a look. A few yards behind Rosie I brought up the rear, and we entered the bungalow gate as a sort of caravan. I felt it would be best to follow their example of silence, and to look just as moody and morose as they. It matched the company very well.

From the top of the veranda he turned to address us. He said, 'It'll not be necessary for either of you to come in.' He went straight into his room and shut the door.

Joseph emerged from the kitchen door, wiping a plate. 'I'm waiting to take instructions for dinner.'

Rosie passed up the steps without a word, moved down the veranda, opened the door of his room, passed in, and shut the door. This utter quietness was getting on my nerves. It was entirely unexpected and I did not know how to respond to it. I thought he would either fight us or argue or do something. But this behaviour completely baffled me.

Gaffur came round, biting a straw between his teeth, to ask, 'What time are we going down?'

I knew this was not his real intention in coming, but to see the drama. He must have whiled away his time gossiping with Joseph; and they must have pooled their information about the girl. I said, 'Why are you in a hurry, Gaffur?' and added with bitterness, 'When you can stay on and see a nice show.'

He came close to me and said, 'Raju, this is not at all good. Let us get away. Leave them alone. After all, they are husband and wife; they'll know how to make it up. Come on. Go back to your normal work. You were so interested and carefree and happy then.'

I had nothing to say to this. It was very reasonable advice he was giving me. Even at that moment, it would have been all different if God had given me the sense to follow Gaffur's advice. I should have gone quietly back, leaving Rosie to solve her problems with her husband. That would have saved many sharp turns and twists in my life's course. I told Gaffur, 'Wait near the car, I'll tell you,' keeping irritation out of my voice.

Gaffur went away, grumbling. Presently I heard him sounding the horn—as irate bus-drivers do when their passengers get down at a wayside teashop. I decided to ignore it. I saw the door on the other side open. Marco showed himself outside the front veranda, and said, 'Driver, are you ready to go?'

'Yes, sir,' said Gaffur.

'Very well then,' said the man. He picked up his bundle and started walking to the car. I saw him through the glass shutters of the hall window. It puzzled me. I tried to cross the hail and go out through the door, but it was bolted. I quickly turned, ran down the steps, and went round to Gaffur's car. Marco had already taken his seat. Gaffur had not started the engine yet. He was afraid to ask about the others, but marked time by fumbling with the switch-key. He must have been surprised at the effect of sounding the horn. God knows why he did it; perhaps he was testing it or idling or wanted to remind everyone concerned that time was passing.

'Where are you going?' I asked Marco, taking courage and putting my head into the car.

'I'm going down to the hotel to close my account there.'

'What do you mean?' I asked.

He looked me up and down with a fierce glance. 'I do not have to explain. I took the room and I am closing the account; that is all. Driver, you may present me your bill direct. Have a receipt ready when you want payment.'

'Is no one else coming?' ventured Gaffur, looking in the direction of the bungalow.

The man merely said, 'No,' and added, 'if anyone else is coming, I'll get out.'

'Driver,' I said with a sudden tone of authority. Gaffur was startled at being called 'driver' by me. 'Take that man wherever he may want to go and bring me back the car tomorrow—and you will make complete settlement of all your bills with him. Keep a separate account for my own trips.' I could have made a further demonstration of arrogance by saying I had brought the car for my own business and so forth, but I saw no point in all that. As I stood watching Marco, a sudden impulse moved me even without my knowledge. I opened the door of the car and pulled him out of it.

For all the heavy helmet and glasses that he wore, he was frail—too much frieze-gazing and cave-visiting had emaciated him.

'What? Are you attempting to manhandle me?' he shouted.

'I want to talk to you. I want you to talk. You can't just go away like this.' I found his breath coming and going sharply. I calmed down and said, softening my style, 'Come in and have your food and speak out. Let us talk, discuss things, and then do what you like. You can't abandon a wife in this place and go away.' I looked at Gaffur and said, 'You are not in a hurry, are you?'

'No, no. Have your food and come, sir. Plenty of time still.'

'I'll ask Joseph to give you food,' I added. I felt sorry that I had not taken charge of the situation earlier.

'Who are you?' Marco asked suddenly. 'What is your business with me?'

'A great deal. I have helped you. I have given a lot of time to your business. I undertook a lot of responsibility for you, these several weeks.'

'And I dispense with your service from this minute,' he cried. 'Give me your bill and be done with it.' Even in his most excited, emotional state, he would not forget his vouchers.

I said, 'Had we better not go into it calmly, sitting down and calculating? I have with me some money that you left with me before.'

'Very well,' he grunted. 'Let us be done with everything, and then you get out of my sight.'

'Easily done,' I said. 'But look here, this bungalow has two suites of rooms, and I can engage one perfectly legitimately.'

Joseph appeared on the steps. 'Will you be wanting a dinner tonight?'

'No,' he said.

'Yes, I may,' I said. 'You may leave, Joseph, if you are in a hurry. If I am staying, I'll send for you. Open the other suite and account it to me.'

'Yes, sir.' He unlocked another door and I strode into it with the air of a proprietor. I left the door open. It was my room and I was free to leave the door ajar if I chose.

I looked out of the window. The sun's rays from the west were touching the tops of trees with gold. It was a breathtaking sight. I wished Rosie could see it. She was inside. I had lost the privilege of walking into their room. I sat down in the wooden chair in my suite and wondered what to do. What was it that I had done now? I had no clear programme. I had no doubt successfully pulled him out of the car. But that took us nowhere. He had gone and bolted himself in his room, and I was in mine. If I had let him go, I might at least have had a chance to bring Rosie round and get her to talk about herself. Now I had made a mess. Could I go out and ask Gaffur to sound the horn again so that the man might emerge from his room?

Half an hour passed thus. There was absolutely no sign of any speech or movement. I tiptoed out of my room. I went to the kitchen. Joseph was gone. I lifted the lids of the vessels. Food was there. No one seemed to have touched it. Heaven knew they were both starving. I felt a sudden pity for the man. Rosie must have completely faded out. It was her habit to ask for something to eat every two hours. At the hotel I constantly ordered a tray for her, if we were out I would stop all along the way to buy fruit or refreshment. Now the poor girl must be exhausted—and add to it the walk up and down to the cave. I felt suddenly angry at the thought of her. Why couldn't she eat or tell me what was what instead of behaving like a deaf-mute? Had the monster cut off her tongue? I wondered in genuine horror. I put the food on plates, put them on a tray, walked to their door. I hesitated for a second—only for a second; if I hesitated longer, I knew I would never go in. I pushed the door open with my feet. Rosie was lying on her bed with eyes shut. (Was she in a faint, I wondered for a second.) I had never seen her in such a miserable condition before. He was sitting in his chair, elbow on the table, his chin on his fist. I had never seen him so vacant before. I felt pity for him. I held myself responsible for it. Why couldn't I have kept out of all this? I placed the tray before him.

'People have evidently forgotten their food today. If you have a burden on your mind it's no reason why you should waste your food.'

Rosie opened her eyes. They were swollen. She had large, vivacious eyes, but they looked as if they had grown one round larger now, and were bulging and fearsome, dull and red. She was a sorry sight in every way. She sat up and told me, 'Don't waste any more of your time with us. You go back. That's all I have to say,' in a thick gruff, crackling voice. Her voice shook a little as she spoke. 'I mean it. Leave us now.'

What had come over this woman? Was she in league with her husband? She had every authority to ask me to get out. Probably she repeated her folly in encouraging me all along. All I could say in reply was, 'First, you must have your food. For what reason are you fasting?'

She merely repeated, 'I want you to go.'

'Aren't you coming down?' I persisted to Marco. The man behaved as if he were a deaf-mute. He never showed any sign of hearing us.

She merely repeated, 'I am asking you to leave us. Do you hear?'

I grew weak and cowardly at her tone. I muttered, 'I mean, you are—or he may want to go down, if it is so—'

She clicked her tongue in disgust. 'Do you not understand? We want you to leave.'

I grew angry. This woman who had been in my arms forty-eight hours ago was showing off. Many insulting and incriminating remarks welled up in my throat. But even in that stress I had the sense to swallow back my words, and, feeling that it would be dangerous to let myself stand there any longer, turned on my heel and went in a stride to the car. 'Gaffur, let us go.'

'Only one passenger?'

'Yes.' I banged the door and took my seat.

'What about them?'

'I don't know. You had better settle with them later.'

'If I have to come again to talk to them, who pays the fare for the trip?'

I beat my brow. 'Begone, man. You can settle all that later.'

Gaffur sat in his seat with the look of a philosopher, started the car, and was off. I had a hope, as I turned to look, that she might watch me from the window. But no such luck. The car sped downward. Gaffur said, 'It's time your elders found a bride for you.' I said nothing in reply, and he said, through the gathering darkness, 'Raju, I'm senior in years. I think this is the best thing you have done. You will be more happy hereafter.'

Gaffur's prophecy was not fulfilled in the coming days. I cannot remember a more miserable period of my life. The usual symptoms were present, of course: no taste for food, no sound sleep, no stability (I couldn't stay put in any one place), no peace of mind, no sweetness of temper or speech—no, no, no, a number of no's. With all seriousness I returned to my normal avocation. But everything looked so unreal. I relieved the boy at the shop, sat there and handed out things and received cash, but always with a feeling that it was a silly occupation. I walked up and down the platform when the train arrived. Sure as anything, I could always get someone to take round.

'Are you Railway Raju?'

'Yes,' and then the fat paterfamilias, wife, and two children.

'You see, we are coming from . . . and So-and-so mentioned your name to us as a man who would surely help us . . . You see, my wife is keen on a holy bath at the source of the Sarayu, and then I'd like to see an elephant camp, and anything else you suggest will be most welcome. But remember, only three days. I couldn't get even an hour of extra leave; I'll have to be in my office on . . .'

I hardly paid attention to what they said. I knew all their lines in advance; all that I paid attention to was the time at their disposal, and the extent of their financial outlay. Even the latter did not really interest me. It was more mechanical than intentional. I called up Gaffur, sat in the front seat, took the party about. While passing the New Extension, I pointed without even turning my head, 'Sir Frederick Lawley . . .' when we passed the statue. I knew exactly when the question would come, 'Whose is this statue?' and I knew when the next question was coming and had my answer ready, 'The man left behind by Robert Clive to administer the district. He built all the tanks and dams and developed this district. Good man. Hence the statue.' At the tenth-century Iswara temple at Vinayak Street, I reeled off the description of the frieze along the wall: 'If you look closely, you will see the entire epic *Ramayana* carved along the wall,' and so forth. I took them to the source of the Sarayu on the misty heights of Mempi Peak, watched the lady first plunge in the basin, the man avowing that he did not care and then following her example. I then took them into the inner shrine, showed them the ancient stone image on the pillar, with Shiva absorbing the Ganges river in his matted locks . . .

I collected my fee, and my commission from Gaffur and the rest, and saw them off next day. I did it all mechanically, without zest. I was, of course, thinking of Rosie all the time. 'That man has probably starved her to death, driven her mad, or left her in the open to be eaten by tigers,' I told myself. I looked forlorn and uninterested and my mother tried to find out why. She asked, 'What has gone wrong with you?'

'Nothing,' I replied. My mother had been so little used to seeing me about the house that she felt surprised and uneasy. But she left me alone. I ate, slept, hung about the railway platform, conducted visitors about, but I was never at peace with myself. My mind was troubled all the while. It was a natural obsession. I didn't even know what had happened, what all the silence and unnatural calm meant. This was a most unexpected development. As I had visualized, I had thought in my dreamy-happy way that he'd present me with his wife and say, 'I'm happy you are going to look after her and her art; I'd like to be left alone to pursue my cave studies; you are such a fine fellow to do this for us.' Or, on the other hand, he might have rolled up his sleeve to throw me out—one or the other, but I never bargained for this kind of inexplicable stalemate. And what was more, for the girl to support him with such ferocity. I was appalled at the duplicity of her heart. I agonized over and over again, piecing together the data and reading their meaning. I deliberately refrained from opening the subject with Gaffur. He respected my sentiment and never mentioned it again, although I was hoping desperately each day that he would say something about them. On certain days when I wanted him, he was not available. I knew then that he must have gone to the Peak House. I refrained from going near the Anand Bhavan. If any of my customers wanted a hotel I sent them nowadays to the Taj. I did not have to bother myself about them unduly. Marco had said he'd settle their accounts direct—well, you could depend upon him to do it. I came into the picture only to collect a commission from them, as from Gaffur himself. But I was prepared to forgo it all. I was in no mood to make money. In the world of gloom in which I was plunged there was no place for money. There must have been some money, I suppose, somewhere. My mother was able to carry on the household as before, and the shop continued to exist. I knew Gaffur's account must also have been settled. But he never said a word about it. So much the better. I didn't want to be reminded of the life that was gone.

I felt bored and terrified by the boredom of normal life, so much had I got used to a glamorous, romantic existence. Gradually I found taking tourists around a big nuisance. I began to avoid the railway station. I let the porter's son meet the tourists. He had already attempted his hand at it before. Of course, the tourists might miss my own speeches and descriptions, but lately I had become dull-witted, and they probably preferred the boy, as he was at least as curious and interested as they in seeing places. Perhaps he was beginning to answer to the name of Railway Raju too.

How many days passed thus? Only thirty, though they looked to me like years. I was lying asleep on the floor of my house one afternoon. I was half awake and had noted the departure of the Madras Mail at four-thirty. When the chug-chug of the train died away, I tried to sleep again, having been disturbed by its noisy arrival. My mother came and said, 'Someone is asking for you.' She didn't wait for questions, but went into the kitchen.

I got up and went to the door. There stood Rosie on the threshold, with a trunk at her feet and a bag under her arm. 'Rosie, why didn't you say you were coming? Come in, come in. Why stand there? That was only my mother.' I carried her trunk in. I could guess a great many things about her. I didn't want to ask her any questions. I didn't feel like knowing anything. I fussed about her, lost my head completely. 'Mother!' I cried. 'Here is Rosie! She is going to be a guest in our house.'

My mother came out of the kitchen formally, smiled a welcome, and said, 'Be seated on that mat. What's your name?' she asked kindly, and was rather taken aback to hear the name 'Rosie'. She expected a more orthodox name. She looked anguished for a moment, wondering how she was going to accommodate a 'Rosie' in her home.

I stood about awkwardly. I had not shaved since the morning; I had not combed my hair; my *dhoti* was discoloured and rumpled; the vest I wore had several holes on the back and chest. I folded my arms across my chest to cover the holes. I could not have made a worse impression if I had tried hard. I was ashamed of the torn mat—it had been there since we built the house—the dark hall with the smoky walls and tiles. All the trouble I used to take to create an impression on her was gone in a moment. If she realized that this was my normal setting, God knew how she would react. I was glad at least I was wearing my torn vest instead of being barebodied as was my habit at home. My mother hardly ever noticed the hairiness of my chest, but Rosie, oh—

My mother was busy in the kitchen, but she managed to come out for a moment to observe the formality of receiving a guest. A guest was a guest, even though she might be a Rosie. So my mother came up and sat down on the mat with an air of settling down to a chat. The very first question she asked was, 'Who has come with you, Rosie?' Rosie blushed, hesitated, and looked at me. I moved a couple of steps backward in order that she might see me only dimly, and not in all my raggedness.

I replied, 'I think she has come alone, Mother.'

My mother was amazed. 'Girls today! How courageous you are! In our day we wouldn't go to the street corner without an escort. And I have been to the market only once in my life, when Raju's father was alive.'

Rosie blinked and listened in silence, not knowing how to react to these statements. She simply opened her eyes wide and raised her brows. I watched her. She looked a little paler and slightly careworn—not the swollen-eyed, gruff-toned monster she had seemed the other day. Her tone was sweet as ever. She looked slightly weak, but as if she hadn't a care in the world. My mother said, 'Water is boiling; I'll give you coffee. Do you like coffee?' I was relieved that the conversation was coming down to this level. I hoped my mother would continue to talk about herself rather than ask questions. But it was not to be. She asked next, 'Where do you come from?'

'From Madras,' I answered promptly.

'What brings you here?'

'She has come to see some friends.'

'Are you married?'

'No,' I answered promptly.

My mother shot a look at me. It seemed to be meaningful. She withdrew her glance swiftly from me, and, looking at her guest kindly, asked, 'Don't you understand Tamil?'

I knew I should shut up now. I let Rosie answer in Tamil, 'Yes. It's what we speak at home.'

'Who else have you in your house?'

'My uncle, my aunt, and—' She was trailing away, and my mother shot at her the next terrible question. 'What is your father's name?'

It was a dreadful question for the girl. She knew only her mother and always spoke of her. I had never questioned her about it. The girl remained silent for a moment and said, 'I have . . . no father.'

My mother was at once filled with the greatest sympathy and cried, 'Poor one, without father or mother. I am sure your uncle must be looking after you well. Are you a BA?'

'Yes,' I corrected. 'She is an MA'

'Good, good, brave girl. Then you lack nothing in the world. You are not like us uneducated women. You will get on anywhere. You can ask for your railway ticket, call a policeman if somebody worries you, and keep your money. What are you going to do? Are you going to join government service and earn? Brave girl.' My mother was full of admiration for her. She got up, went in, and brought her a tumbler of coffee. The girl drank it off gratefully. I was wondering how best I could sneak out and groom myself properly. But there was no chance. My father's architectural sense had not gone beyond building a single large hall and a kitchen. Of course, there was the front *pyol* on which visitors and menfolk generally sat. But how could I ask Rosie to move there? It was too public—the shop-boy and all his visitors would come round, gaze at her and ask if she was married. This was a slightly difficult situation for me. We had got used to common living in that hall. It had never occurred to us to be otherwise. We never wanted anything more than this. My father lived in his shop, I played under the tree, and have received male visitors on the outside *pyol* and left the inner room for mother or any lady that might come. When we slept we went in. If it was warm, we slept on the *pyol*. The hall was a passage, a dressing-room, drawing-room, study, everything combined. My shaving mirror was on a nail; my finest clothes hung on a peg; for a bath I dashed to a chamber in the back yard, half open to the sky, and poured over my head water drawn straight from the well. I ran up and down and conducted my toilet while my mother came into or out of the kitchen or slept or sat moping in the hall. We had got used to each other's presence and did not mind it in the least. But now with Rosie there?

My mother, as if understanding my predicament, said to the girl, 'I'm going to the well. Will you come with me? You are a city girl. You must know something of our village life too.' The girl quietly rose and followed her; I hoped she'd not be subjected to an inquisition at the well. The minute their backs were turned I got busy, ran hither and thither, scraped my chin in a hurry, cut myself a little, bathed, groomed myself, and changed into better clothes, and by the time they were back from the well I was in a condition to be viewed by the Princess of the Earth. I went over to the shop and sent the boy to fetch Gaffur.

'Rosie, if you would like to wash and dress, go ahead. I'll wait outside. We'll go out after that.'

It was perhaps an unwarranted luxury to engage Gaffur for an outing. But I saw no other way. I could not talk to her in our home, and I could not make her walk through the streets. Although I had done it before, today it seemed different. I felt a little abashed to be seen with her.

I told Gaffur, 'She is back.'

He said, 'I know it. They were here at the hotel, and he went by the Madras train.'

'You never told me anything.'

'Why should I? You were going to know anyway.'

'What, what has happened?'

'Ask the lady herself, now that you have her in your pocket.' He sounded resentful.

I told him placatingly, 'Oh, don't be sour, Gaffur . . . I want the car for the evening.'

'I'm at your service, sir. What do I have the taxi for unless it is to drive you where you command?' He winked and I was relieved to see him back in his old cheerful mood. When Rosie appeared at the door I went and told my mother, 'We will come back, Mother, after a little outing.'

'Where?' asked Gaffur, looking at us through the glass. As we hesitated he asked puckishly, 'Shall I drive to the Peak House?'

'No, no,' Rosie cried, becoming very alert at the mention of it. 'I have had enough of it.' I didn't pursue the subject.

As we passed the Taj I asked, 'Would you like to eat there?'

'Your mother gave me coffee; that is enough. What a fine mother you have!'

'The only trouble is she asks you about marriage!' We laughed nervously at this joke.

'Gaffur, drive on to the river,' I said. He drove through the market road, honking his horn impatiently through the crowd. It was a crowded hour. Lots of people were moving around. The lights were up. Shop lights sparkled and lit up the throughfare. He took a sharp turn at Ellaman Street—that narrow street in which oil-merchants lived, the oldest street in the city, with children playing in it, cows lounging, and donkeys and dogs blocking the passage so narrow that any passing car almost touched the walls of the houses. Gaffur always chose this way to the river, although there was a

better approach. It gave him some sort of thrill to honk his car horn
and scatter the creatures in the road in a fright. Ellaman Street ended
with the last lamp on the road, and the road imperceptibly merged
into the sand. He applied the brake under the last lamp, with a jerk
sufficient to shake us out of the car. He was in an unusually jovial
mood today; he was given to his own temperaments and moods,
and no one could predict how he would behave at a given moment.
We left him under the lamp. I said, 'We want to walk about.' He
winked at me mischievously in reply.

The evening had darkened. There were still a few groups sitting
here and there on the sand. Some students were promenading.
Children were playing and running in circles and shouting. On
the river step, some men were having their evening dip. Far off
at Nallappa's Grove cattle were crossing the river with their bells
tinkling. The stars were out. The Taluk office gong sounded seven.
A perfect evening—as it had been for years and years. I had seen
the same scene at the same hour for years and years. Did those
children never grow up? I became a little sentimental and poetic,
probably because of the companion at my side. My feelings and
understanding seemed to have become suddenly heightened. I
said, 'It's a beautiful evening,' to start a conversation. She briefly
said, 'Yes.' We sought a secluded place, away from the route of
promenading students.

I spread out my handkerchief, and said, 'Sit down, Rosie.' She
picked away the kerchief and sat down. The gathering darkness was
congenial. I sac close to her and said, 'Now tell me everything from
beginning to end.'

She remained in thought for a while and said, 'He left by the
train this evening, and that is all.'

'Why did you not go with him?'

'I don't know. It is what I came for. But it didn't happen that
way. Well, it is just as well. We were not meant to be in each other's
company.'

'Tell me what happened. Why were you so rude to me chat
day?'

'I thought it best that we forget each other, and that I go back
to him.'

I did not know how to pursue this inquiry. I had no method of
eliciting information—of all that had gone before. I fumbled and
hummed and hawed in questioning, till I suddenly felt that I was

getting nowhere at all. I wanted a chronological narration, but she seemed unable to provide it. She was swinging forwards and backwards and talking in scraps. I was getting it all in a knot. I felt exasperated. I said, 'Answer me now, step by step. Give an answer to each question. I left you with him to speak about the proposal we had discussed. What did you tell him?'

'What we had agreed—that he should permit me to dance. He was quite happy till I mentioned it. I never spoke about it that whole day or till late next day. I led him on to tell me about his own activity. He showed me the pictures he had copied, the notes he had made, and spoke far into the night about their significance. He was going to be responsible for rewriting of history, he said. He was talking about his plans for publishing his work. He said later he would go to Mexico, and to some of the Far Eastern countries to study similar subjects and add them on to his work. I was full of enthusiasm although I did not follow everything he said. I felt after all an understanding was coming between us—there in that lonely house, with trees rustling and foxes and animals prowling around, some light glimmering in the far-off valley. Next morning I went with him to the cave to have a look at the musical notations he had discovered. We had to pass through the main cave and beyond it into a vault by a crumbling ladder. A fierce, terrifying place. Nothing on earth would have induced me to go to a spot like that, stuffy, fierce, and dark. "There may be cobras here," I said. He ignored my fears. "You should feel at home, then," he said and we laughed. And then he lit up a lantern and showed me the wall on which he had scraped off the lime and discovered new pictures. They were the usual grotesque, ancient paintings of various figures, but he managed to spell out the letters around them, and take them down as musical notations. It was nothing I could make out or make use of. They were abstract verse about some theories of an ancient musical system or some such thing. I said, "If these were about dancing, I could perhaps have tried—" He looked up sharply. The word "dance" always stung him. I was afraid to go on with the subject. But there, squatting on the ancient floor, amidst cobwebs and bats, in that dim lantern light, I felt courage coming back. "Will you permit me to dance?"

'Promptly came his reply, with a scowl, the old face was coming back. "Why?"

'"I think I'd be very happy if I could do that. I have so many ideas. I'd like to try. Just as you are trying to—"

' "Oh, you want to rival me, is that it? This is a branch of learning, not street acrobatics."

' "You think dancing is street acrobatics?"

' "I'm not prepared to discuss all that with you. An acrobat on a trapeze goes on doing the same thing all his life; well, your dance is like that. What is there intelligent or creative in it? You repeat your tricks all your life. We watch a monkey perform, not because it is artistic but because it is a monkey that is doing it." I swallowed all the insults; I still had hopes of converting him. I lapsed into silence and let him do his work. I turned the subject to other things, and he was normal again. After dinner that night he went back to his studies and I to my game-watching on the veranda. As usual, there was nothing to watch, but I sat there turning over in my head all that he had said and all that I had said, and wondering how to get through the business. I ignored all insults and troubles in the hope that if we reached an agreement in the end, it'd all be forgotten. As I sat there, he came behind me, and, putting his hand on my shoulder, said, "I thought we had come to a final understanding about that subject. Did you or did you not promise that you'd never mention it again?" '

The Taluk office gong sounded eight and all the crowd had vanished. We were alone on the sand. Still I'd not learned anything about Rosie. Gaffur sounded the horn. It was no doubt late, but if I went home she would not he able to speak. I said, 'Shall we spend the night at the hotel?'

'No. I'd like to go back to your house. I have told your mother that I'll be back.'

'All right,' I said, remembering my cash position. 'Let us stay here for half an hour more. Now tell me.'

'His tone,' she resumed, 'was now so kind that I felt I need not bother even if I had to abandon my own plans once and for all: if he was going to be so nice, I wanted nothing more—I'd almost made up my mind that I would ask nothing of him. Yet as a last trick I said, encouraged by his tone, "I want you to see just one small bit, which I generally do as a memento of my mother. It was her piece, you know." I got up and pulled him by his hand to our room. I pushed aside the chair and other things. I adjusted my dress. I pushed him down to sit on the bed, as I had done with you. I sang that song about the lover and his girl on the banks of the

Jamuna and danced the piece for him He sat watching me coldly. I had not completed the fifth line when he said, "Stop, I have seen enough."

'I stopped, abashed. I had been certain that he was going to be captivated by it and tell me to go ahead and dance all my life. But he said, "Rosie, you must understand, this is not art. You have not sufficient training. Leave the thing alone."

'But here I committed a blunder. I said haughtily, "Everyone except you likes it."

For instance?"

'"Well, Raju saw me do it, and he was transported. Do you know what he said?"

'"Raju! Where did you do it for him?"

'"At the hotel." And then he said, "Come and sit here," pointing at the chair, like an examining doctor. He subjected me to a close questioning. I think it went on all night. He asked details of our various movements ever since we came here, what time you came to the hotel each day, when you left, where you kept yourself in the room, and how long, and so on, all of which I had to answer. I broke down and cried. He got from my answers enough indication of what we had been doing. Finally he said, "I didn't know that that hotel catered to such fervid art-lovers! I was a fool to have taken too much decency for granted." Till dawn we sat there. He on the bed, and I on the chair. I was overcome with sleep and put my head on the table, and when I awoke he was gone to the caves.

'Joseph had left some coffee for me. I tidied myself up and went down in search of him. I felt I had made the capital blunder of my life. I had been indiscreet in talking to him as I had been indiscreet and wrong in all my actions. I realized I had committed an enormous sin. I walked as in a dream down to the cave. My mind was greatly troubled. I didn't want anything more in life than to make my peace with him. I did not want to dance. I felt lost . . . I was in terror. I was filled with some sort of pity for him too, as I remembered how he had sat up unmoving on the bed all night while I sat in the chair. The look of despair and shock on his face haunted me. I walked down the valley, hardly noticing my surroundings. If a tiger had crossed my path I'd hardly have noticed it . . . I found him sitting in his cave on his usual folding stool, sketching out his copies. His back was turned to the entrance when I went in. But as I got into the narrower entrance the light was blocked and he turned. He looked at me coldly. I stood like a prisoner at the bar. "I have come to apologize sincerely. I want to say I will do whatever you ask me to do. I committed a blunder . . . "

'He returned to his work without a word. He went on as if he had been alone. I waited there. Finally, when he had finished his day's work, he picked up his portfolio and papers and started out. He put on his helmet and spectacles and went past me as if I had not existed. I had stood there for nearly three hours, I think. He had measured, copied, noted down, and examined with a torch, but without paying the slightest attention to me. When he went back to the bungalow, I followed him. That's where you saw us. I went to his room. He sat in his chair and I on the bed. No word or speech. You came into the room again. I sincerely hoped you would leave us and go away, and that we could be peaceful between ourselves . . . Day after day it went on. I stayed on hopefully. I found that he would not eat the food I touched. So I let Joseph serve him. I ate my food alone in the kitchen. If I lay on the bed, he slept on the floor. So I took to sleeping on the floor, and he went and lay on the bed. He never looked at me or spoke. He arranged with Joseph and went down a couple of times, leaving me alone in the bungalow. He returned and went about his business without worrying about me. But I followed him, day after day, like a dog—waiting on his grace. He ignored me totally. I could never have imagined that one human being could ignore the presence of another human being so completely. I followed him like a shadow, leaving aside all my own pride and self-respect; I hoped that ultimately he'd come round. I never left his side even for a moment, whether in his room or in the cave. It was a strain to remain speechless in that vast lonely place. I thought I had gone dumb. Joseph was the only one to whom I could say a word whenever he appeared, but he was a reserved man and did not encourage me. I had spent three weeks thus, in a vow of silence. I could not stand it any more. So one night as he sat at his table I said, "Have you not punished me enough?" My voice sounded strange, and like someone else's to me after so many weeks. It had a booming quality in that silent place that startled me. He started at the sound, turned, looked at me, and said, "This is my last word to you. Don't talk to me. You can go where you please or do what you please."

' "I want to be with you. I want you to forget everything. I want you to forgive me—" I said. Somehow I began to like him very much. It seemed enough if he forgave me and took me back.

'But he said, "Yes, I'm trying to forget—even the earlier fact that I ever took a wife. I want to get out of here too—but I have to complete my work; and I'm here for that. You are free to get out and do what you please."

'"I'm your wife and I'm with you."

'"You are here because I'm not a ruffian. But you are not my wife. You are a woman who will go to bed with anyone that flatters your antics. That's all. I don't want you here, but if you are going to be here, don't talk. That is all."

'I felt too hurt. I thought that Othello was kindlier to Desdemona. But I bore everything. I had a wild hope that in the end he'd relent, that when we left this place he might change. Once we were back in our home, everything would be all right.

'One day he started packing up. I tried to help him, but he would not let me; and then I packed up my things too, and followed him. Gaffur's car arrived. Both of us came down to the hotel. Back in Twenty-eight. The room looked poisonous to me now. He stayed for a day settling accounts; and at train time he went with the baggage to the railway station. I followed him mutely. I waited patiently. I knew he was going back to our home at Madras. I wanted very much to go back home. The porter carried our trunks. He pointed at my portion of the baggage and told the porter, "I don't know about these—not mine." So the porter looked at me for a second and separated my box. When the train arrived the porter carried only his baggage, and he took his seat in a compartment. I didn't know what to do. I picked up my trunk and followed. When I tried to step into the compartment he said, "I have no ticket for you," and he flourished a single ticket and shut the door on me. The train moved. I came to your home.'

She sat sobbing for a while. I comforted her. 'You are in the right place. Forget all your past. We will teach that cad a lesson by and by.' I made a grandiose announcement, 'First, I'll make the world recognize you as the greatest artist of the time.'

Within a short time my mother understood everything. When Rosie had gone in for a bath, she said, cornering me, 'This cannot go on long, Raju—you must put an end to it.'

'Don't interfere, Mother. I am an adult. I know what I am doing.'

'You can't have a dancing girl in your house. Every morning with all that dancing and everything going on! What is the home coming to?'

Encouraged by me, Rosie had begun to practise. She got up at five in the morning, bathed, and prayed before the picture of a god in my mother's niche, and began a practice session which went on for nearly three hours. The house rang with the jingling of her anklets. She ignored her surroundings completely, her attention being concentrated upon her movements and steps. After that she helped my mother, scrubbed, washed, swept, and tidied up everything in the house. My mother was pleased with her and seemed kind to her. I never thought that my mother would create a problem for me now, but here she was. I said, 'What has come over you all of a sudden?'

My mother paused. 'I was hoping you would have the sense to do something about it. It can't go on like this for ever. What will people say?'

'Who are "people"?' I asked.

'Well, my brother and your cousins and others known to us.'

'I don't care for their opinion. Just don't bother about such things.'

'Oh! That's a strange order you are giving me, my boy. I can't accept it.'

The gentle singing in the bathroom ceased; my mother dropped the subject and went away as Rosie emerged from her bath fresh and blooming. Looking at her, one would have thought that she had not a care in the world. She was quite happy to be doing what she was doing at the moment, was not in the least bothered about the past, and looked forward tremendously to the future. She was completely devoted to my mother.

But unfortunately my mother, for all her show of tenderness, was beginning to stiffen inside. She had been listening to gossip, and she could not accommodate the idea of living with a tainted woman. I was afraid to be cornered by her, and took care not to face her alone. But whenever she could get at me, she hissed a whisper into my ear. 'She is a real snake-woman, I tell you. I never liked her from the first day you mentioned her.'

I was getting annoyed with my mother's judgement and duplicity. The girl, in all innocence, looked happy and carefree and felt completely devoted to my mother. I grew anxious lest my mother should suddenly turn round and openly tell her to quit. I changed my tactics and said, 'You are right, Mother. But you see, she is a refugee, and we can't do anything. We have to be hospitable.'

'Why can't she go to her husband and fall at his feet? You know, living with a husband is no joke, as these modern girls imagine. No husband worth the name was ever conquered by powder and lipstick alone. You know, your father more than once . . .' She narrated an anecdote about the trouble created by my father's unreasonable, obstinate attitude in some family matter and how she met it. I listened to her anecdote patiently and with admiration, and that diverted her for a while. Afer a few days she began to allude to the problems of husband and wife whenever she spoke to Rosie, and filled the time with anecdotes about husbands: good husbands, bad husbands, reasonable husbands, unreasonable ones, savage ones, slightly deranged ones, moody ones, and so on and so forth; but it was always the wife, who by her doggedness, perseverance and patience, that brought him round. She quoted numerous mythological stories of Savitri, Sita, and all the well-known heroines. Apparently it was a general talk, apropos of nothing, but my mother's motives were naively clear. She was so clumsily roundabout that anyone could see what she was driving at. She was still supposed to be ignorant of Rosie's affairs, but she talked pointedly. I knew how Rosie smarted under these lessons, but I was helpless. I was afraid of my mother. I could have kept Rosie in a hotel, perhaps, but I was forced to take a more realistic view of my finances now. I was helpless as I saw Rosie suffer, and my only solace was that I suffered with her.

My worries were increasing. The boy at the shop was becoming more clamorous. My sales were poor, as the railways were admitting more pedlars on the platforms. My cash receipts were going down and my credit sales alone flourished. The wholesale merchants who supplied me with goods stopped credit to me. The boy's method of account-keeping was so chaotic that I did not know whether I was moving forward or backward. He produced cash from the counter in a haphazard manner, and there were immense gaps on the shelves all over the shop. The boy was probably pocketing money and eating off the stuff. With my credit at the wholesalers' gone, the public complained that nothing one wanted was ever available.

Suddenly the railways gave me notice to quit. I pleaded with the old station master and porter, but they could do nothing; the order had come from high up. The shop was given to a new contractor.

I could not contemplate the prospect of being cut off from the railways. I grew desperate and angry. I shed tears at seeing a new man in the place where I and my father had sat. I slapped the boy on the cheek and he cried, and his father, the porter, came down on me and said, 'This is what he gets for helping you! I had always told the boy—he was not your paid servant, anyway.'

'Payment for him? He has swallowed all the cash, credit, and every consumable article in the shop. Fattened himself on it! He must pay me for all his gluttony, which has ruined my business.'

'It's not he who has ruined you, but the *saithan* inside, which makes you talk like this.' He meant Rosie, I'm sure; she was peeping out of the doorway of our house. My mother watched from the *pyol* in great pain. It was a most unedifying spectacle.

I did not like the porter's reference, and so said something violent and tried to attack him. The station master appeared on the scene and said, 'If you create a disturbance here, I'll have to prohibit your entry.'

The new shopman watched the scene with detachment. A whiskered fellow—I did not like his leering look. I turned on him fiercely, leaving the porter, and cried, 'Well, you'll also face the same situation, remember, some day. Don't be too sure.'

He twirled his whiskers and said, 'How can everyone hope for the same luck as yours?' He winked mischievously, at which I completely lost my temper and flew at him. He repelled me with a back-stroke of his left hand as if swatting a fly, and I fell back, and knocked against my mother, who had come running onto the platform, a thing she had never done in her life. Luckily, I didn't knock her down.

She clung to my arm and screamed, 'Come away. Are you coming or not?' And the porter, the whiskered man, and everyone swore, 'You are saved today, because of that venerable old lady.' She dragged me back to the house; a few batches of paper, a register, and one or two odd personal belongings which I had kept in the shop were under my arm; with these I entered my house, and I knew my railway association was now definitely ended. It made my heart heavy. I felt so gloomy that I did not turn to see Rosie standing aside, staring at me. I flung myself in a corner of the hall and shut my eyes.

8

MY CREDITOR WAS the Sait, a wholesale merchant in Market Road. He called on me the next day. There was a knock on the door, and there he was. I was watching Rosie at her practice, leaning against the wall and lounging on the mat. I felt abashed at the sight of the Sait at my door. I knew why he had come. He had brought a fat ledger wrapped up in a blue cloth. He seemed pleased at the sight of me, as if he had feared that I had run away from my post. I was at a loss to say anything for a moment. I didn't want to show confusion. After the railway station episode, I was recovering my sense of perspective again. While watching Rosie do her practice, I seemed to get a clearer notion of what I should be doing. The sound of her anklets, and the whispered music she sang, her rhythm and movement, helped. I felt that I was once again becoming a man of importance. My mother, fortunately for me, had not spoken a word to me since the previous evening, and that saved me a great deal of embarrassment and strain. My mother could not help speaking to Rosie; in spite of all her prejudice, she liked the girl really and could not help treating her kindly. She had not the heart to starve her or offend her in any way. She attended on her enough to give her food and shelter, and left her alone. Only she could not trust herself to speak to me after the scene at the railway station. I am sure she felt that I had ruined, by my erratic ways, what her husband had so laboriously built up. But fortunately she did not take it out on the poor girl, but let her alone—after her usual dose of homilies and parables, all of which Rosie took in good humour.

The Sait was a thin man with a multi-coloured turban on his head. He was a prosperous businessman, very helpful with credit, but, of course, expected proper settlement of debts. He was at my door. I knew why. I fussed over him, and said, 'Come in, come in. Be seated. What a rare pleasure!' I dragged him and seated him on the *pyol*.

He was a good friend of mine, and he hesitated to talk about the dues. There was an awkward silence for a moment. Only Rosie's anklet-jingles could be heard for a while. He listened to it and asked, 'What is it?'

'Oh!' I said casually. 'A dance practice is going on.'

'Dance practice!' He was astounded. It was the last thing he expected in a home like mine. He sat thinking for a while, as if putting two and two together. He shook his head lightly. The story of the '*saithan* inside' had evidently reached him. He suppressed any inquiry regarding it as not his business, and said, 'What has come over you, Raju? You have not paid my dues for months and months, and you used to be so regular!'

'Business conditions have not been good, old man,' I said with a sort of affected resignation and cheer.

'No, it's not that. One must—'

'Oh, and that boy whom I trusted cheated completely.'

'What is the use of blaming others?' he asked. He seemed to be a ruthless man, who was bent upon harassing me. He took out his notebook, opened it out, and pointed at the bottom of a column. 'Eight thousand rupees! I can't let this go on very long. You will have to do something about it.'

I was tired of being told to do 'something about something'. My mother started it with regard to the girl, someone else about something else. The girl had started to say, 'We must do something,' and now this man; I felt irritated by his advice and said curtly, 'I know it.'

'What do you propose to do about it?'

'Of course you are going to be paid—'

'When?'

'How can I say? . . . You must wait.'

'All right. You want another week?' he asked.

'Week!' I laughed at the joke. He looked hurt. Everyone seemed hurt by me at this time.

He became very serious and said, 'Do you think it is a laughing matter? Do you think I have come to amuse you?'

'Why do you raise your voice, Sait? Let us be friends.'

'Friendship has nothing to do with this,' he said, lowering his voice. When he raised it the jingling inside could not be heard. But when he lowered it we could hear Rosie's steps in the background. A smile, perhaps, played over my lips as I visualized her figure on the other side of the wall. He felt irritated at this again. 'What, sir, you laugh when I say I want money, you smile as if you were dreaming. Are you in this world or in paradise? I came to talk to you in a businesslike manner today, but it is not possible. All right, don't blame me.' He bundled up his account book and rose to go.

'Don't go, Sait. Why are you upset?' I asked. Everything I said unfortunately seemed to have a ring of levity about it. He stiffened and grew more serious. The more he scowled, the more I found it impossible to restrain myself. I don't know what devil was provoking so much mirth in me at this most inappropriate moment. I was bubbling with laughter. I suppressed a tremendous urge to giggle. Somehow his seriousness affected me in this way. Finally, when he turned away from me in utter wrath, the profound solemnity of this puny man with his ledger clutched under his arm and his multi-coloured turban struck me as so absurd that I was convulsed with laughter. He turned his head, threw a brief glance at me, and was off.

With a smiling face, I re-entered the house and took up my position on the mat. Rosie paused for a second to ask, 'Something very amusing? I heard your laughter.'

'Yes, yes, something that made me laugh.'

'Who was he?' she asked.

'A friend,' I said. I did not want her to know these troubles. I didn't want anyone to be bothered with these things. I did not like to be bothered by anything. Living with Rosie under the same roof was enough for me. I wanted nothing more in life. I was slipping into a fool's paradise. By not talking about money, I felt I had dismissed the subject—a stupid assumption. The world outside Rosie seemed so unreal that it was possible for me to live on such an assumption. But not for long.

Within a week or ten days I found myself involved in court affairs. My sense of humour had completely ruined my relations with the Sait, and he had proceeded directly to get satisfaction through a court. My mother was distraught. I had not a friend in the world except Gaffur. I sought him out one day at the fountain parapet and told him where I stood. I was returning from the court. He was all sympathy, and said, 'Have you a lawyer?'

'Yes. The one there over the cotton godown.'

'Oh—he is the adjournment expert. He can keep the case going for years. So don't worry. Is it a civil suit or criminal suit?'

'Criminal! They have made out a case against me that, when he came to ask for his dues, I threatened to beat him. I wish I had done so!'

'What a pity! If it were a civil case, it could go on for years, and you would be none the worse for it while it lasted. Have you got *that* in your house?' he asked slyly. I gave him a fierce look. And he said, 'How can I blame a woman for what you are? . . . Why don't you look after tourists again?'

'I can't go near the railway station now. The railway staff are going to depose against me, to prove that I beat people up.'

'Is it true?'

'Hm. If I catch the porter's son, I'm going to wring his neck.'

'Don't do such things, Raju; you will not help yourself. You have brought sufficient confusion on yourself. Do pull yourself together. Why don't you do sensible things?'

I thought this over. I said, 'If I had five hundred rupees, I could start a new life.' I outlined to him a plan to utilize Rosie's services and make money. The thought of her warmed me up. 'She is a gold mine,' I cried. 'If I had money to start her with—oh!' My visions soared. I said to him, 'You know Bharat Natyam is really the greatest art business today. There is such a craze for it that people will pay anything to see the best. I cannot do anything about it because I have no money. Can't you help me, Gaffur?' He was amused at my request. It was now my turn to feel upset at laughter. I said, 'I have done so much for your business.'

He was essentially a man of heart. He appealed to my reason. 'I'm not a rich man, Raju. You know how I borrow money for even the upkeep of the car. If I had five hundred, I'd let my passengers ride on better tyres. No, no, Raju . . . listen to my advice. Send her away and try to get back to ordinary, real life. Don't talk all this art business. It's not for us.'

On hearing this, I grew so upset that I said something to hurt him. He got back into his driving seat with a serious face. 'If you like a drive any time, call me; that's all I can do to help you. And, remember, I'm not asking for the old dues from you—'

'Set it off against the commission due to me for all your Peak House trips,' I said haughtily.

'Very well,' he said, and started his car. 'Call me any time you want the car; it's always there. I pray that God may give you better sense.' He was off. I knew here was another friend passing out of my life.

Unfortunately, he was not the last. My mother's turn came soon. I was rapt, watching Rosie do a piece called 'The Dancing Feet'. Rosie said she had introduced a couple of variations, and wanted me to give my opinion. I was becoming a sort of expert on these matters nowadays. I watched her critically, but what I watched were the curves that tempted me to hug her on the spot. But my mother was passing in and out, and nowadays we had to seize our romantic moments and get through with it at odd times—for instance, when my mother went to fetch water. We knew exactly how long she would be away and utilized it. It was all irksome, but very novel, and made me forget my troubles. Whenever I watched her sway her figure, if there was no one about I constantly interrupted her performance, although I was supposed to watch her from an art critic's point of view. She pushed me away with, 'What has come over you?' She was a devoted artist; her passion for physical love was falling into place and had ceased to be a primary obsession with her.

I had a little money still left in the savings, although I gave no hint of it to anyone. A couple of days after the Sait's coming, I drew the entire amount from the bank. I did not want it to be seized. This was keeping us. I had a small lawyer handling my case in the court. I had to give him part of my money for court fees and such things. He had his office in the attic of a cotton shop in Market Road—a choking place with one shelf of books, one table, one chair, and one bench for clients. He had spotted me on the very first day while I was loitering with terror in my eyes, obeying the first summons. He had ingratiated himself into my favour while I waited in the corridor. He asked, 'Did you hit the Sait, really? Speak the truth to me.'

'No, sir. It's a lie.'

'Evidently they want to bring in a criminal motive to quicken the procedure. We will dispute that first, and then the civil; we have a lot of time. Don't worry. I'll deal with all that. How much money have you in your pocket?'

'Only five rupees.'

'Give it here.' If I had said 'two' he'd probably have been content to take that. He pocketed it, held up a sheet of paper for my signature, and said, 'That's right. It fixes all your affairs up nicely.'

At the court I was asked to go behind an enclosure while the judge looked at me. The Sait was there with his notebook, and he had his lawyer, of course; we glared at each other. His lawyer said something; my five-rupee lawyer said something, gesticulating in my direction; and the court-servant patted my back and told me to go. My lawyer nodded to me. It was all over before I could understand anything. My lawyer met me outside. 'Managed to get an adjournment. I'll tell you the next date later. Meet me at my office, over the cotton godown—come by the staircase on the side lane.' He was off. If this was ail the bother there was, I felt I could get through it easily. I was in excellent hands.

I told my mother on returning from the court, 'There is nothing to worry about, Mother; it's going nicely.'

'He may throw us out of this house. Where will you go after that?'

'Oh, all that will take a long time. Don't unduly burden your mind,' I cried.

She gave me up in despair. 'I don't know what is coming over you. You don't take anything seriously nowadays.'

'It's because I know what to worry about; that's all,' I said grandly.

Nowadays our domestic discussions were carried on in the presence of Rosie. No privacy was needed; we had got used to her. Rosie behaved as if she did not hear these domestic matters. She looked fixedly at the floor or at the pages of a book (the only things I managed to salvage from our shop), and moved off to a corner of the hall, as if to be out of earshot. She did not, even when she was alone with me, embarrass me by asking any questions about our affairs.

My mother had adjusted herself to my ways as an unmitigated loafer, and I thought she had resigned herself to them. But she had her own scheme of tackling me. One morning as I was watching Rosie's footwork with the greatest concentration, my uncle dropped in like a bolt from the blue. He was my mother's elder brother, an energetic landowner in my mother's village who had inherited her parents' home and was a sort of general adviser and director of all our family matters. Marriages, finances, funerals, litigation, for everything he was consulted by all the members of the family—my mother and her three sisters, scattered in various parts of the district. He seldom left his village, as he conducted most of his leadership by correspondence. I knew my mother was in touch with him—a postcard a month from him, closely written, would fill her with peace and happiness for weeks and she would ceaselessly talk about it. It was his daughter that she wanted me to marry—a proposal which she fortunately pushed into the background, in view of recent developments.

Here entered the man himself, standing at the door and calling in his booming voice, 'Sister!' I scrambled to my feet and ran to the door. My mother came hurrying from the kitchen. Rosie stopped her practice. The man was six feet tall, darkened by the sun from working in the fields, and had a small knotted tuft on his skull; he wore a shirt with an upper cloth, his *dhoti* was brown, not white like a townsman's. He carried a bag of jute material in his hand (with a green print of Mahatma Gandhi on it), and a small trunk. He went straight to the kitchen, took out of the bag a cucumber, a few limes, and plantains and greens, saying, 'These are for my sister, grown in our gardens.' He placed them on the floor of the kitchen for his sister. He gave a few instructions as to how to cook them.

My mother became very happy at the sight of him. She said, 'Wait, I'll give you coffee.'

He stood there explaining how he came, by a bus; what he had been doing when he received my mother's letter, and so on and so forth. It was a surprise to me to know that she had written to him to come. She had not told me. 'You never told me you wrote to Uncle!' I said.

'Why should she tell you?' snapped my uncle. 'As if you were her master!' I knew he was trying to pick a quarrel with me. He lowered his voice to a whisper, pulled me down by the collar of my shirt, and asked, 'What is all this one hears about you? Very creditable development you are showing, my boy. Anybody would be proud of you!' I wriggled myself free and frowned. He said, 'What has come over you? You think yourself a big man? I can't be frightened of scapegraces like you. Do you know what we do when we get an intractable bull calf? We castrate it. We will do that to you, if you don't behave.'

My mother went on minding the boiling water as if she didn't notice what went on between us. I had thought she would come to my support, but she seemed to enjoy my predicament, having designed it herself. I felt confused and angry. As I moved out I could overhear my mother speaking to him in whispers. I could guess what she was saying. I went back to my mat, rather shaken.

Rosie was standing where I had left her with her hip slightly out, her arm akimbo. She was like one of those pillar-carvings in the temples. The sight of her filled me with a sudden nostalgia for the days when I took people to see the old temples and I sighed for the variety of life and contacts and experiences I used to have. Rosie looked a little scared. 'Who is he?' she asked in a low tone.

'Don't bother about him. He must be crazy. You don't have to worry.'

That was enough for her. My guidance was enough. She accepted it in absolutely unquestioning faith and ignored everything else completely. It gave me a tremendous confidence in myself and seemed to enhance my own dimensions. I told her, 'You need not stop your dance. You may go on with it.'

'But, but—' she indicated my uncle.

'Forget his existence completely,' I said. I was in a very challenging mood, but inside me I trembled still to think what my uncle might have to say. 'You don't have to bother about anyone except me,' I said with sudden authority. (My uncle used to be called in to frighten me when I was a boy.) 'This is my house. I do as I please here. If people don't like me, they need not visit me; that is all.' I laughed weakly.

What was the use of pouring out all these challenging statements to this girl? She resumed her song and dance, and I sat observing her, with extra attention as if I were her teacher. I observed my uncle peep out of the kitchen, and so I made myself more deliberately teacher-like. I issued commands and directions to Rosie. My uncle watched my antics from the kitchen. Rosie went on with her practice as if she were in her private room. My uncle presently came over to watch, his eyes bulging with contempt and cynicism. I ignored him completely. He watched for a moment, and let out a loud: 'Hm! So this is what is keeping you busy! Hm! Hm! Never dreamed that anyone in our family would turn out to be a dancer's backstage-boy!'

I remained silent for a while before mustering courage and resolution to attack him. He mistook my silence for fear and brought out another of his broadsides. 'Your father's spirit will be happy to see you now, literally grovelling at the feet of a dancing girl.'

He was out to provoke me. I turned round and said, 'If you have come to see your sister, you had better go in and stay with her. Why do you come where I am?'

'Aha!' he cried, delighted. 'Good to see some spirit in you. There is still hope for you, although you need not try it on your uncle first. Did I not mention a moment ago what we do to recalcitrant bull calves?' He was squatting on the floor now, sipping his coffee.

'Don't be vulgar,' I said. 'At your age too!'

'Hey, wench!' he cried to Rosie, addressing her in the singular, or something even lower than singular. 'Now stop your music and all those gesticulations and listen to me. Are you of our family?' He waited for an answer. She stopped her dance and simply stared at him. He said, 'You are not of our family? Are you of our clan?' He again waited for her to answer and answered himself. 'No. Are you of our caste? No. Our class? No. Do we know you? No. Do you belong to this house? No. In that case, why are you here? After all, you are a dancing girl. We do not admit them in our families. Understand? You seem to be a good, sensible girl. You should not walk into a house like this and stay on. Did anyone invite you? No. Even if you are invited you should go on staying where you belong, and not too long here. You cannot stay like this in our house. It is very inconvenient. You should not he seducing young fools, deserting your husband. Do you follow?' She sank down at this onslaught, covering her face with her hands. My uncle was evidently gratified at the success of his efforts, and proceeded to drive home his point. 'You see, you should not pretend to cry at these things. You must understand why we say such things. You must clear out by the next train. You must promise to go. We will give you money for your railway ticket.'

At this a big sob burst from her. I was completely maddened by it. I flew at my uncle and knocked the cup out of his hand, shouting, 'Get out of this house.'

He picked himself up, saying, 'You tell me to get out. Has it come to this? Who are you, puppy, to ask me to get out? I'll make you get out. This is my sister's house. You go out if you want enjoyment with dancing girls—'

My mother came running out of the kitchen with tears in her eyes. She flew straight at the sobbing Rosie, crying, 'Are you now satisfied with your handiwork, you she-devil, you demon? Where have you dropped on us from? Everything was so good and quiet— until you came; you came in like a viper. Bah! I have never seen anyone work such havoc on a young fool! What a fine boy he used to be! The moment he set his eyes on you, he was gone. On the very day I heard him mention the "serpent girl" my heart sank. I knew nothing good could come out of it.' I didn't interrupt my mother; I allowed her all the speech she wanted to work off feelings she had bottled up all these weeks. She then catalogued all my misdeeds down to my latest appearance in the court, and how I was going to lose even this house, so laboriously built by my father.

The girl looked up with her tear-drenched face and said amidst sobs, 'I will go away, Mother. Don't speak so harshly. You were so good to me all these days.'

My uncle now interrupted to tell his sister, 'This is your mistake, Sister. That wench is right in a way. Why should you have been so good to her? You should have told her at the beginning what was what.'

I seemed powerless to suppress this man or send him away. He said what he liked and stayed where he liked. Unless I physically pushed him out, there was no way of saving poor Rosie; but he could knock me flat if I laid hands on him. I was appalled at the somersault in my mother's nature the moment she got support in the shape of a brother. I went over to Rosie, put my arm around her to the shock of the two (my uncle cried, 'The fellow has lost all shame!'), and whispered to her, 'Shut your ears to all that they say. Let them say what they like. Let them exhaust themselves. But you are not leaving. I'm going to be here, and you are going to be here. Others who don't like the arrangement are welcome to leave.'

They went on a little longer, and when they could say nothing more they retired to the kitchen. I never spoke a word more. I learned a great secret, that of shutting my ears, and I felt happy that Rosie too could put herself through this hardening process, absolutely relying on my support. She lifted her head and sat up, watching the household coldly. My mother called me in to eat when food was ready. I cook care to see that Rosie was also fed. My mother didn't call us until she had fed my uncle on the vegetables he had brought and had cooked them according to his specifications. After food he went over to the *pyol*, spread out his upper cloth, sat on it munching paan, and then lay down on the cool floor to sleep. I felt relieved to hear his snores. The calm after the storm was absolute. My mother served us food without looking at us. A great silence reigned in the house. It continued until three-thirty in the afternoon.

My uncle renewed the fight by coming in to announce to all whom it might concern, 'An hour more for the train. Is the passenger ready?' He looked at Rosie sitting below a window and reading. She looked up, disturbed. I never left her side that whole afternoon. Whatever people might say, I wanted to be near at hand to support her. As long as my uncle remained in town there could be no relaxation of the vigil. I would have given anything to know when my uncle would be leaving. But he was a man of independent notions and was not affected by my genuine desire to have him go.

Rosie looked up, slightly scared. I held a hand up to give her courage. My mother came out of her corner and, looking kindly at Rosie, said, 'Well, young woman, it has been nice having you, but you know, it is time for you to go.' She was trying new tactics now, of kindliness and a make-believe that Rosie had agreed to leave. 'Rosie, girl, you know the train is at four-thirty. Have you packed up all your things? I found your clothes scattered here and there.'

Rosie blinked unhappily. She did not know how to answer. I intervened to say, 'Mother, she is not going anywhere.'

My mother appealed to me. 'Have some sense, Raju. She is another man's wife. She must go back to him.'

There was such calm logic in what she said, I had nothing more to do but repeat blindly, 'She can't go anywhere, Mother. She has got to stay here.'

And then my mother brought out her trump card. 'If she is not going, I have to leave the house,' she said.

My uncle said, 'Did you think she was helpless, and only a dependant on you?' He thumped his chest and cried, 'As long as I am breathing, I will never let down a sister.'

I appealed to my mother, 'You don't have to go, Mother.'

'Then throw that wench's trunk out and give her a push towards the railway, and your mother will stay. What do you take her for? You think she is the sort that can keep company with all kinds of dancing—'

'Shut up, Uncle,' I said, and I was taken aback by my own temerity. I feared he might repeat his threat to recalcitrant bulls. Fortunately, he said, 'Who are you, puppy, to say if I am to shut up or speak? You think I notice you? Are you sending that . . . that . . . out or not? That's all we want to know.'

'No; she is not going,' I said very calmly.

He heaved a sigh, glared at the girl, looked at my mother.

'Well, Sister, you must start packing, then. We will go by the evening bus.'

My mother said, 'All right. I can pack in a minute.'

'Don't go, Mother,' I pleaded.

'See that girl's obstinacy. She watches it all so calmly,' said my uncle.

Rosie pleaded, 'Mother, don't go.'

'Oho!' said my uncle. 'She has reached the stage of addressing you as Mother. Next she will be calling me Uncle-in-law, I suppose.' He turned to me with a horrible grin and said, 'Your mother needn't quit really. This house is hers for her lifetime- If I had had her cooperation, I'd have shown you a few nice tricks today. She would have stayed on till the end. My brother-in-law was no fool. He made you master of only one half of the home . . .' All of a sudden he entered into legal complexities, arising from my father's will, and described how he would have tackled the whole situation if he had been in my mother's position, and how he would have disputed every inch of the ground and taken the matter to the Supreme Court, and how he would have shown the world what to do with scapegraces who had no respect for family traditions but yet tried to enjoy their ancestors' hard-earned wealth. I was relieved as long as he waxed eloquent over legalities, as it helped him forget Rosie for the time being. True to the tradition of the landed gentry, he found litigation an engrossing subject. But the spell was broken when my mother came in to say, 'I'm ready.' She had picked up a few clothes here and there. Her large steel trunk, which had never been moved from its place in a corner for decades and decades, was packed and ready to be lifted out. She had a basket with a handle into which she had thrown a few copper and brass vessels. My uncle announced, 'These belong to our house, given by my father when this girl, my dear sister, married and was going to set up her own family. It's our gift to her, and so don't gaze on it with such a look.'

I looked away and said, 'She certainly can take what she likes. Nobody will say anything.'

'Aha, you are proud of that, are you?' he said. 'You are showing a lot of liberality to your mother, aren't you?'

I had never in my life seen him so unpleasant. We had always been in terror of him when we were children, but this was the first occasion I had seen so much of him as an adult. My mother looked saddened rather than angry, and seemed almost ready to come to my rescue. She interrupted him sharply to say with extraordinary consideration in her voice, 'I need nothing more. This will do.' She picked up several small prayer books, which she read every day of her life before her midday meal, sitting before the pictures of the god in meditation. I had seen her for years at the same time sitting with closed eyes in front of the niche in the wall, and it now filled

me with sadness that I would not see her there any more. I followed
her about the house as she picked out her articles and packed. My
uncle, as if to keep an eye on me, followed my steps. Apparently he
feared I might induce my mother to stay on.

In spite of his supervision, I asked, 'Mother, when will you be
back?'

She hesitated to answer, and said finally, 'I'll—I'll—let us see.'

'The moment she gets a telegram that the line is clear,' said Uncle
and added, 'We are not the sort to let down our sisters, remember.
That house in the village is always hers to return to; so that she has
not got to be at anybody's mercy. Our house belongs to our sister as
much as to us,' he added boastfully.

'Don't fail to light the lamps in the god's niche,' said my mother,
going down the steps. 'Be careful with your health.' Uncle carried
the trunks and she carried the basket. Soon they were at the end of
the street and turned the corner. I stood on the step watching. At
the threshold stood Rosie. I was afraid to turn round and face her,
because I was crying.

We were a married couple to all appearances. Rosie cooked the
food, and kept the house. I seldom went out except to do a little
shopping. All day long she danced and sang. I made love to her
constantly and was steeped in an all-absorbing romanticism, until I
woke up to the fact that she was really getting tired of it all. Some
months passed before she asked me, 'What are your plans?'

'Plans!' said the sleeper, awakening. 'What plans?'

She smiled at this and said, 'There you are, always lying on
the mat watching me or holding me in your arms. I have now had
good practice—I can manage a show of four hours, although with
accompaniments it would have been much more helpful—'

'I'm here, accompanying and marking time for you. What other
accompaniment do you want?'

'I need a full orchestra. We have stayed indoors long enough,' she
said. I found her so earnest that I had not the courage to joke any more.

I said, 'I'm also thinking. Very soon we must do something.'

'Rosie is a silly name,' I said as a first step after two days of
hard thinking. 'The trouble with you is that although your people
are a traditional dance family, they didn't know how to call you.
For our public purposes, your name must be changed. What about
"Meena Kumari"?'

She shook her head. 'It's no better. I see no reason to change my name.'

'You don't understand, my dear girl. It's not a sober or sensible name. If you are going to appear before the public with that name, they will think it's someone with cheap tricks, such as those we see in gambling side-shows. For a classical dancer, you should call yourself something that is poetic and appealing.'

She realized that there was a point in what I said, and she picked up a pad and pencil and noted down all the names that came into her head. I added my own. We wanted to see how they sounded and also how they looked on paper. Sheet after sheet was filled up and discarded. It became a sort of joke. We seemed to be forgetting our main job in enjoying the fun. Each name had something ridiculous about it, comic-sounding or an impossible association. At dead of night she sat up to ask, 'What about . . .?'

'The name of the wife of a demon-king—people will be frightened,' I said. Eventually, after four days of hard thinking and elimination (a labour which gave us the satisfaction of being engaged in professional duties), we arrived at 'Nalini', a name that could have significance, poetry, and universality, and yet be short and easily remembered.

With the attainment of a new name, Rosie entered a new phase of life. Under the new name, Rosie and all she had suffered in her earlier life were buried from public view. I was the only one who knew her as Rosie and called her so. The rest of the world knew her as Nalini. I bestirred myself, began to go out and meet people in the town. I attended meetings of various groups—at the University, the town hall, and the Club, and watched for a chance. When the Albert Mission boys had their annual social, I mixed in their affairs through the slender link of the clerk in the Union, who had once read with me at the old *pyol* school, and I suggested, 'Why not a dance recital instead of the usual Shakespeare tragedy?' I held forth on the revival of art in India so vehemently that they could not easily brush me aside, but had to listen. Heaven knew where I had found all this eloquence. I delivered such a lecture on the importance of our culture and the place of the dance in it that they simply had to accept what I said. Someone doubted if a classical dance would be suitable for a student assembly. I proved that the classical dance could be viewed as the lightest of entertainments, considering its versatility. I was a man with a mission. I dressed myself soberly for the part in a sort of rough-spun silk shirt and an upper cloth and a hand-spun and hand-woven *dhoti*, and I wore rimless glasses—a present from Marco at one of our first meetings. I wore a wristwatch; all this in my view lent such weight to what I said that they had to listen to me respectfully. I too felt changed; I had ceased to be the old Railway Raju and I earnestly wished that I too could bury myself, as Rosie had done, under a new name. Fortunately it didn't make much difference. No one seemed to bother about my affairs as those in the immediate railway colony did, and even if they knew they seemed to have other things to remember than my career and its ups and downs. I never knew I could speak so fluently on cultural matters. I had picked up a little terminology from Rosie and put it to the best use. I described 'The Dancing Feet' and explained its significance word by word and almost performed the dance act myself. They watched me in open-mouthed wonder. I threw a further bait to the committee: if they liked, they could go with me and see a sample of the show. They enthusiastically agreed. I mentioned her as a cousin who was on a visit, and who was famous in her own place.

The next morning Rosie had tidied up the hall so that it did not look too bad. She had decorated the place with flowers from a gold mohur tree. She had stuck the bunch in a bronze tumbler, and kept it in a corner; it touched up our little home with some sort of beauty. She had also pushed away our rolls of bedding and other boxes, stools, and odds and ends to the farthest corner, thrown a *dhoti* over the heap, and covered it again cunningly with a striped carpet pulled from under a bed. This gave it a mysterious look. She had shaken the old mat and rolled it up so that the tattered portions were invisible. She managed to have ready cups of brown, steaming coffee. All this was an excellent preparation, calculated to win a public for her. The men, two of them, came and knocked on the door. When I opened it there they stood. Rosie had hung a printed sheet over the kitchen doorway and was behind it. I opened the door, saw the men there, and said, 'Oh, you have come!' as if I had thought they wouldn't. Somehow I felt it would be good to give it all a casual air. They smirked foolishly, realizing they had come on an agreeable errand to watch a possible beauty.

I seated them on the mat, spoke to them of world politics for a moment, and said, 'You can spare a little time, I suppose? I'll ask my cousin if she is free.'

I walked through the kitchen curtain and she was standing there. I grinned and winked at her. She stood stock-still and grinned back at me. We were enjoying this piece of stage-management; we felt we had already begun to put on a show. She had tied her hair into a knot, decorated her forehead with a small vermilion dot, lightly sprinkled a little powder on her face, and clad herself in a blue cotton saree—an effect of simplicity produced with a lot of preparation. After five minutes of silent waiting, I nodded, and she followed me out.

The Secretary and the Treasurer gaped. I said, 'These are my friends. Sit down.' She smiled, and seated herself on a small mat— modestly away. I knew at that moment that her smile was an 'open sesame' to her future. There was an awkward pause for a moment and then I said, 'These are my friends. They are having a variety show in the College Union, and were wondering if you would do anything for them.'

She asked, 'Variety? What other items are you having?' and puckered her brow in a superior way.

They said apologetically, 'A few fancy-dress items, mimicry and such things.'

She said, 'How can you fit my programme into that? How much time do you want to give me?' She was taking charge of their programme.

They said, greatly flustered, 'One hour, an hour and a half— anything you like.'

Now she delivered them a homily. 'You see, a dance programme is not like variety, it needs time to be built up. It's something that has to develop even as one is performing and one is watching.'

They agreed with her sentiments absolutely. I interrupted to say, 'Their main idea in coming now is to see you, and to see whatever bit of your art you can show them. Would you oblige us?'

She made a wry face and grumbled, looked hesitant, and gave us no reply.

'What is it? They are waiting for a reply from you. They are busy men.'

'Oh, no. No need to hustle the lady. We can wait.'

'How, how to—manage now—no accompaniments—without accompaniments I never like—' she was saying, and I said, 'Oh, this is not a full-dress show. Just a little—When there is a full-dress show we shall have accompaniments. After all, you are the most important item.' I cajoled her and the other two happily joined me; and Rosie agreed hesitantly, saying, 'If you are so keen, I can't refuse. But don't blame me if it is not good.' She went behind the curtain once again, returned bearing coffee on a plate, and set it down.

Out of formal politeness the gentlemen said, 'Why bother about coffee?' I pressed them to accept it.

As they sipped their coffee, Rosie began her dance, to the accompaniment of a song that she lightly sang. I ventured to beat time with my hands, like a very knowing one. They watched in fascination. She suddenly paused, wiped the perspiration from her brow, took a deep breath, and, before resuming again, said to me, 'Don't beat time; it misleads me.'

'All right,' I said, awkwardly grinning, trying not to look snubbed. I whispered, 'Oh, she is so precise, you know.' They shook their heads.

She finished her piece and asked, 'Shall I go on? Shall I do "The Dancing Feet"?'

'Yes, yes,' I cried, glad to be consulted. 'Go on. They will like it.'

When they recovered from the enchantment, one of them said, 'I must admit I have never cared for Bharat Natyam, but watching this lady is an education. I now know why people are in raptures over it.'

The other said, 'My only fear is that she may be too good for our function. But it doesn't matter. I'll reduce the other items to give her all the time she wants.'

'We must make it our mission to educate the public taste,' I said. 'We must not estimate the public taste and play down to it. We must try to raise it by giving only the best.'

'I think up to the interval we shall have the variety and all such tomfoolery. After the interval this lady can take up the entire show.'

I looked up at her for a second as if waiting for her approval, and said, 'She'll, of course, be pleased to help you. But you must provide the drummer and accompanists,' and thus acquired at last the accompanists Rosie had been clamouring for all along.

9

MY ACTIVITIES SUDDENLY multiplied. The Union function was the start. Rocket-like, she soared. Her name became public property. It was not necessary for me to elaborate or introduce her to the public now. The very idea would be laughed at. I became known because I went about with her, not the other way round. She became known because she had the genius in her, and the public had to take notice of it. I am able to speak soberly about it now—only now. At that time I was puffed up with the thought of how I had made her. I am now disposed to think that even Marco could not have suppressed her permanently; sometime she was bound to break out and make her way. Don't be misled by my present show of humility; at the time there was no limit to my self-congratulation. When I watched her in a large hall with a thousand eyes focused on her, I had no doubt that people were telling themselves and each other, 'There he is, the man but for whom—' And I imagined all this adulation lapping around my ears like wavelets. In every show I took, as a matter of right, the middle sofa in the first row. I gave it out that that was my seat wherever I might go, and unless I sat there Nalini would be unable to perform She needed my inspiring presence. I shook my head discreetly; sometimes I lightly tapped my fingers together in timing. When I met her eyes, I smiled familiarly at her on the stage. Sometimes I signalled her a message with my eyes and fingers, suggesting a modification or a criticism of her performance. I liked the way the president of the occasion sat next to me, and leaned over to say something to me. They all liked to be seen talking to me. They felt almost as gratified as if they spoke to Nalini herself. I shook my head, laughed with restraint, ancl said something in reply, leaving the watching audience at our back to guess the import of our exchanges, although actually it was never anything more than, 'The hall seems to have filled.'

I threw a glance back to the farthest corner of the hall, as if to judge the crowd, and said, 'Yes, it's full,' and swiftly turned round, since dignity required that I look ahead. No show started until I nodded to the man peeping from the wings, and then the curtain went up. I never gave the signal until I satisfied myself that everything was set. I inquired about the lighting, microphone arrangements, and looked about as if I were calculating the velocity of the air, the strength of the ceiling, and as if I wondered if the pillars would support the roof under the circumstances. By all this I created a tenseness which helped Nalini's career. When they satisfied all the conditions and a performance began, the organizers felt they had achieved a difficult object. Of course, they paid for the dance, and the public was there, after paying for their seats, but all the same I gave the inescapable impression that I was conferring on them a favour by permitting the dance. I was a strict man. When I thought that the programme had gone on long enough I looked at the watch on my wrist and gave a slight nod of the head, and Nalini would understand that she must end the show with the next item. If anyone made further suggestions, I simply laughed them off. Sometimes slips of paper travelled down from the back of the hall, with requests for this item or that, but I frowned so much when a slip was brought near me that people became nervous to pass on such things. They generally apologized, 'I don't know. Someone from the back bench—it just came to me—' I took it with a frown, read it with bored tolerance, and pushed it away over the arm of the sofa; it fell on the carpet, into oblivion. I made it look as if such tricks should be addressed to lesser beings and that they would not work here.

One minute before the curtain came down, I looked for the Secretary and nodded to him to come over. I asked him, 'Is the car ready? Please have it at the other door away from the crowd. I'd like to take her out quietly.' It was a false statement. I really liked to parade her through the gaping crowds. After the show, there were still people hanging around to catch a glimpse of the star. I walked ahead of her or beside her without much concern. At the end of the performance they presented her with a large garland of flowers, and they gave me one too. I accepted mine with protest. 'There is really no reason why you should waste money on a garland for me,' I said; I slung it carelessly on my arm or in the thick of the crowd dramatically handed it over to Nalini with 'Well, you really deserve two,' and made her carry it for me.

It was a world of showmanship till we reached the privacy of our house, when she would throw off the restraint and formality of hours and give me a passionate hug with 'Even if I have seven rebirths I won't be able to repay my debt to you.' I swelled with pride when I heard her, and accepted it all as my literal due. Methodically she started wrapping the flowers in a wet towel so that they might remain fresh in the morning.

On programme days she cooked our supper in the afternoon. We could easily have afforded to engage a cook, but she always said, 'After all, for two people, we don't need a cook moping around the house. I must not lose touch with my womanly duties.' She spoke of the evening show all through dinner, criticizing some arrangement or the background accompaniment, how so-and-so just failed to catch up. She lived entirely in the memory of her evening show. Sometimes after food she demonstrated a piece. And then she picked up a book and read on till we went to bed.

In a few months I had to move out of my old house. The Sait managed to score a point of law and secured an attachment of the property before judgment. My lawyer came to me and said, 'Don't worry about it; it only means he will have to pay the house tax, with arrears, if any. Of course, your mother's signature may be required too, but I'll get it. It is just like mortgaging the house to him. You may have to give him rent—a nominal one if you stay here.'

'Paying rent for my own house!' I said. 'If I have to pay rent I prefer a better house.' For our growing stature the house was inadequate. No visitor could be entertained. No privacy. No place for my furniture. My father had designed this house for a shopkeeper, not for a man of consequence and status who had charge of a growing celebrity. 'Moreover, where is the place for you to practise in?' I asked Nalini when she demurred at the notion of moving out. Somehow she was deeply attached to the house, the place which first gave her asylum.

The lawyer went to the village and returned with my mother's signature on the document. 'How did she take it?' I could not help asking.

'Not badly, not badly,' said the adjournment expert. 'Well, of course, we cannot expect elderly people to take the same view as we do. I had to argue and persuade her, though your uncle proved a difficult man.'

Four days later my mother's letter came; she had written on a yellow paper with a pencil: ' . . . I gave my signature not because I was happy about it but because otherwise the lawyer would not go from here, and your uncle would not let him stay in peace. It is all confusing to me. I'm sick of everything. I signed without your uncle's knowledge, when he was away in the garden, so that the lawyer might leave this place without any damage to his person. Anyway, what does it all mean? Your lawyer mentioned that you are looking for a new house for that woman. If it is so, I'll come back to live in my old house. After all, I wish to spend the rest of my days in my own house.' It was good of my mother to have set aside her own anger and written to me. I felt touched by her solicitude. I was troubled by her desire to come back. I could understand it, but I resisted the idea. It seemed best to let the Sait take the home and be done with it once and for all. Who wanted this ramshackle house anyway? To have Mother live in the house, I should have to pay a rent to the Sait. Who would look after her? I was so busy. I rationalized in all possible ways and put away her letter without a reply. I moved to another house and became very busy, and in all the rush quietened my conscience. I felt sorry, but I rationalized: 'After all her brother is dear to her, and he will look after her. Why should she come here and live all alone?'

The stylish house at New Extension was more in keeping with our status. It was two-storied, with a large compound, lawns, garden, and garage. On the upper floor we had our bedrooms and a large hall where Nalini practised her dance. It was carpeted with a thick, deep blue, spun-silk carpet at one end, leaving a space of marble tiles for her to dance on. I had managed to fix up a pedestal and a bronze image of dancing Nataraja in one corner. It was her office. I had now a permanent group of musicians—five of them: a flautist, a drummer, etc. She had a 'dance master' whom I discovered in Koppal, a man who had steeped himself in the traditional dance for half a century and lived in his village home. I ferreted him out and brought him over to Malgudi and gave him an outhouse in our compound to live in. All kinds of people were always passing in and out of our house. I had a large staff of servants—a driver for our car, two gardeners for the garden, a Gurkha sentry at the gate with a dagger at his waist, and two cooks because our entertainments were beginning to grow. As I have said, a miscellaneous population was always passing in and out of the compound: musicians, their friends, those that came to see me by appointment, the servants, their friends, and so on. On the ground floor I had an office with a secretary-in-waiting, a young graduate from the local college, who dealt with my correspondence.

I had three or four grades of visitors. Some I received on the veranda; these were musicians or aspiring musicians who wanted a chance to accompany Nalini. I was offhand with them. About ten such asked for an interview with me every day. They were always waiting on the outer veranda to have a chance to speak to me. I went in and out, hardly noticing them. They respectfully rose at the sight of me and saluted, and if they intercepted me I kept up a show of giving them a hearing, and then said, 'Leave your address with my clerk there. If there is anything that can be done, I'll ask him to call you up.' When they flourished a batch of testimonials I snatched a brief look at them and said, Good, good. But there is nothing I can do now. Leave your name in the office'—and I passed on. My outer veranda was cluttered with benches on which people sat and waited all day to have a chance to speak to me. I treated them with the scantiest attention. I left them to guess when I would come to my table. Sometimes obscure composers turned up with new songs especially created for Nalini's benefit. Sometimes when I sat at the office table I did not mind if they peeped in and took their chance to speak to me. I never offered this class of visitor a chair, but did not mind if he pulled one up and sat down. When I wanted to dispose of him, I pushed my chair back and went in abruptly, leaving it to my secretary to see him off. Sometimes I observed through the glass window in the hall how big a crowd waited for me outside, and I made a strategic exit through a side door, straight on to the garage, and from there dashed to the gate, while the visitors looked on helplessly. I felt vastly superior to everyone.

Apart from those that came as supplicants, there were others who approached me with genuine offers of engagement. They were the higher grade of visitors. I received them on the hall sofa and rang the bell for coffee. I offered my inner circle of visitors coffee day and night. Our coffee bill alone amounted to three hundred a month, enough to maintain a middle-class family in comfort. The appointments in the hall were all expensive—brass-inlaid trays, ivory knick-knacks, group photographs with Nalini in the middle. Sitting in that hall and looking round, I had the satisfaction of feeling that I had arrived.

Where was Nalini in all this? Away and out of sight. She spent a great part of the day in her rehearsal hall: with her musicians. One could hear the stamping of feet and the jingle of anklets on the upper floor. After all, she was living the life she had visualized. Visitors had always a hope that they might get a glimpse of her passing in or out of the house. I knew what they were looking for, with their shifty looks darting at the inner doorway. But I took care to see that no one saw her. I had a monopoly of her and nobody had anything to do with her. If anyone ventured to ask for her I said, 'She is busy,' or 'No need to trouble her. You have told me; that is enough.' I resented anyone's wanting to make a direct approach to her. She was my property. This idea was beginning to take root in my mind.

There were, however, a few friends of the inner circle whom I took upstairs to her room. It was a very eclectic group. They had to be my intimates; I had had no friends at all formerly; my friendship was now sought after by others. I was on back-slapping terms with two judges, four eminent politicians of the district whose ward could bring ten thousand votes at any moment for any cause, and two big textile-mill owners, a banker, a municipal councillor, and the editor of *The Truth*, a weekly, in which an appreciation of Nalini appeared from time to time. These men could come into my hall without appointment, demand coffee, and ask loudly, 'Where is Nalini? Upstairs? Well, I think I'll see her for a moment and go.' They could go up, talk to her, order coffee, and stay on as long as they pleased. They addressed me as 'Raj', familiarly. I liked to hobnob with them because they were men of money or influence.

Apart from them, sometimes musicians or actors or other dancers called on Nalini and spent hours and hours with her. Nalini enjoyed their company immensely, and I often saw them in her hall, some lying on carpets, some sitting up, all talking and laughing, while coffee and food were being carried to them. I occasionally went up and chatted with them—always with a feeling that I was an interloper in that artistic group. Sometimes it irritated me to see them all so happy and abandoned. I signalled to Nalini to come over to the bedroom, as if for a big, important aside, and when she closed the door I whispered, 'How long are they going to stay?'

'Why?'

'They have been here the whole day and may go on till night.'

'Well, I like their company. It's good of them to visit us.'

'Oh, as if we had no one else to visit us.'

'It's all right. How can I tell them to go? And it makes me happy to be with them.'

'Surely; I'm not denying it. But remember, you have to rest and we have a train journey ahead. You will have to pack up, and also practise. Remember you have promised new items for the Trichy show.'

'That's easy to manage!' she said, turning round and going back to her friends, shutting the door on me. I silently fretted. I liked her to be happy, but only in my company. This group of miscellaneous art folk I didn't quite approve of. They talked too much shop and Nalini was likely to tell them all our business secrets. She never missed a chance to get a gathering of such friends, wherever she might be. She said, 'They are people with the blessing of Goddess Saraswathi on them, and they are good people. I like to talk to them.'

'You don't know the world—they'll be a jealous lot. Don't you know that the real artists never come together? These people come to you because they are your inferiors.'

'I'm tired of all talk of superior and inferior. What is so superior about us?' she asked in real indignation.

'Well, you know, you have more engagements than a hundred of them put together,' I said.

'That's more money,' she said. 'I don't care much for that sort of superiority.'

Gradually arguments began to crop up between us, and that, I said, put the final husband-wife touch on our relationship. Her circle was widening. Artists of the first and second rank, music-teachers, dilettantes of the town, schoolgirls who wanted ideas for their school functions, all kinds of people asked to see her. Wherever possible I turned them back, but if they managed to slip through and get upstairs, I could do nothing about it. Nalini kept them for hours and would hardly let them go back.

We had calls from hundreds of miles away. Our trunks were always packed and ready. Sometimes when we left Malgudi we did not return home for nearly a fortnight. Our engagements took us to all corners of south India, with Cape Comorin at one end and the border of Bombay at the other, and from coast to coast. I kept a map and a calendar and tried to plan out our engagements. I studied the invitations and suggested alternative dates, so that a single journey might combine several engagements. Arranging an itinerary for each period took up a lot of my energy. We were out of town for about twenty days in the month, and during the ten days we were in Malgudi we had one or two dates nearer home, and whatever was left over could be counted as rest. It was a strenuous programme, and, wherever I might be, my secretary kept me informed of the mail arriving each day and received instructions by phone. I was committed three months ahead. I had a large calendar on which I marked in red the dates of engagements, and hung it up at first in her rehearsal hall, but she protested, 'It's ugly. Take it away!'

'I want you to keep an idea before you of where you are going next.'

'Not necessary,' she cried. 'What am I going to do, looking at those dates?' She rolled it up and put it in my hand. 'Don't show it to me. It only frightens me to see so many engagements,' she said. When I told her to get ready for the train, she got ready; when I asked her to come down, she came down; she got in and out of trains at my bidding. I don't know if she ever noticed what town we were in or what *sabha* or under whose auspices a show was being held. It was all the same, I think, whether it was Madras city or Madurai, or a remote hill town like Ootacamund. Where there was no railway, a car came to fetch us from the railhead. Someone met us at the platform, led us to a limousine waiting outside, and drove us to a hotel or a bungalow. Our circus of accompanying musicians was taken away in a bunch and berthed comfortably somewhere. I kept this lot in good humour by fussing about their comfort. 'They are our accompanists. I hope you have made proper arrangements for them too.'

'Yes, yes, sir. We've reserved two large rooms for them.'

'You must send them a car later to bring them over to our place.' I always made it a point to collect them and keep them handy two hours ahead of a show. They were a timeless lot, those instrumental players; they slept, or went shopping, or sat around playing cards—never looking at a clock. Handling them was an art—they had to be kept in good humour; otherwise they could ruin a whole evening and blame it on mood or fate. I paid them well. I kept up a show of looking after them, but I kept aloof. I was careful to see that they assumed no familiarity with Nalini.

If the show was at six, I generally insisted upon Nalini's resting until four o'clock in the afternoon. If we were guests in a house, she generally liked to sit around with the womenfolk and chat endlessly with them. But I went up to her and said with a good deal of firm kindness, 'I think you had better rest a while; the train journey last night was not very comfortable,' and she finished the sentence she was uttering or hearing and came up to our guest-room.

She felt annoyed at my interference. 'Why should you come

and pull me out of company? Am I a baby?' I expostulated with her that it was for her own good that I did so. I knew it was only a partial truth. If I examined my heart I knew I had pulled her out because I did not like to see her enjoy other people's company. I liked to keep her in a citadel.

If there was a train to catch after the show, I managed to have a car waiting ready to take us to the station. I had food brought to us on the train in silver or stainless-steel vessels, and we had our supper in the privacy of our compartment. But it was a brief, short-lived relief, as it soon began all over again, getting down at another station, going through another performance, and off again. When we visited places of importance, she sometimes asked to be taken to see a famous temple or a shop or some local sight. I always replied, 'Yes, yes. Let us see if we can fit it in,' but it was never done, as I always had to catch another train so as to fulfil another engagement. We were going through a set of mechanical actions day in and day out—the same receptions at the station, fussy organizers, encounters, and warnings, the same middle sofa in the first row, speeches and remarks and smiles, polite conversation, garlands and flash photos, congratulations, and off to catch the train—pocketing the most important thing, the cheque. Gradually I began to say, not 'I am going to Trichy for a performance by Nalini', but 'I am performing at Trichy on Sunday, on Monday I have a programme . . .', and then, 'I can dance in your place only on . . .' I demanded the highest fee, and got it, of anyone in India. I treated those that came to ask for a show as supplicants, I had an enormous monthly income, I spent an enormous amount on servants and style, and I paid an enormous amount of income tax. Yet I found Nalini accepting it all with a touch of resignation rather than bouncing contentment. She had seemed such a happy creature in our old house, even when my uncle was bullying her.

Nalini cherished every garland that she got at the end of a performance. Usually she cut it up, sprinkled water on it, and preserved it carefully, even when we were in a train. She said, holding up a piece of the garland and sniffing the air for its fragrance, 'To me this is the only worthwhile part of our whole activity.'

We were in a train when she said it. I asked her, 'What makes you say so?'

'I love jasmine.'

'Not the cheque that comes with it?'

'What is one to do with so much? All day long and all through the week you are collecting cheques, and more and more often. But when is the time coming when we can enjoy the use of those cheques?'

'Well, you have a big household, a big car and what not—is that not enjoyment of life?'

'I don't know,' she said, remaining moody. 'How I wish I could go into a crowd, walk about, take a seat in the auditorium, and start out for an evening without having to make up or dress for the stage!'

Some dangerous weariness seemed to be coming over her. I thought it best not to prod too much. Perhaps she wanted fewer engagements, but that was not possible. I asked, 'You are not saying that your legs are aching, are you?'

It had the desired effect. It pricked her pride and she said, 'Certainly not. I can dance for several hours at each show. Only you want me to stop.'

'Yes, yes; true,' I cried. 'Otherwise you would be fatiguing yourself.'

'Not only that; you also want to catch the train—though what will be lost if we catch the next day's, I don't know—'

I didn't allow her to finish her sentence. I flatteringly called her a shrewd girl, laughed and enjoyed it as a joke, fondled her, and made her forget the subject. I thought it was a dangerous line of thought. It seemed absurd that we should earn less than the maximum we could manage. My philosophy was that while it lasted the maximum money had to be squeezed out. We needed all the money in the world. If I were less prosperous, who would care for me? Where would be the smiles which greeted me now wherever I turned, and the respectful agreement shown to my remarks when I said something to the man in the next chair? It filled me with dread that I should be expected to do with less. 'If we don't work and earn when the time is good, we commit a sin. When we have a bad time no one will help us.' I was planning big investments as soon as possible—as soon as we could count on a little more margin. As it was, the style of living and entertaining which I had evolved was eating up all our resources.

Sometimes she said, 'Spending two thousand a month on just the two of us. Is there no way of living more simply?'

'Leave that to me; we spend two thousand because we have to. We have to maintain our status.' After a good deal of thought, I ran the bank account in her name. I didn't want my creditors to get at me again. My adjournment lawyer was proceeding at his own pace, sometimes coming to me for a signature or funds, and managing things without bothering me. Nalini signed any cheque I asked her to sign. One thing I must add: whenever I was in town I gathered a big circle of friends and we played cards pratically twenty-four hours at a stretch. I had set apart a room for the purpose and I had two personal servants serving tea and coffee and even food on the spot; and we had surreptitious drinks too, although there was prohibition in force—well, the prohibition law was not for a man of my influence. I had managed to get a medical certificate to say that I needed alcohol for my welfare. Although I myself cared very little for drink, I hugged a glass of whisky for hours. 'Permit-holder' became a social title in our land and attracted men of importance around me, because the permit was a difficult thing to acquire. I showed respect for the law by keeping the street-window shut when serving drink to non-permit folk. All kinds of men called me 'Raj' and slapped my back. We played Three-Cards sometimes for two days at a stretch; I changed a two-thousand-rupee cheque for the purpose, and expected those who came there to meet me on equal terms. Through my intimacy with all sorts of people, I knew what was going on behind the scenes in the government, at the market, at Delhi, on the race course, and who was going to be who in the coming week. I could get a train reservation at a moment's notice, relieve a man summoned to jury work, reinstate a dismissed official, get a vote for a co-operative election, nominate a committee man, get a man employed, get a boy admitted to a school, and get an unpopular official shifted elsewhere, all of which seemed to me important social services, an influence worth buying at the current market price.

In the glow of this radiant existence, I had practically overlooked the fact that Marco still existed. We hardly mentioned his name. I never took note of the fact that he still inhabited the globe, and I took the only precaution needed—I avoided any engagement near his house. I didn't want to run the risk of facing him again. I had no idea what Nalini had in mind. I believed she still felt embittered at the thought of him, and would rather not be reminded of him.

I supposed that all associations with him were dim, fossilized, or
had ceased to exist. I also thought that under her new name Nalini
she was safely out of range, but I was mistaken. We played for
a whole week at Malgudi. The post one day brought us a book.
Generally I received a miscellaneous collection of mail—catalogues,
programmes, verse, and what not, all of which was seen and
disposed of by my secretary. Some Tamil and English illustrated
journals meant for Nalini were sent up. I hardly looked at anything
except letters offering engagements, and certainly never at books
and journals. I was a man of many preoccupations, and I found it
impossible nowadays to sit down with any book and had instructed
my secretary not to bother me with them. But one day he brought
a packet, saying, 'Would you look at this, sir. I thought it might be
of special interest.'

He held the book open. I snatched it from him. It was a book
by Marco, a book full of illustrations and comments. 'See page
158' said a pencilled message. I turned it over, and there it was, the
heading 'Mempi Cave Pictures'. At the head of the chapter was a
brief line to say, 'The author is obliged to acknowledge his debt to
Sri Raju of Malgudi Railway Station for his help.' The book was
from a firm of publishers in Bombay, with their compliments, sent
by instructions of the author. It was a gorgeous book costing twenty
rupees, full of art plates, a monograph on *The Cultural History of
South India*. It was probably an eminent work on the subject, but
beyond me.

I told the secretary, 'I'll keep it. It's all right.' I turned the pages.
Why did the boy bring it up as a special matter? Did he know who
was who? Or—? I dismissed the idea. It must have been because
he was rather taken by the blue and gold of the binding and the
richness of the material. He must have feared that if he didn't
draw my attention to it, I might probably demand an explanation.
That was all. So I said, 'Thank you, I'll read it.' And then I sat
wondering what I should do about it. Should I take it upstairs
to Nalini or—? I told myself, 'Why should she be bothered with
this? After all, it is a piece of academic work, which has bored her
sufficiently.' I turned it over again, to see if there was any letter
enclosed. No. It was impersonal, like the electricity bill. I turned
to page 158 and re-read his note. It was thrilling to see my name
in print. But why did he do it? I lost myself in speculating on his
motives. Was it just to keep his word because he had promised, or

could it be to show that he had not forgotten me so lightly? Anyway, I thought it would be best to put the book away. I carried it to my most secret, guarded place in the house—the liquor chest adjoining the card room, the key of which I carried next to my heart—stuffed the volume out of sight, and locked it up. Nalini never went near it. I did not mention the book to her. After all, I told myself, 'What has she to do with it? The book is sent to me, and the acknowledgement is of my services.' But it was like hiding a corpse. I've come to the conclusion that nothing in this world can be hidden or suppressed. All such attempts are like holding an umbrella to conceal the sun.

Three days later Marco's photograph appeared in the *Illustrated Weekly of Bombay*, on the middle page. The *Illustrated Weekly* was one of the papers Nalini always read—it was full of wedding pictures, stories, and essays she enjoyed. The photograph was published along with a review of his book, which was called 'An epoch-making discovery in Indian cultural history'. I was looking through my accounts in the hall, free from all visitors. I heard footsteps clattering down in a great run. I turned and saw her coming with the magazine in her hand, all excitement. She thrust the page before me and asked, 'Did you see that?'

I showed appropriate surprise and told her, 'Calm yourself. Sit down.'

'This is really great. He worked for it all his life. I wonder what the book is like!'

'Oh, it's academic. We won't understand it. For those who care for such things, it must seem interesting.'

'I want so much to see the book! Can't we get it somewhere?' She suddenly called my secretary, an unprecedented act on her part. 'Mani,' she said and held the picture up to him, 'you must get me this book.'

He came nearer, read the passage, brooded for a moment, looked at me, and said, 'All right, madam.'

I hurriedly told him, 'Hurry up with that letter, and go in person to the post office and remember to add a late fee.' He was gone. She still sat there. Unless she was called to meet visitors, she never came downstairs. What was this agitation that made her do these things? I wondered for a moment whether I ought not to bring the book out to her. But she would ask me for so many explanations. I simply suppressed the whole thing. She returned upstairs to her room. I noticed later that she had cut out the photo of her husband and placed it on her dressing mirror. I was rather shocked. I wanted to treat it as a joke, but could not find the right words, and so left it alone. I only averted my eyes when I passed the dressing mirror.

It was a long week in town; otherwise we should have been fully occupied in moving about, and probably would have missed that particular issue of the *Illustrated Weekly*. On the third day, while we were in bed, the very first question she asked me was, 'Where have you kept the book?'

'Who told you about it?'

'Why bother? I know it has come to you. I want to see it.'

'All right, I'll show it to you tomorrow.' Evidently Mani must be responsible. I had made it a convention in our establishment that the secretary should have no direct access to her, but the system was breaking down. I decided to punish him properly for his lapse.

She sat reclining on her pillow with a journal in her hand, to all appearances reading, but actually preparing herself for a fight. She pretended to read for a moment and suddenly asked, 'Why did you want to hide it from me?'

I was not ready for this, and so I said, 'Can't we discuss it all tomorrow? Now I'm too sleepy.'

She was out for a fight. She said, 'You can tell me in a word why you did it and go to sleep immediately.'

'I didn't know it would interest you.'

'Why not? After all—'

'You have told me that you never thought his work interesting.'

'Even now I'll probably be bored. But anything happening to him is bound to interest me. I'm pleased he has made a name now, although I don't know what it is all about.'

'You suddenly fancy yourself interested in him, that's all. But the book came to *me*, not to you, remember.'

'Is that sufficient reason why it should be hidden from me?'

'I can do what I please with my own book, I suppose? That's all. I'm going to sleep. If you are not reading, but are merely going to think, you can as well do it in the dark, and put out the light.'

I don't know why I spoke so recklessly. The light was put out, but I found that she was sitting up—and crying in the dark. I wondered for a second whether I should apologize and comfort her. But I decided otherwise. She had been bottling up a lot of gloom lately, it seemed to me. It would do her good to have it all out without my interference. I turned over and pretended to sleep. Half an hour passed. I switched on the light, and there she was, quietly crying still.

'What has come over you?'

'After all, after all, he is my husband.'

'Very well. Nothing has happened to make you cry. You should feel pleased with his reputation.'

'I am,' she said.

'Then stop crying and go to sleep.'

'Why does it irritate you when I speak of him?'

I realized it was no use trying to sleep. I might as well meet the challenge. I replied, 'Do you ask why? Don't you remember when and how he left you?'

'I do, and I deserved nothing less. Any other husband would have throttled me then and there. He tolerated my company for nearly a month, even after knowing what I had done.'

'You talk about a single incident in two different ways. I don't know which one I should take.'

'I don't know. I may be mistaken in my own judgement of him. After all, he had been kind to me.'

'He wouldn't even touch you.'

'Should you taunt me with that?' she asked with sudden submissiveness. I couldn't understand her. I had an appalling thought that for months and months I had eaten, slept, and lived with her without in the least understanding her mind. What were her moods? Was she sane or insane? Was she a liar? Did she bring all these charges against her husband at our first meeting just to seduce me? Would she be levelling various charges against me now that she seemed to be tiring of me—even to the extent of saying that I was a moron and an imbecile? I felt bewildered and unhappy. I didn't understand her sudden affection for her husband. What was this sudden mood that was coming over her? I did my best for her. Her career was at its height. What was it that still troubled her? Could I get at it and find a remedy? I had been taking too much for granted in our hectic professional existence.

'We must go on a holiday somewhere,' I said.

'Where?' she asked in a businesslike manner.

I was taken aback. 'Where? Anywhere! Somewhere.'

'We are always going somewhere. What difference is it going to make?'

'We'll go and enjoy ourselves on our own, without any engagement.'

'I don't think it's going to be possible until I fall sick or break my thighbone,' she said and giggled viciously. 'Do you know the bulls yoked to an oil-crusher—they keep going round and round and round, in a circle, without a beginning or an end?'

I sat up and told her, 'We'll go as soon as the present acceptances are finished.'

'In three months?'

'Yes. After they are finished we'll pause for a little breath.' She looked so unconvinced of this that I said, 'Well, if you don't like an engagement, you can always say no.'

'To whom?'

'Why, of course, to me.'

'Yes, if you would tell me before you accept and take an advance.'

There was something seriously wrong with her. I went over to her bed, sat on it, shook her by the shoulder a little just to make it look personal, and asked, 'What is the matter with you? Are you not happy?'

'No. I'm not happy. What will you do about it?'

I threw up my arms. I really could not say anything. 'Well, if you tell me what is wrong, I can help. As far as I can see, there is nothing for you to be sorry about—you are famous, you have made money, you do what you like. You wanted to dance; you have done it.'

'Till the thought of it makes me sick,' she added. 'I feel like one of those parrots in a cage taken around village fairs, or a performing monkey, as he used to say—'

I laughed. I thought the best solvent would be laughter rather than words. Words have a knack of breeding more words, whereas laughter, a deafening, roaring laughter, has a knack of swallowing everything up. I worked myself into a paroxysm of laughter. She could not remain morose very long in the face of it. Presently she caught the contagion, a smirk developed into a chuckle, and before she knew what was what her body rocked with laughter, all her gloom and misgivings exploded in laughter. We went to sleep in a happy frame of mind. The time was two hours past midnight.

Our life fell into a routine after this little disturbance. After a break of only three days, during which time I steeped myself in the card game, avoiding all discussions with her, our encounters were casual and slight. She was passing through a period of moodiness, and it was safest to keep out of her way and not to rouse her further. The engagements for the next three months were all-important, running, as they did, into the season of music and dance in south India, for which I had taken heavy advance payments. We had ahead of us a travel programme of nearly two thousand miles, from Malgudi back to Malgudi, and if we went through with it there was ample time for her to get over the mood, and then I could push her into another quarter-year of activity. I had no intention of slackening this programme. It seemed so unnecessary, so suicidal. My only technique was to keep her in good humour to the best of my ability from quarter to quarter.

We were getting through our engagements uneventfully. We were back in Malgudi. Mani was away for a couple of days and I was attending personally to an accumulation of correspondence on my table. Offers of engagements I piled up on one side. I had some misgivings about accepting any of them right away as I normally would. I felt I should do well to speak to her before replying. Of course she'd have to accept them, but I wanted to give her a feeling of being consulted. I sorted them out.

Suddenly I came upon a letter addressed to 'Rosie, alias Nalini'. It had on it the address of a lawyer's firm in Madras. I wondered what to do with it for a while. She was upstairs, probably reading one of her inexhaustible journals. I felt nervous about opening the letter. I had half an impulse to take it to her: a sensible part of me said, 'It must, after all, be her business. She is an adult, with her own affairs. Let her tackle it, whatever it may be.' But this was only fleeting wisdom. The letter had arrived by registered post some days ago and Mani had received it and kept it on the table. It had a big seal on its flap. I looked at it with misgiving for a while, told myself that I was not to be frightened by a seal, and just cut it open. I knew she would not mind my seeing her letters. The letter came from a lawyer and said, 'Madam, under instruction from our client, we are enclosing an application for your signature, for the release of a box of jewellery left in safe custody at the Bank of . . . in the marked place. After this is received we shall proceed to obtain the other signature as well, since you are aware that the deposit is in your joint names, and obtain the release of the said box, and arrange to forward it to you under insurance cover in due course.'

I was delighted. So this was going to bring in more jewellery for her? Of course she would be elated. But how big was the box? What were the contents worth? These were questions that agitated my mind for a while. I looked through the letter for some clue; but the lawyer was sparing of words. I took the letter and turned to go and give it to her. But on the staircase I paused. I returned to my room and sat in my chair, thinking. 'Well, let me think it over. Where is the hurry?' I asked myself. 'She has waited for this box so long. Just a couple of days more is not going to matter. Anyway, she never mentioned it, perhaps she doesn't care.' I took the letter to my drink casket and locked it up. A good thing Mani was not there. Otherwise he might have created a mess.

I had some visitors after this. I talked to them and went out in the evening to see a few friends. I tried to distract my mind in various ways, but the packet bothered me. I returned home late. I avoided going upstairs. I heard her jingles upstairs, and knew that she was practising. I returned to my office table with the letter from the drink cabinet. I opened it carefully and read it again. I looked at the enclosed application. It was on a printed form; after her signature was going to be Marco's. What was the man's purpose in sending it now? Why this sudden generosity to return her an old box? Was he laying a trap for her, or what was it? Knowing the man as I did, I concluded that it might not be anything more than a correct disposal of his affairs, similar to his acknowledgement of my help in his book. He was capable of cold, machine-like rectitude; his vouchers were in order; he saw probably no sense in being responsible for Rosie's box any more. Rightly, too. The right place for Rosie's box was here. But how to release it? If Rosie saw this letter she would do God knew what. I had a fear that she would not view it calmly, in a businesslike manner. She would in all likelihood lose her head completely. She was likely to place the wildest interpretation on it and cry out, 'See how noble he is!' and make herself miserable and spoil for a fight with me. There was no knowing what would set off the trigger nowadays. His mere photo in the *Illustrated Weekly* drove her crazy: after that book incident I was very careful. I never showed her the book at all.

Next day I waited for her to ask for it, but she never mentioned it again. I thought it'd be safest to leave it there. I was very careful. I kept her in good humour and engaged, that was all; but I was aware that some sort of awkwardness had developed between us, and I kept myself aloof with extreme care. I knew that if I allowed more time she would be all right. But I felt that to show her this letter would be suicidal. She might refuse to do anything except talk about his nobility. Or (who could say?) she might insist on taking the next train to his place, throwing up everything. But what was to be done with the letter? 'Just let it rest in the company of whisky bottles till it is forgotten,' I told myself and laughed grimly.

During dinner, as usual, we sat side by side and spoke of things such as the weather, general politics, the price and condition of vegetables, and so on. I kept the subject rigorously to inconsequential affairs. If we held on for another day, it'd be perfect. On the third day we should be on the move again, and the bustle and activity of travel would shield us from troublesome personal topics.

After dinner she sat down on the hall sofa to chew betel leaves, turned over the pages of a journal on the hall table and then went upstairs. I felt relieved. The swing was coming back to normal. I spent a little time in my office, looking into accounts. The income-tax statement was due to be sent in a couple of weeks. I was poring over my very personal account-book just to see where we stood, and how to prepare our expense accounts. After brooding over this mystic matter for a while I went upstairs. I knew I had given her enough time either to be steeped in the pages of a book or to sleep. Anything to avoid talk. I was becoming uncertain of my own attitude nowadays. I feared I might blurt out about the letter. I laid my head on the pillow and turned over, with the formula, 'I'll sleep, I think. Will you switch off when you are done?' She grunted some reply.

How much jewellery might be in the box? Was it his present to her or her mother's or what? What a girl! She never gave it a thought! Perhaps they were antiquated and she did not care for them. If so they might be sold now and converted into cash, and no income-tax officer would ever dream of its existence. Must be a substantial lot if it had to be kept in safe custody. But who could say? Marco was eccentric enough to do strange things. He was the sort of fellow to keep even a worthless packet at the bank, because that was the right thing—to—do—the—r-right thing to—do . . . I fell asleep.

Soon after midnight I awoke. She was snoring. An idea bothered me. I wanted to see if there was any time limit mentioned. Suppose I kept the letter secret and some serious consequences arose? I wanted to go down and examine the document at once. But if I got up, she would also wake up and ask questions. Or if I took no notice at all of it, what would happen? The box would continue to remain in safe custody; or the lawyer might write a reminder, which might come in when I was out and slip its way through to her, and then questions, explanations, scenes. This was proving a greater bother than I had thought at first. Nothing that that man did was ever quiet or normal. It led to unbelievable complexities. As I kept thinking of it, it magnified itself until I felt that I had dynamite in my pocket. I slept fitfully till about five o'clock, and then left my bed. I lost no time in going to the drink cabinet, pulling out the document, and examining it. I carefully read through the document, line by line, several times over. The lawyers said, 'per return post', which seemed to my fevered mind an all-important instruction. I took it over to the office desk. I found a scrap of paper and made a careful trial of Rosie's signature. I had her sign so many cheques and receipts each day that I was very familiar with it. Then I carefully spread out the application form and wrote on the indicated line: 'Rose, Nalini'. I folded it and put it in an addressed cover which the lawyers had enclosed, sealed it, and I was the first to appear at the window when our extension branch post office opened at seven-thirty.

The postmaster said, 'So early! You have come yourself!'

'My clerk is sick. I was out for a morning walk. Please register this.' I had walked down for fear that opening the garage door might wake her up.

I had no clear idea as to when or how the jewel box might arrive, but I looked for it every day. 'Any parcel in the post, Mani?' I asked constantly. This almost threatened to become a habit. I expected it within the next two days. No signs of it. We had to go out of town for four days. Before leaving I instructed Mani, 'There may be an insured packet coming. Tell the postman to keep it in deposit till we are back on Tuesday. They keep such things, don't they?'

'Yes, sir. But if it is only a registered parcel, I can sign for you.'

'No, no. This is an insured parcel and it will have to be signed for by one of us. Tell the postman to bring it again on Tuesday.'

'Yes, sir,' said Mani, and I left him abruptly; otherwise he might have started expanding on the subject.

We were back on Tuesday. The moment Rosie went upstairs

I asked Mani, 'Did the parcel arrive?'

'No, sir. I waited for the postman, but there was nothing.'

'Did you tell him that we were expecting an insured parcel?'

'Yes, sir, but there was nothing.'

'Strange!' I cried. 'Per return', the lawyers had written. They probably wanted the signature, that was all. Perhaps Marco planned to appropriate the box himself and had tried this ruse. But as long as that lawyer's letter was with me, I could hang them; none of their tricks was going to succeed. I went to my drink cabinet and re-read the letter. They had committed themselves clearly. 'We shall arrange to forward, under insurance cover . . .' If it meant nothing in a lawyer's letter, where was it going to mean anything? I felt somewhat puzzled, but told myself that it would ultimately arrive; banks and lawyers' offices could not be hustled; they had their own pace of work, their own slow red-tape methods. Slow-witted red-tapeists—no wonder the country was going to the dogs. I put the letter back and locked it up safely. I wished I didn't have to go to the drink cabinet every time I wanted to read the letter; the servants, knowing the contents, might begin to think that I took a swill of whisky every few minutes. My desk would be the right place for the letter, but I had a suspicion that Mani might see it; if he caught me studying the letter so often, he was sure to want to take a look at it by stealing up at my back and pretending to have some question to ask. He had worked for me for months and months without my noticing anything against him, but now he and everyone around appeared sinister, diabolical, and cunning.

That evening we had an engagement at Kalipet, a small town sixty miles away. The organizers were providing a van for the musicians, and a Plymouth for me and Nalini, so that we might fulfil the engagement and return home the same night. It was a benefit show for building a maternity home, and they had collected seventy thousand rupees. The price of tickets ranged from two hundred and fifty rupees in a kind of fancy scale, and officials persuaded businessmen and merchants to contribute. Businessmen ungrudgingly paid up on condition that they were given the nearest seats in the first row. They wanted to sit as near the performer as possible, with a chance of being noticed. In their thoughts, Nalini, while dancing, noted their presence and later inquired, 'Who were those important men in the front row?' Poor creatures, they hardly knew how Nalini viewed her audience. She often remarked, 'They might be logs of wood for all I care. When I dance I hardly notice any face. I just see a dark well in the auditorium, that's all.'

This was a very large-scale function because of official interest in it. The officials were interested because the chief man of the place, who was behind all the shows, was a minister of the state cabinet, and it had been his ambition in life to build a first-rate maternity centre in this area. Knowing the circumstances, I had moderated my demand to a thousand rupees for expenses, which meant it was free of income tax. After all, I too liked to contribute to a social cause, and certainly we would not come out of it too badly anyway. But it was all the same for Nalini. Instead of travelling by train, we were going by car, that was all. She was pleased that we should be returning home the same night.

The show was held in an immense pavilion specially constructed with bamboos and coconut matting and decorated with brilliant tapestry, bunting, flowers, and coloured lights. The stage itself was so beautifully designed that Nalini, who generally ignored everything except the flowers at the end, cried, 'What a lovely place. I feel so happy to dance here.' Over a thousand people were seated in the auditorium.

She began her first movement, as usual, after a signal from me. She entered, carrying a brass lamp, with a song in praise of Ganesha, the elephant-faced god, the remover of impediments.

Two hours passed. She was doing her fifth item—a snake dance, unusually enough. I liked to watch it. This item always interested me. As the musicians tuned their instruments and played the famous snake song, Nalini came gliding onto the stage. She fanned out her fingers slowly, and the yellow spotlight, playing on her white, upturned palms, gave them the appearance of a cobra hood; she wore a diadem for this act, and it sparkled. Lights changed, she gradually sank to the floor, the music became slower and slower, the refrain urged the snake to dance—the snake that resided on the locks of Shiva himself, on the wrist of his spouse, Parvathi, and in the ever-radiant home of the gods in Kailas. This was a song that elevated the serpent and brought out its mystic quality; the rhythm was hypnotic. It was her masterpiece. Every inch of her body from toe to head rippled and vibrated to the rhythm of this song which lifted the cobra out of its class of an underground reptile into a creature of grace and divinity and an ornament of the gods.

The dance took forty-five minutes in all; the audience watched in rapt silence. I was captivated by it . . . . She rarely chose to do it indeed. She always said that a special mood was needed, and always joked that so much wriggling twisted her up too much and she could not stand upright again for days. I sat gazing as if I were seeing it for the first time. There came to my mind my mother's remark on the first day, 'A serpent girl! Be careful.' I felt sad at the thought of my mother. How much she could have enjoyed watching this. What would she have said if she could have seen Rosie now, in her shining costume and diadem? I felt a regret at the rift that had developed between me and my mother. She occasionally wrote me a postcard, and I sent her small sums of money now and then, dashing off a few lines to say I was well. She often asked when I'd get back the house for her—well, that involved a big sum and I told myself I'd attend to it as soon as I had some time. Anyway, what was the hurry? She was quite happy in the village; that brother of hers looked after her very well. Somehow I could never fully forgive her for her treatment of Rosie on that fateful day. Well, we were now on cordial terms, but far away from each other, the best possible arrangement. I was watching Nalini and at the same time thinking of my mother. At this moment, one of the men of the organization came up to me unobtrusively and said, 'You are wanted, sir.'

'Who wants me?'

'The District Superintendent of Police.'

'Tell him I'll be with him as soon as this act is over.'

He went away. The District Superintendent! He was one of my card-playing mates. What did he want to see me about now? Of course, the officials were all here, expecting the minister (a sofa was kept vacant for him), and extra police were posted to control the crowd and the traffic. After this act, when the curtain came down, thunderous applause broke out, and I went out. Yes, the District Superintendent was there. He was in plain dress.

'Hello, Superintendent, I didn't know you were coming; you could have come with us in the car,' I cried.

He plucked my sleeve and drew me aside because there were too many people watching us. We went to a lonely spot under a lamp outside, and he whispered, 'I'm awfully sorry to say this, but I've a warrant for your arrest. It has come from headquarters.'

I smiled awkwardly, partly disbelieving him. I thought he was joking. He pulled out a paper. Yes, it was a true and good warrant for my arrest on a complaint from Marco, the charge being forgery. When I stood ruminating, the Superintendent asked, 'Did you sign any recent document for—the lady?'

'Yes; she was busy. But how can you call that forgery?'

'Did you write "For" or just write her name?' He plied me with questions. 'It's a serious charge,' he said. 'I hope you will pull through, but for the moment I have to take you in custody.'

I realized the gravity of the situation. I whispered, 'Please don't create a scene now. Wait until the end of the show, and till we are back home.'

'I'll have to be with you in the car, and after the warrant is served you can arrange for a surety bond till the case is taken up. That will leave you free, but first I'm afraid you will have to go with me to the magistrate. He has to sanction it. I have no powers.'

I went back to my sofa in the hall. They brought me my garland. Somebody got up and made a speech thanking the dancer and Mr Raju for their help in getting the collection to over seventy thousand rupees. Incidentally he spun out a lot of verbiage around the theme of the dance in India, its status, philosophy, and purpose. He went on and on. He was a much-respected president of the local high school or some such thing. There was tremendous applause at the end of his speech. More speeches followed. I felt numb, hardly hearing anything. I didn't care what they said. I didn't care whether the speech was long or short. When it was over, I went to Nalini's dressing-room. I found her changing. A number of girls were standing around her, some waiting for autographs, and some just looking on. I said to Nalini, 'We will have to hurry.'

I went back to the Superintendent in the corridor, composing my looks, trying to look cheerful and unconcerned. A lot of the First-row men surrounded me to explain their appreciation in minute detail. 'She just towers above all others,' someone said. 'I have seen dancers for a half-century—I'm the sort of man who will forgo a meal and walk twenty miles to see a dance. But never have I seen,' etc. etc. 'This maternity home, you know, will be the first of its kind. We must have a wing named after Miss Nalini. I hope you will be able to come again. We would like to have you both for the opening ceremony. Could you give us a photograph of her? . . . We'd like to enlarge it and hang it in the hall . . . That'll be a source of inspiration for many others, and, who knows, in this very building may be born a genius who may follow the footsteps of your distinguished wife.'

I didn't care what they said. I simply nodded and grunted till Nalini came out. I knew that the men surrounded and talked to me only in the hope of getting a close view of Nalini. As usual, she had her garland; I gave her mine. The Superintendent led the way unobtrusively to our Plymouth waiting outside. We had to walk through a crowd buzzing around us like flies. The driver held the door open.

'Get in. Get in,' I said impatiently to Nalini. I sat beside her. Her face was partially illuminated by a shaft of gaslight from a lamp hanging on a tree. Thick dust hung in the air, churned up by the traffic; all the vehicles, cars, bullock-carts, and *jutkas* were leaving in a mass, with a deafening honking of horns and rattle of wheels. A few policemen stood at a discreet distance and saluted the Superintendent as our car moved away. He occupied the front seat next to the driver. I told her, 'Our friend, the District Superintendent, is coming back with us to the city.'

It was about two hours' journey. She talked for a while about the evening. I gave her some comments on her performance. I told her something of what I had heard people say about her snake-dance. She said, 'You are never tired of it,' and then lapsed into silence and drowsiness, only waiting for our destination, as our car whizzed along the country highway, past long rows of bullock-carts with their jingling bells. 'They sound like your anklets,' I whispered to her clumsily.

The moment we reached our home, she threw a smile at the Superintendent, murmured 'Good night', and vanished into the house. The Superintendent said to me, 'Let us go now in my jeep.' It was waiting at the gate.

I sent away the Plymouth. I said, 'I say, Superintendent, give me a little time, please. I want to tell her about it.'

'All right. Don't delay. We must not get into trouble.'

I went up the staircase. He followed. He stood on the landing while I went into her room. She listened to me as if I were addressing a stone pillar. Even now I can recollect her bewildered, stunned expression as she tried to comprehend the situation. I thought she would break down. She often broke down on small issues, but this seemed to leave her unperturbed. She merely said,

'I felt all along you were not doing right things. This is *karma*. What can we do?' She came out to the landing and asked the officer, 'What shall we do about it, sir? Is there no way out?'

'At the moment I have no discretion, madam. It's a non-bailable warrant. But perhaps tomorrow you may apply for reconsideration of bond. But we can do nothing till tomorrow, till it's moved before the magistrate.' He was no longer my friend, but a frightful technician.

10

I HAD TO spend a couple of days in the lock-up, among low criminals. The District Superintendent ceased to be friendly the moment we were in the Central Police Station. He just abandoned me to the routine care of the station officer.

Rosie came to see me in the police lock-up and wept. I sat for the first time with my eyes averted, in the farthest corner of the cell. After a while I recovered my composure and told her to go and see our banker. All that she asked was, 'Oh, we had so much money! Where is it all gone?'

I went back home three days later, but the old, normal life was gone. Mani worked in a mechanical manner, with bowed head, in his own room. There was no work for him to do. Fewer letters arrived for me. There was a sepulchral quietness about the house. Nalini's feet were silent upstairs. No visitors came. She had had to scrape up a bail bond for ten thousand rupees. If I had lived as a normal man of common sense, it would not have been difficult to find the amount. As it was, I had tied up whatever was left over in several foolish share certificates, on which the banks would not advance any money, and the rest I had spent in show living, including the advances taken for future engagements.

I suggested to Rosie, 'Why don't you go through with your engagements for the next quarter? We should receive the balance of the fees.' I caught her at dinner, because nowadays I spent all my time downstairs and left her alone. I lacked the confidence to face her alone in her room. I even spent my sleeping hours on the hall sofa.

She did not answer. I repeated my question, at which she muttered, when the cook went in to fetch something, 'Must we discuss it before the cook?' I accepted the snub meekly.

I was now a sort of hanger-on in the house; ever since she had released me from police custody, the mastery had passed to her. I fretted inwardly at the thought of it. When the first shock of the affair had subsided, she became hardened. She never spoke to me except as to a tramp she had salvaged. It could not be helped. She had had to scrape together all her resources to help me. She went through her act of help in a sort of cold, businesslike manner. I ate my food in silence. She deigned to spend some time in the hall after food. She came and sat down there. She had a tray of betel leaves by her side on the sofa. I pushed it off and dared to seat myself by her side. Her lips were reddened with betel juice. Her face was flushed with the tingling effect of betel leaves. She looked at me imperiously and asked, 'Now, what is it?' Before I opened my mouth, she added, 'Remember, you should speak nothing before the cook. The servants are gossiping too much. On the first of the month I'm going to send one of them away.'

'Wait, wait. Don't rush,' I began.

'What should I wait for?' Her eyes glistened with tears; she blew her nose. I could do nothing about it but just watch. After all, the mastery had passed to her and if she thought fit to cry, it was her business. She had enough strength in her to overcome it if she thought it necessary. It was I who needed comforting. I was overwhelmed with a sudden self-pity. Why should she cry? She was not on the threshold of a prison. She had not been the one who had run hither and thither creating glamour and a public for a dancer; it was not she who had been fiendishly trapped by a half-forgotten man like Marco—an apparent gazer at cave-paintings, but actually venomous and vindictive, like the cobra lying in wait for its victim. I can now see that it was a very wrong line of thought to adopt. But how could I help it? It was only such perverse lines of thought and my excessive self-pity that enabled me to survive those moments; one needed all that amount of devilry to keep oneself afloat. I could give no time for others. I could not bother to think of her own troubles, of the mess she had been led into, of the financial emptiness after all those months of dancing and working, of the surprise sprung upon her by my lack of—what should we call it, judgement? No, it was something much lower than that. Lack of ordinary character! I see it all now clearly, but at that time I still clung to my own grievances, and could watch without much perturbation her emotional tantrums. I allowed her to have her cry as usual. She wiped her eyes and asked, 'You said something when we were eating?'

'Yes; but you wouldn't let me proceed,' I said petulantly. 'I was asking why you should not go through with the programmes, at least those for which we have received an advance.'

She remained in thought for a while and said, 'Why should I?'

'Because we received only an advance, while what we desperately need is the full fee in every case.'

'Where is all the money?'

'You should know. The account is all in your name, and you may see the bankbook if you like.' It was a cruel thing to say. Some devil was wagging his tongue within my skull. I was suddenly racked with the feeling that after all I had done for her she was not sufficiently sympathetic to my cause.

She spurned continuing this perverse discussion. She merely said, 'Please tell me what those engagements are and I'll return them all their money.'

I knew that this was just a brave statement. Where would she find the amount to refund? 'Why should you? Why should you not go through with them?'

'Is money your only consideration? Don't you see how I can't face the public again?'

'Why not? If I'm under arrest, I'm under arrest; that is all. Not you. Why should you not go about your business normally?'

'I can't; that is all. I can say nothing more.'

I asked coldly, 'What do you propose to do in future?'

'Perhaps I'll go back to him.'

'Do you think he will take you back?'

'Yes, if I stop dancing.'

I laughed in a sinister manner. 'Why do you laugh?' she asked.

'If it were only the question of dancing, he might.'

Why did I talk like this? It hurt her very much. 'Yes; you are in a position to say such a thing now. He may not admit me over the threshold, in which event it is far better to end one's life, on his doorstep.' She remained moody for a while. It gave me a profound satisfaction to see her imperiousness shattered after all. She added, 'I think the best solution for all concerned would be to be done with this business of living. I mean both of us. A dozen sleeping pills in a glass of milk, or two glasses of milk. One often hears of suicide pacts. It seems to me a wonderful solution, like going on a long holiday. We could sit and talk one night perhaps, and sip our glasses of milk, and maybe we should wake up in a trouble-free world. I'd propose it this very minute if I were sure you would keep the pact, but I fear that I may go ahead and you may change your mind at the last second.'

'And have the responsibility of disposing of your body?' I said, which was the worst thing I could have said. Why was I speaking like this again and again? I think I was piqued that she would not continue her dancing, was a free creature, while I was a jailbird.

I said, 'Is it not better to keep dancing than think these morbid thoughts?' I felt I must take charge of her again. 'Why won't you dance? Is it because you think I won't be there to look after you? I'm sure you can manage. And it may after all be only for a short time. Oh, there is nothing in this case of ours. It'll just break down at the first hearing. You take my word for it. It's a false charge.'

'Is it?' she asked.

'How can they prove anything against me?'

She merely ignored this legal rambling and said, 'Even if you are free, I'll not dance in public any more. I am tired of all this circus existence.'

'It was your own choice,' I said.

'Not the circus life. I visualized it as something different. It's all gone with that old home of yours!'

'Oh!' I groaned. 'And you wouldn't let me rest then. You drove me hard to help you come before the public, and now you say this! I don't know, I don't know, you are very difficult to satisfy.'

'You don't understand!' she cried, and got up and went upstairs. She came down a few steps to say, 'It does not mean I'm not going to help. If I have to pawn my last possession, I'll do it to save you from jail. But once it's over, leave me once and for all; that's all I ask. Forget me. Leave me to live or die, as I choose; that's all.'

She was as good as her word. A sudden activity seized her. She ran about with Mani's help. She sold her diamonds. She gathered all the cash she could, selling all the shares under par. She kept Mani spinning around. She sent him to Madras to pick up a big lawyer for me. When the stress for cash became acute and she found we would have a lot to make up, she became somewhat more practical-minded. She swallowed her own words and went through her engagements, shepherding the musicians herself, with Mani's help, making all the railway arrangements, and so forth. I taunted her as I saw her moving around. 'You see, this is what I wanted you to do.' There was no dearth of engagements. In fact, my present plight, after a temporary lull, seemed to create an extra interest. After all, people wanted to enjoy a show, and how could they care what happened to me? It hurt me to see her go through her work, practice, and engagements unconcernedly. Mani was very helpful to her, and those who invited her gave her all assistance. Everything went to prove that she could get on excellently without me. I felt like telling Mani, 'Be careful. She'll lead you on before you know where you are, and then you will find yourself in my shoes all of a sudden! Beware the snake-woman!' I knew my mind was not working either normally or fairly. I knew I was growing jealous of her self-reliance. But I forgot for the moment that she was doing it all for my sake. I feared that, in spite of her protestations to the contrary, she would never stop dancing. She would not be able to stop. She would go from strength to strength. I knew, looking at the way she was going about her business, that she would manage—whether I was inside the bars or outside, whether her husband approved of it or not. Neither Marco nor I had any place in her life, which had its own sustaining vitality and which she herself had underestimated all along.

Our lawyer had his own star value. His name spelled magic in all the court-halls of this part of the country. He had saved many a neck (sometimes more than once) from the noose; he had absolved many a public swindler in the public eye and in the eye of the law; he could prove a whole gang of lawless hooligans to be innocent victims of a police conspiracy. He set at naught all the laboriously built-up cases of the prosecution; he made their story laughable; he picked the most carefully packed evidence between his thumb and forefinger and with a squeeze reduced it to thin air; he was old-fashioned in appearance, with his long coat and an orthdox-style *dhoti* and turban and over it all his black gown. His eyes scintillated with mirth and confidence when he stood at the bar and addressed the court. When the judge's eyes were lowered over the papers on his desk, he inhaled a deep pinch of snuff with the utmost elegance. We feared at one stage that he might refuse to take our case, considering it too slight for his attention; but fortunately he undertook it as a concession from one star to another—for Nalini's sake. When the news came that he had accepted the brief (a thousand rupees it cost us to get this out of him), we felt as if the whole case against me had been dropped by the police with apologies for the inconvenience caused. But he was expensive—each consultation had to be bought for cash at the counter. He was in his own way an 'adjournment lawyer'. A case in his hands was like dough; he could knead and draw it up and down. He split a case into minute bits and demanded as many days for microscopic examination. He would keep the court fidgeting without being able to rise for lunch, because he could talk without completing a sentence; he had a knack of telescoping sentence into sentence without pausing for breath.

He arrived by the morning train and left by the evening one, and until that time he neither moved off the court floor nor let the case progress even an inch for the day—so that a judge had to wonder how the day had spent itself. Thus he prolonged the lease of freedom for a criminal within the available time, whatever might be the final outcome. But this meant also for the poor case-stricken man more expense, as his charges per day were seven hundred and fifty rupees, and he had to be paid railway and other expenses as well, and he never came without juniors to assist him.

He presented my case as a sort of comedy in three acts, in which the chief villain was Marco, an enemy of civilized existence. Marco was the first prosecution witness for the day, and I could see him across the hall wincing at every assault mounted against him by my star lawyer. He must have wished that he had not been foolhardy enough to press charges. He had his own lawyer, of course, but he looked puny and frightened.

The first part of the comedy was that the villain wanted to drive his wife mad; the second part of the comedy was that the wife survived this onslaught, and on the point of privation and death was saved by a humble humanitarian called Raju, who sacrificed his time and profession for the protection of the lady and enabled her to rise so high in the world of the arts. Her life was a contribution to the prestige of our nation and our cultural traditions. When the whole world was thirsting for Bharat Natyam, here was this man slighting it, and when she made a big name for herself, someone's gorge rose. Someone wanted to devise a way of blowing up this whole edifice of a helpless lady's single-handed upward career,

Your Honour. And then the schemer brought out the document—a document which had been forgotten and lain in concealment for so many years. There was some other motive in involving the lady by getting her to sign the document—he would go into it at a later part of the argument. (It was his favourite device to make something look sinister; he never found the opportunity to return to it later.) Why should anyone want to trot out a document which had been kept back for all those years? Why did he leave it alone so long? Our lawyer would leave the point for the present without a comment. He looked about like a hound scenting a fox. The document, Your Honour, was returned without signature. The idea was not to get involved, and the lady was not the type to get caught by jewellery; she cared little for it. And so the document was unsigned and returned, the good man Raju himself carrying it to the post office in order to make sure of its dispatch, as the postmaster would testify. So it was a big disappointment for the schemer when the document went back unsigned. So they thought of another trick: someone copied the lady's signature on it and took it to the police. It was not his business to indicate who could have done it; he was not interested in the question. He was only interested to the extent of saying categorically that it was not his client who had done it; and unhesitatingly he would recommend that he should be immediately discharged and exonerated.

But the prosecution case was strong, though unspectacular. They put Mani in the box and examined him till he blurted out that I was desperately looking for an insured parcel every day; the postmaster was cross-examined and had to admit that I had seemed unusual, and finally it was the handwriting expert who testified that it could reasonably be taken to be my handwriting: he had detailed proofs from my writings on the backs of cheques, on receipts and letters.

The judge sentenced me to two years' imprisonment. Our star lawyer looked gratified, I should properly have got seven years according to law books, but his fluency knocked five years off, though, if I had been a little careful . . .

The star lawyer did not achieve this end all at once, but over a period of many months, while Nalini worked harder than ever to keep the lawyer as well as our household going.

I was considered a model prisoner. Now I realized that people generally thought of me as being unsound and worthless, not because I deserved the label, but because they had been seeing me in the wrong place all along. To appreciate me, they should really have come to the Central Jail and watched me. No doubt my movements were somewhat restricted: I had to get out of bed at an hour when I'd rather stay in, and turn in when I'd rather stay out—that was morning five and evening five. But in between these hours I was the master of the show. I visited all departments of the prison as a sort of benevolent supervisor. I got on well with all the warders: I relieved them in their jobs when other prisoners had to be watched. I watched the weaving section and the carpentry sheds. Whether they were murderers or cut-throats or highwaymen, they all listened to me, and I could talk them out of their blackest moods. When there was a respite, I told them stories and philosophies and what not. They came to refer to me as *Vadhyar*—that is, Teacher. There were five hundred prisoners in that building and I could claim to have established a fairly widespread intimacy with most of them. I got on well with the officials too. When the jail superintendent went about his inspections, I was one of those privileged to walk behind and listen to his remarks; and I ran little errands for him, which endeared me to him. He had only to look ever so slightly to his left, and I knew what he wanted. I dashed up and called the warder he was thinking of calling; he had only to hesitate for a second, and I knew he wanted that pebble on the road to be picked up and thrown away. It pleased him tremendously. In addition, I was in a position to run ahead and warn warders and other subordinates of his arrival; and that gave them time to rouse themselves from brief naps and straighten out their turbans.

I worked incessantly on a vegetable patch in the back yard of the superintendent's home. I dug the earth and drew water from the well and tended it carefully. I put fences round, with brambles and thorns so that cattle did not destroy the plants. I grew huge brinjals and beans, and cabbages. When they appeared on their stalks as tiny buds, I was filled with excitement. I watched them develop, acquire shape, change colour, shed the early parts. When the harvest was ready, I plucked them off their stalks tenderly, washed them, wiped them clean to a polish with the end of my jail jacket, arranged them artistically on a tray of woven bamboo (I had arranged to get one from the weaving shed), and carried them in ceremoniously. When he saw the highly polished brinjals, greens, and cabbages, the superintendent nearly hugged me for joy. He was a lover of vegetables. He was a lover of good food, wherever it came from. I loved every piece of this work, the blue sky and sunshine, and the shade of the house in which I sat and worked, the feel of cold water; it produced in me a luxurious sensation. Oh, it seemed to be so good to be alive and feeling all this; the smell of freshly turned earth filled me with the greatest delight. If this was prison life, why didn't more people take to it? They thought of it with a shudder, as if it were a place where a man was branded, chained, and lashed from morning to night! Medieval notions! No place could be more agreeable; if you observed the rules you earned greater appreciation here than beyond the high walls. I got my food, I had my social life with the other inmates and the staff, I moved about freely within an area of fifty acres. Well, that's a great deal of space when you come to think of it; man generally manages with much less. 'Forget the walls, and you will be happy,' I told some of the newcomers, who became moody and sullen the first few days. I felt amused at the thought of the ignorant folk who were horrified at the idea of a jail. Maybe a man about to be hanged might not have the same view, nor one who had been insubordinate, or violent; but short of these, all others could be happy here. I felt choked with tears when I had to go out after two years, and I wished that we had not wasted all that money on our lawyer. I'd have been happy to stay in this prison permanently.

The superintendent transferred me to his office as his personal servant. I took charge of his desk, filled his inkwells, cleaned his pens, mended his pencil, and waited outside his door to see that no one disturbed him while he worked. If he so much as thought of me, I went in and stood before him, I was so alert. He gave me file-boxes to carry to his outer office; I brought in the file-boxes that they gave back to his table. When he was away, the newspapers arrived. I took charge of them and glanced through their pages before taking them to him. I don't think he ever minded; he really liked to read his paper in bed, after his lunch, in the process of snatching a siesta. I quietly glanced through the speeches of world statesmen, descriptions of the Five Year Plan, of ministers opening bridges or distributing prizes, nuclear explosions, and world crises. I gave them all a cursory look.

But on Friday and Saturday I turned the last page of the *Hindu* with trembling fingers—and the last column in its top portion always displayed the same block, Nalini's photograph, the name of the institution where she was performing, and the price of tickets. Now at this corner of south India, now there, next week in Ceylon, and another week in Bombay or Delhi. Her empire was expanding rather than shrinking. It filled me with gall that she should go on without me. Who sat now on that middle sofa? How could the performance start without my signal with the small finger? How could she know when to stop? She probably went on and on, while others just watched without the wit to stop her. I chuckled to myself at the thought of how she must have been missing her trains after every performance. I opened the pages of the paper only to study her engagements and to calculate how much she might be earning. Unless she wrote up her accounts with forethought, super-tax would swallow what she so laboriously piled up with all that twisting and writhing of her person! I would have suspected Mani of having stepped into my shoes, and that would have provided more gall for me to swallow, but for the fact that in the early months of my stay Mani came to see me on a visitor's day.

Mani was the only visitor I had in prison; all other friends and relatives seemed to have forgotten me. He came because he felt saddened by my career. He wore a look of appropriate gloom and seriousness as he waited for me. But when I told him, 'This is not a bad place. You should come here, if you can,' he looked horrified and never saw me again. But in the thirty minutes he was with me he gave me all the news. Nalini had cleared out of the town bag and baggage. She had settled down at Madras and was looking after herself quite well. She had given Mani a gift of one thousand rupees on the day that she left. She had a hundred bouquets of garlands presented to her on the railway platform. What a huge crowd had gathered to see her off! Before her departure she had methodically drawn up a list of all our various debts and discharged them fully; she had all the furniture and other possessions at our house turned over to an auctioneer. Mani explained that the only article that she carried out of the house was the book—which she came upon when she broke open the drink cabinet and had all the drink thrown out. She found the book tucked away inside, picked it up, and took it away carefully.

'That was my book. Why should she take it?' I cried childishly. I added, 'She seems to think it a mighty performance, I suppose! . . . Did it please him? Or did it have any useful effect?' I asked devilishly.

Mani said, 'After the case, she got into the car and went home, and he got into his and went to the railway station: they didn't meet.'

'I'm happy at least about this one thing,' I said. 'She had the self-respect not to try and fall at his feet again.'

Mani added before going away, 'I saw your mother recently. She is keeping well in the village.' At the court-hall my mother had been present. She had come on the last day of the hearing, thanks to our local 'adjournment lawyer', who was my link generally with her, as he continued to handle the tortuous and prolonged affair of half my house being pledged to the Sait. He had been excited beyond words at the arrival of the glamorous lawyer from Madras, whom we put up at the Taj in the best suite.

Our little lawyer seemed to have been running around in excitement. He went to the extent of rushing to the village and fetching my mother—for what purpose he alone knew. For my mother was overcome with my plight as I stood in the dock; when Rosie approached her to say a few words in the corridor, her eyes flashed, 'Now are you satisfied with what you have done to him?' And the girl shrank away from her. This was reported to me by my mother herself, whom I approached during the court recess. My mother was standing in the doorway. She had never seen the inside of a court-hall, and was overwhelmed with a feeling of her own daring. She said to me, 'What a shame you have brought on yourself and on all known to you! I used to think that the worst that could happen to you might be death, as when you had that pneumonia for weeks; but I now wish that rather than survive and go through this . . .' She could not complete her sentence; she broke down and went along the corridor and out before we assembled again to hear the judgment.

11

RAJU'S NARRATION CONCLUDED with the crowing of the cock. Velan had listened without moving a muscle, supporting his back against the ancient stone railing along the steps. Raju felt his throat smarting with the continuous talk all night. The village had not yet wakened to life. Velan yielded himself to a big yawn, and remained silent. Raju had mentioned without a single omission every detail from his birth to his emergence from the gates of the prison. He imagined that Velan would rise with disgust and swear, 'And we took you for such a noble soul all along! If one like you does penance, it'll drive off even the little rain that we may hope for. Begone, you, before we feel tempted to throw you out. You have fooled us.'

Raju waited for these words as if for words of reprieve. He looked on Velan's silence with anxiety and suspense, as if he waited on a judge's verdict again, a second time. The judge here seemed to be one of sterner cast than the one he had encountered in the court-hall. Velan kept still—so still that Raju feared that he had fallen asleep.

Raju asked, 'Now you have heard me fully?' like a lawyer who has a misgiving that the judge has been wool gathering.

'Yes, Swami.'

Raju was taken aback at still being addressed as 'Swami'. 'What do you think of it?'

Velan looked quite pained at having to answer such a question. 'I don't know why you tell me all this, Swami. It's very kind of you to address at such length your humble servant.'

Every respectful word that this man employed pierced Raju like a shaft. 'He will not leave me alone,' Raju thought with resignation. 'This man will finish me before I know where I am.'

After profound thought, the judge rose in his seat. 'I'll go back to the village to do my morning duties. I will come back later. And I'll never speak a word of what I have heard to anyone.' He dramatically thumped his chest. 'It has gone down there, and there it will remain.' With this, he made a deep obeisance, went down the steps and across the sandy river.

A wandering newspaper correspondent who had come to the village picked up the news. The government had sent a commission to inquire into the drought conditions and suggest remedies, and with it came a press correspondent. While wandering around he heard about the Swamiji, went to the temple across the river, and sent off a wire to his paper at Madras, which circulated in all the towns of India. 'Holy man's penance to end drought', said the heading, and then a brief description followed.

This was the starting point.

Public interest was roused. The newspaper office was besieged for more news. They ordered the reporter to go back. He sent a second telegram to say 'Fifth day of fast'. He described the scene: how the Swami came to the river's edge, faced its source, stood knee-deep in the water from six to eight in the morning, muttering something between his lips, his eyes shut, his palms pressed together in a salute to the gods, presumably. It had been difficult enough to find knee-deep water, but the villagers had made an artificial basin in sand and, when it didn't fill, fetched water from distant wells and filled it, so that the man had always knee-deep water to stand in. The holy man stood there for two hours, then walked up the steps slowly and lay down on a mat in the pillared hall of the temple, while his devotees kept fanning him continuously. He took notice of hardly anyone, though there was a big crowd around. He fasted totally. He lay down and shut his eyes in order that his penance might be successful. For that purpose he conserved all his energy. When he was not standing in the water, he was in deep meditation. The villagers had set aside all their normal avocations in order to be near this great soul all the time. When he slept they remained there, guarding him, and though there was a fair-sized crowd, it remained totally silent.

But each day the crowd increased. In a week there was a permanent hum pervading the place. Children shouted and played about, women came carrying baskets filled with pots, firewood, and foodstuffs, and cooked the food for their men and children. There were small curls of smoke going up all along the river bank, on the opposite slope and on this bank also. It was studded with picnic groups, with the women's bright-coloured sarees shining in the sun; men too had festive dress. Bullocks unyoked from their carts jingled their bells as they ate the straw under the trees. People swarmed around little water-holes.

Raju saw them across his pillared hall whenever he opened his eyes. He knew what that smoke meant; he knew that the they were eating and enjoying themselves. He wondered what they might be eating—rice boiled with a pinch of saffron, melted *ghee*—and what were the vegetables? Probably none in this drought. The sight tormented him.

This was actually the fourth day of his fast. Fortunately on the first day he had concealed a little stale food, left over from the previous day, in an aluminium vessel behind a stone pillar in the innermost sanctum—some rice mixed with buttermilk, and a piece of vegetable thrown in. Fortunately, too, he was able on the first day to snatch a little privacy at the end of the day's prayer and penance, late at night. The crowd had not been so heavy then. Velan had business at home and had gone, leaving two others to attend on the Swami. The Swami had been lying on the mat in the pillared hall, with the two villagers looking on and waving a huge palmyra fan at his face. He had felt weakened by his day's fasting. He had suddenly told them, 'Sleep, if you like; I'll be back,' and he rose in a businesslike manner and passed into his inner sanctum.

'I don't have to tell the fellows where I am going or why or how long I shall be gone out of sight.' He felt indignant. He had lost all privacy. People all the time watching and staring, lynx-eyed, as if he were a thief! In the inner sanctum he briskly thrust his hand into a niche and pulled out his aluminium pot. He sat down behind the pedestal, swallowed his food in three or four large mouthfuls, making as little noise as possible. It was stale rice, dry and stiff and two days old; it tasted awful, but it appeased his hunger. He washed it down with water. He went to the back yard and rinsed his mouth noiselessly—he didn't want to smell of food when he went back to his mat.

Lying on his mat, he brooded. He felt sick of the whole thing. When the assembly was at its thickest, could he not stand up on a high pedestal and cry, 'Get out, all of you, and leave me alone, I am not the man to save you. No power on earth can save you if you are doomed. Why do you bother me with all this fasting and austerity?'

It would not help. They might enjoy it as a joke. He had his back to the wall, there was no further retreat. This realization helped him to get through the trial with a little more resignation on the second day of his penance. Once again he stood up in water, muttering with his face to the hills, and watching the picnic groups enjoying themselves all over the place. At night he left Velan for a while and sneaked in to look for leftover food in his aluminium vessel—it was really an act of desperation. He knew full well that he had finished off the vessel the previous night. Still he hoped, childishly, for a miracle. 'When they want me to perform all sorts of miracles, why not make a start with my own aluminium vessel?' he reflected caustically. He felt weak. He was enraged at the emptiness of his larder. He wondered for a moment if he could make a last desperate appeal to Velan to let him eat—and if only he minded, how he could save him! Velan ought to know, yet the fool would not stop thinking that he was a saviour. He banged down the aluminium vessel in irritation and went back to his mat. What if the vessel did get shattered? It was not going to be of any use. What was the point of pampering an empty vessel? When he was seated, Velan asked respectfully, 'What was that noise, master?'

'An empty vessel. Have you not heard the saying, "An empty vessel makes much noise"?'

Velan permitted himself a polite laugh and declared with admiration, 'How many good sentiments and philosophies you have gathered in that head of yours, sir!'

Raju almost glared at him. This single man was responsible for his present plight. Why would he not go away and leave him alone? What a wise plan it would have been if the crocodile had got him while he crossed the river! But that poor old thing, which had remained almost a myth, had become dehydrated. When its belly was ripped open they found in it ten thousand rupees' worth of jewellery. Did this mean that the crocodile had been in the habit of eating only women? No, a few snuffboxes and earrings of men were also found. The question of the day was: who was entitled to all this treasure? The villagers hushed up the affair. They did not want the government to get scent of it and come round and claim it, as it did all buried treasure. They gave out that only a couple of worthless trinkets had been found inside the crocodile, although in actual fact the man who cut it open acquired a fortune. He had no problems for the rest of his life. Who permitted him to cut open the crocodile? Who could say? People didn't wait for permission under such circumstances. Thus had gone on the talk among the people about the crocodile when it was found dead.

Velan, fanning him, had fallen asleep—he had just doubled up in his seat with the fan in his hand. Raju, who lay awake, had let his mind roam and touch the depths of morbid and fantastic-thought. He was now touched by the sight of this man hunched in his seat. The poor fellow was tremendously excited and straining himself in order to make this penance a success, providing the great man concerned with every comfort—except, of course, food. Why not give the poor devil a chance, Raju said to himself, instead of hankering after food which one could not get anyway. He felt enraged at the persistence of food-thoughts. With a sort of vindictive resolution he told himself, 'I'll chase away all thought of food. For the next ten days I shall eradicate all thoughts of tongue and stomach from my mind.'

This resolution gave him a peculiar strength. He developed on those lines: 'If by avoiding food I should help the trees bloom, and the grass grow, why not do it thoroughly?' For the first time in his life he was making an earnest effort; for the first time he was learning the thrill of full application, outside money and love; for the first time he was doing a thing in which he was not personally interested. He felt suddenly so enthusiastic that it gave him a new strength to go through with the ordeal. The fourth day of his fast found him quite sprightly. He went down to the river, stood facing upstream with his eyes shut, and repeated the litany. It was no more than a supplication to the heavens to send down rain and save humanity. It was set in a certain rhythmic chant, which lulled his senses and awareness, so that as he went on saying it over and over again the world around became blank. He nearly lost all sensation, except the numbness at his knees, through constant contact with cold water. Lack of food gave him a peculiar floating feeling, which he rather enjoyed, with the thought in the background, 'This enjoyment is something Velan cannot take away from me.'

The hum of humanity around was increasing. His awareness of his surroundings was gradually lessening in a sort of inverse proportion. He was not aware of it, but the world was beginning to press around. The pen of the wandering journalist had done the trick. Its repercussions were far and wide. The railways were the first to feel the pressure. They had to run special trains for the crowds that were going to Malgudi. People travelled on footboards and on the roofs of coaches. The little Malgudi station was choked with passengers. Outside, the station buses stood, the conductors crying, 'Special for Mangala leaving. Hurry up. Hurry up.' People rushed up from the station into the buses and almost sat on top of one another. Gaffur's taxi drove up and down a dozen times a day. And the crowd congregated around the river at Mangala. People sat in groups along its sandbank, down its stones and steps, all the way up the opposite bank, wherever they could squeeze themselves in.

Never had this part of the country seen such a crowd. Shops sprang up overnight, as if by magic, on bamboo poles roofed with thatch, displaying coloured soda bottles and bunches of bananas and coconut-toffees. The Tea Propaganda Board opened a big tea-stall, and its posters, green tea plantations along the slopes of blue mountains, were pasted all around the temple wall. (People drank too much coffee and too little tea in these parts.) It had put up a tea-bar and served free tea in porcelain cups all day. The public swarmed around it like flies, and the flies swarmed on all the cups and sugar-bowls. The presence of the fly brought in the Health Department, which feared an outbreak of some epidemic in that crowded place without water. The khaki-clad health inspectors sprayed every inch of space with DDT and, with needle in hand, coaxed people to inoculate themselves against cholera, malaria, and what not. A few youngsters just for fun bared their biceps, while a big crowd stood about and watched. There was a blank space on the rear wall of the temple where they cleaned up the ground and made a space for people to sit around and watch a film show when it grew dark. They attracted people to it by playing popular hits on the gramophone with its loudspeakers mounted on the withering treetops. Men, women, and children crowded in to watch the film shows, which were all about mosquitoes, malaria, plague and tuberculosis, and BCG vaccination. When a huge close-up of a mosquito was shown as the cause of malaria, a peasant was overheard saying, 'Such huge mosquitoes! No wonder the people get malaria in those countries. Our own mosquitoes are so tiny that they are harmless,' which depressed the lecturer on malaria so much that he remained silent for ten minutes. When he had done with health, he showed a few Government of India films about dams, river valleys, and various projects, with ministers delivering speeches. Far off, outside the periphery, a man had opened a gambling booth with a dartboard on a pole, and he had also erected a crude merry-go-round, which whined all day. Pedlars of various kinds were also threading in and out, selling balloons, reed whistles, and sweets.

A large crowd always stood around and watched the saint with profound awe. They touched the water at his feet and sprinkled it over their heads. They stood indefinitely around, until the master of ceremonies, Velan, begged them to move. 'Please go away. The Swami must have fresh air. If you have had your *darshan*, move on and let others have theirs. Don't be selfish.' And then the people moved on and enjoyed themselves in various ways.

When the Swami went in to lie on his mat in the hall, they came again to look at him and stood about until Velan once again told them to keep moving. A few were specially privileged to sit on the edge of the mat very close to the great man. One of them was the schoolmaster, who took charge of all the telegrams and letters that were pouring in from all over the country wishing the Swami success. The post office at Mangala normally had a visiting postman who came once a week, and when a telegram came it was received at Aruna, a slightly bigger village seven miles down the river course, and was kept there until someone could be found going to Mangala. But now the little telegraph office had no rest—day and night messages poured in, just addressed 'Swamiji', that was all. They were piling up every hour and had to be sent down by special messengers. In addition to the arriving telegrams, there were many going out. The place was swarming with press reporters, who were rushing their hour-to-hour stories to their papers all over the world. They were an aggressive lot and the little telegraph-master was scared of them. They banged on his window and cried, 'Urgent!' They held out packets and packed-up films and photographs, and ordered him to dispatch them at once. They cried, 'Urgent, urgent! If this packet does not reach my office today . . .' and they threatened terrifying prospects and said all sorts of frightening things.

'Press. Urgent!' 'Press. Urgent!' They went on shouting till they reduced the man to a nervous wreck. He had promised his children that he would take them to see the Swamiji. The children cried, 'They are also showing an Ali Baba film, a friend told me.' But the man was given no time to fulfil his promise to his children. When the pressmen gave him respite, the keys rattled with incoming messages. He had spent a fairly peaceful life until then, and the present strain tore at his nerves. He sent off an SOS to all his official superiors whenever he found breathing space: 'Handling two hundred messages today. Want relief.'

The roads were choked with traffic, country carts, buses and cycles, jeeps and automobiles of all kinds and ages. Pedestrians in files with hampers and baskets crossed the fields like swarms of ants converging on a lump of sugar. The air rang with the music of a few who had chosen to help the Swami by sitting near him, singing devotional songs to the accompaniment of a harmonium and *tabla*.

The busiest man here was an American, wearing a thin bush-shirt over corduroys. He arrived in a jeep with a trailer, dusty, rugged, with a mop of tousled hair, at about one in the afternoon on the tenth day of the fast and set himself to work immediately.

He had picked up an interpreter at Madras and had driven straight through, three hundred and seventy-five miles. He pushed everything aside and took charge of the scene. He looked about for only a moment, driving his jeep down to the hibiscus bush behind the temple. He jumped off and strode past everyone to the pillared hall. He went up to the recumbent Swami and brought his palms together, muttering, '*Namaste*'—the Indian salute, which he had learned the moment he landed in India. He had briefed himself on all the local manners. Raju looked on him with interest; the large, pink-faced arrival was a novel change in the routine.

The pink visitor stooped low to ask the schoolmaster, sitting beside the Swami, 'Can I speak to him in English?'

'Yes. He knows English.'

The man lowered himself on to the edge of the mat and with difficulty sat down on the floor, Indian fashion, crossing his legs. He bent close to the Swami to say, 'I'm James J. Malone. I'm from California. My business is production of films and TV shows. I have come to shoot this subject, take it back to our country, and show it to our people there. I have in my pocket the sanction from New Delhi for this project. May I have yours?'

Raju thought over it and nodded serenely.

'Okay. Thanks a lot. I won't disturb you—but will you let me shoot pictures of you? I wouldn't disturb you. Will it bother you if I move a few things up and fix the cable and lights?'

'No, you may do your work,' said the sage.

The man became extremely busy. He sprang to his feet, pulled the trailer into position, and started his generator. Its throbbing filled the place, overwhelming all other noises. It brought in a huge crowd of men, women, and children to watch the fun. All the other attractions in the camp became secondary. As Malone drew the cables about, a big crowd followed him. He grinned at them affably and went about his business, Velan and one or two others ran through the crowd, crying, 'Is this a fish market? Get away, all of you who have no work here!' But nobody was affected by his orders. They climbed pillars and pedestals and clung to all sorts of places to reach positions of vantage. Malone went on with his job without noticing anything. Finally, when he had the lights ready, he brought in his camera and took pictures of the people and the temple, and of the Swami from various angles and distances.

'I'm sorry, Swami, if the light is too strong.' When he had

finished with the pictures, he brought in a microphone, put it near the Swami's face, and said, 'Let us chat. Okay? Tell me, how do you like it here?'

'I am only doing what I have to do; that's all. My likes and dislikes do not count.'

'How long have you been without food now?'

'Ten days.'

'Do you feel weak?'

'Yes.'

'When will you break your fast?'

'Twelfth day.'

'Do you expect to have the rains by then?'

'Why not?'

'Can fasting abolish all wars and bring world peace?'

'Yes.'

'Do you champion fasting for everyone?'

'Yes.'

'What about the caste system? Is it going?'

'Yes.'

'Will you tell us something about your early life?'

'What do you want me to say?'

'Er—for instance, have you always been a yogi?'

'Yes; more or less.'

It was very hard for the Swami to keep up a continuous flow of talk. He felt exhausted and lay back. Velan and others looked on with concern. The schoolmaster said, 'He is fatigued.'

'Well, I guess we will let him rest for a while. I'm sorry to bother you.'

The Swami lay back with his eyes closed. A couple of doctors, deputed by the government to watch and report, went to the Swami, felt his pulse and heart. They helped him to stretch himself on the mat. A big hush fell upon the crowd. Velan plied his fan more vigorously than ever. He looked distraught and unhappy. In fact, keeping a sympathetic fast, he was now eating on alternate days, confining his diet to saltless boiled greens. He looked worn out. He said to the master, 'One more day. I don't know how he is going to bear it. I dread to think how he can pull through another day.'

Malone resigned himself to waiting. He looked at the doctor and asked, 'How do you find him?'

'Not very satisfactory; blood pressure is two hundred systolic. We suspect one of the kidneys is affected. Uremia is setting in. We are trying to give him small doses of saline and glucose. His life is valuable to the country.'

'Would you say a few words about his health?' Malone asked, thrusting his microphone forward. He was sitting on the head of a carved elephant decorating the steps to the pillared hall.

The doctors looked at each other in panic and said, 'Sorry. We are government servants—we cannot do it without permission. Our reports are released only from headquarters. We cannot give them direct. Sorry.'

'Okay. I wouldn't hurt your customs.' He looked at his watch and said, 'I guess that's all for the day.' He approached the schoolmaster and said, 'Tell me, what time does he step into the river tomorrow?'

'Six a.m.'

'Could you come over and show me the location?' The schoolmaster got up and took him along. The man said, 'Wait, wait. You'll not mind understudying him for a minute. Show me where he starts from, how he gets up, and where he steps and stands.'

The teacher hesitated, feeling too shy to understudy the sage. The man urged him on. 'Come on, be cooperative. I'll take care of it, if there is any trouble.'

The teacher started from the pedestal. 'He starts here. Now follow me.' He showed the whole route down to the river, and the spot where the Swami would stop and pray, standing in water for two hours. The crowd followed keenly every inch of this movement, and someone in the crowd was joking, 'Oh! The master is also going to do penance and starve!' And they all laughed.

Malone threw a smile at them from time to time, although he did not know what they were saying. He surveyed the place from various angles, measured the distance from the generator, shook the schoolmaster's hand, and went back to his jeep. 'See you tomorrow morning.' He drove off amidst a great roar and puffing of the engine as his jeep rattled over the pits and ditches beyond the hibiscus, until he reached the road.

The eleventh day, morning. The crowd, pouring in all night, had nearly trebled itself because it was the last day of the fast. All night one could hear the voices of people and the sound of vehicles rattling over the roads and pathways. Velan and a band of his assistants formed a cordon and kept the crowd out of the pillared hall. They said, 'The Swami must have fresh air to breathe. It's the only thing he takes now. Don't choke the air. Everyone can have his *darshan* at the river, I promise. Go away now. He is resting.' It was an all-night vigil. The numerous lanterns and lamps created a criss-cross of bewildering shadows on all hedges, trees, and walls.

At five-thirty in the morning the doctors examined the Swami. They wrote and signed a bulletin saying: 'Swami's condition grave. Declines glucose and saline. Should break the fast immediately. Advise procedure.' They sent a man running to send off this telegram to their headquarters.

It was a top-priority government telegram, and it fetched a reply within an hour: 'Imperative that Swami should be saved. Persuade best to cooperate. Should not risk life. Try give glucose and saline. Persuade Swami resume fast later.'

They sat beside the Swami and read the message to him. He smiled at it. He beckoned Velan to come nearer.

The doctors appealed, 'Tell him he should save himself. Please, do your best. He is very weak.'

Velan bent close to the Swami and said, 'The doctors say—'

In answer Raju asked the man to bend nearer, and whispered, 'Help me to my feet,' and clung to his arm and lifted himself. He got to his feet. He had to be held by Velan and another on each side. In the profoundest silence the crowd followed him down. Everyone followed at a solemn, silent pace. The eastern sky was red. Many in the camp were still sleeping. Raju could not walk, but he insisted upon pulling himself along all the same. He panted with the effort. He went down the steps of the river, halting for breath on each step, and finally reached his basin of water. He stepped into it, shut his eyes, and turned towards the mountain, his lips muttering the prayer. Velan and another held him each by an arm. The morning sun was out by now; a great shaft of light illuminated the surroundings. It was difficult to hold Raju on his feet, as he had a tendency to flop down. They held him as if he were a baby. Raju opened his eyes, looked about, and said, 'Velan, it's raining in the hills. I can feel it coming up under my feet, up my legs—' He sagged down.

The World of Nagaraj

1

NAGARAJ FANCIED HIMSELF a man with a mission. If you asked, 'What is your mission?' he would look away and pretend not to have heard your query. He was not quite clear in his mind about his mission, but always felt he must be up and doing. He could not stay in bed after the hall clock struck six, but his wife, who got up first, would say, 'Where is the hurry? Why don't you sleep till seven as others do? None of them to be seen so early except your good self . . .' and, rising, hurry off to the back yard to start her day with a cold bath and the washing of clothes. Nagaraj would stay in bed till all sound from the back yard ceased, when he could be sure she had moved into the kitchen to light the fire and put the coffee kettle on or had entered the *puja* room to mutter a prayer before the gods. Now it was certain she would not cross his path and accost him with, 'Why should you get up so early?' Not in his nature to retort openly, though he would probably mumble within himself, 'Just my wish, and that's that.' He would get up and pass along briskly to the back yard for a wash.

After his morning coffee, he stepped out and strolled along to wake up his friend Jayaraj, the photographer, who slept on a bench in front of his shop at the market archway. Nagaraj sat on the edge of the bench while Jayaraj was still asleep and glanced through a one-sheet morning paper, which Truth Printing published, giving a summary of news items culled from yesterday's papers and radio broadcasts. It cost ten paise a day and, though Jayaraj paid the subscription, the first to read it was Nagaraj, who always arrived with the delivery boy. Nagaraj read through it in four minutes and picked up talking points for the day. 'The minister is going to Bermuda,' Nagaraj would announce to Jayaraj when he opened his eyes.

'Which minister?'

'One of them, there are so many . . .'

'What for?'

'I don't know. How can I guess? No explanation. I must speak to the printer. Only one sheet for ten paise and one side filled with advertisements!'

'What sort of advertisement? Just rubbish. What have we in this town? Manufacturers? Any notable enterprises? Any personality of importance? Nothing to advertise.'

'Not so bad. I wouldn't agree with you,' said Nagaraj. 'We have our own shops and men, our town can grow and develop gradually if a vision is kept up before the public through advertisements. Above all, this paper gives us an idea of what is going on around us, also of shops, marriages, vacant houses, deaths . . .'

'All packed on one side of a sheet!' Jayaraj sneered. 'I'd stop it if the Truth Printing man was not my friend desperately needing support.'

'I don't mind it. Such frugal fare saves us time, and some tit-bits and information are useful for my work . . .'

Jayaraj ignored Nagaraj's mention of work, stood up and said, 'Now wait here, I will dash across to my house for a wash, and come back. I don't want to leave the place unguarded, demons are around ready to break the lock . . .' He indicated the inside of the shop and said, 'Irreplaceable treasures there. Everyone, every blackguard who passes through this market gate has an eye on my camera and equipment.'

'But why do you always borrow the Trustee's imported camera?'

'That's for outdoor purpose only, but the one in there is my own, the best lens. Whether you aim it at a corpse or a bridegroom, it's all the same to it. Have you ever considered how impartial the lens could be?'

'Ah, ah! How profound your thoughts . . .'

'Very few appreciate me; they think I'm just a common photographer, little realizing that the man behind a camera must be a thinker, otherwise he will end up as a lens-wiper.'

'True, true, that's what I want to emphasize in my book too.'

Jayaraj checked himself from enquiring about the book. Otherwise he would have to sit there and listen to Nagaraj's grandiloquent plan to write on Sage Narada. The first time Nagaraj had mentioned the subject, Jayaraj had blundered into asking 'Why Narada?', thereby starting Nagaraj on the celestial sage who had a curse on his back that unless he spread a gossip a day his head would burst. The sage floated along with ease from one world to another among the fourteen worlds above and below this earth, carrying news and gossip, often causing clashes between gods and demons, demons and demons, gods and gods, and between creatures of the earth. Ultimately, of course, such clashes and destruction proved beneficial in a cosmic perspective. Evil destroyed itself. That was Nagaraj's thesis. Jayaraj realized that he often ignored a customer as he was engrossed in Nagaraj's talk, and in course of time became wary whenever Nagaraj showed symptoms of leading on to the subject of his book. He got up and left but was soon back to open his shop.

Nagaraj left his post and ambled along to watch the stalls. The shutters were just going up, the shopmen heaping vegetables and fruits on shelves and on the floor. Nagaraj derived a strange pleasure from looking at the exhibit of farm produce: 'That mound of cabbages looks beautiful,' he reflected as he walked down the narrow space between the stalls. 'Also those brinjals shining green and purple—all these are attractive, like flowers in a garden—but what a pity they are cut up and cooked—when served on the plate, how different, greasy and mangled they seem! Can't say it to my wife, she will take it as a comment on her cooking . . . Have to be careful and diplomatic all the time, the tightrope walking called domestic harmony. Nowadays she is too ready to take offence.' His was a familiar figure in the market. He was hailed here and there as he passed, but he preferred not to do any marketing today. He replied, 'Not today, I have no money now . . .'

'Not at all necessary. I can take it later. You are like our bank . . .' But he kept moving, laughing at the joke, secretly worrying whether he should not stop and carry that bitter gourd which looks like, like what? He fumbled for a comparison and gave it up. Later it occurred to him that the bitter gourd was patterned after a minor crocodile with hieroglyphics on its back. He marvelled for a second at nature's variety. 'No two vegetables alike,' he commented to himself, 'some of them even more grotesque than the bitter gourd. Nature's jokes!'

He walked home, the back of his mind worrying over something. He wished he could define the worry and exorcise it. He found he had nothing to worry about. 'Thank God I don't have to think of money. I'm not greedy, that's why I'm happy. Even after the division of property, I get a thousand rupees from the bank deposits left by my father. Fortunately he specified my share, otherwise it would have been bitter arguments with my brother, who showed a fighting temperament while asking for his share of the property after Father's death. But of that let me not think now; I had enough at that time. Never wish to think of it. If I want more money I could rent out a portion of my house: with the pressure on housing at present, anyone will be happy to give me at least three hundred for a portion and the property is big enough for both parties to co-exist without coming in each other's way. But is it worth it? No,' he told himself. 'My old mother should have her freedom to hobble up and down unrestricted, and my wife must have her freedom to talk, comment, argue and shout uninhibited, without any tenant watching—after all, it is her privilege and I do not have to listen to her full speech; I can move away to the *pyol*.'

When he reached home he didn't knock on the door but divested his feet of the sandals at the doorway and, hoisting himself on the smooth cool *pyol*, sat down leaning against the pillar on the veranda. He loved its cool granite surface and could now watch the goings-on in Kabir Street.

For the next hour or two he would not stir out of his perch. When he sat thus, he was filled with a sense of supreme contentment, never wanting anything more out of life. The activities of his neighbours fascinated him. He could enumerate the timing of every arrival and departure.

The Talkative Man should be out in fifteen minutes. His was the first house in the row. He was the busiest man in the street, fancied himself a journalist and wandered about the town the whole day on his bicycle. Nagaraj wondered what he got out of it. 'None of my business, I suppose. His forefathers have left him the big house and enough money to keep him going. Blessed fellow, never married, unlike me, a prisoner of domesticity. Oh, no! I should not be saying such things—rather unfair and insulting to the poor creature my wife, who has not had a day's rest, serving me and my mother ungrudgingly, though she has moments of nerves when she would flare up at me or my mother, especially my mother, but that'll always pass . . .'

His thoughts turned to Sambu, his immediate neighbour, hardly to be seen outside, a contrast to the Talkative Man. Sambu sat glued to a canvas deck chair beside the street window, reading a book all day as long as the light lasted, and at dusk he switched on a reading lamp and continued. 'What a lot he reads, unsocial fellow: never shows any interest in anyone but just goes on reading; anyway what is there to read all the time, poor fellow, bound to grow flabby and shapeless if he goes on like that. Decent fellow, never interferes with anyone but just goes on reading. Why should I mind? It's his business; only I want him to remain in good shape. He has put on weight after his mother's death. He must at least go for an early morning walk along the river. Lazy fellow. His father was a skinflint moneylender who confiscated a whole library which a poor scholar had built up laboriously, although his monthly budget remained unbalanced all his life. On his death, Sambu's father attached the library along with the rosewood shelves through a court order, and Sambu has done nothing but read all day, after his father's death. Rather unhealthy for the eyes. They should pass a law that one should read only books personally acquired or earned, not an inheritance.'

There was a slight noise at the door on the other side. He knew that his mother was trying to open the door but he knew also that she could not move it. It was massive, of ancient teakwood, tanned through time and weather, the framework with lotus-like carvings, brass knobs on the central panel shaped like virginal breasts, so shining and attractive that, when very young, Nagaraj used to stand on his toes and try to reach those nipples with his lips; his brother, who was taller and always luckier, took his mouth to the knobs and clicked his tongue in appreciations crying, 'Oh, that milk is so sweet,' and made Nagaraj envious. They also played trains standing on the bottom ledge of the door and clutching the brass knobs to push and pull the door.

'Nagu! Nagu!' his mother cried from the other side. 'The water is getting cold, come for your bath.'

'She still thinks I am ten years old, doesn't notice my age that I'm past fifty.' She was frail and wasp-like, and hobbled about the house with a staff in hand.

'Nagu, Nagu,' her thin voice plaintively continued on the other side of the door. He understood his wife's strategy. If she had come out to call him, he would have snapped back (he imagined), 'Don't disturb me now.' But Mother's intrusion was different. He stirred himself and said mildly, 'I know when to bathe, Mother.' He knew he sounded pompous, while he had only been watching and woolgathering, which were important activities in his scheme of living. Watching and brooding had a subtle value which people never realised. Left to himself he was prepared to sit on the *pyol* the whole day, looking on the life and movement of Kabir Street. Now he could not ignore his mother's call. 'How old is she? Must be seventy or eighty or ninety—lost count of her years, as it was the family tradition generally not to celebrate anyone's birthday beyond the tenth. "Happy Birthday" greetings are a western fashion,' he thought. At once he corrected himself. 'What about the elaborate ritual on one's sixtieth year?' His brother, he remembered, had celebrated two months ago his sixtieth birthday like a wedding, with printed invitation and pipe and drum and garland and feast at his village home, having himself and his wife photographed in bridal costume. (Jayaraj was a special invitee.) It was a grand occasion in the village and he had to attend it, leaving his mother behind in the care of the woman who came in daily to sweep the house and was now cajoled into staying all day with a bonus of ten rupees. Mother was delighted because she liked the woman, who had been in their service for years out of count and was a dependable ally against the daughter-in-law. His brother's sixtieth birthday was memorable. He had entertained the entire village, hundreds of guests for each meal—they had spread dining leaves in every corner of their home and also outside on the street, blocking all passage for the day. Nagaraj felt a little awkward about it as he noticed his brother and sister-in-law going through elaborate ceremonies conducted by showy priests from Trichy and then moving around, giggling like newly-weds, with garlands dangling from their necks. Jayaraj had managed to borrow the imported camera from the Trustee, and was in his element, clicking away. A lot of village men surrounded him and ventured to ask to be photographed.

He said, 'Certainly, five rupees a copy and you must come to town to collect it.'

His brother, who overheard it, was in such a jolly mood—unknown in normal days—that he said, 'Jayaraj, take their photos also. I'll pay.'

Nagaraj responded to his brother's good mood by sticking to him all through and laughing at his banal jokes unreservedly. He had brought presents for the occasion, brocades and silks for his sister-in-law from Coomar's and a pair of *dhotis*, lace-edged two inches, for his brother, and silverware and a wristwatch for his nephew Tim. Nagaraj's wife was very solicitous and tried to please her sister-in-law in a hundred ways while she, in turn, pressed sweets, coffee and drinks on her in-laws from the town. They were laughing, joking and smiling at one another endlessly, and sang songs sitting before the holy fire. 'What makes them so happy on a birthday? I'd feel gloomy if I realized I was sixty. Birthdays must be ignored, as occasions, taking one inescapably a step nearer decrepitude and decay!' One must be as innocent as the old watchman at the temple who had to sign a form—with his thumb impression—and declare his age for a pension now and then. He always begged Nagaraj to fill in the columns. It was no use asking his age since he always said, 'I don't know, sir. We poor people are not taught to count. You have wisdom and must know how old I am by looking at me.'

Nagaraj would study his lined face and the bent back and declare, 'Seventy-seven. Next year remember to say seventy-eight and not twenty-four.'

He heard his mother's call again and rose, switching off his reveries. When he pushed the door open she was there like a hovering spirit. He felt annoyed at her persistence and wanted to shout, 'Why don't you leave me alone?' but sublimated his words, 'Yes, yes, it won't take more than five minutes. I'll be ready.' What would be the point in losing his temper? Apart from other considerations she was deaf and never understood a word.

His wife was in the second courtyard and glared at him speechlessly as he passed. 'Why is she scowling? I've done nothing . . . It's becoming difficult to survive in the company of these two women,' he reflected, compressing his lips, sealing his remarks which might rush forth to say, 'If you have no one to heckle, don't choose me.' His wife just said, 'If the water gets cold, I can't light the fire again.'

He took his bath in the back yard, behind the screen of a couple of zinc sheets. Bathrooms were a recent notion; they were unknown earlier. They had always washed and bathed in the river which flowed along the back of their Kabir Street homes. When the chill wind blew from the river they set up a cauldron on a pile of bricks under the mango tree and heated the water with brambles and twigs from the back yard wilderness.

Now the water was the right temperature. His wife had a genius for doing the right thing and he felt a profound gratitude for her attention as he poured water over his head and messed about with the green soap, which as usual smarted at his eyes. 'She has a purpose in hustling me to bathe; otherwise one has to go about collecting faggots again. But should not the matter be left to my good sense too? Can't I judge what I should do in consideration of everyone's welfare? It's not Mother and my wife alone who are concerned. I'm the head of the family. Let no one forget it . . .' At this point he tried to switch off his mind again: too much of thinking is no good, rather fatiguing.

The bath was refreshing and, as always, induced in him a holy mood. After a bath he always picked up an ochre drape and *dhoti* suspended from a nail at the door of the *puja* room. He had acquired them a few months ago after a laborious search. One day he found a bearded sadhu at the Town Hall on the lawn, who wore the ochre robe of a holy man. Nagaraj approached him timidly, the other's appearance being overwhelming, and asked with humility, 'Where can I get cloth similar to yours?'

The sadhu looked at Nagaraj fixedly. 'Why?'

Nagaraj felt confused and said, 'I like it.'

'That is not a good enough reason. This raiment is sacred and meant for one who is a sanyasi. Are you one or do you want to be one?'

Nagaraj felt embarrassed and tongue-tied. 'I've a family . . .'

'How large?'

'I've an old mother and wife.'

'No children?'

Nagaraj shook his head and said, 'But my brother in the village has a son.'

'How does that help you?'

Nagaraj now felt emboldened to sit beside the sadhu on the soft lawn, the only green spot in the town. For some reason or the other the Municipality maintained with care this green patch. Nagaraj said further, 'But I'm fond of my brother's son, Tim . . .'

'Tim! Who gave him such a name? What does it mean?'

Nagaraj felt caught. He had no explanation.

'Every god in Heaven has a thousand names—couldn't you pick up one of them instead of Tim? What does it mean, anyway?'

'When he was a year old the only noise he could lisp was "Tim". It was charming and everyone began to address him as Tim—though his actual name at the naming ceremony was Krishnaji.'

'Ah! Highest God, and you have chosen to call him Tim, which should be the name of only a wandering cat!'

'Such things somehow happen, Swamiji. No one can be responsible for such mistakes. But in all school registers his name is Krishnaji.'

'Do you know why we name children after the gods? So that His name in some form is always on one's lips and the walls echo divine names!'

'Ah! What profound words!' Nagaraj cried.

The sanyasi was flattered and commanded, 'State your business with us.'

'Just wanted to know how I can acquire those ochre robes . . .'

The sanyasi looked down at his chest and said. 'These days people have a craving for fancy clothes.' He swept around his arm to indicate the crowds on the lawn. 'Do you see anyone who is not dressed like a clown in all this crowd?'

'All kinds of flowery patterns and colours! Sometimes I feel those men wear women's sarees instead of *dhotis*. You can't find a white *dhoti* anywhere—all in fancy clothes as your good self remarked a little while ago . . .' echoed Nagaraj. The sanyasi laughed, pleased at the concurrence. Nagaraj felt inspired to continue, 'Did you notice the youth of the country?—in tight pants and jeans and T-shirts and, as I hear it, schoolgirls crop their hair and wear short skirts while boys wear long uncut hair. You must forgive my mentioning these things . . .' He knew he was exaggerating these fashions which were more noticeable in a city like Madras than in Malgudi and actually were known in Malgudi only through photographs in magazines, but it pleased the sanyasi to hear such sweeping statements in support of his own observation and he came back to the question of the ochre robe. 'Now, explain why you want to dress like a sanyasi. There are enough fakes in holy men's garb.'

Nagaraj explained, 'I thought it would give me greater peace of mind at home if I wore a sanyasi's dress in the *puja* room, at least . . .'

Nagaraj met the sanyasi again at the same place two days later. The sanyasi handed him a packet. 'This is ochre dye. Dissolve it in water and soak your clothes in it overnight, and there in the morning you will be ready to look like a sage.'

'I don't want to parade it, but wear it only when I perform a *puja*.'

'Wear it for an hour or a lifetime, I don't care what you do, but only remember when you are wearing this ochre your mind should be only on God, not on money or the family. Your thoughts must be away from all sensual matters, free from *kama, krodha, lobha* and *moha*. You must observe silence, become deaf to other people's voices, never pay attention to it, even if there is an urgent telegram—'

'No one sends me a telegram.'

'Don't interrupt, but listen. Never hear the knock on the door. Don't look at your wife except as a mother, and don't let your mind dwell on your night life—'

'I have none now. For over ten years we have been living like brother and sister.'

'Don't interrupt,' commanded the sanyasi, and Nagaraj was happy to shut up. Even as he was explaining his private life he was not sure he was truthful: he remembered that some nights, in the darkness, at a deep silent hour, he slipped down from his cot and sought his wife's body while she slept on a mattress on the floor. 'Even that must be given up,' he told himself. 'No more . . .'

After his bath he took the ochre *dhoti* and the wrap and briskly dried himself with it as he entered the *puja* room, a cubicle at a corner off the second courtyard, which for generations had been the family prayer room. His wife had already lit the oil lamps before the deity, filled a basket with flowers from the garden in the back yard, and lit incense sticks. Now in his ochre robe he felt transformed. While he was in this dress, his wife was not to bring up any domestic matter or any letter in the post, never call him to the street door, even if an emperor knocked. She had to conduct herself as if he had ceased to exist. His mind worked further on the theme. It was a state of being dead for some moments each day. His guru, the Town Hall sanyasi, had explained, 'It's good to experience death a little each day so that when your time is up you will slip into the state effortlessly. You will realise how noble and welcome it is—then Death will not be dreaded and avoided. You will overcome death itself. . .' Nagaraj sat in his cubicle before the brass images lit up by the flickering oil lamps, and felt elevated. He recited in an undertone fragments of Vedic hymns he had learnt and half forgotten, all the holy verse he knew and the mantras he was taught in boyhood. He showered flowers on the images. The fragrance of incense and flowers gave him a feeling of sitting in a haven of peace, silence, isolation. He felt he had been vouched a rare guidance by the sanyasi. The first time he wore the sanyasi's garb, his wife withdrew into the kitchen and shut the door with a bang. She was sullen. He wanted to assure her that the garb and restrictions were to last only for thirty minutes, but he had no way of communicating the message as he had to observe silence when he was dressed thus. He swallowed back his words and stepped into the *puja* room.

When he finished his *puja* and came out and changed into normal white dress, he asked, 'Why have you shut yourself in?'

'So that your meditation may not be spoilt by the sound of my breathing.'

'The kitchen smoke might affect your eyes,' Nagaraj said.

'Ah! How considerate! So much the better if I'm not able to watch your antics. Anyway, why are you doing these funny things?' He wondered how to explain and if he could tell her the need for a short course of daily death as a rehearsal for the final one. He checked himself as he realized that she might not understand the philosophy but feel shocked and lament at the mention of death and bring the neighbours gate-crashing. And so he hummed and hawed and blinked till she said, 'You don't know the reason yourself! Some fool has put it in your head.'

'Oh, no, don't call him a fool,' he pleaded.

'Whom? Who is "he"?'

He did not wish to betray the source of his inspiration and mumbled inconsequentially. Eventually she got used to the change, realizing it was harmless and that the ochre robe would be on for only thirty minutes. When he emerged from the special garb and dressed normally in a white *dhoti* and banian, she would say, 'Your food is ready.' He followed her and sat down on a wooden plank at his usual place under the window. His oval silver plate would be set down and food served on it. He would eat with relish and feel like expressing some appreciation: 'I'd never have thought that salted cucumber would be so good. Should I fetch some more from the market tomorrow?'

She felt relieved and said, 'Don't bother. The woman who brings a basket offers a good selection—all her vegetables are fresh . . .'

'She gets them probably from the farms direct, while in the market they are carried in lorries from wholesale traders—you must come with me to the market to look at the mounds of fresh cabbage, a great spectacle, I tell you—'

'How can I come? Who will be with Mother? She is restless, moving all the time, and if she has a fall while no one is here—God help us . . .'

'You fear the worst. We could tell her to be careful and not to bolt the door while we are out . . . He realized he was getting into unnecessary detail.

His wife said, 'No need to talk of all that now.' Her secret grievance was that his mother had become her sole concern while Nagaraj went about freely without a care. She often said, when the mood was dark, that she had become a prisoner in the house owing to the old lady's restlessness. He thought it best not to pursue the subject. He terminated the theme then and there and, after uttering a few pleasantries, rose and walked to the back yard to wash his fingers and gargle. He was so satisfied with the meal he had consumed that he felt like uttering a compliment to please his wife. His mind buzzed with ideas but he was hesitant since he had to weigh his words to avoid complicated discussions about Mother once again. He just said, 'Some new patterns seem to have arrived at the Saree Centre. We must make some special arrangement so that you may have a look at them . . .' His wife did not reply; she realized that he was being pleasant without commitment and ignored his offer. Unless they engaged some nurse to guard his mother, it would be impossible to leave home. Even her evening visits to the nearby temple had to be manoeuvred. She had to seek a neighbour's help and get back in a dashing hurry. That always left a feeling that she did not give the god at the temple enough time.

After eating, Nagaraj did not stay in. He dressed briskly before a long mirror hanging by a nail in his room, a family heirloom which reflected one's figure chin down to knee if one stood straight in front of it and the other areas if one stooped. He was satisfied with his looks, his dress and deportment. He wore for his outings a special kind of snow-white *dhoti* with gold thread on the edge, a blue shirt and an upper cloth, also white. He was satisfied that his personality was impressive enough.

His routine first stop was Kanni's stall at the market corner— an old chum of his primary-school days at the municipal free school in Vinayak Street. It was a one-room building with discoloured tiles on its roof. All classes were held in the same hall with four teachers in four corners bawling out their lessons over the children's babble and wielding their canes freely, whacking, as a matter of policy, the nearest child. Nagaraj's father found it practical to send his two children here: it was close by and the children could go up without escort, and it was also cheap, being a municipal school, no fee, except an occasional cash present to the teacher. Nagaraj used to sit on the same bench as Kanni and they were whacked together by their teacher. His brother sat away on a different bench, being in a senior class in that hall. He maintained himself aloof as a superior person and never encouraged Nagaraj to walk beside him to school, preferring the company of boys of the same height. If, by chance, Nagaraj got mixed in his company he ordered him off. Luckily, very soon he demanded to be sent to the Board High School in another direction, and Nagaraj felt happy to he free from his company. But Kanni stuck to him and instead of going home after the classes they played marbles in the street until Nagaraj's father came out to drag him home. Eventually they pursued different careers. Nagaraj went to the Albert Mission School and Kanni became an apprentice under his father, who was a carpenter. Later he built a bunk at the market corner and opened a little shop selling cigarettes, soda, and betel leaves and tobacco for chewing. It was a strategic corner and attracted a crowd while Kanni himself, now middle-aged, sat on a low stool inside the shop and served the customers crowding in front.

Nagaraj stopped, and Kanni greeted him with, 'What's the news?'

'Nothing much . . . floods, droughts, fights and speeches by ministers.'

'Is that all?'

'The minister has left for Bermuda to market our handloom cloth—'

'Which minister?'

'I don't know. I can only repeat the newspaper.'

'Where is Bermuda?' Kanni asked mechanically, holding out a small aluminium spoonful of arecanut and four tender betel leaves smeared with lime. Nagaraj rolled them up with arecanut and stuffed them into his mouth and enjoyed the slight tingling sensation it produced. Little beads of perspiration broke out on his brow and he said, 'Put it on my account, as usual . . .'

'Of course. Even in my dream I can remember who owes me how much.'

'Anytime you want the account settled . . .' said Nagaraj, chewing the paan, lips red with betel juice. You could not find a more contented soul in Malgudi at that moment. In that mood he passed on to his next station. Half a mile along the market road, turning left he got into Grove Street, a mainly residential area, and passed under an arch over a gate announcing in grand style: COOMAR'S BOEING SAREE CENTRE. Raman, the signboard painter, was offered a special fee to make the lettering impressive. It hit the eye the moment you turned the corner.

Earlier in their life, Coomar (a self-made man) had struck a lasting friendship with Nagaraj at the Boardless Coffee House, where they generally met when Nagaraj was studying at the Albert Mission College. Those days, Nagaraj avoided going home when his classes were over for the day. Evening was a dull hour at home with his father poring over accounts or discussing agricultural matters with visitors from the village and his mother was away at the temple listening to a religious discourse, and his brother was in his room chatting with a friend. Nagaraj shared the room with him but was forbidden to enter it when he had friends there. So Nagaraj had to while away his time till about seven o'clock when the visitors would be gone and Mother would be back. He loved her company and followed her around as she busied herself in the kitchen and the other parts of the vast house. At the Boardless, Nagaraj always found enjoyable company in his class-fellows, who guffawed and joked till Varma the proprietor sounded a call-bell on his desk to indicate that it was time for them to vacate the table. Coomar, though not a student at any stage in his life, found himself in their company and ordered more coffee for everybody in order to retain the table. When the company dispersed, Coomar stuck to Nagaraj as he walked down Market Road looking at shops and crowds or strolled along the river. Friendship developed between them. Once, years later, Coomar invited Nagaraj into his house at Ellaman Street. It was a narrow little place with a rice store in front, which was their family business. He confided later while they were alone, 'I don't like our family business—selling rice is dull work.'

'What do you plan to do?'

'I don't know—something more active . . .'

'What really do you want to do?' Nagaraj asked sympathetically. Coomar remained silent for some time.

'I do not know. I wish I had gone to school like you. But I was not interested.'

'It doesn't matter,' said Nagaraj grandly, in a sudden access of blind sympathy. 'I myself would not continue but for the compulsion at home. My brother is a model student, very regular in his studies, and so my parents expect me to follow his example . . .'

Coomar felt slightly impatient with the other's rambling interruption while he was bursting with his own problems and said, 'Parents are all alike. My father wants me to go to school or measure out rice in the shop. I'm prepared to walk out of home if they compel me. I have my own ideas.'

'Tell me,' said Nagaraj, rigorously suppressing his desire to continue his own narration.

'I came across,' began Coomar, 'a fellow at the bus stand. He comes from a village nearby, carrying with him a bundle of sarees, sells them to the women in the city and goes back to his looms in the village. He is a handloom weaver working at home with his family's help. Cheap cotton sarees not costing more than fifteen rupees. At a time three sarees are woven on the loom, in a week he can have six sarees ready. He comes by bus and spreads them out under a tree and sells them. Whenever I go to the bus stand, I find him there, and I have talked to him—'

'What takes you to the bus stand so regularly?' Nagaraj could not help asking.

Coomar felt irritated again at the interruption but felt obliged to explain: 'Impossible to stay at home, must keep away a greater part of the day, otherwise I'll have to measure out rice . . .' At which both laughed. 'Also I like the Central Bus Stand at South End: full of bustle and activity, with a canteen and waiting hall where one can rest. I know many of the bus folk and often help them in some way. I got an idea one day: why should I not sell those sarees rather than our rice? After all, women are ready customers for anything that appeals to them. If I can find two hundred rupees for a start, I can achieve wonders.'

Before the evening was out, Nagaraj fell in with his plans and promised his help. His mother gave him pocket money off and on which he spent at the Boardless for his evening tiffin. His father also gave him money whenever the harvest came. Nagaraj's needs were limited, he never spent the full amount he earned every month. Once a month he took it to the post office on Market Road and put it in the savings bank. He did not recollect the exact amount available but promised Coomar all help.

At their next meeting at the Boardless, when the company was gone, he took Coomar aside and whispered, 'I have two hundred and eighty at the savings bank, I'll give you two hundred, but don't you tell my brother or anyone.' Thus Coomar got a start in business. He kept in touch with the weaver at the bus stand, paid him for six sarees at a time with part of the cash. He hired a bicycle from the Rajan Mart every day, tied the bundle of sarees on the rack and started off on his sales trip. He had an instinct for the right time and place and the phrase. He never started early his daily rounds: he realized that menfolk should not be present during his visit to a customer in her home. Eleven in the forenoon was an hour most breadwinners in the family would be out. After seeing the man off, the lady of the house would have her meal, chew betel leaves, relax and fall into a shopping mood, especially when the shop was at her door.

On the very first day of the venture, he rode through Kabir Street, leaned his bicycle on the front srep and knocked on the door. The door was opened by Nagaraj's mother. Nagaraj, as was his habit even in the early years, was away after his midday meal on a routine visit to Kanni's, and then on to the Town Hall library to be in communion with the librarian. That gave him a feeling of doing research for his magnum opus on Narada, though most of the time was spent sitting on the single stool beside the old librarian's chair exchanging information on the weather, local affairs and the human predicament in general. From time to time he paused to remark, 'There are no authentic references to Narada anywhere and I feel handicapped.'

'Why don't you invent something about the sage?'

'That I can't do. I want to write something which will have authority.'

Nagaraj walked back home and found his friend Coomar squatting in the veranda with all the sarees out of the bundle and his wife preoccupied in selecting one. She said, 'Your friend will not leave without selling me a saree.'

'How can I?' said Coomar. 'This is my first business and I know your wife's hand must be lucky . . .'

'Undoubtedly,' said Nagaraj, pleased.

His mother, standing at the door watching the transaction, added, 'These sarees seem rather costly and the fabric so thin . . . these days . . .'

The daughter-in-law said, 'Seems to me quite good value. We don't want sarees thick as sackcloth.'

'They used to last a lifetime,' Mother retorted.

Nagaraj was anxious to avoid controversy in the presence of his friend. 'Sita, give him something to drink, he has been cycling in the sun.'

Coomar said, 'Just a tumbler of cold water and nothing else. This is my first sale, let me see how lucky your wife's inauguration is going to prove!' Sita fetched from her little shelf in a corner thirty-five rupees for two sarees while the old lady kept looking on with disapproval. After Coomar left, Sita whispered to her husband, 'Why should your mother bother? This is my money.'

'You must not take her seriously, she doesn't mean to hurt you.'

When he passed in, his mother began, 'In our days . . .' He didn't encourage her to continue, but said, 'They are going to arrange a forty-day discourse at the temple,' and diverted her talk.

It was an auspicious start for Coomar. He divided the town into convenient sectors and covered the entire city methodically, day by day. He sat down with a sheet of paper in hand, in the little room available to him when his father was away at his shop, and drew a rough map of Malgudi, marking the areas where his customers could be found. He noted: 'East, West, South and North. East: Vinayak Street, Kabir Street. North: New Extension and Lawley Extension, not at present. First cover where they favour cheap sarees, maximum price twenty-five rupees. When I get a feeling of the market conditions . . .' Thereafter he started on a cycle with his bundle every day according to schedule.

He knocked on a door when he was sure the men were away. When the door opened and the lady appeared, he said, 'Would you like to see new sarees?'

'No,' would be the expected answer, 'I don't want to buy—'

'I never said I'm selling. I just want to show, that's all. Someone suggested that I show you the samples first before they get sold . . .' And as the lady hesitated, he went back to the bicycle and brought out the bundle of sarees, laid it at her feet and spread out his wares. When he left he would have sold at least one saree. On the rare occasion when a man happened to open the door and say point-blank, 'No one is buying any saree . . .'

'But amma has asked me to come—new patterns.' At this point the lady of the house would come on the scene. Before the man could question, 'Did you ask to see a saree?' Coomar had spread and displayed his wares, saying, 'No harm in having a look at these. No need to buy . . .'

'What is the price?' would be the next question.

'If you like the stuff, make your choice, do not bother about the price . . .' By the time he had bundled up and started on his rounds again, he would have made one more sale and collected the cash.

At the end of the day he went to the bus stand, met the weaver and ordered the next lot—at this stage only the twenty-five rupee variety. He felt encouraged to offer clients costlier sarees in course of time. He contacted a silk weaver in another village and acquired sarees of one-hundred-rupee value. He ordered only four at a time; cycling was easier with only four in a bundle. He tried other zones—Lawley Extension, New Extension, and a new housing colony beyond the railway crossing. At the end of the day he met Nagaraj at the Boardless for help in writing up the accounts.

He stopped going in search of custom. Coomar's name became well known when he took a small shop on Market Road. Eventually he returned the two-hundred-rupee loan to Nagaraj, bought the house at the corner of Grove Street and opened the big shop.

Nagaraj felt gratified that the small loan he managed to give had taken Coomar such a long way. When Raman, the painter, had finally fixed the signboard on the arch at the gate, they stood away in the middle of Grove Street and surveyed it with satisfaction. Raman had imparted colour and design to COOMAR'S BOEING SAREE CENTRE. Coomar took Raman in and seated him on the carpet and offered him five hundred rupees tucked amidst green betel leaves, two coconuts and a bunch of bananas on a tray. Raman accepted it gratefully and took his leave. Nagaraj said, 'Good style . . . I mean your payment.'

'Goddess Lakshmi has been kind,' was all that Coomar had to say.

Now Nagaraj uttered the question that had been bothering him all along. 'Why Boeing? What is it?'

Coomar himself was not clear in his mind about it. So he said, 'It's a name which I noticed on a paper wrapped round a yarn sample, and it appealed to me somehow.'

After Kanni's, the retreat to the Grove Street Saree Centre was very pleasant. A spreading margosa tree afforded a cool shade to the building, and Nagaraj found it agreeable and interesting to work for

Coomar. The Boeing Centre had become one of the established institutions of Malgudi. All day it was crowded with shoppers, mainly women, who spent hours and hours choosing sarees. Weavers from the loom areas thronged to gain Coomar's patronage. It was always reputed that Coomar's sarees were created especially for Malgudi women: the stamp of Coomar meant fast colours and unfading lace of the finest gold-coated silver.

'I want you to look over my business and give me your suggestions,' Coomar said one day, and set up a table and chair for Nagaraj at one end of the hall while he himself sat cross-legged on a cushion on the floor, leaning on a bolster. The Saree Centre was a big hall stacked with sarees in almirahs all round. Carpets and mats covered the floor, wall to wall, and several assistants pulled out sarees from the racks and spread them out on the mats for inspection by customers who, unlike customers of other kinds of business, settled down for the day and relaxed.

Attendants heaped on his table registers and ledgers and cash bills, which Nagaraj scrutinized and entered in the appropriate column in his books. He loved this work, alternating red ink and black ink while entering figures. He picked up special penholders at Bari's—paper merchants and stationers at Kalighat Lane which cut across Market Road at some point westward. He loved the stationery shop with its smell of gum and paper and display of pens and pencils under a glass.

'I import pens the like of which you can't see anywhere,' the stationer would claim, being in business second generation on the same spot. 'You might have heard of Hamilton Bond. It's world famous—the best in the world. The chief of that concern was Sir Richard Hamilton, whose signed portrait adorns the wall of our home, which is nearby. He gave it to my grandfather and even today the firm sends us goods on credit without any condition. Is that possible now with others? Impossible, sir. We settle the bills promptly on the sixtieth day . . .' He seemed to Nagaraj like a nonstop gramophone with the needle coming back to the starting point every time to begin all over again.

'This chap's musical refrain is Hamilton. He will not let me examine penholders in peace . . .' Nagaraj loved coloured penholders—green, red, yellow and brown, with nibs in different styles. He would prefer to be left alone to make his choice. The Boeing Saree Centre was a place of colour, a riot of blue and red and mauve and green as sarees were spread out on the mats, and he did not like to hold a pen which might be incongruous in this seeming flowerbed of a million hues. But the lean paper-fellow would not leave him in peace, dressed as he always was in a white *jibba* and jodhpur trousers and an embroidered cap, dogging his steps and chattering about Hamilton.

Coomar had asked him to choose the best stationery he liked and he explained, 'Our Boeing Centre is unique and has distinction, and our stationery must not be inferior. Go ahead and choose without fear or hesitation about the prices.'

'A liberal allowance,' Nagaraj thought. 'But why are these merchants so conceited and talkative, each man thinking he is a special brand of God's creation?'

Nagaraj worked free for Coomar; no pay packet at the beginning of a month. 'I don't need it, and this arrangement leaves me free to come and go when I like, though this bandicoot can afford to pay me, considering that he collects two thousand rupees an hour from those saree-crazed chatterboxes and I don't know what he does with all that cash.'

Facilitated thus by a lack of arrangement, Nagaraj appeared at the Centre regularly but without a feeling of compulsion, and left when he liked, and Coomar never said a word, being polite and enjoying Nagaraj's free services.

Nagaraj liked to be out of the house as far as possible, otherwise he might have to arbitrate between his mother and Sita all day. He sometimes wondered at the transformations time brings about.

Sita was a timid little creature when he married her. How many years ago? He threw his mind back almost twenty years. When he went to approve his bride at their house in Sullivan Street, she looked so small and helpless. At first he felt discouraged. He was under twenty and she was fourteen and looked as if she had just come out of the nursery school. Her personality had not yet developed. Her obscure features could not give one an idea whether she was good looking or not. She had a rotund face, a scraggy slight figure and a long, long braid, with a wheaten complexion over which some kind of face powder stood out challengingly. During that bride-inspection she had to demonstrate her musical ability with a harmonium and sang some song in a feeble voice. Nagaraj, though he could not make up his mind, was favourably inclined. He had just passed his BA exam and was himself stocky and dark complexioned and never hoped he could command a glamorous bride. His qualification was not his personality but his family— that was his Kabir Street home and background, people who were considered aristocratic inheritors of vast rice fields in the village. Sita's father was a retired government servant and was recommended by a well-wisher of both the families. Nagaraj's father could not hope for a better connection, since he was convinced that Nagaraj was wishy-washy and dreamy—a view that he held to the last.

In the early days Nagaraj found his wife too timid and bashful. His mother in those days was like a commander-in-chief and the girl meekly accepted the role of a lackey at home, forever at the beck and call of her mother-in-law, trailing behind her all the time, hardly ever coming into his room while he longed for a tête-à-tête. When she came in she never allowed the door to be shut fully but always left a crack open. 'Mother may not like it,' 'Mother may want to call me,' 'She is all alone in the kitchen, I must be near at hand, she may mistake me . . .'

'Mistake? What sort of mistake—after all, you will be talking to your husband . . .' She hardly gave him her company with a free heart. And he took to the *pyol* habit, to sitting there and watching the street. In the evenings when Mother went to the temple at the corner, Sita relaxed and came to him. She would not sit down for fear that the neighbours might gossip. Nagaraj would try to hold her hand or pull her down to his side. She resisted and drew herself away out of his reach, whereupon he would protest, 'After all you are my wife, what is wrong?'

'Don't talk so loudly—hush, this is not our room.' She would stand beside him fidgeting, allowing enough space between them to make onlookers think that the couple were semi-strangers. Nagaraj accepted the arrangement as inevitable. He could not make any demand on her or anyone. Not in his nature. At a discreet distance from each other, they would discuss the day's events from the time she was up at six a.m. till the moment Mother went down to the temple. How she put the kettle on for coffee, how she almost toppled down the filter while pouring boiling water into it. How lucky Mother was not there! 'She had gone out to fetch wood chips from the back yard. When she came in she could see nothing more than some water spilled on the floor and asked for an explanation. I explained it away somehow, and Mother did not bother about it any more . . .' Nagaraj simpered as if he admired Sita's pluck and resourcefulness, although he did not quite understand what she had done. He added irrelevantly, 'Be careful while handling the boiling water.' They watched for a while in silence the neighbours' children playing in the street and the women returning home from their shopping and visits, throwing sidelong glances at the couple on the *pyol*. 'People are returning from the temple, Mother'll be here soon . . .' said Sita, turning to go in.

Nagaraj would implore, 'Stay,' and try to hold her.

'She told me to grate half a coconut for chutney. She will be upset,' said Sita. Suddenly she would wrench herself free and run in so that when Mother returned she would see him alone and, even while climbing the steps, ask, 'Where is Sita?'

'I think she is scraping coconut, judging from the noise inside . . .' he would say with an innocent look. Mother would hold out a little vermilion and sacred ash—offerings from the temple—and then go in, pleased at the dutifulness of her daughter-in-law.

2

AFTER HIS GRADUATION, Gopu spurned Nagaraj and ordered him about. Nagaraj did not mind it. He continued to be a devoted younger brother.

'You are like Lakshmana in the *Ramayana*, who stood behind Rama, his elder brother, all the time without a murmur or doubt,' remarked his father sometimes. It was no doubt flattering, but it didn't help the younger man very much. The brothers shared the front room in the Kabir Street house; the room in the other wing was occupied by Father and Mother. His mother slept on the floor, while Father occupied the teakwood four-poster which filled the space in the room. When the sons came up to the college level, Mother preferred to go out and sleep in the second courtyard in summer. In the cooler season she slept in the hall. When Gopu's fame as a graduate spread, letters of marriage offers came enclosing horoscopes from parents who had daughters. And Father spent much time in scrutinizing and comparing the charts and finally approved one, the daughter of a 'sub-registrar' from Sembiam, said to be wealthy and influential in that area (the sub-registrar, unofficially, levied a percentage as his share on any property registered and collected much cash from unlettered villagers who were at his mercy).

They locked up the Kabir Street house and chartered a whole bus for the wedding trip. It was a grand occasion, a six-hour journey northward after crossing the river at Nallapa's grove. Nagaraj often recollected with pleasure the occasion as they carried eatables and spiced rice and curds, fruits in large quantity, enough to feed the party of forty relatives and friends in the bus. Nagaraj enjoyed the endless eating all the way. It was very pleasant on the whole. His brother also seemed to thaw a bit. The prospect of his wedding softened him and he chatted with Nagaraj all through the journey and joked and laughed. To Nagaraj, who was already in a state of elation, his brother's patronage was an added pleasure. He kept on humbly agreeing with all that he said, and laughed at his lugubrious jokes as the bus sped along the countryside through coconut avenues and cattle herds, and for some time the babble and chatter among the company resounded over the noise of the running bus. It was a long journey—enough time for them to talk, eat and fall asleep in their seats or lapse into silence, watching the scenery.

When Gopu's wife joined him at Kabir Street about a year later, Nagaraj had to vacate his corner in the front room. Gopu just said, 'Boy, leave my room.' Nagaraj picked up his books and pushed out his dealwood box in which he had kept an assortment of possessions—tinsel pieces, picture books and pencils and clothes. He moved his desk to a corner in the hall. Now his brother isolated himself and kept to his room all day, but his wife emerged periodically and went in again, shutting the door, leaving Nagaraj to speculate what might be going on inside. Gopu did not seem keen on working anywhere after acquiring his BA. His father hinted from time to time, 'Now that you are a BA, it will be easy to get a job. Shall I speak to Mr Menon, our District Collector, who knows a lot of people and will help?'

'Not necessary,' was Gopu's only answer. He showed no inclination to go out of the house or seek work. Father let things drift, unable to divine the other's intention, while he shut himself away with his wife.

All the time Nagaraj sat in the allotted corner of the hall trying to concentrate on his studies, sitting on the floor. They had only two folding chairs in the house, one in his brother's room and one in his father's. Nagaraj had been offered another room in the second courtyard but he preferred to stay in the hall in order that he might watch the traffic there. Watching and speculating what went on behind the door was more interesting than homework. While appearing to be reading his lessons he noted from a corner of his eye his sister-in-law bearing a dish of some eatable to their room, perhaps almond fried in butter with a sprinkling of sugar. After his marriage his brother fancied himself a sultan in his palace chamber, pampered by his wife. Nagaraj also noted how long it took for his brother to eat the stuff. He saw by the old ticking clock on the opposite wall that Gopu consumed whatever came in about twelve minutes. His mouth watered at the thought and he wondered what it could be, *bonda* or *halwa*. Was it sweet or sour? He could not hope to have a taste of it since it was a special preparation created at a special stove which had been commissioned for the sultan in a specially reserved corner of the general kitchen where his mother had cooked for the entire family from the beginning of time (as it seemed). The sultan's spouse concocted specialities for her husband in strictly limited quantities, of which others could enjoy only the fragrance emanating from the stove.

'Why couldn't I have it too?' Nagaraj asked his mother. 'What is it that sister-in-law makes for Gopu?'

'None of your business to talk about it.'

'But I want it too.'

'She goes herself to Chettiar's shop, buys something and comes home. Never heard of any young woman going out to a shop by herself. She has brought from her parents' house her own stove and vessels, and gives her husband what she likes. I never look at her corner of the kitchen.'

'Why don't you make the same thing for us too?'

'All right, all right,' she said to mollify him. 'Now you eat this . . .' When she got a feeling that Gopu was dependent solely on his wife, she would offer her creation to the daughter-in-law. 'Let Gopu taste this too. He will like it.' Sometimes the daughter-in-law would agree and carry a dish to his room, but more often say, 'No, Mother, don't trouble yourself. He'll not eat it.' It was a state within the state.

Nagaraj noticed that the two managed their jurisdictions with tact. Sister-in-law Charu was allotted her corner of the kitchen along the eastern wall. She set up a little stool, and mounted a kerosene stove on it and beside it a little platform on which she arranged a set of aluminium saucepans and ladles, etc., and she stood over her workshop, frying and sizzling delicacies for her husband. This position had the advantage that she could work with her back to her mother-in-law, who squatted on the floor in front of her mud oven at the other end, which was an age-old equipment of her kitchen. It was built once a year with the clay dug from the back yard, kneaded and moulded into an oven.

Mother believed that food cooked over smoky firewood in the mud oven was healthful while a kerosene flame caused throat trouble. To prove it she blew her nose and sneezed when Charu lit her kerosene stove. Charu ignored these symptoms and said, 'Mother, a wood fire leads to cold and eye disease, that's what my mother used to say . . .' and she managed without going in for wood fuel but used only kerosene or charcoal, thus tactfully puncturing her mother-in-law's notions about the kerosene stove. If Mother-in-law asked, 'What are you preparing?' Charu only mumbled without turning round, and if the mother-in-law repeated her question, she mumbled again persistently. After the first few days she ignored all queries and communicated only when it pleased her. 'This time of the year, carrots are in plenty,' Charu might deign to remark occasionally, facing her wall. At which the mother-in-law would feel so pleased that she would elaborate on the state of vegetables and try to stretch the conversation out. 'Well, go and tell Gopu that plates are laid and we are waiting.'

If her mood was right, Charu would fetch her husband from the room to join the family at the meal. His sitting plank would be placed beside the door and there he always sat, after throwing a word of greeting to his mother, which was enough to thrill her, since she saw so little of him all day. His father sat as always at his allotted seat below the first window. Mother served them. Nagaraj had his position of vantage below the second window. Being the juniormost, he was served last, but being Mother's pet, she served vegetables and rice liberally until he protested and Father came to his rescue saying, 'Just give him what he wants, he is old enough, don't overload his plate.' His brother ate in silence, he was not particularly friendly with his father, as he suspected that if he relented Father would renew his offer to take him to the influential collector to find him a job, and it seemed to the observant Nag that he nipped Father's proposal in the bud while Charu kept a watch on his plate and served with measured caution. She took from her mother-in-law's preparations just a small quantity of some item of food and served her husband for the sake of appearances so that it might not seem as if she ignored completely the food meant for the family. The family ate in general silence, only Nagaraj trying to keep up a conversation, undeterred by the absence of response from the rest of the family. He laughed and cracked jokes and narrated his school incidents, unmindful of the indifference of others. Only his mother pretended to listen and appreciate what he said, but always concluded, 'Eat, eat, don't keep talking . . .'

At this stage, when fragments of memory brought back pictures of other people and other days, all that load of experience seemed improbable to Nagaraj. His mother now hobbled about like a frail ghost asking inane questions of the two left at home, himself and his wife; only three in that vast household which stretched from Kabir Street to the river. Mother perambulated about the house unnecessarily, as it seemed to Nagaraj, with weak legs and minimal energy, and she would not rest, although provided with a fan and a cot in the hall.

The old lady kept inspecting and watching every corner of the house and commenting, to the annoyance of Nagaraj's wife who often burst out, 'Please keep your mother in one place. I feel paralysed when she is following me about, questioning and questioning—I can't cook or sweep or clean if I'm bothered like this.' Nagaraj had more tolerance than his wife.

'After all, she is asking some questions, give some answer and be done with it—'

'How many times can I face the same set of questions?'

'As often as necessary,' Nagaraj said and fled from the scene before his wife could retort.

Mother's decline started with Father's death. The fifteenth day after his father's funeral the mourning period was over and all the purificatory ceremonials were gone through. It was past two in the afternoon when the last guest departed after an elaborate feast and the family members were left to themselves. Nagaraj was getting ready to shut himself in his room and sleep. His wife was putting back the vessels on the shelf and sweeping the floor clean of flowers and shreds of banana leaves and spilled food, sharing silently the labours of winding up. The cooks engaged for the feast were taking leave of Nagaraj's mother, who was lost in her own thoughts, leaning on a pillar in the courtyard, away from all company. She was clad in a simple white saree, without lace, and with all jewellery removed, although when her husband was living she used to be radiant with diamonds and clad in gold-laced sarees, never going below a certain standard of dress and decoration, so that the neighbours always remarked, 'She's like Goddess Lakshmi and rules the family like a queen!' Some called her vain and showy—'Wants to impress us with her diamonds and brocade. We know how this family came to be rich—moneylenders, actually . . .'

Nagaraj felt deeply moved by her withdrawal and from time to time went near her to whisper a word of comfort or philosophy. Nagaraj was saying, 'Mother, why don't you go in, and rest? Visitors are gone—I'll also turn in for a couple of hours' rest in my room—' Gopu overheard Nag's words and said at once, 'Nagu, don't try to go away. I have business with you. Come to my room.'

Thus it started. For a month to come, every hour of the day was occupied in drawing up a list of assets, properties, possessions and articles left by his father. He had left a will, which simply declared, 'Everything I have, to be divided equally between my two sons unless they come to some agreement suitable to their needs.' A lawyer friend of the family was to help them come to a decision. Gopu stuck to the expression in the will, 'Some arrangement suitable, etc.', declaring, 'Father himself was aware that equal division was unsuitable—I can't accept anything unless there is a fresh valuation.' Thereafter every item was listed and valued. Such things were beyond Nagaraj's temperament and capacity. They inspected room by room, and every item in the household went into the list 'except the broomstick', as his mother declared when she recovered her mood and speech. Nagaraj's own inclination was to accept whatever came in as his share, but his brother was aggressive and demanding. He insisted upon being given all the land and coconut garden in the village along with the farmhouse and cattle. 'Thank God the fellow wants them. I couldn't have stood the smell of cattleshed even for five minutes . . .' thought Nagaraj.

'What have you to say?' asked the lawyer.

Nagaraj did not want to say anything, having no ideas of his own, and maintained a pregnant silence which the lawyer took to be a state of profound thinking on his part.

His brother lost his patience and cried, 'Nag, understand there is no other way.'

Nagaraj looked despondent and bit his lips and shot off at a tangent, 'What happens to Mother's jewellery?'

'The question does not arise now,' said the lawyer pompously. 'Only to be decided at the appropriate time.'

'What do you mean?' asked Nagaraj, looking outraged and feeling that he should not let the others have their own way. He suspected the lawyer was being bribed by his brother, although he had been his father's chum. His strategy produced results. In return for surrendering his interests in the village holding, he was to have the Kabir Street house as the sole owner. Nagaraj asked, 'What about Mother?'

'Let her have her choice,' pronounced the lawyer. 'After all, only two sons—she'd like to be with one or the other and move when she needs a change.'

'Very well put,' said Gopu.

'All this presupposes that the brothers live separately,' added the lawyer. 'Am I right?'

Gopu went red in the face as he asserted, 'I won't stay here a day after the documents are signed. Who wants to be here? Not my family.'

It only confirmed Nagaraj's suspicion that Gopu's wife was the prompter behind the scene, planning to get away from the mother-in-law.

At the end of the month the partition deed was drawn and signed and registered. Packing up all his share of silver, brass utensils, miscellaneous articles and furniture, and odds and ends (with the exception of the oval silver plate and the wall mirror which Nagaraj stubbornly would not yield), Gopu never knew Nag could be so firm in any matter. After consulting a priest, a day was fixed and a van stood at the door. Gopu loaded all his share, prostrated at Mother's feet and left with his family, while his mother looked on sadly and asked constantly, 'Was this all necessary?' She shed tears at the parting. Nagaraj himself felt overwhelmed. He ran a few yards clutching the door when the van moved, crying to his brother, 'Leave Tim behind, not too late even now. St Stephen's is a good school. I'll look after him—'

His brother just said, 'No, he will be with me.'

Nagaraj was heartbroken.

3

ON THE FEW occasions when Nagaraj visited his brother at the village, he noticed Tim going to a '*pyol* school'—that was a sort of mud platform canopied with thatch and straw and presided over by the local pedagogue who conducted his classes by shouting and flourishing his cane at the children who squatted before him. This teaching method was much appreciated by the village elders, who based their educational philosophy on the proverb, 'The unbeaten child will remain unlearned'. Nagaraj felt sickened: a far cry from St Stephen's in Malgudi, which was a coveted school where Tim was admitted by Nagaraj when the brothers lived together in Kabir Street as an undivided family; and definitely worse than the derelict municipal school in which he and his brother had studied as children. He did not talk about it for fear of irritating Gopu. Luckily the shed collapsed during a storm, and the platform was washed off; the pedagogue could not rebuild it.

Thus ended the educational career of the village children, who turned to performing odd tasks on their farms. Gopu, however, sent Tim to a town school five miles away. The boy had to walk a mile to catch a highway bus after waiting for it under an avenue tree. It was tedious. Some days, if the bus arrived late, he missed it deliberately, since he did not like to be caned for going late to his class. So he just dawdled and wandered about and marked time till he could go back home. Some days, if a bus going in the direction of Malgudi came up, he jumped into it and secretly visited his uncle at Kabir Street. He enjoyed his visits to his uncle as he was received with warmth and feted in their house. Nagaraj saved the boy embarrassment by not questioning him too closely about his movements but took care to return him to his village in the evening bus.

It was a busy hour at the Saree Centre, which meant the noisiest moment with customers, all women, discussing the worth of various types and patterns and their suitability for occasions. Nagaraj was quite used to this din. He could go on with his accounting and entries without feeling disturbed. He sat in his corner bent over his papers, and did not hear the call from across his table, 'Uncle! I've come—' When he looked up he saw Tim standing before him. He almost rubbed his eyes to be sure that it was no apparition.

'Tim! Why did you not tell me you were coming?' Nagaraj put away his books, wiped the pen with the rag which was always in its place on his desk under a glass paperweight. He locked up the ledgers, murmured to Tim again, 'Sit down on that stool. I'll be with you in a minute.'

Nagaraj sensed that this was unlike other visits by Tim. The boy, who usually looked bright and happy during his visits, now looked glum and only muttered, when questioned, 'I've come away with my trunk.' What was the significance of the mention of the trunk? Nagaraj suspected some complication back at the village and only said, 'Wait, sit on that stool. I'll be with you soon.' In a little while he went to Coomar, said something, and joined his nephew.

'Let's go,' he said. The boy stood up and gazed with wonder at the crowd of women and the colourful sarees spread on the mat. Carrying his small trunk, Tim accompanied Nagaraj home. They walked silently. Nagaraj was afraid to open his mouth lest some impossible situation should reveal itself.

Sita, opening the door, was surprised to see Tim. Nagaraj said inanely, 'He is come with his trunk.' While he went in to change and wash, she took charge of Tim and his trunk, and gave him coffee and tiffin, and decided not to question him. Nagaraj's mother was in a far corner of the house in the second courtyard, on her routine wandering, and was not yer aware of her grandson's arrival.

When Nagaraj was ready for a talk, he felt a little anxious and nervous. He seated Tim on the *pyol* and asked, 'Now, tell me what happened. Why are you carrying your trunk?'

'Because I am not going back—'

'Oh!' exclaimed Nagaraj, rather pleased. 'Surely . . . But does your father know?'

'He should know, he saw me walking out with the trunk.'

Nagaraj realized that the boy attached some extraordinary significance to the trunk. He remained silent; some neighbours passing down the street noticed them conversing and slowed down their pace, hoping to overhear their talk. The executive engineer of the last house, returning from the bar, cried on seeing Tim, 'Hello! How you have grown, like the eucalyptus tree which stood around my office in the hills. Say *namaste* to your elders,' and passed on.

Tim volunteered to explain, 'He called me a donkey—'

'Who?'

'Father.'

'Why?' Nagaraj asked aloud, but added within, 'Why not?'

The boy explained, 'He asked me to go to the fields and report to him on the work people were doing. I hesitated, I had to go out to catch the bus, otherwise I would be punished for going late. He called me "donkey". I said, "What's a donkey, Father?" and he slapped my face. My mother was away.'

'Otherwise what would have happened?' Nagaraj asked, his curiosity stirred as to how Charu would confront her husband. He asked, 'Does your mother . . .?' He could not find the right word. He swallowed back the phrase, 'Quarrel with him?' It would have been very pleasing to hear that she did, but he changed his sentence to 'Did she tell you what to do?'

The boy was rather puzzled at the nature of the enquiry, and said, 'I packed up my trunk and left. Mother was returning just as I was leaving. I met her on the way and told her, 'I'm going to Malgudi and will not be back.' She asked many questions but I could not answer them. She tried to hold me back and snatched away my trunk but I shook myself free and ran, crying, 'I won't come back. Don't wait . . .'

Nagaraj felt confused by this muddled account and said, 'Stay here by all means. I'll be happy . . .' He felt his brother was likely to turn up sooner or later and worsen the situation. He felt a terrible responsibility had fallen on him.

Nagaraj was sitting on the *pyol,* spending the evening as usual looking at the coconut trees with crows retiring for the night. Before repairing to the trees they assembled on the roof of the tall house in the opposite row. Scores of them flew down and perched like schoolchildren under the supervision of a convent sister. The crows argued a lot among themselves and hopped and shifted about before dispersing. Nagaraj always felt a fascination for this evening activity of the crows, and wished he knew the language of birds as did the kings of folklore. The crows probably have a leader who allots them treetops for the night and they argue and debate about it before coming to a decision. The leader would probably be saying, 'Don't you see the sky is reddening? Hurry up, darkness will soon be upon us, and remember we are not human beings who light lamps for their night life . . .'

This fantasy was shattered when *jutka* halted in front of him, wheels crunching the gravel. He could not believe his eyes: his brother emerged from the *jutka*. As he stepped down, all the pent-up affection in Nagaraj burst forth, 'Oh, Gopu, come, come. Why didn't you write to me you were coming? I'd have met you at the bus stand—you came by bus?'

'How else? Did you expect me to come in an aeroplane from our village?'

'Why not? Within ten years you may have plane service all over . . .'

'Don't talk nonsense!' Gopu said. He picked up his bag and, thrusting his hand into the inner pocket of a tight buttoned-up grey coat (which Nagaraj had known him to possess for years), fished out an eight-anna coin to pay the fare. The *jutka* driver did not close his fingers on the coin but kept staring at Gopu accusingly. 'That's all. Go,' thundered Gopu. 'The avarice of these fellows has no limit.'

'Grass sells at ten annas a bundle. How can I feed the horse and myself?'

'Go away, I don't care,' cried Gopu. 'These fellows in Malgudi are spoilt by outsiders. Go, you won't get a paisa more,' whereupon Nagaraj took out of a fold at his waist in his *dhoti* four annas and counted it out on the man's outstretched palm. Glaring at the brothers without speaking, the driver declared the general meanness of Kabir Street dwellers, whipped his horse and moved off. Gopu said, 'You are spoiling these fellows. Why did you pay, as if I couldn't afford it? I want to teach these blackguards in Malgudi a lesson.'

'Life is too short for teaching lessons—'

'You and your philosophy,' sneered Gopu, and asked, 'Where is Tim?'

'Gone out,' said Nagaraj, somewhat nervously.

'It's six-thirty! And he is not home yet!' cried Gopu acidly.

'Come in first, have a wash and eat something, and then I will tell you. Come in first. Plenty of time. What time did you leave?'

Gopu ignored the question and said, 'I'm going back in the morning and he must come with me.'

'Where is the hurry?' Nagaraj asked apprehensively.

'He is my son and has to be with me, that's all. I'm not bound to explain. I've tolerated his ways too long,' he said, raising his voice. 'I'm thinking of admitting him at Albert Mission . . .'

'What for? Did you have the sense to ask me first?'

Nagaraj had no reply to this, a part of his mind admiring his wife's cautioning him. She had said, when Nagaraj spoke of it, 'Don't rush without consulting your brother about Tim's studies. He may not like you to take upon yourself all that.'

And Nagaraj had tried to silence her with, 'You always think negatively. I know what to do with Tim.'

And she went away with a toss of her head, saying, 'Surely you know your brother—after all, aren't you brothers?'

'She has uncanny forethought,' he said to himself now. 'I should hereafter leave everything to her—all management and decisions.'

'What are you muttering to yourself, while you have nothing to say to me, and stand there blinking and mumbling like a schoolboy,' sneered Gopu.

Nagaraj realized he could not very well confess that he was secretly admiring Sita's wisdom. 'Come in. Sita will be back from the temple soon. Evenings she visits the temple.'

'Are you trying to divert my thoughts? Tell me first, where is Tim?'

They were both standing on the doorstep. The ex-engineer living in the last house was tottering back from the bar at the market. He halted in front of the house and said, 'Where is my wife? I'm wifeless but not yet a widower, sir. Pity me and yield her if you have kept her here.'

Gopu said, 'Oh, this fellow still going strong! Let's go in.' He turned and went in. Nagaraj led the way, and first took him to Tim's room, flinging the door open. 'You remember we used to be here. Now Tim is in this room.'

'Where is Mother? How is she?' asked Gopu. Nagaraj led him to his mother's room in the second courtyard. He whispered, 'These days she retires before sunset and wakes up before midnight and keeps calling everybody, thinking it is morning.' Gopu stood on the threshold of her darkened room and, finding her asleep, withdrew, saying, 'I will see her later before I leave.'

Sita had meanwhile returned from the temple quietly, without a sound, as a courtesy to her husband's elder brother. Gopu sat in his chair while Nagaraj kept standing. She stood in the doorway and asked, 'Shall I make coffee? Give me five minutes. I was delayed as there was a Friday crowd with their offerings.'

'I had coffee on the way at the canteen in the bus stand.'

'If I had known you were coming—a postcard would have been enough . . .' She was acting the part of junior sister-in-law (younger brother's wife) perfectly. Gopu appreciated it. Whatever might be his attitude to his brother, he was always gentle with Sita. After the formal welcome she withdrew to prepare a dinner befitting the visitor. Before going she somehow managed to signal to her husband and he quietly got up and followed her. In the hall she whispered, 'What shall I make? Should you not have warned me? How can I manage if you sit back as if you were a guest?'

'Be quick and do something,' he said. 'I know you can . . .' He turned round and re-entered the room.

Meanwhile Gopu had taken off his shirt and coat and uppercloth and heaped them on the chair. He settled himself comfortably and remarked, 'So late, and Tim hasn't come yet! You let him loaf like this!'

'He goes out and comes home,' Nagaraj explained.

'Where does he go? Don't you have to keep an eye?'

Nagaraj realized his inability to do such a thing and grinned awkwardly. Gopu glared at him in anger, 'You are strange, impossible. You have no idea what to do, where and when. You exist from day to day like a cow chewing the cud and staring at space . . .'

Nagaraj felt uncomfortable and laughed nervously, treating it as a joke.

Gopu said, 'Whatever may be the reason, he will have to come back with me, that's all. You should have turned him round and sent him to the village on the first day. Instead of that . . .'

Nagaraj had a sinking feeling at the prospect of Tim going away and said, 'I'll see that he comes to the village later.'

'Do you think I'm here to ask for a favour? I can handle him myself. Except these few days, I was the one to handle him. What do you know of boys? If he is growing in your shadow, he will be another Nagaraj. We do not want another Nagaraj in the family.' And he laughed bitterly. Nagaraj was unaffected by this attack, took it all as an expression of Gopu's sense of humour and goodwill. He got up abruptly to go out of the room under the pretext of finding if dinner was ready. His brother, now settled on the easy chair in the room, said, 'Don't get up and try to escape. You have not lost that habit yet! Listen to me. You should have turned him back on the very first day. Instead of that you petted and pampered him, without even asking whether he took my permission before leaving home.'

'Yes, I asked him whether he had your—'

'What did he say?'

'I don't remember,' Nagaraj said.

'I want him with me. I'm adding so many things to our farm—I don't have to explain to you, but anyway you must understand the situation. Also his mother misses him and is crying all the time. He must share my labours and assist me, a grown-up boy must make himself useful. I'm putting up a gas plant which can function with the cattle refuse, which is in plenty with forty animals in the shed— the gas plant will give us light and fuel. My wife has eye trouble now, cooking with firewood, kerosene being scarce, and the smoke has affected her eyes. Also we could have gas lights.'

'Very interesting, but why disturb Tim? He is happy here.'

'If you have not realized why, I don't have to tell you anything more. Even this I have said too much for a fellow like you.'

At this point they had to go and eat. Gopu ate in silence, not wishing to exhibit his irritation before Sita. Sita had managed to provide betel leaves and arecanut on a silver plate for chewing after dinner. Gopu and Nagaraj sat on the bench in the hall and were chewing with the contentment that comes with good food followed by proper betel-chewing.

At ten o'clock Tim knocked on the door. Gopu rushed up to open it, gazed on Tim, and said, 'After all, you found your way home!'

Tim was called in by Sita to eat.

'Is this the hour daily when he comes?' asked Gopu, and added in an undertone, 'You should spank him.'

'No, no,' Nagaraj said, shocked, and added rather idiotically, 'See how tall he has grown!' while his mind clamoured to clear the point as to what made him call Tim 'donkey'.

Tim remained silent while his father was telling him to pack up. Nagaraj felt unequal to the situation. He was afraid that Gopu might assault his son or call him 'donkey' again. If he repeated that awful explosive term, God knew what would happen. He feared that the boy might hit back in some terrible manner. He wished he could don his ochre robe and retreat into the *puja* room, dead for the hour, away from all strife. 'Why don't you get ready? We leave early in the morning,' shouted Gopu.

All that the boy said was, 'No, I'm staying here. I may come there for a few days, later, but now I want to be here. I am not coming home.'

Gopu let out a sigh of despair, unable to do anything else. Nagaraj felt happy to see Gopu, who always had the last word, now helpless. His aggressiveness, conceit and sharp tongue were gone. Nagaraj felt like crying out to Tim, 'Well done, my boy!' but remained silent, looking appropriately solemn. Gopu tried to change his tone. Tried persuasion. Mentioned his mother and her crying. It was also hard for Nagaraj to imagine Charu crying, she who had been so imperious and self-assured as the senior daughter-in-law of the family years ago. Nothing moved Tim. He was adamant. He just kept saying, 'I'll come later and see Mother. I want to be here.'

Next morning Gopu left in a rage, without saying goodbye, carrying his bag and walking off to find a *jutka* at the market corner, Nagaraj following him meekly. Gopu said, 'You go back. You have spoilt him beyond repair: you are Narada, mischief-maker. If he doesn't want to see me, I don't want to see his face either,' and went down the street briskly as Nagaraj turned back home.

Nagaraj was happy that Gopu had called him Narada abusively. He took it as a compliment. 'Narada created strife, no doubt, by passing disturbing gossip from one quarter to another, but it always proved beneficial in the long run, in an eternal perspective. Must write about him from this angle. Must write in English, of course, so that the book is widely read and people understand the concept of Narada. Must start writing on a good day like Vijayadasami, the day of the Goddess of Learning. But I'm not a writer, must be helped by someone in the line. Must consult the Talkative Man, if I can stop him for a moment when he emerges from his home while starting on his rounds. Or Professor Lingham of Albert Mission School.'

Returning, he didn't enter the house but sat on the *pyol* to contemplate further on Narada. The problem was that there was no authoritative source. Narada's birth was controversial. He would take him as one that just happened to be, that was all and that was sufficient. All that mattered was that he was a unique personality, the god of music. He was ever-cheerful and active, always with a song on his lips, and moved with ease among gods and demons. Blessed with extreme mobility, he traversed at a thought the skies and space, through galaxies and the Milky Way, and was welcome in all the fourteen worlds above and below this world. Gods and demons alike were friendly to him, although he was a bearer of gossip from one world to another and created strife. 'Wait till I write my book,' he addressed his brother mentally, sending his thoughts to the bus stand.

4

GOING BACK TO the past, Sita's association with Tim had begun on that day her sister-in-law brought him from her parents' home as a three-month-old baby. She took charge of him and showered on him all the maternal love bottled up within her, being childless. She bathed the child, changed his clothes and nursed him, leaving Charu free to attend to her husband's needs, embroider or read magazines by the light in the back courtyard. Her mother-in-law never ordered her or commented on her activities, as she felt slightly awed in her presence and also grateful to her for bearing a child, unlike Sita.

Various measures to cure barrenness had been suggested to Sita by her mother-in-law, who fancied herself an expert, having inherited medical knowledge from her herbalist grandfather. She would sit before Sita in the veranda of the third courtyard to supervise her chewing of neem leaves every morning, and at that time would also regale her with reminiscences.

'I remember how double-bullock carts arrived to fetch my grandfather to distant corners of the country. He must have cured thousands of cases of barrenness, and I used to enjoy the day-long rides with Grandfather. I can still hear the jingling of the bells around the necks of trotting bullocks. He would not ride in anything less than a double-bullock carriage with proper cushions. If anyone sent an ordinary bullock-cart with a straw-covered seat, he would not come out of his room but ask me or my sister to send away the caller. And many women remained barren thereafter, for he was a determined soul. Once he said, "No", it remained "No", even if the heavens pleased.'

At some stage, Sita refused to eat any more neem leaves, declaring that she preferred to remain childless. Mother-in-law said, 'Very well. Remember that there is no deficiency on our side. Nagaraj is normal. Don't you see Gopu's wife bearing a son within two years? As the proverb goes, what can the hand that holds the plough achieve, if the hand that lifts the rice pot is unlucky?' Sita bore these taunts patiently. She had given up finally after trying other remedies, such as a forty-day penance and special *pujas* and then pilgrimages to remote temples. Nagaraj accepted all these suggestions sheepishly. 'If we do all that Mother suggests and yet fail to breed, nobody can blame us. We will have done our best,' he would whisper to her during their bus journey to a temple sixty miles away where the carved image of a cobra was the presiding deity and had to be anointed with milk and honey from time to time, since an astrologer had analysed from the horoscope that Sita's barrenness was due to a curse on her family, an ancestor having killed a King Cobra . . .

When Tim was five years old, Nagaraj had proposed rather timidly to his brother that he put him in school. Nagaraj feared at first that his brother might turn around and say, 'What business have you to put my son to school?' but he sounded unexpectedly mild and was not averse to the proposal. Nagaraj remarked to himself, 'I do not know how to judge Gopu. He flares up unexpectedly and also listens to reason unexpectedly as he does now—strange fellow!' Gopu just said, is he not too young for school?'

'Oh, no! Stephen's takes in children of three years also, very good nursery and kindergarten. Tim can enjoy the company of other children. Lots of games and playthings.'

They summoned their family priest to fix an auspicious day. Mother wanted a piper and drummer to take the boy to school in a procession after a ceremonial inauguration at home. But it was ruled out, as Stephen's was a Mission School and they might refuse admission to a child arriving in a noisy procession. So they had to be satisfied with performing the inauguration rites at home and then conduct the boy to school dressed properly, rubbing off the sandal-paste caste mark on his forehead. 'St Stephen's is no ordinary school. It was established over a century ago; its students became judges and council members and civil servants all over the country; even in England old students of St Stephen's are found . . .' Nagaraj let his imagination wax, and his brother and mother and others listened to him with interest.

Nagaraj felt victorious on the first day Tim went to school, and escorting him back and forth became his chief occupation. He accompanied Tim while he ambled down to Stephen's, stopping to watch every little object, every crow and street puppy and sparrow on the way, dawdling along. Nagaraj indulged him to the fullest, sharing his joy and wonder. They usually arrived late at the school gate—the sister in charge was tolerant towards the nursery classes. The same process was repeated when Tim was let off at four in the afternoon, once again enjoying the spectacles on the road side. Sometimes he spotted a donkey beside a wall and let out a whoop of astonishment and stood still gazing on it. Nagaraj also stood in wonderment, and when it threatened to prolong, gently pushed and piloted the youngster onward, enjoying fully every moment with Tim and through Tim.

Now Tim's coming promised to make life richer in the Kabir Street home. For his comfort, Nagaraj cleared the front room, furnished it with a table and chair, brought in a camp cot from the loft (which his brother had not noticed in the partitioning of properties). 'Boys must have beds and desks if they are to develop properly, unlike us, who read our lessons in any corner and slept in corridors, if not in cattle sheds. Our parents were indifferent. That's the reason why I am like this . . .' He paused to question his own statement. 'Like what? Nothing wrong with us. Gopu was a first class BA. He has his defects but is a studious fellow—but he always had his room and table: I was the one shunted out hither and thither and had to do my homework in any corner available. No wonder I failed in BA and scraped through a third class later . . .'

After this recollection his thoughts returned to Tim's needs. He told Tim, 'Here is your room, you may shut yourself in and sit at your desk, read, read and read all day, and nobody will disturb you . . .' Next he took Tim to Albert Mission Junior College, saw his friend Jesudoss, the headmaster, and got him admitted, explaining, 'His early years were at Stephen's but his father moved to the village and his studies were interrupted . . .'

Nagaraj's mind was seething with plans for his nephew. Must consult Rajan of Rajan Cycle Mart about a bicycle for Tim and then must take him to Bari, the loquacious stationer, in order to pile on his desk paper and notebooks, and then to watch the young man in his room bent over his studies—a vision which stirred him deeply. This was an ideal place for study, absolutely silent and quiet but for his old mother's constant movement over the whole place. If the door was shut she was bound to knock on it to ask why, and not rest till it was opened. But this was a minor problem. Tim should not mind it. He was fond of his grandmother and was seen now and then sitting on her bed chatting. If he just opened the door and said he was at his studies, she was bound to feel pleased and leave him alone.

The old mother, however, did not live long enough to enjoy her grandson's company. In less than three months after his arrival she was gone. She tumbled down during her perambulation through the vast acreage of the house and was bedridden, with Tim nursing her, without leaving her side even for a moment. To cremate her, Gopu, as the elder son, came down with his family, performed the funeral rites correctly and left in a businesslike manner on the fourteenth day, hardly exchanging half a dozen words with Tim. His mother, Charu, made constant but infructuous attempts to persuade him to return home.

During those days of rituals, Nagaraj enjoyed the crowd at home, though the occasion was grim. After Gopu and family left, life became dull. Without his mother's presence, which seemed to have had the effect, unnoticed all these years, of filling all space, the house seemed to have become suddenly vast and cavernous. With Jayaraj's help, Nagaraj got a bromide enlargement of his mother made out of an early group photo, and hung it up prominently in the ball. He festooned it with flowers every morning, standing on a stool to reach it. Sita became sole mistress of the house, although suffering occasional stabs of regret at the memories of her rudeness to the old lady in recent times.

5

WITHIN ONE YEAR, Tim was well settled in town, and liked it. His father Gopu gradually got reconciled to the idea, and had overcome much of his bitterness against his son. However, he was not able to forgive his brother for, as he fancied, separating son from father. He thought Tim's prejudice against village life was due to Nagaraj's openly expressed aversion to the smell of cattle and cattlesheds and his contempt for *gobar* gas, which sounded blasphemous. He said to his wife, 'Nag is absolutely ignorant. A fellow who cannot appreciate the value of *gobar* gas must be a bigger dunce than I take him to be. And he must have spoken slightingly of our efforts; no wonder Tim is what he is. It is our misfortune that Tim should have come under this fellow's spell. Anyway, thank God this property did not go to him. He would have reduced it to a desert within one week. Now, after all these years of labour, our farm and fields are well developed and proving profitable. We were the first to utilize the facilities the government offered in the shape of pesticides and fertilisers, machinery and, above all, the gas plant. I hope we shall soon acquire tractors, too, and let our neighbours burst with envy.'

Nagaraj felt it his duty to visit the village to see the changes and improvements. 'Otherwise Gopu is likely to mistake me.' When he blurted out this sentiment, Sita just said, 'You know your brother better, and if you demean yourself it's your business. Charu will laugh at us: she is bound to tell her sisters or friends—'

Nagaraj said, 'You imagine things—I won't spend a day more than necessary. I'll come back. If I take Tim along with me, I'm sure it will change the whole picture—'

'I'd like to see you try and get Tim to go with you—'

'Why not?' he asked without any point.

'After Mother's death and their last visit,' Sita remarked at a tangent, 'your brother never cared to ask how you are, and writes only to Tim on a postcard.'

'You must not read other people's letters.'

'You don't have to tell me. One can't help reading a postcard. I look at it just to find out if he has any thought for you, while you keep thinking and talking of him all the time . . .'

Nagaraj was unequal to this kind of talk. Saying to himself, 'She is not in a good mood,' he suddenly turned round and moved off to seek asylum on the *pyol*. He was confident she would not follow, being busy in her world of kitchen and back yard.

He took the bus next day and visited his brother, who became excited when Nagaraj said, 'I could not stay away a minute longer after I heard from some people how the farm is transformed through your recent efforts.' This completely softened Gopu, at least for the time being. He immediately proposed to give Nagaraj a guided tour, but Charu came on the scene and said, 'First let your brother have some food. He has travelled from the town.' She turned to ask Nagaraj, 'Why has Tim not come?'

And Nagaraj said, 'He has a test and said he will come later'—

while Tim had only said, 'Not interested in *gobar* gas, manure and garbage. Tell Mother I'll see her later.' Nagaraj had added, 'I'll also tell Gopu that you'll see him—'

'Yes,' Tim said and added, 'How can I help seeing him when I go there?'

Nagaraj was quite exhausted at the end of the guided tour. His orbit in Malgudi was limited to Kanni's shop, the Saree Centre and the river, and an occasional visit to the Town Hall library, where he used to go regularly at one time, that was before the era of Coomar's Boeing Centre. Now he terminated his outings after the morning meal at the Centre where he remained busy all day; moreover the old librarian had retired and a younger fellow was in charge full of notions about library systems, who did not offer anyone a seat beside his desk or encourage conversation, much less show any interest in Narada. On the first day when Nagaraj introduced himself and broached the theme, he had asked, 'Are you a writer?' Nagaraj could not say yes or no, but replied, 'I live in Kabir Street.'

'I am not asking for your address. I just want to know if you are making a living as a writer.'

Nagaraj suppressed his desire to give an account of his financial status as an inheritor of ancestral wealth like other Kabir Street gentry, which was implied in his mentioning Kabir Street; he alluded to his special interest in Narada, particularly the proposed research into his ancestry. This young, forthcoming librarian dismissed the proposal instantly, 'You will not find it in this library. I am going to change all that. The shelves will be cleared of all antiquated literature. They have no relevance to our culture today. We need more literature on Five Year Plans and their effect on the welfare and economic schemes, political life and so on. India today is on the threshold of a vast social revolution . . .' Nagaraj fled from the library and gave up the habit of visiting it even occasionally. Hence, his walks were of late much reduced and his feet, unaccustomed to a lot of trudging, now ached with the inspection of the farm.

His brother had taken him through coconut groves, guava orchards, and fields where rice and millets grew; he demonstrated the technique of spraying pesticides or chemical fertilizers; he also showed him a few mechanical gadgets for threshing, for slicing and mashing cattle feeds. His masterpiece, however, was the cement gas plant. The government gave a subsidy, cement and technical staff, in order to modernize rural life. He patted the walls of the plant proudly and affectionately. Nagaraj felt he might soon bow before it, prostrate on the ground, and wave a camphor flame. Nagaraj realized that the road to the other's heart lay through the gas plant. He looked impressed with the changes although he did not understand any of it; as he could not find the right terms, he kept murmuring all through the tour, 'Wonderful! Wonderful!' so much so that Gopu said, 'Like a parrot, you are uttering the same phrase. Do you really understand anything?' Nagaraj was slightly worried how he was to come through if cross-examined. He remained silent and thoughtful. They were now in the banana grove with bunches still ripening on their stalks. The green glare from the broad leaves waving seemed to him soothing, and he declared, 'How green is this shade!'

'Banana is always green, what is there to wonder about like a baby?'

Nagaraj felt secretly that he could appreciate cabbage heaps in Malgudi market better. He could think of nothing to say except, 'Do you give it any special manure?'

'If I explain, will you understand?' Gopu asked contemptuously, moving out of the banana corner. He was rather sore that Nagaraj seemed impervious to the value of agriculture, horticulture or any culture. As they walked back home, Gopu walked ahead and Nagaraj followed with a hangdog air. Nagaraj smarted inwardly at Gopu's superciliousness, although he had seemed so enthusiastic, warm and kind at the start of the circuit when Nagaraj had feigned so much interest in the gas plant. One couldn't go on singing the praise of that gas god endlessly. Could one? 'I have gone to the maximum extent possible in appreciating his work, can't do more. Gopu is a rustic who wears a tuft and dabbles in mud and manure like a baby. He takes advantage of my silence. Suppose I turn around and face him with, "What do you know of Narada? Can you attempt a serious work which will be approved by pundits?" If I am indifferent to cattle and dung, it is because I have better things on my mind.'

When saying goodbye next day he felt that he owed his brother a compliment and said, 'You have done very well, especially the cement plant for gas.' As a token of goodwill, a basket of fruits and vegetables was added by Gopu to his baggage at his departure.

Nagaraj's main occupation was watching Tim's movements—unobtrusively, because he was not sure that Tim liked to be watched; so he pretended indifference and preoccupation but kept an eye on Tim from the minute he heard footsteps in his room. He rose earlier than Tim, before seven, in spite of Sita's daily effort to keep him down in bed. As we have noted, he jumped out of his bed the moment Sita was up and busy in the kitchen. He paused before Tim's door to detect the sound of movement inside. When he heard no noise, he told himself, 'The boy is still asleep, God bless him. After all, his classes begin only at ten-thirty. No hurry.' And then he went about his business but came again and again to listen at the door. When he guessed Tim was up inside, he tip-toed away. When Tim showed himself outside, Nagaraj cried, 'Had good sleep?' He ran into the kitchen to warn Sita that the young man was up and to have his coffee ready. Sita generally ignored him but sometimes replied petulantly, 'One would think you were dancing attendance on a rare son-in-law. I know he'll come in for his coffee when he wants—'

'No, no, we should not leave it like that. After all . . .' he drawled, unable to conclude the sentence.

'After all what?' Sita asked.

'Hush!' Nagaraj said, 'he is coming,' and did not stop to hear further comments but moved off as if he did not notice Tim. But wherever he was he seemed to possess a sort of clairvoyance and to know how Tim was sipping his coffee or asking for less sugar or milk. This was the time when the boy spent some time talking to his aunt. Nagaraj followed every word passing in the kitchen. Tim might be saying sometimes, 'I want to give up sugar.'

'Why?'

'They say it is beneficial to health to avoid it.'

'Don't you believe all that story,' Sita would say. 'Without sugar, how can you take in coffee? It is bitter.'

'Americans drink pure decoction without milk or sugar, they call it black coffee.'

'Why do they do that?'

'In order to remain slim,' would be Tim's answer.

6

AT TEN, NAGARAJ was sitting on the *pyol* peering into the darkness of the crossroad from the market. The boy was still away. Rather a puzzle what he was doing with himself. He had got into the habit of borrowing neighbour Sambu's scooter, imitating the Talkative Man. It was parked in the passage of Sambu's house while he was all day poring over a book beside his window. You had only to ask and the scooter was yours for the day. Sambu hardly ever stirred out of his library.

Nagaraj speculated, looking at the stars, whether Tim would have fallen off the scooter somewhere. He groaned at the thought, which brought his wife out at the door. 'What was that noise?'

'Which noise?'

'Some kind of howling.'

'I didn't notice. Perhaps a street dog howling at the moon . . .'

'Where are you? This is the dark half of the month.'

'Perhaps that's why the dog has to howl for it.'

'Why are you sitting there, to catch a cold? The boy will be back. You are too fussy. He is in college and can take care of himself—old enough.'

'That's all right, you go to bed. I like it here. It's cool . . .'

She hesitated a moment to express an opinion. 'You are not. . .' she began.

He knew what she was going to say and tried to divert her thoughts with, 'I heard today tamarind is going to be scarce—remember to buy our year's supply if it is coming in basket headloads from villages.'

'Available in plenty. Why do you worry about it now?'

'Because they are exporting lorry leads to Iraq . . .'

She laughed at the notion, 'Iraq? Where is it? Do they also eat rasam and sambhar? Their food would be different.'

'I only told you what I have heard.'

She burst into a laugh. 'In your Saree Centre you seem to hear strange reports.'

Further talk was not possible as the scooter was heard coming at the market end of the lane. Nagaraj wished he could find more time for a discussion with his nephew and demand an explanation, but it seemed impossible. From the minute he got up from bed the young man moved up and down the house and then constantly

went out on his bicycle or the neighbour's scooter, and returned
home late. Sita did not share her husband's blind leniency towards
the boy. She felt at times that he would benefit from a sound
thrashing. She found it impossible to depend on his words. He was
full of charm but never meant what he said, and proved slippery.
He would promise to be on time for food but could never be found
when others were ready and waiting. He would pick up his college
books and bicycle, open the front door and just vanish while she and
her husband were before their plates in the dining room. Why he
behaved thus could not be understood. Till he was expected in the
kitchen, he would be hanging about his aunt uttering pleasantries
and sometimes also detailing his preference in food matters, and
then suddenly disappear. Nagaraj, though puzzled by his behaviour,
would explain it away. 'He'll be back—must have thought of
something suddenly about his college and will come back . . .'

When he was in, it was impossible to get angry with him. He
displayed such friendliness and dogged his aunt's footsteps in the
vast house, talking and explaining to her scientific wonders, world
events and all kinds of things. He would ask, 'What is the menu
today?' and express his joy at whatever he heard, only to disappear
when they were getting ready to serve him. But not every time.
Sometimes he stayed on and expressed appreciation of his aunt's
culinary genius. That pleased her greatly, but only for the time
being. She had misgivings about him sometimes, rather bewildered
by his manner. On some evenings he would appear unexpectedly
at an odd hour and say plaintively, 'I'm dying of hunger. Give me
anything.' The lady would feel so pleased that she would bustle
about and feed him. Soon after eating he would take his bicycle or
the neighbour's scooter and disappear, much to the bewilderment of
Nagaraj while he was planning a quiet chat with him on the *pyol*.

Today, when the boy passed in, Nagaraj sniffed. He detected a faint
alcohol flavour in the air. That disturbed his mind for a moment.
He wondered if the young fellow was out somewhere sitting up
in evil company. The Talkative Man had mentioned some time
ago that he had noticed his nephew in a group of young men at
Kismet in New Extension. Nagaraj felt disturbed but covered
it up quickly. He wanted to ask if Kismet was such a horrible
place that one should not be seen there, but the Talkative Man,
as ever in a hurry, did not stop to explain. Nagaraj asked him

later, 'What is Kismet?'

'A sort of club and restaurant and bar—started by a North Indian—very popular and fashionable.'

'What do they have there?'

'Anything from ice cream to whisky and soda, and dinner if ordered—'

'Oh, whisky!' Horrible word, not for Kabir Street families, in spite of the engineer in the last house who tottered about muttering imprecations and challenges every evening, abandoned by his family who had left him and moved out of town.

'Do you go there every day?' Nagaraj asked, his curiosity increasing every moment.

'Not every day; sometimes to meet people—it's something new to us in Malgudi.'

Nagaraj left it at that, worrying secretly why Tim should be seen there. Very uneasy thoughts followed. When Tim passed leaving a trail of alcoholic scent, Nagaraj began to sniff every day and felt relieved when he did not detect the smell. However, one evening he could not help asking, 'I find some sort of smell when you pass, something like a spirit stove of a doctor's . . .'

Tim laughed and explained, 'Oh, that! How well you remember old scents, though spirit stoves are abandoned nowadays!'

Nagaraj followed the boy into the passage and could not rest until he got an explanation about it.

Tim explained, 'Some chap sprayed eau-de-Cologne on me.'

'Why?'

'They play that sort of joke in our club.'

'But your breath also smells when you talk.'

'Oh, that chap sprayed it on my lips too . . .'

7

WORRY HAD BEEN a luxury unknown to Nagaraj till now. Nowadays when he sat on the *pyol* he realized that his mind had lost its poise. His thoughts constantly revolved round the subject of Tim, with many questions unanswered, and he found it exhausting. Formerly when he sat down cross-legged on the *pyol* he could watch tranquilly the scenes in the street: not only the men, women and pedlars but also the swarm of sparrows at the rice mill, the school of crows on the roof of the house opposite and, above all, glimpses of a pedigreed white terrier with brown patches around the eyes next door, imported from Singapore, who had his outing on a leash only when the family went out. He was always well groomed and brushed and sheltered comfortably; he had never known the company of other dogs and lived in luxury. But his owners made the mistake of building a mansion in New Extension and the pedigreed terrier did not like the idea: when the affluent family moved, the dog was also led away but he sprang back to Kabir Street, breaking out of his fancy kennel in New Extension within a couple of days. He curled up happily in the road dust in Kabir Street in front of the abandoned house, when he was not trotting in the company of ruffianly mongrels behind any bitch within sight. He apparently preferred vagrancy to a sheltered aristocratic existence, flourishing on scraps and leftovers found in garbage heaps and enjoying the thrill of street fights with intruding dogs. He was bitten and scarred, and became almost unrecognizable as the tramphood developed, his coat turning yellow with grime. Not all the blandishments and efforts of his owners to rehabilitate him were of any avail. Presently one noticed here and there in Kabir Street white puppies with brown patches. All of which reminded Nagaraj of a Tamil verse his grandmother had taught him: 'House the dog in a cage, groom him, splash on him turmeric and perfume, yet you cannot uplift him—underneath it all he will remain a dog.'

While formerly Nagaraj could watch this canine tramp with detachment, philosophizing about him, finding a similarity with certain human beings who gave up worldly pleasures and ties for a life of wandering as scholars or saints, nowadays the sight of that vagrant terrier stirred up uneasy feelings about Tim. Was he rolling in dust and fighting others, driven by the same impulse as moved the terrier? He had preferred Kabir Street to his village, and now went farther, even abandoning Kabir Street to some mysterious existence, coming home late smelling of eau-de-Cologne. He laughed at the notion of eau-de-Cologne. Did the boy take him to be an idiot? Just because he was old-fashioned and moved about in *dhoti* and shirt and upper cloth instead of pants and bush-shirt? Had he not known drinking people in his day? Coomar, who in his youth could outdo all the eau-de-Cologne spraying folk in the world! He laughed at the naivete of his nephew, who took him to be an unobservant fool.

When he was reflecting thus, Sita came out for some minor marketing at the corner shop and stopped short on hearing Nagaraj's laughter. 'What is going on?' she asked, surprised. 'Are you talking to yourself?'

'Why not?' Nagaraj asked. 'I am my best listener: quiet and agreeable and never disputing.'

'One would take you for a crackpot.'

'Why not? People are more tolerant of crackpots.'

'You go on saying "why not" for everything. It's becoming difficult to talk to you nowadays.'

'No such complaint from my side,' he said, and she turned away in exasperation and went down the street.

Nagaraj resumed his speculations about Tim. 'It might after all be actual eau-de-Cologne—such pranks were likely but rather costly; who pays for it?' He pulled his mind back from the theme with an effort. 'After all, Tim smelled of eau-de-Cologne only occasionally—unfair to stick it to him. I am probably exaggerating and misapprehending, bloating the theme by too much brooding. I'm becoming more and more critical of the young man with the soft down on his upper lip, eyes open in perpetual wonder, the same as it used to be when going to St Stephen's. In those days he gaped at any insect or animal which came to his notice—nowadays probably there are other things. Poor boy, trusts in my trust in him. I'm betraying him by this kind of thinking—must not allow this trend. If Sita suspected I harboured suspicion about Tim, God alone knows what she would do. She might fight me, being so fond of him. On the other hand, she might agree with my own evil notions and turn hostile and create difficulties for the boy until he fled to his father in the village, realizing that it was the lesser of the two evils.'

Nagaraj's heart bled at the hostile notions that were seething in his head about the young fellow, who came and went unsuspecting of his uncle's devious, evil notions—all because he stayed away late and brought in a whiff of eau-de-Cologne occasionally. And it would be a sin to draw a parallel between the trusting child who had sought asylum here and that truant dog lying in the road dust. He was appalled at the thought of his own perfidy. All because of lack of proper occupation—except when he was at the Saree Centre. Must attend to that work more seriously and not take advantage of Coomar's tolerance by leaving the Saree Centre before closing hours. Must also start on Narada soon. Pray to Narada to guide him. But Narada was not a god, he was only a sage with divine powers. No one heard of a prayer to Narada; nowhere in the scriptures did one ever come across any prayer supplicating, 'O Narada . . .'

These days Nagaraj never waited for Tim but had his supper at his normal hour. Sita, too, held out for some time, saying, 'I'll wait for Tim. It does not look proper . . .' After realizing that Tim came home only after ten or eleven in the night, she stopped waiting for him and joined Nagaraj at supper, and filled a couple of bowls with rice and vegetables for Tim to help himself to whenever he should come home.

Sitting in the hall they discussed the subject (Tim) at night when the after-dinner calmness had descended on the house. 'What does he do so late in this town?' they asked each other untiringly every night.

'Why not ask him straight away?' she said.

'I don't get a chance. I see only flashes of him before he picks up his bicycle and leaves—I can't hold him for a talk.'

She said, 'You haven't tried. You are his uncle and guardian, you have a responsibility. Your brother can come down on you any time if he finds you are neglecting duty.'

'That's true, you are right,' Nagaraj said ruefully. 'But I don't know . . . What do you think I should do?'

'You must be a little more firm,' she said. 'Why do you quail in his presence?'

'Why don't you ask him yourself? You have been more than a mother to him.'

She rejected the idea and simply said, 'It's a man's job.'

'How do you want me to set about it?'

'As soon as you see him first thing in the morning, tell him, 'Don't go away. I want to talk to you,' and then get him to sit down with you on this bench or in my room, and take care not to go to the *pyol* for this meeting, where the whole street will be listening—'

'But in his room, there is only one chair,' Nagaraj said dolefully. 'I can't keep him standing and lecture to him like a schoolteacher.'

'In that case, this hall bench should do. I promise I'll keep away in the kitchen so as to leave you both alone.'

Nagaraj did not like the idea; he felt he could not face his nephew alone. 'No, you must also be there. It's better two of us talk to him, rather than one,' he told his wife, feeling that an impossible duty was being thrust on him and wishing he could don the ochre robe and go into silence for ever. At the sound of the bicycle being lifted up the front steps, they became alert. Sita ran to the door and Tim entered with a smile, and at that smile all their misgivings vanished, and she deliberately avoided sniffing the air for liquor. 'It is not fair to suspect him.' Nagaraj rose from the bench, cheerily asking, 'Had a good day, Tim? Your dinner is ready.'

The boy just said, 'I'll change and come,' and went to his room.

Next evening they started worrying about him again, and Nagaraj decided, 'Tomorrow or the day after, I'll talk to him . . .' While Tim departed and arrived as usual, without bothering about them, a postcard from the village arrived and created uneasiness. Nagaraj found it under the street door and could not help perusing it. The card, from Gopu, said, 'Boy, what is happening? You never write, and we do not know whether you are studying or wasting your time. If your uncle thinks he can leave you to live the existence of an unleashed donkey, he is mistaken. I'll make him answer for your deeds . . .' And so on, a long letter in pin-point writing, loading on the poor postcard enough words to cover four sheets of notepaper. 'The miser!' Nagaraj muttered to himself, 'why can't he use a large sheet of paper and envelope instead of using a postcard for his epic-length message? If he wrote it properly and sent it sealed, I wouldn't know what he was thinking. However, thank God for the postcard. I know Gopu's mind now . . .'

He somehow wished to avoid mentioning this card to Sita, and quietly took it and left it on Tim's table. 'Food for thought in that postcard. Yes, Sita once again has shown that her premonitions were sound. Must be guided by her advice again in all matters. Didn't she warn me about my brother coming down on me for neglecting Tim? Must talk to Tim as advised by Sita.' But she would not participate in that exercise, and by himself he would not achieve anything. Anyway, he would try to talk to him and not let him go on like an unleashed donkey. 'Gopu was truly ungrateful and ungracious. I must follow Sita's strategy to corner Tim first thing in the day, assuming a tone of authority and firmness.' He rehearsed the scene for a while.

Next morning, he felt feverish sitting on the hall bench, watching and waiting for Tim's door to open. Sita kept an eye on him. She constantly came out of the kitchen with a significant glance in his direction, and passed up and down in front of him, hissing as she passed, 'After the card from your brother, you must act, otherwise . . .'

'We should not have read his card, that's why I placed it on his table. Why did you read it?'

'Have I no right to go into his room?' she asked angrily in whispers. Nagaraj was trying to frame a fitting reply when she cut in with, 'Hush, I hear him moving . . .' in a conspiratorial tone.

Nagaraj asked mentally, 'What on earth do you expect me to do?' She went back into the kitchen and Nagaraj felt more lost than ever, wishing that she had stayed on to lend him support in confronting Tim, who had not emerged yet from his room. Nagaraj felt a brief reprieve, it seemed, from a harsh sentence. If Sita could lend her voice and fill up the pauses and gaps in his own proposed dialogue with Tim, that would he a great help.

While he was brooding thus, Sita made a dash from the kitchen again, to whisper, 'Be firm and clear. After your brother's postcard, it is your duty . . .' 'How,' he wanted to ask, but she turned round and retreated into the kitchen in a flash, as if afraid to be seen in his company. 'Why is she avoiding me?' Nagaraj thought. 'After all, we are lawfully wedded . . .' He wanted to go and tell her firmly, 'You were not expected to read his letter.' But she had taken refuge in the kitchen in a cowardly manner after handing him the dagger. From some unplumbed depths of memory he thought of the dagger scene from *Macbeth*, which he had studied for his BA examination, in a previous incarnation as it seemed. Lady Macbeth, egging her husband on to stab the sleeping king . . . Macbeth had a less difficult job, as he had only to tackle a sleeping king, not a moving target like Tim. Actually Sita was acting more like Narada: creating complications between two parties (himself and Tim).

Following this idea, Nagaraj was happily lost in plans for his magnum opus on Narada, till the door opened and Tim appeared; at the sight of him, fresh from sleep, with his crop ruffled, all the well-rehearsed lines were gone. Tim didn't give him any chance either. He threw a glance at his uncle and swiftly moved off to the bath at the back yard. Nagaraj didn't know what to do now. He felt he had failed in his duty and had let down Sita. She was bound to attack him for his hesitancy. His opening lines would have been, as soon as Tim appeared at the door, 'Tim, don't go away before I have a word with you,' in a firm, unambiguous tone. But one can't fling such a sentence at another just waking up—as bad as stabbing a sleeping king. One should allow a decent margin of time for such things. But Sita was unrealistic and impetuous. Thank God she did not expect him to bawl at Tim's bedside, 'I must have a word with you!'

Half an hour later Tim was returning to his room, after a wash and coffee. He showed surprise at finding his uncle in the hall at this time, when normally he should be out at Jayaraj's or on the *pyol* to observe the street life in the morning. 'Not gone out, Uncle?' he asked.

This would have been the right cue for his rehearsed sentence, 'I'm only waiting for you, don't go away, etc' But Nagaraj could only say, 'Just for a change, that's all, I'll start out later, perhaps . . .' As he was hesitating, the boy was gone. He did not wait for Nagaraj to spin out his sentence. He went into his room, shutting the door behind him, while Nagaraj kept gazing on it not knowing what to do next, dreading lest Sita should come before him again with her sinister looks and hissing commands. Presently she did come out to ask, 'Have you . . .?'

In sheer desperation he nodded 'yes'. It was a lie, of course, but a life-saving one as it seemed to him. She asked him in the same undertone, 'What did he say?'

'Don't ask now, I'll tell everything later,' he said with an air of deep diplomacy. While she was trying to say something, he said in a tone of urgency, 'Begone, here he cometh . . .' feeling vaguely indebted to Shakespeare again though he had lost his own lines ordered by Sita.

He felt victorious when she left him alone: he had achieved grand results this morning. He thought that he now understood the importance of tact and diplomacy in domestic life. 'Ninety-nine per cent of husbands must be practising diplomacy for survival since wives are all alike, thoughtless and commanding. If men weren't crafty, family structure would have crumbled long ago. The greatness of our society lies in its stability, unlike the West, where one reads of divorces . . .' The boy came out dressed in pants and a white shirt. 'Never wears a *dhoti*' Nagaraj commented mentally. 'Nothing wrong with *dhoti*, but these boys are imitating Western fashions.' He felt vaguely bound to greet Tim and establish communion, so he said, 'Going out so soon?'

'Yes,' said the boy, moving towards his bicycle on its stand at the front door.

'What about food?'

'I'll be back . . .' That was his usual answer. Some days he came back, often he didn't. Nagaraj said in an undertone, 'Your aunt will have food ready by nine.'

'I will come back and eat,' repeated Tim in a flat voice.

Nagaraj would have asked next, had he a chance, 'What is the hurry?' and would have gone on smoothly to speak his lines, 'Don't go away, I must speak to you.' But the boy did not give him a chance, he reached his bicycle, took it off its stand, opened the front door and was gone. At least he had been planning an opening gambit, with, 'Let me come to the door and see you off . . .' but he did not get a chance. He knew Sita was keeping a secret watch on him but he defeated her by talking to Tim under his breath so that Sita should hear nothing but infer from appearances that some serious talk was going on.

After Tim was gone, Nagaraj moved on to his *pyol* seat, without going in to report to Sita the substance of his talk with the nephew. 'Good to leave her guessing till she comes out.' Sita was busy cooking and could not leave the kitchen; she had been straining her ears to catch the drift of her husband's conversation with Tim, but it was inaudible, they had been talking in an unusually low key. She could only distinguish two voices overlapping each other: her husband's phlegmatic rambling and the gruff tone of Tim. Unable to contain her curiosity, the moment the rice was ready to be lifted off the fire, she left the kitchen and sought out Nagaraj on the *pyol*. She stood at the door and summoned him to come in. 'Why?' he asked.

'Wish to know what happened. We can't talk there, you know it.'

He was sitting on the platform with his knees drawn up and legs crossed comfortably as in a yoga pose, and was reluctant to uncoil himself but she stood there unrelenting. He was about to say something, but she ordered peremptorily, 'Please be good enough to get up and step in.' He obliged her by crossing the threshold and advancing a few inches, wondering what to say; he was still in the glow of a discovery, namely the unimportance of a direct answer and the peace that comes consequently. But he realized at the same time that the tactic should be adopted with circumspection, otherwise it might lead to disaster. While his mind was thrashing out this question she stood there impatiently, waiting for his report. 'Have you nothing to say?' she asked with forced moderation. 'The kettle is on, I have to get back.'

'What for?' he asked inanely.

She ignored his question and straight away asked, 'What did he say?'

'Well, one wouldn't expect him to say anything, what one had to tell him being more important.'

'Did he listen?'

'Yes, of course, he had to, otherwise . . .'

He sounded so menacing that Sita felt pleased and said, 'I'm glad you are stirring yourself after all.'

'Naturally! You don't understand me. Rome was not built in a day . . .' he suddenly said, another literary tag welling up from some unsuspected depth.

She said, 'Who cares about Rome?' rather taken aback by his sudden dash to Rome. 'What had he to say?' she persisted.

'We should wait and not rush him. I have my own way of managing all situations, as you well know.' He got into a mood of victorious self-analysis, but Sita had no patience to stand there and listen. She turned to go, asking again, 'What did he have to say?'

Nagaraj replied, 'What can he say, after the way I spoke to him? But he is very shrewd. He'll have understood how one feels though he didn't show it . . .'

Apparently Sita was pleased with his answers and left muttering, 'I cannot afford to lounge on the *pyol*, I have things to do . . .'

8

THINKING IT OVER, Nagaraj realized that he had achieved nothing; the problem of Tim remained where it began, although he had appeased Sita. 'Gopu has called his son an unleashed donkey, a thoroughly wrong notion, which shows Gopu knows nothing about donkeys,' he said to himself. 'In the village probably donkeys are found all over the place unless tethered, but here, in an orderly town like Malgudi, they conduct themselves admirably.' He noticed the Kabir Street donkeys, numbering four, always stood like statues beside a blank wall, which was the back of a house opening on the other side of a lane. They belonged to the washermen living in huts, who loaded their backs with soiled clothes collected from the neighbourhood and whipped them on towards the river where they would do their laundering. When they came back from the river, the animals were unleashed, but they always remained standing in a meditative pose and never moved except to chew an old newspaper or a dining leaf blown by the wind in their direction. They occasionally let out a thundering bray in unison, to relieve the tedium perhaps—but move? Never.

'What did Gopu mean by talking about an unleashed donkey loafing about and likening it to Tim? Must be rather hurting to a young soul. Wonder how he could swallow that kind of insult written on a postcard! He was probably used to being called an unleashed donkey by his father, but at some stage rebelled and came here to live with us. I'm honoured to have his trust in me; good boy, so decent in his behaviour, not a day was he ever rude or impertinent. Why should he be rude when we are so gentle with him? Sita never showed any diminution of her love (from the day he came as a three-month-old baby), although she wants me to control him firmly, finding his ways rather puzzling. She wants to know where he goes and spends his time, what has happened to his college studies? It's all, of course, very important, indeed it's my duty to find out. No wonder Gopu threatens to come down on me and hold me responsible. When did I last visit Albert Mission?' It seemed a decade ago.

Even when he came face to face with Professor Jesudoss at the market the other day, it never occurred to him to make any enquiry about the young fellow. After a cursory salutation and some formal remarks about the price of commodities in the market, they parted. The reason why he had to hurry away was that they had met in front of the fish stall and he could not stand the stink, although Jesudoss did not seem to mind it; perhaps he was taking a fish home in his plastic shopping bag. Nagaraj pulled his mind back to Tim. He decided to concentrate on him and not let other thoughts intrude. First thing was to find out whether Tim was attending his classes.

At three in the afternoon, after closing his account book at the Saree Centre, he went up to Coomar to say, 'The Public Prosecutor's account is overdue.'

'We may have to wait a little longer,' said Coomar, looking up from yarn samples he had been examining.

'No,' said Nagaraj, 'don't allow too much time, the marriage took place over a year ago.'

'Nag, give me a couple of weeks more and if they don't respond we'll take whatever steps may be necessary,' said Coomar.

Nagaraj said, as if conceding a point, 'Very well, but don't let it get out of hand.' He felt he had offered sound advice though, if Coomar had asked him to specify the steps to take he would have felt uncomfortable. He would perhaps have suggested that his family lawyer, who was now in dotage, serve a notice on the Public Prosecutor. But would a declining lawyer ever have the guts to challenge a Public Prosecutor to settle a saree account? He concluded they were all of the same gang, including Coomar. 'Who knows?' He said to Coomar, 'I'll see you tomorrow. I have some work now,' making a move. He went down Market Road, saw an autorickshaw in front of the City Hardware Store. He was about to summon it when Gupta, the owner of Hardware, hailed him from his seat inside the shop.

'Nagaraj, why don't you come in? Come and have tea and then go. What have you been doing with yourself all these days?'

'I have to go to Albert Mission before it closes.'

'Have you become a student again? Ha, ha!'

Nagaraj shouted back from the street, 'I have my nephew studying there . . .'

'Oh! Come in, come in. Is he your nephew Tom?'

'No, Tim,' corrected Nagaraj, feeling outraged. They named dogs Tom.

'Yes, yes, sorry for the mistake. My hearing is not at all good these days. Come in for a minute and have a cup of coffee—excellent coffee from New Udupi next door.'

Nagaraj stepped in, reflecting, 'Offered tea, and now coffee! What is he going to give me, really?'

Gupta, the owner of Hardware, seated him on a stool across his table and ordered his servant to fetch coffee with the warning, 'Must be the best coffee, otherwise tell that man I'll pay him off and open my account at Anand.' He explained, 'Malgudi is not what it used to be a couple of years ago—so much competition in every trade.' Sipping his coffee, Nagaraj heard Gupta say, 'Tom is here sometimes—'

'Tim,' corrected Nagaraj.

'Yes, yes, sorry. Timmy comes here—'

'Not Timmy, but Tim,' corrected Nagaraj again, feeling outraged and saying to himself, 'What a fellow! Cannot remember a simple name.'

'What is the meaning of Tim?' asked Gupta irrelevantly.

'Deity in our village temple,' replied Nagaraj on an inspiration.

'What god is that?' asked Gupta with curiosity. Nagaraj gave some answer describing the image as possessing four arms and three eyes.

'Oh!' said Gupta, impressed. 'It must be an aspect of Siva. You must get me a photo for my collection. My walls at home are covered with photographs of gods in their hundreds. I ask for a photograph from any friend who mentions a new god.'

'Very good habit,' Nagaraj commented. 'Nobler than collecting portraits of film stars.'

Gupta confessed, 'Would you believe it? I never see films.'

'I used to see a lot in my youth, yes, even the cinema posters I don't look at now.' How Tim came to be known here bothered Nagaraj but he did not want to talk about him, and looked as if it were the most natural thing for Tim's name to be heard in a hardware shop.

He stood up, saying, 'I must see Jesudoss at Albert Mission before it closes . . .' and hurried out lest he should hear something shocking about Tim if he lingered. The autorickshaw was still there. He got into it and ordered, 'Albert Mission before closing time.'

The driver said, 'Rather far off—you must give me more.'

'More than what?'

'More than what the meter shows—if we get paid according to the meter, we will have to starve, considering the petrol price.'

'But I don't see a meter in your vehicle.'

'There are some vehicles with meters, but the police have . . .' He went on with his rambling account of the problems of running an autorickshaw service. Nagaraj stamped his foot and said, 'Are you going to start or not? I've to go to Albert Mission before their closing time.'

'It's beyond the level crossing.'

'I didn't build the college, whichever side of the level crossing it may happen to be,' said Nagaraj.

'Extra for points beyond level crossing.'

Gupta happened to watch the scene from his seat, and shouted,

'Why are you haggling with my friend? Get going, Muni.'

At this the rickshaw-man said, 'He is the boss and I must obey him. If he interferes and loses, it's his business. I don't care. Do I wait at the school and bring you back?'

'Yes, I live in Kabir Street.'

With all his dallying it was late when Nagaraj reached the college. But Jesudoss was still in his room. They were old friends and could chat for half an hour. Nagaraj did not want to show that he was spying on Tim. He had to conceal his intention and worries and also find out the whereabouts of his nephew, whom he had wildly hoped to meet at Albert Mission. In the midst of their talks, Jesudoss asked suddenly, 'Why have you stopped Krishnaji?'

'We call him Tim.'

'Doesn't matter what you call him, but what is he doing?' Nagaraj was at his wits' end to find an answer while covering up his shock. It would have been easier if he could have afforded to be frank. But his desire to protect Tim was overwhelming. He feared that if he spoke plainly he might have to blurt out his brother's phrase, 'unleashed donkey'. So he gave no direct answer to Jesudoss but just said, 'Oh, as a teacher you must have noticed how young men want to try new experiments and carve careers for themselves.'

'All very well, but education should come first. Krishnaji was a bright student and I went out of my way to give him admission, and you withdrew him even without a word to me!'

Nagaraj felt cowed by his tone and flashing eyes and said, 'I have come now exactly for that purpose!'

'After a whole term?' Jesudoss said cynically, pulling out a register, opening a page and thrusting it forth, with his finger stabbing a line. 'He came first at the last term test!'

'I told you he is a clever boy, above average.'

'And yet you would not force him to continue his studies!' said Jesudoss accusingly.

Nagaraj began to feel guilty. The need to be on the defensive (not really knowing what he was defending) was fatiguing. When he met Jesudoss outside, at the fish market, for instance, the professor was so mild and friendly. But in his official seat within the four walls of Albert Mission, he sounded terrible. How people assumed different *avatars* on different occasions, he marvelled secretly. He had always viewed Jesudoss as his best friend, never as a prosecutor. He was now displaying an aspect which was shocking. Nagaraj

regretted coming out here at all, blamed his brother's postcard and
Sita for his predicament, and sat wondering how to terminate the
interview. At this point, Jesudoss himself rose, saying, 'We call them
"drop-outs" and know fully how helpless parents or guardians can
be anyway . . .'

Nagaraj fled to his autorickshaw, reflecting, 'I had thought of
him as an easy-going friend, what a mistake!'

9

NAGARAJ FELL INTO an introspective state of mind that evening
while he sat on the *pyol* and watched the stars. Sita noticed that
he was unusually moody and silent. Normally, as soon as he came
home for the day, he would have a wash, change his dress, and go
into the *puja* room for half a second, stand before the gods with
his eyes shut, pick up a small pinch of sacred ash from the wooden
bowl, press it on his brow, and then call Sita and ask for something
to eat and drink, and enjoy the usual banter with her. But today his
pattern of behaviour changed, much to Sita's puzzlement. First, he
was late coming home. He flung off his uppercloth and shirt and did
not stop to ask for coffee but repaired to his *pyol* and sat brooding.

Sita felt disturbed, having mostly known him as vivacious
and talkative. Now his silence seemed unnatural. The only other
occasion on which he remained moody was when his mother was
laid up, years ago, with a fractured hip; and another time, earlier,
when Tim was carried away in the tempo van on the day the
brothers separated. Of course, other occasions were minor ones
when they had arguments on domestic matters. But today, thinking
back, Sita felt she had done nothing to upset him. In her turn she
became introspective while cutting some vegetables for dinner. She
was so preoccupied that she hurt her finger, and a drop of blood
oozed out. She came out of the kitchen holding up her finger and
asked Nagaraj, 'Have you got a plaster or something? I have cut my
finger.' At the sight of her bleeding finger, Nagaraj let out a shriek
which brought the lady next door to ask, 'What has happened?'
Nagaraj wailed, 'Oh! She has cut her finger . . .'

'Just a scratch, that's all. Have you any plaster or ointment? We
have nothing in this house,' said Sita.

'I have everything,' said the lady. 'With all the children in the house, one has to keep these things.' She led Sita into her house and stuck a plaster on the hurt finger, Nagaraj trailing behind her anxiously, uttering cries of sympathy. When they were coming back, he asked, 'How did it happen?'

She whispered, 'Please don't go to the *pyol* and mope again. Come into the house—otherwise that lady will not miss a word of our talk. Shut the door and come in.'

'Do you feel any pain?' he asked solicitously.

'It's just a scratch, I tell you. You didn't even come for coffee. What's the matter?' He followed her into the kitchen and sat down on a plank, which pleased Sita. She busied herself scrubbing some utensils and putting them back on a shelf.

'If you make less noise with all those clanging vessels, you can hear me say something interesting.' Her curiosity was aroused. She said, 'Wait till I have done with these vessels. Go and wait in the hall. Whether my finger bleeds or not, I alone have to do things in this house. No one else . . . Now go. I'll be with you in ten minutes.' Her manner was unusually mild; he felt happy she was showing so much concern for his moods. He said, 'No, I'll stay here. Give me a little buttermilk with salt and a squeeze of lime and a dash of asafoetida in it—just the thing for the hot day. Make it thin.' He enjoyed the fuss and affability Sita displayed, and thought that she probably guessed the turbulence in his mind. The buttermilk made him cool and composed, and he said suddenly, 'Sita, listen.' She turned her head slightly from the oven, frying something, and said, 'I'm listening.'

He sat blinking, and toyed with the thought, 'If I pick up my ochre dress, I could remain dumb and Sita won't know a thing.' He was worried how she might react to his news about Tim. She was so devoted to him that she might fall into a fit and froth at the mouth; he might have to call again the lady next door for help, as he had no idea whatever how to handle such a situation. 'Better not tell her anything now,' he decided, but Sita came up and sat beside him on another plank. 'We are like newly-weds; actually these two sitting planks came from your father on the day of our wedding,' said Nagaraj.

'Why do you have to tell me that now? Don't I remember how your father behaved at the time? He insisted on rosewood planks with silver studs at the corners and shouted and lost his temper when he found that the silver studs were rather tiny. My father looked panic-stricken and got a silversmith immediately to make and fix these roses in the corners . . .'

After this digression, she drew her plank closer and said, 'Now go on. I know it is Tim.'

He was taken aback. 'You are uncanny,' he cried. 'How did you guess?'

'What else would you be thinking of? Now tell me. I'm glad you are becoming active about that boy after all. It would have been so good if you had listened to me and acted earlier.'

'Why bother about all that now?' he said, feeling happy that she wasn't giving him any chance to open his mouth. He felt shielded by her garrulity and monologue, and felt he was being given a chance indeed to choose the right phrase to convey the shocking news about Tim. She was bound to turn round and accuse him again of neglecting his duty as an uncle. The important thing was to convey the news properly so that it didn't recoil on him. He was searching, like a writer in the throes of composition, for the precise sentence and the right emphasis. As he sat cogitating, she said with a smile, 'If you want to hide something—don't.'

'Don't what?' he asked, to mark time without having to come to the point. She was very patient and considerate and did not hustle him but humoured him throughout and waited patiently until he told her about Tim's dropping out of school. When he blurted it out, in his own way, he felt relieved, a great burden off his chest. And she said, 'We must decide what to do next.'

They discussed Tim but could come to no decision about the next step.

'Shall I visit my brother and tell him the facts?'

'What facts have you got?' asked Sita.

Nagaraj said, 'That Tim has dropped out.'

'If he asks in his usual style what you were doing all these days before discovering it . . .?'

Nagaraj had no answer. He made some gurgling noise at the throat and she said, 'Will that be your answer?' with a wicked gleam in her eyes. Nagaraj felt she should not heckle him but resume the considerate, gentle manner she had shown a little while ago when he was moody. He wished he could assume the same mood again but found it impossible. Once he had got the matter off his chest, he felt light and cheerful, and he appealed, 'Please help me. Don't go on like this.' She said firmly, 'We must send Tim back to his father if he is not studying. There can be no excuse for holding him back here.'

'No one is holding him back. He is here out of his own free will.'

'Well, try and tell your brother so; let us see what he says.' He appealed again, 'Sita, don't let us be lost in lectures and discussions. Tell me what to do. Help me with your advice. You are gifted . . .'

That compliment won her and she said, 'Let us hear what Tim has to say.'

That seemed such a sensible way out of this problem that he cried, 'Excellent idea, absolutely first class!' and he tapped his head and said, 'Surprised why it didn't occur here.'

Later they sat down to their supper with a sense of relief, feeling that they had found a master key for all problems. That mood lasted till Tim arrived at his usual hour and went about cheerfully demanding, 'Auntie, food, please.' They waited until he finished eating and came back to the hall. Sita joined them in the hall after shutting the kitchen for the day, looking too serious. Tim, who was unusually jovial today, remarked, 'Auntie, thinking of something? Won't you tell me what?' She looked at Nagaraj to open the subject, but he was confused and prayed that Sita would provide the opening lines. She, however, remained dumb—only by her look she tried to goad Nagaraj on. Tim looked from one to the other. Nagaraj cleared his throat and asked, 'How is Albert Mission these days?'

'Must be as bad as ever,' he replied, and added, 'Who knows?'

'Surely, you must know!'

'No,' replied Tim briefly, got up suddenly and said, 'I got a prize in a lottery.'

'How much?' they could not help asking in a chorus.

'Not much, but I share it with a friend,' he said.

'Won't you explain how much you got?'

'I won't know my share yet, some friends are taking care of it.'

'You said "a friend".'

'Did I? My mistake,' and he laughed.

'Where is the ticket?'

'Not with me, otherwise I would have come with sweets for you—Oh, Kismet sweets are so good!'

Nagaraj looked at Sita and simultaneously they came to the conclusion that something was wrong somewhere. Tim suddenly got up and shut himself in his room. Nagaraj felt like banging his fist on the door to get Tim out. But all that he could do was to pace the hall up and down, sunk in thought. Sita left him with a significant glance at the door and retired to the bedroom. Nagaraj would have preferred to go out on to the *pyol*, peer into the silent dark street, and clarify his thoughts, but Sita had bolted and barred the massive door, and would objecr to its being opened, and it could not be opened without its ancient hinges creaking. When he went to bed, Sita asked, 'What do you make of it all?'

'Don't take him seriously, he is joking, that's all.'

She ordered, 'Tomorrow you must take the first bus to the village and tell your brother. It's your duty.'

'What is there to tell Gopu? There is nothing to say.'

'Tim seems to have come home drunk today.'

'I sniffed, but did not smell anything.'

'You don't smell anything because you don't want to. We cannot go on like this . . .It's all wrong. Are you going to talk to your brother or not?'

She looked so firm and determined that he felt like crying out, 'Oh, Lady Macbeth again!' To add to his discomfiture, she added, 'First talk to Tim, and then go to the village and discuss this matter like two normal human beings. It is very serious.' She added, 'If you are not going, I'll go myself, first thing in the morning.'

'Oh! Macbeth!' he felt like crying out, and spent an uneasy night, unable to sleep. He kept questioning again and again, 'Why is she taking such a dreadfully serious view of things while we don't know what he means by "lottery" and "share" and "friends"? We don't have the patience to wait and ask questions but must rush and make it worse. The boy looked unusually cheerful until his mood was spoilt by cross-examination. Who knows the full truth? Perhaps he has a bumper prize, which even as a share might be substantial— these are days when lottery prizes amount to fifty lakhs. Even a share will make Tim rich. What would he do with it?'

Nagaraj's mind conjured up visions of Tim's affluence, and that was very pleasant until he remembered Sita's command to him to leave for the village. Otherwise she threatened to go herself. What are women coming to these days, ordering men about!

Gopu with his wife arrived suddenly next morning. Nagaraj fell into a confused state of mind. As he greeted and received them his mind kept drumming the thought, 'Thank God Sita's scheming to despatch me to the village is dropped now, or will she still insist on driving me to the village even while they are here? Anything is likely with Sita . . .'

There was a great deal of fussing and hospitality and no explanation asked for the visits, or surprise shown, as they might offend the visitors. Sita displayed undiluted ecstasy on meeting her sister-in-law after such a long time. The hubbub of their greetings woke up Tim, who emerged from his room confused and half sleepy. His mother cried, 'Should you not write to us as to how you are—and should you not visit your home at least on a Sunday?' Nagaraj on hearing it wanted to interject with, 'Why only Sunday? All days are Sundays in his case.' But he suppressed it and said, 'Exactly what I have also been trying to tell him . . .' Tim grunted a reply to his mother after a word of greeting and passed on to the bathroom. On the way he ran into his father coming out of the bath, who said, 'Don't run away. I have come to speak to you.'

Nagaraj felt relieved on hearing these words—which he felt, thankfully, were taken out of his mouth—and hoped Sita would leave him alone now and cease to behave like Lady Macbeth. It almost looked as if all his responsibilities were ended with the visit of his brother. He hoped he would take Tim away. Although his heart bled at the thought of his nephew's departure, he felt he needed respite from Sita's heckling and the strain of speculating about the young man.

He allotted the room in the second courtyard for his brother and his wife, feeling very nervous at first lest he should decline to go in there and insist upon sharing Tim's room. But this complication did not arise, the guests not minding where they were put up.

'Gopu, thank God,' thought Nagaraj, 'has grown rather mild in his talk and has refrained from calling his son "unleashed donkey".'

Gopu took the opportunity, when Tim was away in the bathroom, to take Nagaraj aside and whisper to him, 'I have come with a purpose. A man from Delhi has come with the proposal for an alliance with our family, through Tim. The horoscopes are well matched . . . Are you listening?'

'Yes, yes,' said Nagaraj, feeling Gopu's good mood was getting exhausted and that he was reverting to his normal abrasiveness.

'You look sleepy—didn't you sleep last night?'

'Ah, yes. Gopu, now that you ask, I'm not able to sleep continuously nowadays, only broken sleep . . .'

'It's natural. You are not a youth to fall asleep like a log . . . but if you worked in the fields as I do, then it's different. You would sleep as if doped.'

'The king slept too soundly, and Macbeth finished him off in his sleep . . .' He suddenly thought of the line, 'Macbeth shall sleep no more . . .' but he had the self-control to say aloud, 'Sleep is important, of course, and what about the proposal from Delhi which you were mentioning?'

'Now listen, and don't put me to the trouble of repeating.'

Nagaraj sat up deferentially, and Gopu said, 'One Sriram from Delhi has sent his daughter's photo with her horoscope and has written to ask if we would consider a marriage proposal. I don't know how they came to know about us, particularly about our boy, who seems to be quite famous. Ha! Ha! If he had really done well in his studies, how nicely it would have fitted in. I don't want to go into all that now . . .'

'True, true,' echoed Nagaraj, feeling relieved that Gopu was not going into inconvenient details. Gopu turned round to ask, 'What do you mean by "true, true"? You keep saying "true, true" like a parrot, but do you know what the Truth is?'

'"What is Truth?" asked the Jesting Pilate and did not wait for an answer,' thought Nagaraj but shot off at a tangent, 'What about the horoscopes?'

'I told you they are perfectly matched,' answered Gopu. 'An astrologer said no two horoscopes suit each other so perfectly in his experience. They are offering ten thousand rupees dowry, and silver, etc. Excellent in every way, only I hope the fellow will prove worthy of it. The girl will come to Trichy in a couple of days and they want the boy to see her—'

'The girl must see the boy,' Nagaraj said in his desire to show an intelligent response.

'Goes without saying. How can the girl help not seeing when the boy stands before her in solid flesh? You say the most obvious things, unless you fear that the girl will shut her eyes at the sight of our fellow . . .'

Nagaraj felt obliged to laugh at the joke.

'What are you laughing at?' asked Gopu in irritation.

'Nothing, nothing, go on, tell me more,' said Nagaraj mollifyingly.

Gopu said, 'I have to take him to Trichy. Now tickets to be

bought. I have a cousin in Trichy on Charu's side with whom we can stay for a day.'

Meanwhile the young man came out of the room dressed to go out. Gopu said, 'We have an important matter to tell you.'

'What is it?' asked the boy in a surly manner. Nagaraj, feeling that his presence might prove inhibiting, unobtrusively moved off to his seat on the *pyol*, leaving father and son alone to talk. Nagaraj was nervous lest an explosion of tempers might occur, but he was also trying to hear what they were saying to each other. Their voices receded and he guessed that they might have gone into Tim's room and shut the door. Nagaraj wondered what could be going on inside, whether they were going to emerge tearing each other apart in a deadly combat, in a state of what historians were fond of calling 'challenge and response'. To his surprise, both of them came out to the *pyol* veranda smiling, leaving Nagaraj to wonder what miracle had occurred. He had never in his experience seen Gopu beaming and Tim so cheerful. Tim told his father, 'Uncle must also come with us.'

'Why?' asked Gopu. 'Not necessary at this stage. Later . . .'

Tim said, 'He must also come,' persistently, as often as Gopu said, 'Not necessary.' But it was all in the style of pleasant exchange of views, a playful debate. Nagaraj wanted to know what it was all about but lacked the courage to question too much. He just sat smiling and looking pleasant lest his brother should accuse him of being sleepy, if silent, or too inquisitive if he questioned. Gopu came and sat on the *pyol*. Tim turned on his heels, picked up his bicycle and was off without saying a single word. Gopu looked after him and remarked, 'Where is he going so early in the day?'

A difficult question for Nagaraj. He gave a short laugh and murmured, 'Young men these days have so many things to do . . .' and before Gopu should turn around and say something about his studies, asked, 'Where does Tim want me to go?'

'Oh that!' said Gopu indulgently. 'To Trichy when we go there to see the girl.'

'Oh! Why me? What about Sita?'

'You should learn to survive without your wife sometimes. Of course, he wanted Sita also to be present, but I said no. We can't take a crowd at this stage. Later, when the marriage is settled, we may all go together in company . . . But he somehow insists on your coming. I had to agree because I don't want him to be a lost donkey. A marriage will tame him and tether him to a . . .'

'Tether him to what?' asked Nagaraj, unable to contain his curiosity.

'Of course, not to a lamp-post, but to a domestic life—what a question!' replied Gopu.

'Has he agreed? How did you manage?'

'I'm not such an idiot as not to know that he is not going to college. I have sources of information; I know what is going on at this end. You keep things away from me but I know. I know all that goes on here. Do you know that he is working at a shady place called Kismet?'

'No, I don't.'

'He comes home late—and you don't even ask where he is going and what keeps him out so late every day!'

'He won't tell me anything,' confessed Nagaraj pathetically. Gopu laughed at him. 'And you have no . . .' Nagaraj realized that Gopu was getting into his original form. He said admiringly, 'You should have been a detective. How much information you have managed to gather sitting in the village! Clever fellow!'

Gopu felt flattered and said, 'I am in touch with my old friends, who write to me or drop in when they happen to pass my way.' He added, 'I told him all that I knew about his activities but assured him that I don't mind what has happened if he will come on this trip to Trichy, and he at once agreed.'

Sita and her sister-in-law came out. Sita said, 'We want to see the morning *puja* at the temple for the good news that has come our way today.' They left. The engineer at the last house, starting out on his first visit to the bar, halted his steps for a minute to cry, 'Good morning, good brothers, good to see good brothers first thing in the good morning,' and passed on.

10

'MARRIAGES ARE MADE in heaven, but this is no heaven in any sense. Nor are angelic faces to be seen . . .' Nagaraj reflected, as he looked around the small hall in which they were seated on a Persian carpet, which seemed incongruous in these surroundings cluttered with odds and ends of old furniture pieces, and walls covered with scores of fading group photos or pock-marked with nails. Tim wore a blue shirt over his jeans and had tousled his hair to look like an off-stage film actor on the cover of the cinema magazines found on the table at Kismet lounge. His father, Gopu, had donned a silk shirt, wrapping a gaudy shawl around his shoulders, and had splashed his forehead with sandal paste and vermilion, acquiring thus a religious air which seemed to intimidate their hosts, consisting of the man from Delhi, his spouse, and some nondescript cousin hovering around.

Noisy untamed children were running round and round the veranda pillars. Nagaraj felt irritated. 'What would happen if I ordered, "Keep these dreadful children away! We are here to see a bride, not to watch these devils"? How different Tim was when he was a child, although his father sees in him now only an unleashed donkey. Poor boy, how anxiously he is waiting for his girl: rather a discouraging prospect since everyone in their group, men, women, and children, look some obscure foreign types with narrow eyes and high cheekbones, of a shade less than coffee.' Obviously out of the same mould of the man from Delhi. And all those awful children were his displaying the same pattern in various grades, two-year-olds toddling about out to ten-year-olds, boys and girls all alike. Nagaraj felt curious to see their mother, perhaps she might he different, one hoped—and the girl might take after the mother. He noticed Gopu sitting like a yogi on the incongruous Persian carpet and looking imposing; if he could be photographed in colour they might make a calendar picture to hang on a wall.

Nagaraj abruptly asked the Delhi man, just to make conversation, 'Have you a photograph of her?'

The Delhi man, who was fidgeting about nervously, said, 'I had a photograph taken before leaving, but the copy will come by post. Anyway you will be seeing her now.'

Nagaraj did not correct him but said, 'Of course, no hurry.'

Gopu said pontifically, 'Why a photograph, when you can see the person directly? Photographs are, after all . . .'

Tim, who was reclining in an old easy chair, all tense and expectant, murmured, 'They say that the studios in Delhi are hopeless, always rushed and careless.'

The Delhi man did not want to contradict a prospective son-in-law and added, 'Life in Delhi is not what it used to be . . .'

At this point, Nagaraj wanted to question what this man's status was in Delhi, but restrained himself, afraid of Gopu's reaction, since he realized that this whole episode had developed from the magic phrase 'man from Delhi proposing an alliance'. Nagaraj wanted to ask, 'What are we waiting for? Where is the girl?' An incense stick wafting some exotic scent disturbed him. He felt disgusted. Meanwhile, he found Gopu enquiring of the gentlemen, 'Where did you get this carpet?' while Nagaraj would have asked, 'How did you manage to acquire this gorgeous carpet and why, since your cousin seems to live in this house which looks to be an enlarged cowshed?'

At the next stage, fruits and refreshments were served. Tim ate with relish everything placed before him, taking it as a foretaste of the father-in-law's hospitality for the rest of his life. Gopu tasted everything in elegant little doses as an act of graceful formality. Nagaraj had to follow his example though he felt like gorging himself. When it was finished and the dishes were carried away, a silver plate with betel leaves to chew was brought in by a lady and placed before them with a flourish. She was middle-aged and Nagaraj guessed she must be the mother of the bride-to-be, and felt relieved, after studying her face surreptitiously, that she was not foreign-looking; though plain, she had regular features, normal eyes and moderate cheekbones. She suddenly stooped low and whispered in her hushand's ear, and he laughed artificially and said, 'Of course, if she is ready.' And he turned to the visitors and said, 'Saroja is ready, says my wife.'

Nagaraj asked inaudibly, 'Why do you say "my wife"? Is she her mother or not? And who is Saroja, why don't you say "daughter"?'

Presently, as if the curtains rose on a stage, led by her mother the bride-to-be appeared: a thick-set girl in a blue lace saree, bedecked with jewellery head to foot. She entered shyly, with eyes fixed on the ground. 'Oh, her eyes, hardly to be located between the eyebrows and high cheeks, how can we judge? Poor Tim will have no chance of judging her looks if she doesn't lift her chin. How will she know what Tim looks like? Is this how marriages are mismanaged in heaven? She is definitely alien-looking, and I pray Tim will refuse.' Nagaraj watched Tim to know if he would avert his eyes, but found him gazing at her in open-mouthed wonder.

Gopu was staring at her unabashedly to evaluate her personality. Nagaraj commented to himself, 'Whatever she may be, the ten-thousand dowry is the real attraction for Gopu. He doesn't seem to care how Tim is going to spend the rest of his life with a companion possessing the sort of face I used to see in geographical magazines at the Town Hall reading-room.' Coming back to the earth he noticed the girl throwing a lingering glance at Tim who, open-eyed, was drinking in her personality. 'Poor fellow! Never knew he'd be so weak-minded. Must warn him not to say "yes" to this proposal. How to tolerate the girl's presence day in and day out if Tim decides to continue to live in Kabir Street with his wife?'

The girl's father induced her to sit down with a harmonium and sing. She protested coyly at first, but yielded. Her voice was nasal. Nagaraj didn't like the cheap coarse lilt of the tune. He shut his eyes, unable to stand the spectacle of the girl opening and closing her lips, exposing her teeth while singing.

Her father said, 'She is singing a famous song from the latest Hindi film. She has learnt it by herself. Once she hears a tune, that is enough; she doesn't have to be taught, she can repeat it. She knows over a hundred songs, all self-taught. Gramophone companies want her to record but I say, "Not yet." She must complete her MA first.' He seemed extremely proud of his daughter. He added, 'In Delhi young people have opportunities to develop their talents. She is a member of a group, often called to perform at social functions, colleges, schools, and clubs.'

Gopu and Tim were properly impressed. Gopu uttered many sounds of appreciation while Saroja sang, nodding his head appropriately. Nagaraj also imitated him to some extent out of politeness but, as usual, his head was buzzing with other ideas. 'I am no expert in music, but I can distinguish between melody and nasal whining. Poor Tim, I hope he will not be carried away.'

But actually Tim was not only impressed but overwhelmed. As he told his uncle later, 'In Delhi girls are smart.' Nagaraj felt despondent, but restrained himself, just emitting some affirmative noises. Gopu kept talking about the Delhi family and made several complimentary remarks about it. Nagaraj asked, 'When will you get the dowry in hand?'

'Right away, as soon as we give the approval—they'll be coming here tomorrow.'

'Have you spoken to Tim?'

'Not necessary. He said he would come by the next bus.'

Nagaraj understood that from the sales point of view he must have encouraged Tim to stay back.

Two days later Tim was back in Kabir Street and was full of praise for the Delhi family. Nagaraj felt it would be impolitic and futile to express his views or ask formally if Tim liked the girl.

11

NAGARAJ FOUND IT irksome, being used to the silence of his home, where even street noises were muffled by the heavy door and the occasional monologues uttered by Sita in the kitchen fell in tune with the surroundings. Now he found his peace disturbed.

Tim and his wife Saroja occupied the middle room, just as Gopu and his wife had done in the past, with this difference: when the Gopus shut themselves in, one never heard any sound outside, but now one's ears were assailed with the incessant chatter and giggling emanating from the room until Tim left for Kismet (or wherever it might be) at his usual hour. Saroja then started reading aloud from a cinema magazine; followed by a sudden burst of singing to the accompaniment of her harmonium. It was this part of her programme that distracted Nagaraj most. Although the door was shut, her harmonium seemed to pierce the walls and the doors. Nagaraj would say to himself, 'Ganesha be thanked that she is not learning the violin, otherwise . . .' It was his nature to feel grateful for small mercies. He tried to face the trial by staying away on the *pyol*, shutting the main door firmly behind him. But still the music pursued him and he could not watch the street life with abandon.

He wondered if he had an aversion to music itself. 'No,' he reflected, 'I was the founder of the Saraswati Sabha at one time and collected funds for classical concerts held at the primary school hall in Vinayak Street, but had to abandon it eventually for lack of support. But I listen to music now and then and enjoy it. I cannot pursue it as a full-time job like my friend Natesh, who started a rival music association years ago, and still runs it. But he is a music teacher, has contacts at Madras and makes money out of the concerts. It is a full-time job but not for me—one who has so much to do and think constantly on, ah, Narada himself, who was the guardian of music. His music never ceased, heard or unheard.'

Nagaraj suddenly remembered Keats's lines, 'Heard melodies are sweet, but those unheard are sweeter'. Why should he not go up and knock on Saroja's door, and ask if the girl knew Keats and would she make her melody unheard? He suddenly felt like praying to Narada himself, though a part of his mind kept echoing: no one ever prayed to one who was only a celestial wanderer and sage. 'Oh, great divine sage,' he inaudibly appealed, 'please give that girl better sense than to sing, and inspire her not to deafen us with her harmonium and film hits.' As if in response to his prayer, the sound of music ceased, and Nagaraj at once said to himself, 'Narada! You are a god, I now understand. Forgive my doubts. Give me the power to write about you; when it comes out, men and women will worship you. But how am I to proceed? I must find a pundit who knows the subject.'

The pause in music was welcome—but could be temporary. Saroja is perhaps looking through her notebook for more songs or perhaps (this was a more embarrassing prospect) she must be coming out to ask sweetly, 'Uncle, how did you like my singing?' It had happened before and he was torn between candour and diplomacy. He did not want to face a similar predicament now. His mind was made up. He briskly got up, went in, dressed, and left the house after a brief explanation to Sita.

Kavu pundit, who lived in 64, IV Cross, Ellaman Lane, off Ellaman Street, had been recommended to him by the old librarian in the Town Hall. Nagaraj was now undertaking a trip to Ellaman Street, which he had often crossed once upon a time during his evening stroll in Coomar's company. Kavu pundit lived in an ancient tiled shed with two coconut trees framing its entrance over a gutter. The pundit was lying in an easy chair with his feet on its arms and was staring ahead at nothing in particular. Nagaraj announced himself, 'Town Hall librarian has asked me to see you.'

'He is my mother's sister's son. Long time since we met. Did he tell you we are cousins?'

Nagaraj nodded noncommittally and mentioned his purpose. The old man became alert and sat up, lowering his feet from the chair arm. 'Do you know Sanskrit grammar?' he asked suddenly.

Nagaraj shook his head and would have added, 'Why Sanskrit grammar, I am ignorant of any grammar. When I was in Albert Mission, I was . . .'

'You are suddenly lost in thought?' asked the pundit. 'Is it very important?'

'Yes, yes,' said Nagaraj, squirming in his seat—a wooden chair, loose jointed, which rocked precariously when he was seized with a fit of sneezing whenever the pundit inhaled a pinch of snuff. It shook and creaked all through their conversation. He could not complete his sentence, being preoccupied with maintaining his balance in his chair. He had wanted to confess, 'I was thrown out of the classroom once for not explaining the difference between an adjective and an adverb and also between a noun and a pronoun.' But as usual he was discreet enough to remain silent. 'You are quiet,' commented the scholar with a slight smile, which produced on his face a regular web of wrinkles, unsuspected normally as he seemed smooth-cheeked when he did not smile. Nagaraj suppressed his thoughts and said, 'I have not had the good fortune to learn Sanskrit—only English and Tamil.'

The pundit said, 'I am not surprised; Sanskrit is not a bazaar language. It is known as "Deva Bhasha". Do you know what it means?'

'"Language of Gods",' translated Nagaraj promptly, feeling proud of his answer and almost looking as if he expected to be rewarded with an almond peppermint, as was the custom in those days when his father helped him through homework.

'At least you know this much; I am glad. Are you aware Sanskrit cannot be picked up at any wayside shop? You must have performed meritorious deeds in several births to be blessed with a tongue that could spell the Sanskrit alphabet.'

'Ah, what wisdom, perhaps one's ears too must be blessed to hear the Sanskrit sound,' added Nagaraj, much to the delight of the pundit. More wrinkles appeared on his face as his smile broadened. Nagaraj added to the pleasure of this dialogue by saying, 'God creates a scholar like your good self to kindle the flame of knowledge in an ignoramus like me.'

'Ah, do not degrade yourself,' said the pundit. 'You talk like a poet, no wonder you want to engage yourself in *kavya*.' Nagaraj knew enough Sanskrit not to ask, 'What is *kavya*?'

The pundit cross-examined, 'Do you know how the phrase has been formed?'

Nagaraj felt he might step into a trap any minute and diverted the talk into other channels. 'In our schools, Sanskrit is neglected.'

'Do you know why?'

Nagaraj hesitated to answer, wondering if it would prove a trap again. He wanted to blurt out what he had often heard: that Sanskrit was a dead language and no one cared, but he feared it might upset the pundit and so he said, 'Because there are no proper teachers.'

The pundit let out a shout of approval and added, 'Too true! How can any pundit teach with walls around in a classroom? Do you know how many schools have approached me?'

'Must be hundreds,' Nagaraj said, to be on the safe side.

'Not so many, but twenty-five schools and colleges. We do not have more than twenty-five even if we counted the colleges outside ...'

Nagaraj felt he need not listen too intently to his talk, which seemed to stray farther and farther from the purpose of his visit, and he switched off his mind while appearing to be listening. The other added, 'For Sanskrit studies our schools are unsuited; they are all right for English and other mlechcha bhashas ...' Again, Nagaraj knew enough Sanskrit to understand what was mlechcha bhasha ('outcast's language') and he felt an urge to dispute this definition since he loved the English language, though his application to its studies was vague and haphazard and he had obtained only marginal credit for his performance in the examinations.

Meanwhile, the pundit was elaborating, 'Do you know how we used to learn or where we were taught? Always on the steps of the river. When it rained we assembled in a temple hall, sitting beside the stone pillar without leaning back. We had to sit erect when our teacher recited, and we had to repeat after him. We needed no books or pencils—everything had to go through only the ear and stay there.' And he tapped his forehead. 'We recited with our master, even while bathing or washing clothes. We were learning at all hours, our masters never leaving our side—no other occupation for at least twelve years or more until our masters were satisfied.'

'What is your impression of Narada?' Nagaraj asked, realizing that it was time to remind the pundit of the purpose of his visit.

'Who am I to pass a judgement on a great soul?'

Nagaraj realized his phrasing was wrong. 'In your studies you must have—'

The other cut him short with, 'You want to listen to his life story?'

'Yes, that is my ambition, my life's aim, you may call it.'

The pundit said, 'Even if you lived through ten births, you would not reach the end of his life story.'

'What should I do now?' Nagaraj asked, puzzled by his answer.

'Go and sit on the river step and meditate and the answer will come. But you will get nowhere near your theme by wearing a silk shirt with a gold fountain pen peeping out of your pocket. You must observe austerity.'

Nagaraj wanted to protest, 'What I am wearing is not silk but cotton and my pen is not gold but Watermans, my father's, costing ten rupees in those days. If my brother had noticed it he would have claimed it as his share of the property,' but as usual he swallowed his words and remained silent.

'Ah, you are scared of meditation. Why?'

'I have not been taught it but I have ochre robes in my *puja* room.'

'Who gave you ochre clothes?'

'My guru.'

'Who is he? There are so many charlatans around us.'

'I know him only as Swamiji. I have lost sight of him. He probably vanished into the Himalayas.'

The pundit laughed and said, 'Unwise, unwise to believe such nonsense.'

Nagaraj felt confused and annoyed at the turn their talk was taking. He was wondering if he could get up without any ceremony and run away, when the other suddenly got up from his seat, went in, and came back carrying four heavy red volumes in his arms, and placed them on a low stool. 'If you read these, you will understand Narada. You may come here and study them every day.'

'May I look through the pages?'

'Yes.'

Nagaraj timidly picked up a volume and turned the leaves. 'All in Sanskrit!' he cried.

'What did you expect? Bazaar language?'

'I have confessed, I do not know Sanskrit.'

'Of course you did. What if? This is just to indicate that you are a nothing without Sanskrit; it must be a lesson to you.'

'If you will kindly read and explain,' began Nagaraj.

'You think I have nothing better to do?'

'I can pay any fee.'

The master looked outraged. 'Do you take me to be a peddler of knowledge? If you are blind and deaf to Sanskrit, who gave you the idea you should attempt the "Great Sage"?'

'In a dream some voice ordered that I should attempt the subject.'

'Then go back to that dream; do not come here,' said the pundit, picked up his volumes and turned in.

Nagaraj felt desolate and stood transfixed, staring after the retreating scholar, hoping that he might relent and come back. He reappeared on the step only to wave Nagaraj off finally, saying, 'Go and write the fable of the inquisitive monkey who had his balls crushed when he sat on a split log and pulled out the wedge, in any bhasha you please, but leave grand subjects alone.'

Nagaraj retraced his steps, went down the lane, sunk in thought. He turned towards the river, ploughing his way through the sands, still warm with the day's sun. Evening time, habitual loungers at the riverside here and there, a sight which revived his spirits.

He had felt rather shocked at the turn the pundit's mood and words had taken. Such a fanatic for Sanskrit. 'The world is ruined by such fanatics. After all, language has a purpose, which could be served without so much madness. What does the pundit take himself to be—a world teacher, while he seems no better than the humble priest who comes home and recites Sanskrit mantras on ceremonial occasions for a fee of twenty-five paise? Kavu pundit is only a swollen-headed version of that class and perhaps must have performed funeral rites for two rupees in his days, though he professes to be a unique scholar now! He and his four red volumes! Those pages probably contain trash, who can say? Even our priest must be keeping such imposing volumes in his house—must be a part of the show, a standard equipment.' He felt a peculiar satisfaction at the memory of their visiting priest being heckled for unpunctuality in those days when rituals were performed regularly at home. Even that priest must have spent twelve years memorizing lessons on the river steps.

Ah, the river steps. He recollected the advice to meditate on the river steps. Why not try? The only sane thing the pundit had uttered was to direct him there to meditate. Wondering how one meditated he walked on to the river steps, ten granite steps leading down to the water's edge with water flowing along softly.

He went down and sat on the last step with his feet touching the cold water. He felt suddenly a glow of satisfaction at having taken a step forward towards Narada. Age-old banyan trees canopying the river's edge rustled, and birds settling on the branches cackled and chirped. 'Would be difficult to meditate in this uproar,' he thought. He contemplated the flowing river and all his doubts vanished. If he had a sheet of paper, he would have spread it and begun the first line. What would be the first line, he asked himself. 'Narada was a great sage . . .' No doubt it would be some beginning, better than no beginning. Critics might say, 'Ah, what a discovery!' and heap insults on the author for being banal. Difficult profession. 'Why should I bother to write and produce a book when my father has left me a house and enough to live on comfortably? Why did any author produce a book? Because he wanted cash. But I do not care for it—even at Boeing Centre I do free work, declining the money offered; rightly too. Did not some philosopher declare: all money is evil? Somehow I am not attracted to it. Otherwise one would have developed like Coomar, who was once such a simple soul, now earning thousands an hour, but watchful night and day to make more and more money and avoid tax. He has also become showy, wears a lace turban and a buttoned-up silk coat over a lace *dhoti*, and has moved from his ancient home at Ellaman Street to New Extension. Feels too great to be seen in his old surroundings, never walks, always riding in a motorcar with a driver to open the door and all that. No time to chat with anyone. Only weavers from the villages, his companions all day at the Centre. Probably drinks at night, resuming his old habit.'

Nagaraj checked his thoughts, realizing that Coomar could not have been the subject of meditation suggested by the haughty pundit. He had said meditate on the river steps, and not meditate on Coomar, who had his faults, but was still a good friend, a great friend. Meditate? How to meditate? On what?

Nagaraj realized when he tried meditation, whatever it meant, his thoughts wandered in all directions and were in a jumble. Perhaps he should press his fingers to his nostrils; stop breathing and close his eyes. He attempted this course for one second and felt suffocated. His eyes darkened, and he was on the point of abandoning it all when he felt a pat on his back and nearly tumbled into the river. He feared that Narada had responded and was manifesting himself. He turned around and saw his neighbour, the Talkative Man, standing over him with a grin.

'Oh, TM, you! Least expected here. What are you up to?'

The Talkative Man came down and sat by his side, dipping his feet in the running water.

'I had to meet a man in Ellaman Street and thought I could as well visit the river. What brings you here?'

'Oh, this is my favourite retreat, I come here often.'

'Formerly with your inseparable friend Coomar,' added the Talkative Man.

Nagaraj said, 'You notice everything.'

'I can't be a journalist otherwise. I must be everywhere and see a lot—even if my paper publishes only three lines of my report.'

'Can you tell me about Narada?' asked Nagaraj suddenly.

'Which Narada? Who is he?' asked the Talkative Man.

To the tune of the rustling banyan leaves overhead, Nagaraj explained his preoccupation and asked, 'Can you take me to someone who will help me?'

The Talkative Man thought over it and said, 'Why on earth do you want to write about Narada?'

Having once been inspired to mention a dream, Nagaraj felt that it saved much explanation, and said, 'I was commanded in a dream.'

The Talkative Man laughed and said, 'You are becoming quite a mystic really. Next you will be miracle healing with a pinch of sacred ash.'

Nagaraj did not know whether to accept it as a compliment or a joke. The Talkative Man would not let him rest there. He prodded him further and enjoyed it. 'Why not?' he asked. 'After all, most of your time you spend on the *pyol*. Why not gather your devotees there?'

Nagaraj accepted the honour with due modesty although troubled by a doubt that the other might not be serious. 'That will be as God wills it. If I can be of service to our fellow beings, I will not hesitate, though not at present. Later, perhaps when my writing is over . . . Now I have to write about the sage and you must help me find a teacher.'

'Why don't you ask the one who commanded you in your dream? He must be the right person.'

Nagaraj did not appreciate the Talkative Man's frivolous attitude, and regretted mentioning his mission which should have lain as a secret to be imparted only to worthy cars. The pundit's attitude was unhelpful. He began to doubt if he would ever get any help or would have to abandon the subject altogether. He threw his mind back and tried to find out why he had chosen Narada. He said to himself, 'It is probably a divine will.'

The other watched his face and asked, 'Can't you get back to the dream?'

Nagaraj replied, 'I wish I could, but for the moment I need a pundit's help to do research. I ask you, but you also talk like Kavu pundit, who asked me to go back to the dream!' He laughed bitterly at the memory of it.

The Talkative Man pricked up his ears. 'Did you say Kavu pundit? The very person I was about to suggest.'

'He would not help me,' confessed Nagaraj in a sad tone.

'Why not?'

'Because I did not know Sanskrit.'

'Very reasonable objection. He is a firebrand where Sanskrit is concerned. But he is the only man in our town who can help you.'

'But he has rejected me already.'

'When did you see him?'

'About an hour ago.'

'He will have cooled off now. Come with me. I'll talk to him.'

Nagaraj regretted mentioning the pundit. Never expected he would be forced to go back to him. He felt uneasy at the prospect of meeting him again, but the Talkative Man was insistent.

'Come with me, he won't say no to me. You should have told me first.'

'But it is impossible to stop and talk to you when you leave home in the morning, although I see you every day.'

'Never mind all that. Come with me now.' Nagaraj felt panicky.

'Oh no, not now . . .'

The Talkative Man seized his arm and almost pulled him up. Nagaraj wondered what this man's secret was that he should feel so confident of his power over the odious pundit. The Talkative Man said, 'He lives close by.'

'I know it,' Nagaraj cried. 'I have no doubt he will throw me out again.'

'He won't. Come with me, you will see the difference.'

'If he sees my face again, I do not know what he will do.'

'I will be there. Don't fear.' Nagaraj felt helpless as the other piloted him across the stretch of sand and back to 64, Ellaman Lane.

He stayed back beside the two coconut trees over the dry gutter at the entrance. The Talkative Man went up and knocked on the door. The pundit appeared and greeted him with apparent pleasure. 'Oh Ramu!' he cried. 'Where have you been all these months? So rare nowadays!'

'I have to move around all day: visiting courts, police stations and various meetings, etc. Nearly twenty miles a day and then to the railway station to post my report.'

'Do you earn enough for all your trouble, or do they cheat you?' the old man asked, leading him to the wooden chair and lowering himself on the easy chair. 'Back on his throne,' commented Nagaraj, watching from behind the coconut trees. 'What is the secret of the Talkative Man's hold on him? He calls him Ramu, never thought he was Ramu.' The old man was saying, 'You must marry. How long are you going to remain a lone vagrant?'

'Uncle, no one will marry me,' said the Talkative Man in mock sorrow. The conversation was proceeding on these lines when the pundit all of a sudden noticed the figure of Nagaraj beside the coconut trees. He shaded his eyes with his palm and asked, 'I see someone there, who is it?'

The Talkative Man said, 'He is my friend, came with me and is waiting.'

'Oh, your friend! Why do you keep him off? Let him come in.'

Nagaraj never suspected that the pundit could assume such an affable tone and wondered again what secret hold the Talkative Man had on him. The Talkative Man hailed, 'Nagaraj, come here! Pundit wants you.'

Nagaraj hesitated, thinking, 'I am not the pundit's slave to be summoned or thrown out as he pleases.' He tried to shrink out of sight and took a few steps back. At this the Talkative Man dashed forward and caught hold of Nagaraj before he could escape. 'Why is this fellow taking so much interest in me? I had better abandon my project.' The Talkative Man tightened his hold on his shoulder till he cried, 'It hurts, leave me . . .' The other would not be deflected from his purpose. 'What an awful fellow! Delights in tormenting me. I wish I had not set eyes on him today,' reflected Nagaraj.

The Talkative Man propelled him before the pundit. He looked him over and cried, 'This fellow, I have seen him somewhere.'

'Sit down, sit down.' The Talkative Man pushed Nagaraj down on the wooden chair and squatted cross-legged on the floor.

'I have seen him somewhere,' the pundit kept repeating.

The Talkative Man said, 'So many visit you to seek your guidance, but you cannot be expected to remember every face. He is my particular friend and neighbour. Very rich, but he has only academic interests unlike other rich men, who only want to squander their cash.'

'Ah!' cried the old man, turning to Nagaraj. 'Very rare indeed. What's your interest?'

The Talkative Man promptly answered, 'He wants to learn all about the great seer Narada.'

'Narada! Is this the same fellow who came earlier?'

The Talkative Man said casually, 'So many are interested in that sage nowadays, quite a popular subject. Last week alone I heard the subject mentioned by at least seven persons, and I will send a news report if I find some more people having an interest in the subject. It's a new phenomenon.'

'Is that so? Wait a minute,' said the pundit, getting up. He went in and emerged with the four red volumes in his arms, dumped them on the stool and said, 'In here you will find everything about the great saint's birth, growth and achievements.'

'You are the right guru for my friend here. Help him.'

'I suspect he is the same fellow.'

'What if!' cried the Talkative Man. 'This world has many men looking alike and wanting to write on Narada.'

The old man repeated, 'I suspect it is the same fellow.'

'Do not call him "fellow". He belongs to one of the oldest Kabir Street families, aristocrats all of them.'

'All grand families,' agreed the pundit. 'I was once related to one of those families through my wife's uncle. She is no more. I am all alone in this house, depending on a servant for my survival.'

The Talkative Man made sounds of sympathy. Nagaraj remained moody and silent, not being sure what would be a proper remark.

The old man said, 'Take a look at those books and see what you can get out of those pages. But you must come and read here. I won't let the volumes out of sight.'

Nagaraj felt desperate, but felt obliged to pick up a volume and pretend to scan the imposing lines on a page. He was wondering how to extricate himself from the situation when the old man suggested, 'Read it aloud, you will then realize how beautiful the composition is. It is one of those classics composed partly in prose and partly in poetry. Such a composition is known as . . .' He mentioned some technical term.

Nagaraj by now had reached a state of desperation and announced, 'I cannot read this.'

'Why?' asked the pundit.

The Talkative Man came to his rescue. He said, 'Uncle, you

have heard of Dr Sripathy?'

'No,' said the old man. 'I know no doctor. I am not like you, wandering about meeting people.'

Added the Talkative Man, 'No one expects it at your age. But let me tell you that Sripathy is a famous eye surgeon, and he had ordered my friend not to read for some time to come. He is not to strain his eyes.'

'How is he going to write?'

'He can listen to your reading, no time limit to it, and then dictate as he pleases. So I suggest you read out and explain, and he will dedicate the book to you and acknowledge your help, in bold print, and when it is ready I'll make it world news and people will come crowding from Europe and America not only to see the author but more than that his guru responsible for the masterpiece.'

The pundit was pleased to hear it, and the Talkative Man made the scheme acceptable further when he suggested a fee for the tuition: one hundred and fifty rupees to be paid on the first of every month, as long as the lessons lasted. The old man was beside himself with joy. He said, however, 'Money is unimportant. If this fellow listens and understands, it is more than enough, but if he is a dunce and expects me to repeat things, I do not want him.'

'He is very intelligent,' announced the Talkative Man. 'Otherwise I would not bring him before you. Can you expect less from a Kabir Street family?'

'You are right, Ramu. If you had told me at the start his family background, I would not have asked any question.'

The Talkative Man finalized the arrangement. Turning to Nagaraj he asked, 'Do you start tomorrow?'

Before he could answer, the pundit interposed to say, 'Let me look into the almanac and find an auspicious day and hour for starting the lessons.'

'When will you see the almanac?' asked the Talkative Man.

'Tomorrow morning after my *puja*. I won't touch it now.'

'Then tomorrow morning?' and the Talkative Man nudged Nagaraj and whispered, 'Take out your purse and give him an advance.'

The pundit received the advance thankfully and asked, 'What do you call your friend?'

'Nagaraj . . .we call him Nag.'

'Don't. Nagaraj is a holy name, don't spoil it. Nagaraj means

King of Serpents, which means "Adi Sesha", the thousand-hooded serpent in whose coils God's Vishnu rests, though some ignorant upstarts want to maintain that "Nagaraj" means not "Adi Sesha" but "Vasuki".' He laughed at the absurdity of it. The Talkative Man and Nagaraj joined in, the Talkative Man remarking, 'People will go to any length to pervert things.'

They were supposed to start their lessons at an auspicious hour and the day was to be fixed by the pundit. Meanwhile, Nagaraj had to go up daily to see the pundit to know when. His daily routine underwent a change. He had to cut short his stay at the Silk Centre and leave at two-thirty instead of four after rushing through his ledger work. On the way he stopped at the Boardless for coffee. Varma, the proprietor of the Boardless, became curious. 'You were one of those late evening men. Why are you so early?'

Nagaraj felt important while explaining, 'I am going through some Sanskrit studies.'

Varma had no interest in it but uttered a general agreement, 'Very important. If I had the time, I would have joined you. But if I leave this desk, who will take care of things here? One has to watch unwinkingly, otherwise business will suffer, reputation for quality will go. One has to watch unwinkingly . . .'

Nagaraj reflected, 'Like a dozen others in the trade, he begins a monologue on money matters.' He paid for the coffee and left. It was tedious to walk the couple of miles every day, but there was no transport system, except for a handful of autorickshaws, but they congregated at the market gate and no driver would agree to drive in the direction of Ellaman Lane even if a return trip was guaranteed.

'It is good exercise,' he said to himself. 'Walking also stimulates the brain.' He had read this in a magazine. 'Narada moved through the universe on foot. Did he wait for an autorickshaw? Even if there were autorickshaws available for a celestial ride, the driver would probably have said, "I can't come in that direction. No return fare from that *loka*. No one is known to return from that *loka* (if it happened to be Yama's—the god of death)."'

Nagaraj laughed to himself at this fantasy. 'Must lighten my text with such humour. Readers will appreciate it. Otherwise it will be a heavy tome. Anyway, let me hope that I will make a start. I do not know what the pundit has in mind. He has starting trouble like Coomar's motorcar, which has to be pushed every day a good distance before the driver could take the wheel.' The pundit's starting trouble seemed to be the auspicious moment, which seemed to be elusive.

The moment Nagaraj appeared before him, the pundit showed him his seat on the rickety chair and took a pinch of snuff which blew in the air and brought Nagaraj to the point of sneezing and falling off the chair. The pundit always asked, 'Why do you sneeze so much? You must see your doctor . . .' Nagaraj dared not say it was the snuff; in a voice thick with sneezing, he would rumble a reply.

The pundit spent his time airing his views on the state of affairs in general. Nagaraj listened respectfully, hoping that at the end of a particular sentence he would rise, go inside the house and return with the red volumes. But no sign of it happening.

The pundit covered various antiquated subjects. He had no idea what the town looked like beyond Ellaman Street. He spent the time asking for an account of the state of the forest beyond the market. 'We lived in Vinayak Street, which was fairly safe, but never ventured in the evenings beyond the market; on the western side of it the forest began, and we admired the courage of the Kabir Street men who lived so close to the forest, where at dusk one heard the jackals howl and also the roar of a tiger, and quite often cattle in the sheds were carried away . . .' He went on and on in the same strain, ignoring the purpose of Nagaraj's visit. Nagaraj explained how it was now a different town and how New Extension had come up not only on the market boundary but also other developments beyond the railway level crossing.

'Do trains actually pass there?' the old man asked, and added, 'Some day I must go and look at the place. From your account it must be like London.'

Nagaraj could not help asking, 'Have you seen London?'

'Yes, of course, in pictures. My cousin is the librarian at the Town Hall. He used to bring me illustrated magazines. We were so close at one time. Nowadays, alas, I think he does not remember me.'

'Oh, no, he remembers, but he has retired and hardly goes out. The Talkative Man sees him some days, but he feels very old now . . .'

'What if? Who is not old or getting old? Is it something special to him? Tell him that he is a fool, that cousin of mine. Do you know that he is my grandmother's sister's son?'

'Yes, yes,' agreed Nagaraj, although he remembered hearing of some other relationship on the first day.

'You must keep in mind the truth of the proverb . . .' began the pundit.

'Which proverb?' Nagaraj could not help asking.

'Which proverb? I have forgotten. Yes, yes, it comes back to me. My grandmother used to utter it, that is, that librarian's grandmother-in-law's sister . . .'

'Now a new kinship?' Nagaraj thought, but resigned himself to accepting whatever relationship the old man bit upon at a time. 'What is the proverb, may I ask?'

'It says kinship vanishes uncherished and loan vanishes unasked.'

Nagaraj was impressed although he saw no connection between the two ideas. He kept wondering when the pundit would begin the lessons, but hinted, 'Narada, sir.'

'You fear that I have forgotten? Wrong, if you think so. Do not misjudge me.'

'Oh, no, don't mistake me, sir—'

'Because you have given me a hundred rupees, don't ever imagine that I am your slave to do your bidding.'

'Oh, no. I would not dream of such a thing. Since I did not notice the red volume, I was thinking it must be lost . . .' He went on rambling, unable to conclude the sentence fearing anything he might say might go against him and the old man might order him to leave.

But he only said, 'Remember this. You are ignorant and young. How old are you?'

'Not too young,' Nagaraj had the recklessness to say and, inwardly, 'What is that to you?'

The old man said, 'What is the use of your coming at this hour when the sun is going? How can I read in this light?' Nagaraj had not the courage to correct him and assert that he had arrived before four.

'Should I come in the morning, sir?' he asked with humility.

'No, my *pujas* are important in the morning. I don't eat until the *pujas* are performed and all the gods are worshipped. Come in and see my *puja* room and look at the number of images I have to decorate with flowers and anoint with milk and honey.'

Thus ended one day's lessons. Nagaraj did not give up hope. He decided to readjust the hour of his visit. Next morning he went

up to the first house on Kabir Street and knocked on the door. The
Talkative Man opened it. Nagaraj explained his predicament. The
Talkative Man said, 'You will have to persist. Go again and again
until he starts. Once he starts, it will be difficult to stop him. Do you
play cards?' he asked suddenly.

Nagaraj said, 'No, why?'

'He loves cards and card players. If you knew cards, he would
not leave you but follow you about . . .'

'Alas, I do not know. How long will it take to learn?'

'You will have to be born with it.'

Nagaraj looked despondent. The Talkative Man said, 'You may
as well come in and talk.'

Nagaraj tried to excuse himself but the Talkative Man brushed
aside his objection. 'After all, your usual seat in the *pyol* won't go
away.'

Nagaraj's nature had no resistance of any kind in it. The
Talkative Man seated him in his drawing room and brought him
a cup of coffee. 'Ah, you look surprised,' said the Talkative Man. 'I
am quite well provided in the kitchen, able to make a few things for
myself when needed. Otherwise I go to Varma who is my benefactor
at most times. Now I have a little time today. The municipal
meeting is postponed. About the pundit. He is a great scholar, but
rather difficult. You must know how to handle him. Anyway, why
don't you choose some other subject available if you are itching to
write?'

'No, Narada is very important to present-day men and women.
He is a celestial sage who moved with ease among the gods.'

'A sage full of mischief and intrigue like a journalist,' said the
Talkative Man, at which Nagaraj felt slightly upset. 'Wait till you
see my book,' he said.

'Provided Kavu pundit makes up his mind,' sneered the Talkative
Man, and added, 'If you knew cards you could have ordered him
about.'

'Alas, I never learnt card playing.'

'Neither Sanskrit nor the cards. How do you expect to be
accepted by the pundit? Why don't you start off with, "Narada was
the author of card playing," and ask the pundit for confirmation?'

'I do not understand.'

'I must tell you Kavu pundit has spent a whole lifetime playing
cards. I was young when his family lived in Vinayaka Street and I

used to hang around playing with his sons and we always noticed him with three others, seated on the *pyol* of his house, holding cards in their hands and lost in a *samadhi*. He did no work except go out and give readings from sacred texts or the *Ramayana* at a temple in a nearby village four evenings in a week. He was popular and respected by his public; they used to send bullock carts to fetch him. While his evenings were spent in holy readings, his days were spent at cards. His wife, who is no more, suffered because he spent all his time in gambling, but she somehow managed. But after her death he was in a terrible mess. He borrowed from moneylenders, played for high stakes and continuously lost. Came a time when his creditors seized his house and he had to move out. He had a little cash and took on lease the shed in which he lives now in Ellaman Lane. If you wrote his life rather than Narada's you could write a best-seller and share the proceeds with him. The key to his heart lies in a game called "Twenty-Eight". I do not know much about it but you just ask him to teach you and he will be only too happy. In between, you could ask questions about Narada.'

Nagaraj could not decide, as usual, whether the Talkative Man was serious or joking, but pleaded, 'Please help me.'

'You will help yourself best only if you learn "Twenty-Eight" or abandon Narada.'

'Impossible,' said Nagaraj, taking it literally. 'The only difference I know in cards is that some are black and some red. Narada cannot be abandoned. It is my whole life's aim.'

'Well, I was only joking. It is a pity you have no use for cards. But I must confess I myself do not know much except what I picked up sitting behind friends at Kismet when I went there.'

'Do you see Tim at Kismet?'

'Of course, where else can I see him?'

'What does he do there? He is married,' reflected Nagaraj aloud.

'Well, what if? There is talk of his bringing his wife to sing. She will get paid for it.'

Nagaraj felt stunned. He never thought it would come to this. A daughter-in-law of the family to sing to a set of drunkards at Kismet. What would his brother say? His head was in a whirl. For the time being Kavu Pundit and Narada receded into the background. 'Saroja to carry her harmonium to New Extension . . . Will she carry it under her arm?' He remained in thought for a moment and asked suddenly, 'How will she take it there?'

'Maybe Tim will carry it for her.'

'They will look like street singers whom I have seen in a film long ago.'

'That was a good film in which Saigal or someone appeared. How do you remember it, wonderful!'

Nagaraj was in no mood to enjoy the compliment. He was worried what Sita would say or the neighbours or his brother, ever ready to pounce on him. 'You look terrified,' commented the Talkative Man, studying his face and enjoying his predicament. 'Don't worry. Let them do what they like. Young people of these days are different.'

'Can you do something about it? Talk to the manager and explain . . .'

'They see nothing wrong in it.'

Nagaraj rose, unable to contain his agitation. He merely said, 'I will not see the pundit today—another day.'

'Excellent idea. Leave him alone for some time, he must have food for thought. I will talk to him and then you can meet him. Meanwhile, see if you can invent stories around Narada. It will be nice if you can invent a series of short stories of Narada independently of Kavu pundit's lessons. Start with the story on hand: I am Narada bringing you a gossip item, which may develop into a family incident.'

Acting on the Talkative Man's advice, Nagaraj allowed three days to pass before meeting the pundit again. He timed his arrival early so that the pundit might not complain of a lack of sunlight during their session. The moment he appeared, the old gentleman cried, 'So early today. Why do you disturb me at this hour? I generally sleep for some time; if I don't, I feel giddy.' Nagaraj remained silent not wishing to offer any explanation.

'Sit down, sit down.' Nagaraj sat in his usual chair, holding his breath while the old man took a punch of snuff and inhaled. The old man said, 'Why are you afraid of snuff? It is unmanly. Snuff keeps one alert. But for this, I wouldn't be able to talk to you. Do you know in ancient texts snuff is mentioned not as tobacco powder but as ambrosia dust, inhaled before a warrior sets out to fight? Even the gods did it. Karthikeya, before setting out to destroy the asura, took several inhalations. In the *Mahabharata* in certain versions, it is mentioned that a truce was declared between the armies so as to relax with the dust, which would be brought in special vehicles with attendants to dispense it impartially. Their position in the battlefield would be in the centre of the conflicting armies and respected by both sides . . .' Nagaraj was relieved to find the pundit in a mood of communication. In order to keep up the good temper, he expressed appreciation of the old man's wide learning. And then, gradually, he came down to this subject, 'Any reference to Narada in the battles?'

'No. He was peace-loving. His gossips led to wars, but he was himself peace-loving and never had a scratch on him.'

'When do we start?' Nagaraj could not help asking.

'Don't be in a hurry. At an auspicious day and time which must come by itself, like a baby after ten months.' The pundit laughed at his joke and Nagaraj was distraught. Soon it would strike four and the old man would complain of failing light. He did not know how to handle this man. He prayed silently to Narada (though he is not a god but a celestial being) for help.

The old man asked, 'Are you praying?'

'Yes, to Narada.'

'He can't help you unless the time comes,' he said, and added, 'all good things must begin at the ripe moment, otherwise they will rot like a plucked unripe fruit. To find the right time, you must have the right time again. An auspicious moment or day must be sought in the almanac only at an auspicious moment to begin with.'

'Auspicious moment to seek an auspicious moment?' Nagaraj exclaimed, unable to understand the idea. It seemed to him an endless quest, like seeing one's reflection standing between two mirrors. 'Perhaps this man will never find the right moment, the reflection in one mirror only reflecting another mirror, and in a hall of mirrors one could go crazy, never being able to find the door. Shall I ask the man to return my money?' He could not pluck up the courage to ask. After another hour's palaver of the same sort he left, sunk in thought. 'I don't care for the hundred rupees thrown away, but this cannot go on forever, I must do something . . .'

Too early to go home (at this hour the harmonium will be going full blast), Lord, help me or back to Coomar's? Too weary to visit the Boardless again and answer Varma's inane questions, such as why he was coming again after his earlier cup only at two o'clock. 'None of his business, to keep count of my cups. I am tired of trudging

Ellaman Lane for no purpose, leaving the ledger entries incomplete. But Coomar is very uncomplaining—good fellow; he can't complain, also, because I work for free. How can he really? If I accept even ten rupees as salary, I would have to stand before him and seek his permission to go out at his hour, a futile activity in any case. The only useful thing the pundit suggested was to try meditation on the river steps. But I do not know how to meditate. The only subject on which I can meditate is this slippery pundit and his devious ways.'

Unnoticed, his feet turned towards the river steps. He found himself sitting on the last step with his feet in running water. Its cool touch mitigated his agitation. 'I will never see that man again. I am quite sick of him. Everyone thinks he can do what he likes with me, say anything or do anything, little realizing that I have assumed a mild attitude deliberately, in order not to hurt others. There was a time when even my father could not check my fiery temper—remember the old Deepavali, when I flung a whole packet of firecrackers into the street gutter simply because he called me . . . I don't remember what. Not a donkey, that is a favourite phrase of Gopu's when he addresses Tim. Some day he is going to hit back, he has already retorted, "What is a donkey's father?" before running away from home. The boy has become soft-headed after marriage! He deserved a better wife. Should not say this. After all, a good girl, though odd looking; something that can't be helped—but she can certainly stop singing, can't she? Now, if what the TM said comes through, she will make us the laughing stock of the community. I have not mentioned it to Sita yet. When she comes to know, can't say how she will react. Already she has a secret grouse that the girl takes no interest in the kitchen. It is only a grouse; even if the girl tried, she would not be allowed to touch anything in there except her own dinner plate, and Sita would prefer that she goes back to her harmonium . . .

'Life is getting more and more complex. All that I seek is freedom, peace of mind and scope to write my book. For that I have to depend on others . . . The pundit is probably holding out for more money, having been a gambler all his life. I am going to show that the book will be written without his interference. The story of Narada is known to everyone in our country, even a child knows it. One does not have to be a pundit to talk about Narada. I can do it if I sit down and recollect all the stories my grandmother told me, while she held me down on her lap coaxing me to swallow the rice forced between my lips. Alas, I could not note down anything, naturally; how could one at that age?'

Nagaraj realized his thoughts were wandering wildly, while he had come to the river steps to meditate on Narada. Come what may, he was going to start without wasting further time. He recollected an advice of the librarian (old one or the new one, could not remember) to invent stories of Narada. Excellent idea, that was how the Saint's biography grew and became authoritative literature over a range of a million years, each narrator inventing and adding some stuff, the great sage himself inspiring every storyteller in his own way. 'Invent' was a wrong word: nothing was invented, nothing can occur to the mind out of a vacuum—there must have been a spark of something which was blown up into a flame. 'Oh, Sage!' he murmured as a prayer in tune with the murmur of the leaves overhead and the chirping of birds, 'give me an idea and let it grow and flourish.' After the prayer his mind was easy. He was going to look into the almanac and fix an auspicious time to begin his effort. Before that he must go to Bari and buy a good notebook and ink and pen. Before everything else, discuss it with Sita.

He got up. He must hurry before Bari closed. Within one hour he was at the other end of Market Road and was happy to find Bari's open. That itself was a good sign. Bari came up effusively. 'Why have we not met for months?' he asked, holding out his hand.

'I am not going to touch his hand, it will be sticky or ink-stained. I have seen him pour ink out of a big bottle into smaller ones for his customers—that was to get more profit than by retailing smaller sealed bottles directly. Profit at any cost is their religion! They are all alike. Coomar's blouse pieces are cut out of unsold sarees.' His further reflections were interrupted by the embroidered-shirt-clad Bari offering, 'Just say it, and it is yours. Only yesterday, I was telling Gupta, you know our hardware man, that you never came this way nowadays. Now what can I do for you?'

Nagaraj mentioned his purpose slowly and clearly. 'I want some high-class notebooks for some special high-class work.'

'Go up and fetch the Tower-brand books cleared yesterday from the train,' he said to an attendant standing behind him. He turned to Nagaraj. 'Something special from Sweden, cleared only two days back from the Madras Harbour and landed in a goods train, though I had asked them to send the consignment by passenger train only to save time, but they do not care. I stored them up over there specially with you in mind; didn't want to offer to others than Coomar's, whose stationery, like their silks, have to be in a special class.'

Nagaraj was beginning to think, 'This man has begun his chatter and won't leave me in peace to choose as I like. Why is my life plagued by fellows of this type everywhere? People who talk their heads off, like that pundit . . .' They waited, staring upward at the servant on the ladder, who picked up a handful of books, more than he could hold, and dropped them, and then took a false step and came skidding down the ladder, scattering the books on the floor. 'They look like a mass of flowers in their coloured bindings,' Nagaraj reflected while the servant was nursing his elbows. Bari said, 'Not for the first time. I have told this fool so often not to lift more than he can hold, but he wants to save a second trip, lazy beggar. Hey, Sunil! Get up and go next door for a cup of tea and you will be all right. Get up, get up, don't malinger . . .' He gave him a coin. Sunil straightened himself and went out, limping. Looking after him, Bari commented, 'These days we have to be careful with labour—they are not what they used to be. I had ten fellows here at one time, and when they began to form unions, I reduced my staff. I got this fellow from Aligarh, and I keep him busy so that he has no time to gossip with others on Market Road.'

Nagaraj paid no attention to his talk but picked up a couple of notebooks from the floor, examined them and said, 'This is not what I want. These are account ledgers.'

'The best you can get from Sweden. I ordered them especially with Coomar's in mind.'

'The pages are full of debit and credit columns, in colour. I want a plain notebook for my personal use.'

'Why didn't you say so? You want plain or ruled? How many pages? All the details you must give, otherwise difficult. My philosophy is to give complete satisfaction to my customers. Do you like glazed paper or matt? You must make up your mind. I can't make it up for you—that is my philosophy in business.'

Nagaraj thought, 'Talks too much!' and said aloud, 'I want a very good notebook to write in—'

'Tell me whether bound or unbound, how many pages . . .'

'Nicely bound—'

'Nicely bound? We have a good variety . . .' He turned to the boy, who was just limping in after his tea, and cried, 'Hey, go up and fetch the two-hundred-page Crow-brand.' The boy hesitated, whereupon he cried again, 'Go up and fetch. What do you think I am keeping you for? Go up, and take care, don't imagine I'll give you money for tea again! If you fall, I'll pack you off to Aligarh.' The boy went up the ladder sullenly. Bari glared after him and said, 'Troublesome fellow. Communists have filled them with notions.'

It was nearly seven when Nagaraj decided that he did not like any of the samples shown. He explained, 'I am beginning an important work on Narada . . .'

'Ah, Narada! Great saint, and so practical!' cried Bari. 'How much he has done for the universe!'

'You know him?'

'Who doesn't? Every child in our part of the country can tell his story!'

'Your country?'

'In Aligarh.'

'Yes, you told me that already . . .'

'Every child and adult can tell you the story of that great saint. His temple in our village is very old. We have a Narada festival. Once a year I close this shop and visit the temple for a week. It is our family right to conduct the annual festival . . .'

Nagaraj was thrilled. He had reached the end of a quest, seeing the light at the end of a tunnel. He grasped the other's hand and cried, 'I must see you every day. I need your help.'

'Anything you want. If you want a fountain pen with a thick handle and broad nibs, you will have to wait for a week. To tell you a secret, I am planning to bind special notebooks in Hamilton Bond, partly gilt-edged. I am making up an order of a particular individual whose name I can't reveal, but you can have the first choice. I am making only half a dozen now. I'll have them delivered at your door if you can wait for a week. Ideal paper for Narada.'

'Very good, give it at the earliest.'

'I won't offer it to all and sundry, only to special customers.'

'Thank you. Hamilton Bond is the best, I know.'

'We are the only agents; his signed portrait hangs on the wall of my house. You must come and see it . . .'

Before they bade goodnight to each other, Nagaraj asked, 'Did you say that your boy is from Aligarh?'

'Of course, straight from our village, where my real name is "Basi". Someone typed it as "Bari" in an application and somehow it has stayed . . . As I was saying, that boy is from our village. He stays with me. I do not let him out of my sight.'

'Does he speak about Narada?'

In order to demonstrate, Bari summoned the boy and asked, 'Where do you come from?'

He blinked for a moment and said, 'Gotia.'

'Who is the god in the temple there?'

'Narad Maharaj,' the boy said promtly.

At which Bari said, 'I take him with me to Gotia every year, and I don't let him out of sight anywhere. He can tell you more stories of Narada than any pundit can.'

'Pundits are no good,' Nagaraj said dolefully.

He went back home feeling triumphant. 'I went in the wrong direction and wasted my time, meeting the pundit. I should have come to this end of Market Road instead of Ellaman; I could have written the first chapter by now . . .' He was in such a glow of contentment that he hardly noticed Saroja's harmonium at first, and when he did hear it, he said to himself, 'Let the poor girl go on if it gives her satisfaction. After all, it's some kind of music appealing particularly to Delhi folk, who also have ears, but perhaps different from ours.'

He burst in on Sita while she was starting the evening supper. 'I have happy news. I have found a man who is a treasure house on Narada. From tomorrow I am going to be very, very busy.'

'What do you mean by it?' she asked in rather a matter-of-fact way.

'I'll have to start writing on Narada—'

'Oh, that! It's always Narada—I thought you were going to be the Chairman of the Municipality!'

'Why, do you think Narada is less important?'

'Have you had coffee or do you want some? Some decoction is left.'

He felt piqued at her lack of interest, but told himself, 'She is happy about it but won't exhibit it. Likes to tease me, that's all, an old wife's privilege after decades of married life!' He explained at length about his visit to Bari and about his village god in Aligarh. She was duly impressed and mixed his coffee without any further remark about his obsession. After coffee he repaired to his seat on the *pyol* and watched the street in a state of tranquillity, in spite of the harmonium in the background.

Next day, at the end of his work at Coomar's, he went to Bari directly, waited patiently till his closing time, watching his transactions and listening to his remarks, comments and philosophy. When Bari had locked up his shop, Nagaraj followed him to his house at the back of the shop in a side street, an old area known as Sowcarpet, where originally were settled businessmen and moneylenders who had migrated from 'upper India', speaking Hindi and Gujarati and other languages of the North. Bari's was an ancient house, as spacious as Nagaraj's Kabir Street home. It had a hall with old sofas, cushions on the floor, with pictures of gods on the walls in addition to Hamilton of Hamilton Bond. Bari seated him comfortably, offered him tea and fruits and then went in and brought an old volume with dusty edges in a grimy faded binding. 'This is *Narad Puran*, our family heirloom . . .'

They came to an arrangement: Nagaraj to visit him three days in the week, going home with him after the shop. He would read aloud from the book, translate and explain, and Nagaraj to take notes and go home and write it in his own way. 'How should I show my gratitude?'

'You buy the paper for printing the book from me and nowhere else, that must be your promise to me. I can give you white printing, twenty-four or thirty-six pounds as you like, which you won't see anywhere in this part of the world.'

While waiting for Bari to close his shop, Nagaraj kept thinking, 'Although he mentions Narada as being the subject of his ancient book, I'd like him to read out at least ten lines so that I may be sure that the book deals with Narada and not Viswamithra, who was an equally dynamic sage: a warrior king, at one stage, lusting for conquests, but became a sage through fierce meditation. If I wrote about him, I'd not have to depend on Bari or the cards-loving pundit, material could be picked up from the library of my neighbour Sambu himself, who goes on reading all day by his window.' He suddenly asked, 'Bari, what do you think of Viswamithra, who was also a great sage?'

'I know, he is in the *Ramayana*, but not as great as Narada. We don't have a temple for Viswamithra anywhere.'

'I would like to hear you read your big book a page or two, so that I may enjoy the sound of your language and hear about Narada'.

Bari readily agreed, 'Tomorrow evening we'll go home and read: it is a masterpiece. In our place we treat it as high as Valmiki *Ramayana*.'

Nagaraj was impressed and sent up an apology to Sage Narada for the sudden lapse on his part. 'Of course, one has to accept Viswamithra's greatness, but now I am committed to writing on Narada. If I succeed, I'll write a second book on Viswamithra, and maybe a whole series to be called "Sages of India"; quite a lot of material available—there are seven sages, who are the progenitors of mankind.'

Eventually Bari persuaded Nagaraj to make a start on the available paper. 'Blue ledger, which is also excellent but not imported. I have got ready some books—you may start on it and later copy it down on Hamilton when the supply comes.' He summoned Sunil and drove him up the ladder to fetch the 'Crow-brand'. The boy asked from the top of the ladder, 'How many?' Bari turned to Nagaraj and repeated the question. While Nagaraj was considering the question, Bari asked, 'How many pages are you going to write?' Nagaraj did not know, but to end the uncertainty replied promptly, 'One hundred pages first part.'

Bari looked up and shouted, 'Bring two fifty-pages,' adding to Nagaraj, 'When you have used up fifty pages of the notes while you sit up with me, you may use the other fifty for your own composition from the notes.'

While carrying the brown parcel of two fifty-page Crow-brand notebooks, Nagaraj felt he had passed another definite stage towards his mission in life. Next morning after the bath and *puja*, he wore his ochre robe, took the Crow-brand notebooks into the *puja* room, said his prayers as usual, placed the notebooks at the pedestal of gods and consecrated them by sprinkling flowers on them. Sita observed his activities but refrained from questioning him because of his ochre robe.

At Bari's house next evening, after tea, Bari came to business. He brought along the ancient volume and kept it on its stand, opened the cover and began to read the text in a sing-song voice. While he read the first page, Nagaraj watched anxiously to catch the name 'Narada', to assure himself that the other man was not palming off some other sage. From time to time Bari paused to translate the contents in broken English and Tamil. Nagaraj sat bemused, but the other went on with zest. After listening for a

while, Nagaraj ventured to ask, 'How is it there is no mention of
Narada yet?'

Bari explained, 'He is not born yet. He won't be born for a long
time to come. The poet explains how the universe was created by
Brahma from his latus seat poised on the Navel of the Supreme Lord
Vishnu . . . Then comes the deluge. Narada's great-grandfathers and
their ancestors have to be born first . . .'

Nagaraj wanted to dispute this theory. He had read that
Narada was an immaculate conception, created by the Supreme
Lord by a mantra, and sent down to earth and other planets and the
galaxy and Milky Way on special missions. Though he could not
accept Bari's theory, he let him read on without interrupting him.
Ten evenings later Nagaraj found one notebook filled with notes.
When he perused the pages on the morning of the eleventh day,
sitting calmly on the *pyol*, he realized that he had been scribbling
down chaotically and phonetically whatever had emanated from
Bari's throat, who read out in a frenzy in a sort of linguistic cocktail
of Hindi, English and Tamil. Nagaraj sat on the *pyol* in a state of
complete abstraction, trying to make out the notes, unmindful of
the traffic on Kabir Street. So preoccupied was he that he did not
notice the presence of the Talkative Man, who stood below on the
road and had to call out 'Nagaraj!' several times before attracting
notice. 'Ah, come up and see this,' Nagaraj cried on seeing him, as
if a saviour had come.

'What is it? Have you already begun your masterpiece? Or
finished it?'

'I am about to begin. Come up and see!'

TM came up the steps, saying, 'I am in a hurry but your work
seems important. It may be a news item for my paper.' He came
up and sat on the *pyol,* looked through the pages and could not
conceal his amusement. 'Looks like planchette writing. I attended
a seance once at New Extension where they were trying to contact
the dead through a planchette, which scribbled something like this.
What exactly is it?'

'Go on, try to read it.'

'I have not the time today, only came to take the scooter from
your neighbour—but, anyway, where did you acquire these spirit
messages?'

Nagaraj explained, 'Bari translated passages from his book in
broken Tamil and pidgin English and sometimes burst into his own

lingo—and I took it down as I heard it, phonetically. I do not know what to do now . . . Well, I'll persist; he has the great book. I'll get something out of it in course of time. I have hopes. Tell me, should I write my book in English? I am beginning to doubt . . .'

'Why?'

'I do not know enough grammar.'

'Should make no difference.'

'I thought it would be best in English, to reach the wide world. After all, I want Narada's personality to be understood universally, irrespective of caste, creed, nationality or religion.'

'Excellent idea. For this purpose English is the right language— the only language free from the grammarian's tyranny.'

Nagaraj was pleased. 'Just what I thought. I am happy we think alike.'

After a couple of days Bari resumed his reading, and another Crow-brand notebook was filled in the next few days. Nagaraj had to indent for six more books so that he might begin his composition right away. 'Where shall I sit and write?' was the next question. 'The last room in the third courtyard would be out of reach of all noise, and I hope of the harmonium too!' He told Sita, 'When the sweeper comes, get a room cleaned and ready for me. I'll sit there and write.'

Sita swept the room, spread a mat on the floor and put in an old sloping desk on which one could work squatting on the floor. 'Or do you prefer a chair and table? The only ones in this house are in Tim's room. We had a cane chair but it has a hole and has been in the loft for years waiting to be repaired. Do you want it?'

'What is she driving at?' Nagaraj wondered. 'How can I sit in that cane chair with a hole? Is she taking it all as a joke?' He suppressed his doubts about Sita's intentions and said, 'Our tradition is to squat on the floor and write.'

She was unusually light-hearted today. 'I don't know why she is in this mood . . . This is a solemn occasion.' He knew he sounded ridiculous but could not help blurting out, 'Valmiki must have been sitting down on the ground while composing the *Ramayana*.'

'But did they have chairs in those days?' Sita asked, laughing slyly.

'Why is she mocking me?' Nagaraj wondered, but replied with due seriousness, 'This is an important work I am beginning, my dear. I have taken so much trouble to collect information . . .'

She modified her tone and asked, seriously now, 'Will it bring you a lot of fame?'

'If people read it.' He was amazed at Sita's concern. He never suspected that she would be interested in his writing. 'After so many years, I'm discovering her,' he thought. 'I have been doing her an injustice, thinking of her only as companion to feed me and look after my comforts.'

12

HE WAS UP at five next morning, violating Sita's edict that he should sleep till seven, and Sita had to get up earlier and adjust her timing too. Nagaraj went through his morning rituals at great speed, bathed, drank his coffee and performed the *puja*, changed to white *dhoti* from ochre robes, and was at his sloping desk before seven with his pen poised above the Crow-brand notebook on the desk. He kept saying, 'Sita, you don't bother. I can look after myself.'

'How?' she asked. 'Your mother never taught you even how to mix your coffee.' He had no answer to this, and was reminded of an obscure line of poetry from his college days: 'Men must work and women must weep, although the harbour be moaning.' 'I suppose it can't be helped,' he thought and accepted her services as inevitable. 'We must sleep earlier hereafter, I suppose.' He would have to cut short his relaxation on the *pyol* after dinner by half an hour. 'Without proper organization and adjustment, nothing can be achieved,' he kept saying to himself. Aloud, he told Sita, 'This will be only for a few weeks . . .'

'You will complete it?' she asked, and Nagaraj was troubled again by the thought that she was quipping.

He said, 'Not exactly . . .' unable to understand why he had mentioned 'weeks' instead of 'months' or 'years' and he decided to let it rest there, unable to conclude his sentence.

He sat down to it but could not decide what should be the opening lines. 'Once upon a time . . .' was such a handy and sensible beginning for any story in olden days. Now nobody used it; it was a pity that it was considered old-fashioned. How very practical it would be if he could straightaway start, 'Once upon a time there was Narada . . .' Critics would sneer, 'Is this writer a thousand years old? Could almost be a contemporary of Narada . . .'

He abandoned 'Once upon a time', and was biting the pen to think of a fresh start. He was not familiar with modern literature; his knowledge was confined to texts taught by Professor Kumar, out of which an assortment of quotable lines remained like sediments . . . not of much use for his present purpose. Must have a chat with Sambu, whose library might have some clue. 'Lives of great men remind us that we could make ours sublime . . .' came up to the surface. 'Yes, that is true,' he commented, 'but so difficult to write about. Between the card-playing pundit and Bari's muddled translations, so difficult to write . . .'

The literary struggle went on for a week. He constantly pored over his notes, and wrote down in the belief that if you plunged in, the right passage would emerge. He suddenly said to himself, 'Do you think that writers always thought over and then wrote? No sir, just inspiration. What is this thing called inspiration? Something that is churned out of a lot of mental struggle, something that has to be dug out, and at the end it comes out like the spring at the bottom of a well.' This analogy somehow soothed his soul as a piece of discovery, and a clue. 'Plunge straight in and you will come up with a pearl oyster.' So he decided to plunge into 'Once upon a time' and watch for developments. 'One can always erase the first sentence, and put something else in its place to satisfy readers.' So he began briskly, 'Once upon a time all the gods in heaven were agitated . . .' He paused to ask himself, 'What were they agitated about?' He sat thinking for a while and added, '. . . about various things . . . about the state of the universe where Evil was rampant . . .' 'Rampant? I have never used the expression in my life. Must look into a dictionary. Is there one at home? Father used to take out of the cupboard a red-bound dictionary whenever he sat down to help in my lessons. At the Albert Mission they always punished me for my spelling, particularly words like "commit" or "receive". To this day I am never certain whether "receive" should be "ieve" or "eive"; it does not matter at this stage, but in those days they made me write down the word one hundred times and bring it to the class, otherwise they would make me stand outside the classroom and do it. Awful days! I wonder how I survived it at all. Whenever I had to write an imposition, my father pulled out the red-covered dictionary and noted down in bold letters on a piece of paper "receipt", "knowledge" or whatever it was, so that I might not blunder again . . . But where is the dictionary? Have not seen it for years.' He suddenly called out, 'Sita, Sita, will you come for a moment?' He shouted, 'What happened to the dictionary, a red-bound one, used to be in Father's almirah?'

'Ask your brother, or your lawyer . . .' Nagaraj realized that his brother must have cleaned up the almirah at the partition of property. He remembered that the shelf had contained an assortment of volumes—epics, philosophy, a dictionary, and old schoolbooks—though he never could remember his father spending any time with a book in hand. Would it be practical to write to his brother to ask for the dictionary? Or would it start family complications? 'Fellow is looking friendly these days, why endanger it? Better borrow it from Sambu.'

He had spent two hours before his desk, and realized that between his ruminations and reminiscences his actual pen had run on to only a dozen lines. He looked over his quota for the day and let out a sigh at the ocean of work that lay ahead, and rose.

The next day's effort was no better. Reminiscences did not intrude, but his notes from Bari's reading were puzzling. He did not know how to reduce them all to a cogent, relevant narrative. Nowhere could he find a mention of Narada. But he had hopes that he would appear; bound to appear ultimately beyond an enormous jungle of verbiage. After all, the old volume had on it the title *Narad Puran*. He made sure that it was so by asking Bari to read aloud the title page every day as a routine formality at the commencement of each session. That was enough to convince him that the book dealt with the right theme.

Studying his notes, he often came across the phrase 'the Great Egg', which was rather obscure at first. But repeated reading produced visions of an enormous egg spanning earth and heaven. It was the womb of the universe, if he understood it correctly. When it burst . . . who could burst it, actually? Was it to be split with an enormous axe? Questions which had no answer in any form. The egg floated on an enormous sea among giant waves in total darkness. Where was the sun then? That, too, had to wait for the egg to be split. Impossible to conceive the size of an egg which could contain the solar system itself. Nagaraj, sitting at his sloping desk, rewrote it reverently, brushing aside his own doubts. It would be sacrilegious to question too much. Old texts mentioned the egg, and they must have had good reason to say so; the chronicles were inspired and the chroniclers were *rishis,* beings who knew what they were saying. If they mentioned Egg they must have meant it. So he accepted the idea, and integrated it in his own narrative, which read something like the following: 'Once upon a time, a great egg floated on the sea in pitch darkness. The sun was not created yet. It was still within the egg . . .' He read and re-read his composition and commented to himself, 'Not at all bad for a start. I can polish it later with someone's help; who is the best person to look over this? I don't know, perhaps such a person has not come out of the great egg yet.' He allowed himself a heretical smile at the notion, but checked himself immediately. He kept scribbling down strictly till the closing hour, signalled by the hall clock striking nine, when he got up with relief. The next day's notes were all about the unmitigated all-enveloping darkness, through which no sort of outline was visible.

Thus it went on, day after day. He spent three evenings with Bari, which provided him with enough material for four days. Even after filling a couple of Crow-brand notebooks he was unable to assess his work or understand what he was doing. He could have no objective view of his own composition, but went on spinning his yarn, groping in the darkness with the tremendous Egg still intact, wafting in the ocean. When it burst Creation would begin, and surely Narada would be the first to emerge.

Sita asked him one morning when he came out of the writing room, 'How is it coming?'

And he had to confess, 'God's ways are inscrutable.'

She asked, 'What do you mean by that?'

'I can't explain,' he said.

And she looked at him and murmured, 'No one compels you to write.'

'It will all be child's play if the wife is helpful,' he thought as he made his way to the *pyol*. He was happy that he was at his mission, but he was unhappy at the same time at his wife's sarcasm.

Saroja noticed Nagaraj early one morning, and asked, 'Why are you up so early, Uncle?'

Nagaraj examined, 'I have a lot of work; in the calm hours of early morning, one can write better and get through a lot of work easily . . .' He had just finished his quota of writing and was moving towards the street, and Saroja was clutching a bundle of clothes, passing from her room towards the bath in the back yard. He felt he should say something to her. 'Oh, so much to wash!'

She said, 'Yes, most of these are Tim's,' and then she added, 'If I also get up early, I could wash all this early in the morning . . .'

'Why should you get up so early? You should take it easy.'

'No, Uncle. My problem is that I too want a lot of time to finish my work and be free to practise.'

He appealed to Sita some time later, 'Saroja is threatening to get up early. Please tell her to stay in bed as late as possible. If her harmonium is played . . .'

'You can't stop her from playing. After all, she plays only in her room. And you will be in the courtyard.'

'But her harmonium pursues me even there.'

'Shut the door.'

'It becomes dark.'

'Switch on the light.'

He realized that she was teasing him.

'What has come over this woman?' he asked himself. 'Of late she is treating my writing as a joke.' He suppressed, as usual, his inner voice. 'Please advise her . . .'

'About what?'

'To sleep, and not play her harmonium. I wouldn't mind what she does after the clock strikes nine.'

'When I try to keep you from rising before seven, you don't care.'

'How can I sleep till seven and write?'

'Even before you started all this, it was difficult to hold you down.'

'Why are you talking about me now? We were discussing Saroja.' Their domestic talk was carried on in the kitchen, which was away from the traffic routes of the house and assured them privacy. Sita refused to interfere. 'I have got on with her well, so far. I don't want to spoil it.'

Saroja got up early next day and, after allowing an interval for Nagaraj to finish his bath, occupied the bath shed, beat her washing on the granite slab and was ready for the day, just when Nagaraj was warming up to his theme. Of late his notes were very unclear. After a lot of cosmic egg and darkness the world was submerged in a deluge. The deluge and its effects occupied a whole notebook. He felt a little annoyed with the old chroniclers, at their lack of economy. Too much detail, too slow. 'Why don't you get on with the subject and bring Narada in? After all, I am writing about

Narada, not about floods and darkness . . .'

But there was no way of speeding up, partly due to the chroniclers' ways, and partly due to Saroja's early-morning activities. Nagaraj could not keep his mind on the subject. Saroja beat wet clothes on a stone noisily, and until the thunderous pit-pat of washing ceased his thoughts remained scattered. When the disturbance ceased, he heaved a sigh of relief and tried to resume, but the respite was short-lived. It lasted only till she passed through to her room, where she began to hum film tunes while grooming herself before her looking glass. After that came the harmonium. While holding the pen over paper Nagaraj realized that it would not move. His whole attention was only on the harmonium, following and suffering every single note. Not more than a few lines of incoherence could be scribbled. He sat firmly until the clock chimed nine, and rose with a sense of frustration. Thereafter he sat on the *pyol*, brooding, until eleven, when he went into the dining room and remained gloomy throughout the meal. Sita guessed what was troubling him. She refrained from questioning or commenting on his state of mind. He dressed as usual before his oval mirror and went out. While he was passing the market gate, Jayaraj hailed him. Nagaraj could not ignore him. Jayaraj enquired, 'I have marked you absent in the attendance register. What's the matter? Every day I wait for you to come and wake me. I see you rarely.' Nagaraj explained his literary preoccupations these days and the altered timetable. Jayaraj congratulated him and wished him fame and fortune. Nagaraj was preoccupied. Jayaraj said, 'You don't look happy. Why do you write, if it makes you sad?'

'It's a hard task.'

'Then stop it. Who compels you to go on? Your wife?'

'Oh, no. She won't interfere, that's the trouble. She is aloof.'

'I don't understand your complication. She must have her own reason.'

Nagaraj passed on. At Kanni's he held out his hand mechanically for betel leaves. Kanni took notice of his glum mood but was too busy serving others to enquire. Nagaraj reached Grove Street, wondering if he should not shift in the morning to some other place—for instance, the temple hall or corridor, which would be quiet. The old watchman could be persuaded to open the side door and find a quiet corner for him. He brightened up at the idea, gloated over it and attained peace of mind to some extent. In such a tranquil state, he greeted Coomar and others and went straight to his seat and picked up the ledgers and was lost in the columns.

The crowd and bustle dispelled his gloom and he could forget for the time being the pains of composition and the harmonium music of Saroja. Tim seemed to be completely out of it all: he left home early, came back to eat in his wife's company, and left again, came home, threw a word at his uncle and aunt, shut himself in his room and left again—seen off by his wife, the only time when the harmonium ceased. 'I don't mind the harmonium, have got used to it, but not in the morning. Saroja should not rise with the sun . . .' At home, while Sita gave him his coffee in the kitchen, he explained his idea to move to the temple for writing. She said at once, 'Unsound. When you are not able to find silence in your own home, how can you find it in the temple?'

'Only the side door will be opened.'

'It'll make no difference. Worshippers don't care whether the side door or the main door is opened, they will pour in and sound the bells and chant and sing, and shout, worse than the harmonium. No, no, it won't work.'

'Then I have no salvation?'

'I don't know,' she said with undue seriousness. 'You should wear your ochre and plug your ears with cotton wool.'

'Why both?' he asked.

'Ochre will keep people away and cotton wool will keep out all sound.'

He studied her face to find out if she was serious. But she turned away to attend to some work.

Next morning, as usual, he wore the ochre robe in the prayer room. Normally he would change to white clothes after prayer, before going into his work room. Today he crossed the courtyard in the ochre drape and sat down in it at his writing desk. He picked up his notebooks and uttered a brief invocation to Saraswathi, the goddess of learning and enlightenment. He looked over the notes, the source for today's composition. Still the universe was under water, the skies were dark, and it rained without respite. He shivered at the picture of total gloom and soaking dampness with no living organism in sight, under enormous pitch-black clouds. He recollected that years ago a freak monsoon had brought four days of continuous rain in Malgudi. The damp and darkness were depressing; one felt paralysed. He remembered all schools were closed, all shops, and the streets were flooded. All signs of life and movement ceased. In that darkness human outlines were lost. Street dogs were drowned and carried off into storm drains. They said that the Sarayu was rising and would soon submerge the town, and wash it away without a trace. Four days the rains had lashed. Now he read in his notes that the great deluge and storm lasted thousands of years without count. Nagaraj shuddered at the picture of it and felt grateful to be living at the present time. He was reflecting on this gloomy scene, wondering how much of it would be relevant to his theme and how to reduce twenty-five pages of gloom to a few lines in his composition and relate it to the main theme. It was an agonizing exercise because it went on and on when he tried to write it down, repeating the gloom, downpour and the accompanying discomforts and black moods he had experienced during the great rains of Malgudi when young.

Now Nagaraj had ten notebooks full. After digesting these he would resume the sessions with Bari; he would begin the next and after that another session and another; thus it might go on—how long? Seemed indefinite and he felt worried about it; this could not go on forever, early-rising was getting on his nerves . . . While his mind was grappling with these problems, the harmonium was blaring away. He covered his ears with his palms, halting his fountain pen, and remembered Sita's advice (ever the wisest counsellor) about plugging the ears with cotton wool. He had searched for cotton wool yesterday, but not a shred available in the house; he had poked his hand into every almirah and box and shelf, but no use. Finally he requested Sita, 'Ask the lady next door if she has a piece of cotton wool in her first-aid box.'

Sita laughed and said, 'We could if you had a cut or bruise but not for your present purpose. We can't mention the reason.'

'But what shall I do tomorrow morning? I'll wear the ochre, but you have also told me to plug my ears.'

'Tomorrow get it at the medical store.'

'But I can't do it so early in the day.' She gave him no answer, and he realized now that he had blundered in not thinking of cotton wool earlier. 'After all, for a rupee a whole roll is available; it would have lasted for over a year . . .' he thought with regret.

He simply could not stand the harmonium sound any more. He felt unusually irritated, got up abruptly intending to knock or bang on Saroja's door and tell her, 'Stop your music for the next hour or

two. Otherwise things will be bad for you.' When he went up to
knock on her door violently, he found it open; she was sitting on
the floor with her harmonium. When he stood in the doorway,
mustering courage to give her a proper talking down, she herself
said, thinking that he had come to appreciate her music, 'Uncle, I
am trying a new song I listened to on the radio last night. Do you
like it?'

Nagaraj felt knocked out, could speak neither the truth nor
untruth. While he was hesitating she said, 'Oh! You have come in
your *puja* dress. I know you won't talk when you are wearing it, and
won't be disturbed. I hope you don't find my music a disturbance.'
He just attempted a benign smile, took advantage of his ochre not to
speak, turned round and went back to his writing. He was haunted
by her eager face, alien looking, seeking appreciation. Sita told him
later, 'Let that poor girl play her harmonium, why should you mind
it? You are sitting far away in the third court.'

'But the harmonium sound is everywhere . . .'

'You are exaggerating; your ancestors have anticipated all this
trouble and built these walls two feet thick.'

'But I have to get on with my writing.'

'And Saroja has to get on with her music. What else can she do?
She doesn't know what to do in the kitchen, she has nothing to do
all day.'

'Why don't you train her in household work?'

'It's not her line. Anyway, let her actual mother-in-law give her
the training. Why should I? However, if she shows any interest, I
am ready!'

He spent the next afternoon visiting Dr Velu of Velu Medical
Hall on Market Road. It was about five o'clock and the doctor
was not yet to be seen. A late lunch followed by a prolonged siesta
always delayed his evening visit to his clinic, and patients were
sitting, lounging and lying on benches and steps and floor in various
stages of ill health. He was reputed to have the healing touch and
a crowd always waited and swarmed around when he arrived on
his scooter in his striped cotton suit and knitted tie and hat. Such
meticulous dressing took time and he always arrived late, resulting
in a swarm of patients jostling in his clinic.

When he arrived, a servant held his scooter and took it away,
and when he stepped in with the stethoscope dangling from his
neck, he was practically mobbed by patients following him with a

babble of complaints. He stood before them, held up his arms, and said, 'Go back to your seats and stay there. Come one by one when I call you.' The doctor took his seat in the hall with a final threat, 'If you are going to be like this I'll see no one today but leave immediately. I will go out on my round of visits.' The mob withdrew. The doctor sounded a bell. A cadaverous tall man wearing thick glasses materialized, wearing a *khaddar jibba* and white Gandhi cap. The doctor waved a finger, and the man withdrew and went to the waiting hall, looked at Nagaraj and beckoned to him, in recognition of his special standing as a Kabir Street citizen. At the sight of him the doctor rose and advanced with his hand held out. 'Nagaraj, it seems a hundred years since I saw you. What brings you now? Are you keeping well? What's wrong with you today?'

'For a very insignificant reason I have come. I can wait.'

'No, I'll attend to the old friend first. Others can wait, the usual running noses, throat, stomach ache and what not. I hope to go on giving relief with God's grace. Where I feel helpless I send them on to Dr Natwar, who has a polyclinic on Mempi Road with all sorts of gadgets, but he is expensive, I can't send him all my patients, who are poor and illiterate. I don't charge more than two rupees for any prescription . . . The tongue is loosened when old friends meet. Now, what is the matter with you? I am at your service.'

'Nothing important,' Nagaraj said, feeling that he had blundered in coming here for mere cotton wool and that he should give some reasonable explanation. 'I didn't wish to worry over a small matter, but actually I have come to ask if you can give me a little cotton.'

'What for? Any injury or cut?'

'Oh, no, it's something very minor. Of late I feel some sort of noise in the ear, and I wonder if a plug of cotton wool will help.'

'What sort of noise? Do you hear a humming or hissing? Any pain while it lasts? Is it intermittent or continuous?' The doctor came over and tugged his ear and peered in with a torch. 'Any dizziness accompanying the hissing?'

'It's something very minor, of no importance, nothing to worry—'

'You are not to come to conclusions. It's a doctor's business. If you read the medical literature on the subject you will see that there are a hundred causes for noise in the ear. We must assume it is a serious symptom and eliminate the cause. After all, there may be nothing except wax.'

'Yes, yes,' agreed Nagaraj. 'I have frequently taken out wax.'

'Never do that!' cried the doctor in alarm. 'If you injure the tympanum it will affect the brain.' Nagaraj shuddered and remained silent. Everything he said seemed wrong. He was getting a little nervous. He had never thought of his health. Now this doctor's face, held so close and with an expression of being about to pronounce a dreadful verdict, unnerved him. The doctor was asking, 'When did you check your blood pressure last?'

Nagaraj promptly replied, 'About a month ago.'

'What was the reading?'

'Normal.'

'Urine? ECG?'

Though he did not know what ECG meant Nagaraj replied, 'Normal, normal.'

'Who is your doctor?'

'At Madras, related to our family.'

'Is he good?'

'Top-class physician with a lot of practice and a nursing home too . . .' Nagaraj felt it would be impossible to invent further answers to ward off the doctor's interest in him, and feared the doctor would next stretch him on a table and pronounce something dreadful. He got up abruptly saying, 'So many are waiting, I'll be back later,' and started.

The doctor said, 'Wait, wait . . .' He hastily scribbled on a pad, tore off the slip and gave it to him. 'Tomorrow go to Natwar's polyclinic and lab and show this. They will test you and give a report. See me with the report; I'd like to have the latest results.'

Nagaraj fled from the place. 'What evil power inspired me to see the man today! He would have sent me home on a stretcher if I had stayed longer with him!'

On the way he stopped at Ganesh Stores and asked, 'Have you cotton?'

'What cotton?'

'Just ordinary cotton.'

'For what?' asked the shop man.

'Why is everyone so fussy about cotton? What a hard thing to come by!' he thought, and said. 'For this and that, you know! Just simple cotton wool which is applied to wounds and stuffed into ears if there is pain.'

'We don't sell that kind of cotton.'

'Then what kind of cotton do you sell?'

'We don't, but we have these.' He produced a tin box and took out of it a handful of wicks. 'Wicks for oil lamps, especially gods!'

Nagaraj examined a sample and said, 'Give me a handful.' They were all twisted cotton. He said to himself, 'I could untwist and fluff them out again . . .' He walked home through the evening crowd on Market Road, sunk in thought, saying to himself, 'Thank God I left the doctor in good time, thank God that He gave me the sense to get away in good time. Narrowly escaped.'

At home he did not mention his visit to the doctor, and tore to shreds the slip of paper the doctor had given for the pathologist. Otherwise Sita was likely to take the doctor's advice seriously and nag him to go in for the report. She had a holy faith in doctors and would have become hysterical about his health. He said, 'Managed to find some sort of cotton after all. Tomorrow I can plug my ears and write without any disturbance.'

Sita snatched the little package from his hand. 'The very thing I wanted. I promised to the gods in the temple to light a hundred wicks. Did I tell you?' She sounded very pleased.

'I can always read your mind,' he said, looking very clever. 'I'll bring you more,' he said.

'This will be enough now.'

'But I want a small quantity now.'

'What for?'

'It's your suggestion. I'll plug my ears as you advised.'

She looked horrified and held the packet away from him. 'What an evil notion! To misuse God's lamp-wicks! I never thought you would stoop so low. It's a sin to misuse God's wicks . . .'

'Where did you read this? In which *shastra*? You can't appropriate my hard-won cotton!' But as usual he swallowed his words without further argument.

Next day's writing was jerky and chequered. His notes were stagnating at the stage of Cosmology and Cataclysm, without a trace of Creation. He found it difficult to use his notes and organize his essay, worrying at the back of his mind what all this had to do with his theme, with a recurring suspicion that Bari was deluding himself with that ancient volume in Rajasthani or some such language; he was in the throes of composition, in a wilderness of doubts and misgivings—not only about the material and its validity but a fundamental harrowing doubt about his competence to write at all! 'What evil genius impelled me to undertake this task? What conceit? Waste of time. Ages since I sat on the *pyol* with a free mind. Coomar is tolerant, even though I am not giving enough attention to his accounts . . .'

With all the self-criticism on one side, he was still struggling to whip the pen on, not having the heart to stop it. But it was a torment. Into this turmoil and confusion butted the harmonium mercilessly. He flung down the pen and covered his ears. Still the noise persisted and it was agonizing. 'I must have committed the worst sins in my previous life to have to hear this now. If I could have barricaded my ears with cotton wool, even with just a wisp of it, I could have mitigated my misery. But cotton? What has happened to all the cotton in the world? Seems more difficult to get than diamonds. To add to all this, Sita with her notions of the sacredness of cotton wicks. At least a couple of wicks could have helped. But she has deprived me of even that relief! Bad woman, unhelpful . . . No, I should not think of her thus. All day she slogs for my comforts . . .'

Next day he started his routine, but dispensing with the ochre cloth which he felt inhibited him since he had to observe total silence while wearing it. Today he was determined to go on with his writing whatever might happen. If disturbed he would go and tell Saroja to shut up. For this his ochre would be an impediment. So he wore a white *dhoti* as a sort of war preparation.

Just as he feared, the attack came. His struggle to concentrate and progress towards something relevant and sensible was thwarted at the start itself. He had hardly written two lines when his pen jerked and criss-crossed the page involuntarily, driven by a sudden blast of noise from the harmonium. He made up his mind to act. He pushed away his desk and rose to his feet resolutely. He was going to tell her, 'This must stop now,' unambiguously.

Sita had a glimpse of him from her kitchen door as he dashed past with the pen still in his grip, but refrained from asking any question. The moment he appeared at the doorway, Saroja said, 'Oh, Uncle, you are not wearing your ochre dress, and now I can talk to you, and you will speak. I want to try a new piece. I want to know how you like it. It goes like this.' She tapped the keys of her harmonium and read out of a piece of paper, musically, the opening lines of a song which said, 'At midnight I am thinking of you, at dawn I think of you . . .' It seemed all right at dawn and noon, but at midnight? It didn't sound innocent enough. Probably it had a double meaning, in which composers of film songs excelled. He felt a little shy to stand there and listen to such a song from a daughter-in-law of the family. While he was squirming and preparing to get away, the words were drowned in the harmonium noise. 'Thank God the harmonium has no tongue,' he thought, and attempted to sneak away. She stopped the harmonium and said, 'Uncle, you are going away? There are four more stanzas . . .' Nagaraj did not know how to escape. The fury which drove him here from his writing room had evaporated. He did not even remember the strong words he had rehearsed in his room. All that seemed important was to get away before the girl could compel him to utter an appreciative word. While the girl was still singing he slinked away, pretending to have heard a knock on the street door.

He realized that it was going to be impossible to tell the girl to stop. While sitting down to lunch, he whispered to Sita, 'You must come to my rescue. I simply cannot write a single sentence unless Saroja mends her ways. Tell her—'

'Why should I? You do it. I saw you cross the courtyard as if you were going to pick up and smash her harmonium.'

He was pleased that Sita could note his fury and understand that he was not effete. If he was roused, nothing could hold him back. 'Sita should not conclude that I am a smiler at all times. After all the years with me, it's a pity she is beginning to understand me only now.'

The lunch concluded in profound silence. He realized that he would never get any help from Sita. He began to suspect that she enjoyed the harmonium music and Saroja's foolish songs. 'No wonder Sita wants it to go on.' She herself used to play the harmonium once but had to abandon the dreadful instrument when his mother, who had governed the family with a firm hand, advised her that in a crowded family it was unseemly for a girl to isolate herself and practise music.

13

NAGARAJ SAT ON the plank jutting out of Jayaraj's shop, explained his predicament and sought advice. Jayaraj was busy cutting and nailing frames and could only say, 'Why should you mind? After all, it is music, and when the walls of a home resound with music, prosperity will come.'

Nagaraj said, 'I don't care for prosperity but only quiet for writing.'

Jayaraj persisted, 'But music! It's good for a home.'

'But this isn't music'

'How can you say so? After all, she has learnt from a master in Delhi and knows what she is doing. Do you think that her father will have spent his time and money for nothing? How can you say it can't be music? You have no ear for music, that's the trouble. After all, this is no family problem; the real problem in a family is different. Take my case. I feel the curse of age . . . can't go on forever like this . . . hammering nails on picture frames, can't see the nail head but hit my thumb often, but my sons don't care, they don't even peep in to see what is what . . .'

He went on elaborating his family problems and Nagaraj concluded it would be no use consulting Jayaraj. He asked why he should not give up framing and concentrate on his camera profession. Jayaraj replied, 'Everyone possesses a smuggled camera, and my profession is dwindling . . .' The smuggling of Japanese cameras was his favourite theme; before he could go on elaborating that subject, Nagaraj wanted to leave, realizing that Jayaraj was unusually dense.

Nagaraj felt that he was born in an unsympathetic world, unsuspected by him all these days. He decided that he would have to think deeply and find a solution himself. 'God helps those who help themselves,' he reminded himself as he walked away from Jayaraj towards the Saree Centre. Turning into Grove Street, he felt revived. The old lime-washed building in the shade of the margosa tree and the crowd of women passing in and out seemed to him a different world altogether. 'God helps those who help themselves,' kept drumming in some corner of his mind. He nodded to Coomar, lounging on his bolster, talking to a group of customers, mainly women and their escorts, quite a motley crew. On the fringe were silk weavers and yarn merchants waiting for an audience. Nagaraj genially nodded to Coomar and passed on to his seat, suppressing an impulse to enquire of Coomar if he believed in 'God helps those who help themselves', and if so what it meant and why God wanted to wait till the poor fellow helped himself, and was it fair on God's part? And if the help was not superfluous at this stage? His mind seethed with these metaphysical questions as he sat down in his chair and picked up the day book and cash vouchers. He felt more tranquil in this textile crowd and the sight of smug Coomar on his throne holding his court. The solidity of existence seemed restored for the time being; Narada and harmonium and all the travails in an unhelpful home receded into the background, although somewhere a corner of his brain was repeating, 'God helps . . . etc'

After his duties at Coomar's were done, he rose to go, putting away the account books. On the way out he threw a paternal farewell smile at Coomar, who was still busy in his court with a different set of courtiers and audience. He checked himself from uttering the 'God helps' formula. But later in the evening he had full scope to discuss the subject with Bari, whom he had to join for the evening study that day. Bari offered him his usual seat and was busy wrapping stationery and pencils for his customers. When he was free, Nagaraj asked, 'Bari, you are a philosopher. Will you tell me if you believe God helps those who help themselves?'

Without a moment's pause, he replied, 'That's my philosophy, otherwise do you think I could have developed this business? Tell me.' He looked so convinced of the basis of his existence that Nagaraj himself prayed secretly, 'God, please help me to help myself for a start. I do not know how to. It reminds me of an auspicious moment to start searching for an auspicious moment.' While Bari was rushing along with his reminiscences, Nagaraj followed his words to some extent while he was addressing his own prayer to God. Bari was just saying, 'Hamilton Bond sole agency would not have come to us without God's help . . .'

'How did you gain that favour?' Nagaraj asked.

'How?' asked Bari. 'By God's grace, of course. My father got Hamilton's signed portrait, which you still find in my home.'

They walked to Bari's house for the reading.

14

THE MOMENT NAGARAJ appeared before him with effusive words of welcome on his lips, Gopu, sitting cross-legged on the *pyol* with a jute handbag at his side, just said, 'Idiot,' and kept looking at him without further speech. Nagaraj was puzzled and could only ask, 'Who?' Gopu repeated, 'Idiot.' This time Nagaraj did not question but thought, 'Why is he calling me "idiot"? Should I not turn round and ask, "What is an idiot's brother?"' He just said, 'Sita has gone out to see her sister, who has arrived from Ceylon.' Gopu ignored this information. Nagaraj hoped he would not be called 'idiot' again and wished he could plug his ears with cotton wool, though it was hard to find.

Gopu had arrived earlier and, finding the house locked, was a little puzzled, never having seen this house locked before; he hesitated on the step with his jute bag in hand. At that moment the engineer emerged from the last house, obviously just starting for the bar. 'Hello! brother of brother,' he cried cheerily while passing, and Gopu wished he could hide his head somewhere. The engineer stopped to say, 'You are welcome to stay with me, only I am wifeless—but not a widower.'

Gopu was afraid of drunkards and just said, 'I will wait here.' 'The lady went away in the morning,' the engineer said, and passed on.

Gopu said, 'I am not going to ask where is Tim. It is useless to ask you.'

'Yes, yes,' said Nagaraj weakly, feeling that some agreement might propitiate him.

Gopu said, 'Two solid persons, a husband and wife living in your care, leave the house and you don't bother about it. Two solid persons just disappear, vanish into thin air, and you ask no question and have no answer.'

'No, no, I saw them go, but I could not ask questions.'

'Why? What choked your throat? Were you unable to speak?'

'Yes, in a way, you see, I had hardly settled down to my *puja*.'

'So? You didn't have the curiosity to ask, "Where are you going?" when you see someone in the house go out bag and baggage!'

'Yes, I wanted to ask, but I was wearing the ochre robe—'

'Ochre robe! That's another thing in your mad scheme.'

'You won't understand,' said Nagaraj within himself. 'You'll understand only *gobar* gas and cattle refuse,' but said aloud, 'I watched them pack up, I watched them go, but I told myself, "Let them. How far can they go, after all?" They did not know that I watched, did not understand that I had been very watchful, ever since the moment Tim cornered me with a sudden remark when I was coming from the bathroom, no, when I was going in . . .'

Gopu listened with an air of resignation. People passing along the street paused to listen to their conversation but resumed their course when the brothers also paused in their talk.

Gopu said, 'Should we sit here for the whole street to listen to what we say? Can't we go in?'

'Oh, yes, of course, I have a key. Sita took away one and gave me the duplicate. We could not find the duplicate at first, and she became impatient.'

'All right, open the door, let us go in,' said Gopu. 'I do not want to gather a crowd to listen to us. This is not a public meeting,' he said in a surly tone.

'It can't be,' Nagaraj said nervously, feeling that the best course would be to agree with whatever Gopu said. 'I am afraid Sita won't be back soon. She made some food and left it for the night; I think we can manage. If we had known you were coming . . .' Nagaraj said, opening the door.

'Oh shut up, more important things to talk about,' said Gopu, following him into the house.

'About what?' Nagaraj asked with an air of innocence. He wanted the subject of Tim to be delayed as long as possible. He knew he was exasperating the other, but he told himself, 'What have I to say to him? I only saw them leave, that is all I know, not more than what Gopu knows, but he bullies me like a lawyer, what is the use?' He said, 'No wonder you feel anxious, but no need, I know where he is.'

'Where?' asked Gopu anxiously. 'Why are you so excited? You used to say that you have friends who inform you of all that happens here—'

'Oh!' Gopu groaned in despair. 'We don't have to discuss that now. How am I to make you stick to the point?'

'Which point?' asked Nagaraj, still dodging the subject. They were sitting on the hall bench. Gopu changed his tactics. 'Come on, tell me from the beginning what happened . . .' in a conciliatory tone.

Nagaraj appreciated the change of tone arid decided to talk without dodging, but he did not know where to begin. He remained brooding, searching for the right opening line. 'Gopu wants it all from the beginning.' It began with Narada, of course, inevitably. 'You see, I have to go on with Narada . . .'

'I know your obsession, but what has it to do with Tim? We are talking about Tim, if you don't mind . . .'

'Of course, of course. The problem was no cotton wool was to be found anywhere. I began to wonder what had happened to all the cotton wool in the world.'

'Did you say cotton wool? What did Tim have to do with cotton wool? Did he plan to indulge in the cotton business? It is ruinous. I know speculators who have become beggars.'

'Yes, I know. Even Coomar once tried it but withdrew swiftly when he lost ten thousand in one bid. It's a treacherous business, really, and you are right.'

Gopu gritted his teeth and said, 'Yet, knowing it, you allowed him to play with fire. What sort of guardian are you? To think that the fool prefers you!'

Nagaraj felt it safer to let the other continue in his notion than correct him. To mention that he sought cotton bits to seal his ears against his daughter-in-law's music might not be a good policy. He listened quietly while Gopu went on fulminating against the cotton market, at last conceding, 'Left to himself, I knew he would come to grief in some such way.'

'Thank God, you are not calling him an unleashed donkey. If you call him that again I can't say what he might do.'

Realizing that he couldn't get anything out of Nagaraj if he spoke roughly, Gopu swallowed the remarks that came uppermost and asked in a gentle tone, 'Did he have nothing to say while leaving?'

'He might have spoken to Sita—not to me, as he knew when I wore the ochre robe—'

Gopu did not allow him to continue but just asked, 'On the previous day, did words pass between you?'

'I was going for my bath, he came out of his room and blocked my path saying, "Why did you go away while my wife was explaining her song and wanted to sing it to you?" I told him, "There was someone at the door," and he just said, "It is an insult and she wants to go away from here"; that's all he said and he left next morning while I was wearing the ochre robe.'

'You and your robe!' said Gopu severely. 'Has Sita no voice in all this?'

'Of course, he told her the same thing, and I had difficulty in convincing Sita that I did not mean to insult. Sita was unhappy, you know how much she dotes on him.'

'Oh, stop! Why could you not listen to that poor girl's song? Have you no ear, have you no courtesy or feeling? Everyone says that she sings so well. In Delhi she gives public performances . . .'

'True, true,' said Nagaraj, and commented within himself, 'Yes, possible here also, but for the cotton shortage,' while Gopu was completing his sentence, 'You go on saying "True, true", God knows what you mean by it.'

'She is . . .' Nagaraj began, and was not sure what to say. Gopu gave up his attempt to carry on a cogent conversation with his brother and just asked, 'Where are they now? At least tell me that clearly.'

'I have my own source of information. Not as ignorant as you think. The Talkative Man in Number One wanders all over the town, and keeps an eye on everyone. He told me that Tim is in Kismet.'

Gopu looked horrified. 'How can you tell me that so casually? Have you no feeling of any sort? Kismet! How could you let him go there with his wife?'

'I hear that they have given him an outhouse to live in with his family.'

'What for? Did Tim desert his home and parents in order to end up in a tavern? Did he marry only to keep a wife in a teahouse?'

'No, they are paying him a salary, and also to his wife for her music' The more Nagaraj spoke the more excited Gopu became, and in his rage jumped up and gripped Nagaraj by his shoulder. Nagaraj felt panicky. In his boyhood he was thrashed by his brother; would he do it again now? He prayed that Sita would appear miraculously and save him from physical harm. Seeing Gopu's face at close quarters he noted mentally, 'He has greying stubble on his chin and upper lip. Won't he shave at least when he comes into town? These rustics don't shave regularly whereas I can't show my face outside unless . . .' Gopu was shouting, 'What have you to say? Silence is no answer. I'll go to a court to get custody of my son . . .'

Nagaraj said, wriggling out of his grip, 'He is twenty-one and may declare that he likes to be where he is.'

Gopu loosened his grip and was in tears from the strain of talking to Nagaraj, and Nagaraj also felt moved. In the midst of his rage Gopu wondered how to classify his brother—whether as a moron or a crafty intriguer always avoiding the main issue on principle. He went back to his seat while Nagaraj said to himself, 'Almost what Cain did to Abel,' remembering suddenly his weekly

Bible lessons at Albert Mission High School. Observing his silence, Gopu concluded that he had taught him a lesson. They remained silent and Nagaraj suddenly said, 'I do not know how to make coffee. Shall we adjourn to the Boardless, if you don't mind the walk?'

'Oh, God!' Gopu cried, holding his head. 'Coffee be damned.'

Nagaraj said, 'Sita has made some food; it must suffice for both of us, if you feel hungry. You are too excited today, unnecessarily anxious about Tim. I have never seen you like this. I fear you are famished. If you ate, you would feel calmer. As I told you, there's enough for two; Sita always prepares liberally, always believing some extra demand would come unexpectedly—if not a guest, at least some poor soul at the door—never turns away anyone even if it is midnight.'

Gopu totally resigned himself, realizing the impossibility of carrying on any useful talk with Nagaraj about Tim. He said in a quiet voice, as if surrendering to the fate that had thrown him in the company of a man like Nagaraj, 'All right, let us eat.'

Nagaraj cried, 'Ah, that is the right spirit!' and became fussy. He told his brother, 'First change and have a wash.' He ceremoniously threw open the door of Tim's room with, 'Back to your old room—we will talk about Tim tomorrow first thing. Sita will also be here. Now eat and rest.' Gopu felt helpless. He sat down to his supper when Nagaraj laid the plates, called him in, seated him on a silver-studded plank and served his food with many apologies for its inadequacy. 'The food is cold, but I do not dare to light a fire . . .'

'Never mind,' said Gopu and ate in silence. After food, Nagaraj brought him a mug of water to rinse his mouth and wash his fingers. When they went back to the hall bench he produced the silver plate with betel leaves and nut. Chewing, a great state of tranquillity befell them, and this was the right moment for Sita to return. She was relieved to find the atmosphere so calm, having been worrying all along how Gopu would react to Tim's departure. She greeted her brother-in-law formally, with respect, avoiding the subject of Tim, and passed in. When she came out of her room, Nagaraj said, 'We have eaten.'

'It was good,' said Gopu.

Sita said, 'Had I known you were coming . . .'

Gopu merely repeated, 'It was all right.'

'Have you had anything to eat?' asked Nagaraj.

'My sister has come from Ceylon and we had our food.' She turned round and went into the kitchen, beckoned to Nagaraj and whispered, 'Was it all right? Should you not have told me he was coming?'

'I never knew.'

She said, 'I found this postcard on the window sill. It must have been lying there for two days, there is not much dust on it. You never noticed it . . .'

'You did not notice it either, you were away only this morning. How is your sister?'

'I think you must have picked up the card and dropped it on the window sill without reading it . . .'

'Why didn't you read it, when you found it on the window sill . . .?'

'I noticed it only after coming in now. Didn't he mention it?'

'I don't remember, he was talking so much.'

Finding them talking in whispers, Gopu got up and retired to his room.

Morning found them approaching the situation afresh. As soon as they were ready for the day, Gopu sat on the hall bench, subdued because of Sita's presence in the house. Nagaraj was still inaccessible, dressed in ochre and in the *puja* room, while Gopu sat silently fretting on the hall bench. As soon as Nagaraj was available Gopu asked, 'What do you propose to do? You expected to get an inspiration in the morning.'

'Morning hours are the best,' Nagaraj said, in order to keep the conversation at a safe level.

Gopu added a query and an answer. 'For what? For cleaning the cowshed?'

Nagaraj laughed with extra happiness, treating it as a joke and telling himself, 'This fellow will never forget cattle sheds and *gobar* gas even if he is placed in London,' and asked aloud, in continuation of his secret thought, 'Don't you ever wish to see London?'

Gopu was taken aback, but taking it casually as one of the irrelevancies to be expected from his brother, said, 'Yes, if Tim keeps vanishing like this.'

Another burst of laughter from Nagaraj, whose only aim was to maintain a cheerful atmosphere in order to convey an impression to Sita that all was well. Sita came out of the kitchen with relief in her face and asked, 'Will your brother want any special item for lunch?'

Gopu replied directly, 'Oh, Sita, don't bother about all that. Anything will do. My thoughts are on Tim. I must get him back and tell Charu, who has been moping and crying ever since we heard the news—'

'What news? Who is that busybody who tells you unnecessary things?' asked Nagaraj (without uttering a word).

Gopu pleaded, 'Sita, tell me what he said before leaving . . .'

'They left abruptly and there was not much speech. I was boiling water for the rice and when I heard his voice and turned around he was gone; even before I could ask him what was happening, he was gone with his wife. I ran to the door but he had arranged for an autorickshaw and was gone.' She had tears in her eyes when she added, 'I don't know what has upset them. I am praying and promising to the god in our temple to light a hundred wicks if he comes back safe.'

Nagaraj blurted out, 'There must have been more than one hundred wicks in the packet I brought you . . .'

Sita changed the subject immediately. 'You didn't ask for breakfast; have an early lunch?'

Nagaraj said, 'Should you ask? Have it ready. We will eat if we are feeling hungry. I always eat before going to the Boeing Centre, that saves a lot of labour for the lady . . .' in a jocular tone. 'But today I will stay back with you.'

Looking at Sita, who was fuming inside at her husband's way of speech, Gopu just said, 'I must first see the boy, wherever he may be. Other things only later. I will go to Kismet. Where is it?'

'Oh, we can't go there,' said Nagaraj. 'They drink whisky and such things there. Don't worry that he is getting into bad habits—although he has eau-de-Cologne sprayed over his clothes sometimes!'

Gopu frowned and said, 'Eau-de-Cologne! What for? What is it?'

'It's a scent.'

Gopu ignored this as one of Nagaraj's habitual irrelevancies and said, 'He should not be there. I must go there immediately; where is it?'

'I have not been there at all, but I know it is in New Extension.'

'Come with me,' said Gopu peremptorily, and Nagaraj looked at his wife for help.

She said, 'Go and help your brother to bring him home.'

Nagaraj felt let down by his wife, and said weakly, 'I have never been there. I don't know anyone there.'

Gopu looked at him and said in a firm tone, 'You are going with me.'

Nagaraj said, rubbing his chin, 'I have not had a shave today. . .' and threw an apprehensive look at his brother's unshaven state. Gopu was not in a mood to continue the talk. Nagaraj looked at Sita to see if she might have second thoughts and help him out. She looked away, and Nagaraj thought, 'Lady Macbeth! You want your husband to be damned. But Shakespeare has nowhere indicated that Macbeth had to go to a tavern . . .'

Gopu got busy to leave. He went in and came out a moment later wearing his grey coat buttoned up to his neck. He hustled Nagaraj, who pleaded, 'I am hungry, aren't you?'

'Sita, give him a glass of buttermilk. I can't wait.'

Nagaraj appealed, 'Let us go after the meal.'

'Yes, food will be ready soon. It will be better to eat before starting out,' added Sita, 'as you may not know when you will be back.'

After food, Nagaraj had no choice but to go in and groom himself as best as he could before his mirror. He then started out with his brother, looking back at Sita standing at the street door with a last hope that she would pull him back. She was cold and firm and advised Nagaraj in an undertone, 'Tell that poor girl that we miss her music'

'Impossible,' Nagaraj thought. 'That means no Narada ever. . .'

They went down Kabir Street to Market Road, where an autorickshaw could be found, Nagaraj dreading his brother's propensity to haggle and quarrel with the driver over the fare. He said to his brother, 'All the auto-drivers are my friends. Let me pay the fare.'

Gopu did not pay any attention to his suggestion but walked down Market Road in grim silence, looking straight ahead. He seemed determined to walk to New Extension. Nagaraj said, 'It's far off, beyond the level crossing.'

'Do you know how much I trudge in the fields every morning?'

'Must be a lot . . .'

'We have to walk to the next village sometimes.'

'Sturdy fellow!' Nagaraj said. 'But here in the town . . .' he began.

Gopu did not encourage him to continue his sentence, but said, 'When I meet Tim and talk to him, you don't talk.'

'Why?' asked Nagaraj.

'It is so.'

'You could have left me behind. I told you I would wait for you at home . . .' Nagaraj ventured to say.

'Ask someone where is this Kismet.'

There was a passer-by whom Nagaraj accosted. He did not know, much to Gopu's annoyance. Gopu ordered, 'Ask someone intelligent. This man looks a ragamuffin.'

'Why can't you do it yourself? Am I your slave or lackey?' asked Nagaraj inwardly. But he said out loud suddenly, 'We should ask Tim himself! Ah, there he is!'

Gopu could not believe his eyes. There he was: Tim, carrying a shopping bag. He hadn't seen them, was about to turn into a lane. Both the brothers were overwhelmed at the sight of him and shouted, 'Tim! Tim!' Tim turned round, looked at them on the corner, and it was his turn to disbelieve his eyes. He stared at them and stopped. The meeting was emotional. Gopu's cheeks were wet with tears. Nagaraj found himself tongue-tied. Gopu said, 'You live here?' looking around at the narrow lane, littered with rubbish in a colony of thatched huts. Tim gave no direct reply. He led them to a stone bench in a corner and made them sit on it.

'Where do you live?' the brothers asked.

Tim flourished his arm to indicate a direction and asked, 'Why did you come here?'

The brothers answered simultaneously, 'To call you back home.'

'I am not coming,' said Tim, hugging his shopping bag.

Gopu was speechless with rage and disappointment and said, 'I am not going back without you.'

Tim ignored the challenge.

'Where is Saroja?'

'In the house.'

'She is keeping well?'

'How is her harmonium?'

Nagaraj wanted to say, 'If you live in a hut, a harmonium must sound terrible in the narrow space.' But Nagaraj remembered his brother's order not to talk. Still, he managed to say, 'We miss you both. Sita wants Saroja back urgently . . .'

'Why?' asked Tim, and did not wait for an answer. He suddenly turned away from them.

Gopu said, 'We want to see Saroja.'

'She has gone out.'

'Where?'

No answer.

'We wish to visit your home . . .'

'It is far off . . .'

'But you said it was here . . .'

No answer.

Tim suddenly left them sitting on the stone bench. The brothers stared at each other not knowing what to make of it. After waiting and watching the direction in which he went, Gopu said to Nagaraj, 'Stay here, I will find out where he lives.' He followed in the direction in which Tim had gone. Nagaraj sat there brooding. Tim seemed to look well. Then why worry? There were instances in the history of mankind where people walked out suddenly, like Buddha, and became famous, actually doing better than those who stuck to home and followed the conventions. Tim would some day emerge as a world philosopher or leader. Till then, would he be living in one of the hovels? Was it necessary? He could live in Kabir Street and become great. But he remembered with regret that no world figure or even local leader ever came from his street; he remembered that when Mahatma Gandhi passed this way, they could not find anyone to offer him flowers from Kabir Street. Not even a trace of one great personality in a hundred years. But probably Saroja would become a famous singer with her harmonium. Horrible instrument. But for some mysterious reason people seemed to favour it. Why think of people? At home Sita herself seemed to enjoy the harmonium noise, having been a player when he had gone to inspect her, his future bride, years ago. His mother put an end to it. Good mother! What is to happen to Narada in this jungle of harmonium lovers? He stopped thinking, and asked, 'Where is this Kismet? No sign of it anywhere . . .' Was it fictitious? But the Talkative Man seemed to be a regular visitor there. Bachelor and moneyed, and no one to question even if he got drunk every day . . . He sensed a foul smell around and noticed a garbage mound at his back being rummaged by crows and hens. 'Where is Gopu? How long should I wait in this stench?' Thoughtless of Gopu to leave like this. But why blame him while he himself didn't possess enough sense to resist him?

Nagaraj was stuck there much like Casablanca on the deck of the burning ship (Nagaraj's literary allusions floating up from the depths of his subliminal self). He sat on the stone bench attempting to swat the flies attacking him from the garbage pile, and felt choked with the stench. A young goatherd stood in front of him, staring while his animal was nosing in the rubbish heap. Nagaraj felt annoyed. 'Go away, what's your business here?' he said commandingly, surprised at the tone he had assumed. The boy moved off obediently. Nagaraj cried, 'Hey, what about your animal?' The boy ignored his question and hurried away. 'That goat may not be his, or may find its way home,' he reflected.

The sun was scorching. 'Not an inch of shade anywhere . . . Horrible place, never suspected Malgudi could be so bad. Must talk to someone. Chakravarthi, the Municipal Chairman, is lazy and indifferent; also I don't know him at all, and even if I came face to face with him I wouldn't be able to attack him, so what is the use of complaining? But whatever may be the reason, it's his business to see that garbage doesn't develop into a hillock anywhere. But what can anyone do? Quite a lot of junglees have invaded the town, attracted by the promise of work on the new railway line to Mempi. Too much of a dream; they will not take it up in this generation, although ministers make speeches.'

He felt hungry, had never strayed so far away from the Boardless at tiffin time. He guessed that the time must be three in the afternoon, judging from the slant of the western sun. 'What does Gopu mean by leaving me like this? He thinks he can do what he pleases with me, just an order, "Stay here," and I obey like a fool. How long? Till the end of Time when the sun would be extinguished and deluge and darkness overtake the universe, as in the chapters of *Narad Puran.*' And he wouldn't know his way back, and what was to happen to Sita? 'She'd become a petrified statue in Kabir Street.' He shuddered at this vision.

An old man who was passing along stopped to ask, 'Are you in pain?'

Nagaraj smiled and said, 'No, but I heard some noise, must be a strange bird flying low.'

The old man lingered, seemed willing to talk, and Nagaraj felt kindly towards him and asked, 'Where do you live?'

'At the level crossing; they have given me a small shed, and when the train passes I warn people and hold a flag. Even then people get run over sometimes. What can I do? Before the signal comes up people want to dash across and reach the other side in a hurry . . . Oh, after that the crowd and police and the wailing of relatives! . . . I am sick of this life. I have served the railway for thirty years. I was a porter at the station at one time and no worry there.' He was talking and also walking away.

Nagaraj watched him go though he wanted to enquire about Kismet. He let him go. 'I wish he had stopped to talk to me. But everyone is in a hurry and passing on. I am stationary like a milestone. The procession passes. Why can't I also pass instead of being a milestone? People take advantage of my milestone nature. Gopu called me 'idiot' this morning, or was it yesterday? I can't remember; this blazing sun is melting my brain and memory. Gopu was right. If I am not an idiot, who else could be one? Gopu has a genius for coining phrases, 'unleashed donkey' is his term and Tim has proved so, otherwise why would he be carrying a shopping bag in this garbage colony? If we had at least stopped to utter a word of explanation, we could have stuck to him and not let him off so easily. Gopu has messed it up by following him, leaving me behind. How long should I wait here? He has condemned me to live in this stench, and I am powerless to move. I think he casts a spell on an idiot—must have practised it at his *gobar* gas farm. Villagers would be up to anything. Otherwise why can't I use my head and rise and walk off? I fear him. If he comes back and doesn't find me, he'll blow up in anger or miss his way home? Laughable; even before I did, he knew this town and loafed around all day with his friends, driving me off from his company, and Father used to thrash him from time to time. I was not considered fit for their company. Phew! What a notion! I have survived and they have vanished into thin air. Probably his gang is still there, but fat and old and unrecognizable, and secretly in touch with Gopu in the village, spying on me and Tim all the time. Gopu constantly brags, "I know what's going on here. I have my own sources . . ." He means all his toothless, bald friends who have no better business than to spy, crafty beggars!'

Far off a train whistled. Nagaraj thought of the level-crossing watchman and hoped he would have reached his post in good time. 'I forgot to enquire what he was doing here in this stinking place instead of minding the crossing. Must have gone to visit a friend or relative. In his absence who would mind the railway crossing? No wonder people get run over. At this rate he will be responsible for reducing the population of this town, which is already getting crowded with jungle folk. Jungle folk should remain in jungles, otherwise they will get run over at level crossings. Ultimately the authorities will put up gates at the crossing to save the lives of men, not to speak of cattle; it's a sin to kill a cow, so they say in all our *shastras*, and yet we don't protect them. They must put up a gate soon . . .'

He would tell the Talkative Man to write about it to the newspapers. 'What is a journalist for unless he acts as the mouthpiece of the community? Ministers will promise, and we may get it, as well as the Mempi Railway, at the end of Kaliyuga, when a new Avatar of Vishnu called Kalki is expected, riding on a white horse and wielding a blazing sword. "When virtue disappears and evil flourishes, I'll come and destroy the world," has promised God in the Gita.' He paused to verify if he was quoting the scripture correctly, but was not sure. 'Is this the place to recite the scriptures?' Amidst this rubbish and pigs, which he noticed were now rummaging the garbage where the goat had left off a little while ago. 'Why should I stay in these surroundings?—one who has belonged for generations to a Kabir Street family, honoured and respected. Gopu is responsible for reducing me to this wretched state.' He felt furious at this thought and briskly got up, muttering, 'Let him blow up when he comes back. If he can't find his way home, let him stay where he pleases—will serve him right . . . "Am I my brother's keeper?" asked Cain, and Gopu is Cain, he has almost killed me . . .'

He got up resolutely and retraced his steps. 'I was a fool not to have thought of it earlier.' It was tiring, and he had to trudge for nearly one hour before he could reach his familiar world of Market Road east. He looked at Bari's as if he had been lost to this world, and felt reassured. He resisted the impulse to enter Bari's and speak to him of Narada. He had missed his lessons for several days now. There were still five books of notes untouched, thanks to Saroja's harmonium and Tim's walk-out, so he could let Bari alone for a considerable time. Would it not be proper to inform him? He might conclude that Narada was dropped. He thought of arresting his step and shouting into the shop, 'I am still at it, don't imagine I am giving up Narada. As long as I live . . .' The meeting might not end in such a businesslike manner. Bari would invite him in to see some new stock of this and that and talk of Hamilton Bond, and chase Sunil up the ladder or out to fetch tea. All that would take time. He was hungry. First things first. He hurried on to the Boardless. Varma welcomed him, and Nagaraj had a feeling of being restored to civilization after having been abducted by some demon and confined in hell.

Varma, sitting on his throne-like seat at the cash table, asked, 'What has happened to you? I have not seen you for three days.'

Nagaraj wondered for a moment how to explain. 'Oh, home duties. My wife was away to see her sister from Ceylon, and with a daughter-in-law in the house . . .'

'Oh, I didn't know you had a grown-up son.'

'Not exactly, but almost one. I am fond of him . . .' He fumbled on, afraid that he might utter some compromising statement about Tim and his Kismet. He knew Varma held strong views on Kismet but he had a short memory. 'Thank God he doesn't remember Tim, though he has seen him on several occasions.' Varma was muddled enough not to remember anyone among the scores of patrons coming in every day.

Nagaraj thought it best to change the subject. 'From Ceylon my sister's wife has brought cloves, dark and pungent; we don't see such cloves here. Only insipid stuff in our shops.'

'You are right; they extract oil and market only the chaff. For my sweets, I get them directly from Kabul or somewhere: dark ones, thick and oily . . .'

Nagaraj ordered tiffin and coffee and moved to a corner table where he could eat in peace. He noticed the Talkative Man come in and take his seat on a special chair beside Varma's throne, as had been the custom from time immemorial. When he noticed Nagaraj, TM came over and joined him. Drinking his coffee he said, 'Nag, I was busy the whole day with your brother.'

'Where is he?'

'Well, it's a long story . . .'

Nagaraj had to get it off his chest, could not contain himself. 'Fool of a fellow, he made me wait at a stinking place and never turned up. Where is he?'

'Gone back.'

'Home?'

'Yes, to his village.'

Nagaraj said, 'Strange man, to keep me waiting and go away without telling me!'

'Listen to me, let me finish my coffee first and then we will talk in a quiet corner. Too much babble and noise around here.'

They left after coffee. Nagaraj was unable to contain his curiosity. They walked down Market Road towards Ellaman Street. Nagaraj felt he was being teased by the other. He reflected as they walked along, 'Why should I show any interest? I don't care what has happened to a fellow who cast me on the rubbish dump and made me starve under the hot sun . . .'

The Talkative Man said, 'I've to peep in at a house in Ellaman Lane and take some notes and then I am free to talk to you.'

Nagaraj's curiosity was aroused and he asked, 'What, notes for your newspaper?'

'Nag, yes, this man claims to be able to stand on his head continuously for seventy-two hours without food and wants to get into the *Guinness Book*.'

'What is that?' Nagaraj asked, saying to himself, 'I don't care whatever it is; if you do not tell me in a few words about Gopu, I will turn round and go home. I am not keen on your company at the moment. . .' The Talkative Man was elaborating on the subject of the *Guinness Book*, all of which fell on deaf ears.

'You must tell me in six words what has happened instead of keeping me on tenterhooks. I am not interested if someone stands upside-down for a whole lifetime. In a sense, most people manage their lives upside-down: Trisanku inherited a whole heaven which was upside-down, himself permanently suspended at this angle through eternity. But where was Narada when all this happened?'

'How thoughtful you have become these days!'

'Oh, I have to think of—'

'Mostly about Tim, I am sure.'

'How did you guess?'

'One doesn't need to guess; your mind is an open book.'

'You are mistaken, my boy, while I'm myself not sure where my thoughts go,' thought Nagaraj, and decided to conceal the subject uppermost in his mind. He remained glum and silent while TM dashed into a house on the way, leaving him standing under a street lamp. 'Today,' reflected Nagaraj, waiting, 'everyone seems to plan to sentence me to wait. Thank God there is no garbage here; fairly clean, only a little cow dung here and there, which might appeal to Gopu—he might love to take it home to his village and feed the *gobar* gas plant . . .' He trembled at the thought of Gopu, in suspense of what might be in store when TM would speak. Perverse fellow: if he had said whatever it might be over their coffee, where they had all the time, which he spent in local gossip about sales tax corruptions . . .

Till they reached the river steps and sat down with their feet in the cool river, TM avoided the subject, and then began, 'You are dying, I know, to hear about Gopu. I'll tell you only this. He has gone back.'

'Where?'

'To his village home. He went straight to the bus stand.'

'But his bag is in my house. Hasn't he taken it?'

'No. The bus stand was nearby and he left.'

Nagaraj thought, 'You are known as the Talkative Man, but you don't know how to begin and carry on the story.' But he said aloud, 'How do you know that he has left?'

'Because he stuck to me the whole day. Till I saw him off I could not attend to any other work.'

'He left me sitting alone and then stuck to you? It is absurd. Didn't even take leave of me.'

'How could he, while you were so far away? Don't you want to know how I was caught up?'

Nagaraj, for some obscure reason, wanted to seem indifferent, while longing to cry out, 'Oh, tell me, tell me everything—don't delay.'

'I felt a little shocked when I saw him in New Extension, a more incongruous fixture one cannot imagine in that background. I could not recognize him in this setting of villas and avenues, having seen him only in your company in Kabir Street. Moreover, I never had much to do with him. That type of village elder usually puts me off. At the turning of New Extension main street, he was going and he spotted me before I spotted him, otherwise it would have been a different story. I was riding my bicycle and passed him as he came up, wearing his grey coat, striding along resolutely with the look of a man out to smash something. There was a Fierce glint in his eye. I didn't recognize him but said to myself, "Here is a man I would never like to collide with." His face was covered with perspiration. He was swinging his arms like an athlete.'

Nagaraj said, 'He started out without a shave.'

'Yes. I noticed the stubble and his pink-edged *dhoti,* and took my bicycle off in a wide detour—you know why?'

'In order to avoid him.'

'Ah, you have understanding!' cried TM appreciatively. 'You are right, I didn't want to meet him; some instinct, I suppose!'

'Still he has not told me anything,' Nagaraj thought with some irritation. 'Let him go on like this a whole year by this river, and I am not going to ask, "What happened? Why did he leave me baking in the sun beside that rubbish dump on a hot stone?"' Indulging in such private thoughts, he missed some of the connecting sentences that the other had been uttering. He had also spent some moments enjoying the rumble of the river; the low splash and swish and the far-off strains of rough music from cartmen crossing Nallappa's Grove while urging their animals on, the sounds softened by the distance. He thought, 'Birds are just starting to come back to the trees,' while the Talkative Man was concluding, 'And so I had to resign myself to the inevitable and set aside all my plans for the day and guide him to Kismet. After all, I said to myself, he is an old family friend, though he looks tough. But he would not leave, holding on to the handle of my bicycle; he looked mad, I tell you. His eyes were bloodshot from walking in the sun. Was he starving?'

'Oh no, Sita insisted upon feeding us before we left.'

'But he looked fatigued.'

'So was 1, waiting for him . . . Serves him right,' added Nagaraj TM said, 'Listen, don't interrupt me. I lose the thread . . .'

'And also the needle?' Nagaraj asked soundlessly, and laughed within at the quip.

'He created a scene at the door of Kismet. The sentry would not allow him to enter because of a dress regulation in that club)—no one clad in a *dhoti* is permitted to enter the hall. Your brother was just wearing a rough *dhoti* and his grey coat, and he challenged the sentry, "You are descended from which heaven? Are you all Europeans here?" I tried to intervene, "There is a by-law, we will change it soon, till then . . ." "I don't care," he cried. "I must see my son who is held here. I'll inform the police . . . ! You can't stop me. I won't go without him!"

'"There is no one inside at this hour." "Where is he?" he cried. "You are lying, you have hidden him here! I won't go till I see him. Do what you like . . ." He sat down cross-legged right in the middle of the entrance. "You produce my son, or let me in to seek him out . . ." I was respected in the club, where I have been a member since it opened. I regretted I ever showed him the way.'

'Do you drink whisky all day?' Nagaraj wished to know, picturing him in that background, lounging and dissipating. 'No wonder you are hardly to be seen . . .' But aloud, 'Every day! All the time! You must he busy, very busy . . .'

'Indeed I am. I have a corner where I do my reports after news-hunting in the city, before going on to the railway station to despatch the letter. I also meet a lot of people there . . .'

'And more whisky then?' Nagaraj thought, but said, 'You have an interesting life.'

'That we will discuss later. Now, about your brother. While he sat there no one could pass in without jumping over him. The Secretary arrived and asked, "Why are you here? Who are you?" "I have come to take my son, Krishnaji and they won't let me in . . ." The Secretary looked at his dress and unshaven face, and decided that he was dealing with a crazy visitor, and was guarded. He threw a look at me and I nodded. He whispered to the watchman, who went in and brought a chair and placed it in a corner of the veranda, and said to Gopu, "Go and sit in that chair, sir, you should not obstruct . . ."

'"Where is my son?" Gopu demanded without budging.

'"Take that chair, he'll come."

'"No, I don't want any chair. I want to go in and search."

'The Secretary was irritated and said, "Only members are allowed in . . ."

'"Is my son a member? If so, what does he do?"

'"I'm not here to answer your questions. You please go, otherwise . . ." I knew what he meant. There was a strongman on the staff at the bar who had to persuade or push out troublesome customers. I had been passive and quiet, but at this point I beckoned to the Secretary and whispered, "Be kind to him, he is a respectable man; let us be tactful."

'"He must leave before members start coming. Can't be blocking the way . . ."

'I said, "I'll take him in as my guest."

'"Till we change the by-laws about dress . . ." he began.

'The Secretary was a funny man, always concerned with bylaws and daily complaining that the President was too slow and indifferent and would not convene the committee. While he was being eloquent on the subject, I had to keep telling him, "We must do something about that man." Gopu watched us like a bear in a trap. Also I remembered he used to picket liquor shops and stores selling foreign cloth by lying across the doorway in those days when young men joined the satyagraha movement started by Mahatma Gandhi. They called in the strongman when they found Gopu adamant. When the strongman tried to lift him, Gopu proved a match for him. All the peasant strength in him came to the surface. "Keep your hands off. Don't touch me, you fool!" he cried. The strongman was nonplussed, and stood still. The Secretary said, "Take him out, I am ordering you." Members started coming in. They stood about for a moment watching him and passed in, jumping over him to reach the card tables or the bar without waste of time. A man scowled at the obstruction and demanded of the Secretary, "What is this? Who is he? Why don't you clear the way? How do you expect us to get in?"

'Gopu just repeated, "I have come to take away my son."

'The Secretary said, "He has not come yet."

'"You are lying, hiding him; I know he must be inside," said Gopu. Some members stood around in groups. The Secretary told the strongman, "Take this man off the door and put him down in that chair, and keep him there." The strongman, used to obeying only such specific orders, bent down and encircled his arms around Gopu as a preliminary to heaving him up. Gopu shrieked in his ear, "I have told you not to touch me; get away, you fool!" I did not know what to do, so moved away and hid myself behind a pillar. The Secretary repeated to the strongman, "Take him, I say, don't you hear me? What are you waiting for, you fool?" The strongman wailed, "He is like a stone. Can't shake him . . .!"

'"Take him, I say, and throw him out." At this, the strongman tried a stranglehold grip on Gopu; now Gopu disentangled his hand and hit the strongman in the face so hard that the strongman reeled back, and when he recovered and came on again with a war cry, determined to maintain his reputation, Gopu just flicked him off, and the strongman tottered back and fell off the veranda into a flowerbed below. When he picked himself up and tried to make another attempt, I said to him softly, "Don't. He may kill you." The strongman accepted my advice and retreated, somewhat bruised in mind and body. I felt proud of Gopu. Never knew a Kabir Street fellow-being could be so strong.'

'Was my brother hurt?' Nagaraj asked solicitously.

'Far from it,' said the TM. 'The strongman was the one who

was demolished. I am sure he will lose his job, being employed chiefly for clearing the club of members who refuse to leave after closing time. Now Gopu seemed to have damaged his reputation. Gopu sat tight, repeating like a mantra, "Give me back my son . . ." A circle formed around him of some men who were pleading with him to rise and go to the chair and wait for his son. Members were discreet enough not to go too near him. Someone was asking, "Who is his son?"

'"That young fellow who works here, and his wife is the one who plays the harmonium and sings in the evenings."'

'Even here!' reflected Nagaraj.

'"Send for him at once," ordered the President of the club.'

'"He has already arrived and slipped in by the other door."'

'"Call him!"'

'"He refuses to come out!"'

'"Tell him his father is waiting, creating a scene . . ."'

'"We have told him!" The end of it was that Tim refused to meet his father. When Gopu learnt that Tim would not recognize him, he rose to his feet, much to everyone's relief. I was afraid he might dash in and bite someone, but he only stood at the door for a moment, looked for me in the crowd and nodded, then turned and went down the steps. I joined him at the gate. He said, "Take me to the bus stand, I am going back."

'"To Kabir Street?"'

'"No, to my village."'

'I led him to the bus stand. He got into his bus without a word.'

'Did he not want to take his jute bag which he has left behind?' asked Nagaraj, inanely.

15

A WEEK PASSED. Sita went on grumbling about the incident, and the indignity suffered by Gopu, for which she somehow held Nagaraj responsible. She kept saying, 'You should not have left him alone.' Nagaraj thought, 'This woman will not understand my position. No use my repeating that he had asked me to wait for him. Perhaps she doesn't believe my word; she doesn't want to. All the blame on me!' Nagaraj received a postcard from Gopu, with the message: *I have no son. I disown him. You have misappropriated and ruined him completely. You may adopt him and assign your property to him as your successor so that you may have someone who will have the right to ignite the funeral pyre when you die . . . being as you are without an issue even after so many years of married life and I know how you have steadily worked to achieve this purpose all your life, plucking him away from me and Charu when he was only two months old.*

Nagaraj was agitated when he read the card; he resolved to suppress it and not let Sita see it. But she had been the one to receive it from the postman when Nagaraj was away at the Boeing Centre. She shed tears when she read it, but simply dropped it on the window sill and did not refer to it when Nagaraj came home, leaving it to him to discover it.

Nagaraj felt choked while picturing himself on the funeral pyre with Tim as his successor applying the burning faggot, according to the rules, in order to ensure a smooth passage to heaven. He suddenly felt touched by Gopu's solicitude to send him heavenward smoothly, where probably material for Narada would be more directly accessible, or even the sage himself might materialize and guide him. Death has its good points. But a son at the firing point was essential; after all, Gopu's suggestion for adoption might be well intentioned, though crude-sounding. Nagaraj thought he should find out more about the process of adoption. Might not be a bad idea, after all. He decided to discuss it with Sita at an appropriate time. He must consult the old family priest first. Whenever it might happen, he was going to ask to be sent upward in his ochre robes, which had all along prepared him for his final journey in small daily doses . . .

He thought of Sita in this connections widowed and forlorn after being inseparable from him for thirty or forty years, and was filled with pity for her, all alone in this vast house. But she would have Tim as her adopted son, and the harmonium-playing daughter-in-law (through adoption, of course). In any case there was not likely to be any objection or trouble, and she herself loved that horrible instrument. Saroja could tote it around the whole house, sit down anywhere she liked and release the cacophony. He would not be there to bear and suffer, unless he came back as a ghost. Would he have to haunt Kabir Street? He felt somewhat lighter and pleasant while viewing himself as a ghost, but the picture of his body on the funeral pyre, with Sita bewildered and crushed, overwhelmed him with self-pity and tears streamed down his cheeks, and he was convulsed with an involuntary sob just at the moment when Sita came up to the *pyol*. She observed his state, took his hand and suggested, 'Let us go in. People are watching; I see the engineer from the last house coming . . . Let us go in quick.' She led him in to the hall bench. They sat there for a while in silence. She said, controlling the tremor in her voice, 'You must not take it to heart. Your brother has always been somewhat rough with you, but he means no harm; he must be upset with Tim. But what can anyone do with him? I think your brother must be feeling it more keenly for Charu's sake; after all, she is the mother and wants her son. What can anyone do with Tim? He cannot be influenced. Don't bother about his postcard, he has written it in a bad mood. At Kismet Tim should have come out to see him . . .'

For a few days a terrible gloom. Nagaraj felt it acutely. 'It is better to have loved and lost than never to have loved at all,' he kept repeating irrelevantly, another quotation sticking out in some corner of his mind. 'Where is it from?' he speculated constantly. 'Shakespeare? Of course, source of ninety per cent of the world's wealth of quotations. No—ninety-nine per cent. The balance of one per cent shared by the Bible, Koran, Bhagavad Gita, and Palgrave's *Golden Treasury*.' He felt proud that he was familiar with such literary treasures. How? He was a little confounded since he had no memory of any regular studies; whatever he remembered was from cursory, casual browsing. Mostly at the Town Hall library in the early days when he regularly visited the library, actually hanging around the place from morning till evening in the days of the benign old librarian, who allowed him a lot of freedom to pull out a volume from any shelf. More than anything, he let him rummage among book dumps left there by neighbouring families who wanted to clear the space in their homes. There in the dumps were a miscellany of publications, from outdated catalogues and law reports to world classics in tatters. Nagaraj spent much time squatting beside the dump in an antechamber, browsing. Recollecting, he felt he had gathered a jumble of literary tit-bits, and most of them had sunk deep in his mind and floated up at unexpected, irrelevant moments. He was filled with self-admiration, but realized that he could not have continued this practice: the old librarian retired and a hotheaded youngster took his place. Nagaraj remembered with some bitterness how brusquely he had dismissed the study of

Narada. 'Also, I must say in fairness to everyone, after the Boeing Saree Centre came into being, I had no time for library visits.' He chuckled within himself as he thought of his brother Gopu, who had no doubt passed BA—God knows by what miracle!—but an ignoramus, boor, and writer of offensive postcards and one who had made himself ridiculous at Kismet. All that he cared for was his *gobar* gas plant; that was his university and library combined. He had a good memory and could mug up his textbooks and pass, that was all. Did he know a single quotation from anywhere? He chuckled again. At this moment Sita came out and noticed his elation. 'Sita, don't you agree that Gopu is an ignoramus?'

'He is a BA,' she said.

'So am I,' said Nagaraj.

'Why think of it now?' she asked. 'It was so long ago.'

'Wonder how he passed? Must have bribed the professors,' he said mischievously.

'Why don't you think of something else? Always obsessed with your brother . . .'

'But do you think he remembers Shakespeare?'

'Think of something else,' she said and went in.

Nagaraj reflected, 'She is a good girl, won't make things worse by agreeing with me. Good girl, Sita. So is Charu, Gopu's wife, though somewhat haughty. Am I right? No, why should I call her haughty? Unreasonable thought. My anger with Gopu is reflected on her; unfair. One may say the worst things of him and be right, still fall short of the full description. He is like one of those *asuras* in the Puranas, headstrong and haughty and vile. But in every case they had a downfall, if not destroyed totally. Evil destroys itself, say our scriptures. How will Gopu's downfall come?' He gloated over this prospect for a while. 'Maybe by some catastrophe such as a thunderbolt hitting his *gobar* gas plant, or through an obstinate pest attacking his farm or a poisonous seed spreading amongst his grass, laying prostrate his cattle. With his hundreds of coconut, banana, mango and guava trees gone, and his farmhouse attached for unpaid taxes, he will be thrown out, and, carrying his bags, trudge all the distance from his village on foot, a bankrupt in rags with Charu hiding at his back, and knock on my door. What would he my first word of greeting? "Who are you, stranger? Your face is familiar!" Or should I say, "Begone, you hot-headed evil man. If you repent sincerely, you may step in and Sita will give you food . . ."'

After this daydream he felt lighter at heart. He felt he had now got something of his own. One good deed Gopu had performed was to confound the Kismet gang and puncture the strongman. 'Going off to the bus without a word to us, not even taking back his jute bag. What did it contain?' Nagaraj felt an uncontrollable curiosity. He left his seat, softly went in, hesitated for a moment to be sure that the way was clear and that Sita was in the back yard, beyond the third court. Stepped in and shut the door of the middle room where Gopu had been staying. He found Gopu's jute bag kept in a corner. It had no lock and he quickly rummaged through its contents. He found a *dhoti* and a shirt and towel—only one change, apparently for another day's stay; he'd wash his daily set himself and put them out to dry. Nagaraj also found a rosary of sandalwood beads, a little well-thumbed book of morning prayers to address the sun, planets and the gods presiding therein, and all the sacred rivers, and the potent gayatri mantra, a little brass box containing sacred ash, and a packet of incense sticks. This was a revelation. Every morning after his bath Gopu shut himself in his room and prayed. He was not the kind to talk about it, but had a secret channel of communication with God, a private arrangement with eternity . . .

Nagaraj was overwhelmed by this idea and felt he had blasphemed a holy person by his wild, vicious thoughts. He begged pardon of the gods who, he felt, were aware of what was going on in his mind. He noticed a diary and felt tempted to open its pages and learn more of Gopu—if his prayers had any relevance to his daily life and human relationships, if he put on a porcupine exterior to cover an inner timidity . . . But he left the diary untouched as he had a feeling of being watched from the skies. At this moment, Sita called from outside, 'What are you doing?'

Nagaraj hurriedly packed the jute bag, shoved it in a corner and opened the door. Surprised, Sita asked, 'Why have you bolted the door?'

'I thought I might look through my notes for Narada here, quietly . . .'

'Afraid I would come and disturb?' she said rather petulantly, and added, 'I am not so foolish . . . But your notebooks are in the other room!'

'Yes,' Nagaraj said. 'That's why I am not looking through them now.' She could not accept his explanations and stood at the doorway staring at him. He found it disturbing and said with an apologetic grin, 'I can't deceive you. Your eyes pierce through me and see my soul. If I ever wanted to deceive you I had so many occasions, but I never tried it. You are a great wife for a man.'

She was rather amused by his rambling talk but stood firm as if she would get the truth out of him. She said, 'After all these years, you are talking as if we were newly-weds. What is it? Come out with it.'

He confessed.

She said, 'Oh, is that all? You and your brother! It's always that. You looked as if you were stealing someone's jewellery.'

'He is a careful man, won't carry valuables in his bag,' he said.

She lost interest in his enumeration of its contents and said off-tangent, 'Why don't you bring your notebooks to this room and write here, if you must, instead of in the other room?'

He resisted the idea. She said, 'That room in the second courtyard is full of vermin and rats. Some day you will find all your notes on Narada completely eaten up and digested by the white ants which have covered the rafters, if you look up . . .'

'You have also mentioned rats,' Nagaraj said.

'Do you think I'm being funny? What the rats leave over in shreds will be finished off by white ants; they help each other . . .'

It seemed to him a good idea to move into this room for writing. He got busy at once. He strode up and down, carried a bundle of Crow-brand notebooks to the middle room table, adjusted the chair and arranged his Waterman's pen to be handy when inspiration seized him; He was satisfied when he looked around and felt that life's pendulum, which had swung erratically, was coming back to normal, which meant that in the background Narada would once again appear and lend a meaning to daily existence. Anyway, he told himself, it was all for the best. The house was now normal and quiet. No speculations about Tim. No need to watch his movements. No need to glorify and find excuses for the eau-de-Cologne smell. No need to hunt for earplugs. The house had become suddenly quiet; absolute calm prevailed. Sita too looked relieved and had shed her irritations and anxieties. Above all, he was free from responsibilities and custody of Tim. He could pray in peace and write in peace, sitting in a chair and at a table. He had never had the use of this table freely at any time. He threw his mind back. In their student days Gopu usurped the table and chair and drove him to a corner, where he had to crouch over a dealwood box and do his homework. When Gopu married, he shut himself in with Charu, chasing off Nagaraj to a corner in the hall. Later Tim, and still later Tim and Saroja and her harmonium occupied the room. Nagaraj felt he had somehow been kept off that table by fate. Now, for the first time, it was within his reach. He felt it was going to be a luxury for him to be able to place his notes on a table and write sitting in a chair. He had a fresh lease of life.

Next morning, after his prayers, he went straight to the *pyol*, throwing a word of cheer in Sita's direction. He hummed a little song, much to her amusement. She said, 'You have become suddenly young.'

'I have always been so. Only you didn't notice.'

'Maybe you don't need your ochre robe for writing.'

'No need. You will be the only one to talk, and I will answer. I can talk and write at the same time. Only I can't bear the harmonium noise.'

'Oh, that, and your brother! You can't get them out of your mind . . . Sometimes I feel I should play my harmonium again. My father spent fifty rupees a month for my tutor. I feel rather dull, I must say, without Tim and Saroja, and I dream sometimes I could resume my music . . .'

Nagaraj felt embarrassed. He thought, 'Why are these creatures music mad? Unfortunately, my opinion will provoke them.' He never expected Sita to have musical ambitions. He was at a loss for words to continue the conversation, but told himself, 'I must immediately secure cotton wool plugs, and depend on my ochre robe. I had thought I would not need them now.' He remained silent, and then said, 'I must begin my work tomorrow morning. Everything is ready—'

'Except the harmonium accompaniment,' she remarked with a grin.

He felt, 'She is still joking, will not take me seriously. First daughter-in-law and now the adopted mother-in-law! Women are an impediment. Ah, how could I say so? The deity of learning is Saraswathi, the goddess with a veena in one hand, and the book and other things in her four arms. I am condemning the whole race of women. Wrong, I think I am losing my head. Prolonged absence from Narada has affected my mind; I must get back to my work soon.'

He got up briskly from the *pyol* and went into his study, sat at his desk and browsed through his notes in the Crow-brand exercise book. He had filled up five books and it filled him with misgivings now. He had lost touch with the subject for some weeks, thanks to Tim's problems, and much of the notes seemed incomprehensible. He had lost touch with the origins of creation and all the darkness and gloom of Bari's book. Even after five notebooks had been filled there was no trace of the main character. Not even an ant seemed to have been created; still water, water everywhere. 'And not a drop to drink,' echoed a literary oddment from a corner of his vast store of jumbled memory. Today, re-reading his notes and his attempted composition based on them, he found that none of it made sense. He felt desperate, and cried out, 'Sita, come here!' The urgency in his voice made her anxious and she almost came down in a run from the second court, where she was leaning on a pillar and reading some magazine. 'What is it?'

Nagaraj pushed across the table a bundle of notebooks and said, 'If you need paper for lighting the oven, take these, take these away.'

She looked alarmed. Had never seen him in such a mood. She collected the books and held them to her bosom protectively. 'What has come over you?'

'They are useless. I think Bari has been foisting on me some nonsense, nothing to do with Narada.'

'Why don't you ask him really what that mysterious book is about? Ask him to read the later portions and see what comes.'

'Brilliant idea . . . I tried it but . . .'

'Ask him to dip into the old volume here and there to see if the sage is hiding anywhere . . .' And both laughed at this fantastic notion. This outburst relieved his mind and he reflected, 'Sita is not as bad as I think.' And at once he repented his secret thought. He touched his cheeks as was their habit while begging pardon for a mistake when young. Observing the motion of his hand, Sita asked, 'What excuse are you praying for and to whom?'

'Ah, how sharp you are! This man is lucky to have Sita for a wife.'

She blushed at this compliment and said, 'After so many years, you are discovering me. Thank Shiva. At least now you know me. But you have not answered my question, what excuse you were seeking from whom?'

'From God for not understanding you properly. I had thought

you did not like Narada.'

'Still I don't understand your preoccupation with Narada. Everyone knows that he was a great sage—that's all. No one has bothered to want to write his life story. Why should you alone bother?'

He had no answer; he blinked unhappily. He could only say, 'But others have written. Kavu pundit has four volumes in Sanskrit on the subject, and Bari has a big tome, which is over a hundred years old.'

'So why should you take the trouble again over the same subject?'

'So that our people may also know.'

'Why do you take upon yourself this task?'

'I don't know, I have always wanted to do it, felt it my duty somehow.'

She said coldly, 'You will be happier if you overcome it. It's only a notion which has somehow got nailed in your brain. Pluck out the nail. Nothing more; get rid of it.'

He listened in silence, echoing secretly Lady Macbeth's lines:

I would, while it was smiling in my face,
Have pluck'd my nipple from his boneless gums,
And dash'd the brains out, had I so sworn
As you have done to this.

Sita's words sounded similar and had a flint-like sharpness, an inescapable logic and unambiguity, very much like Lady Macbeth's advice. 'She wants to remove Narada from the scene of action in a very Lady-Macbeth-like manner.' His heart bled at the thought of eliminating Narada, abandoning a personality who had occupied his thoughts all his waking hours for years. Sita noted his sudden silence and preoccupation and asked, 'You look suddenly sad. Why?'

He thought, 'Everyone wants my private thoughts and demands them to be exposed. After all, I too have a right to remain silent; if I speak out, no one can bear it. Out of consideration for others, and they assume I am a fool . . .' While these thoughts were racing along thus, she watched his face, and he just said, 'I am not . . .' and checked his sentence before 'fool'.

Sita watched his face with amusement and concluded, 'If you can't drop Narada, I've nothing to say. I only wanted to suggest you could write about God Krishna, his boyhood, childhood, and his championing of the Pandavas in the great battle . . . The subject is everywhere, easier than Narada.'

Nagaraj shook his head, 'What I want to write is something new, not widely known or appreciated. You will realize when it comes out . . .'

She withdrew suddenly, remembering something to do in the kitchen. Nagaraj stared after her for a while and said: 'She wants to avoid the subject, probably hates Narada. Nor will she accept these notes for fuel, which was a handsome offer on my part . . . but she picked up the notebooks and hugged them to her bosom. What does she mean? Difficult, women, difficult to understand. Whatever may happen, tomorrow I will start writing again at seven a.m. The times are propitious, no harmonium to madden me.' He suddenly shouted, 'Sita, tomorrow morning at seven o'clock I am going to continue my writing, even if the heavens fall. We will have to be up at five o'clock as usual, sorry to bother you, my dear.' He added within himself, 'This is a matter in which I alone can have a voice, not you, although in other matters you are welcome to speak your mind.' After this outburst, external and internal, he felt triumphant that he had established his standing not as one married to Sita but as the author of *Narad Maharaj*, as Bari would say. It was possible that the sage might reveal himself to him in a vision. Why not? Visions do not come by one's sweating for it, but unasked, as grace for concentrated meditation. 'I'll meditate on Narada more methodically hereafter.'

He rose with a new resolve and stretched his limbs, whispering to himself: 'You must never listen to women. They will not let you do anything worthwhile, nothing more important than buying brinjals and cucumber, and mustard and rice, and caressing whenever a chance occurred. One who is out to make a mark in any walk of life will have no chance.' His thoughts continued, 'What about my mother? Who knows how she must have nagged and reduced my father to what he became: just a grabber of village produce, bullying the cultivators who brought grains in cartloads. Even otherwise what would he have done, produced more than two brothers, perhaps? Ha! Ha! Wonderful brothers. A sister between us would have made some difference; she would have acted as a buffer. But poor Father had no time, having to browbeat peasants from the village all the time and squeezing out their cash, while Mother kept providing him food hour by hour to satisfy his gluttony during the day and at night perhaps his carnal desires . . .

'Why am I thinking such thoughts of the poor man, who came every evening to the municipal school to take me home safely, although I wanted to play marbles in the street. How concerned he was when he took charge of my school books and carried them home; and then did my homework. I am an ungrateful wretch, indulging in evil thoughts. Poor Father, forgive me and don't send down any punishment from your seat in heaven. Forgive me, please. There is an evil half of me which floats to the surface at unexpected moments and provokes sinful thoughts. Please quell them. If you ever meet the great sage Narada in your heavenly home, please tell him to help and guide me in my effort, tomorrow morning at seven o'clock. Sita will be up at five. When I begin again there will be no stopping—all day I am going to write. I hope Bari is not deceiving me with a bogus Narada in his obscure volume; so far no sign of even that. However, tomorrow is D-Day, as they used to say during the war.'

At this moment, he heard a van stop in front of his house, and opened the door only to let in Tim, Saroja and the van driver who carried in, during several trips to and fro, two trunks, bedding rolls, a basket, a large-sized harmonium (which was known as a 'leg harmonium' and which had a stand, the bellows to be operated by a foot pedal leaving both hands free for the player to produce the maximum noise) and a folding chair. 'Got a good price for my old instrument and I was able to get this and the chair,' she explained to Sita who had come out and was watching the arrivals speechlessly. Nagaraj was confused, though he made several sounds of welcome and moved about between the street door and the middle room excitedly, accommodating and arranging their baggage, saying something all the time, not really knowing what to say. The persistent thought in his mind was, 'If you had brought ten pounds of cotton wool to plug my ears, it would not have sufficed, considering the monster you have brought in.'

Tim went to his room, looked around and at the table and said, 'These your books?'

Nagaraj picked them up apologetically. 'White ants and rats in that room—so Sita said . . .' He hurriedly took them to his bedroom and, unobtrusively, also his brother's jute bag. He wanted to add, 'I asked Sita to burn the notes but she clutched them to her bosom and put them back on your table . . .' But he only said aloud, 'I have not at all been able to write these days . . .'

'So busy?' asked the boy, sneeringly, as it seemed to Nagaraj.

'Not exactly, but I missed you . . . I am glad to see you . . .' He could not say anything more, nor ask why Tim had come back suddenly. He thought it best to avoid the question. Meanwhile Sita and Saroja were in the kitchen talking simultaneously and non-stop. Sita seemed to be particularly happy that Tim was back. She seemed to feel, 'Now our home is back to normal.' And Tim moved about the house as if nothing had happened or changed. Nagaraj had many questions to ask, but Tim gave him no chance. He shut himself in the room. Nagaraj had not the courage to knock on his door and enquire, ask, or investigate. 'He has come back in the same manner as he left—no explanation or any elaborate discussion—not in his nature, why should one expect anything different? I'll take him as he is. If his father wants him, he is welcome to come and take him. I am only a milestone. I stay and others come and pass. I must only watch, not ask questions. Tim's life and actions are, as ever, a mystery. But God has not endowed me with a temperament to solve mysteries. I have to accept them, that's all . . . I do not mind anything except that huge harmonium; when its bellows work, the roof will be lifted off the rafters and beams. I dread it. If I speak about it, they will both walk out again, and then Gopu will come down and badger me. I must be prepared for anything. If Tim walks out again, where will he go? Back to Kismet?'

This question was answered by Sita later that night in the privacy of their bedroom, after Tim had shut himself in with Saroja. Sita sat on the edge of Nagaraj's bed after closing the door and said in an undertone, 'Saroja said they have come to stay and are not going back to Kismet.'

'Why?'

'Because they belong to this house—and nowhere else to go.'

'Should we adopt him?' he wanted to ask but suppressed it, fearing that she might break down at the reminder of Gopu's postcard.

Sita added, 'Saroja said that Tim had a fight with the Secretary of Kismet,' and described it with a lot of admiration for the way Tim waged it. 'She was earning fifty rupees an evening for singing and playing the harmonium for the members. It went on smoothly till they brought in the leg harmonium. The Secretary then came, while she was playing, to move her instrument to a side room, telling her to operate it there as it was too noisy and disturbed the club members who were assembled in the hall for playing cards or chatting. Tim dropped whatever he was doing at the moment, rushed up in a rage and shouted at the Secretary for insulting his wife. There was a lot of commotion while Tim pushed and slapped the Secretary. Saroja was afraid that they might call the police . . .'

'I wish the police had come and seized the harmonium,' Nagaraj said. 'I dread that tomorrow morning it will start blaring. I can have no hope of writing any more. You could as well take the notebooks back to the old room, where at least white ants may relish my notes on Narada . . . And another thing: don't be surprised if I wear the ochre robe when I am at home. It'll force me to remain silent and not speak out and upset the children and drive them out again. I shall also acquire a lot of cotton wool and try and pack it all in my ear so that even a thunderclap may sound like a whisper.'